UNLOCKED BOOKS

THE MAGIC IN HISTORY SERIES

FORBIDDEN RITES
A Necromancer's Manual of the Fifteenth Century
Richard Kieckhefer

CONJURING SPIRITS
Texts and Traditions of Medieval Ritual Magic
Claire Fanger

RITUAL MAGIC
Elizabeth M. Butler

THE FORTUNES OF FAUST
Elizabeth M. Butler

THE BATHHOUSE AT MIDNIGHT
An Historical Survey of Magic and Divination in Russia
W. F. Ryan

SPIRITUAL AND DEMONIC MAGIC
From Ficino to Campanella
D. P. Walker

ICONS OF POWER
Ritual Practices in Late Antiquity
Naomi Janowitz

BATTLING DEMONS
Witchcraft, Heresy, and Reform in the Late Middle Ages
Michael D. Bailey

PRAYER, MAGIC, AND THE STARS IN THE LATE ANCIENT AND ANTIQUE WORLD
Scott Noegel
Joel Walker
Brannon Wheeler

BINDING WORDS
Textual Amulets in the Middle Ages
Don C. Skemer

STRANGE REVELATIONS
Magic, Poison, and Sacrilege in Louis XIV's France
Lynn Wood Mollenauer

UNLOCKED BOOKS
Manuscripts of Learned Magic in the Medieval Libraries in Central Europe
Benedek Láng

The Magic in History series explores the role magic and the occult have played in European culture, religion, science, and politics. Titles in the series will bring the resources of cultural, literary, and social history to bear on the history of the magic arts, and will contribute towards an understanding of why the theory and practice of magic have elicited fascination at every level of European society. Volumes will include both editions of important texts and significant new research in the field.

MAGIC IN HISTORY

UNLOCKED BOOKS

Manuscripts of Learned Magic in the Medieval Libraries of Central Europe

Benedek Láng

THE PENNSYLVANIA STATE UNIVERSITY PRESS
UNIVERSITY PARK, PENNSYLVANIA

Library of Congress Cataloging-in-Publication Data

Láng, Benedek, 1974–
   Unlocked books : manuscripts of learned magic in the
  medieval libraries of Central Europe / Benedek Láng.
      p.   cm.—(Magic in history series)
  Includes bibliographical references (p.   ) and index.
  Summary: "Presents and analyzes texts of learned magic written
  in medieval Central Europe (Poland, Bohemia, and
  Hungary), and attempts to identify their authors, readers,
  and collectors"—Provided by publisher.
  ISBN 978-0-271-03378-5 (pbk : alk. paper)
  1. Magic—Manuscripts.
  2. Manuscripts, Medieval.
  I. Title.

BF1593.L36 2008
133.4'309430902—dc22
2008013593

Copyright © 2008 The Pennsylvania State University
All rights reserved
Printed in the United States of America
Published by The Pennsylvania State University Press,
University Park, PA 16802-1003

The Pennsylvania State University Press is a member of the
Association of American University Presses.

It is the policy of The Pennsylvania State University Press to
use acid-free paper. This book is printed on stock
that meets the minimum requirements
of American National Standard for
Information Sciences—Permanence of Paper for Printed
Library Material, ANSI Z39.48–1992.

Contents

List of Illustrations	vii
Acknowledgments	ix
List of Abbreviations	xiii
Introduction: In Search of Magician Schools	1

PART ONE: MAGIC

1	Definitions and Classifications	17

PART TWO: TEXTS AND HANDBOOKS

	Introduction: The Sociology of Manuscripts	47
2	Natural Magic	51
3	Image Magic	79
4	Divination with Diagrams	123
5	Alchemy	144
6	Ritual Magic and Crystallomancy	162

PART THREE: READERS AND COLLECTORS

	Introduction: The Motives and Intentions of Scribes	191
7	Magic in the Clerical Context	194
8	Magic in the Courtly Context	209
9	Magic in the University Context	241

CONCLUSION: Seven Questions	265
EPILOGUE: When Central Europe Was Finally Close to Becoming a Center for Magical Studies	276
APPENDIXES	281
SELECTED BIBLIOGRAPHY	295
DESCRIPTION OF SELECTED MANUSCRIPTS	319
GENERAL INDEX	329
INDEX OF MANUSCRIPTS	333

Illustrations

1. Magical cure against toothache. Prague, PNK XI C 2, fol. 146v. Courtesy of the Národní knihovna ČR. — 66
2. *Bellifortis*: a military instrument. Göttingen, Universitätsbibliothek, Cod. Philos. 63, fol. 109r. Courtesy of the Universitätsbibliothek. — 73
3. *Bellifortis*: a military instrument. Göttingen, Universitätsbibliothek, Cod. Philos. 63, fol. 38v. Courtesy of the Universitätsbibliothek. — 74
4. *Bellifortis*: summoning of spirits. Göttingen, Universitätsbibliothek, Cod. Philos. 63, fol. 94r. Courtesy of the Universitätsbibliothek. — 75
5. *De septem quadraturis planetarum*. Kraków, BJ 793, fol. 60r. Courtesy of the Biblioteka Jagiellońska. — 84
6. Geomantic divination. Kraków, BJ 793, fol. 67r. Courtesy of the Biblioteka Jagiellońska. — 86
7. Geomantic divination. Kraków, BJ 793, fol. 71v. Courtesy of the Biblioteka Jagiellońska. — 87
8. Geomantic divination. Kraków, BJ 793, fol. 73v. Courtesy of the Biblioteka Jagiellońska. — 88
9. Geomantic divination. Kraków, BJ 793, fol. 75r. Courtesy of the Biblioteka Jagiellońska. — 89
10. *Sphera Pythagorae*. Kraków, BJ 793, fol. 86r. Courtesy of the Biblioteka Jagiellońska. — 90
11. *Picatrix*: planetary figures. Kraków, BJ 793, fol. 190r. Courtesy of the Biblioteka Jagiellońska. — 99
12. *Picatrix*: planetary figures. Kraków, BJ 793, fol. 191v. Courtesy of the Biblioteka Jagiellońska. — 100
13. *Picatrix*: decanic figures. Kraków, BJ 793, fol. 193v. Courtesy of the Biblioteka Jagiellońska. — 101
14. *Picatrix*: decanic figures. Kraków, BJ 793, fol. 197r. Courtesy of the Biblioteka Jagiellońska. — 102
15. *Liber runarum*: magical runes. SLB N 100, fol. 198r. Courtesy of the Sächsische Landesbibliothek. — 111

16 *Liber runarum*: magical runes. BAV Pal. Lat. 1439, fol. 348r. © Biblioteca Apostolica Vaticana (Vatican). 112
17 *Rota runarum*. BAV Pal. Lat. 1439, fol. 199r. © Biblioteca Apostolica Vaticana (Vatican). 113
18 *De imaginibus septem planetarum* by Belenus: karacteres planetarum. BAV Pal. Lat. 1375, fol. 270v. © Biblioteca Apostolica Vaticana (Vatican). 117
19 *Chiromantia delineata*. Kraków, BJ 551, fol. 117r. Courtesy of the Biblioteka Jagiellońska. 127
20 *Ciromantia ex diversis libris collecta*. BAV Pal. Lat. 1396, fol. 91r. © Biblioteca Apostolica Vaticana (Vatican). 129
21 *Sphera Pythagorae* with a cryptographic title. BAV Pal. Lat. 1375, fol. 44r. © Biblioteca Apostolica Vaticana (Vatican). 131
22 Cryptographic alphabets. BAV Pal. Lat. 1375, fol. 19r. © Biblioteca Apostolica Vaticana (Vatican). 132
23 *Sphera Pythagorae*. Prague, PNK I F 35, fol. 60v. Courtesy of the Národní knihovna ČR. 133
24 Magical mirror. Dresden, Mathematisch-Physikalischer Salon, Staatliche Kunstsammlungen. Photo by Peter Müller. 139
25 Drawing on Solomon's rings. Prague, PNK I F 35, fol. 466v. Courtesy of the Národní knihovna ČR. 141
26 The Holy Spirit as the supervisor of the alchemical process. Kraków, BJ 837, fol. 9v. Courtesy of the Biblioteka Jagiellońska. 153
27 Alchemical retort. Kraków, BJ 837, fol. 10r. Courtesy of the Biblioteka Jagiellońska. 154
28 Magical mirror from Rostock. Drawing by W. L. Braekman (*Societas Magica Newsletter*, Winter 2001). Reproduced with the kind permission of W. L. Braekman. 171
29 The prayer book of Wladislas: the king and the crystal. Oxford, Bodleian Library, Rawl. liturg. d. 6, fol. 15r. Courtesy of the Bodleian Library, University of Oxford. 176
30 The prayer book of Wladislas: the king and the angels. Oxford, Bodleian Library, Rawl. liturg. d. 6, fol. 72r. Courtesy of the Bodleian Library, University of Oxford. 177

Acknowledgments

Completing a long-term project offers the pleasure of acknowledging the generous help of all those scholars and friends who participated in the process of its preparation and provided scholarly and personal help, support, and encouragement, and without whom the final version would be less worthwhile to read. Looking at the long list of the names, one might think that this work is more of a communal effort than the fruit of individual research. Indeed, the following book was born—more than most scholarly achievements—as a result of collective work, without implying, of course, that any conscious plagiarism has been committed.

I am first of all indebted to Gábor Klaniczay, not only because he was the supervisor of the doctoral dissertation on which this book was based, but also because it was in his seminars where I first read in the secondary literature that medieval magicians (whoever they were) actually produced written material. I am no less grateful to Paolo Lucentini, who introduced me to the complicated tradition of Hermetic texts, letting me consult his library and giving me access to the unpublished material of the "Hermes Latinus" editorial project. My third guide in the labyrinth of medieval sources was Charles Burnett from the Warburg Institute, who supplied me with a great number of unpublished articles and microfilms.

My chapters on the notion of magic and the Central European use of the *ars notoria*—a medieval genre of ritual magic—owe enormous debts to Claire Fanger, who made an exciting discovery in my own field, a "trouvaille" that I hope I would have made, had I been more thorough in my research (see my chapter on the royal prayer book of King Wladislas). Much scholarly advice was offered by Richard Kieckhefer, who also provided me with helpful instructions on how to restructure the book to make it accessible to an audience that extends beyond a modest circle of specialists. No less helpful and useful were the kind suggestions and corrections of György Endre Szőnyi, who helped me over a number of years, by reading and improving my writings and by introducing me to the vast secondary literature pertaining to Renaissance magic.

The approach to magical sources shown in my work rests on the conviction that no meaningful account can be given on learned magic unless we situate it in the framework of the history of science of that period. This conviction is the fruit of long and regular consultations with the philosopher Márta Fehér, who provided me with philosophical training that has always had a profound influence on my work.

I would also like to express my gratitude to those doctoral candidates who shared their research with me. The help we gave one another with common problems and with finding manuscripts and secondary literature usually proved as useful as reading the oeuvre of the great scholars. I especially profited from reading the theses of Sophie Page and Frank Klaassen, both of whom set an example of how to write on the medieval use and readership of magical texts. My present work owes a great debt to their studies as far as its structure and terminology are concerned. I also benefited from the inspiring conversations with Isabelle Draelants, Håkan Håkansson, David Juste, David Porreca, and Julien Véronèse.

My overview would be much less "Central European" if the doctoral students of the Central European University (CEU) had not helped me in various ways. The most appreciated contribution came from Jolanta Szpilewska, who tirelessly rendered the Polish secondary literature accessible and readable to me. I greatly enjoyed the scholarly and friendly discussions with Renata Mikołajczyk, whose research on the medieval doctors of Kraków was a model for my own work.

Furthermore, I would like to thank my friend Péter Banyó, who helped me in so many ways that I cannot even start recording them here, and to further alumni of the Medieval Studies Department of the CEU, Ottó Gecser, Petra Mutlová, Dóra Bobory, Marek Klaty, and Gábor Kiss Farkas, all of whom have participated in one way or another in my research. I also thank the staff of the Medieval Studies Department. I owe special thanks to Réka Benczes, Andrew Lewis, and Matthew Suff, the lectors of this book, who have a particular gift for raising a text with a few changes to a considerably higher level of elegance.

I am no less indebted to and grateful for the kindness and intellectual help of Krzysztof Bracha, Anna Kozlowska, Mieczysław Markowski, Grażyna Rosińska, and Hanna Zaremska in Poland; Milena Bartlová in the Czech Republic; Christopher Ligota, William Ryan, and Jo Trapp in London; Paul Kunitzsch in Munich; Gerlinde Huber-Rebenich in Jena; and Vittoria Perrone Compagni in Florence, who gave me invaluable advice through personal discussions or e-mail.

A medievalist who wants to see his sources and develop his research in well-supplied libraries has to be either wealthy or very fortunate when applying for grants. Not possessing the former virtue, I had the good fortune to enjoy the financial support of the Central European University, which funded my master's and my doctorate and covered the expenses of several research trips to Kraków, Prague, Florence, Rome, and London; the Norddeutsche Landesbank, Warburg—Wolfenbüttel Fellowship; the Warburg Institute in London; and the Herzog August Bibliothek in Wolfenbüttel. The Warburg Institute and the Herzog August Bibliothek are without doubt the best-equipped centers for researching a topic such as mine. The Warburg Institute—with its fourth floor devoted partly to the history of science and magic—provides the reader not just with books and articles, but thanks to the arrangement of its holdings, inspiration. I would also like to acknowledge the support of three Hungarian grants, the Deák Ferenc Fellowship, the Bolyai János Research Grant, and the OTKA (F-049545), which have provided me with excellent opportunities to finish this book while I was working in the inspiring and friendly milieu of the Department of Philosophy and History of Science (Budapest University of Technology and Economics). This book would not have been completed without the sabbatical I enjoyed for a long semester, thanks to the generosity of my department (special thanks are due my chair Tihamér Margitay, and my colleagues, Gábor Zemplén and János Tanács, for their intellectual support). Finally, I feel obliged to thank the Collegium Budapest, Institute for Advanced Study, where, as a junior fellow, I had the time and excellent research opportunities to transform the manuscript of my dissertation into the present book.

Finally, I wish to thank the one person without whom writing this project would make no sense: the most durable patience and valuable assistance came from my wife, Márta, who put aside her academic career and traveled with me to various cities, towns, and libraries of Western and Central Europe, and who gave birth to our son, Kristóf, while I was working on my dissertation, and to our daughter, Flóra, while I was involved in creating this book.

Versions of several portions of this book have appeared in print: Claire Fanger and Benedek Láng, "John of Morigny's *Liber visionum* and a Royal Prayer Book from Poland," *Societas Magica Newsletter* 9 (2002): 1–4; Benedek Láng, "The Kraków Readers of Hermes: Magical and Hermetic Manuscripts in Kraków," in *Hermetism from Late Antiquity to Humanism*, ed. Paolo Lucentini et al. (Turnhout: Brepols, 2003), 577–600; Benedek Láng, "Angels Around the Crystal: The Prayer Book of King Wladislas and the Treasure Hunts of Henry the Bohemian," *Aries: Journal for the Study of Western Esotericism* 5 (2005): 1–32; Gábor Farkas Kiss, Benedek Láng, and Cosmin Popa-Gorjanu, "The Alchemical Mass of Nicolaus Melchior Cibinensis: Text, Identity and Speculations," *Ambix* 53 (2006): 143–59; Benedek Láng, "Demons in Krakow, and Image Magic in a Magical Handbook, in *Demons, Spirits, Witches, II: Christian Demonology and Popular Mythology*, ed. Gábor Klaniczay and Éva Pócs (Budapest: CEU Press, 2006), 13–44; Benedek Láng, "Research Problems of Magical Texts in Central Europe," in *The Role of Magic in the Past*, ed. Blanka Szeghyová (Bratislava: Pro Historia, 2005), 11–17; and Benedek Láng, "The Criminalization of Possessing Necromantic Books in Fifteenth-Century Krakow," in *Religion und Magie in Ostmitteleuropa*, ed. Thomas Wünsch (Berlin: LIT Verlag, 2006), 257–71.

Abbreviations

A et A	Markowski, Mieczysław. *Astronomica et astrologica Cracoviensia ante annum 1550*. Studi e testi, Istituto nazionale di studi sul Rinascimento, 20. Florence: L. S. Olschki, 1990.
AHDLMA	*Archives d'histoire doctrinale et littéraire du Moyen Age* (Paris).
BAV Pal. lat.	Biblioteca Apostolica Vaticana, Palatinus latinus collection.
BH	Csapodi, Csaba, and Klára Gárdonyi Csapodiné, eds. *Bibliotheca Hungarica: Kódexek és nyomtatott könyvek Magyarországon 1526 elott* (Bibliotheca Hungarica: Codices and Printed Books in Hungary Before 1526). 2 vols. Budapest: Magyar Tudományos Akadémia Könyvtára, 1993.
BJ	Kraków, Biblioteka Jagiellońska.
BnF	Paris, Bibliothèque nationale de France
CBJ	Wlodek, Zofia, Jerzy Zathey, and Marian Zwiercan, et al., eds. *Catalogus codicum manuscriptorum Medii Aevi Latinorum qui in Bibliotheca Jagellonica Cracoviae asservantur*. 8 vols. Wrocław: Zakład Narodowy im. Ossolińskich, 1980–2004.
CLM	Munich, Codex Latinus Monacensis (Bayerische Staatsbibliothek).
HMES	Thorndike, Lynn. *History of Magic and Experimental Science*. 8 vols. New York: Columbia University Press, 1923–58.
JWCI	*Journal of the Warburg and Courtauld Institutes* (London).
KMK	Prague, Metropolitan Library (Knihovna metropolitní kapituly pražské).
L-PC	Lucentini, Paolo, and Vittoria Perrone Compagni, eds. *I Testi e i codici di Ermete nel Medioevo*. Florence: Polistampa, 2001.
MTAK	Budapest, Library of the Hungarian Academy of Sciences (Magyar Tudományos Akadémia Könyvtára)

ÖNB	Vienna, Österreichische Nationalbibliothek.
PNK	Prague, National Library of the Czech Republic (Národní knihovna ČR).
Podlaha	Podlaha, Antonín, ed. *Soupis rukopisů knihovny metropolitní kapituly pražské* (Catalogue of Manuscripts of the Metropolitan Chapter Library of Prague). Prague: Česká Akademie věd, 1922.
Rosińska	Rosińska, Grażyna. *Scientific Writings and Astronomical Tables in Cracow: A Census of Manuscript Sources (XIVth–XVIth Centuries)*. Studia Copernicana 22. Wrocław: Zakład Narodowy im. Ossolińskich, 1984.
SLB	Dresden, Sächsische Landesbibliothek.
T (1947)	Thorndike, Lynn. "Traditional Medieval Tracts Concerning Engraved Astronomical Images." In *Mélanges Auguste Pelzer*, 217–74. Louvain: Institut Supérieure de Philosophie, 1947.
TK	Thorndike, Lynn, and Pearl Kibre. *A Catalogue of Incipits of Mediaeval Scientific Writings in Latin.* Revised and augmented edition. Cambridge, Mass.: Mediaeval Academy of America, 1963. Addenda et Corrigenda in *Speculum* 40 (1965): 116–22, and 43 (1968): 78–114.
Truhlář	Truhlář, Josef. *Catalogus codicum manu scriptorum latinorum, qui in c. r. bibliotheca publica atque universitatis Pragensis asservantur.* 2 vols. Prague: Regia Societas Scientiarum, 1905–6.
WP	Weill-Parot, Nicolas. *Les "images astrologiques" au Moyen Âge et à la Renaissance: Speculations intellectuelles et pratiques magiques (XIIe–XVe siècle)*. Paris: Honoré Champion, 2002.

Introduction:
In Search of Magician Schools

There is a rather curious handwritten note in the first page of the British Library's copy of a printed reference book that was widely read in the sixteenth century, the *Locorum communium collectanea* by Johannes Manlius, "In this interesting book the first authentic notice of the Magician Dr Faustus is to be found at p. 43."[1] On page 43, following a report on Abbot Trithemius (who, according to the author, was a great magician), there are indeed a few paragraphs on the famous figure whose legend soon became a popular literary topic. There it states that Faustus, "when he was a student in Kraków, studied magic, as this art was at the time widely used and publicly practiced there."[2] This statement appears in Manlius's book as part of common knowledge, and it soon became in fact generally accepted. Another, slightly later source relying heavily on Manlius, the *Dies caniculares* by Simon Maiolus, repeats the claims that a Johannes Faustus studied magic in Kraków, where—according to Maiolus—it was publicly taught.[3]

The general approval of a proposition, however, is not necessarily related to its truth value. This sentence, for example, has a number of untrue implications. It asserts, first of all, that the man who was to become the archetype of human dealings with the devil did exist and was called Johannes. Now, philological investigations have established that the historical Faustus did indeed exist, but he was not called Johannes at all, but rather Georgius. Second, Manlius says that he studied in Kraków—at least for a time. Again, this seems to be false, for there is no historical

---

1. British Library, London, 12209.b.1.
2. "Hic cum esset scholasticus Cracoviensis, ibi magiam didicerat, sicut ibi olim fuit ejus magnus usus, et ibidem fuerunt publicae ejusdem artis professiones." Johannes Manlius, *Locorum communium collectanea* (Basel: Johannes Oporius, 1563), 43.
3. "Johannes Faustus qui Cracoviae magiam, ubi ea publice olim docebatur, didicerat." Simon Maiolus, *Dies Caniculares* (Moguntiae: Johannes Theobaldus Schönmetter, 1615), 601.

evidence that Faustus was ever in Poland.[4] Finally, Manlius explicitly states that Faustus went to Kraków to study magic because this art was publicly practiced—in Maiolus's words, even instructed—in the famous university town.

It is widely known that according to certain popular beliefs, magicians were wandering students who learned magic from books by great intellectual effort in special schools.[5] Such schools were located, for example, in Salamanca and Toledo. It is quite understandable why these Iberian towns had such a reputation: they were located at the meeting point of three—the Arabic, the Christian, and the Jewish—cultures, and it was through them that the Latin Middle Ages imported the new learning. This was where the Western world had been confronted with—and started to translate—the Arabic scientific corpus. This cultural import included at least as much astrology, talismanic magic, and alchemy as mathematics, philosophy, optics, and physics. It is not surprising, therefore, that a whole tradition of *topoi* had presented Toledo as an international center of the black arts, divination, and demonic magic, ever since the first scientific and magical texts were translated.[6] This conviction was so strong that the "notory art," described in a widespread text of medieval ritual magic, the *Ars notoria,* was also called the "art of Toledo."[7] To give another example: a source pertaining to the same genre of learned magic, the *Liber iuratus Honorii* (Sworn Book of Honorius) purports to report a general synod of magicians arriving from three cities: Naples, Athens, and Toledo. Even as late as the sixteenth century, François Rabelais wrote of a "faculté diabologique" functioning in Toledo.[8]

However, why Kraków had a reputation as a center of magic is far from being so

---

4. Frank Baron, *Doctor Faustus: From History to Legend* (Munich: Wilhelm Fink Verlag, 1978), 11–16 and 84.

5. See Ladislaus Toth, "Savoir et pouvoir par les livres de magie," *Aries* 15 (1993): 13–25, on folk beliefs. On the literary tradition concerning schools of magic, see P. Jacoby, "Hochschulen der Zauberei," in *Handwörterbuch des deutschen Aberglaubens,* ed. Hanns Bächtold-Stäubli, 10 vols. (Leipzig: Walter de Gruyter, 1927–42). On the image of the magician (especially Virgil, Talesin, Merlin, Michael Scot, and Roger Bacon) in medieval popular beliefs, see Juliette Wood, "Virgil and Talesin: The Concept of the Magician in Medieval Folklore," *Folklore* 94 (1983): 91–104.

6. The first Latin authors responsible for this tradition were William of Malmesbury and Caesarius of Heisterbach; see Klaus Herbers, "Wissenskontakte und Wissensvermittung in Spanien," in *Artes im Mittelalter,* ed. Ursula Schaefer (Berlin: Akademie Verlag, 1999), esp. 244–47, and Jacoby, "Hochschulen der Zauberei."

7. Among other examples, it was thus called by the fourteenth-century Burgundian Laurens Pignon; see Jan R. Veenstra, *Magic and Divination in Burgundy and France: Text and Context of Laurens Pignon's "Contre les devineurs" (1411)* (Leiden: Brill, 1998), 293–94. Since the *Ars notoria* describes exactly the kind of magic that provides better memory and competence in the liberal arts, the association of Toledo with the notory art is a telling indication that proficiency in the new learning and magic were intermingled.

8. François Rabelais, *Pantagruel: Le Tiers Livre,* in *Oeuvres complètes* (Paris: Librairie Gallimard, 1951), 3:433.

obvious. While it might have been a commonplace in Manlius's times that Kraków had once been a center for magical studies, it is far from evident today what the source of this conviction was. Did Kraków really possess a particularly magical milieu?

My book has succeeded if, by its end, its readers feel that they have received sufficient information to answer this question. More precisely, I will focus on not only Kraków but all of Central Europe, as seen through contemporary manuscripts. Even though I cannot promise to identify a public school for the black arts functioning in the medieval territories of Poland, Hungary, or Bohemia—as magic was never instructed officially and openly in any medieval school or university in Europe—a large number of instructive cases will compensate the reader for the frustration caused by the lack of a department of necromancy: among them, a king summoning angels and peering into a crystal ball in order to learn the hidden intentions of his people and the secrets of the material world; an engineer designing terrifying siege-guns and powerful catapults, whose military manual contains the first medieval depiction of the Archimedes' screw, but also various magical methods to occupy castles (one of which requires the fat of a hanged man); an executioner and torturer who starts collecting handbooks on magic and reeducates himself as a magician; an alchemist of a royal court who finds the text of the Christian Mass the most convenient model for describing the secret process of transmutation; and a medical doctor educated in the best schools of Montpellier, on whose advice princes and peasants collected snakes and frogs with their bare hands and consumed them for medicinal purposes. Nevertheless, the main focus will be the university masters whose libraries include—besides a large number of scientific treatises—some surprising items pertaining to the field of learned magic: handwritten notes scattered in the blank pages of the codices on how to learn about the outcome of various enterprises or illnesses; human hands drawn with great care indicating the main lines of fate for the purposes of palmistry; texts of natural magic which include various recipes using animal substances used for magical purposes; the earliest surviving version of the great handbook of talismans and ritual magic, the *Picatrix*, which is in fact the only copy containing the illustrations of the half-animal half-human creatures described in the text; and finally the *Liber runarum* (The Book of Runes) containing the names of angels transcribed in Scandinavian runes, which bear special powers and are supposed to be engraved on talismans in order to activate their benign or malign influence. Thus, although Faustus probably never studied magic in Kraków, Prague, or Buda, it is possible to compile a bibliography of the texts he would have used if he had.

For the sake of clarity, the texts under investigation will be classified into certain categories. The first comprises the relatively innocent practices of natural magic, which operate through the secret correspondences of the world and the hidden properties of objects. Then come the more manipulative methods of image (in other words, talismanic or celestial) magic, which work with names and figures engraved in specific stones and metals. The last is that of ritual (or ceremonial) magic, which relies on the invocation of angels and demons, and which is somewhere on the borderline between magic and religion. These categories, with which I will operate throughout my study, will be carefully defined in the Chapter 1. For the moment, it is enough to emphasize that although the threefold distinction of natural, image, and ritual magic is a helpful framework for the classification of medieval magical texts,[9] the borders between these subcategories will not always be clear.

It is much harder to account for the inclusion of two further categories, the divinatory material (including geomancy and palmistry) and the alchemical sources. These arts share with magic the characteristic of being frequently condemned; nevertheless, they were not necessarily seen as branches of magic, and—as it will be argued in due course—were condemned for reasons different from those marshaled against talismanic and ritual magic. But as the borderlines in the field of magic are fuzzy, I tended to be inclusive rather than exclusive. Therefore, divination is also incorporated in this study, considering the fact that texts on divination often traveled together with texts on natural and image magic. Evidence of alchemy, as provided by a couple of Central European sources, will also be presented, first because it seems to supplement the picture on the readership of magic in that era, and second because I—like most modern readers—am somewhat imprisoned in the modern categorization of magic, which undeniably includes alchemy. It is important to always bear in mind that the modern and medieval categories of magic, science, and religion do not necessarily coincide.

No similar admission is made in this book regarding purely astrological texts, even though nowadays astrology might also seem to be a part of magic. It is of primary importance to remember that there is no necessary link between the two fields. Astrology was taught in certain universities,[10] magic never, or at least not as part of the curriculum. Even though certain elements of astrology provoked serious

---

9. When applying this distinction, I generally follow the structure of two recently defended doctoral dissertations: Frank Klaassen's "Religion, Science, and the Transformations of Magic: Manuscripts of Magic, 1300–1600" (Ph.D. diss., Department of History, University of Toronto, 1999)—its published version is forthcoming in the Magic in History series by the Pennsylvania State University Press, and Sophie Page's "Magic at St. Augustine's, Canterbury, in the Late Middle Ages" (Ph.D. diss., Warburg Institute, University of London, 2000). It is worth adding, however, that Frances Amelia Yates has already applied a somewhat similar threefold typology to her Renaissance material: natural-celestial-ritual magic. See, for example, Frances Yates, *Giordano Bruno and the Hermetic Tradition* (London: Routledge and Kegan Paul, 1964).

10. On general overviews concerning the role of astrology (interrelated with astronomy and medicine) in university curricula and the medieval philosophy of nature, see Richard Lemay, "The Teaching of Astronomy in Medieval Universities, Principally at Paris in the Fourteenth Century," *Manuscripta* 19 (1975): 197–217, and Lemay, "The True Place of Astrology in Medieval Science and Philosophy:

theological debates, such as the concept of the Great Year (which implied that earthly history is fundamentally periodical, which contradicted the teaching of the church)[11] and the effect of the stars on particular events and on human free will,[12] general astrological principles in a more innocent form were relatively well accepted as a part of medical training, and as functional elements of natural philosophy.[13] The idea that the incorruptible, perfect, and divine celestial regions exercise an influence over the corruptible earthly bodies was supported not only by the arguments of Aristotle and Ptolemy—the two main authorities of antiquity in the field of celestial sciences—but also by empirical evidence. Celestial causal superiority is evident in the influence of the sun on temperature, rain, and the cycle of seasons; or the power of the moon on the ebb and flow of the tides; not to mention that a sophisticated system had been worked out relating the sections of the zodiac, the planets, and the various parts of the human body. In addition, experience—understood in the medieval sense of the word—suggested that celestial virtues influenced metals (think of the behavior of the magnet, which was a frequent subject in the discussions of natural philosophy), and the association of planets with metals (the sun with gold, the moon with silver, and so on) was regarded as valid in general, not just in alchemical considerations.

Second, astrology is excluded for regional reasons: although the readers and scribes of magical texts in Central Europe were often concerned with the celestial sciences, and are to be found among the circle of university professors, students of astrology, and courtly astrologers, this correlation does not work in the other direction: the majority of these astrologers were not involved in magic. In brief, astrology was a fully fledged discipline in its own right in the fifteenth century, but magic was never officially studied or practiced, and if certain philosophers (who will be introduced in the next chapter) proved tolerant of some of its forms, magical texts never entered the university curriculum. Therefore, I will frequently touch upon the issue of astrology while looking at the use and the codicological context of magical works, but I will not, however, include astrological sources in the textual analysis.

Towards a Definition," in *Astrology, Science and Society: Historical Essays*, ed. Patrick Curry (Woodbridge: Boydell, 1987), 57–73. On the requirements expected from a doctor to lecture in astrology at Bologna, see Lynn Thorndike, ed., *University Records and Life in the Middle Ages* (New York: Columbia University Press, 1944; repr., New York: Octagon Books, 1971), 282.

11. Edward Grant, *Planets, Stars, and Orbs: The Medieval Cosmos, 1200–1687* (Cambridge: Cambridge University Press, 1994), 498.

12. Krzystof Pomian, "Astrology as a Naturalistic Theology of History," in *Astrologi Hallucinati*, ed. Paola Zambelli (Berlin: Walter de Gruyter, 1986), 29–43.

13. Edward Grant, "Medieval and Renaissance Scholastic Conceptions of the Influence of the Celestial Region on the Terrestrial," *Journal of Medieval and Renaissance Studies* 17 (1987): 1–23; John D. North, "Medieval Concepts of Celestial Influence: A Survey," in Curry, *Astrology, Science and Society*, 5–18.

Further limitations to this study are linguistic. The focus of the research is predominantly on Latin texts. This is not due to the complete lack of vernacular sources. Although no such examples have been found in Hungarian, the fifteenth century no doubt witnessed the translation of divinatory and natural magic texts into German and Czech. Again, these sources will not be ignored completely; however, proper research into the vernacular texts of learned magic (finding the Latin original, identifying the additional elements coming from local sources, and so on) would require a separate study.[14]

Nevertheless, the presentation and close reading of basic texts form only the first objective of my investigations. Once the examples of magic have been collected, and their codicological contexts examined (to determine which texts travel alone in the manuscript tradition, and which ones occur together with other genres), the main concern of the book is to explore and characterize the circle of people who wrote, copied, collected, used, and read these manuscripts to the extent that the evidence will permit. The historian's work is then to identify which texts travel independently in the codices, and—provided two or more magical texts find themselves bound together regularly—what characteristics of theirs made the collector believe that they belong together.[15]

While only in some exceptional cases are the specific owners known, it is often possible to identify the social stratum to which they belonged. Richard Kieckhefer calls the owners and users of manuscripts of magic the "clerical underworld";[16] others attribute this practice generally to the lower clergy.[17] William Eamon speaks about the rise of an "intellectual proletariat, a group composed of university-educated laymen who had failed to find useful or permanent employment."[18] An "underworld of learning," clerics, medical doctors, and members of universities

14. For research on German divinatory texts, see, for example, Elisabeth Wade, "A Fragmentary German Divination Device: Medieval Analogues and Pseudo-Lullian Tradition," in *Conjuring Spirits: Texts and Traditions of Medieval Ritual Magic,* ed. Claire Fanger (University Park: Pennsylvania State University Press, 1998), 87–109.

15. This is one of the main focuses of Frank Klaassen's "English Manuscripts of Magic, 1300–1500: A Preliminary Survey," in Fanger, *Conjuring Spirits,* 3–31. As Klaassen stresses, even the manuscripts without any identified owner "give us access to the world view of their authors, scribes and collectors, and frequently betray a great deal about these individuals their professions, names, education, status, or relative wealth" (3).

16. Richard Kieckhefer, *Magic in the Middle Ages* (Cambridge: Cambridge University Press, 1989), 151–75.

17. See, for example, Stanisław Bylina, "La prédication, les croyances et les pratiques traditionnelles en Pologne au bas Moyen Âge," in *L'Église et le peuple chrétien dans les pays de l'Europe du Centre-Est et du Nord (XIVe–XVe siècles)* (Rome: École française de Rome, 1990), 301–13.

18. William Eamon, *Science and the Secrets of Nature: Books of Secrets in Medieval and Early Modern Culture* (Princeton: Princeton University Press, 1994), 69. Eamon refers to R. R. Bolgar, *The Classical Heritage and Its Beneficiaries* (Cambridge: Cambridge University Press, 1954), 178. See also Alexander Murray, *Reason and Society in the Middle Ages* (Oxford: Oxford University Press, 1978), chap. 9.

could have been the real necromancers and practitioners of magic, or at least the readers of occult texts. Their curiosity in experimental and occult studies, their education, profession, background, convictions, and wishes can be inferred from the books they collected. And then, reconstructing the university careers, training, interests, and libraries of the compilers and owners of the given texts helps us understand the role of the magical books that lined their shelves and the place of magical beliefs in their conceptual schemes.

Similar questions are to be raised in a Central European context. What is known about the people who wrote, copied, and used magical texts? Did Central Europe have its own magicians, or was the presence of sources on magic nothing more than the result of simple incidental curiosity of well-known intellectuals at the universities and the courts? In other words, in what stratum of the social hierarchy should one look for the readers: among the anonymous clerics and ordinary masters, or in the group of highly respected scholars? Did the scribes add their own inventions to the field of magic, or did they merely follow Western practices? Did they belong to the local "clerical underworld"? (And on a more general level: what are the boundaries of this underworld?) Furthermore, were the compilers and the collectors educated at Polish, Bohemian, or Hungarian universities? Did they possess such handbooks for personal use or out of pure curiosity?[19]

Throughout this study, "Central Europe" will designate the geographical and political entity that lies beyond the limits of the first expansion of the Western barbarian peoples, the Carolingian Empire, but which did not belong under the direct sphere of Byzantine influence, and could therefore join Western Europe around A.D. 1000. (This happened simultaneously with the process of the North's inclusion in the enlarged notion of the West, while Southeastern Europe found itself under the aegis of Byzantium.) Central Europe comprises the countries of three Christian states, whose political developments show genuine resemblances: Poland, Bohemia, and Hungary. Strictly speaking, the territory covered here should be referred to as "East-Central Europe," since what is usually understood as "Central Europe" is supposed to include Austria, Italy, and—partially at least—Germany as well. In the following, however, for the sake of simplicity and brevity, I will refrain from operating with such difficult expressions. I will apply the simpler term "Central Europe" when referring to Poland, Bohemia, and Hungary, not denying the fact that this notion has been the subject of long theoretical debates.[20] Since my

---

19. This approach is in many ways similar to that of the scholars dealing with the "history of reading." See Guglielmo Cavallo and Roger Chartier, eds., *Histoire de la lecture dans le monde occidentale* (Paris: Editions du Seuil, 1997), and Roger Chartier, *L'Ordre des livres* (Paris: Alinea, 1992).

20. The classic study on the internal borders of Europe and on the medieval notion of Central Europe is Jenő Szűcs, "The Three Historical Regions of Europe: An Outline," *Acta Historica Academiae Scientiarum Hungaricae* 29 (1983): 131–84. Further considerations on this issue, with special

research is related to the medieval emergence of courts, institutions, and libraries, by and large I will concentrate on Kraków, Prague, and Buda, not neglecting of course towns of lower political significance, insofar as ecclesiastical formations and book collections can be associated with them.

As far as manuscripts are concerned, the eastern boundary of Central Europe is very clear: beyond this region sources are written in a different language; they belong to a different manuscript tradition, even though occasionally this border is permeable.[21] The southern borders are more cultural than political: while the history of medieval Croatia is closely associated with that of Hungary, and consequently falls under the scope of the present inquiry, Istria and Dalmatia had a separate history in the Middle Ages, dominated by Italian influence. Therefore, the famous alchemical text *Pretiosa margarita novella*, composed in Pula by Petrus Bonus, a native of Ferrara, will not be treated together with Bohemian, Polish, and Hungarian sources on alchemy.[22]

---

attention to the patterns of university foundations in the region, are Gábor Klaniczay, "Late Medieval Central European Universities: Problems of their Comparative History," in *Universitas Budensis, 1395–1995*, ed. László Szögi and Júlia Varga (Budapest: Bak-Fisch, 1997), 171–82, and "Medieval Central Europe: An Invention or a Discovery?" in *The Paradoxes of Unintended Consequences*, ed. Lord Dahrendorf, Yehuda Elkana, et al. (Budapest: CEU Press, 2000), 251–64. On the birth of medieval Central Europe, see also Aleksander Gieysztor, *L'Europe nouvelle autour de l'An Mil. La Papauté, l'Empire et les "nouveaux venus"* (Rome: Unione Internazionale degli Istituti di Archeologia, 1997). For a helpful historiographic survey on the formation of the idea of Central Europe in the secondary literature, see Gábor Klaniczay, "The Birth of a New Europe about A.D. 1000: Conversion, Transfer of Institution Models, New Dynamics," in *Eurasian Transformations, Tenth to Thirteenth Centuries: Crystallizations, Divergences, Renaissance*, ed. Johann P. Arnason and Björn Wittrock (Leiden: Brill, 2004).

21. William Francis Ryan has researched Eastern Slavic (especially Russian) magical sources; see especially *The Bathhouse at Midnight: An Historical Survey of Magic and Divination in Russia* (Stroud: Sutton, 1999), and "Magic and Divination: Old Russian Sources," in *The Occult in Russian and Soviet Culture*, ed. Bernice Glatzer Rosenthal (Ithaca: Cornell University Press, 1997), 35–58. See also the following: Ihor Ševčenko, "Remarks on the Diffusion of Byzantine Scientific and Pseudo-Scientific Literature Among the Orthodox Slavs," *Slavonic and East European Review* 59 (1981): 321–45; Mirko Dražen Grmek, *Les sciences dans les manuscripts slaves orientaux du Moyen Âge* (Paris: Université de Paris, 1959); and Grmek, "Les Sciences chez les Slaves au Moyen Âge," in *Histoire générale des sciences*, vol. 1, *La science antique et médiévale*, ed. René Taton (Paris: Presses Universitaires de France, 1966), 557–67.

22. Still, if someone is interested in science and magic in Dalmatia, the following will be helpful: Žarko Dadić, *Egzaktne Znanosti Hrvatskoga Srednjovjekovlja* (Zagreb: Globus, 1991), and Mirko Dražen Grmek, "The Life and Astrological-Medical Ideas of Federik Grisogono of Zadar," *Medical Journal* (Zagreb) 92 (1970): 34–42. For a helpful bibliography of Grmek's further works related to this field, see Danielle Gourevitch, ed., *Maladie et Maladies: histoire et conceptualization: Mélanges en l'Honneur de Mirko Grmek* (Geneva: Librarie Droz, 1992), xvi–xlv. A potential reader interested in Petrus Bonus of Ferrara might want to consult Chiara Crisciani's study, "The Conception of Alchemy as Expressed in the *Pretiosa Margarita Novella* of Petrus Bonus of Ferrara," *Ambix* 20 (1973): 165–81.

The western boundaries of my region are somewhat less clear, and defined according to different, rather practical considerations. Eastern Germany, Austria, and Italy are historically and politically closely related to Hungary, Bohemia, and Poland. Culturally, these countries formed an organic unity; Polish, Bohemian, and Hungarian students frequently studied in German and Italian universities, while German and Italian humanists and professors often came to Central European institutions. Apparently, political boundaries did not present any obstacle. However, the source materials provided by Italy, Austria, and Germany are substantially different both in quantity and quality. In the present study, I intend to rely on a well-defined and delimited Polish, Bohemian, and Hungarian sample. It follows that I will not present a systematic survey of the magical manuscripts of Vienna[23] or Erfurt,[24] for example, because such an attempt would go beyond the scope of a single book, but whenever the traces lead to the West, I intend to follow them naturally, and I will include occasionally material from beyond the western limits of my area. The reason for this is that Central European universities were founded at much the same time and in much the same way as the universities of the German-language area (Heidelberg, Cologne, Leipzig, and Erfurt), and that political boundaries did not stop the wandering students of the fifteenth century. Their "homeland"—the university—was an international formation,[25] and they traveled freely, without paying much attention to national divisions, carrying their books, that is, my sources, with them.

Having thus acquainted ourselves with the idea of Central Europe, it is still not quite clear why this region should be treated separately as far as the texts of learned magic are concerned. In other words: what is so distinctive in this region with respect to the field of magic?

Two answers can be given to this question. The first is related to a tendency already pointed out by the scholarship dealing with the diffusion of Arabic magical texts in Western Europe: copies of magical texts "found an attentive audience only after about . . . 1400 in Central Europe."[26] Put differently, the answers to the questions posed in this book can be found in fifteenth-century manuscripts. The second characteristic feature of this area is a relative tolerance shown toward texts

---

23. The exclusion of Vienna may seem particularly arbitrary, since the University of Vienna was founded roughly the same time as the universities of Prague, Kraków, and Pécs, and Vienna itself lies almost two hundred kilometers east of Prague, and thus must be considered Central European. My reasons, I repeat, are merely functional; Vienna alone possesses more extensive manuscript holdings than all the libraries where I carried out systematic searches.

24. A fruitful field of research might be based on the twenty treatises on magic in the fifteenth-century library of Erfurt. See David Pingree, "The Diffusion of Arabic Magical Texts in Western Europe," in *La diffusione delle scienze Islamiche nel Medio Evo Europeo*, ed. B. Scarcia Amoretti (Rome: Accademia Nazionale dei Lincei, 1987), 58 n. 1.

25. On the metaphor, see Klaniczay, "Late Medieval Central European Universities."

26. Pingree, "Diffusion," esp. 79 and 59.

on learned magic. This tolerance—which I definitely do not want to overstate—is to be understood by Western European standards. While in Paris, statutes and theological declarations condemning various forms and practices of magic were issued one after the other in the later Middle Ages, in Central Europe it was apparently without the slightest sign of fear of prosecution that university students and professors kept magical items in their libraries.

Because the two phenomena are closely related, they can be investigated in parallel. In order to understand why magical texts arrived in Central Europe with such a considerable delay, it is necessary to observe the particular traits of the intellectual history of the area. Roughly speaking, the use and copying of magical texts presupposes the presence of a certain learned culture, and the emergence of a sufficient number of learned scribes, compilers, and book collectors to sustain such a culture requires an intellectual milieu that only universities, monasteries, and royal or episcopal courts can provide.

The date suggested as the arrival of the magical texts in Central Europe coincides with the time of the reorganization of the University of Kraków (originally founded in 1364). After the death of its founder, King Casimir the Great, the university fell into a state of decline that ended only thanks to a new stimulus received from Queen Jadwiga, in the last years of the fourteenth century. This renewal opened up a golden age in the life of the university, in which, in the first half of the fifteenth century, two private chairs were founded especially for the studies of astronomy and astrology. These chairs yielded many new astronomical and astrological works, and provided the history of science with several generations of astronomers, while supplying various clerical and secular courts of Central Europe with thoroughly trained astrologers. Because of this flourishing, the University of Kraków became an international center of astronomy as well as of astrology, and it had an extensive relationship with other centers in Bologna, Paris, Vienna, and the royal court of Matthias Corvinus, king of Hungary. Probably without exaggeration, the contemporaries merely noted that "Kraków is stuffed with astrologers."[27]

The Prague milieu, in contrast, was somewhat less astrologically oriented. On the one hand, interest in alchemy was already present in Bohemia two hundred years before its late sixteenth-century apogee at the time of Emperor Rudolf II. This interest or even practice of the science of alchemy was probably stronger than a pure curiosity on the part of a confined intellectual circle, because we have an alchemical work dating from the middle of the fifteenth century written in the vernacular, that is, in Czech.[28] On the other hand, natural and image magic, as

---

27. "Cracovia astrologis referta est." Aleksander Birkenmajer, *Études d'histoire des sciences en Pologne*, Studia Copernicana 4 (Wrocław: Zakład Narodowy im. Ossolińskich, 1972), 491.
28. See Chapter 5, note 41, and the accompanying text.

well as divination, are well represented in the manuscript collections of the first university of Central Europe in Prague. Apart from the university, the monastic context must have also provided fertile ground for an interest in magic: a number of magical texts have come to us from the Augustinian libraries of Třeboň and Brno.

Finally, the southernmost intellectual center of the time (no less interested in the celestial sciences) was the court of King Matthias of Hungary. King Matthias's enthusiasm for Renaissance Neoplatonic philosophy, his fascination with Hermetism, reflected also by the books of his famous Corvinian Library, his enthusiastic correspondence with Marsilio Ficino, the other Italian humanists staying and working in his court, are described by contemporary sources and researched by modern studies. According to Antonio Bonfini, one of the learned Italians staying in the royal household, members of the court were deeply concerned with Neoplatonism, and the names of Plato, Pseudo-Dionysus the Areopagite, Hermes Trismegistos, Zoroaster, Orpheus, Plotinus, and Pythagoras were mentioned in philosophical discussions on a day-to-day basis.[29] It is also often emphasized that King Matthias invited great experts of astronomy and astrology, such as the Pole Martin Bylica of Olkusz, the Königsberg-born Johannes Regiomontanus, and perhaps even the Italian Galeotto Marzio to the newly founded university in Pozsony (present-day Bratislava), the so-called Academia Istropolitana.[30] Astrology was taken so seriously that Matthias consulted his court astrologer before campaigns and had the horoscope of his new university prepared.

This was the institutional milieu that served as fruitful soil, not only for the development of the celestial sciences, but also for a deep interest in magic. The intellectual centers listed so far copied and produced a considerable number of texts belonging to each branch of magic. In various courts of kings, archbishops, bishops, dukes, and princes, as well as in the newly founded Central European universities, a new type of intellectual found himself in a peculiar and convenient place for satisfying his interest and getting involved in research.

Yet is it possible to claim that Central Europe was the birthplace of a "center of magical studies"?[31]

Anticipating one of the negative conclusions of my research (partly in order to avoid hasty misinterpretations), let me emphasize here that there is no reason to suppose that magic played any genuine role in late medieval Kraków, Prague, or

---

29. Antonius Bonfini, *Symposium de virginitate et pudicitia coniugali,* ed. Stephanus Apró (Budapest: K. M. Egyetemi Nyomda, 1943), 119–20.
30. Ibid.
31. The expression "center of magical studies" is used by David Pingree for the late medieval St. Augustine's Abbey in Canterbury after he had identified a number of manuscripts of learned magic as having belonged to certain identifiable monks of the monastery (Pingree, "Diffusion," 94). Concerning these texts and their owners, as well as the extent to which "center of magical studies" can applied to St. Augustine's Abbey, see Page, "Magic at St. Augustine's," chap. 1.

Buda. Interest in various forms of magic did not constitute a unified or coherent movement either inside or outside the courtly and university life. If we take the extant manuscripts as starting points, and plot their locations on a map of Europe, we will see that Central Europe—especially Kraków—deserves special attention. By pursuing these lines further, we can then address the general issues of who produced and preserved these sources. On the other hand, however, if we proceed in the opposite direction, and wish to provide a general picture of the intellectual activity of the region, we can talk about a strong, consistent concern in astrology, but this claim cannot be extended to the question of magic, examples of which will remain relatively scattered and isolated.

The succeeding chapters follow the former of the two procedures. I start with a careful study of the sources themselves, presenting the main genres of magical literature one by one, then describe the extent to which the categories are represented in the surviving Central European source material, and examine whether the texts are mere imports from the Western manuscript tradition, or whether one can find local products, examples of "original" texts. The codicological context of the particular magical texts will also be questioned as veritable sources: the position of certain kinds of magic in the framework of learning can be better understood on the basis of the tracts that occur or travel together with them. In addition, an *excursus* departing from the main body of the argumentation of the book will focus on the visual material contained in the sources.

Part Two concentrates more on the human and institutional elements. Two chapters will be devoted to the role that magic played in monastic milieus and royal courts, while a third will survey the patterns of the founding of universities and go deeper into the secrets of the personal libraries of university professors and students. Special attention will be paid in two *excursus,* first to the question of the criminalization of practice of magic, and the dangers awaiting those who did not make a secret of their interest in the occult, and second to the transformation of the figure of the magician, as demonstrated by a historical example closely related to the Kraków material. Here is where we return to the person of Faustus.

The present work can expect basically two kinds of readers: the first has a good knowledge of the sources and genres of magic, but is supposedly less acquainted with the history of local universities and royal courts. The second is more familiar with these latter questions but does not necessarily recognize every magical text by its incipit. I have tried to find a way between the Scylla of leaving my audience uninformed and basic subjects unexplained and the Charybdis of boring some readers by too much popularization. I have had to repeat facts that are widely known in the Western scholarship of learned magic in order to introduce and characterize the categories I operate with. In a bibliographical essay, for example, situated at the end of the book, I have provided short overviews surveying the findings and the main tendencies of the secondary literature of the given branches of magic. These fairly conventional summaries are not meant to be significant contributions to scholarship, their purpose is to provide background knowledge for the readers who may need it. Similarly, my description of the foundation and early history of Central European universities will not contribute anything new to what has been said about the intellectual history of the area; however, I still needed to give some information on the milieu before getting to the subject of the private libraries of university people.

Remaining with the question of the readership of this book, I must also take into consideration the linguistic barrier that separates the three Central European countries from their German-speaking neighbors. The secondary literature and the primary sources of Austria, Germany, and Italy are accessible for the well-prepared modern scholar, but the same is not necessarily true for the Polish, Bohemian, and Hungarian material used in my work. One of my intentions and a *raison d'être* of this book is to provide this hypothetical scholar with further research tools.

PART ONE

Magic

1
Definitions and Classifications

Modern Attempts to Define and Classify Magic

Before becoming acquainted with the major types of magic and going through the catalog of magical texts, the reader has every right to expect a concise and exact definition of what is meant in the book by "magic." But it is not just pure courtesy toward the reader that obliges me to dwell upon the meaning of this word; disregarding the issue of a definition may even turn out to be perilous. It has been frequently pointed out that "magic," when applied in secondary literature, expresses the preconceptions, the ethnocentric projections, and the historical distortions of the researcher, rather than the content of what it purports to signify.[1]

Defining magic, however, is not a simple task. Modern experts on the history of magic have emphasized various components of medieval magical practices. Some of them gave general and necessarily true definitions with which one can only agree. The fairly inclusive description for example, given by Lynn Thorndike, the classic authority of the field early in his career, can hardly function as a definition: "Magic appears as a human art or group of arts employing varied materials in varied rites, often fantastic, to work a great variety of marvelous results, which offer man a release from his physical, social, and intellectual limitations, not by the imaginative and sentimental methods of music, melodrama, and romance, nor by religion's

---

1. See, for example, Hildred Geertz's criticism and Keith Thomas's answer concerning the use of the term "magic" in Keith Thomas, *Religion and the Decline of Magic* (London: Weidenfeld and Nicholson, 1971), in Geertz and Thomas, "An Anthropology of Religion and Magic: Two Views," *Journal of Interdisciplinary History* 6 (1975): 71–89 and 91–111. See also Einar Thomassen, "Is Magic a Subclass of Ritual?" in *The World of Ancient Magic: Papers from the First International Samson Eitrem Seminar at the Norwegian Institute at Athens, 4–8 May, 1997*, ed. David R. Jordan, Hugo Montgomery, and Einar Thomassen (Bergen: The Norwegian Institute at Athens, 1999), 55–66.

spiritual experience, but by operations supposed to be efficacious here in the world of external reality."[2]

Since Thorndike, a number of aspects of magic have been offered as definitive. Some scholars follow certain anthropological traditions, and present magic as a nonrational way of thinking, a symbolic system, that has expressive, psychological, and sociological efficacy rather than instrumental rationality and truth value.[3] Others disagree with the statement that magic only expresses hopes and wishes, and put more emphasis on its alternative rationality. Richard Kieckhefer, for example, argues that in the Middle Ages magic was considered as a "rationally explicable practice with objective rationality."[4] Similarly, William Eamon looks for an inner quality of the practice of magic, namely that it serves to understand and manipulate nature through its secret correspondences beyond the abilities of ordinary humans,[5] while Bert Hansen speaks about technology and a special kind of instrumentality emerging in magical practices.[6] It is worth adding that on the north transept fore portal of Chartres Cathedral, magic is portrayed as one of the four mechanical arts.[7] William Ryan, although not intending to give the perfect definition, emphasizes an external, legal point of view: the disapproved (or even criminalized) character of the practice of magic.[8]

To cut this introduction short, I quote William Ryan again, who, in turn, applies to the question of magic what Gábor Klaniczay wrote on the attempts at presenting a general theory of witchcraft: "The wide array of theoretical explanatory tools and comparative sets stand in puzzling contrast to the ease with which each general

---

2. Lynn Thorndike, "Some Medieval Conceptions of Magic," *Monist* 25 (1915), esp. 138–39.

3. Among medievalist magic scholars, Valerie Flint's conception of magic can be classified as being of this type; see Flint, *The Rise of Magic in Early Medieval Europe* (Oxford: Clarendon Press, 1991), 12 and 406. For a critical but helpful review on the book, see Brian Vickers, "On the Rise of Magic in Early Medieval Europe," *History of European Ideas* 18 (1994): 275–87. See also Alexander Murray, "Missionaries and Magic in Dark-Age Europe," review of *The Rise of Magic in Early Medieval Europe* by Valerie Flint, *Past and Present* 136 (1992): 186–205. On Flint's views on medieval magic, see Richard Kieckhefer, "The Specific Rationality of Medieval Magic," *American Historical Review* 99 (1994): 813–36.

4. Kieckhefer, "Specific Rationality," esp. 822. See also Kieckhefer, *Magic in the Middle Ages*, 8–17, and I. C. Jarvie and Joseph Agassi, "The Problem of the Rationality of Magic," in *Rationality*, ed. Brian Wilson (Oxford: Harper & Row, 1970).

5. Eamon, *Science and the Secrets of Nature*, 23. It would be unfair not to mention the fact that Eamon did not intend to define magic; still, this proposition can be viewed as such.

6. Bert Hansen, "Science and Magic," in *Science in the Middle Ages*, ed. David C. Lindberg (Chicago: University of Chicago Press, 1978), esp. 484: "Magic is characterized by the utilization of 'occult forces' (that is, forces either supernatural, or natural but hidden) to accomplish specific desired ends, often by means of words or symbols."

7. See Michael Camille, "Visual Art in Two Manuscripts of the *Ars Notoria*," in Fanger, *Conjuring Spirits*, 135.

8. Ryan, *Bathhouse at Midnight*, 2–5.

proposition can be contradicted."⁹ Apparently, the notion of magic, with all its historical, psychological, ethnological, sociological, and scientific aspects and modifications, eludes every attempt at one final and exact definition.

All expectations of defining magic on the analogy of science and religion and all hopes of demarcating it from their neighboring fields are based on the assumption that science and religion themselves can be defined for all times and places. However, neither religion nor science are static concepts, but rather dynamic constructions with changing frontiers. In any given historical period it is the wider circle of the learned community that determines what counts as a religious ritual, a scientific endeavor, or a magical act.¹⁰

Nonetheless, while theoretically oriented studies have become fully aware that the term "magic" itself is deeply problematical, a strong consensus seems to have emerged on why it should be kept as a useful research category.¹¹ One helpful way of getting out of the labyrinth while keeping this word in the scholarly terminology is to describe specific cases of magical practice (or, to be more precise, genres of the literature of magic), instead of defining sharply what is and what is not magic. Giving up the hope of finding one common constituent in every instance of magic, we can recognize a complicated network of various resemblances that—as Wittgenstein would say—"overlap and criss-cross," linking the particular examples. These examples are without sharp borders and form a family that we can call, for the sake of convenience, magic.¹²

In consequence, I will approach magic through its various textual manifestations. Instead of trying to work these forms into modern definitions, my point of departure will rather be a few medieval attempts at understanding, defining, classifying, and eventually condemning magic (authors such as Richard of Fournival, William of Auvergne, and the author of the great catalog of astrological and talismanic literature, the *Speculum astronomiae* [Mirror of the Celestial Sciences] will be considered here). I resolve magic into three main, but not sharply distinct

---

9. Ibid., 4; Gábor Klaniczay, "Witch-Hunting in Hungary: Social or Cultural Tensions," *Acta Ethnographica Academiae Scientiarum Hungariae* 37 (1991–92): esp. 67.

10. On the problems of defining magic as opposed to religion, see Henk Versnel, "Some Reflections on the Relationship Magic-Religion," *Numen* 38 (1991): 177–97, and Jan N. Bremmer, "Appendix: Magic *and* Religion," in *The Metamorphosis of Magic from Late Antiquity to the Early Modern Period*, ed. Bremmer and Jan R. Veenstra (Leuven: Peters, 2002), 267–71, as well as the publications listed in note 11.

11. On the notion of magic in antiquity and on the potentialities of defining it in relation to religion, see Jens Braarvig, "Magic: Reconsidering the Grand Dichotomy," in Jordan, Montgomery, and Thomassen, *World of Ancient Magic*, 21–54, and Thomassen, "Is Magic a Subclass of Ritual?"

12. Ludwig Wittgenstein, *Philosophical Investigations* (Oxford: Blackwell, 1992), §§ 66–67. I had come to this conclusion before I read Versnel's article, "Some Reflections," in which the author also finds the Wittgensteinian concept of family resemblances a most helpful aid in keeping magic as a practical category.

categories—natural, image, and ritual magic. This will not cover all the occurrences of magic; still, it will help us understand what texts were considered magical in the Middle Ages.

Religion or Science?

Medieval commentators understood magic in one of two ways. The first saw magic as another, socially disapproved form of religion. If the approach was condemnatory, magic was seen as a perversion of religion, one that also operated with ritual tools, but one that, instead of abiding by the true aims of religion, tended to turn to demonic forces. The second tradition associated magical practice with science, and often presented it as an alternative, or mistaken (even bastard) science, emphasizing—in contrast to demonic intervention—the occult powers, natural forces, universal sympathies, and secret correspondences that it utilizes.[13]

Advocates of the first approach usually went back to Augustine's theory, which was indeed the first attempt at a sophisticated and comprehensive model of magical action.[14] In this model, magic appears in the context of the theory of signs as an act of communication with demonic powers (while Christian rituals are also acts of communication, but only with the divine sphere). Thus, all superstitious practices, including divination and astrology, presuppose an implicit or explicit pact with demons. This is valid even in the case where the operator—deceived by the demons—is not aware of the pact, because this pact is secured by the magical language, signs, and rituals he has applied. For a reader of Augustine, basically every instance of magic—however innocent it may seem—seems to be ultimately associated with idolatry and demonolatry, and becomes consequently harmful. Augustine was well aware of the common features and elements of the rituals of magic and those of religion (prayers, sacraments, and the cult of relics). It is true—he wrote—that what magicians do is often similar to what saints do: the difference lies not in the visible realm but in what is secretly implied. While saints communicate with divine powers for the greater good, magicians seek their own, selfish ends.

This categorical rejection of a wide range of magical practices as ultimately demonic prevailed in the early Middle Ages, and remained a strong conviction even after new theories challenged its monopolistic position. A vast debate developed in the theological and scientific discourse on the nature and power of demons, on how they can be compelled, and on the dangers threatening the invoker. A certain

---

13. On the parallel histories of these two conceptions, see again Kieckhefer, "Specific Rationality," 814–21, Kieckhefer, *Magic in the Middle Ages*, 8–17; and Robert A. Markus, "Augustine on Magic: A Neglected Semiotic Theory," *Revue des Études Augustiniennes* 40 (1994): 375–88.

14. His fullest account on magic is to be found in book 2 of the *De doctrina christiana*, and in the *De civitate Dei*, bks. 8–10. For a helpful semiotic analysis, see Markus, "Augustine on Magic."

tension behind the debate was caused by the fact that the medieval concept of "demon" was born of two different traditions: the Christian notion of "demon" as a fallen angel working under the Devil, and the Greco-Roman concept of a more material "daimon," who is a neutral (occasionally even benign), powerful, and knowledgeable spirit who, in certain circumstances, may obey its invoker.[15] Thus, it is not primarily the existence or the efficacy of demons that was debated, but their willingness to cooperate with humans.

As early as the seventh century, Isidore of Seville (ca. 560–636) acknowledged the competence of demons: he taught that demonic magic should be avoided, precisely because demons were effective—but harmful—agents. Johannes of Francofordia, a professor of theology at the University of Heidelberg (between 1404 and 1440), added an interesting point to the subject when treating the question whether demons can be compelled with the help of characters, figures, or words.[16] He pointed out that the demon—thanks to his extensive knowledge in the field of herbs, stones, and other elements of the world—is the best doctor.[17] A native of Poland and a former student of Padua, the thirteenth-century Witelo, who is otherwise known as the author of a comprehensive work on optics, also arrived at a noteworthy conclusion.[18] In his long and philosophical letter on the nature of demons, Witelo put forward the idea that demons are intermediary creatures between human beings and the angels, that they are mortal but very long-lived, and that they have an exceptional knowledge of the world and possess superhuman power.[19] There is

---

15. On the history of medieval conceptions of demons, see Richard Kieckhefer, *Forbidden Rites: A Necromancer's Manual of the Fifteenth Century* (Stroud: Sutton, 1997), 154–60, and Jeffrey Burton Russell, *Lucifer, The Devil in the Middle Ages* (Ithaca: Cornell University Press, 1984).

16. "Questio, utrum potestas cohercendi demonis fieri possit per caracteres, figuras atque verborum prolationes." See Joseph Hansen, ed., *Quellen und Untersuchungen zur Geschichte des Hexenwahns und der Hexenverfolgung im Mittelalter* (Bonn: Carl Georgi, 1901), 71–82.

17. "Ex quo sequitur quod demon est optimus medicus valde cognoscens rerum naturas scilicet herbarum lapidum et huiusmodi." Ibid.

18. Witelo's *Perspectivorum libri decem* is an important source on medieval optics, which he wrote in his years spent in the papal court of Viterbo (1269–73). For Witelo's life and his *Perspectiva* in English, see Sabetai Unguru, ed., *Witelonis perspectivae Liber primus: An English Translation with Introduction and Commentary and Latin Edition of the Mathematical Book of Witelo's "Perspectiva,"* Studia Copernicana 15 (Wrocław: Zakład Narodowy im. Ossolińskich, 1977).

19. On Witelo and his *De natura daemonum* in French, see Birkenmajer, *Études d'histoire des sciences en Pologne*, 97–434; the text itself is reproduced on 122–36. For a later analysis of Witelo's life, sources, historical context, and cosmological conceptions, in Polish, with a second publication of the letter, see Jerzy Burchardt, ed., *List Witelona do Ludwika we Lwówku Śląskim* (Vitelo's Letter to Ludwig in Lwówek), Studia Copernicana 19 (Wrocław: Zakład Narodowy im. Ossolińskich, 1979). See also Renata Mikołajczyk, "*Non sunt nisi phantasiae et imaginationes:* A Medieval Attempt at Explaining Demons," in *Communicating with the Spirits,* ed. Éva Pócs and Gábor Klaniczay (Budapest: CEU Press, 2005), 40–52, and Eugenia Paschetto, "Witelo et Pietro d'Abano à propos des demons," in *L'homme et son univers au Moyen Age,* ed. Christian Wenin, vol. 2 (Louvain-la-Neuve: Editions de l'Institut supérieur de philosophie, 1986), 675–82.

no reason to be afraid of them, since although occasionally they do bad things, this is against their essentially good nature.[20]

This positive theory on the functioning of demons, however, was by no means shared by the mainstream. Instead, the consensus of theologians echoed the famous 1398 conclusions issued by the theology faculty of the University of Paris: it is not true that good, benign, and omniscient demons exist, nor is it true that demons can be bound by magic arts: they just pretend to be compelled.[21] A few years later, Jean Gerson (1363–1429), the chancellor of the University of Paris and a man of great learning, arrived at the same conclusions in his systematic study on magic: demons cannot be compelled by magic arts; they only pretend that they are compelled so that they will be adored like gods, and will be able to deceive their invokers.[22]

While the demonic understanding of magic had a privileged position in the early Middle Ages because of the twelfth- and thirteenth-century impact of the transmission of Arabic magical and divinatory works, the condemnations became more differentiated, and the classifications more elaborated.[23] This was the age when the second, scientific interpretation of magic emerged. As a result, every magical text had the opportunity to pretend to be less demonic than it was in reality, and they could consequently find toleration in some calm and unnoticed area of the complicated typologies. But from where did this scientific reading of magical texts arrive?

The Arabic tradition provided the West not only with various practices of magic but also with some theoretical background. As a matter of fact, there was only one text (known to the Latin readers from the thirteenth century) that offered a comprehensive theory of magic, *De radiis stellarum* (On the Rays of the Stars),

---

20. The letter is not really a Polish source: it was written in Padua toward the end of Witelo's legal studies, and its four surviving copies are in London, Vatican, Paris, and Naples (see Burchardt, *List Witelona*, 19, 43–54); and in them the text occurs together with other sources of natural philosophy, but two quite similar texts also appear in these codices: Roger Bacon's *Epistola de secretis operibus artis* and Arnaldus de Villanova's *De improbatione spirituum*.

21. Henricus Denifle and Aemilio Chatelain, *Chartularium Universitatis Parisiensis*, vol. 4 (Paris: Culture et Civilisation, 1897), 32–35. Article 23: "Quod aliqui demones boni sunt, aliqui benigni, aliqui omniscientes, alii nec salvati nec damnati, error." Article 17: "Quod per tales artes daemones veraciter coguntur et compelluntur et non potius ita se cogi fingunt ad seducendos homines: error." On the condemnations of September 19, 1398, see also Jean-Patrice Boudet, "Les Condamnations de la magie à Paris en 1398," *Revue Mabillon*, n.s., 12 (2001): 121–57.

22. Jean Gerson, *De erroribus circa artem magicam*, in *Oeuvres complètes*, ed. Palémon Glorieux, vol. 10, *L'oeuvre polémique* (Paris, Desclée, 1973), 77–90. See also Gerson's *Trilogium astrologiae theologizatae*, in *Oeuvres complètes*, 10:90–108, Prop. 14: "Addens daemones non cogi per artes magicas, sed ita fingere se cogi ut colantur sicut dii et hominis fallacia multiplici decipiant." On the relationship of the 1398 condemnations and Gerson's works, see Boudet, "Les Condamnations de la magie."

23. On the gradual "positivization" of magic in the later Middle Ages, see Claire Fanger and Frank Klaassen, "Magic III: Middle Ages," in *Dictionary of Gnosis and Western Esotericism*, 724–31, ed. Wouter J. Hanegraaff et al. (Leiden: Brill, 2005).

attributed to Al-Kindi (ca. 800–ca. 870), the famous Arabic philosopher of Baghdad.[24] (It is true, however, that various chapters of the *Picatrix* also offer some theoretical explanation of how magic works; nevertheless, the text as a whole is not primarily philosophical.) The treatise *De radiis stellarum* presents a world of universal harmony. This world functions according to rational norms: the celestial bodies (planets and constellations) regulate earthly events through the rays emanating from them. Since it is their influence that is responsible for the terrestrial variety of things, the magician who is familiar with the condition of the celestial realm will have sufficient knowledge about the objects of the lower world. But he will know even more than that: a close reading of the celestial realm will also reveal the past and the future. In addition, sufficient knowledge about the constitution of one individual in the lower world will mirror—thanks again to the universal harmony—the structure of the celestial world. The book also contains chapters devoted to prayers addressed to God, to the virtue (that is, the inner power) of words,[25] and to magical figures, characters, and images. Nonetheless, this philosophical explanation does not go into detail regarding the actual practice of magic; the technical part is left to texts such as Thebit's *De imaginibus* and the *Picatrix*.

Al-Kindi's *De radiis stellarum* had a wide distribution in Europe. As a rule, it was copied together with philosophical and scientific texts.[26] However popular it was, and however complete its theory might have been, for obvious theological and philosophical reasons the Christian West could not accept its purely astrological explanation without any further modifications and without any reference to demonic involvement. The Kindian principles were rejected by the authorities of the University of Paris on two occasions; they were on the list of condemned articles both in 1277 and in 1398.[27]

24. Al-Kindi's *De radiis stellarum* was published with an extensive and helpful introductory study by Marie-Thérèse d'Alverny and Françoise Hudry, *AHDLMA* 41 (1974): 139–260. See also d'Alverny, "Kindiana," *AHDLMA* 47 (1980): 277–87, and WP 155–74.

25. On the power of words, see Claire Fanger, "Things Done Wisely by a Wise Enchanter: Negotiating the Power of Words in the Thirteenth Century," *Esoterica* 1 (1999): 97–132, http://www.esoteric.msu.edu/esoteric.msu.edu/Fanger.html.

26. Three copies of *De radiis stellarum* can be found today in Central European libraries, but they all come from German cities. Two different versions occur at the end of the Prague manuscript KMK L LXXVII (Podlaha 1323). The first, copied in the thirteenth century, was supplemented by a second one by a fourteenth-century owner in Goslar. It is not known how the manuscript arrived in Prague. The other copy is kept today in the University Library of Wrocław, somewhat isolated among theological and moral tracts. Originally, it belonged to Johannes Gode de Baudissin, the rector of the University of Leipzig, and was inherited later by the Dominican monastery of Wrocław. D'Alverny and Hudry doubt that the Dominicans noticed the presence of this text of magical theory at all among the rich collection inherited from Johannes Gode. Al-Kindi, *De radiis stellarum*, 178.

27. The articles concerned with theories of celestial causation, such as that of Al-Kindi, in 1277 were *articuli* 74us, 133us, 162us, and 167us; in 1398, they were 26us and 27us. See Denifle and Chatelain, *Chartularium Universitatis Parisiensi*, 4:32–35; Boudet, "Les Condamnations de la magie";

The Greek and Arabic traditions offered a huge corpus of astrological and magical texts that could be partly, but not fully, incorporated into Christian natural philosophy. These texts, providing astrological techniques, divinatory devices, alchemical transmutations, and magical manipulations, were quickly and widely disseminated, read, copied, and collected from the early thirteenth century on. Christian intellectuals were somewhat ambivalent about these works; all testify to a certain cautiousness, as we will see. As time progressed, there was a growing tendency to differentiate, categorize, and tolerate; as a rule, however, we can say that the Christian reception of magical literature was more complicated than a simple import of the theory of Al-Kindi. Thomas Aquinas (1225–74), for example, in his letter to an unknown Italian soldier, admits the licit function of certain astrological causality and accepts the occult power of some earthly objects (such as the rhubarb, the magnet, or the relics of saints), but ascribes the effect of images and formulas to the activity of demons.[28]

Aquinas's impact is undeniable. However, if we want to observe the reception of the magical works in a more detailed way, and if we want to set up a thorough taxonomy of these texts, the best possible method is not to turn to the great theologians, because even though they expressed their opinion on magical texts, they rarely had firsthand knowledge about them. Instead, we should rather rely on the works of those—perhaps lesser known—authors who had the opportunity to study the texts carefully, and had consequently a direct acquaintance with the sources they wrote about.

Licit or Forbidden? William of Auvergne and the *Speculum Astronomiae*

In order to define the categories with which we will operate throughout this study, let us turn to two thirteenth-century authorities who had detailed knowledge of the freshly imported texts: William of Auvergne, bishop of Paris (ca. 1180–1249), and the mysterious author of the *Speculum astronomiae* (who had long been identified with Albertus Magnus).[29] The intentions of the two authors are quite similar: both want to defend the licit and innocent scientific literature from the contaminating proximity of necromantic works, since—as they say in a worried tone—

---

and Roland Hissete, *Enquête sur les 219 articles condamnés à Paris le 7 mars 1277* (Louvain: Publications Universitaires, 1977).

28. Joseph Bernard McAllister, ed., *The Letter of Saint Thomas Aquinas "De Occultis Operibus Naturae"* (Washington, D.C.: The Catholic University of America Press, 1939). For a more recent edition, see *Opera Omnia* (Léonine edition), vol. 43 (Rome: Editori di San Tommaso, 1976), 159–86. See also WP 223–59.

29. On the main arguments of the scholarly debate over the identity of the author of the *Speculum astronomiae*, see the bibliographical essay in appendix 1.

even philosophers and learned men who are not acquainted with magic and astrology tend to label innocent books and practices necromantic.[30] Demarcating science from nonscience, both authors provide exhaustive lists of titles, text *incipits*, and content descriptions.

But—one may inquire—if the necromantic books are so harmful, how is it that these authors know so much about them? As they hasten to clarify, their familiarity with the books of magic dates from a much earlier date. The bishop of Paris had inspected them when he was still a young man;[31] the author of the *Speculum* says that he had studied them long before he decided to write about this issue, and because he shrank with horror from them, he did not have a perfect memory regarding their number, titles, *incipits*, contents, or even authors.[32] As we will immediately see, the reliability and meticulousness of their work seriously undermine these disclaimers.

William of Auvergne does not follow Augustine in rejecting all magic as a demonic enterprise.[33] In his *De legibus* (On the Laws, 1228–30) he introduces the term "natural magic," and declares that it is the eleventh part of natural philosophy.[34] William admits that there are learned people who reject this classification, but asserts that they do so because they are unfamiliar with the texts of natural magic and think that demons are involved in all magical practices. Such learned

---

30. William of Auvergne, *De legibus*, chap. 24, 69bD–70aE, in *Opera Omnia* (Paris: Andraeas Pralard, 1674; rpr., Frankfurt am Main, 1963); Paola Zambelli, *The "Speculum Astronomiae" and Its Enigma: Astrology, Theology, and Science in Albertus Magnus and His Contemporaries,* Boston Studies in the Philosophy of Science 135 (Boston: Kluwer Academic Publishers, 1992), 208–9.

31. William of Auvergne, *De legibus*, chap. 25, 78aF: "haec omnia in libris iudiciorum astronomiae, et in libris magorum atque maleficiorum tempore adolescentiae nostrae nos meminimus inspexisse." Secondary literature refers usually to two editions of William of Auvergne's *Opera Omnia:* the first published in 1591 by Zenarus in Venice (which Thorndike used in *HMES*, 2:338–71), and the second in 1674 in Paris by Andraeas Pralard. The latter was reprinted in Frankfurt am Main in 1963. I will refer to the pages of the second edition while giving also the chapter numbers. As Thorndike mentioned, the chapter titles figuring in both printed versions are not very helpful.

32. For the Latin text, its English translation, and a detailed study of the *Speculum astronomiae*, see Zambelli, *The "Speculum Astronomiae" and Its Enigma*, 242–43. I use the English translation established by C. Burnett, K. Lipincott, D. Pingree, and P. Zambelli. The text was first published, together with the description of the manuscripts, in Paola Zambelli, Stefano Caroti, Michela Pereira, and Stefano Zamponi, eds., *Speculum astronomiae* (Pisa: Domus Galileana, 1977). Also see *HMES*, 2:577–92, 692–719, and Lynn Thorndike, "Further Consideration of the *Experimenta, Speculum astronomiae*, and *De secretis mulierum* Ascribed to Albertus Magnus," *Speculum* 30 (1955): 413–43.

33. Steven P. Marrone, "William of Auvergne on Magic in Natural Philosophy and Theology," in *Was ist Philosophie im Mittelalter?* (Akten des X. Internationalen Kongresses für mittelalterliche Philosophie der Société Internationale pour l'Étude de la Philosophie Médiévale 25. bis 30. August 1997 in Erfurt), ed. Jan Aertsen and Andreas Speer (Berlin: Walter de Gruyter, 1998), 741–48.

34. William of Auvergne, *De legibus*, chap. 24, 69bD: "Et de operibus huiusmodi est magia naturalis, quam necromantiam, seu philosophicam philosophi vocant, licet multum improprie, et est totius licentiae naturalis pars undecima."

people, however, are mistaken—William continues—natural magic operates simply and innocently with natural virtues (*virtutes naturales*) of the objects of nature.

William of Auvergne returns to the issue of natural magic in his more extensive work, *De universo* (On the Universe, 1231–36). Here he reports a number of experiments relying on the hidden power and secret correspondences of herbs, stones, and animals, all belonging to the field of natural magic, which do not imply demonic intervention, or rely on curiosity. (We should bear in mind that curiosity for the medieval theologian is not identical with the positive and appraisable attitude of the scientist who questions the natural world, it is rather viewed as a vain desire to accumulate knowledge of things that are not necessarily meant to be known.)[35] He concedes that not every branch of magic is as innocent as natural magic. Divinations performed with the help of demons and judicial astrology, which purports to predict particular events falling under free will are to be condemned, as Augustine insisted, because they do not function according to the order of nature.[36]

The bishop is also very critical of magical operations that make use the power of images, figures, and characters.[37] Those, for instance, who attribute virtue to the images and try to expel scorpions with the image of a scorpion are mistaken. These methods belong to what he calls *magisterium imaginum*,[38] and what we will call image magic.[39]

William condemns image magic because, in his opinion, images and talismans have no power in spiritual matters or over earthly objects. Under this category, he lists a number of texts attributed to Hermes, Belenus, and Toz Graecus in what amounts to a bibliography of the medieval Hermetic corpus. This was first mention in the Christian West for some of the titles in his list.[40] The numerous and scattered references he provided proved to be particularly useful for posterity: based on this inventory it became possible to reconstruct the library of Hermetic works available in the thirteenth century. These works were translated in the twelfth century, some from Hellenistic Greek texts, but the majority from ninth-century Arabic sources on talismanic magic. Among them, William mentions not only the rather philosophically oriented *Asclepius* but also a number of technical-operative works on Hermetic magic, such as the *Liber lunae* (Book of the Moon), the *Liber*

---

35. "Curiositas, quae est libido sciendi non necessaria." See William of Auvergne, *De universo* II 3 22, 1059–61.
36. Marrone, "William of Auvergne on Magic," 746–47.
37. William of Auvergne, *De legibus*, chap. 23, 67aB. See also WP 175–213.
38. William of Auvergne, *De universo* II 2 76, 929bA–930bE.
39. "Talismanic magic," "celestial magic," or "texts on engraved images" are also widely used labels for this category.
40. David Pingree, "Learned Magic in the Time of Frederick II," in *Le scienze alla corte di Federico II, Sciences at the court of Frederick II*, 39–56, Micrologus Library 2 (Turnhout: Brepols, 1994), 41.

de quattuor confectionibus (The Book on the Four Recipes), the *Liber de annulis septem planetarum* (The Rings of the Seven Planets), the *Antimaquis,* and the *Libri septem planetarum* (The Book of the Seven Planets), practical texts that will be discussed further.[41]

For our present purposes, it is enough to say that William of Auvergne set up two major categories for the newly imported magical texts (besides judicial astrology and the openly demonic items): that of accepted natural magic, the operations of which rely on *virtutes naturales* and follow the order of nature (even if they somewhat accelerate natural processes), and that of image magic (*magisterium imaginum*), the underlying principles of which he condemns as implicitly or explicitly demonic.

The second category, that is, the manipulation of operative images, becomes a principal subject and a place for further differentiation in another important source on the history of magic, the *Speculum astronomiae*. The *Speculum* is a detailed annotated bibliography providing the titles, *incipits,* and occasionally summaries of the contents of astrological and magical texts.[42] This example of the otherwise rather boring genre of bibliographies provoked huge attention in philological circles. Its author intended it as a guide to the medieval reader through the labyrinth of the sudden bounty of astrological literature, and offers—unintentionally— to the modern historian an excellent research tool for identifying sources that are not—or hardly—known. His explicit purpose was to differentiate between useful astrological works on the one hand, and harmful necromantic books on images, illusions, characters, rings, and sigils on the other. This latter category—he writes—has become too closely associated with the first, innocent one, as necromancers had borrowed certain astronomical observations in order to render themselves more credible. These necromancers pretended to be concerned with astrology only in order to disguise their necromancy. However, the author of the *Speculum* promises, God willing, to disclose their poison.[43]

It is obvious that the unknown author of the *Speculum* belongs in the company of the best Latin connoisseurs of magic of the thirteenth century, such as William of Auvergne and Michael Scot.[44] Not only did he have the education to compile

---

41. Paolo Lucentini, "L'Ermetismo magico nel sec. XIII," in *Sic itur ad astra: Studien zur mittelalterlichen, insbesondere arabischen, Wissenschaftgeschichte. Festschrift für Paul Kunitzsch zum 70. Geburtstag,* ed. Menso Folkerts and Richard Lorch (Wiesbaden: Harrassowitz Verlag, 2000), 409–50; Antonella Sannino, "Ermete mago e alchimista nelle biblioteche di Guglielmo d'Alvernia e Ruggero Bacone," *Studi medievali* 40 (2000): 151–209 (see 166–79 for a list of the works mentioned or alluded to in *De legibus,* especially in chaps. 23–27).

42. For the text, see Zambelli, *The "Speculum Astronomiae" and Its Enigma.*

43. Ibid., 208, "Proemium," and 222, "Caput quartum."

44. Michael Scot was an astrologer from the court of Emperor Frederick II, whose acquaintance with the texts of magic is documented in his *Liber introductorius*. On his report on astrological and magical literature, see Lucentini, "L'Ermetismo magico," esp. 420–24. The *Liber introductorius,* this huge trilogy summarizing the new science, is still unedited. An edition of its "Prohemium" can be

such a bibliography, he must have also had access to a well-equipped library. As it has been recently pointed out, the author was most probably consulting the exceptionally rich book collection of Richard of Fournival (ca. 1201–ca. 1260), astronomer, physician, mathematician, poet, book collector, and the chancellor of the cathedral of Amiens. The catalog of his library has come to us from the pen of Richard himself. In the *Biblionomia* (again a bibliography!), Richards guides his reader through his collection, displaying his thematically arranged books. Though not explicitly, and certainly without the intention of its author, the *Biblionomia* happens to be a classification of science and magic, just like the *Speculum*. Reading it, we can imagine accompanying the owner, who shows us his books classified into the categories of philosophy, rhetoric, arithmetic, medicine, law, and theology. However, at a certain point he brings the tour to an abrupt halt: he bars us from his collection of secret books, kept in a special section of his library. These books, he explains, cannot be exposed to the public eye because of their "profundity"— a term probably meant to refer to their dangerous magical content. We can only wonder what this dangerous content may have looked like, given that the *Liber vaccae* (The Book of the Cow) for example—with all its recipes for generating bees and cows one from another, for fecundating the latter in order to give birth to homunculi, for turning a man into the shape of a beast, and for other unusual experiments[45]—was not off-limits; indeed, it was classified with the medical books.[46] Fortunately, modern philology has established that the secret book section in Richard of Fournival's library was a primary source for the author of the *Speculum*,

---

found in Glenn Michael Edwards, "The *Liber Introductorius* of Michael Scot" (Ph.D. diss., University of Southern California, 1978). Hans Meier, a former librarian of the Warburg Institute, prepared a transcription of the *Liber introductorius* (CLM 10268, fols. 1–78) in 1928, when he was still a student in Hamburg. Although he was killed when his house was bombed in 1941, and his paper partly destroyed, a copy of his transcription (partly in proof copy, partly typed, and partly handwritten) is preserved in the library of the Warburg Institute.

45. From the extensive literature on the *Liber vaccae*, I have found the following particularly useful: David Pingree, "Plato's Hermetic *Book of the Cow*," in *Il Neoplatonismo nel Rinascimento*, ed. Pietro Prini (Rome: Istituto della Enciclopedia Italiana, 1993), 133–14; Pingree, "From Hermes to Jābir and the *Book of the Cow*," in *Magic and the Classical Tradition*, ed. Charles Burnett and W. F. Ryan, 19–28 (London: The Warburg Institute, 2006); Page, "Magic at St. Augustine's," chap. 3; Dag Nikolaus Hasse, "Plato arabico-latinus: Philosophy—Wisdom Literature—Occult Sciences," in *The Platonic Tradition in the Middle Ages*, ed. Stephen Gersh and Maarten J.F.M. Hoenen (Berlin: Walter de Gruyter, 2002), esp. 52–58; and William R. Newman, *Promethean Ambitions: Alchemy and the Quest to Perfect Nature* (Chicago: University of Chicago Press, 2004), 177–81.

46. It is not clear whether all or only part of the *Liber vaccae*—also known in the Middle Ages as *Liber anguemis*—was included in the book collection of Richard de Fornivale. It is listed in the following context: "Item epystola Ameti filii Abraham filii Macellani de proprietate, et est extracta de libro Galieni qui dicitur Anguemiz, et est ex dictis Humayni." See Léopold Delisle, ed., *Le Cabinet des manuscrits de la Bibliothèque Nationale*, vol. 2 (Paris: Imprimerie Nationale, 1876), esp. 533. On the medical section of Richard's library, see Eduard Seidler, "Die Medizin in der "Biblionomia" des Richard de Fournival," *Sudhoffs Archiv* 51 (1967): 44–54.

and the list of these books—which Richard never revealed—might have been fairly similar to what we find in the famous eleventh chapter of the *Speculum*.[47]

Elaborating his purifying enterprise in this eleventh chapter, the author of the *Speculum* gives us a detailed list of suspicious talismanic works of Arabic origin. If we took the author's claim seriously, that he did "not have a perfect memory"[48] regarding this literature, we would be puzzled by the quantity and accuracy of the references. He classifies these works into the abominable and the detestable, on the one hand, whose images derive their power from demonic influences, and the acceptable, on the other, whose images obtain their virtue solely from the celestial figures. Nevertheless, the author declares—rather surprisingly and somewhat inconsistently—that even the truly necromantic works should be preserved, not destroyed, until the time arrives when it will be useful to have them inspected. But even then, their inspectors should be wary of using them.[49] With the birth of modern philology this time has apparently arrived. Historians of science and scholars of magic find it most useful to inspect that small portion of the "abominable" and "detestable" magical texts which has not perished, and consequently the eleventh chapter of the *Speculum* containing their titles and descriptions enjoys today a noble position in every citation index of medieval studies.

As it has been previously mentioned, the threefold distinction of this chapter takes place within the category that is called *magisterium imaginum* by William of Auvergne, *scientia imaginum* by the author of the *Speculum*, and image magic throughout the present book. The abominable branch is considered such because it requires suffumigations (ritual burning of various essences, literally: from below) and invocations, and therefore cannot be anything but demonic. The second category—"somewhat less unsuitable, nevertheless detestable"—is only slightly better; it is "effected by means of inscribing characters which are to be exorcised by certain names," and regarding this practice "it is suspected that something lies under the names of the unknown language, which might be against the honor of the Catholic faith."[50] Much scholarly work has been done to find the reasons why— and according to what principles—the author differentiates between the two, rather similar categories. On the basis of their references to the talismanic texts, an attempt has been made to identify the first, abominable division with Hermetic magic, and the detestable one with Solomonic magic, the texts of which are usually attributed to the wise Solomon.[51]

---

47. On the relationship of the *Biblionomia* and the *Speculum*, see the bibliographical essay in appendix 1.
48. Zambelli, *The "Speculum Astronomiae" and Its Enigma*, 242.
49. Ibid., 270, "Caput Decimum Septimum."
50. Zambelli, *The "Speculum Astronomiae" and Its Enigma*, 240–41.
51. Pingree, "Learned Magic"; see also WP 40–62.

Taking a look at the abominable (or Hermetic) category, we see immediately why medieval Christian philosophers recoiled from it. It comprises the two famous books of talismanic magic that flirt openly with demonic help, the *Liber prestigiorum* (The Book of Talismans)[52] and the *Liber lunae* (The Book of the Moon), as well as a number of lesser known technical texts attributed to legendary authorities such as Hermes or Belenus. Many of these sources are not explicitly demonic; they just give precise instructions on the preparation of talismans or magical rings. These usually correspond to the seven planets, and they are supposed to be manufactured out of the proper metal, by engraving the appropriate image in the corresponding material, whether this material is the metal itself or an inlaid gem. Some of the Hermetic texts, however, go deeper into the realms of demonic magic: suffumigations and invocations to spirits are not entirely missing in the preparation process of certain planetary images, and these details may well account for the critical approach of the *Speculum*.

While the *Speculum astronomiae* condemns a great number of talismanic texts, it also saves two items, and the tolerated texts may prove to be even more informative about the author's classificatory schemes than the ones condemned. Besides the abominable and detestable categories, there is a third one created precisely for those images which do not require suffumigations, incantations, or the use of unknown words: their power is taken *only* from celestial signs.[53] Thus, the author gives a certain leeway to natural talismans (a notion without any meaning for William of Auvergne), that is, to image magic relying on exclusively natural powers. This space, however, is not too large: only two—albeit quite widely disseminated—texts find refuge here.[54]

The first is the *De imaginibus* (On Images, or in a probably better translation, On Talismans) of Thebit ben Corat in the translation of John of Seville. Its attribution to the historical Thābit ibn Qurra, ninth-century scientist and philosopher of the city of Harran,[55] is still an unsettled issue. Even though two, rather different, Latin translations of the work have survived—the *De imaginibus* by John of Seville,

---

52. When translating *prestigium* as "talisman," I am following Charles Burnett's suggestion in "The Arabic Hermes in the Works of Adelard of Bath," in Lucentini, *Hermetism from Late Antiquity to Humanism: La Tradizione Ermetica dal mondo tardo-antico all'umanesimo*, ed. Paolo Lucentini, Ilaria Parri, and Vittoria Perrone Compagni (Turnhout: Brepols, 2003), 369–84.

53. Weill-Parot devotes a considerable part of his book to proving that the notion of *imago astronomica*—which is the notion that becomes the *differentia specifica* separating the last, relatively innocent, and licit category from the dangerous and illicit necromantic works—was created by the author of the *Speculum;* see WP 27–219. See also Nicolas Weill-Parot, "Causalité astrale et 'sciences des images' au Moyen Age: Éléments de réflexion," *Revue d'histoire des sciences* 52 (1999): 205–40.

54. For a detailed analysis of this category, see WP 62–83.

55. I use the Latin form "Thebit ben Corat" when discussing the Latin texts attributed to this Arabic scientist, and the Arabic form "Thābit ibn Qurra," when discussing the historical figure.

to be found in the natural category in the *Speculum astronomiae,* and the *Liber prestigiorum* by Adelard of Bath, with a considerably more demonic content, classified in the first, abominable category—the Arabic original has not.[56] As the Latin text of *De imaginibus* stands now, it is a rather ambitious talismanic work. In its introductory paragraph, it refers to no lesser authority than Aristotle and claims that the "science of images" is higher and more precious than geometry and philosophy.[57] Following this statement, the author gives the procedures (under what constellation, with what words uttered) for preparing and using magical images, or statuettes. These images serve rather common purposes within the genre of image magic: to drive away scorpions, to destroy a city, to find missing objects, to influence a king, and to stimulate love or hatred between two persons. Indeed, there is no explicit reference to demons. The second tolerated text bears the rather similar title *Opus imaginum* (The Book of Talismans), and is falsely attributed to Ptolemy. Pseudo-Ptolemy's talismans are described in a more elaborate way than those of Thebit, and arranged according to different principles, but they are otherwise very similar in their function and significance.[58] In this case, however, the author of the *Speculum* gives his seal of approval more carefully; he considers it innocent for the time being, but views it as virtually useless, and warns us that if there is any, thus far hidden necromantic (that is: demonic) detail in it, this text will also be intolerable.

Finally, a few words on the impact of the classification of the eleventh chapter. It has been noted that the two talismanic works accepted (and, in the case of Thebit's *De imaginibus,* excessively quoted) by the *Speculum* can be found much more frequently than the condemned ones; they occur not only together but adjacent in several manuscripts.[59] On our part we can add to this list a partly astrological, partly magical handbook from Kraków, BJ 793, in which both texts occur (the *De imaginibus* even twice)[60] without any of the condemned abominable or detestable books. Could it be that the fifteenth-century compiler of this codex (or the scribe of the manuscript from which this one was copied) included them because he respected the judgment of the *Speculum astronomiae?* It is true that the *Speculum* was widely copied in Europe. Two copies have even survived from medieval Kraków.[61]

---

56. On the two translations of the text, see appendix 1, "Bibliographical Essay on Current Debates."

57. "Pretiosior geometria et altior philosophia est imaginum scientia." For an edited version of the text, see Francis J. Carmody, ed., *The Astronomical Works of Thabit ben Qurra* (Berkeley and Los Angeles: University of California Press, 1960), 180–94; for this quotation, see 180.

58. T (1947) 256–59; Pingree, "Diffusion," 75–76; WP 77–79.

59. These two works of image magic appear together in BnF lat. 16204, Florence, Laurentianus 30, 29.

60. The two occurrences are the same redaction, but the second one lacks the final sections.

61. In the manuscript tradition of the *Speculum* (comprising sixty surviving manuscripts), its context is usually astronomical-astrological, and occurs very rarely together with talismanic texts (WP 99–102). The two copies in Kraków are BJ 1970, a partial version containing only the first five

Either directly or indirectly, the taxonomy of its author could have influenced the attitudes of scribes and collectors; it might have had decisive impact on what texts were considered decent and suitable for copying, and what talisman descriptions were seen as inappropriate and undesired in scientific manuscripts.

LATE MEDIEVAL CLASSIFICATIONS AND BOOKLISTS

Until the time of Abbot Trithemius (1462–1516),[62] no medieval classification of magical texts can be compared, in sophistication and amplitude, to those found in William of Auvergne's works and the *Speculum astronomiae*. However, there were authors of perhaps lesser significance whose classifications and booklists might be informative about the late medieval distribution of magical works, and who may have played some role in the legitimization (or rejection) of the translated magical corpus. Let us take a closer look at two such examples.

The first, a short enigmatic treatise extant in a manuscript from Prague (which is, however, not necessarily a Central European product)[63] resembles *De legibus*, *De universo*, and the *Speculum* in intent, but goes even further in tolerance.[64] The author takes as the starting point of his argument the often quoted ninth premise of the *Centiloquium* (Hundred Statements) attributed to Ptolemy: "The images of the lower world are subjected to the images of the sky." Numerous works were based on these words—proceeds the author—which were falsely considered necromantic by their ignorant posterity, even though they contain the great secrets of the ancient philosophers.[65] Among these misinterpreted but valuable books, he lists

---

chapters, copied in the thirteenth or fourteenth century (the year 1298 is mentioned), in a mathematical context; and BJ 2496, from the fifteenth century, in an astronomical-astrological context; the latter manuscript also contains the *Epistola de iudiciis astrorum* of Thomas Aquinas. For a description of these manuscripts, see Zambelli, Caroti, Pereira, and Zamponi's edition of the *Speculum astronomiae*, 142–44, and Agostino Paravicini Bagliani, *Le "Speculum Astronomiae" une énigme? Enquête sur les manuscrits*, Micrologus Library (Turnhout: Brepols, 2001), 26–27.

62. I discuss Trithemius's *Antipalus Maleficiorum* in greater detail in Chapters 3 and 9.

63. PNK VIII G 27 (Truhlář 1609), fifteenth-century, fols. 37r–40v. Marianne Reuter describes another, incomplete copy of the same text from early fifteenth-century southern Germany—Universitätsbibliothek München, Q 738, fols. 37r–38r—in *Die lateinischen Mittelalterlichen Handschriften der Universitätsbibliothek München* (Wiesbaden: Harrassowitz, 2000), 189–97.

64. Following references in TK 157, and Lynn Thorndike, "Some Little-Known Astronomical and Mathematical Manuscripts," *Osiris* 8 (1949): esp. 59–60, Paolo Lucentini and Antonella Sannino located this text and published it together with an introductory study in "*Recommendatio astronomiae:* un anonimo trattato del secolo XV in difesa dell'astrologia e della magia," in Burnett and Ryan, *Magic and the Classical Tradition*, 177–98. I am grateful to Paolo Lucentini for letting me consult his transcription before publication.

65. PNK VIII G 27, fol. 38v; see also Lucentini, "L'Ermetismo magico": "Ad idem est Ptholemeus in Centiloquio verbo nono: 'Vultus huius seculi vultibus celestibus sunt subiecti.' Super quod

the title and incipit of Hermes' *Liber lunae,* the *Liber de imaginibus diei et noctis* (The Book on the Images of Day and Night) of Belenus, and—for the first time in medieval sources known to us—a rare work combining image magic with magical Scandinavian runes, the *Liber runarum* (The Book of Runes).[66] According to this author, these are the books that contain the greatest secrets of the ancient philosophers.[67]

The second is a short text surviving in a codex kept today in Dresden, and copied in 1488 in Kraków, probably by a student of the university, Egidius of Corintia.[68] Egidius's book contains a wide range of texts written by his professors of astronomy and astrology at Kraków University. At first sight it is an ordinary handbook of an average student. However, inserted between the scientific treatises, Egidius copied many works of image magic as well,[69] and on one folio he even left a booklist, which sheds some light on his interests. This list is unknown to us from other sources, and it seems very likely that Egidius compiled it himself. It starts with a fourfold classification of the occult and "exceptive" arts into the divinatory, the necromantic, the magical, and the natural.[70] This term, the *ars exceptiva,* was introduced in a basic text of ritual magic, the *Ars notoria,* and refers to the magical arts.[71] Since the term is not used to mean anything else in medieval Latin, its appearance in the Dresden text seems to indicate that Egidius knew something of the notory art.

What is more exciting, however, is that after finishing with the four types of divination, the author proceeds to the other magical categories listed in the incipit, and introduces a number of book titles as belonging to *nigromantia, magica,* and *naturalia.* This list is a particularly rich collection of magical works, including often enigmatic titles. Among these, we find the following:

---

verbum fundantur multa secreta sapientium celantium artem de talibus ymaginibus per multos libros qui ad nos non pervenerunt, et per ignaros et socios philosophantum, qui tardi fuerunt ad perscrutandum secreta nature, attribuuntur nigromancie."

66. Since two of the four extant copies of the *Liber runarum* have come to us from Kraków, I describe this text in detail in Chapter 3.

67. PNK VIII G 27, fol. 38v: "Isti sunt libri qui ceciderunt nominandi propter tum raritatem tum eciam quia maxima secreta philosophorum antiquorum comprehendunt."

68. On Egidius and his codex, SLB N. 100, see Chapter 3. For the sake of simplicity, in the following I will refer to the scribe of the Dresden codex as Egidius, even though it is not completely certain that he inscribed the whole codex or authored the booklist.

69. On these texts of image magic, see Chapter 3.

70. "Arcium exceptivarum et ocultarum quedam dicuntur communi nomine divinacionis, quedam nigromantice, quedam magice, quedam naturales." SLB N. 100, fol. 173v.

71. On the meaning of the exceptive arts in the *Ars notoria,* see Claire Fanger, "Plundering the Egyptian Treasure: John the Monk's *Book of Visions* and Its Relation to the *Ars notoria* of Solomon," in Fanger, *Conjuring Spirits,* esp. 238 n. 22.

Clavicula Salomonis (The Lesser Key of Solomon),
Liber Semphoras (The Book of Semphoras, which, according to the author, is full of unknown characters and miraculous operations),
Liber veneris (The Book of Venus),
Liber quattuor annulorum Salomonis (The Book of the Four Rings of Solomon),
De arte eutonica (On Eutonic Art, whatever that is),
Liber novem candariarum (*sic*) (The Book of the Nine Candles),
Liber ad demoniacos (Book for Those Possessed by Demons),
Liber machometi de septem nominibus (The Book of Machomet on the Seven Names),
Liber institutionis Raziel (The Book of Instructions of Raziel),
Liber de capite Saturni (On the Head of Saturn),
Liber Lunae (The Book of the Moon),
Liber Martis (The Book of Mars),
Liber Iovis (The Book of Jupiter),
Liber Almandel (The Book of Almandel),

and some further Hermetic and Solomonic works, until we finally arrive at the category of *naturales*. The similarity between this text and the eleventh chapter of the *Speculum astronomiae* is striking. Not only do they belong to the same genre; but also Egidius's list follows—with some minor alterations—the order in which the *Speculum* presents the titles of the magical books. It seems evident that he was acquainted not only with the *Ars notoria* but also with the *Speculum astronomiae*.

As we have seen, the Dresden text operates with four categories, but in the first of these, consisting of the four kinds of divination, book titles are not mentioned. The remaining three groups (magical, necromantic, and natural works) by and large correspond to the three (abominable, detestable, and natural) categories of the *Speculum*. The necromantic and magical groups include most of the rejected texts of the *Speculum*, following its attitude rather faithfully, but in the natural category there is an important difference. In both cases two texts are called natural, the first of which is Thebit's *De imaginibus;* however, the author of the Dresden text is not interested in the other text, the *Opus imaginum* of Ptolemy, about which the author of the *Speculum* had already expressed his ambivalence. Instead, Egidius gives—as the most perfect among all books—a text unknown to the author of the *Speculum* for simple chronological reasons, the great and famous handbook of magic, the *Picatrix*.

While the author of the Dresden text follows the text of the *Speculum* relatively closely, he occasionally gives titles that do not appear in his main source (such as the *Clavicula Salomonis* and the *Liber Semphoras,* as well as, of course, the *Picatrix*), and indicates the content in cases when the *Speculum* gives only the incipit. These signs imply that besides being acquainted with the text of the *Speculum,* he had probably also a direct knowledge about some of the books attributed to Solomon, Hermes, Muhammed, and Thebit, and in all probability he knew the content of the *Picatrix.* It is also worth mentioning that there is one more major difference between the *Speculum* and the Dresden text: the latter does not show the slightest sign of condemning the books it lists. It admits that most of them are magical or necromantic and contain demonic magic, but there is no reprobation in these lines.

What William of Auvergne, the *Speculum astronomiae,* the *Biblionomia,* the Prague treatise, and the Dresden text have in common is that they show an explicit effort to systematize and classify the literature of magic, and to find a convenient place for those magical items that accompanied the huge scientific corpus offered by the Greek and Arabic tradition. These authors have a secure and firsthand knowledge of the magical texts, but apart from the authors of the Prague treatise and the Dresden text, they abstain from legitimizing all what they have read. A growing tendency toward differentiating, categorizing, and tolerating certain kinds of magic is apparent, however. William of Auvergne accepts only natural magic, while rejecting image magic and Hermetism. Richard of Fournival satisfies his curiosity with collecting magical works, but he does not make them accessible to the public, and he remains silent about their titles and content. The *Speculum astronomiae* is no longer silent about the same sources, and it even accepts some of the least dangerous examples of image magic. More than a hundred years later, the Prague manuscript seems to accept even the hitherto rejected items, but avoids discussing the most demonic ones, while the Dresden text, written probably by Egidius of Corintia in 1488, approaches them in a completely neutral manner. If we trace a line from Augustine through the thirteenth-century authors to the late medieval classifications and booklists, it seems reasonable to talk about an articulate tendency of "positivization" of magic,[72] as a result of which late medieval intellectuals

---

72. See Claire Fanger's discussion in Fanger and Klaassen, "Magic III": "While 'magic' was used as a term of opprobrium from antiquity, by the later middle ages it begins to be possible for intellectuals to argue in a limited fashion for the positive benefits of some types of theory and practice that are connected to the idea of magic (though the word 'magic' might still be avoided by some writers interested in praxis, and negative uses of the word continued as before). . . . It should be taken as axiomatic that in any era alongside any positivized view of magic there will be found negative views, and that positive and negative views, varyingly configured, can coexist in the same time period, the same social circles, and even in the same person. Thus in the early modern period, when arguments for positivized forms of magic were more common than they had been before, the condemnation of magic (as 'maleficium') was also harsher than it had been before. . . . In outlining the 'positivization' of magic in the later middle ages, we will thus be describing the recasting of an old problem, not its elimination. If the voice of condemnation is often the loudest voice heard, the intellectual climate in the later middle ages nevertheless undergoes an alteration in its attitude to magic on a deeper level, recuperating from Arabic and Hebrew sources some of the bases on which the syntheses of magic with philosophy and theology are constructed in the early modern period."

could safely incorporate a growing portion of magical texts in the framework of science.

Toward a Typology of Magical Texts

Taking into consideration the overcharged connotations of the word "magic," in the following chapters we will try to stick to more neutral (or at least less burdened) expressions and categories, which were—with a single exception—established by medieval authors.

We will use the expression "natural magic" in a scientific sense of the word, close to William of Auvergne's usage. The practices of this branch are based on the conviction that different parts of the world are in occult correspondence with each other. Thus, through the secret relations between various items of nature (that is, celestial configurations, days of the week, parts of the day, parts of the human body, herbs, animals, metals, stones, gems, and so on), it becomes possible to learn about their hidden but natural virtues. With a strong understanding of natural magic, one can even go further and use the correspondences to manipulate the objects of the world. This genre of magic finds its sources in the Greco-Roman tradition of notions of occult powers and processes in the natural order, its main ideas and components occur in medieval encyclopedias, works of natural philosophy and medicine, lapidaries, bestiaries, books of marvels, books of secrets, and even weather predictions. The most widespread text of natural magic is the *Experimenta* (or *Liber aggregationis*) attributed to Albertus Magnus, which became the source of many other texts belonging to this branch, such as the *Experimenta* of Nicholas of Poland and the *Bellifortis* of Conrad Kyeser, to name two Central European examples.

As a rule, we can say that natural magic makes use of the natural power of earthly entities rather than demonic forces. Since this understanding of magic is connected with its "scientific" interpretation, sometimes—as expected—it is difficult to decide whether a certain experiment belongs to the field of manifest powers, that is, the area of natural philosophy and medicine, or falls into the domain of occult powers, that is, natural magic.

Reading further into William of Auvergne and the *Speculum astronomiae*, we arrive at the world of talismans, that is, at image magic, which is situated halfway between natural and demonic magic, and between tolerated and illicit practices. The works devoted to magical images—as we have seen in the case of the *De imaginibus* of Thebit and the *Opus imaginum* of Ptolemy—apply magical characters, small statues, seals, numbers, combinations of letters, and strange circular and quadrangular figures that were to be engraved on rings, metals, and gems under well-defined astrological circumstances.

Interest in image magic is inseparable from natural philosophy and astrology;

indeed, the chief—and usually rather short—texts on image magic are often inserted in the space left free between treatises in these genres.[73] The astrological orientation of this category is also underlined by its favorite attributions: Thebit and Ptolemy were famous authorities on the celestial sciences.

But there was no consensus on the exclusively astrological orientation of image magic, and debates emerged about whether all talismans rely entirely on astrological principles and natural powers. The *Speculum astronomiae* was certainly right to distinguish several subclasses of this branch. Although procedures of image magic are usually not explicitly demonic, they often flirt with demonic forces and incorporate suffumigations and invocations addressed to spirits—as is, for example, unambiguous in the *De imaginibus* of Belenus. Consequently, just as between science and natural magic, it is difficult to distinguish between image magic and demonic magic (sometimes called necromancy), and indeed astrological images were occasionally called necromantic. There are, however, a number of basic differences between talismanic texts using spiritual help and handbooks containing invocations to demons. One of them is the codicological context, which is rather informative about the attitude of the scribes and collectors: as a rule, talismanic texts and demonic handbooks did not travel together.[74] A second reason to make a distinction is internal: the degree of involvement of demons is certainly much greater and more explicit in texts of demonic or ritual magic, and the methods of invoking and binding them are more elaborated, while texts of image magic may often present themselves plausibly as purely astrological works. Third, while the prerequisites for successful magical practice involve previous learning and scientific education in the case of image magic,[75] they involve ritual and religious activities in demonic and angelic magic, such as chastity, confession, periods of silence, fasting, and meditation.[76] In short, image magic and ritual magic are two distinct literary genres.

---

73. Klaassen, "English Manuscripts of Magic."
74. Ibid.
75. In the introduction of Thebit's *De imaginibus*, "astronomia" and "imaginum scientia" are mentioned as crucial parts of scientific learning; see Carmody, *Astronomical Works*, 180. The *Picatrix* emphasizes the point that previous learning is necessary for understanding the secrets contained in it: "Quare scias quod hoc secretum quod in hoc nostro libro intendimus discooperire acquiri non potest nisi prius acquiratur scire. Et qui scire intendit acquirere studere debet in scienciis et eas ordinatim perscrutari quia hoc secretum haberi non potest nisi per sapientem et studentem in sciencia ordinatim." *Picatrix. The Latin Version of the Ghāyat al-hakīm*, ed. D. Pingree, Studies of the Warburg Institute 39 (London: The Warburg Institute, University of London, 1986), 4; unless otherwise indicated, all references to the *Picatrix* in the notes are to this edition. See also 31–32: "In quo ostenditur quomodo potest attingi ad istam scienciam."
76. Kieckhefer, *Forbidden Rites*, 256–57: "opus istum . . . dei nominibus est consecratum et confirmatum ne aliquis operator falli possit, si spem et fidem bonam habeat et certam in domino Ihesu Christo. . . . Sic ergo fideliter credere unicuique operatori est necesse, ne fallatur. . . . In primis,

As the author of the *Speculum* listed a number of Hermetic texts as an (abominable) subtype of talismanic magic, we will also devote a section in our image magic chapter to the texts attributed to Hermes, Belenus, and Toz Graecus—bearing in mind, of course, that geomancy, pure astrology, and natural magic are also represented in the Hermetic literature, and thus, medieval Hermetism cannot be altogether included in the wider category of image magic.

The categories of both divination and alchemy—the subjects of Chapters 4 and 5—were considered separate fields by medieval authors, partly connected, partly unrelated to the other fields of magic. Divination was understood as including geomancy, palmistry, name magic (onomancy), and the numerical and combinatorial practices contained in the books of fate. Since the main objective of these techniques was to foretell future events that are hidden but foreordained, one can easily understand the unanimous rejection of divination by Latin authors, starting with Varro (ca. 116–ca. 27 B.C.) and Isidore of Seville, through the *Speculum astronomiae* until Johannes Hartlieb (ca. 1400–1468), who viewed its methods as a usurpation of divine prerogatives. While Varro and Isidore did not make much effort to distinguish the divinatory arts from magic, and became subsequently responsible for a close association of the two fields, the canons of early medieval church councils, as well as several later medieval authors, such as Hugh of Saint Victor and Thomas Aquinas, treated them separately. However, they saw in both of them the operation of demons, and consequently condemned their use.[77]

Interestingly, alchemy is the art where Central Europe proved to be the most original. While texts belonging to other genres are usually imports from the West, alchemical texts are rather regional products and bring up interesting local issues. It is important to emphasize, nevertheless, that alchemy is not connected to natural, image, or ritual magic with regard to its codicological context and readership; nor was it necessarily seen as a part of magic by the medieval authors (as it has already been mentioned): still I believe—and I hope to be able to prove—that excluding it from an overview of Central European magical texts would deprive the final picture of one of its crucial elements.

Up to this point we have been operating with categories that were partly or entirely constructed in medieval discourse. Conversely, the expression "ritual magic"—which is the focus of our last chapter on the genres of magic—is a modern product, and we will stick to it only for pragmatic reasons. What is common in most

---

quicumque hoc opus sit facturus ad quod vocatur liber consecrationum, ab omni pollucione mentis et corporis se debet abstinere in cibo et potu, in verbis ociosis sive inmoderatis, et sit mundis indutus vestibus, novem diebus ante opus inceptum."

77. Thérèse Charmasson, "Divinatory Arts," in Hanegraaff et al., *Dictionary of Gnosis and Western Esotericism*, 313–19.

ritual magic texts, and what differentiates them from other branches of magic, is that the procedures they provide rely on spiritual, demonic, or angelic help, and that they usually address the spiritual powers through prayers and conjurations. This is the category where the distinction of Augustine between the two acts of communication with invisible powers, between the true, Christian, and the perverted, magical way of using religious rituals, seems to be the most legitimate. Because of its apparent similarity to the liturgy, the expression "magic in a Christian framework" was also introduced as a helpful and rather precise description of ritual magic.[78] Indeed, the most basic texts of this branch resist any comparison with scientific and astrological works; they clearly belong to the domain of religion. They were rarely copied with texts of science, natural, and image magic; they rather occur by themselves, or they are bound together with other texts of the same genre.[79]

It would be easy, but quite misleading to apply the term "demonic magic" to this category, because this would express only half of the truth. The pseudonymous magician-authors—hiding themselves behind names such as Solomon, the Apostle Paul, Apollonius, Euclid, or Honorius—often use the deliberately ambiguous term "spirits," and claim that these spirits are not demons, or at least not malign creatures. It is no wonder that a whole debate developed on the issue of the identity of spirits between the magicians, who were experts in the invocations, and their opponents, who carefully analyzed the conjuring handbooks before eventually burning them. Plenty of testimonies survive on the critical standpoint of the church authorities, while there is only one explicit account that shows the conflict from the magicians' point of view. This can be read in a curious book, the *Liber iuratus Honorii* (Sworn Book of Honorius), which reports of a great gathering of eighty-nine magicians from Naples, Athens, and Toledo, who reject the unfair accusations of the pope and his cardinals, and emphasize that the principles of their magical art are "in the cause of truth." As this apology of necromancers implies, it is not the magicians but the representatives of the church who are led by demons, and that this demonic inspiration is the reason why they spread false and unlikely stories about their adversaries.[80] Hopefully, we will not be accused of siding with

---

78. "Magic in a Christian framework" is an expression Sophie Page uses in "Magic at St. Augustine's," chap. 6.

79. See Klaassen, "English Manuscripts of Magic."

80. See *HMES*, 2:283–90; Robert Mathiesen "A Thirteenth-Century Ritual to Attain the Beatific Vision from the *Sworn Book* of Honorius of Thebes," in Fanger, *Conjuring Spirits*, 143–62; and Richard Kieckhefer, "The Devil's Contemplatives: The *Liber Iuratus*, the *Liber visionum* and the Christian Appropriation of Jewish Occultism," ibid., 250–65. See also Jean-Patrice Boudet, "Magie théurgique, angélologie et vision béatifique dans le *Liber sacratus sive juratus* attribué à Honorius de Thèbes," in "Les Anges et la magie au Moyen Âge: Actes de la table ronde, Nanterre, 8–9 décembre 2000," ed.

the eighty-nine magicians if we reserve a certain place within the category of ritual magic for texts that are not demonic, and that make serious efforts to convince their readers that the addressees of their prayers are actually angels. In this subtype we will classify such books as the widespread *Ars notoria,* its derivative, the *Liber visionum* (The Book of Visions) of brother John, a monk of Morigny, and the relatively rare *Liber iuratus Honorii,* which also relies in part on the text of the *Ars notoria.*

Nevertheless, there are books that do not even pretend to be nondemonic. While texts belonging to the tradition of the *Ars notoria* situate themselves in a holy context, call the beings invoked spirits or angels, and aim to obtain seemingly innocent abilities such as better memory or knowledge in the liberal arts, other authors provide openly demonic techniques of all kind. These techniques serve for treasure hunting, for the discovery of thieves or stolen goods, for obtaining a horse, a boat, or right away a castle, for obtaining a woman's love, or for conjuring a spirit who refuses to appear. The texts do not refrain from giving advice on how various destructive and harmful aims can be achieved: the reader may learn how to make someone lose his senses, or how to foment hatred between friends. While methods are usually similar to those found in the *Ars notoria* (prayers and invocations), the objectives and the intentions are so different that modern secondary literature tends to differentiate between two subdivisions: "angelic" and "demonic" magic.[81] Both refer to the art of obtaining various kinds of benefits with the help of spiritual beings, but while angelic magic puts great emphasis on the ritual preparations for the magical act, such as confession, fasting, and meditation, claims not to use demonic help, and tends to bring divine entities down to earth with the help of prayers to God, Christ, the Holy Spirit, and the order of benign angels, demonic magic involves the invocation of demons, and uses magic circles, powerful words, secret seals, suffumigations, sacrifices, and conjurations in order to obtain benefits, to cause harm or disease, to become invisible, or to manipulate the emotions of others.

Even this superficial acquaintance with their content makes it easy to understand why manuscripts with explicit demonic content had a much lower chance of survival.[82] In Central Europe, for example, no example of this genre is known at the moment; therefore, we will not elaborate the subject of demonic magic further. However, the *Ars notoria* and its various derivatives are relatively widespread,

---

Henri Bresc and Benoît Grévin, *Mélanges de l'École Française de Rome, Moyen Âge* 114 (2002): 851–90. For a text edition, see Gösta Hedegård, *Liber iuratus Honorii: A Critical Edition of the Latin Version of the Sworn Book of Honorius* (Stockholm: Almqvist and Wiksell International, 2002).

81. Fanger, *Conjuring Spirits,* vii–ix.

82. Kieckhefer, *Forbidden Rites,* publishes and discusses an instructive example of demonic magic found in CLM 849; Klaassen, *Religion, Science,* chap. 5, sec. 4, describes another such example found in the Bodleian manuscript Rawl. d. 252.

and probably thanks to their seemingly innocent religious character, they were able to survive in some Central European libraries. In Western Europe their pietistic character and devoutness did not convince the representatives of the church, the *Ars notoria* was frequently condemned, its revision, the *Liber visionum* even burned;[83] whereas in Central Europe various long paragraphs of the *Liber visionum* were inserted into another piece of ritual magic (which—we can rightly claim—is the derivative of the derivative of the *Ars notoria*), namely the prayer book of King Wladislas, and there is no sign of anybody finding its prayers borrowed from the notory art or from John of Morigny vain and worthy of condemnation.

To sum up, we have described five categories into which medieval magical texts can be classified: natural, image, and ritual magic (the latter comprising demonic and angelic magic), divination, and alchemy. One important term remains unexplained, however, which is perhaps one of the most often used expressions: *necromantia*. This term, which originally served simply to refer to divination by the dead, became a much richer expression in the Middle Ages.[84] By the thirteenth or fourteenth century the meaning of necromancy had become at least threefold. It was used first as a rhetorical designation of something illicit, harmful, and rejected. This meaning was emotional rather than conceptual; it was practically independent of the content of the text, and said more about the standpoint and intentions of the person applying the term: he sees demonic intervention or wicked aims in a certain practice which he calls accordingly forbidden magic, that is, necromancy (the term "black magic" was not used until the Renaissance).

The second meaning has more to do with the content of a text called necromantic, and refers to what we have just defined as the second, demonic subtype of ritual magic. It should be added, however, that secondary literature uses the term "necromancy" sometimes in a wider sense, including the other, "angelic" branch of ritual magic, or even certain demonic practices of image magic.

It might sound surprising, but "necromancy" in its third meaning was long a successful applicant for denoting a widely accepted part of science. The great summary of Arabic magic, the *Picatrix*, defines it in a rather wide and naturalistic sense

---

83. See Nicholas Watson, "John the Monk's *Book of Visions of the Blessed and Undefiled Virgin Mary, Mother of God*: Two Versions of a Newly Discovered Ritual Magic Text," in Fanger, *Conjuring Spirits*, esp. 164.

84. This is why Jean-Patrice Boudet suggests that a distinct modern form, *nigromancy*, should be used as the synonym of black magic, while *necromancy* would remain to refer to the original meaning, that is, the invocation of the spirits of the dead. Jean-Patrice Boudet, "La Genèse médiévale de la chasse aux sorcières: Jalons en vue d'une relecture," in *Le mal et le diable: Leurs figures à la fin du Moyen Age*, ed. Nathalie Nabert (Paris: Beauchesne: 1996), esp. 38. Others do not accept this proposition because it would imply that the two words existed in medieval discourse when in fact the distinction Boudet proposes is a strictly modern phenomenon. See, for example, Kieckhefer, *Forbidden Rites*, 19 n. 14.

as the science dealing with all the things that are hidden from the senses or from the intellect, the functioning of which most people do not understand.[85] What is more, it was not just the magical texts themselves that understood necromancy in such a wide and permissive sense. In an early twelfth-century work on the education of clerks (*Disciplina clericalis*), written by Petrus Alfonsi (fl. after 1106), a Jewish convert to Christianity, necromancy appeared as one of the seven liberal arts. Another work, written especially on the classification of sciences by Dominicus Gundissalinus (fl. 1140), mentioned "the science of nigromancy according to physics" as a subdivision of natural science together with medicine, astrological judgments, the science of images (meaning talismans), agriculture, navigation, the science of mirrors (that is, optics), and alchemy.[86] Petrus Alfonsi and Dominicus Gundissalinus are by no means atypical; their works were not peripheral pieces of the literary production of the twelfth century. Alfonsi's text served the education of clerks, while the work of Gundissalinus was used in the university curriculum; and therefore, the authors' views on the importance of necromancy gained no little publicity. Taking a look at their background, the source of these strange views will quickly become obvious. The idea that necromancy might be considered as a part of science is a conceptual import from the Arabic tradition. Petrus Alfonsi was a translator of Arabic scientific texts, while the *De divisione philosophiae* by Gundissalinus relied heavily on *De ortu scientiarum* attributed to al-Farabi (870–950). Nevertheless, this friendly reception of the word was not universal among the Latin philosophers and theologians. It took quite a while to decide which parts of the Arabic knowledge could be admitted into the Christian scientific corpus, and necromancy was not among the lucky candidates. The two previous meanings of necromancy are better indicators of the European fate of this discipline than the one used by Alfonsi and Gundissalinus.

Instead of getting lost in the labyrinth of the complex implications and undertones of the words "necromancy" and "magic," the chapters that follow will rather stick to the five categories introduced above, categories which hopefully will not become so easily misleading. Nevertheless, while we attempt to classify our sources in these categories, we should always bear in mind that this typology of the various

---

85. See *Picatrix*, 5: "Scias quod ista scientia nominatur nigromancia. Nigromanciam appellamus omnia que homo operatur, et ex quibus sensus et spiritus sequuntur illo opere per omnes partes et pro rebus mirabilibus quibus operantur quod sensus sequatur ea admeditando vel admirando. . . . Et generaliter nigromanciam dicimus pro omnibus rebus absconditis a sensu et quas maior pars hominum non apprehendit quomodo fiant nec quibus de causis veniant." See also WP 129.

86. For the latter two examples, see Edward Peters, *The Magician, the Witch, and the Law* (Philadelphia: University of Pennsylvania Press, 1978), 63–67, and Charles Burnett, "Talismans: Magic as Science? Necromancy Among the Seven Liberal Arts," in Burnett, ed., *Magic and Divination in the Middle Ages: Texts and Techniques in the Islamic and Christian Worlds* (Aldershot: Variorum, 1996), I, 1–15, and WP 139–45.

genres of magical literature is far from being perfect, its inner limits are vague, one can easily find texts that could be classified under more than one category. Even such a basic work of medieval learned magic as the *Picatrix* cannot be satisfactorily classified into any one of them, in view of the fact that it cuts through the frontiers, containing a vast range of magical practices, including image and ritual magic, while offering also a theory of magic and some attempts at its classification.

PART TWO

Texts and Handbooks

Introduction:
The Sociology of Manuscripts

Identifying a medieval codex with the group of texts recorded on its folios would be rather misleading. It is more than that, just as a library is more than a mere collection of books (which difference will be explored in greater detail in Part Three). Books are more talkative than the texts contained in them; they tell different—and sometimes more interesting—stories.

Magic can be the subject of a book, and a book can be a magical object. Books are not merely containers of secret studies and arcane knowledge; they are often regarded in their physical existence as magical objects, amulets, or relics and, consequently, as dangerous entities in their own right.[1] They may function as instruments of power, having special abilities to protect, help, instruct, or deceive their readers.[2] Subsequently, the very possession of magical books is often criminalized: as it happened in the cases of Henry the Bohemian and Nicholas, the Kraków hangman, whereas monks of various orders were repeatedly threatened with severe punishments for possessing alchemical writings.

---

1. On the religious and magical uses of writing and the relationship between books and magic, see Gábor Klaniczay and Ildikó Kristóf, "Écritures saintes et pactes diaboliques. Les usages religieux de l'écrit au moyen âge et temps modernes," *Annales, Histoire, Sciences Sociales* 56 (2001): 947–80; Krzysztof Bracha, "Pismo, słowa i symbole" (Writing, Words, and Symbols), in *Inskrypcje toruńskie* (Toruń Inscriptions), ed. Irena Sawickiej (Toruń: UMK, 1999), 7–25; and the studies in Peter Ganz, ed., *Das Buch als magisches und als Repräsentationsobjekt* (Wiesbaden: Otto Harrassowitz, 1992), esp. William Brashear, "Magical Papyri: Magic in Bookform"; Jean Vezin, "Les livres utilisés comme amulettes et comme reliques"; Alain Boureau, "Une épisode central dans la construction de la magie noire du livre: de la rivalité des exégèses à la crémation du Talmud (1144–1242)"; and Brian P. Copenhaver, "The Power of Magic and the Poverty of Erudition: Magic in a Universal Library." For a more general overview, see Rudolf Hiestand, ed., *Das Buch in Mittelalter und Renaissance* (Düsseldorf: Droste, 1994).

2. For example, the books themselves might become divinatory devices: a random opening of a holy book transmits the divine message about future and hidden phenomena. Thus, a book might serve as a form of communication with supernatural powers. See Klaniczay and Kristóf, "Écritures," 962–63.

Books of magic require special care, attention, and respect: examples of the literature on ritual magic claim to be sacred objects, and are supposed to be consecrated according to well-defined ceremonies.³ In the *Liber consecrationum* (Book of Consecrations), detailed instructions are given to the owner to keep the book in a secret place sprinkled with holy water, binding it appropriately, and also to fast, dress in clean clothes, and pray to the heavenly powers before approaching the book with the intention of using it. The royal prayer book of Wladislas—the subject of Chapter 6—attests to have been written and composed with special orations, fasting, with the utmost reverence, and with all sorts of ceremonies.

A Kraków codex of encyclopedic content and of necromantic fame, the *Liber viginti artium* (Book of the Twenty Arts) of Paul of Prague, was believed to bear the traces of the touch of the devil.⁴ Its demonic power was so feared even in the eighteenth century that the book was hidden under a stone for some years so that it could not be read; other reports claim that it was chained to the wall in the library of Vilnius. From time to time, the book is believed to possess sinister powers as if malign demons might reside in it. Various descriptions have come to us reporting that when such books were burned, bystanders heard the voices of escaping demons. Opponents ascribed a certain personality to them and viewed them as agents. Nicholas Eymeric, the Catalan inquisitor who had a close acquaintance with necromantic books, since he read, condemned, and burned a great number of them, handled these codices as if they were active participants in the sinister rites they described. The burning of such books might have been perceived as a kind of exorcism, as well as an imitation of the punishment that magicians deserved.⁵ Thus, the controversy on magic is also a battle of books in which they either succeed and survive, or fail and perish.

However, we do not necessarily need to hear escaping demons to view magic codices with a certain interest (or suspicion). As the main vehicles of secret and forbidden knowledge, they are responsible for the dissemination of learned magic, and their destruction or survival greatly depends on the picture they construct. Sometimes their attempt at legitimating their magical content by creating a most holy image remains unsuccessful and leads to the formation of an opposite, diabolical impression. We will see this (at least partly) failed effort in the case of the *Ars notoria* and the *Liber visionum,* the latter of which was not only condemned but also burned in Paris. However, in a different region and a different century, a

---

3. A most telling example of this is the *Liber consecrationis* (Kieckhefer, *Forbidden Rites*, 8–10 and 256–76), but the alternative title of the *Liber iuratus Honorii*, the *Liber sacratus*, reflects a similar tendency, too. The *Liber visionum* of John of Morigny also gives instructions for the consecration of the text; see Fanger, "Plundering the Egyptian Treasure."

4. BJ 257, fol. 150r.

5. Kieckhefer, *Forbidden Rites*, 1–22; Klaniczay and Kristóf, "Écritures," 960–62.

further revision of the same *Ars notoria* and *Liber visionum* paragraphs in the royal prayer book of Wladislas met a considerably more favorable reception in Kraków.

Handbooks on natural and image magic follow different strategies from those of manuals on ritual magic. They portray themselves as scientific works, inserting the magical texts between practical works on astronomy and natural philosophy. Thanks to this structure, they identify their scribes' and owners' interest, even if they do not identify the men themselves. They tell us whether the texts were intended for daily use or copied by simple coincidence, in abhorrence of blank space (a special kind of *horror vacui*) left between the longer pieces of scientific literature. They represent the conceptual scheme of the scribe, his tacit classification of sciences, and the place he assigned to magic within the framework of a system of sciences. Occasionally, this classification is not even tacit. For example, Conrad Kyeser's work on magical warfare, the *Bellifortis*, ends with a detailed taxonomy, in which the author places magical sciences among the less questionable disciplines. Kyeser's *Bellifortis* is furthermore a good example to illustrate the foregoing premise: the text is not a prisoner of the book containing it. Whereas the original version of the *Bellifortis* insulted the greatest enemy of Kyeser, Emperor Sigismund, one later copy of this work, surviving in a codex in Buda, became disassociated with the *intentio auctoris* to the extent that it was eventually dedicated to the emperor himself. Apparently, the two versions of the same text adopted different strategies of survival in the complicated political contexts of those decades.

The chapters that follow have two aims: first, to describe the content and the history of magical texts found in Central Europe, and second, to show what the manuscript codices that—primarily or accidentally—comprise them can add to this history. In a separate section I will address the question of how the writing and visual decoration of a book of magic determine its character as a "representational object."

We will concentrate on the historical and sociological context of the given epoch's scientific knowledge. An attempt will be made to determine what counts as scientific knowledge in a particular age, where its boundaries are drawn, and what can be found within and outside these boundaries. Thus far, we have gotten acquainted with the theoretical arguments of accepting or rejecting a text that wished to enter the domain of legitimate science. We witnessed how a group of scholars struggled with the question of demarcation, that is, the problem of drawing the frontiers of accepted science and of establishing what can be considered a part of it. In Part Two, in contrast, we will examine the mechanism of acceptance and rejection as it can be reconstructed from the manuscripts themselves. We have perhaps less sociological evidence than the historians of later epochs have to find out how the scholars who accepted the demarcation criteria established by a larger community of intellectuals were rewarded and how those who were reluctant to accept them were excluded (the sporadic evidence we do have will be presented in Part Three). Yet we can apply a somewhat analogous approach that can be labeled as the *sociology of manuscripts*. Instead of reconstructing the norms followed by a learned society or an academy when accepting or rejecting an applicant, in the following five chapters, we will rather examine the norms a medieval codex followed when accepting a text on its folios, and a library followed when tolerating a book on its shelves. Exploring which texts survived in many copies and which ones only in a few, and taking a look at the texts neighboring a given treatise of magic will perhaps be more informative about where the limits of science and magic were in fact drawn than reading the explicit theoretical literature on the demarcation issues.

2

Natural Magic

Eating Frogs and Snakes in Kraków:
The Case of Nicholas of Poland

A small medical scandal took place in 1278 in a region of "Lesser Poland" near Kraków. A certain Nicholas from the local Dominican monastery did not follow the proper and accepted way of examining and curing medical problems: he did not inspect the urine of the sick, but instead turned to less established methods. He suggested that people should consume snakes (*serpens*), lizards (*lacerta*), and frogs (*rana*) in order to cure the various illnesses they suffered from. Instead of properly examining human urine, which was indeed a most widespread method in medieval medicine, he used a closed pouch, the contents of which nobody was allowed to check, and he hung this pouch at night above the bed of the sick person (or perhaps around his neck like an amulet). If the patient sweated and had dreams during the night he stood a chance of being cured; otherwise, he was doomed.

These methods were taken seriously; and with Nicholas's encouragement, people collected reptiles and amphibians with their bare hands. He acquired some followers in the circles of the local Dominicans at the monastery of Kraków, and even Leszek the Black, the duke of Sieradz, and his wife Griphina became convinced of the advantages of the new approach. However, maintains the chronicler Rocznik Traski, who recorded these events in 1341, some people were horrified by all that Nicholas did and initiated.[1]

---

1. August Bielowski, ed., *Monumenta Poloniae Historica*, vol. 2 (Lwów: Nakładem własnym, 1872), 844–45: "Eodem anno surrexit quidam religiosus nomine Nicolaus nacione Theutonicus, ordinis fratrum Predicatorum, qui docuit homines comedere serpentes, lacertas et ranas contra quamlibet infirmitatem a qua detinebantur, sive fuit dolor oculorum vel aliud. Urinam autem hominis infirmi nunquam inspiciebat, sed habebat quasdam bursiculas clausas. Quid autem in eis clausum fuisset, aspicere prohibebat. Suspendebat autem illas bursiculas singulas super singulos infirmos per

The eccentric man who became the focus of these rumors was called Nicholas of Poland (Nicolaus de Polonia) or Nicholas of Montpellier by the sources. He was born in Poland of German—probably Silesian—origin, and he had spent twenty years in Montpellier before returning to Poland to puzzle his compatriots.[2] As the historians reconstructing Nicholas's career have emphasized, this controversial person "was neither an untrained empiric nor a charlatan."[3] He was probably trained in the Dominican *studium generale* of Montpellier in the period when this town hosted one of the best medical centers of Europe. Though it is not known whether he earned a doctoral degree there, his works witness a deep familiarity with the academic medical tradition and a good mastery of the Latin idiom. However, he was by no means a follower of the mainstream tradition.

Two Latin texts are known to have been written by him. His theoretical work, the *Antipocras*, is a versified critique of the conventional Hippocratic system taught in the university curriculum at that time, the rejection of which is spelled out in its very title: *anti hippocras*.[4] In this polemic text, he lays down the theoretical foundations of his alternative medicine, the practical aspect of which is illustrated by a collection of actual cases in his second work, the *Experimenta*.[5] In addition, there is also a German collection of recipes attributed to him, the *Cyrurgia*, which

---

noctem, et qui sudabunt ex huius suspensione et quedam videbant sompnia curabantur, et qui non, non. Capiebantur autem serpentes nuda manu ab hominibus in nomine predicti Nicolay, non in nomine Christi. Nam si quis in nomine Christi vellet capere serpentem, eciam si habuit manum tectam cum cyroteca, statim momordit eum serpens. Ab hoc autem informati quidam fratres de ordine Predicatorum comedebant serpentes. Dominus eciam Lestco dux Syradie cum uxore sua Griphina per mandatum eiusdem Predicatoris eodem anno cepit comedere serpentes, lacertas et ranas, propter quod fuit abhominabilis omni populo, licet fuerint eis valde medicinales."

2. Nicholas of Poland was discovered for the modern scholarship by Ryszard Ganszyniec, who prepared a thorough and most helpful edition of Nicholas's works, supplied with introductions, a great number of notes, and the published version of a few related texts that might have served as the sources of his works. See Ganszyniec, *Brata Mikołaja z Polski pisma lekarskie* (The Medical Writings of Brother Nicholas of Poland) (Poznan: Czcionkami Drukarni Zjednoczenia, 1920). After a long silence, interrupted by *HMES*, 2:768–70, and a short Polish article, Stanisław Szpilczyński, "*Antipocras* Mikołaja z Polski, 13. w." (*Antipocras* by Nicholas of Poland, the Thirteenth Century), *Kwartalnik Historii Nauki i Techniki* 4 (1959): 605–19. William Eamon and Gundolf Keil rediscovered this case: see Eamon and Keil, "*Plebs amat empirica:* Nicholas of Poland and His Critique of the Medieval Medical Establishment," *Sudhoffs Archiv* 71 (1987): 180–96; Eamon, *Science and the Secrets of Nature*, 76–79; and Keil, "*Virtus occulta:* Der Begriff des 'empiricum' bei Nikolaus von Polen," in *Die okkulten Wissenschaften in der Renaissance*, ed. August Buck, Wolfenbütteler Abhandlungen zur Renaissanceforschung 12 (Wiesbaden: Otto Harrassowitz, 1992), 159–96. For a highly critical opinion on the last article, see the review by Brian Vickers in *Annals of Science* 52 (1995): 77–84.

3. Eamon and Keil, "*Plebs amat empirica*," 180.

4. Published in Karl Sudhoff, "Antipocras, Streitschrift für mystische Heilkunde in Versen," *Archiv* 9 (1916): 31–52, and in Ganszyniec, *Brata Mikołaja*, 44–71.

5. John W. S. Johnsson, ed., "Les Experimenta magistri Nicolai," *Bulletin de la société française d'histoire de la médicine* 10 (1911): 269–90; for a more complete version, see Ganszyniec, *Brata Mikołaja*, 136–57.

supplements the *Experimenta* with experiments from other sources.⁶ Both Latin works—written by him while he was away from his home country—are rather rare in the European libraries,⁷ and almost completely absent from the Central European collections.⁸

In the focus of the *Experimenta* we find yet again snakes and frogs. Nicholas gives detailed instructions on how to pulverize them, how to mix them with oil, wine, and various other liquids, which the patient is supposed to drink in turn, and how to prepare pills and other medicaments from these ingredients. Different kinds of snakes, scorpions, lizards, and frogs are good for different medical problems: toothache, difficult childbirth, deafness, illnesses of the eye, and so forth. To cure an open wound, he recommends taking an "aquatic frog," cutting open its stomach, and attaching the animal together with its innards to the injury, which will eventually heal.

It is obvious even for those who are not familiar with the finer details of the medieval history of science, that snakes and frogs in such a concentration do not constitute the procedures of Hippocratic medicine. Indeed, in his poem *Antipocras,* Nicholas expresses his skepticism regarding the methods of the scholastic, "rational," and academic physicians, who rely on authorities such as Galen and Hippocrates, instead of following a "natural" and "experimental" practice.⁹ The importance of his personal experience as opposed to the purely theoretical methods is also emphasized in the not very modest incipit of the *Experimenta:* "Here begin the *Experiments* on animals of friar Nicholas, *medicus* [medical practitioner] from Poland, who spent twenty years in Montpellier, and who was a person of such experience [who was so proficient in *experientia*] that no similar person is believed to have lived before him, nor is that hoped in the future—as it appears from his miraculous works while performing great and unexpected cures in various lands and regions."¹⁰

6. Ganszyniec, *Brata Mikołaja,* 171–222.
7. The *Antipocras* survives in only one manuscript: Berlin, codex Philipps 1672.
8. There is, however, one copy of the *Experimenta* in KMK M XIV (Podlaha 1367), fols. 9r–18v. In this manuscript, as in some other surviving copies of the text, Nicholas is called Nicolaus de Bohemia. Neither Nicholas's works nor their sources can be found in the Dominicans' library in Kraków, where he had been a medical practitioner, which is not surprising, since this collection of medieval manuscripts was almost entirely destroyed in a fire in 1850; only forty-five codices survived. Zofia Włodek, "Inventaire des manuscrits médiévaux latins, philosophiques et théologiques de la bibliothèque des pères dominicains de Cracovie," *Mediaevalia Philosophica Polonorum* 14 (1970): 155–86.
9. Ganszyniec, *Brata Mikołaja,* 46: "Hic improbat actor actoritatem Galieni, que dicit, medice quomodo sanas, si causam ignoras? Hoc in sermone sine cause cognitione monstro, posse bene curam fieri, Galiene." Sudhoff, "Antipocras," 41, transcribes the same sentence with "seu" instead of "sine," which would not have the same sense.
10. Sudhoff, "Antipocras," 32: "Incipiunt experimenta de animalibus fratris Nicholai medici de Polonia, qui fuit in Monte Pessulano 20 annis, qui tante fuerat experiencie, quod ante ipsum non creditur similis ei fuisse nec speratur de futuro, ut patet in miris operibus suis in diversis provinciis et regionibus curas magnas et subitas faciendo."

And this is directly followed by the first cure, the wording of which seems to support the claim that the recommendations had certain experimental background. For dissolving a calculus, either vesical or renal, "take some serpent-powder, put it in wine, and give it to the patient to drink in the morning and in the evening. If it works efficiently, do the same with toad-powder, and if that works too, try scorpion-powder, but always the suitable quantity." To illustrate what the adequate quantity is, we are provided detailed instructions on the pulverization process. "Take three or four toads, put them in a new pot, close it with clay so that they cannot evaporate, and then put it close to the fire, in a way that its content does not get singed just desiccated, and if you shake the pot, you will know from its sound when it is desiccated enough to get pulverized. Than take it from the pot, and if it is not dry enough, desiccate it perfectly in a shadow in the wind, and then smash it minutely in a mortar, and finally put it in a closed glass vessel so that it cannot evaporate. You can prepare serpent or scorpion powder in a similar way."

The *Antipocras* offers a clear explanation of why Nicholas is so fascinated by snake flesh, and why he recommends eating or drinking it—if possible—twice a day: occult virtue is conferred in all earthly things, especially in snakes, frogs, and scorpions. The ultimate source of this spiritual virtue is the goodness of God.[11] Similar to the claims of William of Auvergne on natural magic, the *Antipocras* specifies that demons are not involved in the occult relationships of the objects of the world.[12] Nicholas accuses scholastic medicine of attributing too much importance to the causes; indeed, he does not attribute any, and admits that he does not know why the celestial and divine virtues exercise any effect on the earthly material.[13] However, he emphasizes that the path leading toward the secrets of nature is definitely not that of *ratio* but *empirica,* and the people to whom God revealed his secrets are not the academic physicians but the ordinary people of villages, who are closer to empirical matters.[14]

Does it follow from his critique of Hippocratic medicine that Nicholas was an outsider with no serious sources and with no connections to any theoretical tradition? Not quite. Although he was far from being an ordinary person, and it is rather understandable that the historians of medicine found him remarkable and amazing enough to publish his writings as early as the beginning of the twentieth

---

11. Ganszyniec, *Brata Mikołaja,* 48, and Sudhoff, "Antipocras," 41: "Hic ostenditur virtus occulta inesse multis rebus per modum forme spiritualis. Virtus nempe dei vim celestis speciei confert sepe rei meritis sive materiei. Hiis elementalis non es neque materialis quam terre natis sic dat bonitas deitatis, immo formalis ac si sit vis animalis." (Sudhoff has "bis" instead of "vis.")

12. Sudhoff, "Antipocras," 42: "Has bene qui sciret fieri sine demone, quiret factor mirorum, que fiunt arte magorum."

13. Ibid., 48: "Cur hoc sit, non legis in me. Qualiter aut quare virtus fluit ex aliqua re, dum res est clausa, non est michi cognita causa."

14. Eamon and Keil, "*Plebs amat empirica,*" 189.

century, we can certainly identify a medieval group of texts that describe the worldview in which Nicholas believed, and with which he was probably familiar. Among his direct sources could have been various "snake-tracts" (*Schlangentraktate*) that circulated in the medical circles of Montpellier in his time, the most famous of which is the *Experimenta duodecim* (Twelve Experiments) of Johannes Paulinus, a collection of twelve experiments with snakeskin.[15] An indication of the close relation between Nicholas's and Paulinus's *Experimenta* is that they appear one after the other in a Prague manuscript.[16]

Nevertheless, we can also describe a wider context of Nicholas's beliefs in occult virtues and in the medical efficacy of amulets, and this context is the tradition of natural magic articulated in the "*experimenta*" literature, the most widespread piece of which was the *Experimenta* or *Secreta* attributed to Albertus Magnus.

The Common Tradition of Natural Magic

The three anonymous texts that I somewhat arbitrarily chose as representing a "common tradition"—the *Experimenta Alberti* (Albert's Experiments), the *Kyranides*, and the *Secretum secretorum* (The Secret of Secrets)—share a few basic features: a worldview based on correspondences and secret virtues, a tendency to describe magical or miraculous recipes and "experiments," and the fact that all of them were relatively well known and read by a wider circle of medieval readers.

The pseudo-Albertian *Experimenta* or *Secreta Alberti* is a compilation of medical and magical elements, partially (especially concerning the virtues of stones) based on Albertus Magnus's authentic works, and it was written in the years shortly before or after the death of the Dominican master (1280).[17] Most often it is referred to as *Liber aggregationis* (The Book of Collections), but since this title first

---

15. Ibid., 190, and *HMES*, 2:794–96. Descriptions of the occult properties of snakes might appear even in the context of mainstream medical texts: in a Kraków manuscript of purely medical content, there is a short tract on *De virtutibus serpentis*. See BJ 774, fol. 82v.

16. KMK M XIV (Podlaha 1367), fols. 9r–18v and fols. 18v–19v.

17. The *Experimenta* is under research by Isabelle Draelants, who is working on establishing the sources, textual connections, diffusion, and authorship of the text as well as on characterizing its literary and disciplinary genre. See Isabelle Draelants and Antonella Sannino, "Albertinisme et hermétisme dans une anthologie en faveur de la magie, le *Liber aggregationis*: prospective," in *Mélanges d'histoire des sciences offerts à Hossam Elkhadem à l'occasion de son 65e anniversaire par ses amis et ses élèves*, ed. Fr. Daelemans, J. M. Duvosquel, Robert Halleux, and David Juste, 223–55, Archives et Bibliothèques de Belgique, numéro spècial 83 (Brussels: n.p., 2007), Draelants, "La virtus universalis: un concept d'origine hermétique?" in Lucentini, Compagni, and Parri, *Hermetism from Late Antiquity to Humanism*, 157–88 and Draelants, *Le liber de virtutibus herbarum lapidum et animalium (Liber aggregationis)*, Florence: Sismel, 2007. From the not too abundant secondary literature, we can also mention *HMES*, 2:720–30, and Thorndike, "Further Consideration," esp. 413–23.

appears only in the fifteenth- or sixteenth-century printed editions of the text, I will refrain from using it. Further alternative titles appearing in the manuscripts indicate its main subject rather expressively: *De uirtutibus herbarum, lapidum et animalium* (On the Virtue of Herbs, Stones, and Animals) and *De naturis et proprietatibus herbarum et animalium et lapidum* (On the Nature and Properties of Herbs, Animals, and Stones).[18] This text, which was very widely disseminated and extremely popular, opens by invoking no less an authority than Aristotle himself: "As the Philosopher said in several places, every science is of good kind. Nevertheless, its operation is sometimes good sometimes bad, as science becomes good or bad according to the aims it is used for. Two conclusions can be drawn from this, the first being that the science of magic is not bad [evil], because thanks to its cognition bad things can be avoided and good things can be pursued."[19]

Then follow the three main sections of the book, which are devoted respectively to the description of plants, stones, and animals (primarily birds). Each paragraph in the first part starts as a proper encyclopedia entry: we are provided with the Chaldean, Greek, and Latin names of the given herb. Having clarified the terminology, we learn the *virtus mirabilis* (marvelous virtue) attributed to the plant that may be applied for a wide variety of personal objectives. Collecting and preparing the herb appropriately, the user can achieve various interesting results: he will be addressed only with friendly words, he will become invisible, a sick person about to die will sing loudly, dogs will lose their ability to bark, and so on. The second book is more formal; its sections start with the aims to be achieved and then explain how a certain stone might be used to attain that given wish. For example, a magnet—the stone which has the most obvious *virtus mirabilis*, and which subsequently appears in every lapidary—has the property of revealing whether one's wife is chaste or not. Besides the usual objectives such as becoming invisible, defeating the enemy, pacifying the tempest, acquiring wisdom and getting rid of folly, seeing the future, and curing melancholy in someone, we find other wishes too, which are not as benign as the apology for magic in the prologue had promised, and which recommend specific stones if we want to burn someone's hand without using

18. See Draelants, *Le liber de virtutibus herbarum*, and Pseudo Albertus Magnus, *Liber aggregationis seu liber secreto[rum]; de virtutibus herba[rum] lapidum [et] animalium quorumd[am]* (London: Wilhelmus de Mechlinia, 1483), and Pseudo Albertus Magnus, *De secretis mulierum. De virtutibus herbarum, lapidum et animalium* (Amsterdam: Iodocus Ianssonius, 1648), 127–65. Michael R. Best and Frank H. Brightman have edited an English translation from 1550, which has been published under the title *The Book of Secrets of Albertus Magnus of the Virtues of Herbs, Stones and Certain Beasts; also A Book of the Marvels of the World* (Oxford: Clarendon Press, 1973), 1–61.

19. Albertus Magnus, *Liber aggregationis*, 1; *De secretis mulierum*, 127: "Sicut dicit Philosophus in pluribus locis, omnis sciencia est de genere bonorum. Verumtamen eius operatio aliquando bona aliquando mala, prout sciencia mutatur ad bonum vel ad malum per finem ad quem comparatur. Ex quo duo concluduntur quorum unum et primum est quod scientia magicalis non est mala, nam per eius cognicionem potest evitari malum et prosequi bonum."

fire or if we want to bring about sadness, fear, or terrible fantasies in others. The third part finally presents experiments operating with particular animal parts and substances, such as the tongue of the sea cow, the skin of the lion, the eyes of the hoopoe, the heart of the owl, and the brain of the eagle. The tongue of the sea cow, for example, may be used to prevent the bad opinions of others,[20] while the heart of the owl is an efficient aid when we want to interrogate someone.[21]

When looking for the direct sources of the theories and practices of the *Experimenta Alberti*, we are informed immediately in the prologue that the author had taken all these truths from the book titled *Kyranidis* (*veritatem suppono ex libro Cyranidis*). The *Kyranides*, which has been addressed here, is a Late Antique collection translated—after an eventful and complicated history—into Latin in 1169 in Constantinople. Claiming to contain knowledge originating from Kiranus, king of Persia, from Harpocration of Alexandria, and ultimately from Hermes Trismegistos himself, it offers recipes for the medical application and magical properties of the elements of nature.[22] As a systematic catalog of the natural world, the first book of the *Kyranides* groups a bird, a fish, a plant, and a stone under each letter of the Greek alphabet. It specifies their therapeutic virtues, and explains how a talisman based on these virtues should be prepared. The three remaining books concentrate on remedies made from quadrupeds (including serpents!), birds, and fish.

While the *Experimenta* offers a great variety of methods that were by no means conventional in medieval science, legitimate natural philosophy, medicine, magic, and revelation are utterly mixed in the *Kyranides*. Among its goals we find clearly medical ones (curing baldness, encouraging erection, making a woman conceive, ensuring that a woman does not conceive) besides others which could rather be called magical (to expel demons, to perform a miracle so that someone will seem robust and glorious to all, to make a dream come true).

Even within the realm of magic, this work can be classified as easily under natural magic as under image magic, since besides describing the specific occult virtues, it also explains systematically the preparation of talismans. What is more, the *Kyranides* even contains a few invocations: for example, having caught an eagle and bound its feet, you should whisper in its ears the following words: "O aquila, amica hominis, nunc macto te ad omnis infirmitatis curationem, coniuro te per Deum caeli et terrae et per quattuor elementa ut efficaciam habeas ad unumquamque

20. Albertus Magnus, *De secretis mulierum*, 160–61.
21. On this question, see also L. C. Mackinney, "Animal Substances in Materia Medica," *Journal of the History of Medicine and Allied Sciences* 1 (1946): 149–70.
22. The text is published in Louis Delatte, ed., *Textes latins et vieux français relatifs aux Cyranides* (Paris: Droz, 1942), 4–206. In the secondary literature, see the following: *HMES*, 2:229–35; Ryszard Ganszyniec, "Studien zu den Kyraniden," *Byzantinisch-neugriechische Jahrbücher* 1 (1920): 353–57, and 2 (1921): 445–52; and Ernest Wickersheimer, "Un Manuscrit non encore identifié de la traduction Latine des Cyranides," *Revue du Moyen Age Latin* 9 (1953): 261–66.

curationem ad quam oblata fueris" [O eagle, friend of man, I sacrifice you now for the purpose of curing all the infirmities, I conjure you by the help of the God of heaven and earth, and by the four elements so that you have efficiency in any kind of treatment for which you will be offered up]. Having uttered this invocation, you cut off its head with an iron sword that had been plunged previously into honey.

Not only its details but also its structure reminds the reader of the *Experimenta*. Contemporary book collectors and scribes also noticed this connection, and thus the two texts appear frequently in the same manuscripts, their traditions are often interrelated. As a result of traveling together from codex to codex—and even to printed editions, borrowing elements from each other—they contained mutual interpolations, adaptations, and contaminations.

The *Secreta,* one of the alternative titles of the *Experimenta Alberti,* expresses the debts of this text to the genre of the literature of secrets.[23] The most paradigmatic piece of this literature is no doubt the third handbook to be presented here, the *Secretum secretorum,* attributed again to a celebrated authority of philosophy, Aristotle.

The form of the *Secretum secretorum* is a long fictitious letter from Aristotle to his pupil Alexander the Great, while the latter was away conquering Persia. To the casual observer it is a usual piece of "Mirror for Princes" literature, in which the philosopher gives advice to the ruler on various political and moral topics. These include issues such as a taxonomy of kings according to their generosity, the way a ruler should conduct himself, the importance of justice, the ministers (of whom a ruler should have five), the ambassadors, the army officers, and the strategy and tactics to be followed in a war. And it was indeed seen by many as a summary of the art of ruling: among the few codices surviving from the library of the Angevin Louis the Great, king of Hungary (1342–82) and Poland (1370–82), there is a copy of the *Secretum secretorum* depicting the king in the first initial, H.[24]

---

23. The basic work on the books of secrets is Eamon, *Science and the Secrets of Nature.* For the *Secretum secretorum,* see 45–53, and *HMES,* 2:267–78; and from among the countless studies I would recommend those in William F. Ryan and Charles B. Schmitt, eds., *Pseudo-Aristotle, the "Secret of Secrets": Sources and Influences* (London: The Warburg Institute, 1982), and Steven J. Williams, *The "Secret of Secrets": The Scholarly Career of a Pseudo-Aristotelian Text in the Latin Middle Ages* (Ann Arbor: University of Michigan Press, 2003). See also Williams, "The Early Circulation of the Pseudo-Aristotelian *Secret of Secrets* in the West: The Papal and Imperial Courts," *Micrologus* 2 (*Sciences at the Court of Frederick II*) (1994): 127–44, and "Esotericism, Marvels, and the Medieval Aristotle," *Micrologus* 14 (*Il Segreto*) (2006): 171–91. The reference edition of the *Secretum secretorum* is still R. Steele, ed., *Opera hactenus inedita Rogeri Baconi,* vol. 5, *Secretum secretorum* (Oxford: Typographeo Clarendoniano, 1920).

24. Hertford College 2 (E.N. 2.), Pseudo Aristoteles *Secretum secretorum* (1371–1382), 66 fols. There is a microfilm copy at the Országos Széchényi Könyvtár (National Széchényi Library, Budapest), FM I/1785. See also *BH,* 2:132; Edit Hoffmann, *Régi magyar bibliofilek* (Old Hungarian Bibliofiles), ed. Wehli Tünde (Budapest: MTA Művészettörténeti Kutató Intézet, 1992), 224; and Emil Jakubovich, "Nagy Lajos király oxfordi kódexe, a Bécsi Képes Krónika kora és illuminátora"

The *Secretum secretorum* is, however, much richer than a handbook of state matters: in addition to the moral, political, and administrative advice on statecraft, it incorporates many other useful things, as one of its translators put it briefly and quite rightly: it "contains something useful about almost everything."[25] We are told on several occasions why the science of astrology is useful, we are introduced to the art of physiognomy, and we are provided with a detailed health regimen (a so called *regimen sanitatis*), which promises to be so useful that it "makes recourse to a physician unnecessary" and contains practical instructions on conserving our health, such as brushing the teeth, walking after a meal, and consuming raisins in order to improve memory. The book "On ministers" includes a detailed cosmogony explaining the place of God, man, the minerals, the vegetables, and the animals, while in the chapter titled "On the conduct of war," Alexander is provided with a name-magic formula, with which he can calculate from the number of the letters of the opposing generals' names, who will win the battle (though this section of the Arabic original does not occur in the Latin translations). Finally, book 10 of the Arabic version (the content of which is scattered in books 2 and 9 in the Latin texts) is entirely consecrated for the occult sciences, starting with an apology of the science of the talismans, continuing with alchemy, and arriving at what can be called the essence of natural magic: a lapidary and a herbal listing of the occult properties of the particular stones and herbs.

All in all, the *Secretum secretorum*—with all its teachings on political matters, medicine, physiognomy, astrology, magical gems, the virtues of herbs, amulets, and recipes—was an exhaustive compendium of general information as useful for a ruler as for anyone else. The name of Aristotle, the pretense of secrecy, and the encyclopedic character all equally contributed to the process, which had the result that the *Secretum* was viewed as a reference work. It circulated in two Latin versions, a longer and a shorter one, translated first only partially by John of Seville in the twelfth century, and later on completely by Philip of Tripoli in the thirteenth.

What is common in the three texts described? Their histories are quite different. The *Secretum* claims to be of Greek origin, but apart from the Latin copies only its two Arabic versions have survived, and we do not know whether there was any Greek original; the *Kyranides* is originally a Hellenistic product, which was then translated from Greek into Arabic,[26] and in turn into Latin; while the *Experimenta*

(The Oxford Codex of King Louis the Great, the Age and the Illuminator of the Viennese Illuminated Chronicle), *Magyar Könyvszemle* 37 (1930): 382–93.

25. For the introduction of Philip of Tripoli written before his translation, see Williams, *The "Secret of Secrets,"* appendix 1; for a detailed description of the content of the *Secretum*, see 7–16.

26. An edition of the Greek text can be found in D. Kaimakis, *Die Kyraniden,* Beiträge zur klassischen Philologie 76 (Meisenheim am Glan: Hain, 1976). An edition of the Arabic version of the Kyranides can be found in Isabel Toral-Niehoff, *Kitāb Ǧiranīs: Die arabische Übersetzung der ersten*

is a compilation of texts already circulating in Latin translations. Nonetheless, all three contain certain Greek elements, and are mainly based on Arabic material interpolated with Christian components.

As it has been pointed out, the matter of these texts cannot be sharply demarcated either from the content of works on medicine, or from that of medical formularies. Recipes, experiments, the use of animal substances, and the objectives to be achieved relate them to medical literature. Furthermore, in their organization they follow the structure of encyclopedias, bestiaries, *herbaria,* and other works on natural philosophy. However, the emphasis on the marvelous, occult, and secret elements, on the *virtus mirabilis* and *occulta,* as well as on the universal sympathy linking all the terrestrial and celestial bodies, and finally the undeniably (and even by medieval standards) magical purposes for which they provide help, detach them from the genre of purely scientific literature and assign their place in the realm of "magic dealing with the natural world." Because of the impact of the twelfth- and thirteenth-century Arabic translations, and in contrast with the earlier trends of natural philosophy, texts on natural magic insist on their experimental and practical character, a trait that is rather alien from the mainstream medical and scientific works that found their main reference in theoretical principles and previous authorities.

One last point needs to be especially emphasized here, because it has often been misinterpreted. Curiously enough, the *experimenta* literature is not particularly experimental! *Experimenta,* that is, the "experiments," should not be interpreted as being analogous to our modern concept, which implies the personal observation of the author of a scientific publication and his special attitude to systematically question the elements of nature. The main source for *experimenta* and *secreta* in the Middle Ages remains what ancient books and authorities claimed; actual experience, repeated experiments, and concrete counterexamples do not play a considerable role in judging the authenticity of the recipes.[27] Therefore, this textual tradition should not be defined as a practical genre, but as "theoretical literature that speaks about practice."[28]

It is exactly this bookish character of the experiments, recipes, and laws (going back to ancient authorities such as Galen, Hippocrates, and Aristotle) that Nicholas

---

Kyranis des Hermes Trismegistos und die griechischen Parallelen herausgegeben, übersetzt und kommentiert (München: Herbert Utz Verlag, 2004).

27. For the assertion of the fifteenth-century chancellor of the University of Paris, Jean Gerson, that "experience teaches us that demons exist," see Gerson, *Opera omnia,* ed. Du Pin (Antwerp, 1706), "Trilogium," col. 196, Prop. 21: "Oppositum posuerunt qui negaverunt daemones esse, . . . fuerunt etiam experientiae multae in oppositum."

28. I borrowed this characterization from Isabelle Draelants, "The *Liber aggregationis (Experimenta/Secreta)*: Another Link between Albert the Great and Arnoldus Saxo?" (paper presented at the Warburg Institute, May 1, 2002).

of Poland rejects. He undeniably relies on the literature that has been defined as natural magic, he probably read all three of these texts, and in his person we can perhaps see the first author demonstrating the influence of Pseudo-Albertus's ideas; yet the reader of his methods will find something unknown from these sources, something really experimental and well-tested. It seems from his texts that Nicholas not only copied and adopted the reports on the medicinal virtues of snakes, but actually also worked with serpent's flesh, grounded his *Experimenta* in direct experience, and probably prepared his own snake powder and snake oil.[29]

The Dissemination of Manuscripts

Few medieval sources enjoyed a wider dissemination in the medieval era than the *Experimenta Alberti* and the *Secretum secretorum*. Full versions and fragments of the *Experimenta* have survived in more than a hundred manuscripts,[30] and a further indication of its popularity is its one hundred and twenty distinct printed editions from the fifteenth through seventeenth centuries. There was only a little exaggeration involved when the *Secretum* was claimed to be the most popular book in medieval Europe,[31] with one hundred and fifty copies of its first, and more than three hundred and fifty copies of its second Latin version,[32] still extant, not to mention its translations into basically all the vernacular languages, among them Provençal, Dutch, Middle High German, and Hebrew.[3] A copy of this handbook could be found on a shelf in virtually every library; the relatively small town of Lőcse (Levoca, in present-day Slovakia) in Upper Hungary alone possessed two copies of it, one belonging to a chapel library and the other to the book collection of the hospital.[34] The *Kyranides* that has come to us in about forty manuscripts seems to be somewhat less widespread but was still widely dispersed in the medieval libraries.[35]

29. Eamon and Keil, "*Plebs amat empirica*," 190–91.
30. Draelants and Sannino, "Albertinisme et hermétisme."
31. *HMES*, 2:267.
32. Ryan and Schmitt, *Pseudo-Aristotle*, 2; Williams, *The "Secret of Secrets*," 2.
33. Williams provides an inventory of the extant Latin manuscripts of the *Secretum secretorum* only up to 1325. After that date the number of the manuscripts and the quantity of evidence on the *Secretum*'s diffusion increases radically. See Williams, *The "Secret of Secrets*," 5 and appendix 3.
34. The Lőcse codices are kept today in the Batthyány library in Alba Iulia (Romania; Gyulafe-hérvár in medieval Hungary); the two manuscripts in question are R I 36 and R I 64. See Eva Selecká Mârza, *A középkori lőcsei könyvtár* (The Medieval Library of Lőcse) (Szeged: Scriptum, 1997), nos. 53–54, and Robertus Szentiványi, *Catalogus concinnus librorum manuscriptorum Bibliothecae Batthyányanae* (Szeged: Hungaria, 1958), nos. 36, 64. In both cases the *Secretum* appears among texts of religious orientation.
35. For a list of extant manuscripts, see L-PC 34–37. Manuscripts of the *Kyranides* are still turning up; for an updated list, see http://www.iuo.it/dipfp/ATTIVITA_DI_RICERCA/HermesLatinus/index.html.

(For the sake of comparison, we do not consider a magical text rare if we possess fifteen or twenty surviving Latin manuscript copies of it. When a scientific treatise has one hundred extant copies scattered in different manuscript collections, we can claim with certainty that it was well known and widely distributed in the Middle Ages, and two hundred copies are the sign of extreme dissemination that may be the characteristic of certain works forming part of the university curriculum, but rarely of magical texts.)[36]

In order to turn to the Central European dissemination and audience of books on natural magic, we should take a closer look at the surviving codices and at their owners.[37] In the manuscripts, the *Experimenta Alberti*, the *Kyranides*, and the *Secretum secretorum* usually occur in a medical-astrological context. In two manuscripts, for example, which once belonged to a medical doctor from Kraków, Andrzej Grzymala of Posnania (ca. 1425–66),[38] we find the *Secretum secretorum* and the *Experimenta* surrounded with medical treatises. Both BJ 813 and 805 are the fruits of the first golden age of the University of Kraków; they were collected around 1364 and owned first by another medical doctor, Professor Herman z Przeworska. In addition to our two tracts of natural magic, they contain mainstream texts of the medical curriculum written by—or attributed to—Hippocrates, Galen, Philaretus, and Arnald of Villanova. Besides these classics, there are also a few practical works on the inspection of urine, on the pulse, on the interpretation of dreams, on human anatomy, and also astrological and astronomical items on comets, on the use of astrolabes, and on constellations. We find in them, finally, the three

---

36. Interesting quantitative studies on medieval manuscripts can be found in Uwe Neddermeyer, *Von der Handschrift zum gedruckten Buch: Schriftlichkeit und Leseinteresse im Mittelalter und in der frühen Neuzeit. Quantitative und qualitative Aspekte,* 2 vols. (Wiesbaden: Harrassowitz Verlag, 1998), particularly in vol. 2, pp. 725–47, and in Ezio Ornato et al., *La face cachée du livre médiéval: L'histoire du livre* (Rome: Viella, 1997).

37. It is important to emphasize that the weirdest example of the genre of natural magic, the *Liber vaccae*, which explains the artificial generation of various animals and *homunculi*, cannot be found in the medical manuscript from Prague, PNK X H 20, even though a text copied on the folios 230v–238v—in fact, *De sexaginta animalibus* of Rasis—is entitled *Liber vacce* in the codex. See TK 1688, incipit: "Verbum Aristotelis et Diascoridis est in collo leonis," and *HMES,* 2:762. This text in the Prague codex includes a number of recipes on how and for what purpose various animal parts may be used. Among the animals, we find cows, sheep, leopards, bees, elephants, deer, hoopoes, camels, eagles, and basically every living being that populated the medieval world. Various substances made out of the members (eyes, tongues, horns, and so on) and fluids (blood and semen) of these animals serve for medical and magical goals. None of this differs radically from the common tradition of natural magic. David Pingree, in his "Plato's Hermetic *Book of the Cow,*" mistakenly lists this text as one of the twelve surviving copies of the *Liber vaccae.*

38. *Polski Słownik Biograficzny* (Polish Biographical Dictionary), ed. Władysław Konopczyński et al. (Kraków: Polska Akademia Nauk, 1935–), 9:114–16; *A et A* 25–27. On Grzymala's library, see Part Three. Grzymala left his books to his colleague, Jan Oswiecim (d. 1488). See Jerzy Zathey, *Historia Biblioteki Jagiellońskiej* (The History of the Biblioteka Jagiellońska), vol. 1 (Kraków: Uniwersytet Jagielloński, 1966), 106–7.

astrological *Centiloquia* (Hundred Aphorisms) of Hermes, Pseudo-Ptolemy, and Albategni that were rather popular in scientific codices.[39] It is again in a medical handbook (BJ 788) that we find a text closely related to the tradition of *Kyranides*: the *Compendium aureum* (Golden Compendium, also known as the Book of Seven Herbs and Seven Planets), attributed to Flaccus Africanus. This "compendium" describes the therapeutic properties and the astrological correspondences of seven plants.[40] The *Compendium aureum* is linked to the *Kyranides* by its subject matter, but the connection between the two works is further underscored by the fact that the *Kyranides* itself explicitly states that a book on seven herbs and seven planets should precede it.

In a fourth medical codex from the Jagiellonian library, BJ 817—owned by the astronomer and medical doctor Matthias of Miechów, who traveled to Italy in 1483, the year of the birth of the codex—Kyranides (or rather Kiramidis) plays a central role as a personified authority. In addition to the integral version of the *Kyranides* itself, this manuscript also contains Thebit's *De imaginibus* and—as a starting text—the *De tonitruis libellus* (Small Book on the Thunders) by the Venerable Bede.[41] What is interesting here is first the exceptional attribution of Bede's work: "Incipit Kiramidis de iudiciis tonitruorum" [Here starts Kiramidis's book on the assessment of thunders],[42] and second, that at the beginning of Thebit's work on talismanic magic, instead of "Dixit Thebit ben Chorat" [Thebit ben Chorat said], we read "Dixit Kyramidis" [Kyramidis said]. When looking at this version of the name, we should bear in mind that the original name of the alleged author of the book was Kiranus or Kiranis, and the word "Kyranides" is already a derivation of this form referring to the text, not to a particular king of Persia. Thus, "Kyramidis" used as a personal name is a derivation of an already derivative form.

In this manuscript, whoever "Kyramidis" might be apparently took over the authorship of the texts surrounding his own! A possible explanation for the confusion caused by the occurrence of Kiramidis as the author of the *De imaginibus* might be provided by the prologue of the *Experimenta Alberti* that lists the *Kyranides* and Thebit one after the other as the main sources of its content ("veritatem subpono quo ad aliqua ex Chyramdis libro et libro Alcorat").[43] The impression that the profound connection of these two texts was recognized by the medieval scribes

---

39. For BJ 813, see also Zathey, *Historia Biblioteki Jagiellońskiej*, 15–21, and *CBJ*, 6:213–23; for BJ 805, see *CBJ*, 6:178–85; for the contents of both manuscripts, see the "Description of Selected Manuscripts" below.

40. For BJ 788, fols. 71r–72r, see *CBJ*, 6:100–107. For a published version of the text, see L. Delatte, *Textes latins et vieux français*, 209–33; the text contained by our codex is to be found at 213–22. See also *HMES*, 2:233.

41. *CBJ*, 6:242–53.

42. A similar title appears in KMK M XXI (Podlaha 1374), fols. 193r–195r.

43. Albertus Magnus, *Liber aggregationis*, 1; *De secretis mulierum*, 127.

is strengthened by a further codex from Kraków, BJ 793, which contains parts of the *Experimenta* copied just after the *De imaginibus* of Thebit.[44]

Generally speaking, we can say that works of natural magic tend to travel together with other texts of the same genre as well as with less magical—rather medical and astrological—texts on the natural world. This is, however, not an exclusive rule: texts of image magic, such as Thebit's *De imaginibus*, might be also associated with natural magic. Let us finally take a closer look at two manuscripts, one from Prague, one from Kraków, to explore more in detail how natural magic is connected to the nonmagical contents of the codices.

The Prague manuscript PNK XI C 2 (Truhlář 2027) is a compilation from around 1440 on various subjects of the natural world.[45] It contains both medical and magical material, in both Latin and Czech. The Czech portion comprises recipes on balms, descriptions of the celestial signs, comments (which are in Latin) on several *herbaria*, a lapidary,[46] and a few medical formulas. Among the Latin texts, we find calendars, a number of astrological and astronomical treatises, a treatise on wine and vinegar, an illustrated and comparative system of urine samples, and a table indicating under which zodiacal sign it is suitable to erect buildings, castrate animals, start a journey or dispute, and so on.[47] There are also a few texts of divination: some geomantic tracts with explicatory tables,[48] and a rather common onomantic device, the *Rota Pythagorae*, the methods of which are based on the letters of the name of the questioner and on the numbers belonging to the planets.[49] The divinatory material finally includes an important piece of the literature of geomantic divination, *Sortes regis Amalrici* (Prophecies of King Amalricus).[50]

The practices of natural science and natural magic are practically inseparable.

---

44. *Experimenta*, fols. 143v–148v; *De imaginibus* of Thebit, fols. 140v–143v; another copy of the same text being on fols. 61r–63r. See *CBJ*, 6:120–37. This manuscript will be analyzed in the following chapter in greater detail.

45. Pavel Spunar, *Repertorium auctorum bohemorum provectum idearum post universitatem Pragensem conditam illustrans*, 2 vols., Studia Copernicana 25 and 35 (Wrocław: Ossolineum, 1985, 1995), 2:245, 247, and 249. For a more detailed description of the codex, see Isabelle Draelants, "Un encyclopédiste méconnu du XIIIe siècle: Arnold de Saxe. Oeuvres, sources et reception" (Ph.D. diss., Université catholique de Louvain, 2000), 1:31–39. I am grateful to Isabelle for providing me with the microfilm copy of the manuscript. See also Draelants, "Une mise au point sur les oeuvres d'Arnoldus Saxo," pts. 1 and 2, *Bulletin de Philosophe Médiévale* 34 (1992): 163–80; 35 (1993): 130–49. Apart from the use of Czech, the mention of saints particularly venerated in Prague, of King Sigismund, and of the Saint Wenceslas chapel equally indicate Prague as the provenance of the codex.

46. Fols. 292r–295r.

47. Fols. 7v.

48. Fols. 70r–71r; 72v–77r; 78r–85v.

49. Fol. 86r–v.

50. Fols. 88v–104v. The text in this manuscript had not been previously identified. It was published erroneously under the title *Experimentarius* of Bernardus Silvestris, but is now referred to as *Sortes regis Amalrici*. On the text and its secondary literature, see Chapter 4.

To complicate the problem further, spirits and demons are not lacking either from the manuscript. A series of recipes against toothache, for example, provide both medical and magical methods. The recipes belonging to the first kind operate with herbal materials that should be placed on the tooth in question, while the second type of procedures apply ligatures, special names, and magical characters: "These are the names of the seven sleepers. Maximianus ⊞ Martinianus ⊞ Malchus ⊞ Constantinus ⊞ Dionisius ⊞ Serapion ⊞ Johannes. For toothache ⊞ Job trayson ⊞ Job zorobantes ⊞ Job connubia ⊞ Job ⊞ And attach this ligature to the teeth or on the neck. And then write this figure three times on the earth while the sick person watches it. And make him tell three paternoster while you write."[51]

Before we continue reading the text, it might be useful to look at this interesting formula more carefully. Apparently, it invokes the names of the saints known as the Seven Sleepers of Ephesus, who were walled up in a cave during the reign of Emperor Decius. They fell asleep and woke up miraculously two hundred years later, during the reign of Theodosius. Their story is described by Gregory of Tours, and it is included also in the Golden Legend. Their names must have been believed to bear magical power, because this formula, or its close variants, appear in many other magical recipes at least from the thirteenth century onward.[52] One of these is a fourteenth-century Czech example found in the Saint George Basilica of the Prague Castle. This time, the text does not occur in a codex, but on a small piece of parchment, which must have been used as an amulet. In this text, the same seven names, together with the form "pax + nax vax," were used again for the purposes of healing magic, this time against fever.[53]

Coming back to the codex, later on the same page we find a prayer, in which a short story concerning Saint Peter and his aching tooth is incorporated (fig. 1). In the margin, a drawn finger calls the reader's attention to this paragraph, while the previous and following methods are also commented upon at length in the main body of the text, which testifies about a certain practical interest in these procedures.

---

51. Fol. 146v: "Ista sunt nomina septem dormiencium. Maximianus ⊞ Martinianus ⊞ Malchus ⊞ Constantinus ⊞ Dionisius ⊞ Serapion ⊞ Johannes. Ad dolorem dencium ⊞ Job trayson ⊞ Job zorobantes ⊞ Job connubia ⊞ Job ⊞ Et istam ligaturam liga ad dentes sive ad collum. Item in terra scribe hac figuram ter vidente infirmo. Et fac eum dicere tria pater noster interim quod scribis."

52. See Willy L. Braekman, ed., *Middelnederlandse geneeskundige recepten* (Middledutch Medical Prescriptions) (Ghent: Koninklijke Vlaamse Academie voor Taal- en Letterkunde, 1970), 255 and 367–68. See also Don C. Skemer, *Binding Words: Textual Amulets in the Middle Ages* (University Park: Pennsylvania State University Press, 2006), 206–7 and 253.

53. "+ In nomine + patris + et filii + et spiritus + sancti + In monte + Celion + requiescunt septem dormientes + Maximianus + Martinianus + Malcus + Constantinus + et Dionisius + Seraphion + et Johannes. Domine Jesu Christe liberare digneris hanc famulam Dobrozlauam a febribus quintanis. pax + nax vax sit huic famule dei remedium Amen." See V. J. Nováček, "Amulet ze XIV. století, nalezený v chrámu sv. Jiří na hradě pražském" (A Fourteenth-Century Amulet from the Saint George Basilica of the Prague Castle), *Český lid* 10 (1901): 353–54.

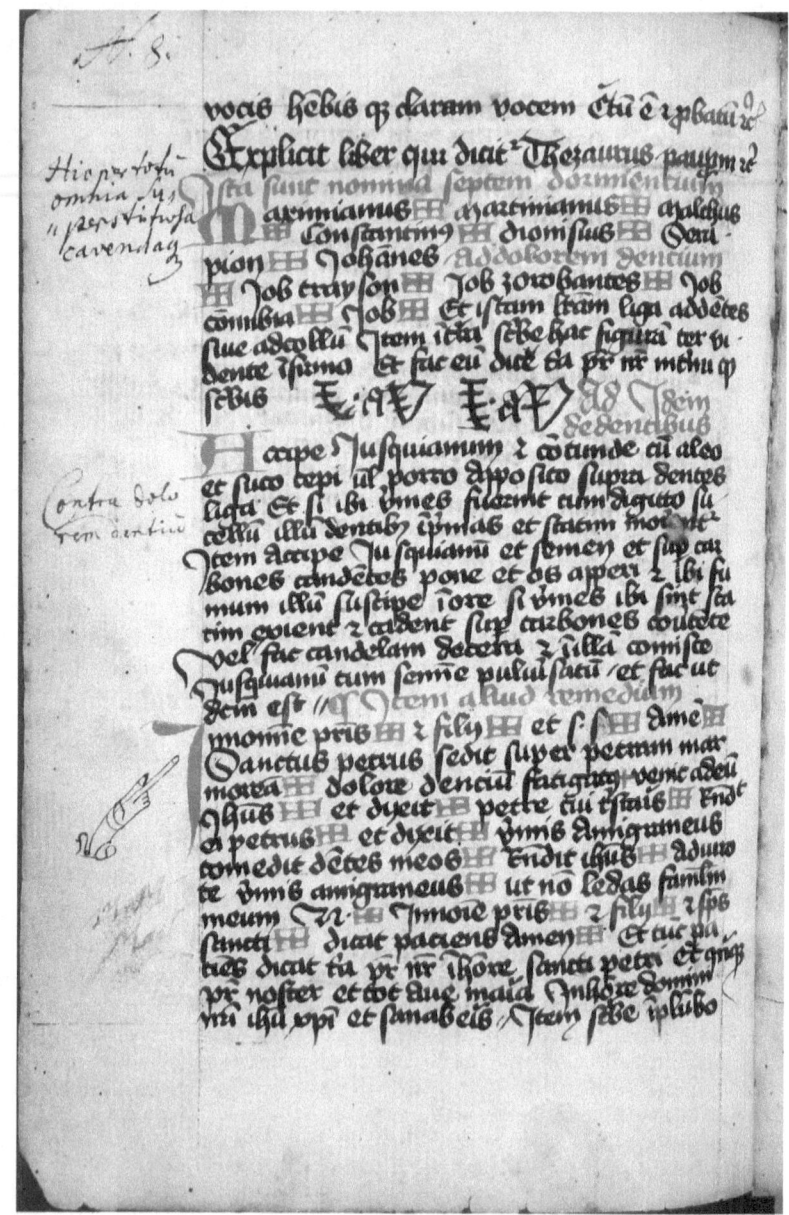

FIG 1   Magical cure against toothache. Prague, PNK XI C 2, fol. 146v. Courtesy of the Národní knihovna ČR.

The next page offers a new mixture against toothache, but the instructions finish by attributing a broader competence to the material: "Contra demonia et omnes incantationes et insidias dyaboli" [Against devils, all incantations and against being bedeviled].[54] Finally, all this is followed by a prayer, or rather a summoning of various spirits who seem to be the personified versions of the traditional seven gifts of the Holy Spirit: "May the spirit of the fear of the Lord dispel from me all demonic influences ☩ may the spirit of piety protect me ☩ may the spirit of knowledge instruct me ☩ may the spirit of fortitude arm me ☩ may the spirit of counsel guide me ☩ may the spirit of understanding inflame me ☩ may the spirit of wisdom teach me ☩."[55]

The various *herbaria* contained in this Prague codex acquaint the reader with the medical properties of the plants, and with the purposes for which they can be used. These purposes include a few similar to those of natural magic, such as expelling serpents and scorpions.[56] It is not surprising that a few folios after this description of the plants, there is a lapidary explaining the virtues of the stones, the second book of the *Experimenta Alberti*.[57] This text—as we can recall—is already beyond the limits of purely natural science, as it contains undeniably magical objectives, such as becoming invisible, causing fear, burning another's hand without using fire, divination of the future, calming tempests, and so on.

This magical lapidary is preceded by another closely related text on stones.[58] This is the lapidary of Arnaldus Saxo, the third part of his encyclopedia, the *De floribus rerum naturalium* (The Flowers of Nature).[59] We have here the fullest version of this encyclopedia containing all its three books: the *De virtutibus lapidum* (The Virtues of Stones), with an alphabetical description of the stones, their virtues and the aims they can be used for; the *De sigillis lapidum* (The Seals of Stones), with the instructions on how talismans might be created by engraving images on the stones; and

---

54. PNL XI C 2, fol. 147r. The Hungarian *Peer Codex*, on which see more in Chapter 7, also contains a number of medical charms. On medical incantations, see Michael R. McVaugh, "Incantationes in Late Medieval Surgery," in *Ratio et Superstitio: Essays in Honor of Graziella Federici Vescovini*, ed. Giancarlo Marchetti, Orsola Rignani, and Valeria Sorge (Louvain-La-Neuve: Fédérations Internationales des Instituts d'Études Médiévales, 2003), 319–46.

55. PNL XI C 2, fol. 147r. "Spiritus timoris domini abigat a me omnia demonia ☩ Spiritus pietatis tueatur me ☩ Spiritus sciencie erudiat me ☩ Spiritus fortitudinis armet me ☩ Spiritus consilii regat me ☩ Spiritus intellectus inflamet me ☩ Spiritus sapiencie doceat me ☩."

56. Ibid., fol. 162v.

57. Ibid., fols. 250r–255v. This book is transcribed in Draelants, "Un encyclopédiste méconnu," 2:862–69.

58. PNL XI C 2, fols. 238v–250r. For Arnoldus Saxo and his lapidary, see Draelants, "Un encyclopédiste méconnu."

59. For a description of the structure of this encyclopedia, see Draelants, "Une mise au point," pt. 1, 175–77. "Flores," that is, "flowers," appearing in titles of scientific works refer to a series of text-excerpts or citations collected by an author.

finally the *De coloribus gemmarum* (The Colors of Gems) with a content corresponding to the title.[60] The objectives include a number of magical ones: the stones can be used against demons, night fears, and diabolical illusions, and also for divinatory aims, acquiring wisdom, achieving victory, and obtaining a good reputation.[61]

The manuscripts presented here are rather typical and allow us to conclude that lapidaries tend to travel in the medical literature together with other works of natural magic. This claim is supported by a further medical handbook (BJ 778) from around 1425, owned and partly copied by Johannes of Dobra, a professor and rector of the University of Kraków.[62] Countless marginal notes, addenda, remarks, short recipes, and excerpts sketched by the owner confirm the impression that it was used as a manual and as a notebook for actual medical practice.[63] The codex contains among other works two short Hermetic herbaria related again to the *Kyranides*: the *Liber de septem herbis* (Book of the Seven Herbs), attributed to Alexander Magnus,[64] and *De virtutibus herbarum* (On the Virtue of Herbs) of Thessalus.[65] It has already been mentioned that the former work describes a correspondence between the medical and magical properties of the seven herbs and the qualities associated with the planets. The information provided by the second work is quite the same, but the presentation is different. This time, the virtues of the planetary and zodiacal herbs are presented in the framework of a revelation given by the god Asclepius to the doctor Thessalus.

Just as it happened in the case of the Prague manuscript, magico-therapeutic *herbaria* are accompanied by magico-therapeutic *lapidaria*. In some folios, before

---

60. An edition of the first, most common book is published in Valentin Rose, "Aristoteles de lapidibus und Arnoldus Saxo," *Zeitschrift für deutsches Altertum* 18 (1975): esp. 424–47. The two other books are published in Claude Lecouteux, "Arnoldus Saxo: Unveröffentliche Texte, transkribiert und kommentiert," *Eupkorion: Zeitschrift für Literaturgeschichte* 76 (1982): 389–400.

61. As Isabelle Draelants pointed out, there are systematic parallels between the second book of the *Experimenta Alberti* and the lapidary of Arnoldus Saxo. See Draelants, "Un encyclopédiste méconnu," 2:553–63. It should be added that both texts bear detectable similarities to an authentic work of Albertus Magnus, the *De mineralibus* (written between 1245 and 1263), which is usually believed to be a source for the Pseudo-Albertian *Experimenta*, while its source, in turn, had been Arnoldus's lapidary. As far as we know, Arnoldus Saxo (or Arnoldus Luca) was one of the encyclopedists and natural philosophers of the thirteenth century, active in the middle of the century in Germany and France. As is probable after Isabelle Draelants's research, he might have been one of the collaborators of Albertus Magnus (although one should note that while we can identify the intellectual circle in and with which Thomas Aquinas worked, very little is known about the *socii* of Albert the Great), and it is also likely that Albert borrowed from Arnoldus Saxo's lapidary when compiling information for his own *De mineralibus*.

62. *Polski Słownik Biograficzny*, 10:449–50.

63. *CBJ*, 6:36–55.

64. PNL XI C 2, fol. 211r (TK 517, 1088); for a synopsis of the content and a list of manuscripts, see L-PC 40–42.

65. Ibid., fol. 211v (TK 1572, 969); for a summary of the contents and a list of the manuscripts containing a copy of *De virtutibus herbarum*, see L-PC 42–44.

reading about the virtue of the herbs arranged in an alphabetical list, the reader comes across the magical properties of the stones and the aims for which they might be used. This lapidary was usually and falsely attributed to Aristotle, and claimed to have been composed in honor of Wenceslas II, king of Bohemia (1278–1305).[66] After all this, we should not be surprised that the following paragraphs speak about certain animals whose pictures should be engraved in the stones in order to produce talismans.[67]

And yet this manuscript has further interesting details to tell us about what its owner, Johannes of Dobra, found remarkable enough to record. He left a few notes on a leaf attached to the codex, one on Dante, and a second one on what he discussed with the astrologer Henricus Bohemus. This latter note deserves more attention, since Henricus—as we will see in Part Three—was imprisoned for years for being a Hussite and for possessing necromantic books. The note informs us that he spoke to Dobra about an Armenian who had been alive for four hundred years. He also mentioned—the note continues—that Master Johannes of Ragusio also talked with this Armenian, and inquired about the way he preserved his life for so long, and the Armenian answered that he used a certain medicine, which (probably the medicine) Johannes of Ragusio did not understand how to make.[68] All in all, Johannes of Dobra's medical interest was closely neighboring the realm of natural magic.

Techniques of Magical Warfare: The *Bellifortis*

A frequent objective of natural magic recipes is to gain victory over one's enemies. Many experiments start with the words: "si vis devincere hostes" [if you want to

---

66. BJ 778, fols. 200r–209r. The text was identified by Isabelle Draelants and Slawek Zsyller. I am grateful to Isabelle for informing me about this identification. See also Chapter 8; TK 160; *HMES*, 2:266; and Maria Kowalczyk, "Wróżby, czary i zabobony w średniowiecznych rękopisach Biblioteki Jagiellońskiej" (Divinations, Superstitions, and Sortileges in the Medieval Manuscripts in the Biblioteka Jagiellońska), *Biuletyn Biblioteki Jagiellońskiej* 29 (1979): esp. 16–17.

67. Ibid., fols. 209r–210v: "Nunc de lapidibus animalium repiculando breviter est dicendum. Quedam enim de numero animalium tam perfectorum.> <Et dicitur signum serpentarii. Ceterum si insculpatur virgo genu flexo clava in manui primus, etc. Et cetera. Sequitur."

68. BJ 778, fol. II. Published in Maria Kowalczyk, "Przyczynki do biografii Henryka Czecha i Marcina Króla z Żurawicy" (Appendices to the Biography of Henry the Czech and Marcin Król of Żurawica), *Biuletyn Biblioteki Jagiellońskiej* 21 (1971): 87–91. "Dominus Henricus astronomus Bohemus dixit michi de quodam Armeno, qui morabatur in Bauoria, qui vixit 400 annorum. Et magister Johannes de Ragusio cum eodem Armeno loquebatur, quomodo sic diu vitam conservaret, qui respondit, quod utebatur medicina quadam, quam idem magister Johannes de Ragusio nondum intellexit. Et hoc michi dicit idem dominus Henricus Bohemus anno Domini MCCCCXL." This Johannes de Ragusio was probably the theologian and ecclesiastical reformer Johannes Stoyci de Ragusio who was born in 1395 in Ragusa (present-day Dubrovnik) on the Dalmatian coast, studied in Padua and Paris, and participated in the Council of Constance. He died in 1443 in Lausanne.

defeat enemies] or "si vis essere victoriosus contra adversarios" [if you want to be victorious over adversaries]. But it is not only natural magic that concerns itself with such objectives; Thebit's *De imaginibus* provides talismanic methods for conquering territories and destroying cities. Thus, we should not be surprised if we find military technology and magical means side by side in certain handbooks. There is no real contradiction in the mixture of such remote interests; in the Middle Ages and in the Renaissance, the combination of medical astrology, engineering, and magic was viewed as rather natural. Mechanical inventions often had supernatural connotations. Medieval popular imagination attributed a certain magical notoriety to technological interest: one may think of the miraculous inventions of Roger Bacon, which are not independent of his later reputation as a magician, but we can also mention the legends surrounding Virgil or Gerbert d'Aurillac (later Pope Sylvester II), in which the alleged magician uses his power for creating automata and miraculous mechanical devices.

The same association of craftsmanship and engineering with magic can be documented in official education, too. Medical astrology was a well-established discipline in the universities, which successively became connected with a technological problem, the improvement of the clock—which was needed, *inter alia,* for casting more accurate horoscopes. It was not exceptional that the mechanical interest of medical astrologers culminated in military technology, as the works of the fourteenth-century Italian physician Guido da Vigevano and those of his contemporary, the medical astrologer Giovanni de' Dondi testify. Since these two works are the only technological texts surviving from the fourteenth century, the combination of these fields is certainly more than a simple coincidence. Further examples for *some* kind of combination of astrology, medicine, technology, military engines, alchemy, clockworks, magic, and metallurgy can be found in the fifteenth century in the works of Giovanni Fontana of Venice, Jean Fusoris, and Henry Arnault of Zwolle, until we arrive to the last famous meeting of medicine and technology on the pages of *De re metallica* by Georgius Agricola in 1556.[69]

Technology—not a university subject in the Middle Ages, as a matter of fact, not even *scientia* in the Aristotelian sense of the word—had always been surrounded by the aura of secrecy and mystery. In addition, it shared with magic the feature of being practical and manipulative, unlike mainstream science (or rather, *philosophia naturalis*), which did not tend to interfere in the natural processes it studied, and which relied more on observation than on manipulation and experimentation. The

---

69. William Eamon, "Technology as Magic in the Late Middle Ages and the Renaissance," *Janus* 70 (1983): esp. 173–76; Lynn White, "Medical Astrologers and Late Medieval Technology," *Viator: Medieval and Renaissance Studies* 6 (1975): 295–307.

Natural Magic   71

engineer, through his technical inventions and mechanical devices—just like the magician through his application of nature's hidden forces and virtues—explicitly aspired to interfere in the course of nature, to alter and ultimately control it.

One of the most beautiful and paradigmatic encounters of technology and magic takes place in a long, illustrated military handbook, the *Bellifortis*. This exceptional work presents important devices and methods of military technology together with magical recipes and necromantic amulets.[70] If we open the book at random, we might find an Archimedes' screw (actually, its first depiction in the Latin Middle Ages) or a magic ring. On one page, we see colorful astrological symbols, on others terrifying siege machines, on one page bathhouses, on another demons.

The author of the *Bellifortis*, Conrad Kyeser (1366–1405), was a German mercenary captain and probably a trained physician and engineer. He composed his work in exile in the first years of the fifteenth century.[71] He was not a nobleman, but born of burgher parents he acquired a university education, and his profession was originally medicine.[72] As a practicing engineer he was present at the Battle of Nicopolis in 1396, where the Turkish armies triumphed over the united Christian forces. He blamed—not entirely unfairly—Sigismund, king of Hungary, for the defeat.[73] He lived at several courts, including that of Wenceslas, Holy Roman Emperor and king of Bohemia, as a free intellectual, an engineer, and probably affecting a bit the role of a magician. For political reasons, and supposedly accused of sorcery, Kyeser was forced into exile in a small community in the Bohemian mountains in 1402. This happened when Sigismund deposed his brother, Wenceslas, and started the systematic dismissal of the latter's supporters from the Imperial court as potential menacing factors.[74] Fortunately for Kyeser, some unemployed

---

70. For the text, see Conrad Kyeser, *Bellifortis*, ed. Götz Quarg, 2 vols. (Düsseldorf: Verlag des Vereins Deutscher Ingenieurie, 1967). This edition contains a facsimile of the text of the *Bellifortis* in MS Göttingen, Universitätsbibliothek, Cod. philos. 63, as well as a transcription of the Latin text, a German translation, and a detailed introduction, all by Quarg. For further secondary literature, see Lynn White, "Kyeser's 'Bellifortis': The First Technological Treatise of the Fifteenth Century," *Technology and Culture* 10 (1969): 436–41; White, "Medical Astrologers"; Eamon, "Technology as Magic"; Eamon, *Science and the Secrets of Nature*, 68–71; and Rainer Leng, *Ars belli: Deutsche taktische und kriegstechnische Bilderhandschriften und Traktate im 15. und 16. Jahrhundert* (Wiesbaden: Reichert Verlag, 2002), 19–21 and 109–49.

71. For Kyeser's life, see Quarg's introduction, in Kyeser, *Bellifortis*, xix–xxv.

72. Subsequently to Quarg's edition, Josef Krása identified a collection of medical recipes by a certain Conrad of Eichstätt, in a miscellany that can be related to the court of Wenceslas, king of Bohemia. See White, "Medical Astrologers," 302. Krása's study was published in *Dějiny a současnost* (1968): 25–29. Leng, however, argues against the identification of Conrad of Eichstätt with Conrad Kyeser (*Ars belli*, 113).

73. See Quarg's introduction, in Kyeser, *Bellifortis*, xxii.

74. We will come back to the reasons for Kyeser's dismissal in Chapter 8.

German illuminators passed through his mountain village, and he was able to hire them to help him prepare his book.

The *Bellifortis* is above all a treatise on warfare. Whether it was to be used as a manual in military conflicts or simply to entertain its peaceful reader with its technical, literary and magical material, is still a matter of debate.[75] In any case, it describes and depicts a number of martial instruments, ladders for the siege of castles, machinery to help horses cross a river, catapults, rockets, arrows, arbalests, nails, scissors, clasps and horseshoes, and recipes for preparing various kinds of fires (for one of the instruments, see fig. 2). The reader is also shown some—at least in the context of engineering—unexpected pictures that seem to be somewhat less related to military affairs: a female chastity device, a tool for castrating men, the black queen of Sheba, a goose fastened to an anchor, and a few pictures on how to prepare a bath appropriately. Some of the machineries bear fantastic features; among them a huge wheeled cat with a long destructive pike in its mouth that might have served to frighten the enemy (fig. 3).

Further elements are explicitly magical, and this is where the *Bellifortis* is greatly indebted to the *experimenta* literature, that is, to the genre of natural magic. Kyeser's familiarity with this literature originates probably from the time of his studies in medicine. He takes paragraphs word for word from the pseudo-Albertian corpus, not just from the *Experimenta Alberti*, which we examined earlier, but from a text that often traveled together with it, the *De mirabilibus mundi* (On the Marvels of the World).[76] This pseudograph starts with a theoretical introduction to magic, continues with random recipes incorporating material from the *Liber vaccae*, and finishes with more systematic paragraphs taken from the *Liber ignium* (Book of Fires) of Marcus Graecus. Among the experiments of the *De mirabilibus mundi*, Kyeser is mostly concerned with those which provide methods for preparing magical lamps that cannot be extinguished either by water or by wind. These recipes make use of various animal substances, such as the flesh of a frog, the tail and blood of a serpent, the blood of a turtle, the tail of a dog and of a wolf, not to mention the brain of a bird.[77] As fire is usually a crucial element in late-medieval warfare, and tracts on fires were consequently important sources of military technology, it is not surprising that the *Liber ignium*—a collection of instructions on

---

75. Leng, *Ars Berlli*, 109–49.

76. Its printed edition also often follows the *Experimenta*. In Albertus Magnus, *De secretis mulierum*, the *Experimenta* appears on pages 127–65, the *De mirabilibus mundi* on pages 170–218. See also Best and Brightman, *Book of Secrets*.

77. "Accipe ranam viridem et decolla eam super pannos" (MS Göttingen, Universitätsbibliothek, Cod. philos. 63, fol. 93v); "Accipe sangwinem testudinis" (fol. 95r); "de pingwedine serpentis" (ibid.); "cerebrum avis" (ibid.); "Accipe cutem serpentis, cutem lupi et canis" (ibid.); "Recipe fel canis" (fol. 96v). For lamps and torches, in general, see fols. 90r–97r.

Natural Magic

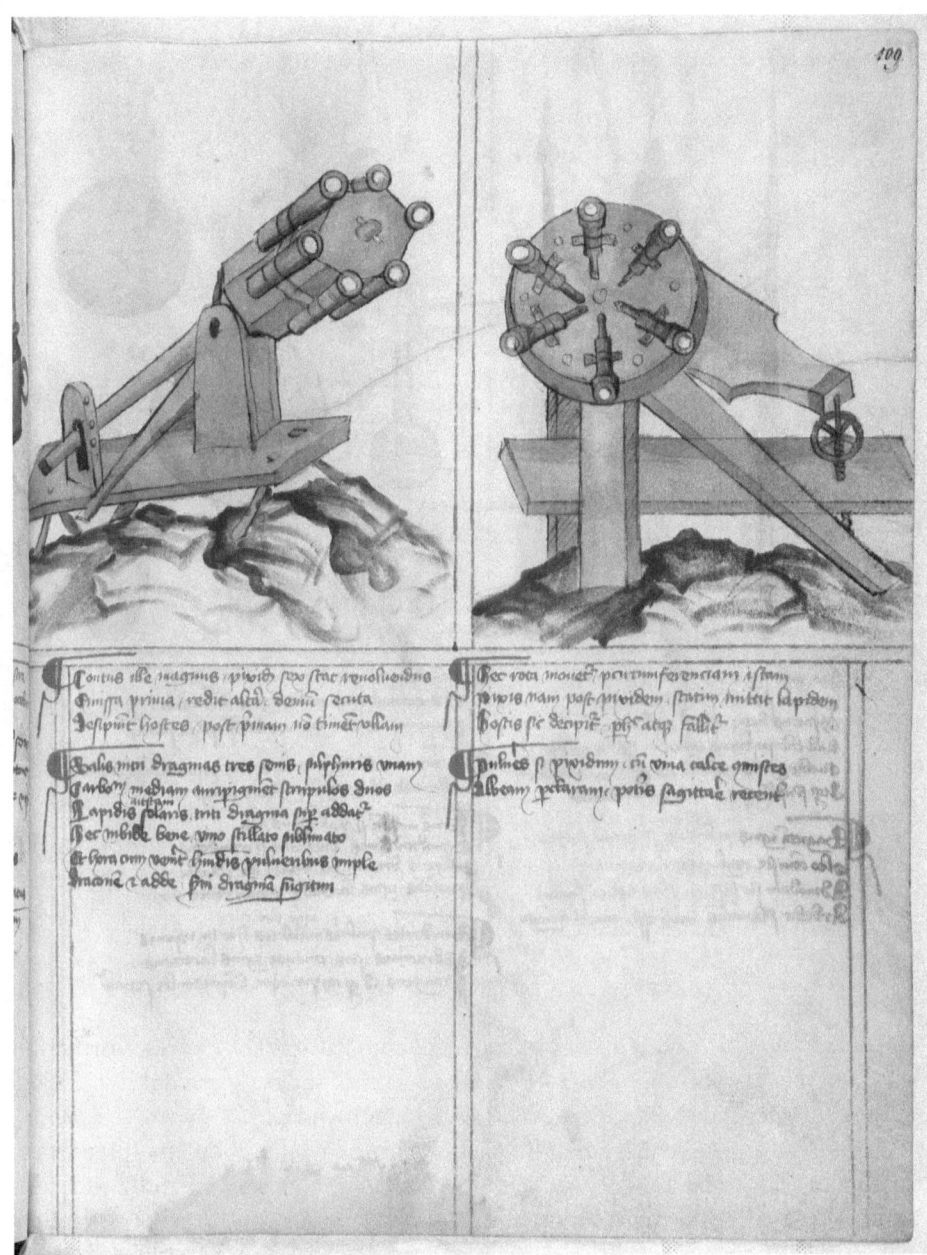

FIG 2 *Bellifortis*: a military instrument. Göttingen, Universitätsbibliothek, Cod. Philos. 63, fol. 109r. Courtesy of the Universitätsbibliothek.

FIG 3 *Bellifortis*: a military instrument. Göttingen, Universitätsbibliothek, Cod. Philos. 63, fol. 38v. Courtesy of the Universitätsbibliothek.

the preparation of various kinds of fires out of combustible substances, instructions which have magical components—became a source of the *Bellifortis* not just through the *De mirabilibus mundi*, but also directly in its own right.[78]

Later sections of Kyeser's handbook instruct the reader about the preparation of magical rings and amulets against demons, dogs, and wolves, and also against fever. The inscription to be engraved in this latter ring is composed of the following enigmatic magic words "Goll Gott Goray," which may be derived from the

78. The *Liber ignium* served also a source for the *Kyranides*, the *Experimenta Alberti*, and the *De mineralibus* by Albertus Magnus. See *HMES*, 2:785–87.

Natural Magic

FIG 4 *Bellifortis*: summoning of spirits. Göttingen, Universitätsbibliothek, Cod. Philos. 63, fol. 94r. Courtesy of the Universitätsbibliothek.

names for God in Hebrew and German.⁷⁹ A full-page colored picture shows a man in the tower of a castle with a horn in his hands, invoking demons, who arrive in the form of naked goblins, one riding a broomstick, the other carrying, as the text informs us, the fat of a hanged man (fig. 4). Secondary literature identifies the person summoning the demons from the tower with Kyeser himself, comparing the picture with his portrait on the last page of the manuscript.⁸⁰ But this identification is only one of the many reasons why we can view Kyeser not only as an active engineer but also as a practicing magician.

With this information, we should not be astonished by how Kyeser closes the book—he casts his own horoscope—or by his inclusion of the magical arts among the sciences. In this classification, after having listed the seven liberal arts, and before getting to the mechanical sciences, Kyeser mentions theurgy and the "exceptive" arts as basic branches of science.⁸¹ The use of the word *ars exceptiva* implies—as we saw in Chapter 1—that the author was familiar with the terminology of the notory art. One more feature supporting this impression is that Kyeser gives the list of sciences in the same order as the *Ars notoria:* liberal, exceptive, and mechanical arts. In the next paragraph, he explains each of the liberal arts briefly; after the description of *loyca, rhetorica, arismetrica, geometria, musica, astronomia,* we read about a method of divination, *geomancia.* All this is again followed by *theologia, philosophia, leges, jus canonicum, phisica,* and then comes *alchimia.* The list of sciences are completed by the *artes theurgice,* that is, magic, which is called "the most sophisticated branch of the mechanical arts," and finally—since we are actually reading a book on military techniques—by the *ars militaris*.⁸² The university subjects, the mechanical sciences, and the magical arts merge into each other rather organically, without any attempt to condemn or exclude the latter ones.

It is not just modern philologists who consider Kyeser's book noteworthy; according to all indications, it provoked considerable interest among its contemporaries, too. Rather exceptionally in the distribution of medieval manuscripts, at least four early drafts from the time of the very composition of the *Bellifortis* have survived, and a relatively large number of copies and excerpts from the following decades have come down to us.⁸³ This shows that however isolated Kyeser might have felt

---

79. MS Göttingen, Universitätsbibliothek, Cod. philos. 63, fols. 132r–133v. In the Golem stories, *Gol* is sometimes the word that the Golem-homunculus has to bear in his mouth in order to be activated. See Kyeser, *Bellifortis,* 98.

80. See the articles of White and Eamon.

81. "Maior quoque theurgica ast minor exceptivas / Obtinent pitagoricas iam artes expletivas / Ac mechanorum practicas sic tradunt inventivas / Militares quoque strages docentes adoptivas." See Kyeser, *Bellifortis,* 101.

82. Kyeser, *Bellifortis,* 102–3.

83. For a list of manuscripts, see Quarg's introduction, in Kyeser, *Bellifortis,* xxx–xxxi, complemented by White, "Kyeser's *Bellifortis,*" 437, and by Leng, *Ars belli,* 134–49.

himself physically in the mountains, he was by no means isolated intellectually, and news of his ideas spread rather quickly.

One of the copies of the *Bellifortis* belonged to the library of Emperor Sigismund, and most probably it was prepared especially for him.[84] From this codex, only the first eight consecutive folios have survived, belonging to the first, astrological, chapter. The extant pages—kept in Budapest at present—contain illustrations depicting the astrological planets symbolically, as human figures on horseback with flags in their hands.[85] Fortunately, Kyeser had died before he could have faced the trauma that the illuminator of this fragment depicted his greatest enemy, the emperor, as the knight symbolizing the sun (the Budapest fragment is the only *Bellifortis* manuscript known to us that contains the portrait of Sigismund). Nothing could have been further from the author's intent. Kyeser belonged to the court of Wenceslas IV, whom Sigismund deposed; moreover, he dedicated the *Bellifortis* to Ruprecht of Pfalz (briefly emperor between Wenceslas and Sigismund, and far from friend of his successor). Kyeser's hatred of Sigismund dated from the time of the military failure in Nicopolis, and his expulsion from the Imperial court did nothing to improve his attitude. To ensure that the reader would not misinterpret his true feelings, he characterizes Sigismund in the opening pages of the *Bellifortis* as "false-hearted and good-for-nothing" (*fallacem et nequam*). It should be added that this passage is missing from those copies of the *Bellifortis* made after Ruprecht's death (1410) and Wenceslas IV's reconciliation with his brother in 1411. They were probably omitted from the Budapest manuscript as well.

Sigismund is not the only Central European monarch with whom these surviving pages can be linked; we have all the reasons to suppose that they spent a few decades on the shelves of the famous Corvinian Library of King Matthias of Hungary. These fragments of the *Bellifortis* were found in the nineteenth century in the archives of Constantinople. The only way they could have gotten there was if they had belonged to the Corvinian Library, a great portion of which was brought to Constantinople in the sixteenth century, when the Ottomans occupied Hungary. Consequently, it is plausible to consider the Budapest fragments of Kyeser's military handbook as the remains of a Corvinian codex. And it must have been magnificent: the artistic quality of the images of the fragment is higher than that of the other versions of the *Bellifortis*,[86] including the beautiful Göttingen

---

84. Hungarian Academy of Sciences, MTAK Cod. Lat. K 465. *BH*, 1:699, in Csaba Csapodi, ed., *Catalogus Collectionis Codicum Latinorum et Graecorum, K 393–K 500* (Budapest: MTAK, 1985); Csapodi, "Az úgynevezett 'Liber de septem signis': Kyeser 'Bellifortis'-ának töredékéről" (The So-Called *Liber de septem signis*: On the Fragment of Kyeser's *Bellifortis*), *Magyar Könyvszemle* 82 (1966): 217–36; Csapodi, "Ein Bellifortis Fragment von Budapest," *Gutenberg Jahrbuch* (1974): 18–28.

85. Reproduced in Csapodi, "Az úgynevezett 'Liber de septem signis.'"

86. The following microfilm and photocopies of the *Bellifortis* may be found in the collection of the Hungarian Academy of Sciences: D 11236/2–3 and D 626–36: MTAK Cod. Lat. K 465 (fifteenth

copy.[87] In Matthias's book collection, works on military techniques played a rather crucial role,[88] and as did works on astrology,[89] thus Kyeser's book would not have felt alone or isolated in this environment.

---

century); Mf A 256/IV: BAV Pal. lat. 1986; Mf A 239/II: ÖNB Cod. lat. 5518; Mf A 207/IV: ÖNB Cod. lat. 3068; Mf A 1604/II: Göttingen, N.S.U.B. Cod. MS Philos., 63 (fifteenth century); Mf A 1604/III: Göttingen, N.S.U.B. Cod. MS Philos., 64 (fifteenth century); and Mf A 139/V: ÖNB Cod. lat. 5278 (sixteenth century).

87. Csapodi, "Az úgynevezett 'Liber de septem signis,'" 226–27. More precisely—the argument continues—several signs (folios are made of paper instead of parchment, verses are not copied in straight lines, and so on) indicate that this version was not the very copy dedicated to Sigismund, just a final draft of it.

88. According to Galeottus Martius Narnensis, *De egregie, sapienter, iocose dictis ac factis regis Mathiae*, ed. Ladislaus Juhász, vol. 3 (Budapest: Egyetemi ny., 1934), 9, Matthias praised the works of Frontinus and Vegetius. See also the following extant manuscripts: (1) Kraków, Biblioteka Czartoryskich, Cod. 1514, Frontinus, *Stratagemata*, (1467), Italy (Florence), see also *BH*, 2:1909; (2) Budapest, Országos Széchényi Library, Cod. Lat. 444, Frontinus: *Stratagemata* (fifteenth century), Italy, *BH*, 1:949; (3) Flavius Vegetius, *De re militari*, see *Bibliotheca Corvina*, (Budapest, 1927), 82. Further military sources from Matthias's Corvinian Library: Robertus Valturius: *De re militari;* Paulus Santinus: *De re militari;* Alexandri Cortesii: *Laudes bellicae Matthiae Regis;* Leon Battista Alberti: *Filarete*. On these titles, see Jolán Balogh, ed., *A művészet Mátyás király udvarában: Adattár* (Art in the Court of King Matthias: Database) (Budapest: Akadémiai Kiadó, 1966), 642; János Csontosi, "Hadtudományi munkák Mátyás király könyvtárában" (Military Works in King Matthias' Library), *Hadtörténeti Közlemények* (1890): 199–210; and Csaba Csapodi and Klára Csapodiné Gárdonyi, *Bibliotheca Corviniana: The Library of King Matthias Corvinus of Hungary*, 4th ed. (Budapest: Helikon, 1990).

89. On the role of astrology in King Matthias's court and library, see Chapter 8.

3

Image Magic

Monsters in the Castle

A notable Flemish mathematician, engineer, and architect of the sixteenth century, Simon Stevin of Bruges (1548–1620), who was actually the first scientist to make consistent use of decimal fractions in mathematical operations, resided in Kraków from 1570 to 1575. During his stay, he took the opportunity to visit the Polish royal castle, the Wawel, and described some strange pictures he admired there: "J'ay veu une partie d'autres signes en peinture contre les parois d'une chambre, à la court du Roy de Pologne en Craco qui éstoient de forme monstrueuse, dont les membres éstoient composez de diverses espèces d'animaux, et éstoit écrit auprès Signa Hermetis, c'est à dire les signes d'Hermes."[1]

We are not in the position anymore to verify what exactly Stevin saw when he wrote of the monstrous figures, because these decorations perished in a fire twenty years later. On the basis of the written source material, however, it becomes possible to reconstruct what the "signs of Hermes" may have looked like. The zoomorphic creatures composed of various different animals described by the Flemish savant are most probably the depictions of certain planetary figures, the so-called decanic spirits. These demons of Egyptian origin are supposed to rule the decans, arcs of ten degrees, thirty-six of which constitute the ecliptic. The artist may have had various different astrological models for his work, since the concept of decans—originally introduced in Europe through Arabic astral magic—was quite widespread; it appears not only in works of image magic of Arabic origin, such as the

---

1. Simon Stevin de Bruges, *Les oeuvres mathématiques* (Leiden: Elsevier, 1634), 107. For the source and its analysis, see Stanisław Mossakowski, "La non più esistente decorazione astrologica del castello reale di Cracovia," in *Magia, astrologia e religione nel Rinascimento: convegno polacco-italiano, Varsavia, 25–27 settembre 1972,* ed. Lech Szczucki (Wrocław: Zakład Narodowy im. Ossolińskich, 1974), 90–98.

Picatrix, but also in the astrological writings of various Latin authors. However, it is worth underlining that it is exactly the *Picatrix* which introduces the decans with the following words: "Modo sequuntur imagines Hermetis," and it is exactly a Kraków copy of the *Picatrix*, which—singularly—not only describes the decanic spirits but even provides pictures of them. Therefore, it is highly possible that the *Signa Hermetis*, after which the zoomorphic figures of the Wawel were modeled, were exactly the decanic figures of the Kraków *Picatrix*, extant in the collection of the University of Kraków, on the folios of the codex BJ 793.[2]

Before concentrating our attention on this particular codex, it is worth surveying its wider contexts—first, the science of talismans as it can be learned from the literature of image magic and from the Hermetic texts, and second, the extant manuscripts which incorporate image magic in a scientific—astronomical-astrological—context, and which help us figure out how far the monstrous figures of the *Picatrix*, the runic spirit names of the *Liber runarum*, and the demons enclosed in magical rings of the Hermetic *Liber de spiritibus inclusis* (The Book of Enclosed Spirits) were taken seriously.

The Science of Talismans

"The earthly figures are subjected to the figures of the sky, and this is why the wise men who construct images observe the entry of the stars in the celestial figures."[3] Shorter than the philosophical explanations of the *De radiis stellarum* of Al-Kindi, more concise than the definitions of the *Speculum astronomiae*, this single sentence can be seen as the quintessence of the underlying assumptions of every practice of image magic. And the source of this statement is not a magical work, nor is it an apology of magic, but hardcore science. It enjoyed serious legitimacy, being the famous and often quoted ninth sentence in the collection of the hundred aphorisms, the *Centiloquium* of—or so it was believed during the Middle Ages—the great authority of astronomy and astrology, Ptolemy.[4] Teaching that wise men actually make images, that is, talismans, and that while doing so, they study the changes of the celestial constellations, it provided astrological justification for all operations with talismans and lent authority to all texts of image magic.

Getting acquainted with the philosophy behind them, we can now ask a rather practical question: how can we recognize the talismanic texts at first glance when

---

2. Mossakowski, "La non più esistente decorazione," 95–97.
3. "Vultus huius seculi vultibus celestibus sunt subiecti et ideo sapientes qui imagines faciebant stellarum introitum in celestes vultus inspiciebant et tunc operabantur quod debebant." "Centiloquium," in Ptolemaeus, *Quadripartitum* (Venice, 1493), fol. 107v.
4. On medieval commentaries of the *verbum nonum* of the *Centiloquium*, see WP 416–18.

we open the codices containing them? Paradoxically, what seems to be their main common characteristic, namely the use of images and the preference for using pictorial representations, cannot be employed as a *differentia specifica* of image magic.[5] Visual elements play a rather important role in simple divinatory texts that have little to do with talismans, necromantic circles are typical elements in demonic magic, and *notae*—comprehensive charts representing the relations of notions and serving as tools for meditation—are extensively applied in the tradition of *Ars notoria*. Strangely enough, images seem to be less characteristic of works on image magic than of works in these other fields of magic.

What texts of image magic truly have in common is their origin. A library of texts on the use of talismans was formed in the twelfth and thirteenth centuries and consisted almost entirely of Latin translations of Arabic works. The sources arrived in Spain in several waves, the first in the twelfth century, the second—including the *Picatrix* itself—through the court of Alfonso X, king of Castile (1252–84).[6] From a purely scientific point of view, these texts were regarded as fairly acceptable; and even though some of them raised serious theological concerns, as we have seen in the *Speculum astronomiae*, this genre supplied astrological and scientific codices with a range of relatively well-tolerated and keenly copied tracts.

The second common element in these texts is the *imago* (talisman or seal) itself, around which the instructions are organized. In modern terminology, one might differentiate between amulets and talismans. An amulet takes its power, not from the image engraved on it, but from the material of which it is made. The use of the appropriate material (usually a metal) is no less important in the case of the talisman, but the main source of the force of this second type of object is the image engraved on it, and the manner of the act of engraving itself.[7]

In medieval sources, the most often used term is *imago*, frequently spelled *ymago* and abbreviated as "y" or "o" in the manuscripts. An *imago* is not necessarily a two-dimensional image drawn or imprinted as a seal; the term can also refer to a sculpted, three-dimensional object, a statuette, as it does in Thebit's *De imaginibus*. Further elements of the medieval terminology of talismans are the *sigillum* (an image engraved or imprinted, in other words, a seal), the *character* (a letter, a planetary symbol, or a geometrical form), the *figura* (a *character* constructed using geometrical principles), and the *anulus*, often spelled *annulus* (a ring or an image of one).[8]

The classic tracts on image magic are first of all the two texts accepted by the

---

5. For a detailed characterization of the genre of image magic, see Klaassen, "Religion, Science," chap. 2.
6. Charles Burnett, "Translating Activity in Spain," in Burnett, *Magic and Divination*, III, 1036–58; Pingree, "Diffusion"; WP 123–38.
7. For the distinction between talismans and amulets, see Pingree, "Diffusion," 58, and WP 102–3.
8. On the terminology, see WP 91–109 and Skemer, *Binding Words*, 6–19.

author of the *Speculum astronomiae* as depositories of good talismanic magic operating solely with celestial powers: the *De imaginibus* attributed to Thebit, and the *Opus imaginum* of Pseudo-Ptolemy. This very short list might be supplemented by the *Liber sigillorum* (Book of Seals) by Thetel, the *De lapidibus* (On the Stones) ascribed to Ptolemy, the Hermetic *Liber lunae,* and a number of tracts ascribed to Hermes Trismegistos, Toz Graecus, and Belenus, among which the *Liber de xv stellis, xv lapidibus, xv herbis, et xv imaginibus* (The Book of Fifteen Stars, Fifteen Stones, and Fifteen Images) is the best known.

As a historian of image magic has remarked, "These texts do not make for exciting reading."[9] They are usually short, strictly practical, and very systematic pieces. As a rule, they are organized according to the purposes for which the talismans can be applied, but in some cases their structure follows the sequence of the materials out of which the talismans are constructed, and occasionally—as it happens in the case of the Hermetic *De imaginibus sive annulis septem planetarum* (On the Images or Rings of the Seven Planets)—the succession of the celestial bodies with which those materials are associated. Each paragraph specifies the material (stone or metal) of the given image, the exact moment and the astrological conditions under which it is to be prepared, the words to be uttered when creating or burying the figure, and the effects of the talisman. From time to time—as the author of the *Speculum* rightly noticed—angelic names, orations, and suffumigations are also involved. This happens quite explicitly, for example, in Belenus's *De imaginibus septem planetarum* (On the Images of the Seven Planets), where the preparation of the talismans includes the uttering of various charms addressed to the planetary spirits.

What might the medieval collectors of these texts have had in mind? What were the motivations of the scribe copying a given list of talismans: an aversion to blank folios, or genuine interest in the practice?[10] While no definite answers can be given to these questions, we can at least underline a common feature of the texts on image magic: their brevity and the relative ease with which they might be inserted between longer texts in a manuscript. What we see on the final pages of a printed book from Prague can only happen to such short practical talismanic texts. At the end of a printed book from the first years of the sixteenth century that once belonged to the Franciscans of the monastery of Krumlov, and which included the *De scientia motus orbis* (On the Science of the Orb's Motion) of Messahala and the *De vita libri tres* (Three Books of Life) by Marsilio Ficino bound together, eleven folios were attached with a rather considerable selection from the bibliography of image magic. On these few pages, we find the *Liber de quindecim stellis* (Book of Fifteen Stars) of Hermes, the *Liber de lapidibus* (Book of Stones) of Ptolemy, the

---

9. Klaassen, "Religion, Science," chap. 2.
10. On this issue, see ibid., esp. chap. 2.

De septem quadraturis planetarum (On the Seven Squares of the Planets) where unusual spirit names—known also from the *Liber runarum*—appear next to the magic squares (Acerlacayl, Mamariol, Behomydyn, Machunent, Lyeleyl, Anrhyym, Rantayebil),[11] and finally a less talismanic, rather astrological *Tractatus de duodecim signis* (Treatise on the Twelve Signs).[12]

In many codices image magic is a later insertion with hasty and less elaborated handwriting, which would indicate that a user of an already written book found something interesting (practical?) and short enough to incorporate in his book. In other cases the scribe's original intention to copy a text can be obvious; in BAV Pal. Lat. 1375, sufficient space is preserved for the full text of Hermes' *De imaginibus*, although the scribe, for unknown reasons, did not finish the transcription.

The neighboring texts are good indicators of the scribe or collector's intentions. Texts of image magic are usually compiled with practical astrological and astronomical works, books of experiments, and lapidaries, which is a telling correlation concerning the place of talismans in the framework of medieval science. The codicological context leads to the conclusion that scribes "regarded magical images as a potentially legitimate part of natural philosophy, a practical extension of astrology, an adjunct to lapidaries or alchemical works, or a feature of the natural world."[13] While we cannot claim with confidence that the prescriptions for the use of talismans were always followed in practice, and that our manuscripts were once used as handbooks, we still might be able to judge how serious the involvement of the scribes was when incorporating such a text. This requires, obviously, an analysis of specific manuscripts.

Image Magic and the *Picatrix* in Kraków

The theoretical principles behind image magic were not unknown in medieval Kraków. Although the *De radiis stellarum* of Al-Kindi was not a frequent work in the region, the *Speculum astronomiae*[14] and the *Centiloquium* of Pseudo-Ptolemy were definitely known. As for the *Centiloquium*, it was a widespread and often translated text, and the belief that it was authored by Ptolemy himself was not questioned in the Middle Ages.[15] The topics touched upon by the "hundred wise

---

11. For a list of the seven planetary angels in the *Liber runarum*, see Gerrit Bos, Charles Burnett, Thérèse Charmasson, Paul Kunitzsch, Fabrizio Lelli, and Paolo Lucentini, eds., *Hermes Trismegistus: Astrologica et divinatoria* (Turnhout: Brepols, 2001), 416 and 428.
12. PNK adlig. 14 H 208 (Truhlář 2764).
13. Klaassen, "Religion, Science," esp. chap. 2.
14. See Chapter 1.
15. The basic secondary literature on the *Centiloquium* and its translations can be found in Richard Lemay, "Origin and Success of the Kitāb Thamara of Abū Ja'far Ahmad ibn Yūsuf ibn

FIG 5 *De septem quadraturis planetarum.* Kraków, BJ 793, fol. 60r. Courtesy of the Biblioteka Jagiellońska.

sentences" embrace the teaching of the horoscope, methods for finding hidden objects, the significance of comets and constellations, and various kinds of medical advice and diagnoses of various diseases. This collection of aphorisms, inspired by Hermetic and Ptolemaic conceptions (it claimed to be the summary of the *Quadripartitum* of Ptolemy), enjoyed a noteworthy success in Latin scientific literature: more than one hundred and fifty copies survive, nine of which are from the astrological school of Kraków, where it was part of the university curriculum.[16] It occurs, for example, in a medical codex (BJ 805) belonging to a doctor, Andrej Grzymala, which codex we will remember as containing the *Experimenta Alberti*, various medical texts, and two other *Centiloquia:* those of Hermes and Albategni.

Given that the ninth sentence in the *Centiloquium* legitimates the practice of talismans in the astrological-medical context, it seems natural to find texts on image magic in Kraków in the medical and astrological codices. Let us start our survey with a most famous manuscript, kept in the Biblioteka Jagiellońska, BJ 793. This manuscript is a typical handbook, a compilation of practically oriented texts arranged with great care, supplied with many charts, figures, indices, and cross-references in the margins, as well as with special green (a rather rare color in codicology) and red notes helping the reader to find what he is looking for. Large geomantic tables composed of point-diagrams help the user to find answers to his questions, and concentric movable wheel systems provide combinatorial and mnemotechnic methods for remembering the truth once learned. The rich variety of circular and quadrangular figures, mystical characters, and letter-combinations make the handbook visually appealing as well (see figs. 5–10).[17]

Bound together around 1460, this selection comprises common astrological texts on the one hand, and treatises of a magical nature belonging mostly to the area of image magic on the other.[18] The long list of the works starts with texts on nativities and astrological medicine (*De urina non visa*—On Urine Not Inspected, *De aegritudine*—On disease) and continues with considerations on the nature of the signs of the zodiac and the effects of the moon on human life. So far nothing is exceptionally magical; the codex seems to be one of the many astrological and medical items held in the Biblioteka Jagiellońska compiled or written in the fifteenth century. The following texts, however, are devoted to the practices of image magic.

Ibrāhīm: From the Tenth to the Seventeenth Century in the World of Islam and the Latin West," in *Proceedings of the First International Symposium for the History of Arabic Science* (Aleppo: Aleppo University, 1978), 91–107.

16. Richard Lemay, "The Late Medieval Astrological School at Cracow and the Copernican System," in *Science and History: Studies in Honor of Edward Rosen*, ed. Pavel Czartoryski et al., Studia Copernicana 16 (Wrocław: The Polish Academy of Sciences Press, 1978), 337–54.

17. On the visual elements occurring in the magical manuscripts, see Chapter 4.

18. For the list of the texts and their sources, see *CBJ*, 6:120–37, and the "Description of Selected Manuscripts" below.

FIG 6 Geomantic divination. Kraków, BJ 793, fol. 67r. Courtesy of the Biblioteka Jagiellońska.

Image Magic

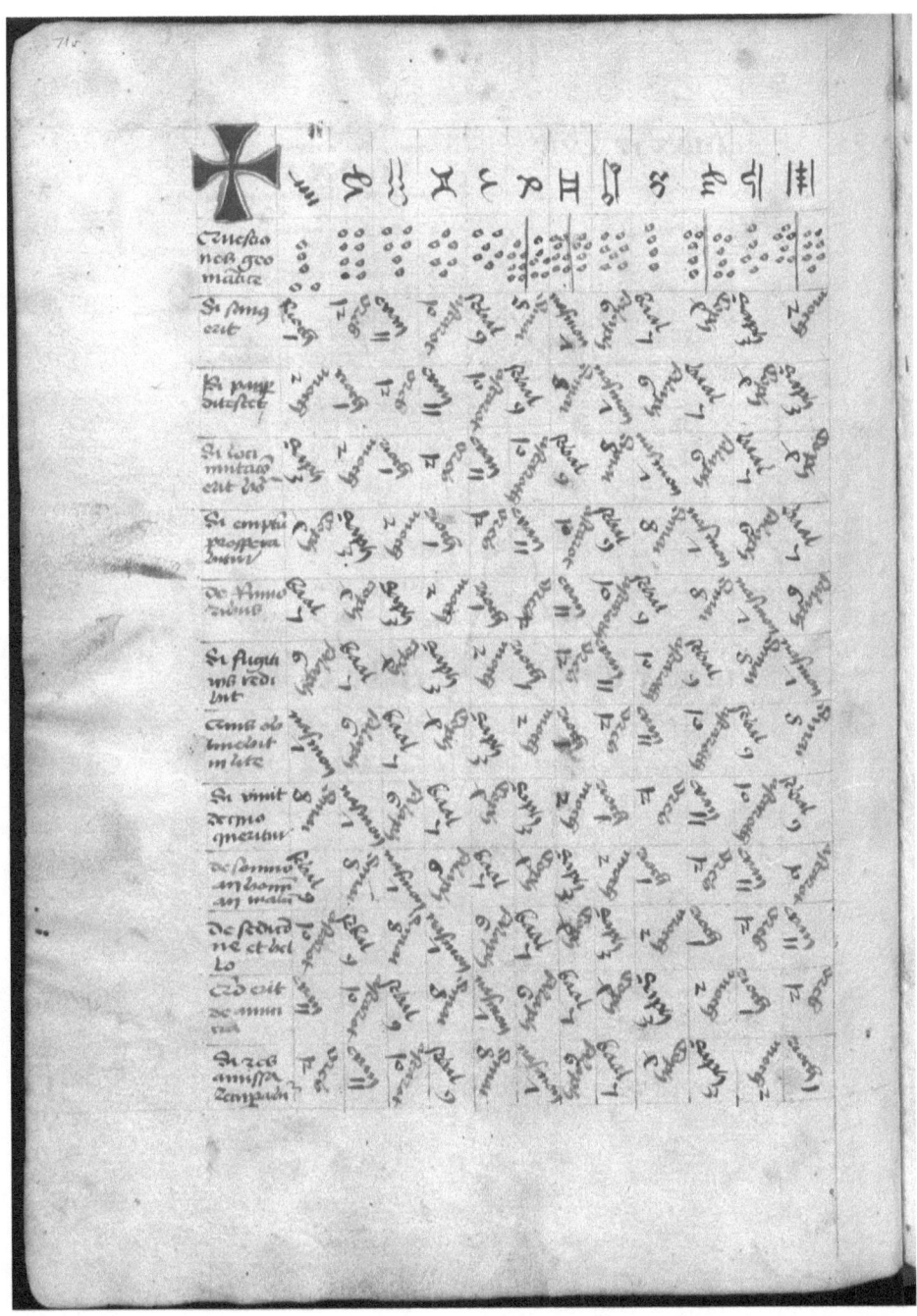

FIG 7   Geomantic divination. Kraków, BJ 793, fol. 71v. Courtesy of the Biblioteka Jagiellońska.

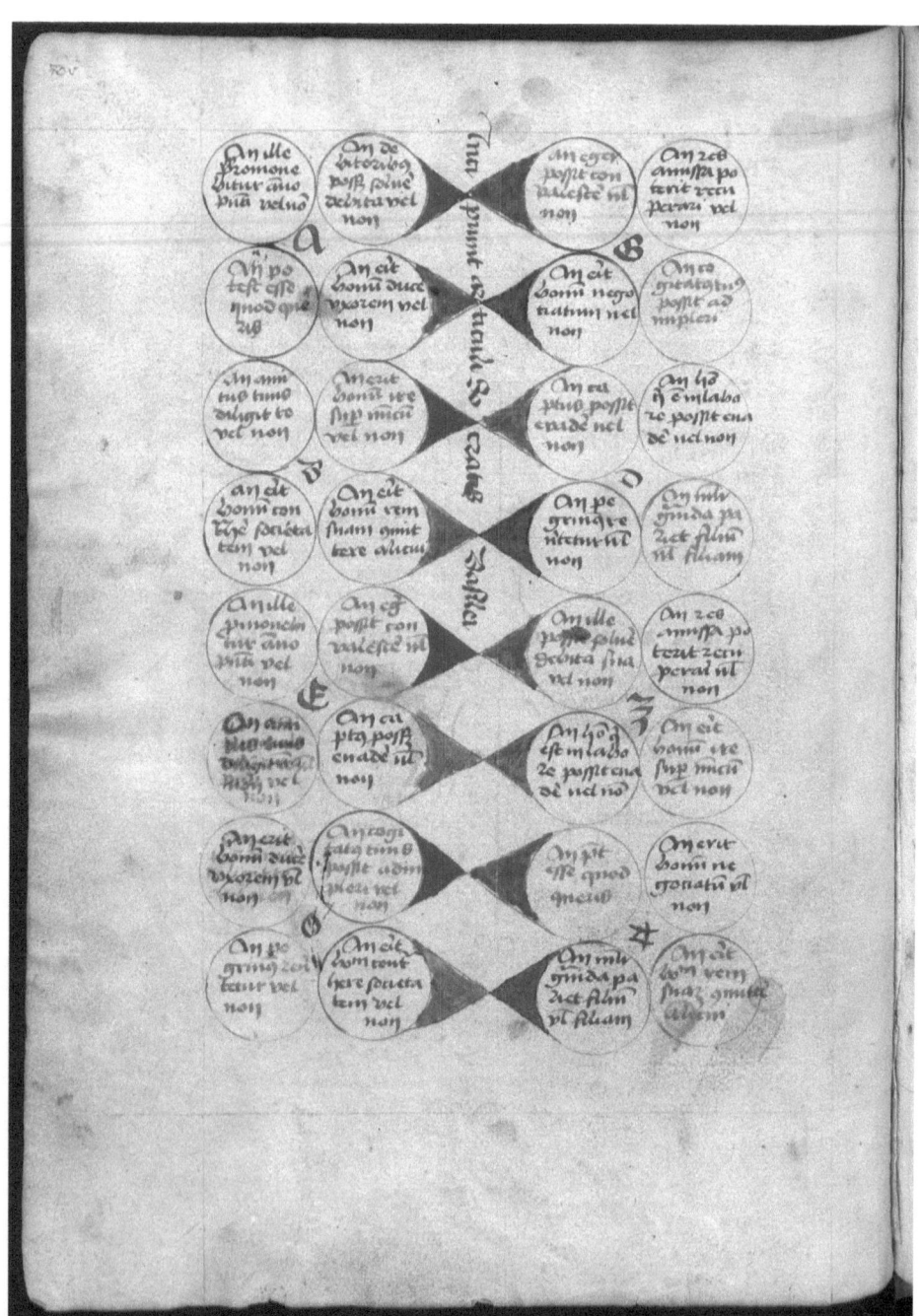

FIG 8 Geomantic divination. Kraków, BJ 793, fol. 73v. Courtesy of the Biblioteka Jagiellońska.

Image Magic

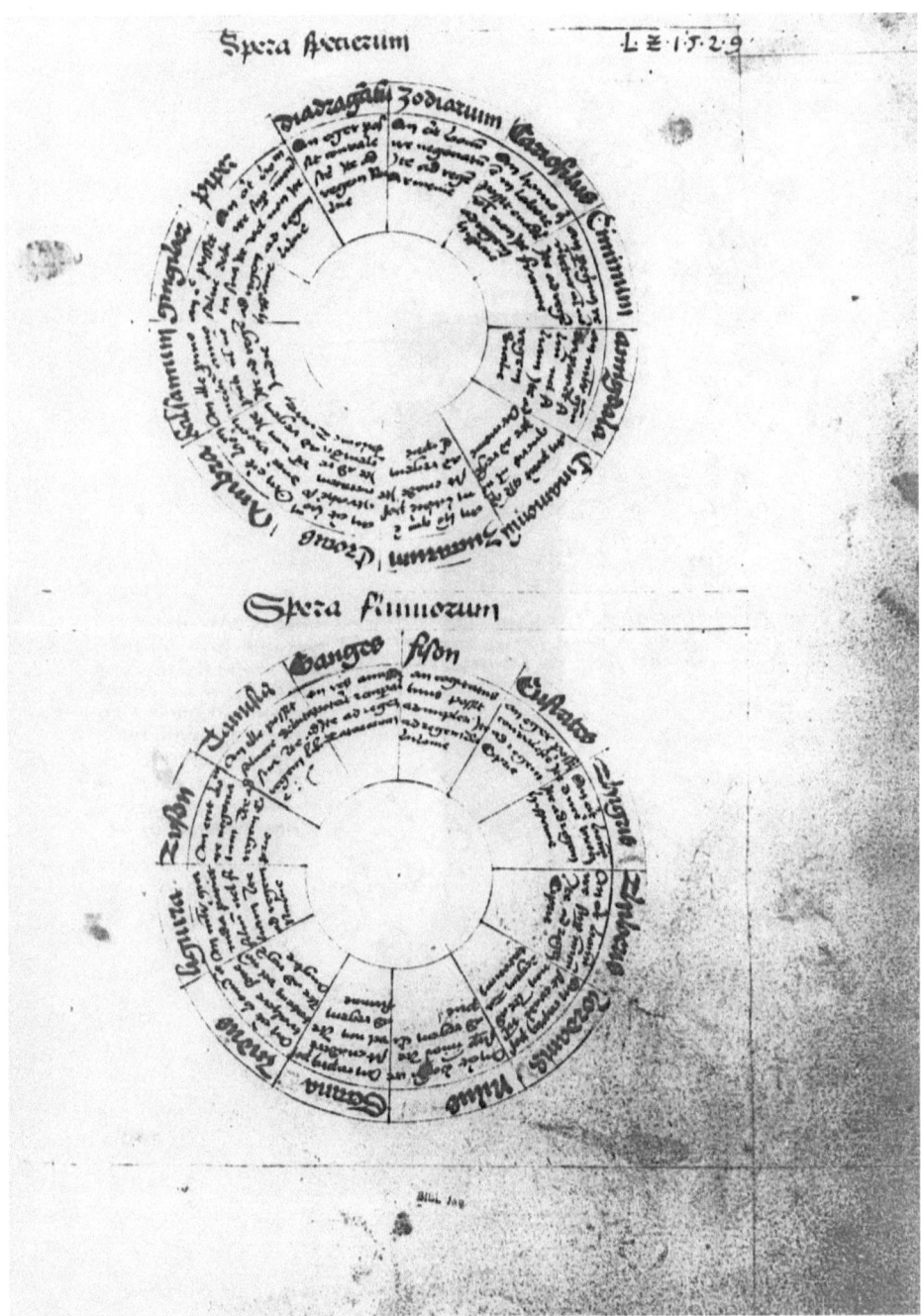

FIG 9 Geomantic divination. Kraków, BJ 793, fol. 75r. Courtesy of the Biblioteka Jagiellońska.

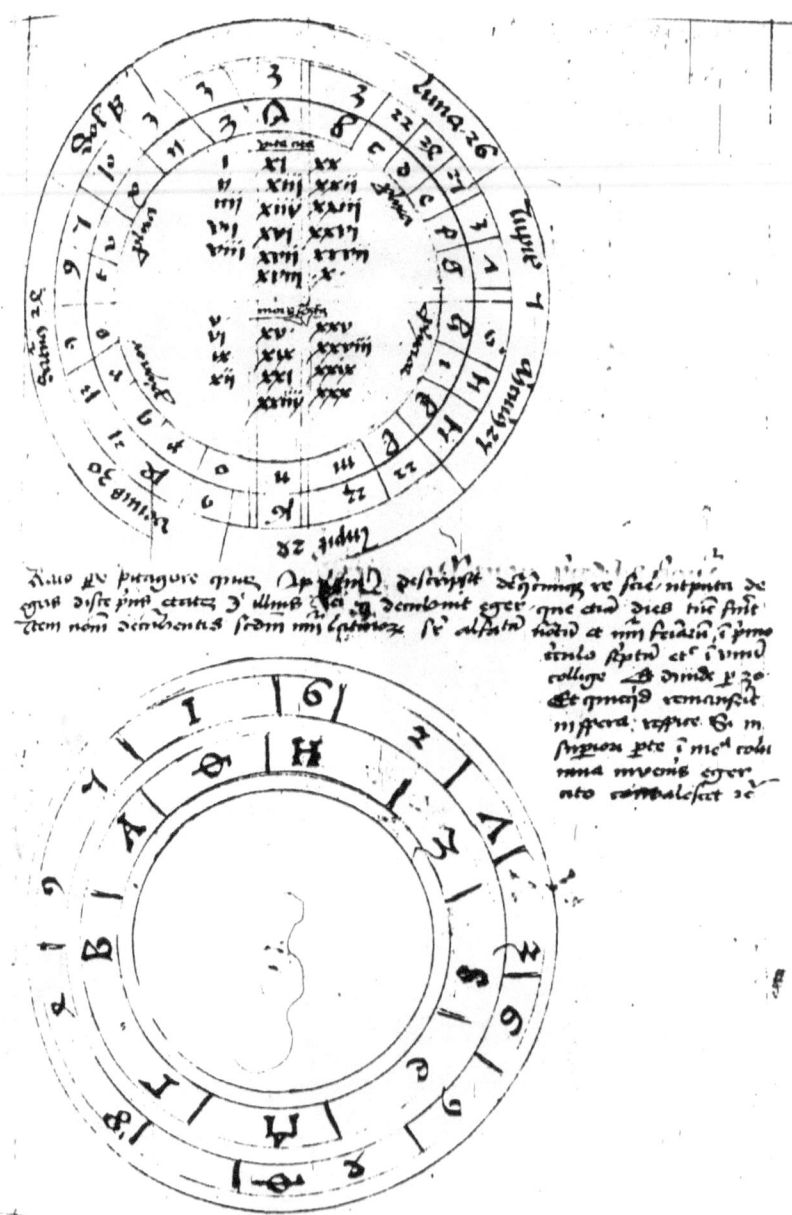

FIG 10 *Sphera Pythagorae*. Kraków, BJ 793, fol. 86r. Courtesy of the Biblioteka Jagiellońska.

In the first of them, *De septem quadraturis planetarum seu quadrati magici* (On the Seven Squares of the Planets, or Magic Squares, reproduced in figure 5), we find magic squares of nine, sixteen, or more cells, each containing a number from one to n^2, where n is the order of the given square. A square of nine cells is a third-order square, for example. These numbers in the cells are arranged in a way that if we add them up in any direction—horizontally, vertically, or diagonally—we are supposed to obtain the same total (in the first square the sum is 15). Each of the squares corresponds to a metal and a planet and represents their secret qualities.

The history of magic squares can be traced back to India and China, and a number of cases can be mentioned from the Islamic and Byzantine worlds until they made their famous appearance in the works of such Renaissance magicians as Cornelius Agrippa and Girolamo Cardano, not to mention the well-known square of four turning up in Dürer's engraving *Melancolia I*.[19] Even though BJ 793 is not the earliest or only Latin occurrence of the magic squares associated with the seven planets before Agrippa, Cardano, and Dürer,[20] the *De septem quadraturis* with its half-dozen identified copies in medieval manuscripts certainly cannot be called a frequent text.[21]

As the power and operability of such talismans depends greatly on how precisely they are prepared, one would expect serious consistency in the instructions provided by the extant copies on the composition of the squares. And yet, one would be disappointed. In the textual tradition, the order in which the squares are

---

19. H. E. Stapleton, "The Antiquity of Alchemy," *Ambix* 5 (1953): 1–43; Schuyler Cammann, "Islamic and Indian Magic Squares," *History of Religions* 8 (1969): 181–209 and 271–99; Vladimir Karpenko, "Magic Squares in European Mysticism," *Hamdard Medicus* 34 (1991): 39–51; Karpenko, "Between Magic and Science: Numerical Magic Squares," *Ambix* 40 (1993): 121–28; Karpenko, "Two Thousand Years of Numerical Magic Squares," *Endeavour*, n.s., 18 (1994): 147–53.

20. Schuyler Cammann, "Islamic and Indian Magic Squares," 292, wrote that the BJ 793 contains the "earliest known instance in Europe of magical squares dedicated to the seven planets." This claim is outdated; see note 21.

21. Thorndike (T 1947, 259–60) mentions two manuscripts where the text is attributed to Ptolemy: Oxford Corpus Christi 125, fols. 76r–77v, and BAV Ottob. Lat. 1809, fols. 21r–25v. For a study on MS Corpus Christi 125 and a larger list of medieval examples on the use of numerical magic squares, see Page, "Magic at St. Augustine's," chap. 4, n. 15. See also Charles Burnett, "The Conte de Sarzana Magical Manuscript," in Burnett, *Magic and Divination*, IX, 1–7. For an analysis and publication of another version of the text (very similar to the Kraków example), see Juris G. Lidaka, "The Book of Angels, Rings, Characters and Images of the Planets: Attributed to Osbern Bokenham," in Fanger, *Conjuring Spirits*, 32–75. In this version (Cambridge University Library MS Dd. 11. 45, fols. 134v–139r), the text on magic squares can be found together with texts of different origin: several *experimenta*, a treatise on the secrets of the planetary spirits, another one on the images of the planets, and several invocations of spirits. A close variant of our text is included in an old English magical compendium from the sixteenth century (British Library, MS Sloane 3826). In this manuscript, the description of the planetary squares follows the *Liber Lunae*. See www.esoteric.msu.edu/Liber/LiberLunae.html. Even in the Central European region there is one more occurrence of the squares: in PNK adlig. H. 208.

associated with the planets varies. In Cardano, the smallest square belongs to the Moon; while Agrippa,[22] the Kraków manuscript, and a rather similar Cambridge copy start with Saturn.[23] The composition of the squares differs, too, in the various copies of the text. While there is only one arrangement of numbers for constructing a third-order magic square (discounting its mirror images and rotations, obviously), there are 880 ways to make a fourth-order square; and this number increases dramatically with the larger squares.[24] Most of these complicated arrangements can be composed only with the help of a computer, medieval and Renaissance scribes could use only algorithmic methods to construct the simpler squares. As a consequence, we often find similar squares in the sources; the fourth-order square of the Kraków manuscript, for example, is identical with that of Dürer's engraving. However, few copies of this text are identical as far as all the seven squares are concerned.

While the scribes enjoyed a certain freedom while constructing the squares, some combinations are simply not correct. This is the case in the Kraków manuscript with the square of five belonging to the planet Mars and with the square of nine corresponding to Mercury, where sums of the rows and columns do not always match the sum indicated in the text. What is even worse, the same number occurs more than once in some of the squares, violating one of the basic rules of the construction—in an nth-order square, each number from 1 to n^2 may be used only once. These errors suggest that the scribe did not really understand the way the numbers are arranged. At first glance, even stronger statements seem justified: as a historian of magic squares claimed, the scribe of the Kraków text "did not have the slightest idea how the system was supposed to work, . . . obviously he was copying something that he failed to understand."[25] However, if we read the Kraków text to its end, we will find a paragraph attached to the instructions that explains how the scribe may double-check at the end whether the construction of a square was successful or not.[26] As the explanations testify, the scribe or the author of the given copy was apparently aware that the sum of the numbers should be identical in every direction, that the largest number occurring in a square is supposed to be the square of the order of the given square, and also, apparently, that each number is to be used only once. This clearly shows that he was familiar with the rules at least on a theoretical level. Perhaps he failed to apply these rules in practice, but he certainly had some ideas about the functioning of the system. Either he made the errors himself, or—more probably—he simply copied what he had in front of

---

22. Girolamo Cardano, *Practica aritmetice et mensurandi singularis* (Milan, 1539), and Cornelius Agrippa, *De occulta Philosophia* (Cologne, 1531).
23. For a transcription of the Cambridge MS, see Lidaka, "The Book of Angels."
24. Karpenko, "Magic Squares in European Mysticism," 39.
25. Cammann, "Islamic and Indian Magic Squares," 292.
26. BJ 793, fol. 61r: "Nota quod iste figure sic debent verificari: in quolibet latere cuiuslibet figure . . ."

him. He may have identified the inconsistency, but he probably did not dare to correct any part of the talisman, exactly because a talisman is supposed to work only in the form given by the sources.

Even though a complicated arithmetical procedure is involved in the construction of such a talisman, the magical content of the squares is not rooted in numerology; the secret properties of numbers play a relatively small role. Magic resides elsewhere in the procedure. Having inscribed each square on a thin metal plate or coin, one can reach a number of aims, not all of them harmless. The figure of Mars, for example, is made for war, battles, and destruction. It is to be engraved on a thin piece of copper in its hour and on its day (which is Tuesday, of course), and then it should be suffumigated with some menstrual blood, or with the clothing of a man hanged or killed with a sword, or—in the event that neither menstrual blood nor such clothing is available—with mouse or cat excrement.[27] As a result of these preparations, the talisman is ready to exert its powers: if it is placed in a building, the building will not be inhabited but left deserted, and it can be equally well used to destroy a business or to cause hatred between two merchants who were fond of each other. And these are just the powers of the figure of Mars engraved on a metal plate and suffumigated appropriately; there are six more talismans, each with its own uses. The last figure—composed of nine rows, and associated with the moon in the Kraków manuscript—for example, if written on parchment and prepared according to the instructions, is appropriate against evil and thieves, and it is also good for expelling someone you hate, provided cucumber and watermelon seeds are applied properly in the procedure. Its preparation requires both conjuration and suffumigation. For expelling someone from a city, the teaching goes as follows: "And speak thus: May N, the son of N leave, and then name the village or the city from where he should be chased away, and say that he shall never return to that city, village or country."[28] Although demons are not named explicitly, this text goes too far. It contains far too many beheaded cocks, ritual instructions, suffumigations, and conjurations, which leave no doubt that the author of the *Speculum astronomiae,* if he had known about it, would have found it intolerable or unnatural.

These multifunctional planetary seals are followed by the great classic of image magic, the *De imaginibus* by Thebit ben Corat (or as the manuscript calls him, Thebith Benthorath), which is no less ambitious than *De septem quadraturis planetarum seu quadrati magici* in its claims—as we have seen in Chapter 1. The main difference is, rather, that the images of Thebit are not ordinary talismans but three-dimensional figures. The version on folios 61r–63r of BJ 793 is almost complete—

27. BJ 793, fol. 60r: "et sculpes predictam figuram et suffumigabis eam cum sanguine menstruoso vel panno suspensi vel cum gladio interfecti vel cum stercorino murium vel munirilegum."
28. BJ 793, fol. 61r: "Et dic sic: Exeat 'N' talis filius 'N', et nominabis villam et civitatem a qua debeat perfugari. Et dicas ab ista civitate vel villa vel patria neque unquam revertatur."

it encompasses the descriptions of all the powerful talismans—only its last paragraph is missing, which is rather an appendix, giving instructions on the preparation of the basic component of the images, the mold.[29] An indication of the scribe's strong fascination with this work is that somewhat later in the manuscript, the same—but this time complete—version of the same text appears, following the *De lapidibus* and the *Opus imaginum* of Pseudo-Ptolemy, the latter of which was the only talismanic text besides Thebit's own to be tolerated by the *Speculum astronomiae*. Regarding this tolerance, it should be added that although this translation of Thebit's images does not include inscriptions on rings, suffumigations, and invocations of spirits (as Adelard's translation does), the author of the *Speculum* apparently overlooked the fact that conjurations are not completely missing.[30]

This classical selection of image magic is followed in the manuscript by a short (fragmented) text attributed to Albertus Magnus, the *Secretum de sigillo Leonis* (Secret on the Seal of Lion),[31] and another short note again on the image of the lion, which refers to Hermes Trismegistos.[32] As "Albertus" instructs the reader in the *Secretum de sigillo Leonis*, when worn around the neck or on the body the *sigillo Leonis* cures various medical problems and protects the wearer against wild beasts, necromancy, demons, and curses. The brief notice ends with explicit references to the secret books of Ptolemy and Hermes on stones and gems. Hermes' teaching on the lion is even shorter than that of Albertus; it is in fact the borrowed first paragraph of a longer text on twelve therapeutic talismans, entitled *De duodecim imaginibus Hermetis* (On the Twelve Images of Hermes) or *Liber imaginum signorum* (The Book on the Images of the Signs).[33]

---

29. See Carmody, *Astronomical Works*, 180–94. Our version terminates on p. 193 in Carmody's edition. For a list of secondary literature on Thebit's work, see the bibliographical essay on image magic.

30. Paragraphs 7 and 17 in Carmody, *Astronomical Works*. For a systematic comparison of the two translations, see Charles Burnett, "Thābit ibn Qurra the Harrānian on Talismans and the Spirits of the Planets," in *The Proceedings of the al-Furqān Conference on Thābit ibn Qurrah, November 2001*, ed. R. Rashed and R. Morelon (forthcoming).

31. Incipit in BJ 793, fol. 63r: "Ego Albertus commentator, in omni experiencia expertus, cum diligenti et vehementi studio perquirerem et discuterem secreta philosophorum antiquorum." The same text can be found in Truhlář 1832, fol. 15v, and in BJ 610, fol. 312v (on this source, containing an excerpt from the *Picatrix*, see more in the next section). See also TK 485. I have found another version of the same text in SLB N. 100, fol. 201v. On the next folio, interestingly, a modern hand transcribed Albert's tract. See also Rosińska 369.

32. Incipit in BJ 793, fol. 63v: "Hermes Trismegistos commemorat in libro suo De ymaginibus, quod sic fit ad calculum: Recipe aurum purum et fac sigillum ubi scribas figuram Leonis Sole existente in Leone." See Rosińska 801 and TK 1319.

33. L-PC 52–53 and WP 477–96. The original *De duodecim imaginibus Hermetis* includes the image of the lion twice: once in the starting paragraph and once in the following list of the twelve signs of the zodiac. In many cases this text of medical astrology occurs in its entirety, such as in a codex copied by a Kraków student, Egidius de Corintia, which contains astrological books by the

The lion enjoyed a privileged position among talismans not only in BJ 793, where two successive texts are consecrated entirely to its preparation and usage, but also in general. Being so widespread, the lion as a seal used for medical practice and therapeutic purposes provoked serious concerns in theology. Jean Gerson, the chancellor of the University of Paris, devoted a whole treatise of his series of polemical works to the question of this particular talisman. In his *Contra superstitionem sculpturae leonis* (Against the Superstition of the Lion's Engraving),[34] he attacked a doctor practicing in Montpellier, who used a seal with the image of the lion for curing renal pains. The main reason behind his attack on this practice was that he suspected an expressed or occult pact with demons in the functioning of astrological seals. The philosophical debate, in which Gerson's intervention was only one element, was not the first in the medical circles of Montpellier. Roughly one hundred years earlier, another controversy along the same lines took place, and this was also the time and the place when and where Jewish doctors introduced the *De duodecim imaginibus Hermetis* into medical discourse.[35] Such an interest in the talisman with the image of the lion left not only written evidence: a medieval seal kept in the Kunsthistorisches Museum of Vienna depicts the sun in the sign of the lion, with the inscription *astronomicum sigillum leonis ghoe* around it.[36]

Returning now to the contents of BJ 793, the series of talisman descriptions is followed by a new thematic section, a set of geomantic texts and tables, which reinforce our impression that the book was copied for actual use.[37]

Whoever the owner of the codex was, he must have been interested not only in manipulating the objects of the world by magical procedures, and not only in predicting the future, but also in the conservation of youth (*De consideratione quintae essentiae*—On the Fifth Essence, by Johannes of Rupescissa), in the water of life (*De aqua ardenti*—On the Ardent Water),[38] in the secret power of stones (*De lapidibus*, attributed to Ptolemy, and the anonymous *Lapidarius Mercurii*—The

---

professors of the university as well as shorter hermetic tracts (SLB N. 100, fols. 172r–173r). However, the first paragraph of this text had a tendency to travel separately, and achieved a much wider dissemination. In addition, the whole *De duodecim imaginibus Hermetis* was also incorporated in the *Picatrix;* therefore, the same instructions on the seal of the lion circulated in various medieval manuscripts under three different redactions. As for the *Picatrix*, see *Picatrix*, 82–83. The translation of the *Picatrix* was finished in 1258, but there are good reasons to suppose that the section *De duodecim imaginibus Hermetis* was inserted only after 1300. The *De duodecim imaginibus* is also quoted in full in Hieronymus Torrella, *Opus praeclarum de imaginibus astrologicis non solum medicus verum etiam litteratis viris utile ac amenissimum* (Valencia: Alphonso de Ortu, 1496), fols. miir–miiiv.

34. In Gerson, *Oeuvres complètes*, 10:131–34.
35. On these controversies and Gerson's intervention, see WP 595–602.
36. WP 893.
37. Since geomantic tracts were used to divine the future, I describe them in Chapter 4, which is devoted entirely to divination.
38. *De consideratione quintae essentiae* and *De aqua ardenti* often traveled together.

Lapidary of Mercury), and also in various experiments to produce a mixture for invisible writing[39] and to find hidden objects and treasure.

Such a comprehensive anthology of readings in practical magic would be somewhat incomplete without the greatest work on talismanic magic, the *Picatrix*, which is the closing text of the codex. The *Picatrix* was translated from Arabic into Castilian at the court of Alfonso the Wise sometime between 1256 and 1258, and from Castilian into Latin probably shortly thereafter. It is more than a collection of works on talismanic magic or a simple compilation of recipes. It contains a great variety of other elements too: theory of science and magic, classification of magic, theoretical justification of amulets, prayers to planetary spirits, and methods for constraining demons, not to mention further rituals.[40]

The circulation of the *Picatrix* in medieval Europe is by no means ordinary. Although it was translated in the mid-thirteenth century, mysteriously no textual quotation of it can be identified in Latin authors before the humanists, and only a few of its copies survived from before the second half of the fifteenth century.[41] One of them is the version preserved in BJ 793. The first two hundred years of this basic handbook of astral magic are practically hidden from our eyes.

Earlier extant instances of the Latin *Picatrix* are without exception short fragments and excerpts, and the majority of the copies come from the sixteenth and seventeenth centuries.[42] Interestingly, one of these fragments happens to be today

---

39. BJ 793, fol. 121v: *De nonnullis experimentis* "si vis habere scripturas in aliquam corporis parte invisibilem"; "si vis in die scripturas invisibiles nocte vero visibiles habere." On the question of secret writing, see also John B. Friedman, "Safe Magic and Invisible Writing in the *Secretum Philosophorum*," in Fanger, *Conjuring Spirits*, 76–86.

40. For the text and the secondary literature of the *Picatrix*, see Vittoria Perrone Compagni, "*Picatrix latinus*. Concezioni filosofico-religiose e prassi magica," *Medioevo* 1 (1975): 237–77; the Pingree edition of the Latin text; Perrone Compagni, "La magia ceremoniale de *Picatrix* nel Rinascimento," *Atti dell'Accademia di scienze morali e politiche di Napoli* 88 (1977): 279–330; David Pingree, "Some of the Sources of the Ghayat al-Hakim," *JWCI* 43 (1980): 1–15; and Pingree, "Between the *Ghâya* and *Picatrix*, 1: The Spanish Version," *JWCI* 44 (1981): 27–56. See also the bibliographical essay, as well as WP 125–34.

41. Apart from a fragment dating from the thirteenth century—see Alfonso el Sabio, *Astromagia*, ed. A. d'Agostino (Naples, 1992), 28 n. 51—most of the surviving copies seem to derive from an Italian manuscript of the middle of the fifteenth century, while the rest go back to a copy made near Liège in the 1380s, which has not survived. See Perrone Compagni, "La magia ceremoniale"; Pingree, "Description of Manuscripts," in his edition of *Picatrix*; and Charles Burnett, "The Scapulimancy of Giorgio Anselmi's *Divinum opus de magia disciplina*," in Burnett, *Magic and Divination*, XVI, 63–64.

42. Three fragments or excerpts of the *Picatrix* are known to have been copied in Central Europe. One is kept in the Vatican library (BAV Pal. lat.1354, fols. 243v–246r) and was copied in Prague by a Czech scribe, Johannes de Bazyn, around 1470. See *Picatrix*, xlvi–li (Pingree edition), and Lynn Thorndike, "Notes upon Some Medieval Astronomical, Astrological and Mathematical Manuscripts at the Vatican," *Isis* 49 (1958): esp. 45–47. The second excerpt is not included in Pingree's edition. It can be found in BJ 610, fols. 312v–316r. Originally it was bound together in a twenty-folio long

remarkably near Kraków. It survived in the binding (as fragments usually survive) of an unknown book, and is kept at present in the Literárny Archív in Martin (a town in the present-day Slovak Republic).[43] While the Kraków copy is the earliest surviving *Picatrix* that is longer than a few folios, the Martin copy is one of its earliest fragments, dating from the fourteenth century. It is possible that the fragment has a local origin and was copied somewhere in the region (meaning Upper Hungary, or southern Poland). The binding comes from the Piarists of Podolin (Podolinec), which was part of the historical Szepes County, given by the Hungarian king Sigismund to Kraków as a mortgage. Can we conclude from this historical connection between Upper Hungary and Kraków that there is a connection between the Martin and the Kraków copies of the *Picatrix?* It is not out of the question that the Martin copy was the source for the Kraków codex, though it would not be easy to prove this connection, especially because the fragment contains exactly those parts of the text (the end of book 2 and the beginning of book 3) which were not included in BJ 793. At the moment, there is more evidence for an Italian origin for the Kraków text.

As it has been mentioned, the Kraków version is unfinished; it contains only the first two parts of the *Picatrix,* including the chapter on the meaning of necromancy, the description of images serving various magical purposes (eternal love, destroying cities, expelling snakes, and separating friends), and the chapters on how one can learn the science of images. Although the Prologue promises all four books, the text is interrupted in the middle of chapter 10 of the second.[44] Before the break, the text describes and the pictures depict the images of the seven planets according to various different traditions. The illustrations match the text perfectly. However, after the first figure of the last planet but one, the text breaks off, only the images are provided, still faithfully depicting what the text—as reconstructed on the basis of other manuscripts—contains.

Now, what is unique in our manuscript, and what brought it worldwide repute, is that although the text stops unexpectedly, the following folios contain the pictures of the planetary and decanic figures—just as the text instructs. This Kraków manuscript is the only illustrated *Picatrix* known to us; indeed, when illustrating his critical edition, the editor could not but borrow from this copy of the text (see

---

fasciculum with astrological and talismanic material, such as the Pseudo-Albertus Magnus's *Secretum de sigillo leonis,* and an excerpt from Hermes's *Centiloquium,* and these folios were later inserted in a longer codex containing astronomical charts, tables, and celestial coordinate systems (see *CBJ,* 6:252–74). The third fragment from Martin (not known to Pingree either) is described in the main text.

43. Martin, Literárny archív Matice slovenskej, J 2042. For a detailed codicological description of the fragment, see Július Sopko, ed., *Codices Ac Fragmenta Codicum Bibliothecarum Slovaciae* (Martin: Matica Slovenská, 1986), 168–69.

44. *Picatrix,* 67, line 15.

figs. 11–14).⁴⁵ Not just the modern scholars, but contemporaries as well found the pictures worthy of interest, as we saw in the beginning of this chapter. Thanks to Simon Stevin's testimony, it can be claimed with confidence that the frescos of the Wawel depicted similar—if not the same—zoomorphic decanic representations as our manuscript. In the history of medieval manuscripts, rarely if ever can the cultural impact of one single codex be detected so directly.

The rich pictorial material of BJ 793 also helps us trace its history. According to the art historian, the clothes in the pictures point to the fourth decade of the century, depicting the Bohemian style.⁴⁶ In contrast—as it happens—the text editor supposes that the codex was copied from one or several Italian sources.⁴⁷ The only certain fact is that the manuscript was copied by a Polish scribe, because he refers to his Polish environment and also because the codex contains a few texts of Polish origin, such as the astro-meteorological work on the disposition of the airs by Petrus Gaszowiec, a Polish astronomer-astrologer.⁴⁸ In the absence of any concrete indication of the owner of the manuscript, we can only speculate about him. On the basis of the character of the collected texts, we can conclude that he was a learned person, probably a professor of the university. If the assumption that the codex is the copy of an Italian book is correct, then it must have been brought to Kraków by one of the many students and professors who had traveled to Italy. According to the most convincing conjecture this person was Petrus Gaszowiec, the author of one of the works inscribed in it, *De mutatione aeris* (On the Changes of the Air).⁴⁹

Petrus Gaszowiec (before 1430–74) was an astrologer, astronomer, and physician, and served as rector of the University of Kraków on three occasions.⁵⁰ He came from a noble family, and was one of the many wandering students of the fifteenth century. He received a doctorate in medicine in Perugia (1452–54), continued his medical studies until 1456 at the University of Cologne, and then returned to Kraków just before the creation of the manuscript. Two copyists accompanied him

---

45. Ibid., tables 3–18. For the iconography of decans, see Ewa Śnieżyńska-Stolot, *Astrological Iconography in the Middle Ages: The Decanal Planets* (Kraków: The Jagiellonian University Press, 2003).
46. Zofia Ameisenowa, *Rękopisy i pierwodruki iluminowane Biblioteki Jagiellońskiej* (Illuminated Manuscripts in the Biblioteka Jagiellońska) (Wrocław: Zakład Narodowy im. Ossolińskich, 1958), 180–84. For a reproduction of the pictures, see figures 242–45.
47. *Picatrix*, xvi.
48. BJ 793, fol. 38v; see also Rosińska 616.
49. *CBJ*, 6:136, "Codicis origo et fata."
50. Birkenmajer, *Études d'histoire des sciences en Pologne*, 457–59 and 527–29; *Polski Słownik Biograficzny*, 7:294–95; *A et A* 161–82; Z. Pauly, B. Ulanowski and A. Chmiel, eds., *Album studiosorum Universitatis Cracoviensis* (Kraków: typis, C. R. Universitatis, 1887–1904), 2:114, 178–79, 198; Josephus Muczkowski, ed., *Statuta nec non liber promotionum philosophorum ordinis in universitate studiorum Jagellonica* (Kraków: Uniwersytet Jagielloński, 1849), 40, 43; Hermann Keussen, ed., *Die Matrikel der Universität Köln* (Bonn: P. Hanstein, 1928–81), 1:570.

Image Magic

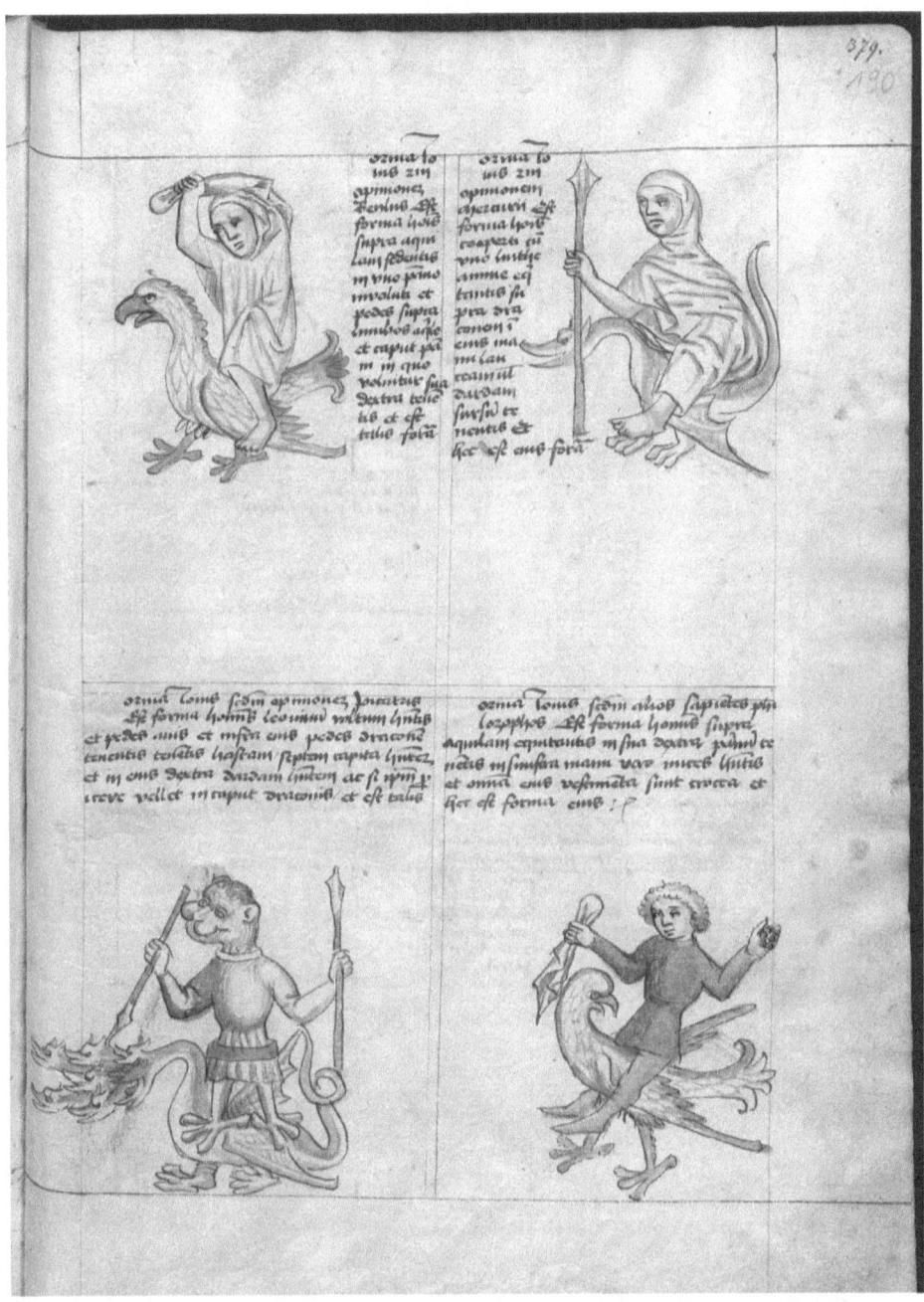

FIG 11 *Picatrix*: planetary figures. Kraków, BJ 793, fol. 190r. Courtesy of the Biblioteka Jagiellońska.

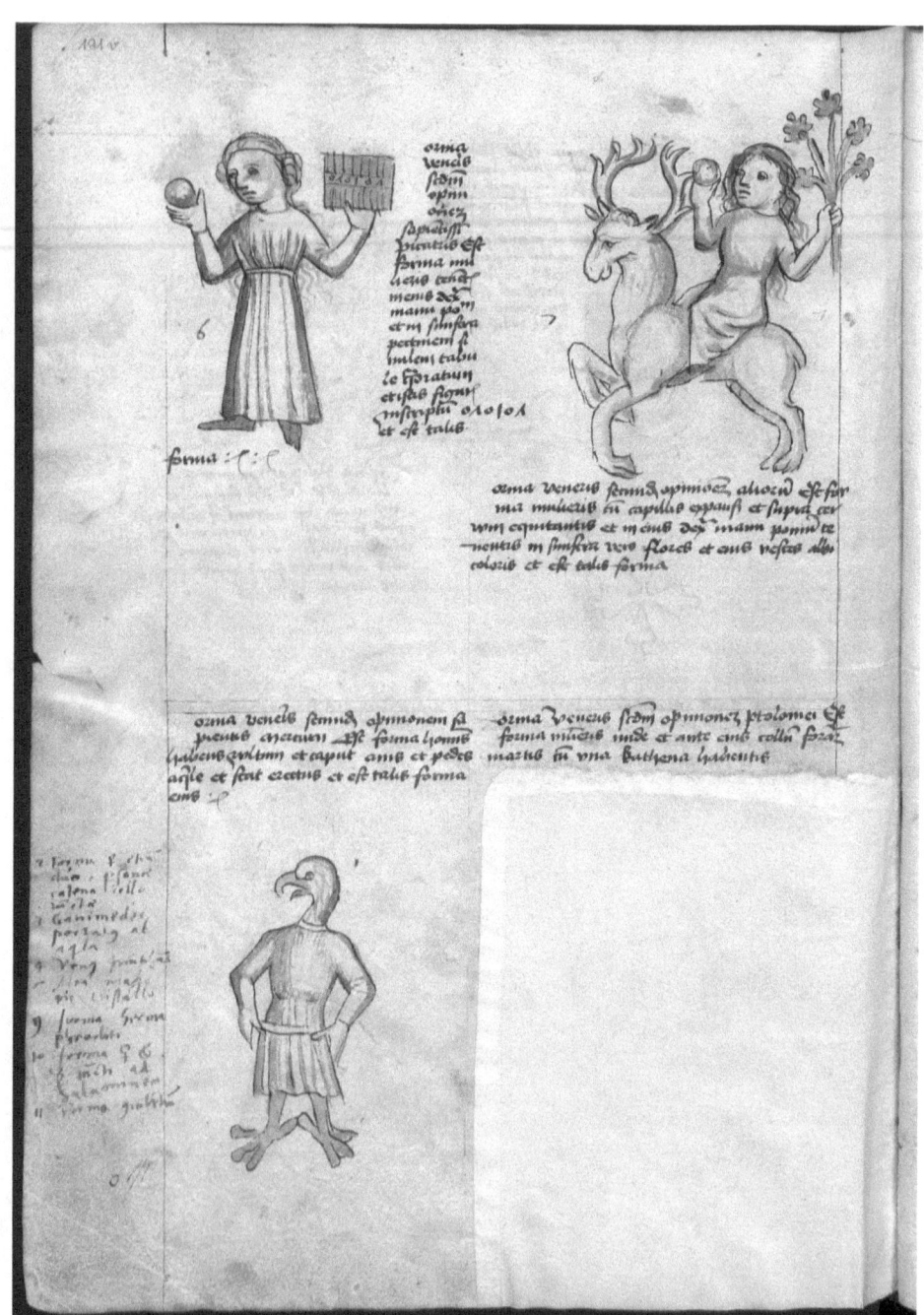

FIG 12   *Picatrix*: planetary figures. Kraków, BJ 793, fol. 191v. Courtesy of the Biblioteka Jagiellońska.

Image Magic

FIG 13 *Picatrix*: decanic figures. Kraków, BJ 793, fol. 193v. Courtesy of the Biblioteka Jagiellońska.

102 PART TWO: TEXTS AND HANDBOOKS

FIG 14   *Picatrix*: decanic figures. Kraków, BJ 793, fol. 197r. Courtesy of the Biblioteka Jagiellońska.

on his travels, which helps us understand how the contents of such a handbook could have been transmitted.

The book itself, as an object, was not a simple import from Italy or Germany. It was bound in Kraków around 1460, and written by a Polish hand. However, most of the texts are undeniably reproductions of well-known Western writings. The whole codex might be viewed as a selection of Gaszowiec's favorite treatises, either because they were connected with his own *De mutatione aeris*, or simply because he found them stimulating. In a word, if Gaszowiec was not the owner of this codex, the real author was probably a man of similar background, another master of astronomy or medicine at the University of Kraków.

To sum up, BJ 793 can be seen as a representative handbook of image magic, a good starting point for anyone wishing to familiarize himself with the science of talismans. In a scientific and astrological context, the scribe included a long list of divinatory methods, the classic texts on images. But why did he not choose to include the whole *Picatrix* in this anthology?

Perhaps, consciously or not, he was following the distinction made in the *Speculum astronomiae* between natural and demonic talismans—that is talismans which take their power only from the heavens, and talismans which use demonic help. The system of the *Speculum* was known and to a certain extent adhered to in Kraków. We may recall furthermore that Egidius of Corintia's booklist deviated from the system of the *Speculum* on one occasion, when he referred to the *Picatrix* as one of the two tolerated and natural texts on image magic.[51]

If we accept that there was a nondemonic understanding of the *Picatrix* in fifteenth-century Kraków, we will not be surprised by the fact that the scribe of BJ 793, while compiling a representative handbook of image magic, included those sections of the *Picatrix* which contain the general reports on the classification and learning of magic and the instructions on the preparation and functioning of images, but omitted the third and the fourth books containing the more risky ritual elements: suffumigations of the seven planets and guidelines on how the planetary spirits and demons should be addressed.

While modern secondary literature does not seem to emphasize this difference between the first and second half of the *Picatrix,* a fifteenth-century reader of the text was apparently aware of it. The Florentine philosopher Marsilio Ficino, when compiling the third book of his *Liber de vita tres,* titled *De vita coelitus comparanda* (On Obtaining Life from the Heavens)—which was the most magical in content among the three books—relied heavily on the *Picatrix*. However, even in the

---

51. Needless to say, the *Picatrix* does not appear in the classification of the *Speculum astronomiae*, since it was translated from Arabic into Castilian in 1256–58, just a few years before the *Speculum* was written, and although the Latin translation quickly followed the vernacular one, its dissemination—as we have seen—was very slow in the first centuries.

Florentine milieu, where Hermetic philosophy gave certain legitimacy to talismanic magic, the reception of the *Picatrix* was not simple. There was no problem with the "natural" explanation for the functioning of talismans—as it is explained in the second book of the *Picatrix,* talismans are objects into which the influence of the celestial bodies has been introduced—but when more ritual elements emerged, such as suffumigations, orations, and open invocations to spirits, fifteenth-century readers became more ambivalent.

The critical point is exactly where the decans are described, not only because it is exactly around the decanic pictures where the shift of emphasis takes place in the text of the *Picatrix,* but also because these strange beings seem to leave the safe territory of the natural planetary influences and bear too much resemblance to planetary spirits. And these spirits, not to say demons, apparently require animal sacrifices, suffumigations, invocations, and veneration in exchange for their willing cooperation.[52] These features of the decanic spirits are exactly those which the *Speculum astronomiae* viewed as explicit signs of demonic intervention.

It seems plausible to suppose that the mid-fifteenth-century scribe of BJ 793 and his contemporary, Ficino, had fairly similar reservations concerning talismans. These reservations—going back to the arguments of the *Speculum*—account for the fact that Ficino introduces in his book the images of the planets, the images of the zodiac, but abstains—with one single exception—from describing the decanic figures, the so-called faces of the signs. He is—as Frances Yates put it—"not sure whether it is right to use" them. The same reservations account, I believe, for the sudden ending of the illustrated *Picatrix* in the Kraków manuscript. Concentrating on planetary images and avoiding decanic images, Ficino and the Polish scribe start hesitating at the same place, and this hesitation is "related to the avoidance of demonic magic."[53]

Operative Hermetic Talismans

The Latin texts[54] that comprise medieval Hermetism were attributed to such legendary authors as Hermes, Toz Grecus, Belenus, Thessalus, and Kyranus, as well

---

52. As it is detailed in *Picatrix,* bk. 3, chap. 9.
53. Yates, *Giordano Bruno,* 72; on Ficino's use of the *Picatrix,* see 69–83.
54. The hermetic texts are under publication in the *Hermes Latinus* series by Brepols. The editorial project directed by Paolo Lucentini resulted the following titles: Simonetta Feraboli and Sylvain Matton, eds., *De triginta sex decanis* (1994); Françoise Hudry, ed., *Liber viginti quattuor philosophorum* (1997); Bos et al., *Hermes Trismegistus;* and Paolo Lucentini and Mark D. Delp, eds., *Hermetis Trismegisti De sex rerum principiis* (2006). The next volume is edited by Vittoria Perrone Compagni and will include the hermetic magic texts (among others, the *Liber lunae, De imaginibus sive annulis septem planetarum,* and the *De imaginibus* of Belenus). See also the *Hermes Latinus* web site for further text editions, secondary literature, manuscripts, forthcoming publications, and administrative information: http://www.iuo.it/dipfp/attivita_di_ricerca/hermeslatinus/varie.htm.

as to historical figures such as Aristotle[55] and Alexander. This group is not to be confused with the somewhat more celebrated Renaissance Hermetism. The philosophical-religious Renaissance *Corpus Hermeticum,* translated by Marsilio Ficino from the Greek in the fifteenth century, originates in Late Antique Hellenism. In contrast, the medieval Hermetic texts, which had a stronger accent on pragmatic material, were translated during the twelfth-century renaissance, from the Arabic, mostly by anonymous authors.[56] The major part of these tracts is the fruit of not a Late Antique, but a later redaction, produced by a group of Neoplatonizing Arabic intellectuals, one of whom was Thābit ibn Qurra, who worked in ninth-century Baghdad. Most of the anonymous Arabic authors, however, were not active in Baghdad; they were probably ninth-century Sābians, who lived in the town of Harrān at the Upper Euphrates, and who claimed Hermes as their god.[57] The philosophers of this town played a crucial role in the history of Arabic science; first, as translators from Greek and Syriac into Arabic, second, as authors of new works on natural philosophy and astral magic, and third, as being responsible for the fusion of Persian, Syrian, Greek, and Arabic theories of nature. These are the Harrānian cosmological beliefs, their cult of planetary spirits, and the rituals of the Sābian religion that are mirrored in the medieval Hermetic and pseudo-Aristotelian literature as well as in the *Picatrix,* and these elements differ substantially from the Hellenistic Egyptian-Greek doctrines on nature, astrology, and Hermes, which reemerged in the Renaissance. There is also a divergence in the attributions: Aristotle and Belenus, favorite authors in the *Arabic Hermetica* do not appear in the Renaissance *Corpus Hermeticum.* The only work that was included in both the medieval corpus and the fourteen texts translated by Ficino was the *Asclepius.*[58]

---

55. On Aristotle as an alleged author of hermetic texts, see Charles Burnett, "Arabic, Greek, and Latin Works on Astrological Magic Attributed to Aristotle," in Burnett, *Magic and Divination,* III, 84–97.

56. On the medieval hermetic texts, see the following overviews: Paolo Lucentini, "L'edizione critica dei testi ermetici latini," In *I moderni ausili all'Ecdotica (Atti del Convegno internazionale di studi, Fisciano—Vietri sul Mare—Napoli, 27–31 Ottobre 1990),* ed. Sebastiano Martelli and Vincenzo Placella (Naples: Edizioni scientifiche italiane, 1994), 265–85, and Charles Burnett, "The Establishment of Medieval Hermeticism," in *The Medieval World,* ed. Peter Linehan and Janet L. Nelson (London: Routledge, 2001), 111–30. The few known translators of medieval hermetic texts are Adelard of Bath, Hermann of Carinthia, and Hugo of Santalla.

57. Pingree, "Some of the Sources," 15.

58. On the *Asclepius,* see Paolo Lucentini, "L'Asclepius ermetico nel secolo XII," in *From Athens to Chartres. Neoplatonism and Medieval Thought. Studies in Honour of Edouard Jeauneau,* ed. Haijo Jan Westra (Leiden: Brill, 1992), 398–420. On the Christian reception of Hermetic texts, also see Antonella Sannino, "La tradizione ermetica a Oxford nei secoli XIII e XIV: Ruggero Bacone e Tommaso Bradwardine," *Studi filosofici* 18 (1995): 23–56; Sannino, "Ermete mago e alchimista"; and Pinella Travaglia, "Note sulla dottrina degli elementi nel De secretis naturae," *Studi medievali* 39 (1998): 121–57.

The texts belonging to medieval Hermetic literature comprise both philosophical-religious texts[59] and technical-operative works on astrology, magic, and alchemy. In the latter category there is a strong concern for talismans, often involving ritual actions—a feature found abominable by the author of the *Speculum*. As Charles Burnett emphasizes, "It is a measure of the success" of such critiques and attacks on the operative Hermetic texts that virtually none of them survived in thirteenth- or fourteenth-century copies.[60] As a paradoxical consequence, if we want to read the *Arabic Hermetica* translated in the twelfth century, we have to turn to manuscripts from the second half of the fifteenth century, that is, to sources contemporary with Ficino and other Renaissance philosophers. And we will find that an important portion of these texts had been copied in Kraków.

The name of Hermes Trismegistos was more than well known to the masters of the University of Kraków in the fifteenth century. In a vast number of scientific treatises, they frequently made reference to Hermes. Quoted in an astronomical and astrological context, he was first of all a legendary authority, an expert in the field of astral studies. Along with Ptolemy, Hali, and Guido Bonatus, he was seen as one of the recognized *prisci astrologi* (ancient astrologers).[61] His *Centiloquium* in particular was frequently quoted, copied, and commented upon in the astronomical production of the university.[62] We have already recorded the success of Hermetic texts belonging to the area of natural magic: the *Kyranides*, the *Compendium aureum* of Flaccus Aureus, and the *Liber de septem herbis* ascribed to Alexander the Great. Entering the field of image magic, we should add to this list the basic compilation on talismans, the *Picatrix*, which is not strictly speaking Hermetic in attribution; however, it incorporates a variety of Hermetic material.[63] In the following, we will concentrate on the fate and the codicological context of some other, less widespread Hermetic or quasi-Hermetic practical texts on images that appear in three manuscripts: the Dresden SLB N. 100, and the Vatican's BAV Pal. lat. 1439 and BAV Pal. lat. 1375.

Putting aside for a moment their common talismanic content, there are other connections among these codices that reinforce the impression that they belong

---

59. The *Asclepius*, the *Liber de viginti quattuor philosophorum* (Book of the Twenty-four Philosophers), and the *Liber Hermetis de sex rerum principiis* (The Book of Hermes on the Six Principles) all belong in this category.

60. Burnett, "The Establishment of Medieval Hermeticism," 126.

61. Rosińska 936, 2312.

62. Copies of and commentaries on the *Centiloquium* are to be found (among other places) in the following manuscripts: BJ 601, fols. 47r–48v; BJ 610, fols. 316r; BJ 793, fols. 149r–151r; BJ 805, fols. 392r–393v; BJ 1939, pp. 135–37; BJ 1963, fols. 121v–123r; BJ 2252, pp. 251–52; and BJ 2620, pp. 133–36.

63. We do not have any proof whether the other classic text on the correspondences of herbs, stones, stars, and talismans, the *Liber de quindecim stellis*, was read in Kraków, since the only Central European copy we have of it comes from Prague.

in one category. All three sources contain mostly the works of Polish astrologers, and were copied in Kraków by university students; Egidius of Corintia probably inscribed the whole Dresden manuscript,[64] and Johannes Virdung of Hassfurt the Vatican codices.[65] The extent of our biographical knowledge could not differ more than in the case of these two. About Egidius, the scribe of the Dresden manuscript, virtually nothing is known apart from the fact that he graduated in Kraków.[66] Johannes Virdung of Hassfurt (ca. 1463–1538), in contrast, left to us a whole library of books (kept in the Palatine collection of the Vatican), which not only testify to his scientific and magical interest, but also contain a number of autobiographical notes that provide us with a detailed account of his curriculum. Virdung—who became the court astrologer of the elector palatine—was a well-known figure of his time, and was often mentioned in the correspondence of his contemporaries. The abundance of evidence allows us to devote a separate section in the third part of our study to the reconstruction of the life and scholarly concerns of this complex personality.

The nonmagical texts that comprise the bulk of these three manuscripts also share some basic features. By and large, they are astrological works by professors of the University of Kraków, such as the astrological compilations of Johannes of Glogovia, a lecturer of the Faculty of Arts, and *De mutatione aeris,* by Petrus Gaszowiec. Johannes of Glogovia (1445–1507)[67]—like Gaszowiec—was a paradigmatic figure of the University of Kraków. His works were popular, widely read, and keenly copied by the students and the professors of the University. He taught in Kraków for forty years continuously (apart from a sabbatical at the University of Vienna), and was twice dean of the Faculty of Arts. He was an author of extraordinary erudition;

64. Franz Schnorr von Carolsfeld and Ludwig Schmidt, eds., *Katalog der Handschriften der Königlichen Öffentlichen Bibliothek zu Dresden,* vol. 3 (Leipzig: B. G. Teubner, 1906), 39–42. For an article devoted exclusively to this manuscript, concentrating primarily on its astrological and astronomical content, see Mieczysław Markowski, "Krakowskie dzieła astronomiczne w rękopiśmiennych zbiorach Saskiej Biblioteki Krakowej w Dreźnie" (Kraków Astronomical Works in the Manuscript Holdings of the Saxon Library in Dresden), *Studia Mediewistyczne* 22 (1983): 19–28.

65. Ludwig Schuba, ed., *Die Quadriviums-Handschriften der Codices Palatini Latini in der Vatikanischen Bibliothek* (Wiesbaden: Reichert, 1992), 88–93 and 236–44; Zofia Włodek, ed., *Polonica w średniowiecznych rękopisach bibliotek niemieckich: Aschaffenburg, Augsburg, Bamberg, Eichstätt, Harburg, Moguncja, Norymberga* (*Polonica* in the Medieval Manuscripts of German Libraries) (Wrocław: Zakład Narodowy im. Ossolińskich, 1974), 82–91. BAV Pal. lat. 1375 is mentioned with other Vatican manuscripts of hermetic content in Lynn Thorndike, "Vatican Latin Manuscripts in the History of Science and Medicine," *Isis* 13 (1929): 53–102. Thorndike published several articles on Virdung's manuscripts, for these see Chapter 9.

66. *A et A* 6–7. Egidius of Corintia was also the author of *Expositio Cracoviensis "Theoricarum novarum planetarum" Georgii Peurbachii.* See SLB N. 100, fols. 87r–120v.

67. Marian Zwiercan, "Jan of Glogów," in *The Cracow Circle of Nicholas Copernicus,* ed. Józef Gierowski, Copernicana Cracoviensia 3 (Kraków: The Jagiellonian University Press, 1973), 95–110. For data on Glogovia's curriculum and for a list of his works, see also Mieczysław Markowski, "Repertorium bio-bibliographicum astronomorum cracoviensum medii aevi: Ioannes Schelling de Glogovia," pt. 1, *Studia Mediewistyczne* 26 (1989): 103–62.

his academic activities embraced practically all the subjects of the "liberal arts." Besides numerous treatises in the fields of grammar, logic, philosophy, and geography, he was the author of more than fifty astronomical and astrological works—or rather compilations. One of them is the unfinished *Summa Astrologiae*,[68] various parts of which can be found in the Dresden and the Vatican manuscripts.[69] As for Gaszowiec's *De mutatione aeris*, it is a scientific treatise on the astrological rules of weather forecasting, dedicated to his professor at the University of Cologne, Gerardus of Hamont. Generally, it seems that any codex containing a copy of Gaszowiec's treatise will also contain works on the topic of image magic. Consequently, Gaszowiec's presence is a good index of magical treatises, while his text itself seems to be rather "innocent."[70]

Further astrological and astronomical elements common to the three manuscripts are the works of Italian (Johannes Bianchini)[71] and Central European (Johannes Regiomontanus, Georgius Peurbach, Albertus of Brudzewo) astrologers, the *Sphaera* of Johannes Sacrobosco, texts by Guido Bonatus, and some treatises on the composition of astrolabes that were important readings in the Kraków curriculum. Both BAV Pal. lat. 1439 and SLB N. 100 contain an astrological text attributed to Hermes, the *Liber de stellis beibeniis* (Book on the Fixed Stars),[72] translated into Latin by Salio of Padua,[73] which is a traditional treatise on the qualities of persons

---

68. The comprehensive work was originally intended to embrace all the important areas of astrology, its definition (*Introductorium in artem astronomiae*), the changes of weather (*Opusculum de mutatione aeris*), the horoscopes (*Introductorium in scientiam nativitatum*), and the choice of lucky days (*Tractatus de electionibus*). The second book of the *Summa* was published separately: Johannes Glogoviensis, *Tractatus in iudiciis astrorum de mutationibus aeris* (Kraków: Florian Ungler & Wolfgang Lern, 1514). For the manuscripts, see *A et A* 62–67; BJ 570 (1467–87), fols. 147–76; BJ 1838 (1485), fols. 69r–115r; and BJ 2703 (ca. 1493), fols. 34r–36r; see also BJ 2703, fols. 75r–77v, Glogoviensis, *Defensio astrologie*, and 2729 (ca. 1486–99), fols. 33v–55v, *Summa Cracoviensis de astrologia*.

69. SLB N. 100, fols. 192r–196v, 230r–266r, and 268v–288r; BAV Pal. lat. 1439, fols. 122r–152r, and 211r–239v.

70. The codices in question are BJ 793, fols. 116v–120v and 155r–156r; BJ 2252, fols. 200–214; BAV Pal. lat. 1439, fols. 336r–344r; and SLB N. 100, fols. 174r–185r and 223r–225v. See also *A et A* 176–79. On the genre of astro-meteorology, see the first chapter of Gerrit Bos and Charles Burnett, eds., *Scientific Weather Forecasting in the Middle Ages: The Writings of Al-Kindi* (London: Kegan Paul International, 2000). Al-Kindi's classic works on weather forecasting were also keenly copied by the Kraków scribes. His *De planetis sub radiis* appears in BJ 793, fols. 47v–48v; BJ 2252, pp. 220–24; CLM 125, fols. 292r–292v; and BJ 551, fols. 121v–122r. For its further occurrences, see Rosińska 1896; Carmody, *Astronomical Works*, 81–82; and TK 1383. Finally, his *De mutatione temporum* (or *De pluviis*) occurs—among others—in BJ 793, fols. 109v–115v; see also Rosińska 1875; Carmody, *Astronomical Works*, 79–81; and TK 1364.

71. Lynn Thorndike, "Giovanni Bianchini in Italian Manuscripts," *Scripta Mathematica* 19 (1953): 5–17.

72. BAV Pal. lat. 1439, fol. 344v–345v; SLB N. 100, fols. 228r–229r.

73. For a critical edition and an introduction by Paul Kunitzsch, see Bos et al., *Hermes Trismegistus*, 9–52. See also "Origin and History of *Liber de stellis beibeniis*," in Lucentini, Parri, and Compagni, *Hermetism from Late Antiquity to Humanism*, 449–60.

born under certain stars.[74] Moreover, our two scribes were also keenly copying texts on divinatory techniques, including the *Sphera Pythagorae* (The Sphere of Life and Death) (see fig. 10),[75] as well as short geomantic tracts and tables.[76] All in all, these manuscripts copied in Kraków by Egidius of Corintia in 1487 and Johannes Virdung of Hassfurt in 1488 are close relatives. (For a visually expressive account on the comparison of the manuscripts, I recommend consulting the comparative table in Appendix 2.)

After this digression on the parallel structure, codicological context, and historical background of the manuscripts, we finally turn to the texts on the operative talismans they contain. Let us start our examination with a rare tract on the magical use of Scandinavian characters, the *Liber runarum* (The Book of Runes).[77] The *Liber runarum* explains how to write the names of the spiritual forces of certain planets in a cryptic alphabet, the letters of which are called *runae* by the author. The names constructed from these clearly recognizable runes carry magical power. The complete versions of the text go fairly deep into the field of astral magic and give detailed directions on how to inscribe the angelic names on the metals and stones associated with every planet.[78] Such practices are, of course, based on the idea that each planet has a spirit through whom it influences the objects of the lower realms.

---

74. The third Kraków copy of the *Liber de stellis beibeniis* occurs in BJ 2252, pp. 252–56, where on pp. 200–214 we also find the *De mutatione aeris* by Petrus Gaszowiec (which is not surprising, since its presence is in strong correlation with magical texts), an astrological work by Arnald of Villanova (pp. 185–99), some notes on Hermes (pp. 251–52; see also Rosińska 800), and a smaller work on the construction of astrolabes that was also included in the two previous manuscripts. There are finally some very interesting pages on astrological magic, which explain how to find hidden or stolen objects by looking at the ascendant and following a detailed set of instructions (pp. 229–35). The codex was copied and occasionally commented on by a certain Clemens of Piotrkow, again a student who graduated from Kraków (in 1473). See also Rosińska 348.

75. SLB N. 100, fol. 203v; BAV Pal. lat. 1375, fol. 44r (Plate 21); see also Rosińska 794. For the *Sphera Pythagorae*, see Chapter 4 herein.

76. BAV Pal. lat. 1375, fol. 44r; SLB N. 100, fol. 203r.

77. The Latin text of the *Liber runarum* and an introduction by Paolo Lucentini can be found in Bos et al., *Hermes Trismegistus*, 401–50; all page references are to this edition. The first study on magical runes occurring in a Hermetic context was written by Charles Burnett, "Scandinavian Runes in a Latin Magical Treatise. Postscript by M. Stoklund," *Speculum* 58 (1983): 419–29; reprinted in Burnett, *Magic and Divination*, VIII. In his source (Sloane 3854, a manuscript of Italian origin, now in the British Library), the *Liber runarum* seemed to be an appendix of the *Liber antimaquis qui est liber secretorum Hermetis*. Later, however, three more—actually longer—copies of the *Liber runarum* not associated with the *Liber antimaquis* were found, one in Vienna (ÖNB Cod. lat. 12834, fols. 1r–6r), and two in our two codices in question: BAV Pal. lat. 1439, fols. 346r–347v, and SLB N. 100, fols. 198r–200v.

78. *Liber runarum*, 444–45: "Habitis nominibus spirituum planetarum, videndum est quomodo ipsa nomina metallis sive lapidibus planetis attributis insculpi debeant per figuras, ita quod nature figurarum sequantur se ad invicem sicut et signa et triplicitates." SLB N. 100, fol. 199v; BAV Pal. lat. 1439, fol. 346v. For a detailed explanation of the method, see Lucentini's introduction to the *Liber runarum*, in Bos et al., *Hermes Trismegistus*, 403–28.

To help those readers whose interest is not purely theoretical, the text ends with a concrete example, using the planet Venus. We are told that if one wants to operate with the power of the planets, he has to inscribe the name of the appropriate angels on the proper metal, and invoke the angels and ask them for help to achieve the given aim—which is, obviously, in the case of Venus talismans, winning the love of another.[79] The list of runes corresponding to their planets and angels appear next to the main body of the text, and in the case of the Vatican manuscript, they also appear on a *rota runarum*, which is copied quite separately, one hundred and fifty folios before the main text (for the runes, see figs. 15 and 16; for the *rota*, see fig. 17).[80]

The originality of the *Liber runarum* does not consist in the magical use of Scandinavian characters. Revealed to the Scandinavians by the god Odin, runes were generally believed to have sacred power and occult virtues. These magic signs were often applied on talismans, amulets, and on all sorts of other objects and written sources from the early Middle Ages onward.[81] In a peculiar German manuscript from the late fifteenth century, runic characters are used extensively for transcribing various names and notions of the medical, divinatory, prognostic, and occasionally demonic, material of the book. Apart from the content of the manuscript, however, the magic of the runes also lies in their cryptographic application. In a demonic invocation written in normal German, for example, those terms which are supposed to remain secret are spelled in runes. If we decipher them, we will see that these terms include the most dangerous names of the devil to be invoked, such as *boes geist* (malign spirit), *diabolo diabolicziio, satana sataniczno,* and the major performative terms, such as *kum her zuo mir.*[82]

But the author of the *Liber runarum* went beyond simply using runes as a secret alphabet; he offered a unique combination of Scandinavian runes with Hermetic elements. Not only did he use runes to refer to planetary angels, he also applied them

---

79. *Liber runarum*, 447: "Nunc restat dare exempla sculpturarum ex premissis, et ego non ponam nisi unum, scilicet de Venere, secundum quod poteris per quamlibet planetarum, sicut predictum est, operari si volueris. Et hoc est ut sculpas nomen angeli Lune et Veneris et nomen puelle sive mulieris in lamina stannea vel ergentea, quod melius est, quibus scriptis sepeli laminam in loco ignis ut continue caleat, ita tamen ne calor ignis sculpturam destruat. Et dum hoc facis inuoca angelos sicut supra dictum est, et subinfer: 'Nunc cor talis N. igne mei amoris ita exuratis, sicut ab igne hec tabula inflamatur.' Sic sepcies inuocabis, et effectum tui operis, si bene operatus fueris, obtinebis." SLB N. 100, fol. 200r; BAV Pal. lat. 1439, fol. 347v.

80. SLB N. 100, fol. 198r; BAV Pal. lat. 1439, fol. 348r, and 199r (*Rota runarum*).

81. On the magical use of Scandinavian runes and on theories why runes are especially suitable for magical application, see Klaus Düwell, "Runen als magische Zeichen," in Ganz, *Das Buch,* 87–100, and Stephen E. Flowers, *Runes and Magic: Magical Formulaic Elements in the Older Runic Tradition* (New York: Peter Lang, 1986).

82. Hartmut Beckers, "Eine spätmittelalterliche deutsche Anleitung zur Teufelsbeschwörung mit Runenschriftverwendung," *Zeitschrift für deutsches Altertum und deutsche Literatur* 113 (1984): 136–45.

Image Magic

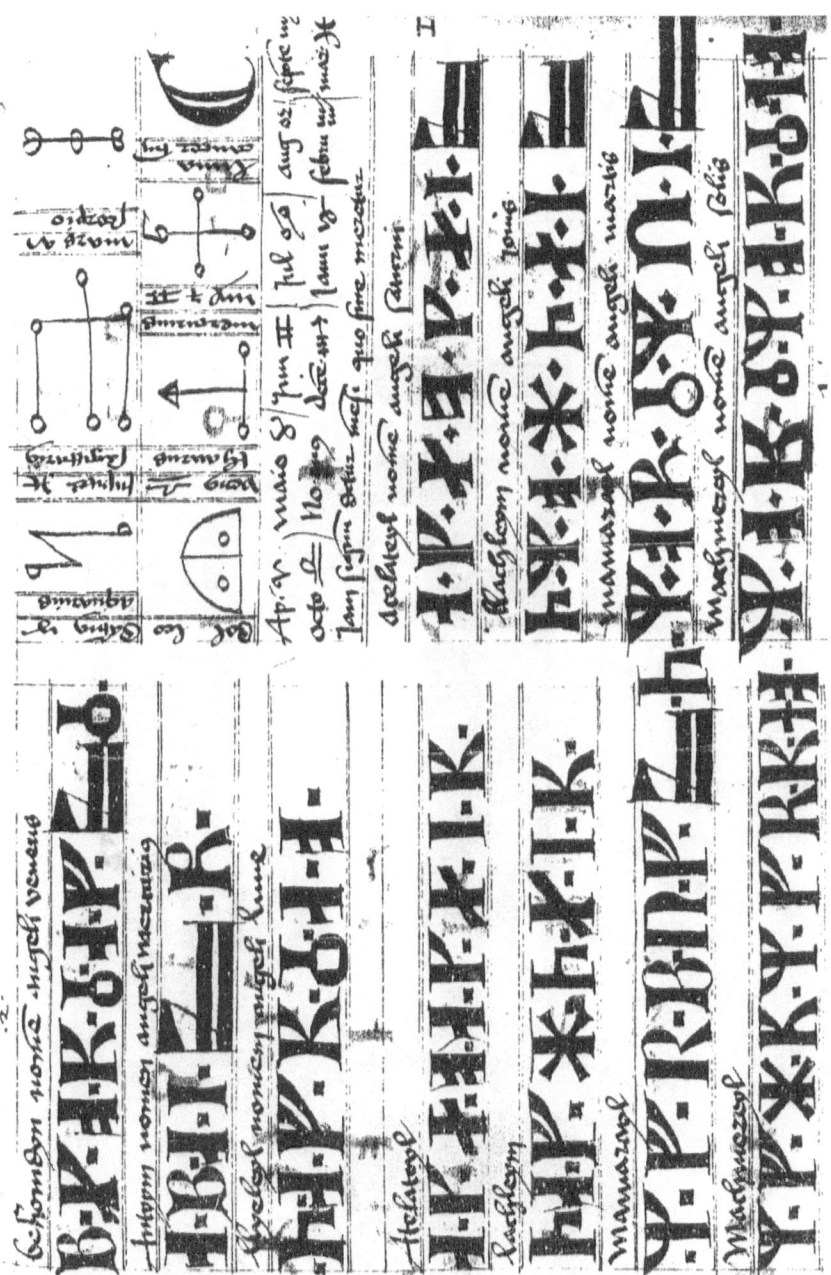

FIG 15 *Liber runarum*: magical runes. Dresden, Sächsische Landesbibliothek N 100, fol. 198r. Courtesy of the Sächsische Landesbibliothek.

FIG 16 *Liber runarum*: magical runes. BAV Pal. Lat. 1439, fol. 348r. © Biblioteca Apostolica Vaticana (Vatican).

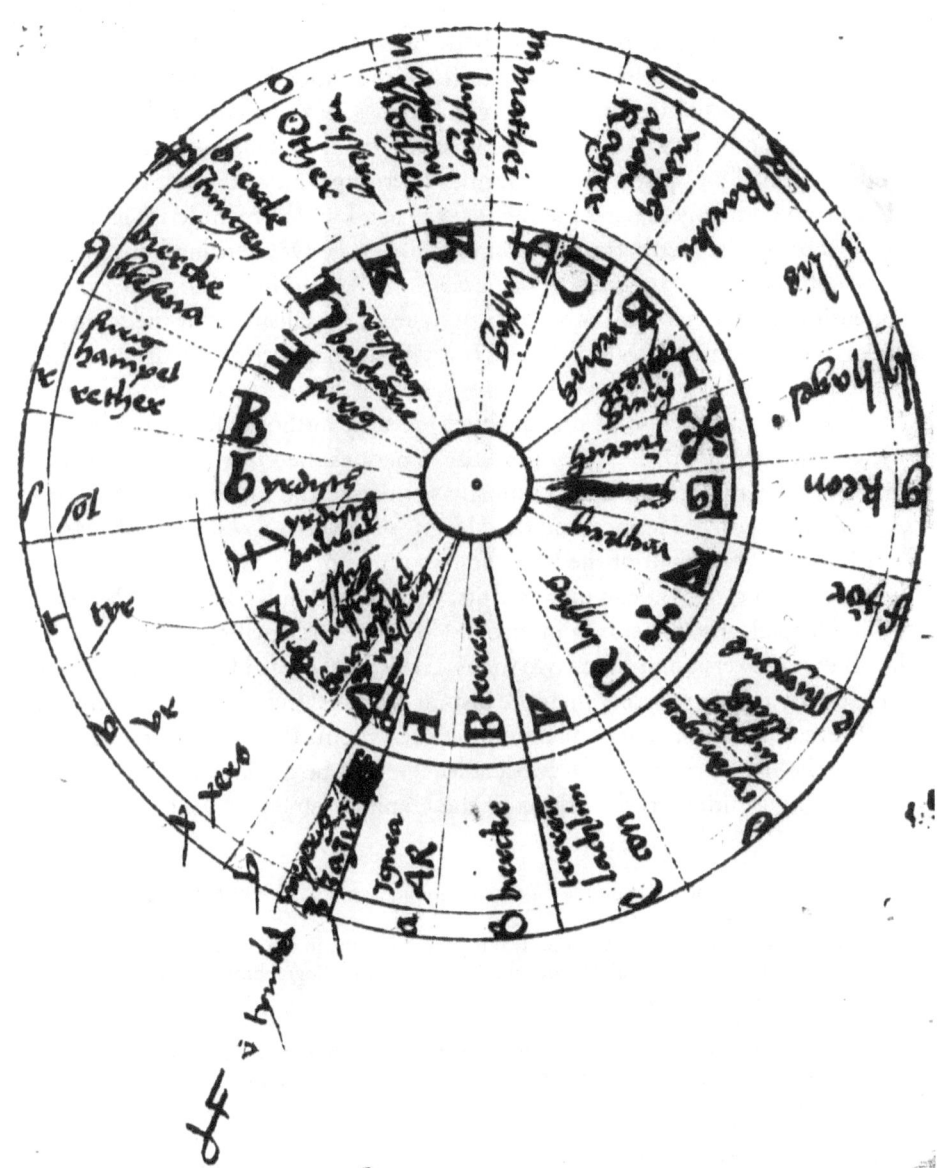

FIG 17 *Rota runarum.* BAV Pal. Lat. 1439, fol. 199r. © Biblioteca Apostolica Vaticana (Vatican).

to Arabic and Hebrew spirit names, and thus he extended the principles of astral magic to encompass the sacred qualities of the runic alphabet.[83] As Charles Burnett wrote about the anonymous author, "It must have been a rare person who could combine a knowledge of the runic alphabet with the oriental secrets of Hermes."[84]

Strictly speaking, however, the *Liber runarum* is not a Hermetic treatise; it does not contain the usual attribution either to Hermes, or to Belenus and Toz Graecus, and what is more, instead of being a translation from Arabic, it seems to be a Latin product probably inspired by the Hermetic writings. Nevertheless, it occurs generally in the company of basic Hermetic texts: in a London manuscript it appears as an appendix of the Hermetic *Antimaquis,* while in the Dresden and Vatican codices it was copied next to the *Liber de stellis beibeniis.*[85] In addition, the *Liber runarum* is mentioned together with other Hermetic texts on talismans in the apology for image magic found in PNK VIII G 27, a Prague manuscript discussed in Chapter 1 in connection with medieval taxonomies of magic texts.[86] The tract on the use of Scandinavian runes is one of those texts the author defends as falsely considered necromantic by ignorant posterity.[87] Besides the *Liber runarum,* he names three other Hermetic works also unjustly slandered: the *Liber lunae,* the *Liber de imaginibus et horis* of Hermes, and the *Liber de imaginibus diei et noctis* of Belenus.[88]

It is striking that half of the four extant sources of the *Liber runarum,* namely, the Dresden and the Vatican manuscripts, were copied in Kraków. On the grounds of philological proofs—common errors, wording, and spelling forms—it can be shown that the versions in these two manuscripts were copied from the same source, while the two other versions are more distant relatives. Indeed, the table in Appendix 2 reveals a very strong connection between them. If we compare one specific page of the list of runes in the two codices, it will be obvious that although the handwriting is different, the setting of the graphic elements and the arrangement

---

83. Lucentini's introduction to the *Liber runarum*, in Bos et al., *Hermes Trismegistus,* 415.
84. Burnett, "Scandinavian Runes," 424.
85. This is why Paolo Lucentini published it as an appendix in the edition of hermetic texts.
86. PNK VIII G 27 (Truhlář 1609), fols. 37r–40v. For bibliographical data and secondary literature, see Chapter 1.
87. Another, less patient medieval report on the *Liber runarum* is written by Johannes Trithemius (1462–1516), who, in his *Antipalus Maleficiorum,* refers to it as a vain and superstitious text. I am grateful to Paolo Lucentini for calling my attention and giving me access to this rare edition. Ianus Busaeus, ed., *Paralipomena opusculorum Petri Blesensis et Joannis Trithemii aliorumque* (Mainz: Balthasar Lippius, 1605), 299: "Item est alius liber de compositione nominum atque characterum malignorum sprituum, similiter vanus et superstitiosus, cuius nomen autoris non inveni, et sic incipit. Ad habendum scientiam, experimentum." The text has recently been edited by Paola Zambelli, "Pseudepigrafia e magia secondo l'abate Johannes Trithemius," in Marchetti, Rignani, and Sorge, *Ratio et Superstitio,* 347–68.
88. See Lucentini's introduction to the *Liber runarum*, in Bos et al., *Hermes Trismegistus,* 406–7, for descriptions of L-PC 70–73, 64–66, and 76–78.

of the inserted words appear in a completely parallel structure.[89] Furthermore, although both scribes promise to give only one single example at the end of the text,[90] unlike the two other copyists they add in fact four instances of invoking planetary angels, using practically the same words. Such small details[91] make it certain that these two students of the university copied their codices around 1487–88 from each other, or, what is more likely, from a common source, which seems to have been an astrological-magical handbook circulating among the Kraków students.

The interest in technical Hermetism attested by one of these scribes, Johannes Virdung of Hassfurt, can be further demonstrated by the third codex under investigation, BAV Pal. lat. 1375. Like BAV Pal. lat. 1439, Virdung copied this one in Kraków in 1488 when he was a student at the university. Its content is also quite similar: classics of astrology and astronomy, planetary tables, and descriptions of astronomical devices. Since the exploration of Virdung's scholarly and magical career and his concern with magic will be the focus of another chapter, here we will concentrate only on a few folios of this manuscript.

BAV Pal. lat. 1375 contains four, similarly structured tracts on talismanic magic, two of which are clearly Hermetic, one ascribed directly to Hermes, the other to Belenus.[92] The Hermetic one, *De imaginibus sive annulis septem planetarum*—which we will remember as having been found abominable by the author of the *Speculum*—is in its complete version a systematic description in seven paragraphs of how the magician is to prepare a talismanic ring for each of the seven planets, using the metal and the precious stone associated with that planet.[93] An image, described in detail in the manuscript, is to be engraved on the stone, or occasionally in the metal, in order to make the talisman capable of certain magical goals that are always in harmony with the well-known properties of the given planet.[94] The version of

---

89. SLB N. 100, fol. 198r; BAV Pal. lat. 1439, fol. 348r; see Plates 15 and 16.
90. SLB N. 100, fol. 200r–v; BAV Pal. lat. 1439, fol. 347v: "Ego non ponam nisi unum <exemplum>."
91. To which we can add the presence of Albicus's *Pronosticationes infirmo secundum dies incensionis*—a relatively rare work—in both manuscripts: in SLB N. 100 at fol. 161v, and in BAV Pal. lat. 1439 at fol. 198r.
92. These two texts are not identical with those of Hermes and Belenus mentioned by the Prague text and quoted earlier; however, they are rather similar in content and structure, and it is instructive that the *Liber runarum* can be associated in one way or another with such texts.
93. BAV Pal. lat. 1375, fol. 270v, in L-PC 59–61, TK 1517, and T (1947) 247. Vittoria Perrone Compagni has produced an edition of the text for the next volume of *Hermes Latinus* (*Textus magici*). I am grateful to her for letting me consult the unpublished materials of this forthcoming volume.
94. A very similar list of talismans is contained in the *Picatrix* (bk. 2, chap. 10). We should note that the *Picatrix* is originally a compilation, and therefore it is not surprising that it incorporates various familiar materials.

the Vatican manuscript contains only two images, those of the sun and the moon. However, the following page is left entirely blank, most probably exactly with the intention of providing enough space for the rest of the text. Comparing this version with other surviving examples of the same two paragraphs, we find that Hassfurt's text places more emphasis on the astrological circumstances of the fabrication of the ring, but makes no mention of which gems to use for the sun and the moon.

This tract is preceded by a work of a virtually identical title that the author of the *Speculum* should have found even more abominable had he known it: the *De imaginibus septem planetarum*, attributed this time to Belenus (or as the manuscript calls him, Belemith).[95] This text, occupying one folio in the manuscript,[96] once again follows the order of planets as an organizational principle, and indicates the hour in which each talisman should be prepared, as well as the materials of which it is to be made. Unlike the previous text, it contains explicit ritual elements, certain actions should be performed "*cum flexis genibus*" (with bent knees), while suffumigations, orations, and summonses to planetary spirits are also involved.[97] The aims are the usual ones of image magic: to appear powerful in battle with the help of a talisman of Mars; to retain a woman's love with the help of a talisman of Venus; to make someone appear abominable with the help of a talisman of Saturn, and so on. The novelty here is that the name of the person on whom the benign or malign effect of the spirits should be exercised is to be written on the image. The text ends with a list of the "ymagines et karacteres planetarum" (the planets' images and characters), consisting of an alphabet of magical signs (not runes this time) most of which is crossed out and made unreadable by a later hand in the Vatican manuscript (see the partial copy of BAV Pal. lat. 1375, fol. 270v, on fig. 18). This caution is not surprising; the characters are most powerful. As the text instructs, they play a rather crucial role in the functioning of the talismans, being the chief factors of constraining the spirits of the planets.

Much longer sets of the same magical characters—crossed out again—may be found in the third of our four texts under study, the *Liber de spiritibus inclusis* (The Book of Enclosed Spirits). This text has never been described or transcribed elsewhere; indeed, this may be its only copy in existence.[98] It belongs to the same genre as the *De imaginibus sive annulis septem planetarum* and the *De imaginibus*

---

95. L-PC 80–83; TK 450; T (1947) 243. An edition of this work is forthcoming in the next volume of *Hermes Latinus*.

96. BAV Pal. lat. 1375, fol. 270r–v.

97. For example, on fol. 270r: "O spiritus fulgens Saturni a superioribus locis descendes hunc N in vilitatem et odium detrudite, tristes adestote, inquetans hunc iracunda." And on fol. 270v: "O Iovis benignissimi spiritus, adestote meque ut hunc N in honorem et dilectionem populi ad maximam potestatem sublevate corda potentium et voluntatem hominum meae voluntati convertire."

98. BAV Pal. lat. 1375, fols. 269v–270r (TK 427). Thorndike mentions it in his "Johann Virdung of Hassfurt Again," *Isis* 25 (1936): 363–71, on 365.

FIG 18 *De imaginibus septem planetarum* by Belenus: karacteres planetarum. BAV Pal. Lat. 1375, fol. 270v (lower part of the page). © Biblioteca Apostolica Vaticana (Vatican).

septem planetarum, but the instructions it contains are even more explicit than those in the work attributed to Belenus, and the information it provides is even more systematically arranged: the words made of the signs are called the "exorcisms" of the given planet. A whole world of correspondences can be inferred from it. After a short and general description of what is common in the methods of fabrication of the seven planetary rings, the text—rather economically, in a three-column table—indicates the specific ingredients to be used and the special instructions to be followed in order to create each ring. Under each planet the author lists, in order, the animal to be sacrificed, the material to be suffumigated, the metal of which the ring is to be made, the figure to be engraved on the ring (which are similar to those described in the tenth chapter of book two of the *Picatrix*), the character of the planet (later crossed out), and a list of exorcisms of the spirits to be invoked. The names of the spirits seem to be angels' names and greatly resemble the names of the *Liber runarum* and the pseudo-Greek, pseudo-Arabic, and pseudo-Hebrew *verba ignota* (unknown names) of the *Ars notoria*. This work—which is most likely a general annotated extract of all talismanic methods—ends with a description of the results the magician should expect from each talisman.

The fourth, and shortest,[99] of these works is an anonymous text on talismanic magic, purportedly by a certain Thomas, who names himself in the incipit: "Ego magister Thomas omnium arcium et omnium scienciarum perfectus" [I, Master Thomas, perfect in all arts and sciences].[100] Like the *Liber de spiritibus inclusis*, it seems to have survived only in this manuscript. Fortunately, it can be identified with an item in Johannes Trithemius's contemporary bibliography of necromancy, the *Antipalus Maleficiorum*: "And there is also the *Liber prestigiorum* [*Book of Talismans*] of a certain Thomas, in which miraculous things are promised to be produced from rings constructed in characters according to the eight mansions of the moon and with vain fumigations, and which starts like this: 'Ego Thomas omnium scientiarum amator. . .' [I, Thomas, friend of all sciences . . .]."[101] Much like the others, it describes the making of talismanic rings, and calls for various invocations and rituals (certain actions are to be performed with "bent knees" as usual), but it is less systematic than the previous works discussed.

What is remarkable is that Trithemius names exactly these texts: the *De imaginibus septem planetarum* of Belenus, the *De imaginibus sive annulis septem planetarum* of Hermes, the work on talismans of "magister Thomas," and the *Liber de spiritibus inclusis* by an anonymous author, "whose name—says Trithemius—I did not find."[102] Of the last two, we have only the copies found in Virdung's manuscript. From where Trithemius might have known these texts (and the equally rare *Liber runarum*), all present in his friend's library, is a question that cannot be entirely answered. The two were friends, but the incipits provided by Trithemius for these works do not completely correspond with the initial sentences of the versions in Virdung's codex. On the other hand, it is most unlikely that Trithemius and Virdung were interested in the same talismanic texts independently. As we will see in detail in Chapter 9, they took ample opportunity to discuss various magical issues, and thus we can take it for granted that they did not abstain from consulting each other's library.

It is time, however, to return to the initial themes: that of the Vatican codex in particular, and that of medieval operative Hermetism in general. To sum up the

---

99. BAV Pal. lat. 1375, fol. 272r.

100. The editors of the Polish catalog read *Hermes*, instead of *Thomas*, misreading the manuscript. Włodek, *Polonica*, 90.

101. Et est *Liber prestigiorum* cuiusdam Thomae, in quo miranda promittentur, ex annulis compositis secundum 8 mansiones Lunae in characteribus et fumigationibus vanis, qui sic incipit: *Ego Thomas omnium scientiarum amator.* Zambelli, "Pseudepigrafia e magia," 366.

102. Ibid.

available evidence, we can claim with confidence that just as BJ 793 represents a reliable handbook of image magic, BAV Pal. lat. 1375 incorporates a good selection of readings from a somewhat narrower category, that of Hermetic talismans.

If we look at the extant texts of Hermetic image magic, we can see a rather strange phenomenon. Because most of our copies of Hermetic texts are from the fifteenth century, it seems that the dissemination of the *medieval* texts ascribed to Hermes is contemporary with the rise of *Renaissance* Hermetism. Although the texts belonging to these two realms are different in nature and orientation, the new concern raised by the humanists and particularly by Ficino might have indirectly encouraged the copying of the texts of the Arabic Hermes in the late fifteenth century. A few decades later, however, the picture changed, and Hermetism started to gain a more philosophical sense, the meaning given by Ficino.[103] For example, in his anthology compiled in the opening years of the sixteenth century, Bernard of Lublin included extracts from the *Asclepius* and certain elements of the *Pimander* from the Ficinian *Corpus Hermeticum,* together with parts of Plato's dialogues, translated again by Ficino, and some works by Aristotle.[104] Both the texts individually and the character of the anthology as a whole demonstrate a preference for the syncretic and the theoretical in keeping with the Renaissance and quite different from the late medieval interest in operative Hermetism. Similarly, King Matthias of Hungary did not include practical tracts of image magic in his library, but—partly as a consequence of his correspondence with Ficino himself—he was more open to the newly translated works of Renaissance philosophical Hermetism.[105] As a result of these changes, the word "Hermetism" (used sometimes in the form "Hermeticism") became synonymous with a post-Ficinian, religious-philosophical preoccupation with the originally Greek corpus of Hermes Trismegistos, and lost slowly its association with the Arabic-medieval Hermes.

The Talismans and the Scribes

We have the clues we need to reconstruct the interest in Hermetism and operative talismans in the university circles of Kraków. Relying on the evidence examined, it seems that—at least for some students of the university—this interest was neither

---

103. From the immense literature, let me mention Yates, *Giordano Bruno;* Yates, "The Hermetic Tradition in Renaissance Science," in *Art, Science and History in the Renaissance,* ed. Charles S. Singleton (Baltimore: John Hopkins University Press, 1968); and the overview given in György Endre Szőnyi, *John Dee's Occultism: Magical Exaltation through Powerful Signs* (Albany: SUNY Press, 2005).

104. Janusz S. Gruchała, "Biernata z Lublina Antologia Filozoficzna z Początku XVI. w" (A Philosophical Anthology of Bernard of Lublin at the Beginning of the Sixteenth Century), *Biuletyn Biblioteki Jagiellońskiej* 38 (1988): 63–77.

105. See Chapter 8.

secondary nor accidental. Even though the texts of Hermetic image magic are often inserted in the space left blank between longer scientific treatises, and occur usually in the last quarter of the manuscripts, this rule has more to do with the nature and shortness of the talismanic texts than with a lack of interest and respect. In many cases (such as for example in BJ 793), long continuous sections were devoted to image magic, which became an organic element of the composition of the codex. In other cases (BAV Pal. lat. 1375, for example) a folio is deliberately left blank for the second part of a Hermetic text on talismans, and whatever the reason was for the omission of this part, apparently it did not follow the original intention. The scattered, sporadic arrangement is most explicit in the Dresden manuscript; however, in this case, the inclusion of works about talismans in the codex is clearly a result of the coherent curiosity of its scribe. He copied (or perhaps rather, wrote) a short notice on magical arts, with the intention of helping the reader in the orientation, in which—as we have discussed in Chapter 1—he attested a deep familiarity with the text of the *Speculum astronomiae,* he seemed to have consulted a great range of Hermetic and Solomonic magical books, and finally, he referred to the *Picatrix* as a work of image magic.

Before closing this chapter on the texts of image magic, one last point is to be addressed on a more general level. What could be the place of this category of magic in the conceptual framework of those scientists who filled their codices with these texts? Where did they put Thebit's *De imaginibus,* Hermes' invocations of spirits, and the *Picatrix* on their bookshelves? Did they consider the works on operative talismans to be at the same level of reality as the astronomical and scientific tracts of the same manuscripts?

The question is obviously *not* whether medieval people generally took talismans seriously, because the answer to that question would be a simple "yes." Various pieces of pictorial evidence depicting powerful objects hanging from the neck or carried elsewhere on the body, and a large number of talismans, amulets, and rings—containing stones, teeth, crosses, shells, hair and bones, and other herbal and animal materials—have survived from medieval times,[106] indicating that people in the Middle Ages—just as today—constructed and used talismans. These objects are often inscribed with numbers, letters, and sacred characters, or engraved with images (magical circles, squares, stars, and demonic figures) and seem to indicate an actual application of the teachings of Thebit, Hermes, the *Picatrix,* and other texts on image magic.

However, this well-documented fact does not answer the initial question; while

---

106. Such medieval and early modern objects are shown in great number in Liselotte Hansmann and Lenz Kriss-Rettenbeck, eds., *Amulett und Talisman: Erscheinungsform und Geschichte* (Munich: Verlag Georg D.W. Callwey, 1966), while textual amulets are presented in Skemer, *Binding Words.*

Image Magic   121

it is obvious that people used talismans with a *general* assumption that these objects would protect them, we may still ask ourselves whether university students and professors could have believed that a given image, engraved and suffumigated properly, might function in *specific* cases too. Did they believe, for example, that it really served for the destruction of a given city, the defeat of a given army, or the failure of a given business in a well-defined moment?

Literature might have provided certain legitimization for image magic. Together with the instructions on the creation of talismans, the Latin Middle Ages imported remarkable stories about the actual use of images from the Arabs. The commentary of Haly on the ninth sentence of Pseudo-Ptolemy's *Centiloquium* (a text that accompanied the hundred aphorisms most of the time) tells of a soldier who also had the fame of a sage, and who knew the nature of stones and herbs very well. Thanks to his expertise, this soldier-savant saved the life of a person stung by a scorpion, with the help of a golden ring with a Bezoar stone in which a picture of the scorpion was engraved. Upon inquiry he was ready to explain in which hour and under what constellation he prepared this ring.[107] Another story, related to the person of Thābit ibn Qurra himself, involves the intervention of personal planetary spirits and the use of powerful talismans against the ill will of enemies, for making oneself invisible, and also for acquiring marvelous powers of sight.[108]

Nevertheless, it seems logical to suppose that for the medieval reader these old Arabic stories were as fabulous, and as difficult to credit, as they are for a modern audience. This is why certain anecdotes written in the Latin world at the end of the fourteenth century deserve serious attention, and may shed more light on what the scribe may have had in mind. These anecdotes have a surprisingly similar content to that of the Arabic stories, involving the application of images for expelling enemies from kingdoms, cities, and castles.[109] The difference is that they are told by a contemporary Italian author (living in France actually), who situates the stories in a "modern," that is, late medieval, context, and does not claim to have recycled them from ancient mythical reports.[110] The events of the first story are related to Thomas of Pizan living in the second half of the fourteenth century, father of the famous Christine of Pizan, and doctor of astrology and medicine in the service of the French king, Charles V. The story informs us that he used planetary talismans engraved with the names of angels under given astrological constellations, which are described in great detail in the manuscripts, for expelling the English army from

---

107. WP 82.
108. For the story, see Burnett, "Thābit ibn Qurra the Harrānian."
109. WP 605, and Jean-Patrice Boudet, *Le "Recueil des plus célèbres astrologues" de Simon de Phares édité pour la société de l'Histoire de France*, vol. 2 (Paris: Champion, 1999), 257.
110. MSS Vatican, Vat. lat. 4085, fols. 104r–105r; BnF lat. 7337, pp. 45r–46v. The text is edited in WP 897–900.

French territory (and one should remember that the story purports to have happened in the middle of the Hundred Years' War).

The relevant conclusion is not necessarily that these images were really used with considerable military success, but rather that the successful application of talismans *for concrete purposes* did not exclusively belong to the realm of ancient legends; a story about their use had a certain credibility. Although we will return on a more philosophical level to the questions of applicability, success, and failure of the different magical procedures in our conclusion, we should accept for the time being that talismanic texts in the Middle Ages were copied with the assumption that they were applicable, and also that talismans were usually believed to possess not only a general protective power, but also concrete efficacy that could be put into operation in specific, say military, cases.

4
Divination with Diagrams

Divination: Definitions and Attitudes

The term "divination" will be used to denote the procedure of foretelling the future and discovering hidden knowledge through the interpretation of signs.[1] These signs might be at one's disposal in several ways. In many cases, they are written somewhere in the natural world, most often encoded on various zones of the body. Thus, among the popular divinatory techniques, we find the reading of the lines on the palms of human hands—this art being called palmistry or chiromancy—as well as the interpretation of the signs occurring in particular divisions of a sheep's shoulder blades (scapulimancy).[2] The justification of such divinatory procedures is that God created a world of universal correspondences, in which, through the interrelation and necessary connection of all things, future events and hidden secrets might be revealed by deciphering various indications.[3]

In other cases, the signs are generated artificially by the inquirer himself—or perhaps herself, since we are speaking of widespread techniques, not privileged by written culture, and equally present in folk beliefs. This happens in the art of *sortilegium*

---

1. A wider understanding of divination is also possible. Laurens Pignon, for example, in his fifteenth-century *Contre les devineurs*, includes a wide range of magical practices besides the interpretation of signs in order to reveal future and occult phenomena. This particularly wide category of divination involves every kind of prognostication, judicial astrology, practices of ritual magic, invocation of demons, and the use of stones, herbs, and words for curing diseases. Pignon seems to understand divination as a synonym for magic and superstition in general. See Veenstra, *Magic and Divination*.

2. For this latter practice, see Charles Burnett, "Scapulimancy (Divination by the Shoulder-blades of Sheep)," in Burnett, *Magic and Divination*, XII, 1–14, and "Arabic Divinatory Texts and Celtic Folklore: A Comment on the Theory and Practice of Scapulimancy in Western Europe," ibid., XIII, 31–42.

3. For a general overview on divination, see Charmasson, "Divinatory Arts."

and geomancy, where the signs to be interpreted were not placed in nature by the Creator, but are drawn by the operator right on the spot. Halfway between the naturally and the artificially created codes, we find a form of divination that operates with the numerical value of human names. In this case, the signs are rooted to a certain extent in the human will (that of the name giver), but are independent of the actual conditions of the inquirer. Gazing into crystal balls (crystallomancy) and other ways of scrying (such as catoptromancy, that is, divination by means of a mirror) are also frequently listed as branches of divination. However, since these practices rely on much more sophisticated rules, and—unlike the previous forms of divination—they use spiritual aid explicitly, they will be discussed separately.

Divination was considered a distinct category of magic; it was usually treated, classified, and eventually condemned in distinct tracts. When looking for the medieval secondary literature on divination, we do not turn to Augustine or William of Auvergne. Neither is it helpful to read Isidore or Hugh of Saint Victor. Even though these latter authors listed the methods of divination according to the four elements (geomancy, hydromancy, aeromancy, and pyromancy), they rather relied on Classical authors (Cicero and Varro) than on actual practice or concrete texts.[4]

For a more realistic and detailed description of divinatory techniques, we have to wait for the later Middle Ages, when discourse on divination became more differentiated. An instructive source is *Das půch aller verpoten kunst* by the early fifteenth-century author, Johannes Hartlieb (ca. 1400–1468).[5] Hartlieb wrote his handbook between 1456 and 1464 in Munich, and described the divinatory methods of the seven forbidden arts—geomancy, hydromancy, aeromancy, pyromancy, chiromancy, scapulimancy, and necromancy—in great detail, illustrating his descriptions with exhaustive reports on concrete practices. In his categorization, Hartlieb went back to a text of an alumnus of Prague University, Nicolaus Magni of Jawor (d. 1435), who had written a treatise on superstitions (*Tractatus de superstitionibus*) while living in Heidelberg.[6]

---

4. Isidore of Seville, *Etymologiae*, bk. 8, chap. 9, in *Patrologia Latina* 82, col. 310–14, or in W. M. Lindsay, ed., *Isidori Hispaliensis Episcopi Etymologiarum sive Originum Libri XX* (Oxford: Clarendon Press, 1911); Hugo de Sancto Victore, *Didascalicon*, VI/XV. "De magica et partibus eius," in *Patrologia Latina* 176, col. 810.

5. Johann Hartlieb, *Das Buch aller verbotenen Künste des Aberglaubens und der Zauberei*, ed. Falk Eisermann and Eckhard Graf (Ahlerstedt: Param, 1989). Helpful secondary literature on Hartlieb can be found in Frank Fürbeth, *Johannes Hartlieb: Untersuchungen zu Leben und Werk* (Tübingen: Max Niemeyer Verlag, 1992).

6. On Hartlieb's adaptation of Nicolaus Magni de Jawor, see Fürbeth, *Johannes Hartlieb*, 100–108. No one has published a modern edition of Nicolaus Magni's text. For a classic text and a recent monograph, see Adolph Franz, *Der Magister Nikolaus Magni de Jawor: ein Beitrag zur Literatur- und Gelehrtengeschichte des 14. und 15. Jahrhunderts* (Freiburg, 1898), and Krzysztof Bracha, *Teolog, diabeł i zabobony: Świadectwo traktatu Mikołaja Magni z Jawora "De superstitionibus"* (The Theologian,

The primary justification for writing about the methods of divination in both works was obviously not to give a comprehensive picture of contemporary popular superstitions, but to provide a severe theological critique of how divination works. Theologians saw in every branch of divination first of all a demonic enterprise, and the abuse of divine privileges (that is, foreknowledge of the future). They did not allow themselves to be persuaded that most of these branches, such as palmistry and geomancy, could function without any visible application of demonic help. They agreed that prognostications, with their rigid determinism and fatalism, seriously threatened the concepts of human free will and divine omnipotence. Obtaining knowledge of hidden and future things that are known only to God requires the implicit or explicit help of the devil; and therefore, theologians felt obliged to depict divination as a most dangerous and demonic practice. Etienne Tempier, in the prologue of his famous condemnations in 1277, explicitly condemned a geomantic tract, the *Estimaverunt Indi* (The Indians Estimated), rejecting it together with books containing necromancy and invocations of demons.[7]

It is worth mentioning that the fourteenth chapter of the *Speculum astronomiae*, devoted solely to the problem of prognostications, was somewhat more ambiguous. It did not condemn categorically all kinds of interrogation concerning whether someone is alive or dead, or whether rumors are true or false; as far as they concern the truth already determined, these queries are acceptable. And even those interrogations which concern contingent things subject to free will, queries that do not seek for advice but want to learn facts about the future are compatible with free will, just as divine providence is reconcilable with it. Still, after this apology for divination, the author admits that these methods aim at learning those things that God wanted to keep hidden from our eyes; and therefore, this art is not to be followed. (The author speaks primarily about astrological prognostications, but the theological concerns he raises are similar in the case of other genres of divination.)[8]

Despite such tolerant views, the rather unanimous negative attitude of theology toward the art of divination exercised such an influence on medieval codices that divinatory techniques copied on the folios were often later rendered unreadable by pious hands. In a manuscript from Kraków (BJ 551), for example, a short Latin text of palmistry and a picture of a human hand are thoroughly crossed out (fig. 19), while on the previous folios we find various magical recipes in Latin and German, among them a text that belongs to the tradition of the *Ars notoria* and involves explicit invocations to spirits. Paradoxically, none of these forms of magic

---

the Devil and the Superstitions: The Testimony of the Treatise of Nicolaus Jawor, *De superstitionibus*) (Warsaw: Instytut Historii PAN, 1999).

7. Denifle and Chatelain, *Chartularium Universitatis Parisiensis*, 1:543 (see Chap. 1, n. 21).
8. Zambelli, *The "Speculum Astronomiae" and Its Enigma*, 260–67.

annoyed the interactive reader; he found only the *chiromantia*, the divination of the marks and lines of the palm, worthy of destruction.

Divinatory Techniques: Geomancy, Chiromancy, *Sortilegium*, and Onomancy

Among the diverse forms of divination that populate medieval manuscripts, geomancy is by far the most widespread.[9] Geomancy has little to do with the element of earth from which it received its name. It consists of marking down a number of points on a piece of parchment or in the soil; then after arranging these points in a special order of pairs and single points, .we obtain graphic figures that can be represented numerically as sets of four binary elements. The result, therefore, can be 1111, 1212, 2212, and so on. Altogether, there are sixteen such groups of digits. The construction of these figures from the projected points is the last moment when random chance might interfere; the subsequent steps follow well-defined instructions mechanically. We construct first four such figures, called "mothers," then by means of combination and addition we further deduce similar figures from them—so-called daughters, witnesses, and the judge—and finally we arrange all of them in a downward-pointing triangle. By complicated rules which involve a lot of turning the pages of the book, the interpretation of these figures will lead to an answer to precise questions that concern mostly everyday life, health, death, wealth, voyages, inheritance, imprisonment, marriage, and enemies, or more concrete issues, such as whether one should enter the clergy or remain a layman, whether a rumor is true or false, whether to buy a certain thing or not, whether a journey will be dangerous, whether a child will be born or not and of which sex it will be.

The first Latin geomantic treatise that spread in the West, the twelfth-century *Ars geomancie* (The Art of Geomancy) by Hugh of Santalla, purports to be a translation from Arabic; and even though its original is not known, extensive evidence supports the theory that this kind of divination derives from Arabic methods. In the following centuries, Latin geomancy achieved a highly complex textual tradition, which has not yet been completely mapped.[10] From the long list of ascribed authors and translators, we can name Al-Kindi, Bernardus Silvestris, Gerardus of

---

9. The first and last systematic analysis of the genre of geomancy is Thérèse Charmasson, *Recherches sur une technique divinatoire: la géomancie dans l'Occident médiéval* (Geneva: Librarie Droz, 1980). See also Charmasson, "Les premiers traités latins de géomancie," *Cahiers de civilisation médiévale* 21 (1978): 121–36.

10. Many of the texts, authors, and translators have been identified by Charmasson's thorough survey (she examined approximately two hundred manuscripts); there are, however, more versions than she managed to describe.

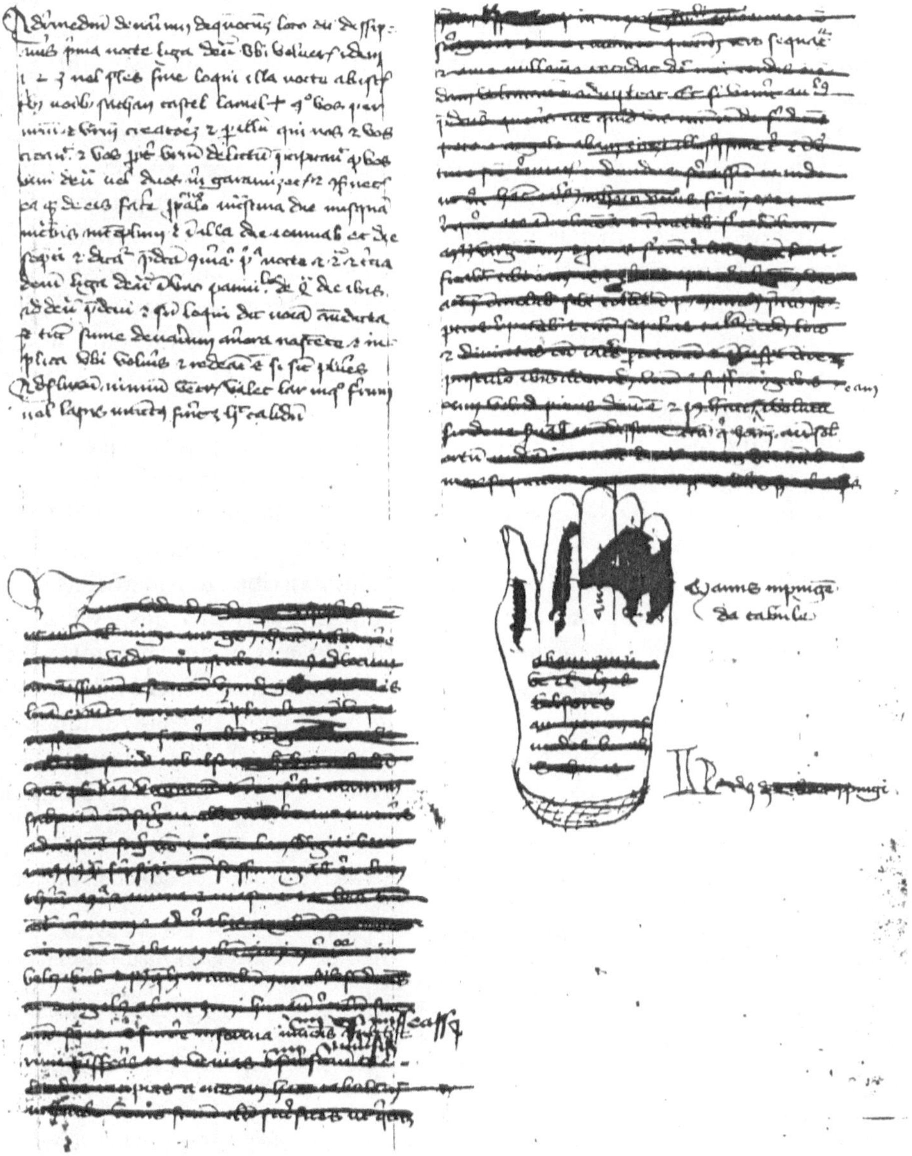

FIG 19 *Chiromantia delineata.* Kraków, BJ 551, fol. 117r. Courtesy of the Biblioteka Jagiellońska.

Cremona, William of Moerbeke, Hermes, Hugh of Santalla, Michael Scot, Pythagoras, and even Socrates. Discouraged by the complexity of the field, catalogs often do not attempt to identify texts of geomancy or do not report their appearance in a manuscript, while in other cases, in spite of the clearly recognizable geomantic figures, they fail to recognize them.[11] An indication of the popularity of this genre is that shorter or longer geomantic texts occur in most of the codices examined thus far in this study; they have a tendency to fill the spaces between longer tracts.[12]

Less frequent, although still quite popular, items in the medieval codices are the texts of chiromancy. The art of reading the lines, marks, and other patterns of the palms appeared in Latin manuscripts from the mid-twelfth century onward.[13] This practice aims at drawing conclusions about the fate, career, family life, and death of a given person: "Chiromancy is the art of learning about men's natural character and inclinations from the signs of the hand," as a manuscript of a Kraków student explains.[14] The reputation of this art is indicated by the fact that some of the chiromantic texts are ascribed to Aristotle and Albertus Magnus.[15]

Central European occurrences of the genre are of a rather practical nature: they usually contain neither theoretical introductions to, nor apologies for, this art. In the manuscript owned by the aforementioned Kraków student, Nicholas of Marienwerder (Nicolaus Wodka de Kwidzyn, 1442–1494, later the astrologer of the Prince of Urbino), there is a technical treatise on palmistry ascribed to Albertus Magnus. This tract concentrates on the lines of the hand, and starts and finishes with two drawings of hands indicating the main lines.[16] The text occurs in a completely nonmagical context: it is copied together with tracts on disciplines of the *trivium* (logic, *ars predicandi, ars dictandi, tractatus de ente*), with Thomas Aquinas's *De generibus scientiarum* (On the Kinds of Sciences), and with Marienwerder's own work on a "cyclical" calendar covering the years 1439 to 1803. An interesting

---

11. In BJ 805 (fols. 405r–409v), for example, the otherwise very reliable catalog of the Biblioteka Jagiellońska calls *De constellationibus* a tract of geomancy. *CBJ*, 6:185.

12. For example: PNK XI C 2, fols. 70r–71r, 72v–77r, and 78r–85v. See also BJ 839, fols. 23rb–36vb (*Liber de Geomantia* of Hugh of Santalla); SNB N. 100, fol. 203; and Brno, Augustinian Library, A 48, fols. 71v–149r (unidentified "practica geomantiae").

13. Charles Burnett, "The Earliest Chiromancy in the West," in Burnett, *Magic and Divination*, X, 189–97, and "Chiromancy Supplement," ibid., 1–23.

14. "Chyromantia est ars cognsocendi mores naturales et inclinationes hominum per signa manuum." ÖNB Cod. lat. 4007, fol. 73v.

15. Lynn Thorndike, "Chiromancy in Medieval Latin Manuscripts," *Speculum* 40 (1965): 674–706; Roger A. Pack, "Pseudo-Aristoteles: Chiromantia," *AHDLMA* 39 (1972): 289–320; Pack, "A Pseudo-Aristotelian Chiromancy," *AHDLMA* 36 (1969): 189–241.

16. ÖNB Cod. lat. 4007, fols. 73r–77r. This version does not contain the ascription to Albert the Great, but other versions of the same text do. See TK 291 and 350; *HMES*, 5:674–75; and Thorndike, "Chiromancy in Medieval Latin Manuscripts," 676. Copernicus's name can be found on fol. IVr: "Magistri Nicolai de Thorun."

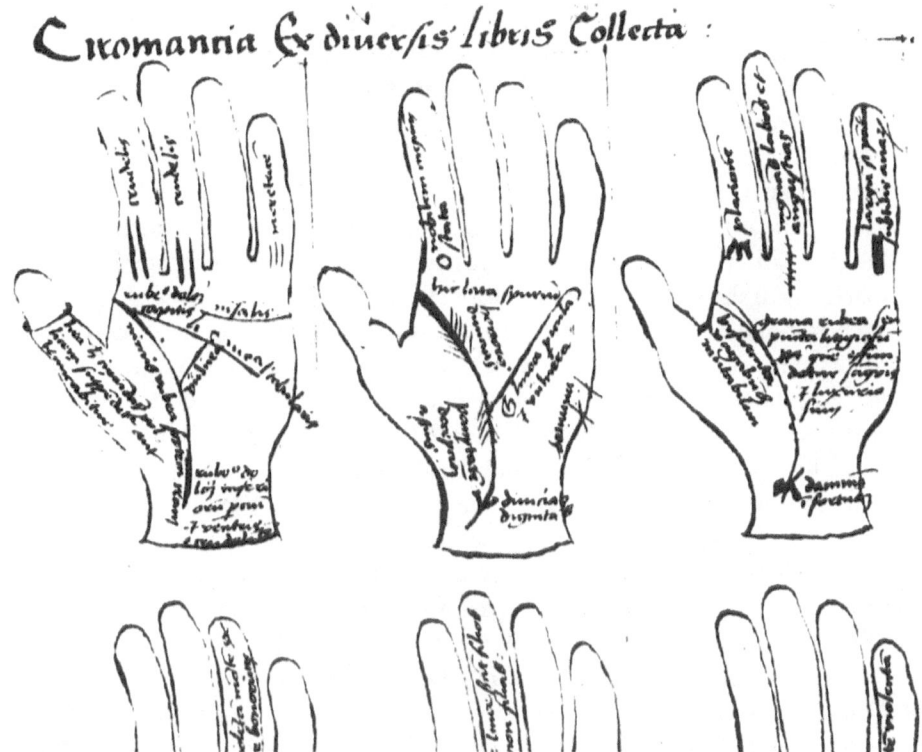

FIG 20 *Ciromantia ex diversis libris collecta.* BAV Pal. Lat. 1396, fol. 91r (superior part of the page). © Biblioteca Apostolica Vaticana (Vatican).

detail in the history of this manuscript is that after Marienwerder's death it went to the library of Nicolaus Copernicus.[17]

Another alumnus of the University of Kraków, Johannes Virdung of Hassfurt, was even more interested in the practice of palmistry. He was already living in Heidelberg as a court astrologer in 1500, when he copied thirty human hands— six on each of five consecutive pages—most of them with lines, figures, and indications (fig. 20).[18] There is no doubt that this is not a separate work but a compilation based on the methods of several texts, since we read on the first page "Ciromancia ex diversis libris collecta" [Chiromancy collected from various books]. Virdung

---

17. *BH*, 1:173; *A et A* 158–59, 320. *Tabulae codicum manu scriptorum in Bibliotheca Palatina Vindobonensi Assservatorum*, vol. 3 (Vienna: Carolus Gerold, 1868), 134–35 (available on microfilm at the Hungarian Academy of Sciences, Mf 3437/II). For more details on Marienwerder and this codex, see Chapter 9.

18. BAV Pal. lat. 1396, fols. 91r–93r.

must have consulted a number of texts of palmistry, and he sketched as many as thirty hands to provide a visually expressive basis for the notes he made from his readings. But he made more hands than he needed, and the last couple of palms are left blank.[19]

An odd case of "chiromancy" can be found in another of Virdung's codices, copied when he still resided in Kraków (BAV Pal. lat 1375). On a folio, just below a set of geomantic figures there is a circle filled with numbers and notes (fig. 21).[20] This circle and the text belonging to it have a title, ciphered in secret letters. Fortunately, with the help of alphabets scattered throughout the manuscript that show the corresponding real and secret characters (fig. 22, for example),[21] we can decipher it: "Hec est operacio ciromancie" [This is the operation of chiromancy]. We should be careful not to believe immediately what this title declares: the circular figure is a divinatory device indeed, but it has nothing to do with the figures of the human hand; it operates with the numerical value of names, and indicates whether the person inquiring about his own fate will die or recover from his illness. It can be equally well used for any other issue that might have a positive or negative outcome, such as a battle, an examination, a marriage, or any other enterprise. The numerical equivalents for each letter are arranged in a circle, where it was possible to find the numerical value of the name of the client. This value is then subjected to a series of mathematical operations, the result of which we should find either in the upper or in the lower hemisphere of the inner part of the circle: if it is in the upper part, the patient will survive (the length of his recovery being determined by the column in which the number occurs), but if it is in the lower part, he will die (sooner or later, depending again on the column). This diagrammatic device of onomancy (divination based on the numerical value of someone's name) is usually attributed to Pythagoras or Apollonius; as a matter of fact, the Latin text of the Vatican manuscript copied by the circle gives a proper title: "Hec est spera Pythagore platonici quam descripsit Apollonius in libro ethicorum" [This is the Sphere of the platonic Pythagoras which Apollonius describes in his books of ethics]. This—obviously false—attribution could have seemed quite plausible in the Middle Ages: Pythagoras was famous for the numerological nature of his philosophy, and the theory that numbers (or numerical values of letters) might correspond to aspects of reality appeared as a residue of the Pythagorean worldview.[22] Thus, the Sphere of

19. Ibid., fols. 92v–93r.
20. BAV Pal. lat. 1375, fol. 44r.
21. Ibid., fols. 19r, 44r, 284r, 285r; see also BAV Pal. lat. 1391, fol. 288. The cryptographic alphabets of BAV Pal. lat. 1375, fol. 19r, are reproduced on plate 22.
22. For the Sphere of Life and Death, see Ernest Wickersheimer, "Figures médico-astrologiques des IXe, Xe, XIe siècles," *Janus* 19 (1914): 1–21; Linda Ehrsam Voigts, "The Latin Verse and Middle English Prose Texts on the Sphere of Life and Death in Harley 3719," *Chaucer Review* 21 (1986): 291–305; Henry Sigerist, "The 'Sphere of Life and Death' in Early Mediaeval Manuscripts," *Bulletin*

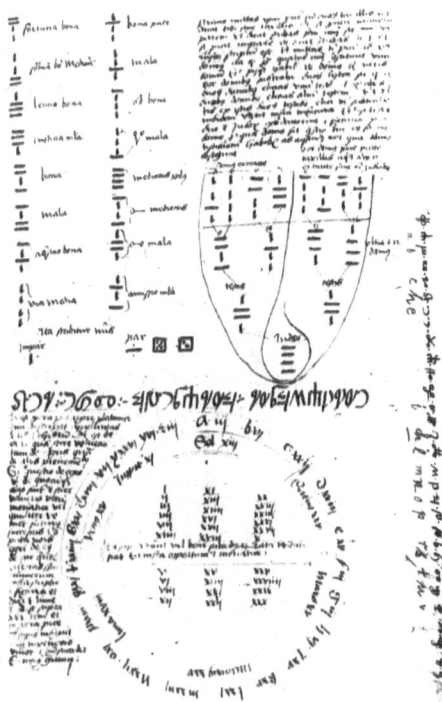

FIG 21 *Sphera Pythagorae* with a cryptographic title. BAV Pal. Lat. 1375, fol. 44r. © Biblioteca Apostolica Vaticana (Vatican).

Pythagoras, also called the Sphere of Life and Death, occurred in medieval manuscripts from the earliest times. Thanks to its visually expressive character, practical nature, and brevity, scribes often included it in astrological and divinatory collections in Central Europe as well (see figs. 10, 21, and 23).[23]

Just as not everything is chiromancy that is called so, not everything is geomancy that seems to be. In BJ 793, following the set of talismanic works described in Chapter 3, we find a series of texts with parallel content: full-page tables and charts with clearly recognizable geomantic figures, and instructions on how to use

---

of the History of Medicine 11 (1942): 292–303; and *HMES*, 1:682–85 and 692–94. See also David Juste, *Les Alchandreana Primitifs: Etudes sur les plus anciens traités astrologiques latins d'origine arabe (Xe siècle)* (Leiden: Brill, 2007).

23. See, for example, PNK XI C 2, fol. 86r; PNK I F 35, fol. 60v (Plate 23); BJ 793, fol. 86r (Plate 10); SLB N. 100, fol. 203v; and BJ 550, fol. 69v–70v; for the two last examples, see Rosińska 794, 1877. Michaelis de Kefira from Kraków copied the *Sphera Pythagorae* in the final part of his astrological compilation containing works by Alkabicius, Albumasar, Al-Kindi, and some Kraków professors, together with three tracts of chiromancy: see CLM 125, fol. 310r. For the texts of chiromancy, see ibid., fols. 301r–309v. For this manuscript, see also *A et A* 315–16.

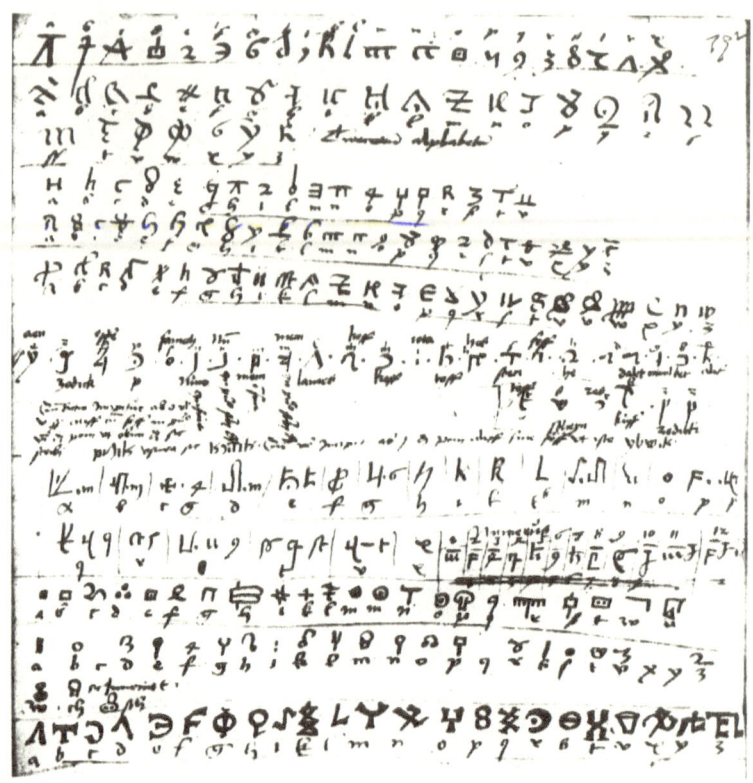

FIG 22 Cryptographic alphabets. BAV Pal. Lat. 1375, fol. 19r. © Biblioteca Apostolica Vaticana (Vatican).

these figures (for a selection of the tables and circles, see figs. 6–10). Some of the texts are anonymous,[24] while others are attributed to Albedatus,[25] Socrates Basileus,[26] or King Amalricus.[27]

24. BJ 793, fols. 63v–67r; 67v–69r; 69v–71r; 71v–73r; Johannes Bolte, "Zur Geschichte der Losbücher," in *Georg Wickrams Werke*, ed. Bolte, vol. 4 (Tübingen: Litterarischen Verein in Stuttgart, 1903), esp. 289; and *HMES*, 2:110–23.
25. BJ 793, fols. 81r–85v (*HMES*, 2:119), and Bolte, "Zur Geschichte," 299–300.
26. BJ 793, fols. 73v–81r (*HMES*, 2:116–17), and Bolte, "Zur Geschichte," 296–98.
27. BJ 793, fols. 88v–104v. This text, long known as the *Experimentarius* of Bernardus Silvestris, is now referred to as the *Sortes regis Amalrici*. Charles Burnett, "What Is the *Experimentarius* of Bernardus Silvestris? A Preliminary Survey of the Material," *AHDLMA* 52 (1977): 79–125; reprinted in Burnett, *Magic and Divination*, XVII; Burnett, "The *Sortes Regis Amalrici*: An Arabic Divinatory Work in the Latin Kingdom of Jerusalem?" *Scripta Mediterranea* 19–20 (1998–99): 229–37. As Burnett pointed out, the work which was edited by Brini Savorelli is in fact a compilation of texts of different origin, and the whole collection was mistakenly called the *Experimentarius* of Bernardus

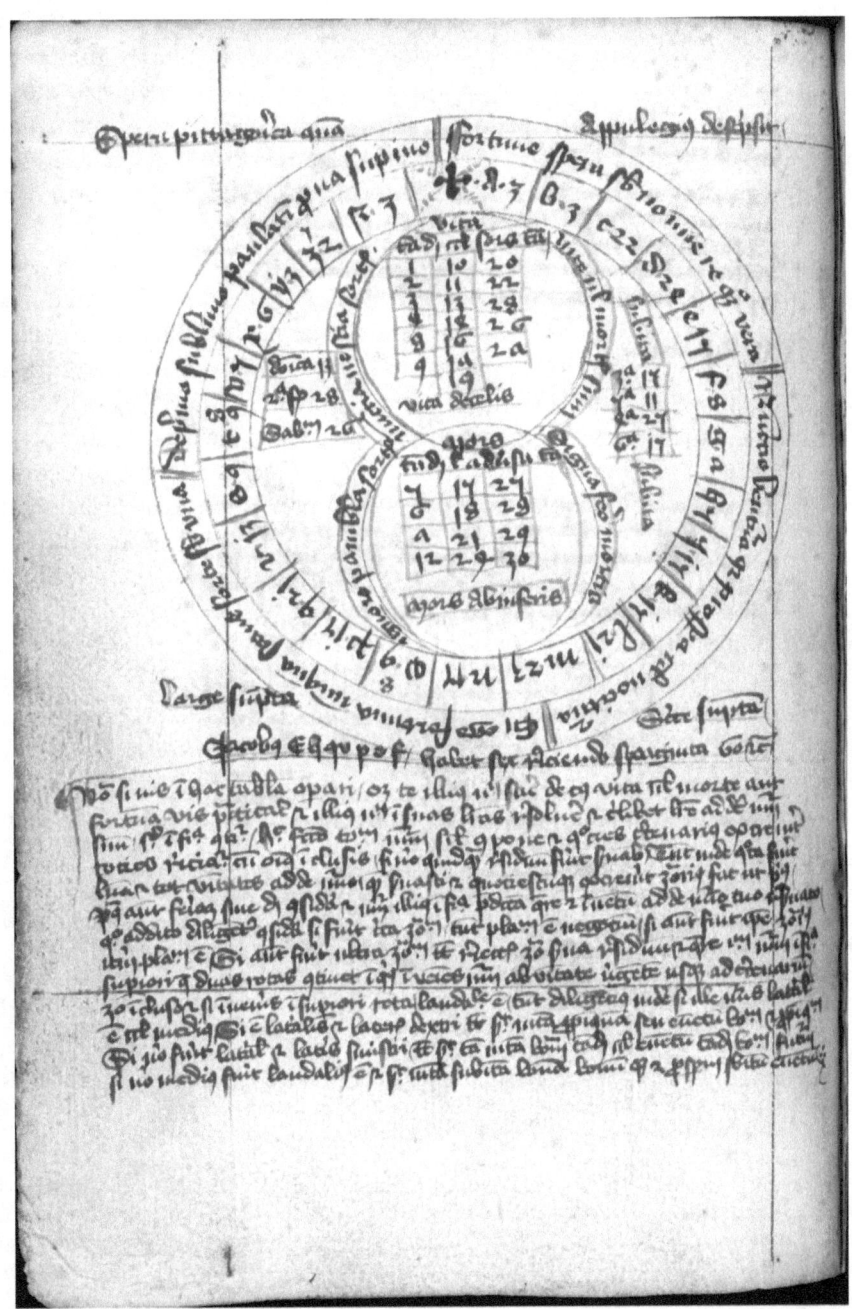

FIG 23 *Sphera Pythagorae*. Prague, PNK I F 35, fol. 60v. Courtesy of the Národní knihovna ČR.

However geomantic they may seem, strictly speaking, these texts do not belong to the tradition of geomancy; instead of long textual considerations, they are mere lists of questions and tables. Known as books of fate and belonging to the genre of *sortes* literature,[28] they use techniques less complex than those of geomancy, on which they are ultimately based. As T. C. Skeat puts it, books of fate are simply "systems comprising a fixed table of specific questions with a fixed number of alternative answers to each question."[29]

Let us finally take a look at a codex in which pieces belonging to the genre of *sortes* literature appear in great concentration: an early fifteenth-century Hungarian manuscript currently kept in Munich.[30] The greater part of this codex is taken up by Guido of Columna's *Historia Destructionis Troiae* (History of Troy's Destruction), which is followed by a medical and a divinatory division, both of them composed of several short pieces.[31] The opening piece of the first, medical, section is titled *Regimen sanitatis* (Health Regimen), and it is an abstract of the "De conservatione corporis" (On the Conservation of the Body) chapter of the Arabic version of the Pseudo-Aristotelian *Secretum secretorum* translated by John of Seville in the twelfth century. In addition, the medical part also includes some recipes and food descriptions, to include a passage on the virtues of the cheese. The second division starts with a text of onomancy, generally referred to in the Middle Ages as Albandinus's *Divinationes;* it continues with astrological treatises on the signs of the zodiac (in which we find a Hungarian word: *pisces id est hall*—"*pisces,* that is, 'fish'") and on the moon (with one more Hungarian word meaning God: *est isten got*), and ends with the *Prognosticon* of Socrates Basileus, which is also found in BJ 793.[32]

The text that the catalogs usually call Albandinus's *Divinationes*[33] is misnamed,

---

Silvestris. Silvestris Bernardus, *Experimentarius,* in Mirella Brini Savorelli, "Un manuale di geomanzia presentato da Bernardo Silvestre da Tours (XII secolo): l'*Experimentarius,*" *Rivista Critica di Storia della Filosofia* 14 (1959): 282–342; see also Bolte, "Zur Geschichte," 298–99.

28. For the differentiation between geomantic treatises and sort-books, see Charmasson, *Recherches,* 222. On the *sortes* literature, besides Bolte's study and Burnett's articles cited in the previous note, see T. C. Skeat, "An Early Mediaeval 'Book of Fate': The Sortes XII Patriarcharum, with a Note on 'Books of Fate' in General," *Mediaeval and Renaissance Studies* 3 (1954): 41–54. Although the BJ 793 has the richest collection of geomantic books of fate in Central Europe (see fols. 63r–103v), they also appear in other codices; for example, a table of geomancy occurs in PNK XI C 2, fols. 72v–73r, while the *Sortes regis Amalrici* is in the same codex on fols. 88v–104v.

29. Skeat, "An Early Mediaeval 'Book of Fate,'" 54.

30. Munich, Universitätsbibliothek 2° Cod. ms. 738; *BH,* 2:2017; Natalia Daniel, Gerhard Schott, and Peter Zahn, eds., *Die Handschriften der Universitätsbibliothek, München,* vol. 3/2 (Wiesbaden: Otto Harrassowitz, 1979), 186–87. See also András Vizkelety, "Ismeretlen magyar vonatkozású kódexek Münchenben" (Unknown Munich Codices of Hungarian Interest), *Magyar Könyvszemle* 95 (1979): 198–202.

31. For a list of the contents, see the description of manuscripts at the end of the book.

32. Both Hungarian words occur on fol. 184v.

33. TK 616; *HMES,* 1:716; Daniel, Schott, and Zahn, *Die Handschriften,* 187.

since Albandinus's name appears in only one of its dozen extant examples.[34] Our text refers to itself as *Liber similitudinum*[35] (The Book of Similarities), and what interests us here is that the method of divination it describes resembles that in the *Sphera Pythagorae,* but it is more astrological in nature. Observing the sign of the client's nativity and the numerical value of the name of the town where he was born, the operator can conclude—after performing some mathematical operations— whether the client is facing good fortune or bad, life or death, success or failure.[36]

Apparently, we are again faced with a collection of texts providing the reader with the useful tools of practical magic. The manuscript has special Hungarian interest, not only because of the Hungarian words it contains, but also because of its scribe, who calls himself Stephanus of Rivulo Dominarum (Asszonypataki István).[37] Philological research has arrived at the conclusion that the codex was copied on Hungarian territory around 1406.[38] The coherently chosen divinatory and onomantic treatises that were attached to the history of the fall of Troy were either gathered by Asszonypataki István himself, or copied from an already existing collection. It would be of great interest to find out why he copied these particular texts, and whether he himself was interested in magical arts or whether he was just asked to collect such methods by someone else; however, for this, we would need more details about his life.

Excursus: Visual Material in Magical Manuscripts

The richest variety of nonartistic pictorial material in the Middle Ages can be found in manuscripts of scientific content. Encyclopedic and scientific handbooks often used visual devices and tabulated information in order to facilitate learning and render the text more easily comprehensible. Among the standard schemata, we find trees, wheels, charts, and other figures.

Trees (*arbores*) served for classifying and dichotomizing elements belonging to a certain topic. Each branch of this organic diagram represented a division in the system of logic: an element in the classification of virtues (*arbor virtutum*), or a part of science (*divisio scientiarum*). The structure of trees populating the medieval

---

34. It appears in BnF lat. 7351. For a partial edition of the text and its analysis, see Juste, *Alchandreana*. In addition, there *is* a divinatory text called *Liber Albandini,* the methods of which are based on the month and day of birth, but it is a different one. See also TK 339.

35. Munich, Universitätsbibliothek 2° Cod. ms. 738, fol. 178r: "Hic est liber similitudinum fortuniorum."

36. The prologue of the *Liber similitudinum* also appears in PNK XI C 2, fol. 17r–17v.

37. Asszonypataka is the name of the place later called Nagybánya (now Baia Mare, in present-day Romania).

38. See Vizkelety, "Ismeretlen magyar vonatkozású kódexek."

manuscripts matched well the demand of scholars, scribes, and students whose preference toward a dichotomizing way of argumentation was expressed, *inter alia*, by the most famous medieval tree, the *Arbor Porphyriana*.

Circular diagrams were useful for classifying things and setting them in order, but also for representing the contrary nature of the elements displayed at the opposite spokes of the wheel, and the common components of the neighboring elements. The advantage of the circle was well exploited in the best-known wheel representing the analogies of the macrocosm and microcosm; the four elements (*ignis, terra, aqua, aer*) correspond to the seasons (*aestas, autumnus, hiemps, ver*), the humors (*colera, melancolia, humor, sanguis*), and the combinations of their characteristics (*siccus, calidus, humidus, frigidus*).[39] Wheels play such a crucial role in Isidore's *De natura rerum* (On the Nature of Things) that it was often referred to as the *Liber rotarum* (Book of Wheels). Wheels were subsequently used to represent the cycles of months and seasons, to calculate the date of movable ecclesiastical feasts, and also as a pedagogical tool for visualizing the order and the orbit of planets. Combinations were easily expressible in circular form too; certain *rotae* helped determine the validity of a syllogism; the combinatory wheels of the Catalan philosopher, Raimundus Lullus, functioned as thinking automata, generating new combinations of letters and concepts, and ultimately directing the user to new theories and truths. Finally, a special case of visual aids arranged the text itself in a tabular or chart form. This could happen with the intention of visualizing, for example, the combination of the four elements of which the whole world is constructed, or simply for didactic purposes in a table of contents, or by listing the major points and headings of a text.[40]

Magic texts applied virtually the same diversity of diagrams and figures, often with similar purposes: for facilitating the understanding of a method, for didacticism, for the representation of combinations and the classification of the elements of an area, for helping to memorize the material, or—an objective unknown in scientific handbooks—for meditative purposes. In the following paragraphs, we are not going to deal with those pictorial representations which possess a certain artistic value—such as the pictures of the planetary spirits in the Kraków *Picatrix*, and the colorful illuminations of Conrad Kyeser's *Bellifortis*—discussed in the previous chapters; instead, we will concentrate on figures and diagrams that are usually less artistically elaborated and often left without mention by the catalogs, and which, nevertheless, play an essential role in magical procedures.

39. Wickersheimer, "Figures médico-astrologiques," 157–59.
40. On the application of graphic representations, classificatory schemes, diagrams, and figures in medieval scientific manuscripts, see John Murdoch, ed., *Album of Science: Antiquity and the Middle Ages* (New York: Charles Scribner's Sons, 1984), and Michael Evans, "The Geometry of the Mind," *Architectural Association Quarterly* 12 (1980): 32–55.

The tabulation of texts is used primarily in books of fate. The practitioner of geomantic techniques is supposed to follow a mechanical procedure through a number of complicated charts and circles until he finds an answer to his initial questions concerning various aspects of daily life. The possibilities of reading such a combinatorial chart according to certain alphabetical keys is much more numerous than the options of reading the sentences in a linear way (see figs. 7 and 8).[41]

The same texts of divination also make use of *rotae*, which play an intermediary role in the process of finding the proper answer to a given question (see figs. 6 and 9).[42] The combination of letters inscribed on colored wheels helps to simplify (or perhaps complicate?) the methods that the client has to follow when trying to find an answer to his question (see fig. 10).[43] In late medieval and Renaissance magical texts, the old Arabic circular methods were mated with the combinatorial wheels of the Pseudo-Lullian and Kabbalistic traditions, giving birth to various sets of alphabets and notions displayed on movable disc systems which could be used to generate a large number of new combinations and permutations. The wheel seemed to be such an adequate representational form of corresponding letters that it was also applied by the copyists of the *Liber runarum*, who displayed the runic and the Latin alphabets together with the corresponding angels' names in a circular arrangement (see fig. 17).[44] Yet the most widespread medieval *rota* remained that of Pythagoras, the Sphere of Life and Death, and its equivalents under different names: the Sphere of Petosiris and that of Democritos. It is worth adding, however, that for the mere functioning of this procedure, the figure would not necessarily need to be a circle; as a matter of fact the same method is sometimes presented in a noncircular form, the *tetragonus subjectus*.[45] Nevertheless, onomantic circles were much more widespread and perhaps more appealing throughout the Middle Ages than tetragonal figures of name magic.

A special subclass of pictorial elements within the literature of magic is the alphabet of secret letters, which might be applied not only as a cryptographic means, but also to designate spirits. Hence, secret alphabets are often called *sigilla spirituum*—the seals of the spirits, and *scriptura coelestis*—celestial writing.[46] We have

41. For the use of tabulation in divinatory texts, see PNK XI C 2 and BJ 793, fols. 71v, 72r, 73v, 74v, 88r.
42. BJ 793, fol. 75r.
43. For wheels in books of fate, see BJ 793, fols. 67r, 86r, 86v. For a helpful overview on the application of wheels in magical texts, especially books of fate, see Wade, "Fragmentary German Divination Device."
44. BAV Pal. lat. 1439, fol. 199r.
45. Wickersheimer, "Figures médico-astrologiques," 172–74.
46. For a comprehensive typology of seals and characters in scientific and magical manuscripts, see Linda Ehrsam Voigts, "The Character of the *Carecter*: Ambiguous Sigils in Scientific and Medical Texts," in *Latin and Vernacular: Studies in Late Medieval Texts and Manuscripts*, ed. A. J. Minnis (Cambridge: Brewer, 1989), 91–109.

already seen the mechanism of applying secret characters and sigils to spell the names of spiritual beings in the *Liber runarum,* where Nordic runes were associated with angels, and we have also seen the short tracts of image magic in BAV Pal. lat. 1375, where strange letters were used for the exorcism of spirits of quite similar names (see fig. 18). A Kraków excerpt from the *Picatrix* also offers a list of such letters, which are called signs of planets (*signa, sigilla,* or *figurae planetarum*—the planets' signs, seals, or figures) and serve for various magical aims (to expel flies and mice, to bless a place, and so on).[47] By the time of the Renaissance—partly because of the impact of the tradition of the Jewish Kabbalah—alphabets of celestial letters proliferated in such great diversity that Cornelius Agrippa felt obliged to offer a whole typology of them in his comprehensive handbook of magic.[48]

Similar letters appear in a circular arrangement alongside names that seem to refer to angels on a metal disc fashioned in the first half of the fifteenth century (fig. 24).[49] This object, kept today in the Mathematisch-Physikalischer Salon in Dresden, bears the inscription "Floron" in its inner circle, a name indicating that we are faced with one of the famous magical Mirrors of Floron. It corresponds almost completely to the description of the Mirror of Floron in the Munich necromantic handbook published by Richard Kieckhefer, an object that should be prepared in the name of the spirit Floron according to detailed rituals involving suffumigations, clean clothes, and virgin boys. If prepared properly, an armed knight sitting on a horse will appear in the mirror, and then the master might ask him about the past, the present, and the future.[50] Although the secret characters and the spirit names of the Dresden metal disc are not identical with those given by the Munich manuscript, their number is the same (ten) and the arrangement of the elements as well as placement of the inscription "Floron" are analogous.[51]

We can conclude that texts on divination supplied the manuscripts with a more abundant collection of diagrams and figures than other genres of magic. Paradoxically, image magic is not so rich in depicted visual elements. The *imago astronomica,* which is the central element of this genre, is quite rarely depicted (the magic squares and the Kraków *Picatrix* being exceptions to this rule). The texts concentrate

47. BJ 610, fols. 312v–316r; see also *Picatrix,* 63.
48. Cornelius Agrippa, "De characteribus et sigillis spirituum," chap. 39 of *De occulta Philosophia,* ed. Vittoria Perrone Compagni (Leiden: Brill, 1992), 490–95.
49. Karel Fischer, "Věda na scestí," *Dějiny a současnost* 9 (1967): 30–32.
50. Kieckhefer, *Forbidden Rites,* 104–6 and 236–38: "Fac fieri speculum de puro calibe, ad mensuram palme unius in rotundo; habeatque manubrium ad tenendum, et sit illuminatum et lucidum ut ensis. Sitque factum in nomine Floron, et in circuitu istius peculi ex alia parte non lucida sint hec decim nomina, cum hiis decem caracteribus descripta, et nomen spiritus predicti sit in medio scriptum." For a picture of the mirror, see ibid., 363.
51. On the use of the Mirror of Floron for various purposes in the Middle Ages, see Armand Delatte, *La Catoptromancie grecque et ses dérivés* (Paris: Librairie Droz, 1932), 44–46.

Divination with Diagrams

FIG 24   Magical mirror. Courtesy of the Mathematisch-Physikalischer Salon, Staatliche Kunstsammlungen, Dresden. Photo by Peter Müller.

rather on textual descriptions of the images that should be engraved on the gems and talismans.

Sources of ritual magic are more interesting from the point of view of pictorial representations. Magical circles—frequently appearing in modern literature and films—are the most famous tools from the inventory of the magician who wishes to invoke demons. These circles serve to protect him from the harmful intentions of the spirits, provided, of course, that in or around the circle he draws the other necessary elements, such as angelic names, swords, pentagrams, and various astronomical characters correctly. Unfortunately, apart from one single small magic ring in a Prague manuscript (fig. 25), this particular inventory item does not figure in any medieval Central European manuscript, and therefore we shall not go into more detail here.[52]

The other subbranch of ritual magic, the notory art, attributes a completely different significance to diagrams. The *notae*, as its geometrical figures and characters are called, are not just auxiliary elements of the rituals. A set of diagrams of circular, triangular, and tree forms are assigned to each branch of learning. These *notae* not only serve to represent the links between the different elements of the text, but also function as visual aids for meditation, through which the operator is able to communicate with the celestial powers. This twofold operation corresponds to the double intentions of the notory art: it promises to provide knowledge of all the liberal arts, while offering a means of communication with the spirits. None of the few Central European examples of the *Ars notoria* is supplied with *notae*, and consequently we will not concern ourselves more with this issue.[53]

But before we leave the *notae* for good, a third function of theirs deserves more attention, because it leads us closer to the functioning of scientific and magical diagrams. The geometrical arrangement of the elements of the main text of the *Ars notoria* in these figures might have helped the operator to remember the details when he tried to reconstruct the structure of the procedure without having his handbook in his hands. Hence, it is not a pure coincidence that the work known as the *Ars notoria* often appeared with the title *Ars memorativa*. In a parallel way, the use of *arbores* and *rotae* in all kinds of scientific and magical literature had much to do with the art of memory in a culture when the importance of remembering played a different and more fundamental role than it has since the invention of printing. As the wheel of the macro- and microcosm helped the user memorize the corresponding seasons, humors, elements, and combinations, the sphere of Pythagoras,

---

52. A detailed description of the use of circles can be found in Kieckhefer, *Forbidden Rites*, 170–85.

53. PNK I F 35, fol. 466v. For a deeper analysis of the *notae* of the *Ars notoria*, see Camille, "Visual Art," 110–39. Further details and considerations may be found in other studies on this genre of ritual magic, listed in Chapter 6.

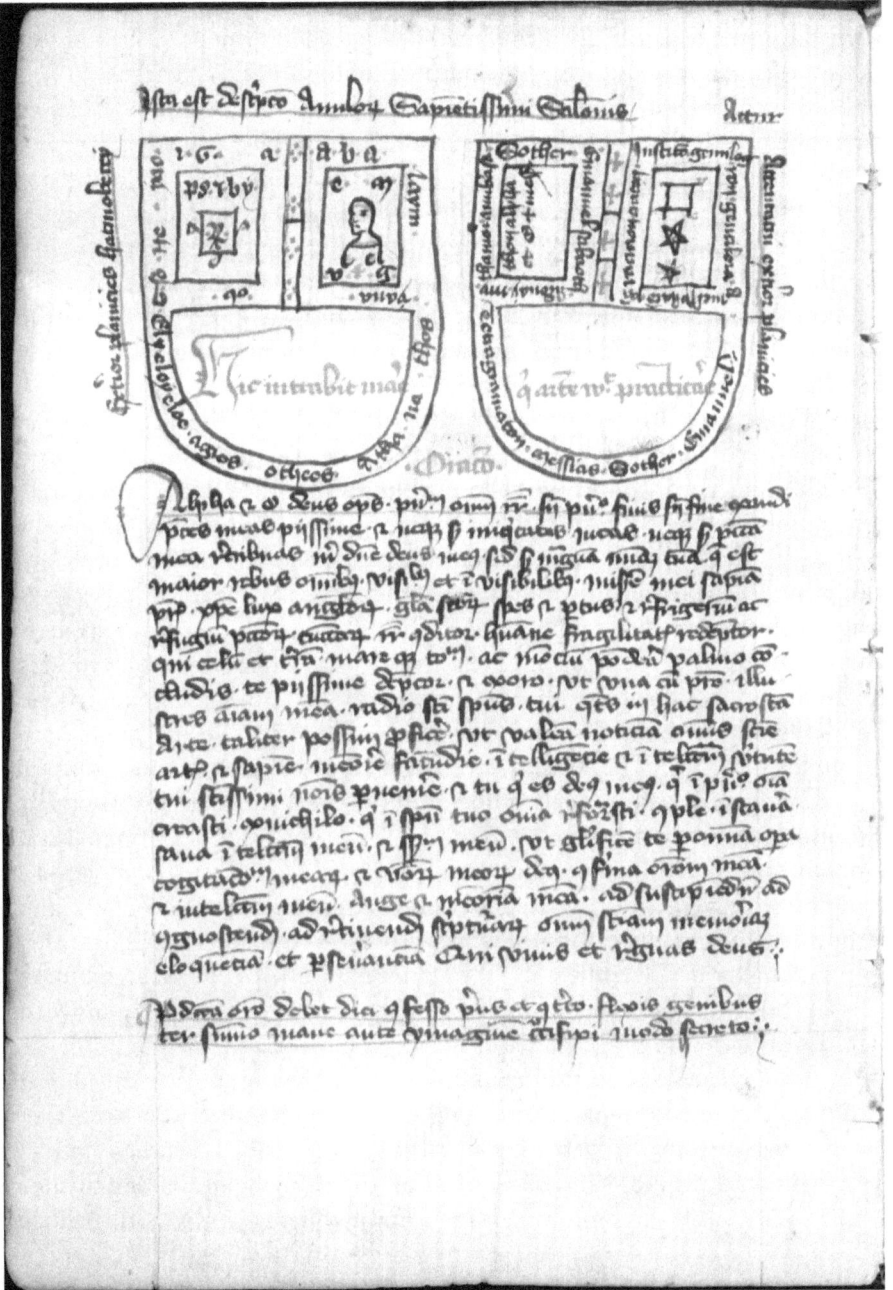

FIG 25 Drawing on Solomon's rings. Prague, PNK I F 35, fol. 466v. Courtesy of the Národní knihovna ČR.

for example, could have facilitated the reproduction of the onomantic calculations, while the arrangement of divinatory methods in a chart form or in another geometric figure might have also served the purposes of the art of memory.[54]

The mnemotechnic function of the pictorial material might also explain a strange habit of figures. Observing the general tendencies in the tradition of diagrams, we see that they often lost their links to the texts that explained their functioning: they started a new and independent life on the folios of manuscripts. It is hard to explain how those charts and circles were used when the scribes copied them without the quite complicated textual instructions. One can only speculate whether the methods were so well known that the explanations were seen as superfluous, whether the figures could be reproduced in an easier way from memory than from the accompanying texts, or—a third option—whether darkness and mystification formed such a crucial element of divinatory methods that the lack of instructions was only one of the elements that rendered the actual employment of the diagrams difficult. Whichever answer we choose, it seems that the history of pictorial representations in magic is related to, but not subject to, the history of magical texts.

Pictures and diagrams can teach us something about which the texts are usually silent. They provide us with information to a certain extent whether the given magical text was used or simply copied. The difference is crucial. We are very well aware that from the mere presence of a specific magical text in a collector's library not much can be concluded about his interest in magic or his secret practices. The problem has not changed much since the Middle Ages. No one could correctly reconstruct my scientific interest merely on the basis of the books that can be found in my private library. What does it mean, for example, that a book on practical astrology on my bookshelf is in the company of a work of German literature? Does that mean that I like reading about astrology? Does it mean that I even practice it occasionally? Did I receive this book as a present for my birthday? Can there be any conclusions drawn from what other books occur in its immediate vicinity? Was it situated in the context of German literature with some specific purpose? Or is it there just by chance? It would be rather hazardous to give any answer without directly asking me, the owner of the given volumes.

In medieval manuscripts, of course, we have a few more external indications that may help us answer these questions. Among such indications is the fact that copying two texts beside each other reveals a stronger association than simply putting them on the same shelf, not to mention that copying something by our own hands shows a deeper commitment than simply buying a book. Still, difficulties

---

54. See John B. Friedman, "Les images mnémotechniques dans les manuscrits de l'époque gothique," in *Jeux de mémoire: aspects de la mnémotechnic médiévale*, ed. Bruno Roy and Paul Zumthor (Paris: Librairie philosophique J. Vrin, 1985), 169–83, and Mary Carruthers, *The Book of Memory: Memory in Medieval Culture* (Cambridge: Cambridge University Press, 1992).

concerning the initial question are quite similar, and this is where the visual material might offer some help.

In this chapter, we have witnessed several strategies of how this help is provided. Extensive use of divinatory tables and charts in a manuscript that is full of cross-references and indications in the margins seem to testify that the given scribe prepared his book with the definite purpose of concrete use, that is, foretelling the future. Copying prognostic diagrams without including their instructions seems to imply an operator who is skilled or experienced enough to use the diagram without referring to the instructions. Sketching thirty human hands for the purpose of collecting chiromantic information from other handbooks is equally a sign of active interest.

In other cases, the attempt to destroy a figure, not the figure itself, may be of relevance. Crossing out spirit names spelled in secret characters is a telling indication of the conviction that such signs possess hidden powers of unpredictable and dangerous effect. Making a text of palmistry unreadable and leaving the adjacent angelic invocations undamaged refers to the fear that the actual use of divination by another reader was a real possibility.

All in all, it seems that the visual material scattered in the magical texts, even more than the codicological context of the same texts, helps us reconstruct a certain interest in operative talismans and divinatory procedures. It is obvious that— at least for some book owners—this interest was neither secondary nor accidental. These examples provide insight into the readership and impact of the magical literature. These pieces of evidence show a manifest and active magical concern by the readers and owners, who apparently used these books, followed the instructions they read in them, or wanted to hinder other readers from following these instructions by eliminating certain elements of the rituals. The presence of the talismanic and divinatory material on the folios of these codices reveals a stronger commitment to using them than their accidental presence on a bookshelf.

5
Alchemy

The Alchemical Mass

The text of the Holy Mass opens with the following, startling announcement meant to be sung to the tune of the Gaudeamus: "The basis of the Art is the dissolution of the bodies." A few lines later, a Kyrie follows: "Our Lord, fount of goodness, inspirer of the sacred art, from whom all good things come to your faithful, have mercy. Christ, Holy one, blessed stone of the art of the science, who for the salvation of the world hast inspired the light of science, for the extirpation of the Turk, have mercy. Kyrie, divine fire, help our hearts, that we may be able, to your praise, to expand the sacraments of the art, have mercy."

It must be obvious even for a nonbeliever whose acquaintance with the Christian liturgy is only superficial that this is not how the Mass is supposed to be celebrated. Indeed, the text, the beginning of which we have just quoted, was not issued by the church authorities but from an entirely different source. A mysterious author from early sixteenth-century Transylvania, Nicolaus Melchior Cibinensis, found this most religious and rather unusual literary genre for elaborating his ideas on alchemical science. His *Processus sub forma missae* (Process in the Form of the Mass), dedicated to Wladislas, king of Hungary and Bohemia, is a curious incorporation of the alchemical process in the framework of the Mass. The headings of his text are the usual components of the Christian liturgy (Introitus Missae, Kyrie, Graduale, Versus, Offertorium, Secretum, and so on), but under them we find some rather unorthodox material: vitriol, saltpeter, the philosopher's stone, marriage with the moon, and the sperm of philosophers wishing to copulate with the Virgin. The Sequentia Evangeli contains an elaborate alchemical process in which the *prima materia* perishes, revives, copulates, conceives, and rejuvenates. Whether the whole text is a treatise on the manipulation of various metallic substances enciphered in secret religious symbols, or is a long prayer rich in alchemical metaphors, is hard to tell. The only certainty is that this is a fertile and a rather organic combination of two kinds of rich symbolism.[1]

The *Processus sub forma missae* and its author were not unknown to the alchemists of the early modern era. The text was printed in the famous anthology of alchemical literature, the *Theatrum Chemicum* (Chemical Theater), by Lazarus Zetzner in 1602.[2] This point needs to be emphasized because the confusion in the literature concerning both the person and the work of Melchior is so great that it is hard to differentiate between evidence and legends even with regard to such simple things as the bibliographical data of his published text.[3] Melchior's portrait appears on the title page of the *Symbola Aureae Mensae Duodecim Nationum* (The Symbols of the Golden Table of the Twelve Nations) by Michael Maier (1568–1622), the alchemist of Emperor Rudolf II. In this international history of the royal art, Melchior is chosen to represent Hungary among the twelve most famous alchemists of the world, and thus he appears in the noble company of Hermes Trismegistos, Maria the Jewess, Avicenna, Albertus Magnus, Roger Bacon, and Raimundus Lullus.[4] He is mentioned and quoted by such authors and editors of the sixteenth and seventeenth centuries as Daniel Stolz von Stolzenberg, Petrus Borelius, Libavius, and Athanasius Kircher. Even Isaac Newton was acquainted with Melchior's name; relying on Maier's description, he incorporated a number of Latin notes on a wide range of alchemical authors and myths in one of his many alchemical manuscripts, among these a few references to the alchemist of Transylvania.[5]

Last but not least, the alchemical Mass was deeply analyzed by Jung as an example

---

1. To my knowledge this is the only example in medieval and early modern times of using the Catholic Mass for alchemical purposes. However, there are cases of using it for other magical aims. See, for example, Lea Olsan's paper delivered at the Thirty-ninth International Congress on Medieval Studies at Kalamazoo, "The Appropriation of Liturgy for Healing Charms and Amulets," on a case of healing magic in Lincoln Cathedral MS 91, fol. 296r–v (ca. 1425–50). I am grateful to her for providing me with a written version of this paper. See Chapter 7 for an example in the Hungarian *Peer Codex* of the Mass being used to cure illness.

2. "Addam et Processum Sub Forma Missae a Nicolao Melchiore Cibinensi Transiluano, ad Ladislaum Ungariae et Bohemiae Regem olim missum," in *Theatrum Chemicum*, vol. 3, ed. Lazarus Zetzner (Ursel, 1602), 758–61. In another copy of the *Theatrum Chemicum* I consulted, this work appears on pages 853–55.

3. For example, Melchior's work is not to be found in *Musaeum Hermeticum* (Frankfurt: Lucas Jennisius, 1625), as Stephanus Weszprémi claims in his *Succinta Medicorum Hungariae et Transilvaniae Biographia*, vol. 2 (Vienna: Johannes Thomas Tratnem, 1774), 128, and as many further authors have erroneously repeated. Melchior's portrait appears in this collection (on 271), but not his text.

4. Michael Maier, *Symbola aurae mensae duodecim nationum* (Frankfurt: Antonius Hummius, 1617), 507–52; the portrait appears on 509.

5. Cambridge, King's College Library, Keynes MSS, MS 29 (SL32/R19). See also B.J.T. Dobbs, *The Foundations of Newton's Alchemy or "The Hunting of the Greene Lyon"* (Cambridge: Cambridge University Press, 1975), 131.

of the analogy between the *lapis* and Christ.⁶ As it is well known, Jung—recognizing a strong correlation between alchemical symbolism and the motifs of dreams and hallucinations—supposed that the symbols of alchemy were the projections of the "archetypes" of the "collective unconscious." What is important here is that in elaborating this theory, Jung attributed great importance to the analogy of Christianity and the alchemical process, and identified a number of corresponding motifs between the royal art and religion. Indeed, Christ appears in the pages of the alchemical Mass as the "blessed stone of the art of science who for the salvation of the world [hath] inspired the light of science, for the extirpation of the Turk."⁷ Melchior's work provides Jung with weighty evidence for the *lapis*–Christ identity, and also for the concept that the *arcanum* of alchemy is somehow concealed in the Virgin. In fact, Melchior's alchemical paraphrase appears as a hymn to Mary, in which a correspondence is made between alchemical transmutation and Christian transubstantiation.

On the circumstances of the birth of this exceptional text, virtually nothing can be established with complete certainty. Who was the author, how could this work be dedicated to a king, and how could it happen that alchemy was chosen as the theme of such a basic liturgical genre as the text of the Mass? Before speculating on the authorship and origin of the alchemical Mass, let us briefly survey the prestige the royal art enjoyed in late medieval intellectual circles. Establishing the status of alchemy might shed more light on the question of how seriously the alchemical Mass could have been taken.

Alchemy in University and Monastic Libraries

Not counting a few early medieval sources, alchemy enters the history of Latin literacy in the mid-twelfth century, as a result of the translation movement from the Arabic.⁸ However, like learned magic, its first Central European traces are only from

---

6. See Carl Gustav Jung, *Psychologie und Alchemie* (Zürich: Rascher, 1944), 536–48. For a more extensive discussion, see Jung, "Erlösungvorstellungen in der Alchemie," *Eranos Jahrbuch* (Ascona), 1936, 13–111.

7. For the English translation, see Carl Gustav Jung, *Psychology and Alchemy* (London: Routledge, 1968), 397.

8. Here, I restrict myself to listing two richly annotated bibliographies on the history of alchemy that are excellent starting points for further research: Claudia Kren, *Alchemy in Europe: A Guide to Research* (New York: Garland, 1990), and Robert Halleux, *Les textes alchimiques* (Turnhout: Brepols, 1979). William R. Newman, *The "Summa Perfectionis" of Pseudo-Geber* (Leiden: Brill, 1991), also provides a helpful overview on medieval attitudes toward "the royal art"; and Vladimir Karpenko, "The Chemistry and Metallurgy of Transmutation," *Ambix* 39 (1992): 47–62, may be consulted for the technical side and the chemical reconstruction of the alchemical transmutation. For a concise and useful survey of medieval alchemy, see Herwig Buntz, "Alchemy III: 12th/13th–15th Century," in Hanegraaff et al., *Dictionary of Gnosis and Western Esotericism*, 34–41.

around 1400. But there is one important peculiarity of the local spread of this discipline: it inspired more original works than the fields of magic did.

Although the "royal art"—unlike astrology—was never incorporated into the university curriculum, it was by no means a neglected topic in codices belonging to clerics, students, and professors. In order to see what might have induced a university master or a monk to deal with alchemy, and to examine what strategies the alchemical texts themselves applied to become integrated in the medical, technological, or religious content of the codices, let us briefly survey a few concrete manuscripts from the libraries of university masters and clerical practitioners.

In many cases, the reason to include alchemy in a scientific manuscript was clearly its medical relevance. In our often-cited magical handbook, BJ 793, we find a crucial source of alchemical medicine: Johannes of Rupescissa's *De consideratione quintae essentiae* (On the Fifth Essence).[9] Rupescissa's text was a frequent item in medieval manuscripts; it was also printed several times in the sixteenth and seventeenth centuries. Although he is undeniably speaking about alchemy, he does not aim to explain the secrets of transmutation; instead, he concentrates on a medical issue, the preparation of the elixir of youth, the *aqua vitae*.[10] Taking into consideration a number of scientific and philosophical arguments, Rupescissa comes to the conclusion that the human body cannot be preserved with the help of something corruptible, but only with a material that is the terrestrial correspondent of the eternal and perfect element of the heavens: the fifth essence, the *quinta essentia*. This terrestrial equivalent of the fifth essence, which has strong preservative virtues, is nothing other than the *aqua ardens,* the "ardent water," that is, alcohol. Now—and here comes alchemy strictly speaking—*aqua ardens* cannot only be prepared as a result of repeated distillations, but can be also extracted from organic and inorganic materials, for example from minerals: inter alia, from gold. This theme explains why this treatise of Rupescissa is followed in the Kraków codex—as well as in many other sources—by a short recipe for preparing *aqua vitae*.[11]

A different way of applying alchemy for medical purposes can be detected in BJ 823, where a great number of short alchemical recipes are scattered among a wide range of medical instructions and theoretical writings on medicine.[12] Similarly, in a codex originally from Buda alchemical and medical recipes follow a number of medical texts—a "health regimen," Zacharias's *De passione oculorum* (On Eye Disease), Bruno Longoburgensis's *Chrirurgia magna* (Surgery)—as well as Albertus Magnus's *De mineralibus* (On Minerals) and Roger Bacon's *Epistola de retardatione*

---

9. BJ 793, fols. 127r–138r; Rosińska 613. The same text also occurs in BJ 3344, fols. 1r–102v, where the name of the author is spelled *Ihannes recepissa*.
10. *HMES*, 3:347–69; for a list of manuscripts, see 725–30.
11. BJ 793, fol. 138r, "De aqua ardenti seu Excerpta de aqua vitae"; Rosińska 1039.
12. BJ 823, fols. 18v, 19r, 28r–50v; *CBJ*, 6:268–80; Rosińska 1840.

senectutis (Letter on the Delaying of Old Age).[13] Frankly, it is often hard to decide whether a formula should be considered a medical technique to prepare a drug, or an alchemical procedure to manufacture the water of life. This ambivalent character of the medical-alchemical content may account for the ownership of these two codices. The mostly fourteenth-century folios of BJ 823 were bound together in the German Cistercian abbacy of Riddagshusio, then—as marginal notes and glosses testify—the manuscript journeyed to Bohemia, and came finally in the mid-fifteenth century to one of the masters of University of Kraków. The Buda codex traveled in an opposite, western direction; it was copied in 1427 in Felhéviz (a small place near Buda) by a certain scribe called Michael Harsch of Geppingen (alias Furndow), who was staying at that time in the house of Ladislaus of Tschitnek (László Csetneky), "magister cruciferatus" of the local Church of the Trinity.[14] In the mid-fifteenth century, the book made its way to Austria and came into the possession of the Carthusian order of Aggsbach. Although the severe punishment of the monks for various kinds of disobedience is a fairly recurrent issue in the records of the exceptionally rigorous charterhouse of Aggsbach, there is no trace that the arrival of this particular codex or the practice of alchemy in general caused any anxiety.[15]

The scientific context that hosts alchemical recipes is not, however, always and necessarily medical. Ninety percent of the texts in BJ 551 are astronomical or astrological, but in it we find a number of alchemical recipes preceding and following a text derived from the *Ars notoria* tradition.[16] Some folios later, there is a text on chiromancy,[17] and a short text on how to extract the heart of a bird in order to prepare a talisman.[18] The alchemical recipes lack any theoretical character; they concentrate on the manipulation of metals and other materials. Some of the recipes are written in German, which might suggest that the book was used—or even prepared—as a practical manual in a German-speaking area. The supposition of the

---

13. The codex, Hs 168, is currently in the Germanisches Nationalmuseum in Nuremberg. See also *BH*, 2:2317 and 3:1190, and *Kataloge des Germanischen Nationalmuseum,* Nürnberg, vol. 2, pt. 1 (Wiesbaden: Otto Harrassowitz, 1983), 5–9.
14. On the scribe Michael Harsch de Geppingen, see János Csontosi, "Magyarországi könyvmásolók és betűfestők a középkorban" (Scribes and Illuminators in the Hungarian Middle Ages), *Magyar Könyvszemle* (1881): esp. 206–7.
15. Karl Thir et al., eds., *Die Kartause Aggsbach* (Salzburg: Universität Salzburg, 2000). For the records, see James Hogg, "The Charterhouse of Aggsbach and the Carthusian General Chapter," ibid., 19–56; and for the manuscripts kept in the library of the monastery, see Heribert Rossmann, "Die Geschichte der Kartause Aggsbach," ibid., esp. 269–84.
16. BJ 551, fols. 109r, 111r–v; Rosińska 24, 1584; *CBJ,* 3:333–45. On fols. 127v–128v there is an unidentified *Liber alchimisticus* (incipit: "Post sim sum [sic] sequitur ultima luna, subest calcio sublimo tere finge gurgulo solvo") that ends with a paragraph in German.
17. BJ 551, fol. 117r.
18. Ibid., fol. 116r.

manuscript catalog that the codex was written in Prague in 1388, and traveled through Vienna or Erfurt to Kraków, where it was owned by the masters of the university, seems to support this speculation. The conclusion to be drawn is that practical alchemy did not need any external medical justification for its appearance in a scientific codex.

Besides its association with various university disciplines, such as medicine, astronomy, and astrology, alchemy was also considered a mechanical art. As a matter of fact, many scholastic authors were convinced that alchemy, with its practical orientation, experimental character, eagerness to manipulate the objects of the world, and motivation to replicate natural products, was alien from the theoretically oriented *scientia* taught at the universities, and belonged—if anywhere—rather to the realm of technology, the *ars mechanica*.[19] It is instructive that alchemy could appear as a noble branch of human knowledge in a technical and military work, Conrad Kyeser's *Bellifortis*. And Kyeser's concern for alchemy was not limited to its mere inclusion in his classification of useful sciences. Since the recipes for Greek fire and other incendiary weapons were closely related to the tradition of alchemy, the royal art played a central role both in Kyeser's chief source, the *Liber ignium* of Marcus Graecus, and in his own descriptions of the different kinds of fire.[20]

To be sure, alchemy might have also occurred in medieval codices alone: we have examples of anthologies consecrated exclusively to either anonymous alchemical recipes (as, for example, in the case of a Prague codex from the fourteenth century),[21] or to the writings of the great authorities of the field (Hortolanus, Bubaccarus, Raimundus Lullus, and Roger Bacon), as it happens in the case of a codex compiled by a Kraków student, Johannes Adam of Bochnia (BJ 5465).

The examples presented thus far were owned by either independent intellectuals or university masters.[22] However, in two cases—those of BJ 823 and the Buda manuscript—we identified monks belonging to the Cistercian and Carthusian Orders as possessors of alchemical texts. We should not forget either that Johannes of Rupescissa, the author of the first text discussed here, was a Franciscan. One can also add that the first genuine alchemical texts from Bohemian territories, the *Processus de lapide philosophorum* (On the Philosophers' Stone) and the *Aenigma de lapide* (Enigma on the Stone), were also written by a monk, Johannes Ticinensis

---

19. William Newman, "Technology and Alchemical Debate in the Late Middle Ages," *Isis* 80 (1989): 423–45; see also his *Promethean Ambitions*.
20. See "Techniques of Magical Warfare: The *Bellifortis*" in Chapter 2.
21. KMK M XVII (Podlaha 1370).
22. Although outdated in many respects, it might be useful to consult Włodzimierz Hubicki, "Chemistry and Alchemy in Sixteenth-Century Cracow," *Endeavour* 17 (1958): 204–7, and Hubicki, "Fuitne olim alchimia in Academia Cracoviensi lecta?" *Kwartalnik historii nauki i techniki* 9 (1964): 199–210. Despite its Latin title, this article is in Polish.

(Jan Těšínský).[23] Finally, the *Annales* of the monastery of Menedékkő in Hungary reports in the early sixteenth century that an earlier prior of the cloister, Johannes of Transylvania, was so deeply interested in alchemy that he spent all the goods of the monastery on the *quinta essentia*, "composed gold, and dissipated the argent," thus pauperizing his community, until he was finally removed from office in 1484.[24]

We would expect monks, especially members of a mendicant order, as Rupescissa was, to direct their thoughts toward less worldly matters than alchemy, an important aspect of which (besides its philosophical, spiritual, psychological, and other dimensions)[25] is the art of making gold. Should we see the cases of Rupescissa and Johannes of Transylvania as signs of a general tendency, or rather as simple coincidences?

Several condemnations issued by the Orders support the impression that the monks' preoccupation with alchemy was a serious problem throughout the Middle Ages.[26] The General Chapter of the Franciscans in 1260, the General Chapter of the Dominicans in 1273,[27] the Cistercians in 1317, and the Curia throughout the pontificate of Pope John XXII (1316–34) issued increasingly threatening prohibitions forbidding monks to study, teach, or practice alchemy.[28] Although the sanctions became more and more severe, and were verging on imprisonment and excommunication, it seems that actual practice was discouraged neither in Western nor in Central Europe.

But it was not just the average monks who were exposed to such accusations. Manuscript no. 3457 in the Sloane collection of the British Library contains a

---

23. They have not survived in their original copies or in their sixteenth-century Czech translations; they have come to us in a seventeenth-century German version. *Drei vortreffliche chymische Bücher des Johann Ticinensis, eines böhmischen Priesters* (Hamburg, 1670).

24. "Priori Patri Gabrieli de Rivulo-Dominarum successit D. Ioannes de Transilvania, Monachus Professus in Maurtacho, qui per Alchimiam et quintam essentiam consumit omnem substantiam, conflavit aureum, et dissipavit argentum, depauperavit domum valde, et patrimonium Iesu Christi et S. Iohannis Baptistae inaniter expendit, ob quam rationem ab officio Prioratus depositus est." See Weszprémi, *Succinta Medicorum Hungariae*, 2:135–37, who quotes Carolus Wagner, ed., *Analecta Scepusii sacri et profane* (Vienna: Trattnern, 1774), 2:77 and 330.

25. For a good summary on the many faces of alchemy arguing against a monolithic understanding of this art, see Lawrence M. Principe, "Alchemy I. Introduction," in Hanegraaff et al., *Dictionary of Gnosis and Western Esotericism*, 12–16.

26. See W. Theisen, "The Attraction of Alchemy for Monks and Friars in the Thirteenth to Fourteenth Centuries," *American Benedictine Review* 46 (1995): 239–53.

27. Benedictus Reichert, ed., *Acta Capitulorum Generalium Ordinis Predicatorum*, vol. 1 (Rome: Polyglotta, 1898), 170: "Acta capituli generalis apud Pest: . . . Magister ordinis de voluntate et consilio diffinitorum precepit districte, in virtute obediencie, fratribus universis, quod in alchimia non studeant, nec doceant, nec aliquatenus operentur, nec aliqua scripta de sciencia illa teneant, sed prioribus suis restituant quam cito poterunt, bona fide per eosdem priores prioribus provincialibus assignanda."

28. See, for example, Reichert, *Acta Capitulorum*, 1:170, 238–39, 252, and 2:65–66, 147, 322, 446, concerning the Dominicans who condemned alchemy eight times between 1273 and 1378.

short alchemical tract with a strange attribution: "The *Practica* of Conrad, Archbishop of Prague, which enabled him to live for many years while he was fighting against the Bohemians with three hundred horses."[29] It purports to originate from the very years of the fifteenth century that saw Johannes Ticinensis writing his tracts on the philosophers' stone. Sloane 3457 is a collection of alchemical formulas and a number of basic works attributed to such authorities as Arnald of Villanova, Ortolanus, and Albertus Magnus—some of which survived only on these folios. As Thorndike observed, "It appears to be the combined library and casebook of an actual alchemist."[30] The fifteenth-century scribe (the manuscript was mainly written by a single hand) occasionally included German notes in the recipes, which suggests that this was his mother tongue.

The one-page work attributed to Conrad is of a strictly practical nature, and contains no "Prague-specific" detail; therefore, it is impossible to tell whether it was really written by Conrad of Vechta, the archbishop of Prague during the reign of Emperor Sigismund. However, we do know that Conrad was the target of severe envy because of his rapid rise in the hierarchy and the great favor he enjoyed at the imperial court; many rumors were spread about his magical practices, which are not otherwise supported by any historical evidence.[31] Consequently, it is possible that his name was used in the same way, though to a lesser extent, as that of Raimundus Lullus, who did not write a single alchemical tract, yet became the ascribed author of a large corpus of such literature.

While it is possible that the archbishop of Prague was unjustly suspected of practicing alchemy, there is ample evidence to suggest that members of both the regular and the secular clergy were indeed interested in the field.[32] Among the usual testimonies, we have the repeated condemnations, the surviving alchemical handbooks, and further written materials. The archaeological type of evidence, however, that survived from an alchemical-metallurgical laboratory unearthed in a place called Oberstockstall, forty miles northwest of Vienna, counts as fairly exceptional.

29. British Library, Sloane 3457, fols. 168v–169r: "Practica Conradi archiepiscopi Pragen qui stetit cum ista practica per multos annos in civitate preliando contra Boemos cum ccc equis et vivebat de eadem practica quia redditus suos receperant Boemi." See also Dorothea Waley Singer, *Catalogue of Latin and Vernacular Alchemical Manuscripts in Great Britain and Ireland*, vol. 1 (Brussels: Maurice Lamertin, 1928), 308. Instead of Waley Singer's transcription of the incipit, I have accepted that of Thorndike ("preliando" instead of "philosophando," for which see the next footnote) because it makes more sense. Merely on the basis of the manuscript, it is hard to decide who is right.

30. Lynn Thorndike, "A Study in the Analysis of Complex Scientific Manuscripts: Sloane 3457: An Important Alchemical Manuscript," *Isis* 29 (1938): 377–92; for the quoted statement, see 378. For one section of the same manuscript, see Pearl Kibre, "An Alchemical Tract Attributed to Albertus Magnus," *Isis* 35 (1944): 303–16.

31. See Chapter 8.

32. See the long list of authors and practitioners from various regular orders, among them mendicants, in Theisen, "The Attraction of Alchemy."

As the excavated retorts, vessels, trays, alembics, phials, glass pieces, wooden and metal objects, and the great quantities of char and bricks witness, the laboratory was active for a period of at least fifty to sixty years in the sixteenth century. And this laboratory, where in all probability numerous attempts were made to transmute metals, was not located in a secret cellar of the town, but in the fireproof chamber of its chapel, while the whole activity was supervised—if not performed—by the local parish priests.[33]

But why did churchmen find alchemy so attractive?

Besides the application of alchemical recipes and theories for medical purposes, the sheer and often condemned desire of making gold, and the somewhat less threatening wish to prepare various amalgams, a further reason might have motivated a cleric to study the royal art. Alchemical symbolism offered fertile ground for a Christian reinterpretation,[34] an instance for which can be found in BJ 837. This is a collection of medical readings, both of theoretical and practical nature, brought to Kraków in the 1420s, either from France (Montpellier) or from Italy, where it was copied and illuminated. It includes, furthermore, texts and marginal notes by two Kraków professors, Johannes of Dobra and Petrus Gaszowiec.[35] These notes imply that the codex was used as a handbook in the *Collegium Maius* of the university.[36]

What interests us are two unusual illuminations found in the manuscript (see figs. 26 and 27).[37] One of them depicts the Trinity in two ways. First it appears in the form of three, separate beings (the Holy Spirit being a young man), and later appears in an integrated form, as a solitary regal figure with three faces. This picture is followed by another one on the next folio, dominated by a crowned alchemical retort standing on a lion's foot, a moon, and two human heads: one bearded and one shaved. The retort, surrounded by the fire of the alchemist, is the home of the *Opus magnum:* it contains a dragon biting its own tail, the symbol of the *prima materia,* an eagle standing on the dragon, and a phoenix surmounting the eagle.[38]

---

33. On the alchemical laboratory of Oberstockstall, see the epilogue. See also Sigrid von Osten, *Das Alchemistenlaboratorium Oberstockstall: Ein Fundkomplex des 16. Jahrhunderts aus Niederösterreich* (Innsbruck: Universitätsverlag Wagner, 1998), and Rudolf Werner Soukup and Helmut Mayer, *Alchemistisches Gold—Paracelsistische Pharmaka: Laboratoriumstechnik im 16. Jahrhundert* (Vienna: Böhlau, 1997).

34. The analogy of religion and alchemy echoes of course the theories of Carl Gustav Jung. Being aware that there are various other contestant theories for the correspondences between the two fields besides Jung's archetypes, we will concentrate only on the parallels and not on their causes.

35. On Johannes of Dobra, see also Chapter 2; on Petrus Gaszowiec, Chapter 3.

36. See *CBJ,* 6:338–44.

37. BJ 837, fols. 9v and 10r.

38. On the two illuminations, see Ameisenowa, *Rękopisy i pierwodruki iluminowane,* 178–80, and Ameisenowa, "Średniowieczne ilustracje alchemiczne w rękopisie Biblioteki Jagiellońskiej" (Medieval Alchemical Illustrations in a Manuscript of the Biblioteka Jagiellońska), *Kalendarz ilustrowango kurjera codziennego na rok 1939,* 1938, 216–18. I consulted a German translation of this

FIG 26   The Holy Spirit as the supervisor of the alchemical process. Kraków, BJ 837, fol. 9v. Courtesy of the Biblioteka Jagiellońska.

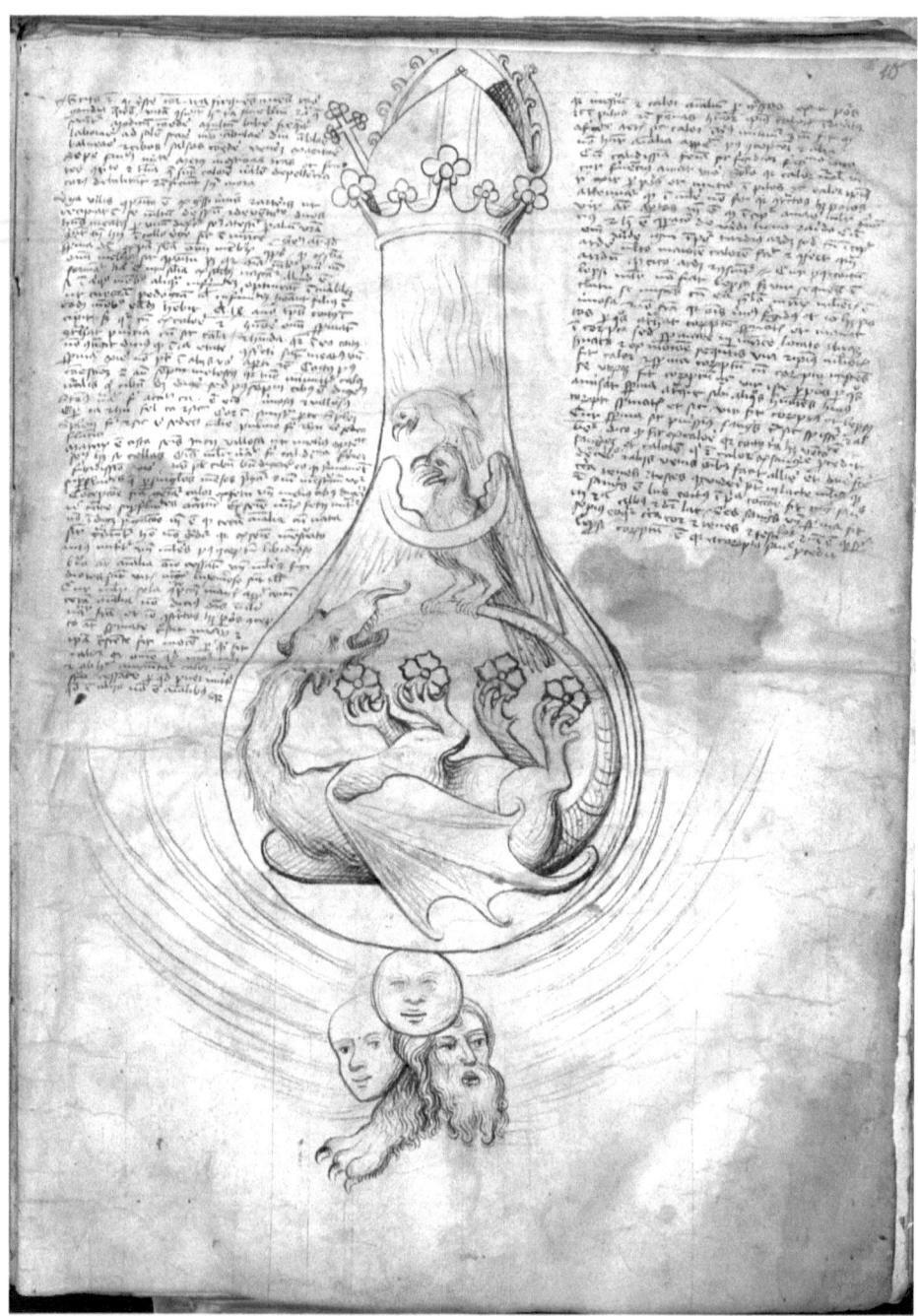

FIG 27   Alchemical retort. Krákow, BJ 837, fol. 10r. Courtesy of the Biblioteka Jagiellońska.

Both birds symbolize immortality and resurrection, and correspond to the act of sublimation in the process of alchemy: the *prima materia* does not perish, but is reborn during the process, just as the phoenix is reborn in the flames. The retort is crowned in a way that is reminiscent of the depiction of the Trinity. What is striking here is that the Holy Trinity, represented as both One-in-Three and Three-in-One, has replaced Hermes Trismegistos as the protector of the *opus magnum*.[39] This religious reinterpretation of the alchemical *processus* takes the transmutation of metals from its suspect context and situates it in the framework of orthodoxy.

While abundant analogies may be found between alchemical imagery and Christian iconography, associating the *opus magnum* directly with the Christian Trinity is a rare iconographic theme in the intellectual history of medieval Europe. Three versions of a German text from 1400, *Das Buch der heyligen Dreyvaldekeit* (Book of the Holy Trinity) contain the same correspondence: the crowned Trinity stands guard over the process of transmutation.[40] Christ's death and resurrection become associated with the putrefaction and sublimation of the philosophers' stone, while the *prima materia* appears as Christ's body and flesh. The illustrations stem from the same tradition, and what is more, probably from the same period: the first decades of the fifteenth century.[41] All in all, we can see that religion and alchemy were not as distinct and as we might have expected.

A crucial piece of evidence concerning the actual practice of the art of alchemy in Prague is the existence of a treatise in Czech from the mid-fifteenth century. This choice of language implies that interest in alchemy in the Bohemian territories had exceeded by that time the circle of those who were able to read Latin. The anonymous manuscript written in 1457 is titled *Cesta spravedlivá*, that is, "The Rightful Way."[42] A later copy of the same text—preceded by an anonymous Latin introduction that explains its origins—is included in a manuscript containing a collection of sixteenth- and seventeenth-century alchemical material.[43] "The Rightful Way" was generally attributed (among others, by the sixteenth-century introduction) to a Bohemian alchemist, Johannes Lasnioro (John of Laz).

---

article, handwritten by Ameisenowa herself, which I found in the library of the Warburg Institute in London.

39. Ameisenowa, "Średniowiecyne ilustracje alchemiczne."

40. Gustav Friedrich Hartlaub, "Signa Hermetis: zwei alte alchemistische Bilderhandschriften," *Zeitschrift des deutschen Vereins für Kunstwissenschaft*, 1937, 93–112.

41. Ameisenowa, "Średniowiecyne ilustracje alchemiczne."

42. Prague, Library of the National Museum, V H 21. On this text and its alleged author, see Vladimír Karpenko, "The Oldest Alchemical Manuscript in the Czech Language," *Ambix* 37 (1990): 61–73. The original title page of the manuscript, with a crowned alchemical vessel containing a scorpion, is reproduced in Karpenko's article on page 63.

43. Prague, Library of the National Museum, III H 11. See Karpenko, "Oldest Alchemical Manuscript," and Karpenko, "Greek Fire in a Czech Alchemical Manuscript," *Centaurus* 30 (1987): 240–44.

Very little is known about John of Laz. Among the few—reliable and less reliable—testimonies about his life, there is a story that he met the widow of Emperor Sigismund, Barbara of Cilly, on several occasions:

> I heard the rumor in various languages about the queen of the king of divine memory, Sigismund, that she was skilled in the art of physics. I went to her to make an assessment with her in the art of physics, and she answered me cleverly. I saw that she took mercury and arsenic and other things she knew well, and she made a powder, which whitened the copper, but did not pass well the test with the hammer, and with that she made many deceptions among the people. I also saw that she made a different powder, and on whatever metal she sprinkled it, warming the metal the powder entered in the mass of the material and in the burnt clay assimilated to pure argent. But when it was cast, it changed back to copper, what it had been earlier, and thus I saw a lot of falsehood performed by her. Again I saw, that she took some saffron of Mars, some saffron of Venus, and other powders, and mixed them, and made cement out of them, and grasped it together with pieces of gold and argent, and united them, it appeared pure gold both from outside and inside. And when she cast the whole thing, it lost its red color, and thus many traders were deceived with that. I saw many tricks and deceptions carried out by her, and corrected her in words. She however wanted to jail me, but I could leave with peace, because God helped me.[44]

We see a queen and empress heavily involved in alchemical experiments, but during her practices she did not aim to perform real transmutation, but to forge false

---

44. The story can be found in the introduction to Nicolaus Petraeus, ed., *Fr. Basilii Valentini Chymische Schriften* (Hamburg, 1717, reprinted in 1740), and it is reproduced in Hermann Kopp, *Die Alchemie in älterer und neuerer Zeit,* vol. 1 (Heidelberg: Carl Winters Universitätsbuchhandlung, 1886), 160–61: "Ego audiens ex variis linguis loqui de regina divae memoriae regis Sigismundi, quod esset perita in arte physica, intravi ad eam et feci examen cum ea de arte physica; astute autem respondit mihi quae mulier. Vidi ab ea quod cepit mercurium et arsenicum, et alias quas ipsa scivit bene, et ex illis fecit pulverem, qui cuprum dealbavit, optime probam sed malleum non sustinuit, et ex eo multas deceptiones fecit inter homines. Item aliud vidi ab ea quod fecit pulverem, et quodcunque metallum desuper aspergebat, calefaciens tunc pulvis ingrediabatur in massam corporis, assimilebatur argenti puri in testa combusti, verum cum fundebatur, versum est in cuprum ut prius fuit, et sic vidi ab ea multas falsitates. Iterum vidi ab ea, quod accepit crocum Martis, crocum Veneris et alios pulveres, et miscebantur simul, et ex eo fecit cimentum, et cum cepit pars cum parte auri et argenti et in hoc junctabatur, apparebat aurum purum intus et exterius, et cum fundebatur totum rubedinem amittebat, et sic multi mercatores per hoc erant decepti. Multas autem ab ea vidi truffas et deceptiones, correxi eam verbis. Illa autem voluit me incarcerare, sed discessi ab ea cum pace quia Deus juvavit me."

gold and to cheat people. When John, the honest alchemist, recognized the abuse of the royal art and reproached her, Barbara attempted to have him imprisoned, and he escaped only with great difficulty. This story—printed in the eighteenth century and allegedly originating in 1440[45]—is not independent of or unconnected with the malign rumors concerning Empress Barbara, and even if it has little to do with what actually happened, it is quite informative about the usual conflicts between alchemists and their protectors (or protectresses).[46]

If we are looking for more contemporary and more trustworthy sources about this alchemist's life, the last paragraph of another of his works, the *Tractatus secundus aureus de lapide philosophorum* (Second Golden Treatise on the Philosophers' Stone) written in 1448, tells us that he was a pupil of a certain Antonius of Florence, who was killed in Bohemia because of his chemical art.[47]

The most important conclusion that we can draw from this piece of information is certainly not that fifteenth-century Bohemia—where John was said to be prosecuted by Empress Barbara and where Antonius was murdered—was particularly unsafe for alchemists, but rather that Italy constituted an important intellectual resource of Bohemian alchemy. The fact that John was a disciple of Antonius of Florence is also supported by the text of "The Rightful Way."[48] Here Antonius appears as a prospector searching for ore in the Bohemian mountains, but apparently he was also involved in transmutations. Now, whether John was really a pupil of this person or just claimed to be so, the role that the Italians and the activity of mining played in the Central European reception of magical arts is quite striking. In Bohemia, we can refer to Antonius, while in Kraków—as we shall see in Chapter 8—a certain Monaldus de Luca seems to have been involved in treasure hunting, undertaken together with Polish university masters who were also associated with gold mining.

What these stories teach us is that the three conceivable ways of searching for gold—the practice of alchemy, the hunting of treasure, and mining—were closely related to each other in the fifteenth century, and this threefold activity seems to have been fostered by Italian masters both in Kraków and in Prague.

---

45. Petraeus, *Fr. Basilii Valentini Chymische Schriften,* quotes the paragraph from a no longer extant parchment manuscript allegedly dating from 1440 titled *Via universalis, composita per famosum Joh. de Laaz, philosophum peritum in arte alcymiae.*
46. Karpenko, "Oldest Alchemical Manuscript," 62.
47. Joannes de Lasnioro, *Tractatus secundus aureus de lapide philosophorum,* in *Theatrum Chemicum,* vol. 4 (Argentorati: Zetzner, 1659), 579–84: "Hic Joannes superius subscriptus de Lazionoro fuit discipulus ipsius Antonij Itali de Florentia oriundi, qui hic in Bohemia propter eam artem Chymicam ab hominibus impiis est trucidatus, prout in Bohemico de lapide Philosophorum scripto testatur ita accidisse."
48. The crucial paragraphs are translated in Karpenko, "Oldest Alchemical Manuscript."

The Identity of Nicolaus Melchior

Having concluded our survey of the Central European sources of alchemy, we should not be surprised to find that practitioners and students of alchemy were concentrated in the university communities, the clergy, and royal households. Thus, it does not seem very striking either that an alchemical Mass could have been written by a leading intellectual and dedicated in all sincerity to a king.

It remains now to clarify who Nicolaus Melchior Cibinensis really was: this author whose immortality was secured through his alchemical Mass, and who was chosen by Michael Maier as one of the most illustrious alchemists of the world. First of all, he was definitely not Cardinal Melchior Brixiensis, the author of the text *De flavo et rubeo viro* (On the Golden and Red Man).[49] Apart from this negative statement, very little can be said for sure about Melchior. As the adjective Cibinensis in his name indicates, he was from the town of Nagyszeben (Hermannstadt, Sibiu, Cibinium)[50] in Transylvania.[51] Hereafter we can only rely on speculations.[52]

In his biography of Hungarian medical doctors, Stephanus Weszprémi identifies Melchior with Nicolaus Oláh (1493–1568), a most important personality in sixteenth-century Hungarian history.[53] Oláh was a counselor to Queen Mary of Habsburg, for a short period the regent, and in the last decades of his life the archbishop of Hungary (1553). He was not only an influential politician and an ecclesiastical leader, but also a well-known humanist of his time, in frequent correspondence with other humanists of Europe, among them Erasmus. He was indeed born in the town of Nagyszeben, just as Melchior was, but there is no evidence that he was interested in alchemy, even though he explored as broad a variety of topics as any humanist and was proficient in many literary genres.

The question remains whether we should really view the *Processus* as a text written by a future archbishop and addressed to his king. Is that not too ambitious from an alchemical treatise? In her recent study, the Romanian scholar Cristina Neagu provides convincing arguments to support Weszprémi's conviction that Melchior

---

49. On Cardinal Melchior Brixiensis, see *HMES*, 4:348.

50. Founded in the twelfth century by a Saxon population on the site of an abandoned Roman settlement known as Cibinium, Nagyszeben became one of the Saxon seats in Transylvania in the medieval kingdom of Hungary. In German it was called Hermannstadt, in Hungarian Nagyszeben, and its present-day Romanian name is Sibiu.

51. His alchemical Mass, however, is not mentioned in the scholarly study on the Sibiu missals. See Karl Reinerth, *Missale Cibiniense. Gestalt, Ursprung und Entwicklung des Messritus der siebenbürgischen Kirche im Mittelalter* (Cologne: Böhlau Verlag, 1972).

52. For the speculations and a text edition of the *Processus*, see Gábor Farkas Kiss, Benedek Láng, and Cosmin Popa-Gorjanu, "The Alchemical Mass of Nicolaus Melchior Cibinensis: Text, Identity and Speculations," *Ambix* 53 (2006): 143–59.

53. Weszprémi, *Succinta Medicorum Hungariae*, 2:128.

was simply a pseudonym under which the young Olah wrote this work.⁵⁴ Bringing together the few indirect pieces of evidence that we have on Melchior, she comes to the conclusion that although there is no final proof *pro* or *contra,* it at least cannot be excluded that the famous archbishop was our author. Melchior was from the same place as Olah, and he was probably also a man of the church, a cleric of higher rank, because, as Neagu points out, "The viewpoint taken by the *Processus* is that of a priest saying Mass."⁵⁵ They must have been more or less contemporaries: while the *Processus* was dedicated to a certain (not specified) Wladislas, king of Hungary and Bohemia, we know that Olah arrived in Buda in 1510 and spent six years at the court of Wladislas II, who reigned in these two countries between 1490 and 1516. In addition, both authors were concerned with the threat of the Turks, and both were committed to acting against this threat on a political level. Finally, Cristina Neagu supports the possible identification of the two persons by pointing out stylistic resemblances between Melchior's alchemical Mass and writings known to be by Olah.

In fact, it was by no means inconceivable in the Middle Ages to associate clerics at the higher levels of the ecclesiastical hierarchy with the royal art, at least at the level of gossip, rumors, and accusations. We have already mentioned an alchemical text attributed to another Melchior, the bishop of Brixen, and another attributed to Conrad of Vechta, the archbishop of Prague. We can now add that Abbot Trithemius, in his *Chronicle of the Monastery of Hirsau,* lists several bishops and archbishops who either supported alchemists financially or practiced the royal art themselves.⁵⁶ Therefore, Nicolaus Olah would not have been the only archbishop of the region who appears as an assigned or real author of an alchemical work.

However, while there is indeed a strong correlation between the data we have about Melchior and Olah, there is further evidence—not known to Neagu—that should also be taken into account. László Szathmáry, a Hungarian historian of chemistry and alchemy, examined the issue of their identity as early as 1928, but since his book was published only in his mother tongue, his considerations remained virtually unknown to historians of alchemy outside Hungary.⁵⁷ Szathmáry collected

---

54. Cristina Neagu, "The *Processus sub forma missae:* Christian Alchemy, Identity and Identification," *Archaeus: Études d'Histoire des Religions* 4 (2000): 105–17. *Archaeus* is an English-language periodical published in Romania. For a review of this specific issue that includes an assessment of Neagu's study, see Radu Dragan's article in *Aries: Journal for the Study of Western Esotericism* 2 (2002): 106–9. Neagu's article was the first study on the issue of Melchior accessible to international scholars, not counting a short mention by Vladimír Karpenko in "Alchemy as donum dei," *HYLE—International Journal for Philosophy of Chemistry* 4 (1998): 63–80 and n. 43.

55. Neagu, "The *Processus,*" 112.

56. Johannes Trithemius, *Annales Hirsaugiensis,* vol. 2 (St. Gall: Georgius Schleger, 1690), 286–88.

57. László Szathmáry, *Magyar alkémisták* (Hungarian Alchemists) (Budapest: Királyi Magyar Természettudományi Társulat, 1928; repr., Budapest: Könyvértékesító Vállalat, 1986), 302–25.

a long list of counterarguments to refute Weszprémi's theory. First, he argued, the *Processus sub forma missae* was dedicated to King Wladislas II, and if Melchior was really Oláh, he could not have been older than twenty-three (his age when Wladislas died), and pages at this age hardly dedicate their writings to their king. (Neagu is aware of this counterargument, and claims that the gifted and ambitious Oláh, who was appointed as the canon of Pécs as early as 1518, must have had a higher position in the previous years than that of a mere page.) Second, as Szathmáry went on, Oláh did not mention alchemy in his extensive correspondence with other humanists, nor was any alchemical work in his library.

Nevertheless, Szathmáry's third argument is the strongest one. The *Processus sub forma missae* survived not only in its printed edition, as Weszprémy supposed in the eighteenth century and as Neagu maintains today, but also in two early modern manuscripts kept today in Vienna.[58] One of these manuscripts, which seems to originate from 1604 and contains a wide range of alchemical literature, provides some new information about the life of Melchior.[59] A short, though fairly obscure, notice preceding the text of the alchemical Mass claims that the *Processus Chymicus* was offered by the last Bosnian king, Stephen (d. 1463), to the Hungarian and Bohemian king, Ladislaus V Posthumous (1440–58), whose (unnamed) chaplain redacted it. The text was allegedly found many years later by Melchior (in the manuscript he is called Nicolaus Matzerus Cibinensis Transsylvanus), who, together with a Bohemian nobleman, Andrea Schampasa, forged coins which were more valuable than those of the king. As a result of the fakery, he was executed in 1531 by Ferdinand Habsburg, who was king of Hungary between 1526 and 1564, after the reign of Wladislas's son, Louis II (1516–1526). If we accept this report—which is the most contemporary thus far—as authentic, Melchior could obviously not have been the same person as Oláh, and he was not even the author of this text of Bosnian origin, only its reader, transmitter, and unfortunate user.[60]

---

58. ÖNB Cod. lat. 11133 and 11347. For the text, see Kiss, Láng, and Popa-Gorjanu, "Alchemical Mass."

59. ÖNB Cod. lat. 11133, fol. 308r: "Processus Chymicus. Serenissimo Hungariae et Boemiae Regi Ladislao a Stephano ultimo Bosniae rege communicatus et a Ladislai Capellano in hanc theoriam redactus. Cujus praxin expertus dominus Nicolaus Matzerus Cibinensis Transsylvanus qui summe erat familiaris Bohemo Andrea Schampasa Pattenstati, cum quo res illorum thesaurorum arcanum propalaretur, taleros excussit bonitate et regios superantes quibus delatis aufugit nobilis et compraehensus presbiter. Divo Ferdinando regnante hic Pragae proxima die Veneris post Phil. Jac. Anno 1531 capite plectitur. Post ejus exitum repertum est hoc opus chymicum sub forma myssae descriptum. Rex Ladislaus natus est anno 1440. Mortuus 23 novembris hora 23 anno 1458. Anno aetatis 18."

60. Interestingly, Jung gives somewhat similar details about Melchior without referring to any primary or secondary source (*Psychologie und Alchemie*, 536). Jung declares that a "Nicolaus Melchior Szebeni" was the chaplain (!) and astrologer at King Wladislas's court from 1490. He stayed at the court after Wladislas's death (1516) under Louis II. After the defeat at Mohács, he fled to the court of Ferdinand I in Vienna, and he was executed in 1531 by the latter monarch. Since this information

Relying on the present evidence, it is impossible to determine who Nicolaus Melchior really was. He was definitely from Cibinium, and he seems to have been a cleric who played some role at the court of the Hungarian king Wladislas II. Furthermore, he was apparently concerned about the Turks, and he tried to use his political influence—however great or small it was—to exhort his fellow Hungarians to resist the Turkish threat. He does not seem to have been an outsider, a fool, or an anonymous magician, but rather a respected figure of his time, who dedicated his work to the king. If the name Melchior was the pseudonym of a sixteenth-century humanist, we may infer that this person is known to us under a different name. On the other hand, if this was not a pseudonym, the task is to identify a new actor in late medieval Hungarian courtly culture. In this case, however, it may be possible to find the person who was actually called Nicolaus Melchioris Cibinensis on the basis of the source evidence provided by his home town.[61]

To come to a conclusion, as far as the practice of alchemy is concerned, we can record a serious involvement of the clergy on all levels. Simple monks were often found pursuing the royal art, but even clerics of higher ranks were concerned with alchemy both in the West and in Central Europe. Melchior, the bishop of Brixen, our Melchior, the Cibinensis—whether he was a simple chaplain or the archbishop of Hungary—and finally Conrad, archbishop of Prague, were all real or assigned authors of alchemical works. It can be probably assumed that this preoccupation with alchemy might provide some explanation of how alchemical thought was incorporated in the Christian liturgy (or perhaps how Christian motifs were integrated in the framework of alchemy) both in textual and pictorial sources.[62]

(particularly the Hungarian place name Szeben and the idea that Melchior was a chaplain) does not appear anywhere in the literature, and nor is it completely identical with the statements of the manuscript quoted above but agrees well with the account of Szathmáry, who simplified what he found in the Vienna source, it seems reasonable to suppose that Jung might have taken this piece of information directly or indirectly from Szathmáry's *Magyar alkémisták,* probably through the intermediary of their mutual friend Károly Kerényi.

61. This was the aim of the research carried out by Cosmin Popa-Gorjanu. In the city archives of Nagyszeben, he identified several individuals bearing the name Melchior whose profession was goldsmith and who could have authored the *Processus.* See Kiss, Láng, and Popa-Gorjanu, "Alchemical Mass."

62. It should be added to the Central European history of alchemy that two fragments, each four pages long and originating from the same alchemical manuscript, have survived in two different Hungarian libraries. The remains of a copy of Pseudo-Plato's *Liber quartus cum commento Hebuhabes Hamed* (Budapest: Egyetemi Könyvtár U. Fr. l. m. 60) and those of Pseudo-Geber's *Summa perfectionis* (Központi Szeminárium S. Fr. l. m. 36) were found hidden in the binding material of two different early modern printed books. Interestingly, a portrait depicting Plato in the first fragment is partly blackened by later hands. The fourteenth-century manuscript that originally contained these two fragments was in Hungary in the early decades of the seventeenth century. However, we do not know its earlier history; that is why I did not include them in the main text on medieval Hungarian alchemy. For further details, see Benedek Láng, "Két fragmentum művelődéstörténeti értékéről" (On the Historical Background of Two Fragments), *Magyar Könyvszemle* 115 (1999): 211–16.

6
RITUAL MAGIC AND CRYSTALLOMANCY

Angels Around the Crystal: The Prayer Book of King Wladislas

King Wladislas, the unworthy sinner and servant of God, kneeling in front of the crystal, prays for the angels to clarify and illuminate it so that he may learn all the secrets of the world and the hidden intentions of his subjects. In his long prayers, we hear a number of unusual requests:[1]

> I Wladislas, unworthy sinner, confident in none of my merits, but burdened with the charge of sinners, cry out to you, ask you humbly and devotedly . . . (68)

1. Ludwik Bernacki and Ryszard Ganszyniec, eds., *Modlitewnik Władysława Warneńczyka w zbiorach Bibljoteki Bodlejańskiej* (Wladislas Warnenczyk's Prayer Book Kept in the Bodleian Library) (Kraków: Anczyc i Spółka, 1928), 68, 16, 17, 21, 16–17, 42, 42, and 15. Specifically, 68 ("Ad vos clamo, rogo humiliter et devote Ego Wladislaus, indignus peccator, nullis meis meritis confidens, sed peccatorum mole gravatus . . ."), 16 ("Da et huic Cristallo et michi indigno famulo tuo Wladislao ad exercendum in eo cunctipotencie tue omnipotencieque virtutem . . ."), 17 (". . . ad videndum in illo Cristallo omnia secreta, que sub quatuor elementis contenta sunt, et omnia que scire voluero . . ."), 21 ("Quatenus super me respicere digneris, indignum famulum tuum Wladislaum, et michi in hoc Cristallo veram visionem per sanctos angelos ostendere digneris . . ."), 16–17 ("Da michi, domine . . . hunc Cristallum . . . ut in eo videre possum Omnia, quecumque voluero, que sub quatuor elementis continentur secreta . . . et impartire michi hanc graciam super hunc Cristallum, sicut Impartitus es regi Salomoni et posteris suis artibus . . ."), 42 ("Mitte michi sanctos angelos tuos ad huius cristalli clarificationem et illuminacionem ut omnia huius mundi secretissima secreta sub quatuor elementis contenta, et precipue illam rem quam pronunc scire voluero, sine omni fallacia et lesione mentis, corporis et anime, per sanctos angelos tuos michi manifesta erunt . . ."), 42 ("Mittat sanctos angelos suos ut me instruant ad videndum in eo omnia que in mundo, in terra vel sub terra sunt, sub quatuor elementis contenta . . ."); and 15 ("Digneris hodie inspirare in cor meum clementer et permamenter perspicacitatem huius Cristalli, per sanctos Angelos tuos, ad clarificandum et illuminandum, ut in eo videre valeam et considerare omnia que sub quatuor elementis contenta sunt, et secretissima mundi, sine nocimento et omni lesione mentis et corporis, per spiritus sancti graciam").

Bestow the virtue of omnipotence and all-powerfulness on this crystal and on me, your unworthy servant Wladislas . . . (16)

. . . in order to see in that crystal all the secrets contained under the four elements and everything that I would like to know . . . (17)

in so far as you consider me, your unworthy servant Wladislas, worthy of it, condescend to reveal for me in that crystal the true vision through your blesséd angels . . . (21)

Give me my Lord . . . this crystal . . . so that I can see in it everything that I would like to, the secrets that are contained under the four elements . . . and bestow me that grace on this crystal, as you bestowed it on King Solomon and on the art of his descendents . . . (16–17)

Send me your blesséd angels for the clarification and illumination of this crystal so that all the most secret secrets of this world contained under the four elements, and particularly that thing, which I would like to know now, will be manifested for me through your blesséd angels without any deceit or injury of the mind, body, and the soul . . . (42)

May he send his blesséd angels so that they [might] teach me to see in it everything that is in the world, on the earth or under the earth, contained under the four elements . . . (42)

Condescend please today to implant in my heart mercifully and eternally the penetrating sight of this crystal through your blesséd angels in order to clarify and illuminate [it] so that I might see and inspect in it everything that is contained under the four elements, and the great secrets of the world, without any damage or injury of the mind or of the body, through the grace of the Holy Spirit . . . (15)

And so the petitions go, with one variation after another on the themes of the unworthiness of the petitioner,[2] God and his angels, and the ways the secret knowledge may be revealed. These excerpts have been taken from an illuminated prayer book now preserved in the Bodleian Library[3] known as the *Modlitewnik Władysława*

---

2. The emphasis on the unworthiness of the operator is a common motif not only in prayer books but also in texts of ritual magic. See, for example, Kieckhefer, *Forbidden Rites*, 264: "Ita quod me famulum tuum, N., licet indignum."
3. Oxford, Bodleian Library, MS Rawlinson liturg. d. 6. Its number in the Summary Catalogue is 15857. See Falconer Madan, *A Summary Catalogue of Western Manuscripts in the Bodleian Library*

Warneńczyka (Wladislas Warnenczyk's Prayer Book), which was at the center of scholarly interest as early as 1928, not only because of its peculiar content, prayers, miniatures, and instructions on pursuing crystallomancy, but also for the mystery surrounding its history and its owners.[4]

Probably originating in fifteenth-century Poland, this is one of the eight prayer books known to have belonged to the famous Jagiellonian royal family.[5] It is, however, the most complex and enigmatic of them all. Its eighty parchment folios contain prayers of various provenance—most derived from prayers in common use— addressed to Christ, the Virgin Mary, and the Holy Spirit. However, in most of the seemingly innocent prayers, we find inserted a stereotypical crystallomantic formula with reference to Wladislas, that is, the person for whom the book was meant, a crystal ball, and various angels. In the following, we will concentrate on three particularly problematic issues: the text of the prayers, the crystal, and the identities of both the owner and the author of the manuscript

Text and Sources

In his detailed study introducing his edition of the Prayer Book of King Wladislas, Ryszard Ganszyniec identifies the provenance of roughly two-thirds of the prayers.[6] Most of these are from standard liturgical texts, the Mass, and private devotionals

---

at Oxford, vol. 3 (Oxford: Clarendon Press, 1895), 521; Otto-Alexander Pächt, *Illuminated Manuscripts in the Bodleian Library* (Oxford: Clarendon Press, 1966), 175; and Csaba Csapodi and Klára Csapodiné Gárdonyi, eds., *Bibliotheca Hungarica: kódexek és nyomtatott könyvek Magyarországon 1526 előtt* (*Bibliotheca Hungarica:* Codices and Printed Books in Hungary before 1526) (Budapest: Magyar Tudományos Akadémia Könyvtára, 1993), 2336. In Hungary, the manuscript is available on microfiche as Magyar Tudományos Akadémia Könyvtára, Mf. 5119/IV.

4. For a published edition of the Latin text and a detailed analysis in Polish, see Bernacki and Ganszyniec, *Modlitewnik Władysława Warneńczyka.* See especially the chapters by Ryszard Ganszyniec, "O Modlitewniku Władysława" (On Wladislas's Prayer Book), and József Korzeniowski, "Modlitewnik Warneńczyka."

5. For a description of the contents of this and the other Jagiellonian prayer books, see Urszula Borkowska, *Królewskie modlitewniki* (Royal Prayer Books) (Lublin: Towarzystwo Naukowe Katolickiego Uniwersytetu Lubelskiego, 1999), esp. 64–76. See also Marta Miśkowiec, "Związki aniołów z magicznym znaczeniem kryształów" (Angels and the Magical Meaning of Crystals), in *Księga o aniołach* (The Book of Angels), ed. Herbert Oleschko, 440–49 (Kraków: Wydawnictwo WAM, 2002), and Barbara Miodońska, "Historyk sztuki o datowaniu tzw. Modlitewnika Władysława Warneńczyka w Oksfordzie" (Art Historian's Dating of the So-called Władysław Warneńczyk Oxford Prayerbook), in *Kultura œredniowieczna i staropolska* (Medieval and Early Modern Polish Culture), 703–14 (Warsaw: PWN, 1991).

6. Ganszyniec, "O Modlitewniku Władysława," esp. 52–67. I am grateful to Jolanta Szpilewska (who received her doctorate in 2003 in the Medieval Studies Department, CEU, Budapest) for letting me consult her unpublished translation of Ganszyniec's introduction.

collected from the core of medieval prayer books. However, Ganszyniec found the source of one prayer ("Summe deus pater piissime") in the *Ars notoria*.[7]

The *Ars notoria*, which is ascribed to Solomon and his "friend and successor" Apollonius, is a fairly widespread work of medieval ritual magic and theurgy.[8] If we are not trained in the field of learned magic, we will easily mistake it at first glance for an innocent religious text, because the ritual of the *Ars notoria* is nothing other than an elaborated liturgical program composed of prayers and orations addressed to transcendent agents. Only a closer look reveals that the text, by means of its large variety of prayers, invocations of divine and angelic names, and numerous rituals, actually promises intellectual perfection, learning, the acquisition of memory, and the ability to understand difficult books. To use its procedures one must first practice a course of confession, fasting, chastity, penitence, and the cultivation of physical and psychological purity lasting several months. However pious this text may seem, its emphasis on the efficacy of words and names of God to help the user attain power, and the purposes for which a user might turn to it—the acquisition of absolute knowledge, moral perfection, and unlimited memory—bring it close to other magical arts.

Being an "ars artium, scientia scientiarum," the notory art is a metascience through which all the other sciences can be mastered: the seven liberal arts, as well as the mechanical and the so-called exceptive—that is, divinatory and magical—disciplines. The last, exceptive category comprises necromancy as well, even though it is reserved to those adepts who would use it only for good aims. To be sure, ritual magic is not the only art that claims to be such a metascience; every mnemotechnic method that helped the reader remember and reproduce textual and visual data in a culture where books were rare and precious did so as well.[9] Hence, it is not a pure coincidence that the *Ars notoria* was called *Ars memorativa*, among other places, in a Kraków fragment.[10]

---

7. See Bernacki and Ganszyniec, *Modlitewnik Władysława Warneńczyka*, 13–16. From the growing literature on the *Ars notoria* (on which also see Appendix 1), I only refer here to the following: J. Dupèbe, "L'«Ars Notoria» et la polémique sur la divination et la magie," in *Divination et Contreverse Religieuse en France au XVIe siècle* (Paris: Centre V. L. Saulnier, 1987), 123–34; the articles in Fanger, *Conjuring Spirits*; Jean-Patrice Boudet, "L'*Ars notoria* au Moyen Age: une résurgence de la théurgie antique?" in *La Magie: Actes du colloque internatonal de Montpellier 25–27 Mars 1999*, vol. 3 (Montpellier: Université Paul-Valéry, Montpellier III, 2000), 173–91; and Julien Véronèse, *L'Ars notoria au moyen age: introduction et édition critique*, Micrologus Library 21 (Florence: Sismel, 2007) and his "Les anges dans l'*Ars notoria*: Révélation, processus visionnaire, et angélologie," in Bresc and Grévin, "Les Anges et la magie," 813–49.

8. Briefly, theurgy is the art of bringing down celestial beings (angels) through the use of prayers on the one hand, and of ecstatic ascent toward union with God, on the other.

9. Among mnemotechnic metasciences, the *Ars magna* of Raimundus Lullus is no doubt the most famous.

10. BJ 2076, fol. 1r: "Item vocatur ars memorativa, quia in profundo oracionis eius adhibetur memoria." See also Jerzy Zathey, "Per la storia dell'ambiente magico-astrologico a Cracovia nel

The *Ars notoria* prayer borrowed by Wladislas's book ("Summe deus pater piissime") was also aimed at increasing intelligence and strengthening memory, but in its new context it contains a petition to God to send his angels to illuminate the crystal. This text is not present in the earliest versions of the *Ars notoria*, but was added later. It appears as a closing prayer in the first printed version, which can be read in a sixteenth-century edition of Cornelius Agrippa's *Opera Omnia*.[11] What is interesting here, and what leads us to certain speculations, is the fact that the very next prayer in the prayer book of Wladislas also contains an excerpt from the *Ars notoria* ("O lux mundi"),[12] which can be found in Agrippa's edition but fifty pages earlier than the "Summe deus," not right next to it.[13] However, the two prayers do appear together another Polish codex, BJ 551, in a short version of the *Ars notoria*.[14] Thus, either there was a direct relationship between BJ 551 and the prayer book, or—more likely—a short version of the *Ars notoria* containing these two prayers next to each other was in circulation, and the compiler of the prayer book worked from a text similar to that of BJ 551.[15]

Ganszyniec left a number of prayers unidentified, but he claimed that the author worked in a continuous and uniform way, borrowing pieces of texts from his sources, but did not compose a single prayer himself. The author, who is consequently rather a compiler, seems to have been satisfied with introducing formulaic paragraphs into the imported texts. More recently, Urszula Borkowska examined the prayers of Wladislas in the context of other prayer books of the Jagiellons, and she noted that "Marian devotion is particularly developed in it, and the angelological texts, rarely developed in prayer books, are extremely interesting."[16]

Ganszyniec and Borkowska cannot be blamed for failing to identify the most important source of the royal prayer book; they were simply not in a position to

---

Quattrocento," in Szczucki, *Magia, astrologia e religione nel Rinascimento*, esp. 102; MS Cambridge, Trinity Coll. 1419, *Liber de arte memorativa sive notoria*.

11. Cornelius Agrippa, *Opera Omnia*, vol. 2 (Lyons: Beringos Fratres, ca. 1620), 657–59.
12. Bernacki and Ganszyniec, eds., *Modlitewnik Władysława Warneńczyka*, 17. This short prayer, not identified by Ganszyniec, was found by Claire Fanger, who kindly drew my attention to it.
13. Agrippa, *Opera omnia*, 2:605.
14. BJ 551, fols. 109v–111r.
15. It may be added that it was Ganszyniec's impression that the compiler downplayed magic as much as possible. He omitted the obviously forbidden elements, the methods of suffumigations, and the most explicit rubrics of magic, since these were condemned by medieval penitential books as *vane superstitiones*. Thus, the compiler constructed the appearance of a regular prayer book, making use at the same time of the ritual character of this genre. As a result of this cautious balance, the magic contained in the book was invisible to everybody except the compiler. See Ganszyniec, "O Modlitewniku Władysława," 78–82. Although this conclusion seems to have become outdated, since scholarship has established the category of ritual magic and since it has been exploring the purifying methods of John of Morigny, Ganszyniec was certainly right in identifying a conscious program of reinterpreting magical texts in a Christian framework.
16. Borkowska, *Królewskie modlitewniki*, 346.

find it, since the *Liber visionum* (Book of Visions) of John of Morigny was not at the center of scholarly interest at the time they were working.[17] John of Morigny was a French Benedictine monk with some university training. As he describes himself in the prologue of his *Liber visionum,* he had been a poor student in his youth, and unable to afford books, he turned to the methods of the *Ars notoria,* which thus became for him a real instrument of learning.[18] Later, however, after becoming a monk, he became convinced that the *Ars notoria* was inspired by demons and abandoned it. His doubts concerning the *Ars notoria* arose when malign spirits began tormenting and terrifying him and his sister, a certain Gurgeta, who was also practicing the nortory art, in her case to learn more quickly to read and write. But even after these visitations, it took a while for even the Virgin and Christ himself to convince him of the wickedness of these arts (before that he had even turned to necromancy, and had written a book on the topic and and prepared a "ring of Solomon").[19] At last, inspired by the Virgin Mary, he decided to prepare a purified version of the *Ars notoria,* and thus he compiled an exceptional collection of Marian visions, the *Liber visionum.*

Brother John was apparently positive that by omitting the suspicious unknown words (*verba ignota*) of the notory art, and by sticking to understandable Latin, he had—with the Virgin's help—resolved all the difficulties of the *Ars notoria,* and expunged every demonic element.[20] Indeed, he was so sure of this that he wrote under his own name and did not attempt to keep his work secret. However, while the prayers and the invocations of angels became more or less orthodox, the dependence of the *Liber visionum* on the *Ars notoria* was still undeniable. Its structure mirrored that of the "Flores aurei" (the first of the two principal chapters of the *Ars notoria*); it used the same technical vocabulary, and above all, promised the same results: the swift acquisition of a stronger memory, greater eloquence, and

---

17. On the *Liber visionum,* see more in Appendix 1. See also, among others, Sylvie Barnay, "La mariophanie au regard de Jean de Morigny: magie au miracle de la vision mariale," in *Miracles, Prodiges et Merveilles au Moyen Age* (Paris: Publications de la Sorbonne, 1995), 173–90; Watson, "John the Monk's *Book of Visions*"; Fanger, "Plundering the Egyptian Treasure"; and Kieckhefer, "Devil's Contemplatives."

18. Fanger, "Plundering the Egyptian Treasure," esp. 244; Claire Fanger and Nicholas Watson, "The Prologue to John of Morigny's *Liber Visionum:* Text and Translation," *Esoterica: The Journal of Western Esoteric Studies* 3 (2001), http://www.esoteric.msu.edu, 137.

19. Fanger, "Plundering the Egyptian Treasure," 245; Fanger and Watson, "Prologue," 145: "Ego, frater Iohannes, postquam dimisi artem notoriam declinavi ad artes nigromancie, et in ipsa preualui tantum quod nouam nigromanciam componerem et quod Annulos Salomonis fabricarem."

20. Thomas Aquinas, for example, condemned the notory art for its use of figures and unknown words (*verba ignota*), assuming that it was through these that the practitioner communicated with demons. Thomas Aquinas, *Summa Theologiae,* 2a–2ae, q. 96. See also Christian Trottmann, "*Studiositas* et *superstitio* dans las Somme de Théologie de Thomas d'Aquin, enjeux de la défiance à l'égard des 'sciences curieuses,'" in Marchetti, Rignani, and Sorge, *Ratio et Superstitio,* 137–54.

deeper understanding.[21] Thus, it is not surprising that the church authorities were not convinced by John's claim that the Virgin Mary had approved his work, and in Paris, in 1323, they ordered it burned.[22] (It is interesting that the *Ars notoria* never suffered the same fate.)

It seems that Brother John's attempt to create a genre of ritual magic acceptable from a Christian point of view had failed. However, if we take a look at the constantly growing list of surviving copies of the *Liber visionum*, we see a considerable distribution of the work in the libraries of the following centuries, which indicates an increasing interest on the part of readers and collectors. John of Morigny would have certainly been pleased to see this, but he would also have been puzzled to realize that one of his readers not only copied his work, but—situating it in a new context, reinterpreted and somewhat restructured it—and actually further purified his already purified book.

As Claire Fanger and I discovered, almost one-third of the prayers in Wladislas's prayer book go back to Brother John's text.[23] These prayers are addressed to God,[24] the Virgin Mary,[25] the four archangels ("I ask you Archangels Michael, Gabriel, Raphael, and Uriel, and invocate you, that you illuminate this crystal"),[26] and the hierarchy of angels ("Oh all of you, blesséd spirits and benign, glorious, kind, and gentle angels, who stay in the order of angels, in the lower ranks and stages of the hierarchy").[27] Although the borrowings are somewhat unsystematic and in most cases the author did not adapt complete prayers, but rather mixed, interpolated, and abbreviated excerpts from various parts of the *Liber visionum*, nevertheless, the order of the extracts more or less follows the original sequence.

Interestingly, the author of the prayer book incorporated those parts of the *Liber visionum* where John describes how he—blindly—used to practice the notory art,

---

21. On the question of how John of Morigny revised and reinterpreted the *Ars notoria*, see Fanger, "Plundering the Egyptian Treasure."

22. Jules Viard, ed., *Les Grandes Chroniques de France*, vol. 9 (Paris: Librairie ancienne Honoré Champion, 1937), 23–24.

23. Claire Fanger and Benedek Láng, "John of Morigny's *Liber visionum* and a Royal Prayer Book from Poland," *Societas Magica Newsletter* 9 (2002): 1–4. The discovery (that the author of the Polish prayer book had borrowed a considerable number of prayers from the *Liber visionum*) was made by Claire Fanger. See also Benedek Láng, "Angels Around the Crystal: The Prayer Book of King Wladislas and the Treasure Hunts of Henry the Bohemian," *Aries: Journal for the Study of Western Esotericism* 5 (2005): 1–32.

24. "O Rex regum, qui es fortissimus." Bernacki and Ganszyniec, *Modlitewnik Władysława Warneńczyka*, 18

25. "Ave, salve gloriosa mea amica, virgo maria," and "O Gloriosa regina angelorum." Ibid., 28 and 30; see also 29 and 32.

26. "Et rogo vos Archangelos Michael, Gabriel, Raphael, et Uriel, et invoco vos, ut illuminetis Cristallum illum." Ibid., 59–60.

27. "O vos omnes spritus sancti angelici, benigni, gloriosi, dulces et mites, qui in ordine angelorum, in inferiori Yerarchia loca et mansiones habetis." Ibid., 59.

before turning away from this wicked and demonic practice.²⁸ As a matter of fact, this is the first text in the prayer book borrowed from the *Liber visionum* (in which it was not a prayer), and the compiler positioned it in the prayer book next to the two *Ars notoria* prayers. It is mainly this positioning that seems to indicate that the author of the prayer book must have known John's whole text, and consciously imitated the structure of the *Liber visionum*, as well as John's passage from the Solomonic art in his own angelic system.²⁹ The impression that John and consequently our author are no longer offering diabolically motivated magic in their books, but are trying to do something nondemonic and divinely inspired, is reinforced by many later claims in the text, among them: "Let me be able to avoid and powerfully overcome all diabolic temptations, all frauds and magic arts."³⁰

Another interesting motif of the prayer book borrowed from the *Liber visionum* is the emphasis on the care with which the book itself had been prepared. Relying on the text of the *Liber visionum,* although somewhat altering it, our author also stresses that the book was written, made, and composed with great diligence and that he prepared himself for the endeavor with several days and nights of vigilance, fasting, special orations, complete reverence, and many ceremonies.³¹ This ritualistic attention to the preparation of the book is unknown in the tradition of the *Ars notoria*. For parallels we have to turn to other magical sources, either to the *Liber consecrationis,* in which the book is not only prepared with such care, but is also consecrated,³² or to the *Liber iuratus Honorii,* at the center of which we find again a consecrated book. The latter one—as we have already seen—narrates a great synod of necromancers and magicians where they chose from among themselves a leader, Honorius, son of Euclid, who wrote a book on the magical arts which contains the hundred sacred names of God. This book is called the sacred or sworn book of Honorius, because—as the text stresses—it is consecrated by God and His angels.³³

---

28. "Oro te, supplico tibi, rogo te toto corde meo, quia prius et antea, quodam suffocacione demoniaca tentatus decepcione, illo prevalente, cecatus, quasi hesitans, non credendo revelaciones sacras et moniciones michi ex bono spiritu, operacione et arte, quibus ignoranter vacaveram esse factam, et in detrimentum anime mee ad diversas peccatorum operaciones quasi scienter cucurri et, prochdolor, adhesi mei in contumeliam creatoris." Ibid., 18–19. Although there are many smaller differences, this section was apparently based on John's text, see Fanger, "Plundering the Egyptian Treasure," 239, for the Latin text, and 226 for an English translation.

29. Fanger and Láng, "John of Morigny's *Liber visionum,*" 2.

30. "Et omnes temtaciones dyabolicas omnesque fraudes et artes magicas valeam devitare et viriliter superare." Bernacki and Ganszyniec, *Modlitewnik Władysława Warneńczyka,* 59; see also 62, 64, and 66.

31. Ibid, 34: "Liber iste cum summa diligencia recta disposicione, debitis diebus, horis et noctibus, vigiliis, ieiuniis, oracionibus specialibus, summa reverencia et omnibus cerimoniis [sic] scriptus, factus et compositus est."

32. Kieckhefer, *Forbidden Rites,* 257–59.

33. On this curious text, see Boudet, "Magie théurgique," and Mathiesen, "A Thirteenth-Century Ritual."

The Crystal

Nevertheless, there still remain a few prayers in Wladislas's prayer book that are not derived from either common devotional texts or the *Liber visionum*. One of these is a prayer addressed to Adonay ("Most potent king, ruler of all visible and mortal creatures"),[34] which appears in a significant position—between the prayer taken from the *Ars notoria* and the first passage borrowed from John, while it also incorporates the "O lux mundi" excerpt from the *Ars notoria*. This prayer is rich in magical elements; among them we find a main motif of natural magic: the occult virtue of gems and herbs induced by God ("You, who implant the virtue in all the gems and herbs, give to this crystal the virtue of your omnipotence).[35] These paragraphs are either composed by the compiler himself, or borrowed from an as yet unidentified magical source. One more reason why they are of interest for us is that they contain some interesting details about "the crystal," details that are not to be found in the other parts of the book. Fairly surprisingly, the crystal appears here as a quadrangular object ("who illuminates this quadrangular crystal"), and functions—as the text goes—through the "holy" (or perhaps rather, magical) names of God: *Agla, Sabaoth, Tetragrammaton, Emanuel,* and *Messias*.[36] It is widely known that these names of God are often used in magical rituals.[37] It may be plausible to suppose—although it is far from being explicitly stated—that these divine names that offer their virtue to the crystal and function as powerful catalysts of the process are physically engraved either directly on the gem or on a metal frame surrounding it.[38]

Although the crystal is undeniably at the center of the practices described by the prayer book, we can only conjecture about its appearance. Since there is no crystal involved in the practices of the *Ars notoria*, nor in those of the *Liber visionum*, the sources of the prayer book identified thus far do not offer much help. Nevertheless, a recently found and exceptionally well preserved object may help us in our speculation. In 1999 German archaeologists excavated an elaborate magical mirror

---

34. "Rex potentissime, omnium creaturarum visibilium morabilis dispositor." Bernacki and Ganszyniec, *Modlitewnik Władysława Warneńczyka*, 16–18.
35. "Qui virtutem das cunctis gemmis et herbis, da et huic Cristallo . . . cunctipotencie tue virtutem." Ibid., 16.
36. "Qui quadrangularem hunc Cristallum illuminet." Ibid. See also ibid., 17: "Manifesta michi secreta quecunque voluero in hoc Cristallo, ut in illo videre valeam, per hec sancta nomina tua, quorum efficacia celum et terra et omnia que in eis sunt, contremiscunt Agla, Sabaoth, Tetragrammaton, Emanuel, Messias," and "ut in cristallus sit illuminatus per sacros angelos tuos et per vim et virtutem illorum verborum essenciam divinam attinencium." Ibid., 21. "Ut tu cristallus sis illuminatus per sanctos angelos, per virtutem et vim illorum verborum." Ibid., 23.
37. See Kieckhefer, *Forbidden Rites*, 139 and 261.
38. See Bernacki and Ganszyniec, *Modlitewnik Władysława Warneńczyka*, 1: "Coram presenti figura, tuo nomini reverenter fabricata et conscripta."

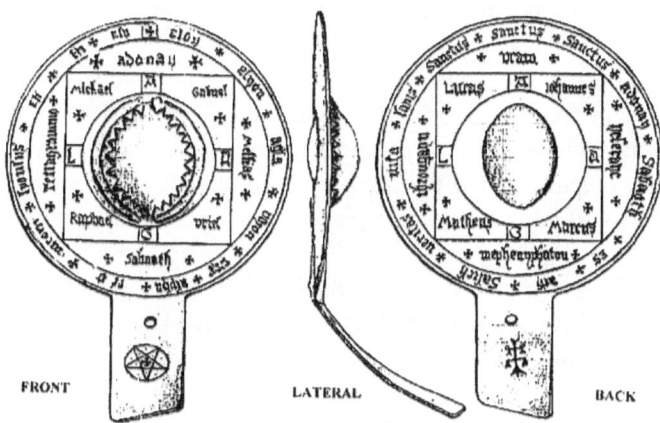

FIG 28   Magical mirror from Rostock. Drawing by W. L. Braekman (*Societas Magica Newsletter*, Winter 2001). Reproduced with the kind permission of W. L. Braekman.

from the sixteenth century near Mecklenburg (fig. 28).[39] The small object (twelve centimeters high) has a handle and a circular main part, in which in the middle of a drawn square we find a three-centimeter rock crystal. Around the crystal, in the—quadrangular!—square, we read the engraved names of the four evangelists on one side, and those of the four archangels on the other. Outside the square we see those divine names which are familiar from the prayer book: *Adonay, Messias, Tetragrammaton,* and *Sabaoth,* while along the perimeter of the outer circle there are further powerful names, such as *Agla, Eli, Eloy, Rex, Alpha et O,* and *Sabaoth* again. No doubt this object once served magical purposes, but who can tell today what (or whom) the practitioner saw when looking at the crystal, and the source from which he read the instructions and the prayers?

Written evidence on the medieval practice of crystal magic is rather scattered and fragmentary; still, its basic rules can be reconstructed.[40] In his survey of magic, William of Auvergne, bishop of Paris, presents the use of crystal balls (more precisely the inspection of shining bodies) in order to see revelations as a method of natural magic, which nevertheless may turn out to be dangerous and demonic, partly because looking into the transparent or shining body may damage the viewer's eyes, and partly because malign spirits may interfere even if the operator

---

39. For a short note and three drawings of this object, see W. L. Braekman, "A Unique Magical Mirror from the Sixteenth Century," *Societas Magica Newsletter* 8 (2001): 5–6.

40. The most comprehensive and reliable work on medieval crystallomancy and catoptromancy—in spite of its title and its date of publication—is still the one by Armand Delatte, *La Catoptromancie grecque.*

did not intend to invoke them. It is clear from this report that the practices of seeking visions or knowledge in crystal balls (*crystallomancy*), magical mirrors (*catoptromancy*), and other shining bodies (such as fingernails, swords, ivory objects, and basins filled with water) were not viewed as mere subbranches of natural—that is to say, nondemonic—magic or pure divination. The detailed methodology, the well-defined procedures of ritual invocations of angels and demons, and the use of young male and female mediums place these practices squarely in the realm of ritual magic.[41]

In 1376, Nicolaus Eymeric, the famous Catalan inquisitor, reported about invocations performed "by tracing a circle in the earth, by placing a boy in the circle, by fixing a mirror, a sword, an amphora, or other small body before the boy, and with the necromancer himself holding a book, and reading, and invoking the demon."[42] In his exhaustive catalog of divinatory techniques, *Das půch aller verpoten kunst*, the German Johannes Hartlieb, mentioning basically the same elements, reports cases of scrying with steel mirrors: these should be consecrated, and then—according to the magicians—angels and not demons appear in them. Interestingly, Hartlieb classifies catoptromantic and crystallomantic experiments under the heading of "pyromancy," that is, originally, the divination with fire.[43]

The anonymous necromantic manual published by Richard Kieckhefer, usually referred to as the "Munich handbook," also contains accounts of experiments based on gazing into crystals, which aim at obtaining information about uncertain things, such as identifying a thief.[44] This crystal is put to work, or rather "switched on," by the various names of God (*Adonay, Sabaoth, Hel, Hely, Sother, Emanuel, Alpha et O*, and so on), and if all the indispensable ingredients are at the disposal of the magician, he may start conjuring angels who will tell him the truth.[45] One of these

---

41. William of Auvergne, *De universo* II 3 20 and 21, 1053bC, 1054aH, 1057bC. See also Marrone, "William of Auvergne on Magic," esp. 745–47; as well as A. Delatte, *La Catoptromancie grecque*, 28–40.

42. Nicolaus Eymeric, *Directorium inquisitorum* (Rome: F. Peña, 1587), 338; quoted and translated by Michael D. Bailey in "From Sorcery to Witchcraft: Clerical Conceptions of Magic in the Later Middle Ages," *Speculum* 76 (2001): 973.

43. Hartlieb, *Das Buch aller verbotenen Künste*; see also A. Delatte, *La Catoptromancie grecque*, 49–55.

44. Kieckhefer, *Forbidden Rites*, 107 and 244–45. One can further add five experiments with mirrors (called the Mirror of Floron, and the Mirror of Lilith) presented by the same source, because mirrors function in the same way for similar purposes, with the involvement of angels and virgin boys. Ibid., 104–6.

45. The endurance of these traditions is well demonstrated by an interesting seventeenth-century book written in Hungarian on ritual magic, which contains instructions on how to find treasure, money, and precious stones hidden under the earth with the help of prayers and invocations. Summoning the appropriate angels and archangels (a different one for each day), the operator is to turn to the sun, give a mirror or a crystal to a virgin boy or girl, and iterate (*flexis genibus*, as usual) a long list of prayers and a set of divine names (*Agios + Otheos + Yschiros + Athanatos + Eleyzon + Ymas +*

elements necessary for the crystallomantic and catoptromantic activities (as well as for a wide range of other divinatory experiments and invocations described by the necromantic handbook) was a virgin boy.[46] That young boy mediums are essential in many magical rituals is testified by other sources as well. John of Salisbury, Johannes Hartlieb, and Nicolaus Jawor all mention the use of virgin boys as mediators of the divine message,[47] John of Salisbury having the most personal experience among them, since he himself was used in his youth by a priest as a recipient of divinatory information (*Policraticus,* bk. 2, chap. 28).[48]

As it is apparent from the sources, a comprehensive and detailed procedure of crystallomancy had been constructed by the High Middle Ages. Very probably, this is the real context in which we are to imagine how the Mecklenburg magical crystal was used by its owner. The angels summoned by the practitioner were supposed to appear in the crystal to answer his questions, which was usually about the location of hidden treasure or stolen articles but occasionally concerned much more important matters, such as "the highest truths" about the world. Virgin boys served as mediums, magical handbooks provided the appropriate formulas to be read, and consecrated crystals were engraved with the secret and powerful names of God. These elements went far beyond the "legitimate science" of natural magic (as William of Auvergne defined it); consequently, they provoked serious attacks from the side of official theology. Inquisitors and university statutes condemned crystallomancy; and its practitioners—as we will see in Chapter 8, examining the trials of Jean de Bar and William Byg—were arrested, forced to confess their error, and even occasionally executed. Thus no historian should expect to find a handbook of crystallomancy that was not only tolerated but used by official authorities and kept in a royal library. Yet the royal prayer book of Wladislas is just such a handbook.

We read very little into the text when we suppose that the crystal—if it actually existed—looked very much like the Mecklenburg mirror. Although we cannot be certain that it existed, we have every right to suppose so. There are no instructions in the prayer book on how to prepare the crystal, and what is more, at one point—

Szentczeges Isten). His objectives extend beyond the simple wish to find treasure; he wants the angels to satisfy all his wishes and requests, provided—the text hastens to stress—that his goals are not malign, vain, or indecent. See János Herner and László Szörényi, "A Tudás Könyve. Hasznos útmutató haladó kincsásóknak" (The Book of Knowledge: A Useful Guide for Advanced Treasure Diggers), in *Collectanea Tiburtiana: tanulmányok Klaniczay Tibor tiszteletére* (Collectanea Tiburtiana: Studies in Honor of Tibor Klaniczay), ed. Bálint Keserű (Szeged: József Attila Tudományegyetem, 1990), 9–33.

46. See Kieckhefer, *Forbidden Rites,* 112–13, 140–42, 240–42, 244, 246–54, and 329–39.

47. For these and many further examples of the use of virgin boys in magical rituals, see Veenstra, "The Confession of Master Jehan de Bar," in *Magic and Divination,* esp. 352 n. 3, and Kieckhefer, *Forbidden Rites,* 98 and 107.

48. See also A. Delatte, *La Catoptromancie grecque,* 15–18.

where the operator invokes the angels for the "composition of the crystal" (whatever this means)—he speaks about the crystal as a *present,* that is, already existing object.[49] The text leaves no doubt that these are the angels who are responsible for preparing it, but seemingly they have already done their duty in the past, and they are not being asked to do so in the present.[50]

Further crystallomantic instructions that we find scattered throughout the folios of the prayer book are not very helpful when we try to imagine how the object functioned. The picture put together from these small bits of information is rather obscure. The angels invoked through the prayers enter and amplify the crystal,[51] then clarify, illuminate, and illustrate,[52] and at the end of the preparatory stage for the vision, they even open it.[53] A last important detail is provided by the statement that the angels are also supposed to consecrate the crystal.[54] Now, the consecration of a magical object, be it a crystal, a sword, or a book, can be easily accounted for, and the clarification and the illumination of a crystal by the angels in the very moment when it becomes a means of communication between terrestrial and celestial agents would still be understandable. But what do amplification (*dilatare*) and opening (*aperire*) mean?

Taking a look at the fourteen miniatures inserted among the prayers does not shed much light on this obscure picture. On most of them, we see a young man wearing a crown with a white eagle on his coat of arms, which is indeed the symbol of the Jagiellonian family. He is kneeling and praying in front of the Madonna (the orientation of the *Liber visionum* is faithfully adapted), to the crucified or the resurrected Christ, or to various saints.[55] One of these illuminations—filling the space exactly between the *Ars notoria* prayer and the first *Liber visionum* text, which tells how Wladislas turned away from his previous magical practices—depicts the young crowned man with a sword (an important part of the magician's inventory)

---

49. Bernacki and Ganszyniec, *Modlitewnik Władysława Warneńczyka,* 60: "Vos ad presentis Cristalli compositionem et illustracionem invito et voco."

50. *Preparare* seems to mean in this context "making it ready for being used," instead of "creating." Ibid., 31: "Ut in illo Cristallo per sanctos angelos tuos illuminatum et preparatum." See also ibid., 35.

51. "Intretis illum Cristallum et dilatetis eum." Ibid., 61. For *dilatare,* see also 21, 38, and 40.

52. Ibid., 42: "Mitte michi sanctos angelos tuos ad huius cristalli clarificacionem et illuminacionem"; "ut omnia huius mundi secretissima secreta sub quatuor elementis contenta . . . et precipue illam rem quam pronunc scire voluero, sine omni fallacia et lesione corporis et anime . . . per sanctos angelos tuos michi manifesta erunt." See also 22, 23, 26, 27, and 43. Ibid., 42: "ut ad illum Cristallum pro illustracione at illuminacione istius." See also 20 and 21.

53. Ibid., 21–22: "Quatenus dilatare et aperire digneris hunc Cristallum per sanctos angelos tuos." Ibid., 23: "Ut tu cristallus scindas te et clarificas."

54. Ibid., 22: "In illo Cristallo per sanctos angelos tuos consecrato."

55. The miniatures are reproduced at the end of Bernacki and Ganszyniec, *Modlitewnik Władysława Warneńczyka.*

in his hand, standing next to a table with a strange object on it that resembles three intersecting circles (fig. 29). The next to last miniature shows the same man kneeling in his chamber in front of the same object on a table, and behind the table three winged angels appear, while a Godlike figure seems to supervise the whole procedure (fig. 30). These angels are supposedly just in the process of illuminating, clarifying, and entering the strange object, which does definitely not resemble the crystal as it is described in the text, but looks like a trefoiled bowl, a frequent object in royal households, often made of precious materials, such as alabaster or quartz for example. Since the illuminator worked several decades after the text had been written, such discrepancies between the pictures and the text are not surprising.

Another late medieval magical text might hold a clue to why the object depicted in the prayer book does not bear any resemblance to the German mirror, and why it is not even quadrangular as the text claimed. The shape of the depicted object is not very far from the "circles" described in the *Clavicula Salomonis* (The Lesser Key of Solomon), in which four smaller circles are situated at the four corners of a square.[56] In its chapter on the construction of the circle, the *Clavicula* first instructs the operator to draw a circle with a consecrated magical sword,[57] and then recite several prayers to God (Lord Adonai) asking Him to *enter* and *consecrate* the circle, which is marked out with His most powerful and holy names, and also to *magnify* and *extend* upon the operator.[58]

I do not want to imply, of course, that the author of the prayer book had an early copy of the *Clavicula Salomonis* in front of him. The point I am trying to make is simply that while the prayers mix three traditions (the *Ars notoria*, the *Liber visionum*, and common prayers), the crystallomantic formulas inserted in them integrate at least two different sets of terminology: on the one hand, that of the actual practice of divination by means of a crystal, as represented by the Mecklenburg mirror, and on the other, that of magical circles used for the invocation of angels—a practice similar to what is described in the *Clavicula*—where entering and magnifying by angels makes more sense than in the case of a crystal.[59] In both traditions there are divine names written on the object, but while the metal frames of the crystal which survived in Mecklenburg may more easily rationalize why our crystal is "quadrangular," the tradition of the Solomonic circles may better explain the circular form depicted on the pictures, as well as the strange terminology of the text.

---

56. For a not very reliable English translation of the text, see Liddell MacGregor Mathers, ed., *The Key of Solomon the King (Clavicula Salomonis)* (London: Kegan Paul, 1909). Joseph H. Peterson's revised translation can be found at http://www.esotericarchives.com/solomon/ksol.htm/.
57. British Library, add. MS 10862, fol. 12v.
58. Ibid., fol. 14v.
59. As an analogy, we can add that the Munich necromantic handbook also uses the words "clarescere" and "crescere" in connection with crystals; see Kieckhefer, *Forbidden Rites,* 239.

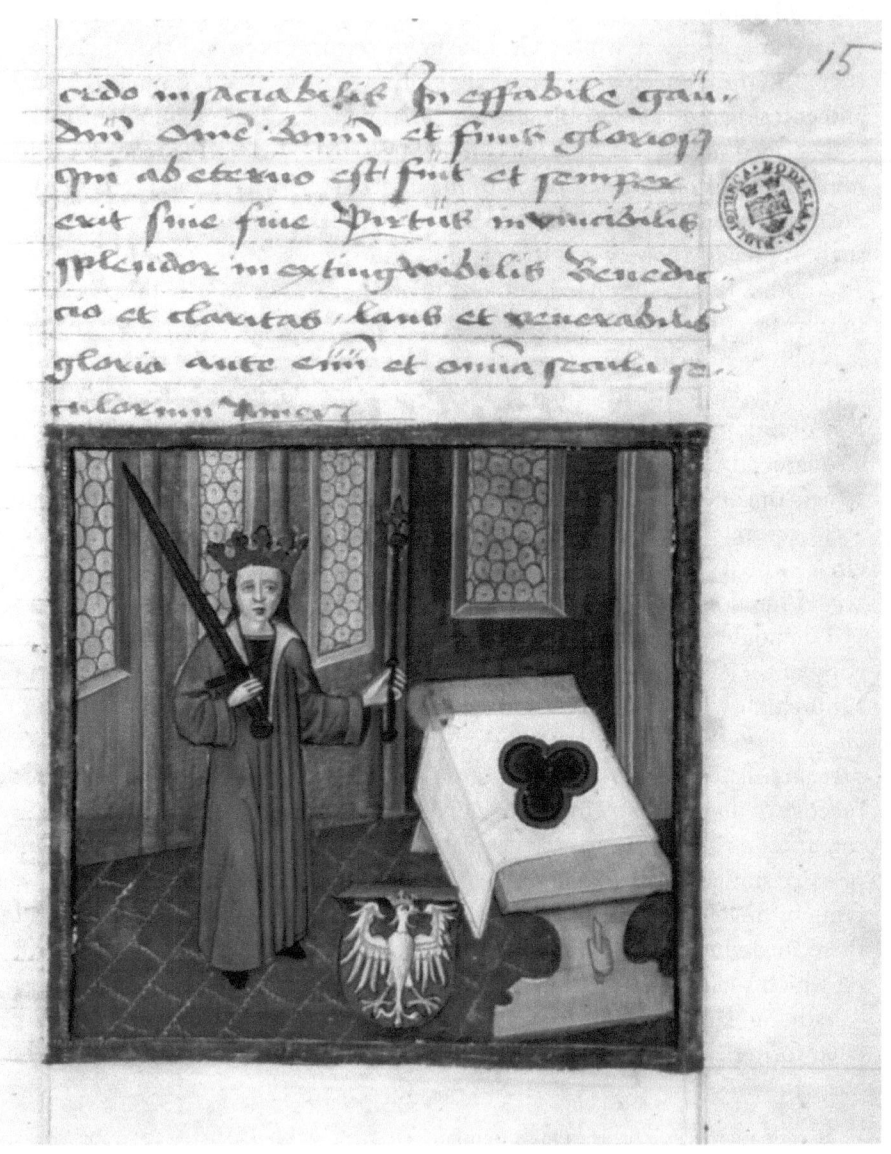

FIG 29 The prayer book of Wladislas: the king and the crystal. Oxford, Bodleian Library, Rawl. liturg. d. 6, fol. 15r. Courtesy of the Bodleian Library, University of Oxford.

FIG 30 The prayer book of Wladislas: the king and the angels. Oxford, Bodleian Library, Rawl. liturg. d. 6, fol. 72r. Courtesy of the Bodleian Library, University of Oxford.

The Owner, the Author, and the Use of the Prayer Book

The fate of the codex is as mysterious as its contents. In 1630 we find it in Besançon in the possession of a certain Jacobus Prive.[60] Twenty-four years later it is still in the same town, owned by a medical doctor called Guerinet, who asks for the Jesuit Johannes Ferrandus's opinion on the manuscript. The Jesuit's answer survives on the blank folios of the prayer book immediately following the text.[61] These folios initiated a long scholarly debate that has not yet concluded. Ferrandus clearly recognized that the codex had been owned by a Polish king, Wladislas, and suspected that among the many Polish kings called Wladislas, it must have been the first one, Jagiello, the grand duke of Lithuania from 1377 to 1401, king of Poland from 1386 to 1434, and creator of the Polish–Lithuanian commonwealth. He gives four reasons for believing this, but admits that it is no more than a conjecture. Just like the modern reader, the Jesuit was puzzled by the magical content of the seemingly devotional book. Furthermore, he did not see how the crystal might have been quadrangular,[62] and he also found the crystallomantic practices to be in opposition with the Christian faith. His main concern was similar to the worries of the Paris authorities who had ordered the burning of the *Liber visionum* in 1323, namely the curiosity and vanity of the operator who asks for total, divine, and eternal knowledge.

The great book collector, Richard Rawlinson (1690–1755), purchased the codex at some point between 1719 and 1726, while traveling on the Continent. He left it to the Bodleian Library together with a huge collection of medieval manuscripts, medals, and coins in 1755, in the year of his death. The sudden growth of the quantity of books in the Bodleian was a real shock for the librarians; for more than a century they could not even catalog the Rawlinson manuscripts.[63]

But all this evidence is secondary to the question of who may have first commissioned the compiling of this text, that is, who Wladislas was. This name in the fifteenth century would not yet have crossed the borders of Poland, and the coat of arms present on all the miniatures clearly belongs to the Jagiello family; consequently every scholar agrees that the owner of the book was one of the several kings of Poland of that name and family.

Traditionally, the codex is associated with the Jagiellonian king of Poland and Hungary who died in 1444 in the Battle of Varna (hence it is called the Prayer Book of Wladislas Varnenczyk).[64] This attribution is supported by the evidence that the handwriting of the codex dates indeed from the 1430s, and that the young

---

60. His name appears on fol. IIr.
61. Fols. 78v–79v. Bernacki and Ganszyniec, *Modlitewnik Władysława Warneńczyka*, 73–76.
62. Ibid., 74: "Crystallum nescio quam quadrilateram."
63. Madan, *Summary Catalogue*, 3:177–78.
64. Ibid., 3:521; Bernacki and Ganszyniec, *Modlitewnik Władysława Warneńczyka*, 69–70.

crowned person depicted on the miniatures resembles the king, who died as a young man in the battle: he is short, almost a child's height, and he has thick hair. This is clearly not the portrait of Wladislas II (1456–1516), king of Bohemia and Hungary, a corpulent bald man who otherwise is also often identified as the owner of the prayer book. The miniatures, however, in contrast to the script, seem to date from the 1490s, and the reign of this Wladislas.[65] As both of these kings were also Hungarian rulers, Hungarian codicologists have contributed, unfortunately, to both sides of this debate.[66]

The text of the prayer book, especially the ceaseless repetitions of crystallomantic formula, is to some extent revealing about the owner, but at the same time it adds further confusion to the picture. Most of the prayers—in the first person singular—let slip some information on Wladislas, not very consistently, however. In the crystal Wladislas wants to see the intentions and acts of not only his subjects, that is, people of lower rank who like or hate him, but also of his equals and superiors, among them kings and princes.[67] We learn that he has both spiritual (ecclesiastical) and secular superiors,[68] which implies that his is not the highest place in the political hierarchy, and he is not a ruling king. Among his equals, he lists mainly dukes,[69] but on one occasion—rather inconsistently—even kings.[70] Dismissing this as an error on the part of the scribe, Ryszard Ganszyniec came to the conclusion that the owner of the original text, which was, according to him, later copied in our codex, was a duke, more precisely a Silesian duke (as Ganszyniec identifies a number of Germanicisms in the text), probably Wladislas of Opole (1356–1401).[71]

It would be difficult at the moment to offer a scenario for the fifteenth-century story of the text (and the codex) that could be satisfactory in every respect; any of the possible solutions leaves open at least as many questions as it answers. On the one hand, Wladislas II, under whose reign the codex was illuminated, definitely cannot be the first owner of the book, since it had been written before his time. On the other hand, the problem with the Opole duke is that once we accept that

65. Władysław Podlacha, "Miniatury modlitewnika Warneńczyka" (On the Miniatures of the Prayer Book), in Bernacki and Ganszyniec, *Modlitewnik Władysława Warneńczyka*, 93–141.
66. See Edit Hoffmann, *Régi magyar bibliofilek* (Old Hungarian Bibliophiles) (Budapest: Magyar bibliofil társaság, 1929), 49 and 164, and Csaba Csapodi, *The Corvinian Library: History and Stock* (Budapest: Akadémiai Kiadó, 1973), 923. Csapodi attributes it to Wladislas I, Hoffmann to Wladislas II.
67. "Acta vel facta superiorum dominorum meorum, regum et principum, eciam michi equalium et inferiorum subditorum meorum, qui me diligunt vel odiunt." Bernacki and Ganszyniec, *Modlitewnik Władysława Warneńczyka*, 31, 35, 38, 40.
68. "Acta vel facta dominorum meorum superiorum spiritualium vel secularium." Ibid., 46.
69. "Eciam michi equalium ducum." Ibid., 40.
70. "Acta vel facta omnium superiorum meorum, dominorum regum et principum, eciam michi equalium regum inferiorum et subditorum meum." Ibid., 35.
71. Ganszyniec, "O Modlitewniku Władysława," 70.

the text we have is a copy made in the 1430–40s of an earlier original, why should we assume that the name Wladislas was present in the original? If our text is a copy, then the owner of the original could have been anyone. However, if we choose Wladislas I, who was in power during the period from which the handwriting can be dated, then the question is who and for what purpose did illuminate the codex with his picture and coat of arms fifty years after his death. And finally, if we want to arrive at a compromise between these solutions, proposing that the text and the book can be related to more than one king called Wladislas, perhaps even to three of them—this series of owners might account for the confusing terminology of kings and dukes in the text—but then the number of other problems only multiply.[72]

Solving the problem of ownership might shed some light on the no less obscure issue of authorship, and vice versa. More precisely, it is not an author we are looking for in the sense that he composed the prayers, but rather a compiler, who had a number of magical and devotional texts in front of him, and who interpolated them in one final collection, incorporating the short crystallomantic formula, and substituting the usual "N," which stands for the operator in the magical literature, with the name Wladislas. Although we do not know his identity, we do know something of how he worked and what kind of person he was.

His work reveals first of all that the *Liber visionum*—which, despite its French origin, has survived primarily in copies of North Italian, German, and Austrian provenance[73]—had a certain Polish (or Silesian, or eastern German) circulation in the late fourteenth or early fifteenth century. Not only did our compiler know it, he knew it well, and apparently even recognized its close relationship with the *Ars notoria*. It is possible that he put the two texts next to each other on his table (he may have owned only a shorter version of the *Ars notoria*), or had one manuscript

---

72. The Jagiellonian coat of arms was probably added to the miniatures in the prayer book in the 1490s. As it is generally known, several unfinished codices of the library of King Matthias were completed in Buda under his successor, Wladislas II. The royal workshop, of course, replaced the Corvinian raven with the Jagiellonian eagle on the decorations. For further details, see Csaba Csapodi, "Quando cessò l'attività della bottega di miniatura di Mattia?" *Acta Historiae Artium Academiae Scientiarum Hungaricae* (1968): 223–33; Csapodi and Csapodiné Gárdonyi, *Bibliotheca Corviniana*, 29–30. For examples of the Polish white eagle inserted in the codices of the Corvinian library, see ibid., plates 41, 51, and 57. Either this prayer book was one of these inherited codices or one that the new king brought with him from Kraków to Buda, in which case it was never in the Corvinian Library. Wladislas II, however, was certainly not the first owner of the codex. It was written or copied during the reign of a previous king, Wladislas I (the "Varnenczyk"), adapted perhaps for his purposes. Now, either the identity of the copyist and the author coincide, and in this case we have arrived at the point of origin of the text, or the prayer book was copied from an earlier example, which may have been commissioned by a Jagiellonian duke, Opole, or the grand duke of Lithuania.

73. On the surviving copies of the *Liber visionum*, see the lists of manuscripts in Fanger and Láng, "John of Morigny's *Liber visionum*," and in Claire Fanger and Nicholas Watson, "Some Further Manuscripts Containing Copies of the *Liber visionum* of John of Morigny," *Societas Magica Newsletter* 12 (2004): 4–5.

in front of him containing both works.⁷⁴ These two works, however, cover only part of the magical content of the prayer book. From that we may conclude that he also had a profound acquaintance with other magical experiments involving crystals, mirrors, and circles. He managed to combine two components: prayers to angels borrowed from the *Ars notoria* and its derivatives on the one hand, and the practice of crystallomancy on the other. What makes his literary product remarkable is that for this combination we had known no earlier example than the angelic conversations of John Dee in the late sixteenth century.⁷⁵

This person, an attentive reader of the *Ars notoria* and the *Liber visionum*, followed the terminology of his sources (as far as his own terminology can be observed at all, since he constantly incorporated alien paragraphs in his texts): he used the rare expression *ars exceptiva* to designate the magical arts;⁷⁶ he used the term "spirits" in order to avoid mentioning demons, used *ars* to refer to the notory art,⁷⁷ and emphasized the power of words and divine names.⁷⁸ He was, furthermore, committed to the goals of his sources (for which the *Liber visionum* had been condemned): he sought perfect knowledge, and he wanted to know "all the secrets which are contained under the four elements."

The scribes of texts of ritual magic tended to make new works by combining, rearranging, and revising material taken from one or more older ones.⁷⁹ Thus, the author of Wladislas's prayer book used material from the *Liber visionum*, which in turn had been constructed using material taken from the *Ars notoria*. And just as the *Ars notoria* was considered heretical, so too was the *Liber visionum*. If this is so, then why was Wladislas's prayer book, made up as it was from materials taken from both, not condemned as well? The difference lies in the reception and the distribution of each. Unlike the other two, the prayer book was intended for a readership that was much smaller than that of the *Ars notoria* and much more tolerant than that of the *Liber visionum*.

The compiler of Wladislas's prayer book, like John of Morigny,⁸⁰ was a

---

74. Such as the Vienna, Schottenkloster, MS Scotensis-Vindobonensis 140 (61), a codex copied in 1377 in which the *Liber visionum* (fols. 1r–106v) is followed by various short versions of the *Ars notoria* (fols. 107r–156r). Albert Hübl, ed., *Catalogus codicum manu scriptorum qui in bibliotheca monasterii b. m. v. ad scotos vindobonae servantur* (Vienna: Otto Harrassowitz, 1899), 74–75.

75. Provided we accept the theory of Stephen Clucas that one of John Dee's sources was the Solomonic art. Stephen Clucas, "John Dee's Angelic Conversations and the *Ars notoria*: Renaissance Magic and Mediaeval Theurgy," in *John Dee: Interdisciplinary Essays in English Renaissance Thought*, ed. Clucas, 231–73 (Dordrecht: Springer, 2006).

76. Bernacki and Ganszyniec, *Modlitewnik Władysława Warneńczyka*, 19: "Quod per illam artem et scienciam exceptivam errore seductus."

77. Ibid., 16, 17, 19.

78. "Vim et virtutem illorum verborum." Ibid., 21, 23, 17.

79. Klaassen, "English Manuscripts of Magic, 1300–1500."

80. See Fanger, "Plundering the Egyptian Treasure."

well-educated cleric, well versed in the language of the church. Both seem to have been practitioners, and although the fifteenth-century compiler is not as forthcoming about his own experience as the fourteenth-century Brother John (or, more precisely, says nothing in his own words), both offer an insight into the world of the readers and operators of the techniques of the *Ars notoria*. Finally, neither of them intended to write a popular handbook of magic aimed at the satisfaction of dubious needs. Instead, they created a genre in which it is hard to decide whether magic or religion plays the more important role. Beyond this, of course, there are also many differences between them—one of them was a real author, while the other was a compiler, among other things—which I will not go into here.

As to who the compiler of the prayer book was, or where he lived, it is possible to speculate with some confidence. From what we know about the dissemination of magical texts in this part of Europe, I think it unlikely that the references and resources he would have needed would have been available at the court of a Polish or Lithuanian duke in the fourteenth century. However, if this text was written in the fifteenth century, then we have a candidate for its authorship. In 1429 a member of the household of King Wladislas I, Henry the Bohemian (Henricus Bohemus), was accused of and condemned for practicing crystallomancy and keeping necromantic books. Like Conrad Kyeser, the author of the *Bellifortis,* Henry was a respected figure at a royal court whose political influence was greater than his rank. And as an influential member of the royal court, he was present at the birth of Wladislas I and stayed close to the future king when he was yet a child, that is, when Wladislas still had superiors. And finally, he was from Bohemia, which might account for the Germanicisms in the text. At any rate, in the 1440s he was again living freely in Kraków, where he had plenty of opportunity and the necessary references at his disposal, as well as a background in crystallomancy to compose a royal prayer book for Wladislas I.

Before completing our analysis, we can pause for a moment to speculate about the reasons why such a source was copied at all. Was it meant to serve actual practice or a mere reading? In the case of the magical manuscripts, usually no definite answer can be given to the question of whether the inclusion of magic in a given codex indicates actual practices or simple curiosity. These texts do not specify whether their scribes tried to test their instructions, and fabricated talismans. As a rule, medieval folios do not tell us the intentions of their scribes. Fortunately, the prayer book of Wladislas is not so silent, and contains internal evidence indicating actual application. In the texts of ritual magic the operator is usually designated merely by the letter "N" (implying that the actual user has to substitute his name wherever he reads "N"): in the royal prayer book, "N" is always replaced with "Wladislas." In the *Liber visionum* John of Morigny explains that each person who wishes to use the prayers of his book must copy his own volume by his own hand, substituting his name for that of John, and then consecrate the copy. Of course, John is aware that his name is fairly frequent, and therefore he stresses that even those persons who are also called John must reproduce the book with their own hands if they really want to use it.[81] Indeed, most of the extant copies of the *Liber visionum* are not mere copies of the original version, but handbooks copied and used by a certain Albertus (of Judenberg),[82] a Petrus,[83] a Bernardus,[84] and other medieval readers with different names. Thus the substitution of the name Wladislas in the prayer book seems to imply that it was made for real use, it was consecrated, and its crystallomantic formula and angelic prayers were probably indeed applied by a certain Wladislas.[85] It is not likely, of course, that a king copied the text with his own hands in order to render the prayers effective, but this is not a problem, because according to John, the actual work of copying may be done by another, as long as it is done under the name of the prospective user.[86] In consequence, certain copies of the *Liber visionum* and the prayer book of King Wladislas constitute those few cases when magical texts themselves expose the fact that the books containing them were consecrated and used as real manuals.

Use and Abuse of Magical Prayers

We have manuscripts and testimonies on the notory art in Western Europe that date back to the early years of the thirteenth century. Some time during that period, two texts of divergent origin, the *Flores aurei* and the *Ars nova*, were combined to produce a work henceforth called the *Ars notoria*. And despite the repeated and severe condemnations of the genre of magical theurgy in general and the *Ars notoria* in particular,[87] numerous copies of this work quickly found their way into medieval libraries.

Church authorities were by no means pleased by the wide dissemination of the

---

81. Graz, University Library, MS 680, fol. 137v, col. 1: "Quamvis liber iste sub hoc nomine iohannes conponatur et plures alij homines vocantur hoc nomine iohannes tamen nullus alius potest operari per eum nisi ille pro quo fuerit specialiter libri conpositus."
82. British Library, MS 18057.
83. Graz, University Library, MS 680.
84. Hamilton, Calif., McMaster University Library, MS 107.
85. I thank Claire Fanger for all these pieces of information, including the quotation from the Graz manuscript.
86. See the text of the vow demanded of anyone who wished to recopy the book in Watson, "John the Monk's *Book of Visions*," 213–14: "Ego, nomen Christianus, famulus sive famula Yhesu Christi, ex meo libero arbitrio et voluntate propter salutem anime mee promitto omnipotenti Deo et beate Marie virgini et omnibus sanctis et electis Dei quod ego hunc librum volo met rescribere, vel alium fidelem sub nomine meo, et secundum hoc librum et institutiones suas volo facere at agere."
87. See Dupèbe, "L'«Ars Notoria» et la polémique."

prayers in the *Ars notoria*. As usual, the closer something is to orthodoxy, the more vigilant resistance it provokes. Official Christianity saw the magical reinterpretation of its own prayers as an intolerable abuse, refused to accept the notory art as a holy procedure, and found its aims—intellectual and mental perfection—dangerously ambitious. Nonetheless, the condemnations rarely turned into actual prosecutions (the case of John of Morigny being one exception), a fact that explains how a number of high-quality manuscripts survived. When we compare this rate of survival and the beauty of the illumination of some *Ars notoria* manuscripts with those of demonic magic, the difference is striking. Contrasted, for example, with the relatively schematic drawings of the necromancer's manual published by Kieckhefer, the artistic value of the *notae* of many of the surviving copies of the *Ars notoria*—as well as the regularity of the handwriting—indicate that they were made with great care and patience, which was only possible in the professional circumstances provided by a *scriptorium*.[88]

The artistic quality and the breadth of dissemination of these texts indicate a persistent interest in a nonscholastic way of acquiring knowledge. But whose interest is this? Where are we to look for the practitioners of the notory art? The undeniably religious nature of the *Ars,* its devotional goals, as well as its emphasis on ritual preparations, purity, confession, and abstinence, point to the monasteries. Indeed, owners of *Ars notoria* texts can be identified among the monks of the Saint Augustine monastery in Canterbury, who incorporated this art in volumes of devotional collections. The prologue of the *Liber visionum* by John of Morigny also offers—from a unique and personal perspective—evidence to support the suspicion that monks and students were among the enthusiastic readers of works on ritual magic, and particularly of the *Ars notoria*. His account also supplements our picture on how ritual magic was transmitted: John practiced it in the company of Johannes, a Cistercian monk, and Gurgeta, his own sister. Apparently, the notory art was taught and learned in a monastic community, one monk introducing the other to the practices, and it was indeed seen as a ritual system of acquiring knowledge. The presence of the *Ars notoria* in such religious contexts may make us think, nonetheless, that its pious aspects were taken as seriously as its magical components, if not more so.[89]

But monks and clerics were not the only ones who read (and recited?) its prayers. There were copies of the *Ars notoria* in royal and ducal libraries, among them, the libraries of Charles V and Charles VI of France. It was also found appealing by the dukes of Milan: as their three book lists testify, they had at least two copies of the *Ars*

---

88. A telling example of a beautifully illustrated, carefully prepared, and well-preserved manuscript is the BnF lat. 9336, transcribed by Véronèse in Véronèse, *L'Ars notoria au moyen age*.
89. Page, "Magic at St. Augustine's," chap. 6; Dupèbe, "L'«Ars Notoria» et la polémique," 132–34.

notoria, as well as a copy of another text of ritual magic, the *Clavicula Salomonis.*[90] Finally, we also find copies of it in book collections of late medieval universities, which is surprising, given that the *Ars notoria* promises quick mastery of university disciplines.[91] In short, the *Ars notoria* was far from being a marginal phenomenon in the Middle Ages.

In Western Europe, texts of ritual magic are distributed fairly uniformly, and we have evidence concerning the sociocultural background of this genre of magic,[92] but similar materials are much less abundant in Central European libraries. Despite the fact that most of the extant *Liber visionum* manuscripts were written only a few hundred kilometers to the west of the region studied here, that is, in the Holy Roman Empire, apart from the sections in the prayer book of Wladislas, no copies of John's text are known to have been made in Poland, Bohemia, or Hungary. As for the *Ars notoria,* only one example of it was known until recently: the aforementioned one-page-long Kraków fragment, which was written in the fourteenth century and survived in the binding of a medieval codex.[93]

Yet we should not forget that versions of the genre of ritual magic are highly divergent, they occur under numerous titles and incipits, and we have every hope that an increasing number of new sources will be identified in the future. Indeed, two more copies of the *Ars notoria* have been found recently, one in Prague and one in Kraków.

The Prague manuscript (PNK I F 35) contains the first part of the *Ars notoria,* the *Flores aurei.* This text is unique in the region for two reasons: first, it is the only version that is longer than a few folios; and second, it is the only version with an illustration—a drawing of the most wise Solomon's magical rings (Plate 25). The *Flores aurei* is followed by a text called the *Ars memorativa,* a usual alternative title for the *Ars notoria,* but this time it refers to the real art of memory.[94] Both texts were copied by the owner and actual author of some of the works in the codex, Frater Mattheus Beran, in 1431. That the inclusion of the *Flores aurei* in this collection of useful texts was not accidental, but a result of conscious editorial work, is

---

90. Pellegrin, *La Bibliothèque des Visconti et Sforza,* 1:135–36, nos. 282 and 286 in the book list of 1426, and 322; nos. 696, 697, and 698 in that of 1459. For the appearance of the *Ars notoria* in monastic and lay libraries, see Boudet, "L'*Ars notoria* au Moyen Age," 183–84. It remains to be decided whether this copy of the *Clavicula Salomonis* is identical with the late sixteenth-century text under the same title. If it is, the book list of the dukes of Milan provides an important piece of evidence for the early history of this magical text.

91. Boudet, "L'*Ars notoria* au Moyen Age," esp. 183–84.

92. Ibid.

93. BJ 2076; Zathey, "Per la storia," 102.

94. This copy of the *Ars notoria*—PNK I F 35 (Truhlář 267)—was identified by Julien Véronèse. Fols. 464v–476v.: "Incipit liber Eirohtonsitra—vetis notorie—sanctissime." Fols. 477r–484r: "Ars memorativa."

confirmed by several small details. In the *explicit* of the text, for example, Beran makes it clear that he himself copied "this most holy divine art," and calls the reader's attention to what has frequently been emphasized in the text, namely that anyone who wishes to practice it must go to confession, lead a chaste life, fast, and pray with bent knees in front of the cross. In addition, though the prayers included in the text are something of a departure in tone from the scientific orientation of the volume, the promises of this art to introduce its user to the liberal arts fit the general character of the whole book perfectly, and its emphasis on the art of memory makes it a suitable neighbor to the survey on the methods of remembering that follows it.

The Kraków *Ars notoria* occurs in a codex that has already been examined on several occasions in the previous chapters. BJ 551 is an otherwise astronomically oriented collection of scientific texts compiled in Prague in the last quarter of the fourteenth century, which came after some travels into the possession of a Kraków student at the end of the fifteenth century. (It is an interesting coincidence that Erfurt and Vienna, two places mentioned in relation to the history of the manuscript, are also the cities where Mattheus Beran, the owner of PNK I F 35, seems to have studied.)[95] On the empty folios between the astronomical treatises, however, someone has inscribed alchemical recipes, Latin and German magical formulas, a treatise on chiromancy later crossed out, parts of the *Secretum mulierum* of Pseudo-Albertus Magnus, and finally, embedded in this magical context, a relatively short work belonging to the *Ars notoria* tradition.[96] The rituals presented in this excerpt are supposed to start at a new moon, and the practitioner—having fulfilled his duties concerning fasting, chastity and physical and mental purity—is to settle himself with bent knees while reciting prayers to *Eloy, Adonay, Athanatos, Tetragrammaton, Pantheon,* and other names of God in order to attain the usual objectives of the notory art: intellectual perfection, learning, the strengthening of memory, the ability to solve scientific problems, and the ability to understand difficult books. To achieve this last-mentioned goal, for example, the practitioner is to write the letters alpha and omega on his right palm before starting the rituals. This action will give a dream telling him where he should open the book the next morning to acquire its content directly.[97] Naturally, all these practices are strictly mandated under the control of Christ and God.

This four-page-long section on understanding difficult books is not found in the earliest extant versions of the *Ars notoria,* but seems to constitute a slightly later addition, which apparently did not always travel with the *Flores aurei* and the

---

95. *CBJ,* 3:344–45.
96. Fols. 109v–111r and 117v.
97. BJ 551, fol. 109v.

Ars nova.⁹⁸ Containing similar methods, prayers, and words, however, it was ultimately attached to the earlier tradition of *Ars notoria* texts. This codex is another example of the tendency of abbreviated versions, and excerpts, of the *Ars notoria*, to travel in the company of works on astrology, alchemy, natural philosophy, and chiromancy, unlike full-length versions, which tended to travel alone, or in the company of other works of ritual magic.⁹⁹ Indeed, this is what happens in BJ 551: excerpted *Ars notoria* prayers and rituals are integrated into a scientific, medical, and alchemical context.

Before we conclude our chapter on the magical use and misuse of Christian formulas, it is worth mentioning a text that does not belong strictly to the tradition of *Ars notoria*, one which, however, constitutes a completely original piece of Christian ritual magic. In a one-page-long fourteenth-century manuscript bound to a codex of the Biblioteka Jagiellońska,¹⁰⁰ a woman called Elisabeth prays to God to secure—or perhaps to regain—the love of her husband Theoderic.¹⁰¹ The text starts rather innocently, as an ordinary prayer: God, Christ, and the Holy Trinity are begged to assure the feelings of the couple so that neither man, woman, nor the devil can stand between them. After this, however, the prayer turns into a conjuration: Elisabeth conjures her own husband with the power of divine names, such as *Ely, Eloy, Eloe, Yosdy, Sabaoth, Adonay, Tetragrammaton, Saday, Messyas, Sother, Emanuel*, and even *Yskyros, Athanatos, Arethon, Melchar*, and *Stramchon*, so that—as a deer wishes to come to the fountains—Theoderic may desire to come to Elisabeth, and act according to her wishes.¹⁰²

The uniqueness of this text lies in its alleged author: it is a woman who performs a Latin conjuration; it is she who uses Christian formulas for the purposes of love magic. Why is that so exceptional? Because, while love magic was mostly attributed to women in the Middle Ages, the actual manuscripts, paradoxically, tend to take the viewpoint of men, except for perhaps this single source. It is very likely that this Latin text, signed in a rather official way by both spouses, may have been

---

98. They do not appear in the early version transcribed by Véronèse, but similar paragraphs appear in Latin manuscripts from the thirteenth century; for an example, see Sloane 1712. (I thank Julien Véronèse for this information.) They are identical with the final pages of the text of the *Ars notoria* as it appears in Agrippa's *Opera omnia*, 2:647–60. However, the paragraphs are in a different order, and there are smaller textual differences.

99. This theory is put forward in Frank Klaassen, "Religion, Science," chap. 4.

100. BJ 655, fol. Iv.; *CBJ*, 4:415–17.

101. The text is published in Jerzy Zathey, "Modlitwa z XIV wieku o charakterze zaklęcia, mająca zapewnić żonie miłość męża" (A Fourteenth-Century Magical Prayer Which Is to Guarantee the Love of a Husband to His Wife), *Biuletyn Biblioteki Jagiellońskiej* 34–35 (1984–85): 63–64. One should not forget that there is no proof that this source was originally written in Poland, even the names of the principals, "Elisabeth" and "Theoderic," can be found in many languages in Europe.

102. Ibid.: "Ut sicuti cervus desiderat venire ad fontes aquarum, ita tu, Theoderice, desideras venire ad me Elisabeth ad faciendam omnem meam voluntatem."

written by a cleric at Elisabeth's request.[103] Therefore, it must have been this learned man who incorporated a conjuration into an orthodox prayer, who used or abused (depending on the viewpoint) Christian elements for the purpose of love magic, and finally, who indicated that the text was written by a woman. If we are looking for anonymous members of the clerical underworld who were responsible not only for some texts but also for whole genres of magic, it seems that we have finally found one.

103. This argument is put forth in Richard Kieckhefer, "Erotic Magic in Medieval Europe," in *Sex in the Middle Ages*, ed. Joyce E. Salisbury (New York: Garland Publishing, 1991), esp. 42–43.

PART THREE

Readers and Collectors

Introduction:
The Motives and Intentions of Scribes

Up to this point, we tried to read the magical literature first and then identify the persons related to it. Now we will concentrate on how scribes and book collectors associated the theme of magic with their other interests, where exactly they located the magic books in their collections, and whether they hid them behind rows of scholarly manuals or exposed them to the curiosity of their guests.

Modern scholarship has very limited access to the motives and intentions of medieval scribes and book collectors. Book owners usually did not make explicit the reasoning behind the selection and classification of their books. The famous case of Richard of Fournival's *Biblionomia,* or that of the *Speculum astronomiae* where we can reconstruct an elaborate system of criteria according to which one of the richest libraries of the thirteenth century, containing basically the whole spectrum of the new Arabic learning, was cataloged, are fairly exceptional.

Such favorable cases are unfortunately unknown in Central Europe in the Middle Ages; instead of a direct understanding of the motives of readers and collectors, we have to look for indirect means to the same end.[1] Three methods offer themselves. First, we may try to find explicit statements scattered in the manuscripts by the scribes and readers.[2] An instructive example of this can be found in a codex that once belonged to the monks of Canterbury. An early fifteenth-century reader left a note on the endleaf of this magically oriented manuscript giving a short summary of the prologue of the condemnations issued by Etienne Tempier in 1277; he testified to a certain awareness of the dangers entailed by necromantic books, including this very codex. As Sophie Page stresses, it is significant that the

---

1. For various Western examples of approaching the motives of the readers and collectors by means of the notes, indices, table of contents, and other traces left in their books, see the studies in Cavallo and Chartier, *Histoire de la lecture.*

2. For general examples of personal notes left by scribes in scientific manuscripts, see Murdoch, *Album of Science,* 10–12.

author of the note did not destroy the codex, but instead decided to leave this warning about the dangers of its contents to other readers.³

My Central European examples of marginal notes are never this explicit; yet they contain some hints about the attitudes of the collectors. Andreas Costen, for example, a student at the University of Kraków and the scribe of a Prague codex that contains texts on astrology, weather forecasting, and the *Centiloquium* of Hermes, made his copying principles fairly clear in the *explicit* of the text. While collecting and copying these texts, Andreas remarks, he omitted the mystical and theological sense, and concentrated consequently on the practical side.⁴ Mattheus Beran, a monk from the monastery of Rudnicz and a former student of medicine at the University of Prague, concludes his great *Confundarius*, containing medical and magical readings, with the following words: "This has been written with my own hands, through many years, in different countries and various places, and from marvelous exemplars."⁵ That is to say that he made considerable effort to collect all these works on the occult power of stones, herbs, and animals, as well as a copy of the *Ars notoria* from various sources and lands, which effort—as it is implied—makes his collection of texts a rather rare and precious reading. To give a further example of how the interest of a book owner may be reconstructed, we can refer to the case of Jan Oswiecim (d. 1488). Oswiecim, a master of the University of Kraków, purchased a number of books with mostly medical and astronomical, but partially magical content. These books belonged formerly to Oswiecim's older *confrère*, Andrzej Grzymala, and were sold when Grzymala died in 1466. Oswiecim prepared accurate tables of contents in each of his new acquisitions, but interestingly, he omitted the divinatory texts from the list of titles. It seems, therefore, that the magical content of these medical codices reflects the interest of the former owners (for example, that of Grzymala) rather than that of Oswiecim.⁶

Usually, however, scribes and collectors did not want to divulge to us what their viewpoint was when selecting their sources. In the absence of a suitable quantity of such records, we can—and as a matter of fact, we did—approach the issue of the motives of scribes in another way. This consists of observing the tendencies of magical texts to occur together or in the company of texts of certain, well-defined scholarly genres, for example, astrology. Nevertheless, this codicological approach, which we attempted to follow in the previous part of the present work, may be misleading

---

3. Page, "Magic at St. Augustine's," chap. 1. This manuscript—MS Corpus Christi 125—is a famous one, rich in magical content.

4. PNK VI F 7 (Truhlář 1144), fol. 98v: "et sic est finis huius materie que quidem materia scripta ac collecta est per me Andream de Costen baccalaureum Cracoviensem in eodem studio in bursa pauperum .misticum sive theologicalem."

5. PNK I F 35 (267), fol. 484r: "manu mea propria scripta per multa annorum tempora, per diversas terras et loca per varia et mira exemplaria."

6. For further details on this question, see Chapter 9.

Introduction: The Motives and Intentions of Scribes 193

if applied by itself. This is first because we do not have a clue why certain magical texts were copied, and it would be certainly an overinterpretation to suppose that, say, a work on image magic in a given codex indicates that the scribe or the collector actually used talismans. Second, as Frank Klaassen has put it, "It would be hazardous to assume that any codex containing a single magical work represents a compiler or scribe with active and practical magical interests." In addition, "The existence of a particular manuscript version of a work of astrological image magic tells us only that someone wanted a copy of it and does not, in itself, suggest the scribe's attitude towards it. The question remains as to why it was copied, what the other interests of those responsible might have been, and how they chose to interpret, categorize, and employ the treatise."[7]

The manuscript evidence on its own does not tell us whether a text of magic was just an accidental part of the codex containing it or whether it was included there with a specific and active interest in the topic.

Looking for a satisfactory answer to these questions—an answer not provided by the examination of the manuscript context of the magical works—leads us to a third strategy of approaching the motives of scribes. In the following chapters, I will attempt to proceed along this line of investigation: instead of single manuscripts, I am going to concentrate on book collections; instead of individual scribes and collectors, I am going to focus on their social context. This means that formerly discussed sources and persons will occasionally turn up again in the three following chapters; the approach, however, will be different. First, I will summarize the scarce evidence on magic copied or practiced in a monastic context, and then, in two considerably richer chapters, I will discuss manuscript and other sources on the interest in magic detected in courtly and in university contexts. This latter part of my work will, hopefully, help to contextualize those sources that we have discussed until now. In two *excursus,* two interesting side-problems will be discussed. First, we will examine to what extent and in which cases the interest in and the practice of learned magic became an issue in court cases, in other words, to what extent the use of magic was criminalized. Second, we will take a closer look at a phenomenon little known in the Middle Ages but which thrived in the Renaissance: we will see how self-appointed magicians consciously constructed their image, and then—with conscious manipulation of their public—increased their fame as magicians and spread reports of their magical expertise and achievements.

7. Klaassen, "Religion, Science," chap. 2.

7
Magic in the Clerical Context

When a Necromancer Turns Monk

In his *Formicarius* (The Anthill), the German Dominican theologian and reformer, Johannes Nider (1380–1438) mentions a Benedictine monk by the name of Benedictus who lived a religious life in Vienna in Nider's time, but who a decade earlier had been a real necromancer.[1] From the following chapter of the *Formicarius*, we learn further details about Benedict. It is specified that he stayed in the Schottenkloster of Vienna and that he was gigantic and frightening as far as his physical features were concerned. Before he entered the monastery

> he possessed necromantic demonic books, and following their teachings he lived rather miserably and dissolutely for a long time. And he had a most devoted virgin sister who was from the Order of Penitents, with the help of whose prayers—as I believe—her brother was saved from the throat of the demons. Inspired by this devotion, he came to various reformed monasteries in various places, wishing to get engaged in monastic life. But because he was of gigantic height and terrible appearance, and a leading necromancer and charlatan, hardly anyone had faith in him. Finally, however, he was accepted in the above mentioned monastery, and upon entering he changed his name and his life, and he started to be called

---

1. Johannes Nider, *Formicarius*, bk. 5, chap. 3: "Contuli insuper etiam cum domino Benedicto monacho sancti Benedicti ordinis, qui licet modo sit religiosus multum Wienne in reformato monasterio, tamen ante decennium adhuc in seculo degens fuit nigromanticus, ioculator, mimus et truphator apud seculares nobiles insignis et expertus." Richard Perger, "Schwarzkünstler und Ordensmann: Aus dem Leben des Schottenpriors und Seitenstettner Abtes Benedikt," *Wiener Geschichtsblätter* 32 (1977): 175. Perger's text is based on the 1474 Augsburg and the 1517 Strasbourg editions of *Formicarius*.

Benedict. He made such an improvement following the rules of the blessed Father Benedict, that in a few years he became a pride of the religion, he was chosen as prior, and he was put in charge in the pulpit for the seculars and became a beloved preacher among the people.

When he was still a novice—as I have heard about him—he sustained many vexations from the demons whom he had abandoned. One day, for example, when he made confession, and got rid of the poison of his perverted life in the hope of receiving pardon, the following night while carrying a lamp in his hands, he felt a demon approaching him. With a violent strike, the demon cast out the lamp from the hands of the novice, and started hurting him considerably. But the soldiers of the Christ overcame the tyranny of this bear, because thanks to holy prayers he was provided with the support of courage, by the help of which he was deliberated from the mouth of the beast.[2]

In spite of these novelistic details, various other sources confirm that Brother Benedictus really lived.[3] He was accepted in the Schottenkloster of Vienna in 1427.

---

2. Ibid., bk. 5, chap. 4: "Fuit et hodie vivit Wienne in monasterio, quod ad Scotos dicitur, frater, de quo precedenti retuli, sancti Benedecti ordinis. Hic in seculo existens famosissimus fuit nigromanticus. Nam libros demonum de nigromantia habuit et secundum eosdem satis miserabiliter et dissolute vixit plurimo tempore. Habuit autem sororem virginem devotam multum de ordine penitencium, cuius ut puto precibus frater a faucibus demonum erutus est. Conpunctus enim ad diversa loca diversorum reformatorum monasteriorum venit, petens sibi sancte conversationis tradi habitum. Sed quia gigantee stature et terribilis aspectu erat et in maleficis et ioculationibus princeps aliorum, fidem vix aliquis viro dabat. Tandem autem receptus in antedicto monasterio, in ipso ingressu nomen mutavit et vitam Benedictus commune vocari cepit et secundum beati patris Benedicti regulas adeo profecit, ut infra paucos annos speculum religionis effectus in prioratus ponerent officium et in ambone pro secularibus praefectus gratiosus est predicator factum ad populum. Hic cum adhuc esset novitius, prout eo referente audivi, multas vexationibus a demonibus, quos reliquerat, sustinuit. Cum enim confessus fuisset sacramentaliter quadam die et virus sue perverse vite emovisset ob spem venie, sequenti nocte lucernam in manibus deferens demonem adesse sensit. Eandem namque lucernam violento ictu de novitii manibus demon excussit et eum non modicum ledere molitus est. Sed vicit Christi miles huius ursi tirannidem quia virtutum alas iam assumpserat quibus per orationes sacras ab ore bestie liberatus est." See Perger, "Schwarzkünstler und Ordensmann," 175.

3. The life and activity of Benedictus was reconstructed by Richard Perger on the basis of the surviving historical evidence collected from various sources. See Perger, "Schwarzkünstler und Ordensmann," and Georgine Veverka, "Der merkwürdige Fall 'Benedikt'—Biographie oder Predigtmärlein," *Wiener Geschichtsblätter* 32 (1977): 177–80. Also see Kieckhefer, *Magic in the Middle Ages*, 156; Werner Tschacher, *Der Formicarius des Johannes Nider von 1437/38: Studien zu den Anfängen der europäischen Hexenverfolgungen im Spätmittelalter* (Aachen: Shaker Verlag, 2000), 400–403; Martine Ostorero et al., eds., *L'imaginaire du sabbat: édition critique des textes les plus anciens (1430 c.–1440 c.)* (Lausanne: Université de Lausanne, 1999), 164–68; and Michael D. Bailey, *Battling Demons: Witchcraft, Heresy, and Reform in the Late Middle Ages* (University Park: Pennsylvania State University Press, 2003), 39 and 130. On the *Formicarius* in general, see Gábor Klaniczay, "The Process of Trance, Heavenly and Diabolic Apparitions in Johannes Nider's *Formicarius*," Discussion Paper Series 65, June 2003, http://www.colbud.hu/main/PubArchive/DP/DP65-Klaniczay.pdf.

His original name and his previous dwelling places are unknown; we only know that he came from Bavaria. He became a prior in 1432, and five years later he was elected the abbot of the Benedictine monastery of Seitenstetten, which is a remarkable ecclesiastical career for someone who had had such an intimate relationship with demons. He died as abbot of Seitenstetten in 1441.

From the *Formicarius* it seems that the conversation between Nider and the monk took place at some point when Benedictus was already a prior but before he became an abbot. Since Nider was in Vienna between 1434 and 1436, this is probably when they met, which furthermore means that the future abbot had practiced necromancy around 1424–26 (that is, a decade earlier), just slightly before he became a monk. Nider's account is corroborated in other small details, too: for example, Benedictus must really have been a gigantic man, as his large tombstone testifies to this. Various further reports, data, and pieces of information have survived about this strange individual; his name is mentioned in the *Catalogue of the Seitenstetten Abbots,* in the *Necrology Notes* of the Vienna Schottenkloster, and—rather understandably—on his tombstone in Seitenstetten.[4]

If all this weren't enough, he appears once again in a curious story, but only in a supporting role. The story is told this time by Martin von Leibitz, abbot of the Schottenkloster between 1446 and 1461. A certain Pilgrimus, the baron of Puecham, was dying. When he was given the last sacraments, he asked the monks around him, one of them being Benedictus, why they were in such a hurry when he still had fourteen days to live. Benedictus asked him how he could be so sure about that, to which he replied that the Virgin Mary had appeared to assure him that he had fourteen more days. The monks were naturally puzzled, and started wondering whether the sickness had attacked his mind. However, although everybody had expected him to die earlier, he really lived fourteen more days before he finally passed away.[5]

---

4. These texts are published in Perger, "Schwarzkünstler und Ordensmann," 175–76.

5. Martin von Leibitz, *Senatorium,* vol. 2 (Lepzig: Hieronymus Pez, 1725), 654; quoted in Perger, "Schwarzkünstler und Ordensmann," 175–76: "Adhuc aliud tibi dicam in eodem monasterio factum. Fuit in es novitandus quidam Pilgrimus baro de Puecham, quem dico novitandum, quia in proposito fuit induere habitum novitiorum, quem praeoccupatus morte non induit; alias si induisset eum, dicerem novitium. Hic cum in lecto aegritudinis iaceret et jam sacramentum Eucharistiae recepisset, quadam die Dominica venit ad eum cum aliquis fratribus frater Benedictus, qui postea abbatem in Seitenstetten (cujus memoriam fecit Formicarius) et hortabatur eum, ut reciperet sacramentum unctionis. Respondit Pilgrimus de Puecham: 'Quare festinatis mecum, cum adhuc habeam per 14 dies vivere?' Ad quem frater Benedictus: 'Si haberetis des hoc literas?' Cui ille: 'Certus sum; nam Beata Maria Virgo apparuit michi et certificavait me, quod habeo adhuc vivere, ut dixi, 14 dies, et quod sum filius perpetuae felicitatis.' Nichilominus obedivit et suscepit sacramentum. Tractaverunt fratres praesentes postea apud se verba audita ab eo; alii interpretantes, quod forte ex valida infirmitate pestilentiae suae laesus esset in capite; alii habuerunt pro sumnio; alii ad literam crediderunt verbis illius devotissimi viri, omnes tamen exitum rei exspectabant. Et licet non fuit consuetum, quo

It is perhaps not too obvious on first reading, but there are some analogies between Benedictus's break with his former dissolute life and John of Morigny's turning away from the demonic *Ars notoria*. In both cases, the necromancer's sister plays a central role in motivating him to give up the necromantic practices. The fact that John's sister Gurgeta was tortured by demons was an argument against the demonic and wicked notory art. The prayers of Benedictus's sister helped persuade him to become a monk; the only difference is that the demons in this latter case chose to torture the necromancer and not his sister. The Virgin Mary's role in the *Liber visionum* is more than central and primary, while in the Vienna story she is rather incidental. Still, there is something magical in her appearance: by telling the nobleman the exact date of his death, her role—however blasphemous it may sound—is somewhat similar to the functioning of the famous onomantic device, the Sphere of Pythagoras, which is used to foretell whether someone will die or not, and whether death will arrive in one, two, or three weeks.

Nevertheless, the Virgin Mary, the involvement of the sisters, and the tormenting demons would certainly not constitute parallels strong enough for supposing that there is more here than pure coincidence. The main reason why the question of these analogies should be raised at all is that the cloister where Benedictus became a prior, the Vienna Schottenkloster, hosts one of those few monastic libraries where the *Liber visionum* of John of Morigny and the *Ars notoria* survived. The codex, which contains the first and some excerpts from the second, is dated to 1377, that is, before Benedictus's lifetime.[6] (It is even more remarkable that the monastery of Seitenstetten, where Benedictus later became abbot, also keeps a fairly early copy of the *Liber visionum*; this one, however, was acquired by the abbey much later, in all probability, not before modern times.)[7] On the basis of all this, I would not exclude the possibility that the *Liber visionum* and the *Ars notoria* could be among those *libri demonum de nigromantia* that Benedictus, the former necromancer and future abbot, possessed according to the account of Johannes Nider, and I would even conjecture that he himself might have played some role in the chain of events that brought these texts to Schotten Abbey.[8]

---

pestilenci tam diu aegrotarent et tandem morerentur, quin infra convaluerunt; tamen sicut dixit ita factum fuit. Transactus 14 diebus, 15. die de hac vita sublatus est et sepultum circa altare Sancti Andreae. Et unus de fratribus, qui fuerunt secum tempore unctionis, Leonardus subprior, homo totus reliquiosus et Deo deditus, praevenit eum moriendo plusquam in octo diebus."

6. Vienna, Schottenkloster, MS 140 (61).

7. Seitenstetten, Seitenstetten Stiftsbibliothek, MS 273. I thank Claire Fanger, who is currently doing research on the Austrian manuscripts of John of Morigny, for the information concerning when the Seitenstetten library acquired this manuscript.

8. Given the present state of knowledge on the dissemination of the *Liber visionum* manuscripts, all this is no more than speculation. However, since further research will be carried out on the Austrian John of Morigny manuscripts, it is more than probable that further details will clarify whether

How typical is Benedictus's case? We certainly have no statistics on how many former necromancers became monks, or on how many of them brought their handbooks with them. The question should rather be posed on a more general level: under what circumstances can a magic book arrive in an ecclesiastical or monastic library, and whose—scientific, religious, or magical—curiosity accounts for such an arrival?

Magic and the Clerics

Medieval monasteries are obviously not the only ecclesiastical entities to which the topic of magic can be related. Interest in learned magic is apparently detectable in the church on a higher level, too. As we have seen, in Abbot Trithemius's *Chronicon Hirsaugiensis* there is a whole list of bishops and archbishops whose names were—rightly or not—associated with alchemy, to which list of alleged or real "alchemists" the names of Conrad of Vechta, the archbishop of Prague, and that of Nicolaus Olah, the archbishop of Esztergom, can also be added.[9]

A certain theoretical interest in the functioning of magic can be reconstructed in the case of the fourteenth-century Hungarian archbishop of Csanád, Jacobus of Piacenza. Jacobus's curiosity lay not so much in the actual practice of magic as in its "secondary literature." The archbishop, who was also a medical doctor, led quite an eventful life. He studied medicine in Bologna, where in 1319 he was accused of having participated in stealing a corpse—supposedly in order to satisfy his interest in anatomy. Returning to Hungary, he became the doctor of King Charles Robert in 1332, somewhat later he was elected to be the archbishop of Csanád, and he died in 1348 as the archbishop of Zagreb.[10] An indication of his high standing at the royal court was that he accompanied the king on his travels to Italy, and that he was sent on a diplomatic mission to meet the pope in Avignon in 1343. It was in Avignon that he ordered the copying of a number of manuscripts of medical content, which he brought to Zagreb, possibly with the intention of founding a medical school.

One of these codices contains the earliest surviving copy of Arnald of Villanova's *Letter on Necromancy*.[11] This letter was written around 1280 to the bishop

---

there is a real link between Benedictus's necromantic interest and the presence of the *Liber visionum* in the two monastic libraries.

9. See Chapter 5.

10. Pál Engel, *Magyarország világi archontológiája 1301–1457* (The Lay Archontology of Hungary, 1301–1457), vol. 1 (Budapest: MTA Történettudományi Intézete, 1996), 67, 79, 91, 450.

11. *Epistola ad espiscopum Valentinum de reprobatione nigromantiae fictionis,* Zagreb Metropolitan Library, MR lat. 154, fols. 81v–83v. For a text edition, see Sebastià Giralt, ed., *Arnaldi de Villanova, Opera medica omnia, VII.1, Epistola de reprobacione nigromantice ficcionis (de improbatione maleficiorum)* (Barcelona: Fundació Noguera, Universitat de Barcelona, 2005). On the Zagreb text,

of Valence, to answer questions he had raised concerning the invocation of demons. Arnald, the Catalan doctor, theologian, and alchemist, whose name was also often associated with necromancy, discusses the powers of necromancers and whether or not it is possible for a magician to invoke and constrain a demon to act according to his will.[12] He arrives at the usual conclusion of the official theology: demons cannot be compelled in a natural way by any human being, primarily because the human mind—being attached to a mortal body—is of necessity inferior to the minds of purely spiritual beings.[13] Although certain monks are convinced that demons can be invoked in various ways, Villanova rejects this view, and explains in great detail why gems, inscriptions, planets, and artificial figures and characters cannot possess any special virtue enabling one to coerce spirits.[14] This theoretically oriented letter also provides a detailed refutation of the methods of image magic, at least to the extent that it entails the help of planetary spirits. Whether the archbishop of Csanád (and later that of Zagreb) was really interested in Villanova's arguments on dismissing demonic magic or simply had the text copied because of the medical fame of its author is impossible to determine. All that we can say is that from the mid-fourteenth century on a theoretical work on magical operations was accessible in the library of the archbishop of Zagreb.

Descending slowly the ecclesiastical ladder from the rank of archbishop, we have evidence suggesting that secular clergy were also involved in certain magical practices. In a sermon on clerical superstitions, originally written in a Bohemian environment by the famous preacher Jan Milíč (Johannes Milicius de Chremsir, d. 1374), but also available in Kraków,[15] the author reports that priests and clerics practice magic, and perform—alone or together with certain women—conjurations and incantations. Abusing the sacraments, the liturgy, the host, the text of the evangelists,

---

the codex, and its possessor, see Mirko Dražen Grmek, "La lettre sur la magie noire et les autres manuscrits d'Arnaud de Villeneuve dans les bibliothèques yougoslaves," *Archives Internationales d'Histoire des Sciences* 42 (1958): 21–26. For the codex, see also *BH*, 2:2940.

12. On Villanova and his letter generally, see *HMES*, 4:848–50, and Juan A. Paniagua, *Studia Arnaldiana: Trabajos en torno a la obra médica de Arnau de Villanova c. 1240–1311* (Barcelona: Fundacion Uriach 1838, 1994). For an early edition of the letter, see Paul Diepgen, "Arnaldus de Villanova De improbatione maleficiorum," *Archiv für Kulturgeschichte* 9 (1911): 385–403. For a second critical edition of the text that takes the earliest copy (the Zagreb text) into consideration, see Mirko Dražen Grmek, "Rasprava Arnalda iz Villanove o crnoj magiji" (The Letter of Arnaldus de Villanova on Black Magic), *Starine Jugoslavenska Akademija Znanosti i Umjetnosti* 48 (1958): 217–29. I am grateful to Marina Miladinov for finding and copying this rare publication for me.

13. Grmek, "Rasprava Arnalda iz Villanove," 221.

14. Ibid., 224–25.

15. On Milíč, see Peter C. Morée, *Preaching in Fourteenth-Century Bohemia: The Life and Ideas of Milicius de Chremsir (+ 1374) and His Significance in the Historiography of Bohemia* (Slavkov: EMAN, 1999). Among the Kraków codices, BJ 1175, BJ 1396, and BJ 1645 contain Jan Milíč' sermons. Concerning them, see Kowalczyk, "Wróżby, czary i zabobony," 9–10.

and so on, they prepare belts, ligatures, and amulets for the purpose of healing or participating in superstitious activities. These men, however—adds Milíč—who allow or even perform such practices are the servants not of God and Christ, but of Baal and Belial.[16]

Should we consider all this a reliable description of what priests and clerics actually did in contemporary Bohemia? Only with reservations. The reasons for skepticism are to be found in the author's life. Milíč was by no means an ordinary preacher. A former member of Emperor Charles IV's chancery and a self-appointed preacher, Milíč had quite a strange career. Among the many novelistic events of his life, we can mention that he—together with his ex-prostitute disciples—managed to take over a famous brothel in Prague known as "Venice," consecrate it, and rebaptize it as "Jerusalem."[17] He then decided it was necessary to share his views of church reform and the coming of the Antichrist with the highest church authorities as soon as possible. He went to Rome, but when he began to preach publicly in Saint Peter's, he was arrested by the Inquisition. He summarized his apocalyptic ideas in a small book titled *Libellus de Antichristo* while still in prison. He was later released, went back to Prague, but returned to the eternal city with his reform ideas several times in the following years. He died on the return leg of his final journey, this time to Avignon, where he met Pope Gregory XI.

Such motifs were not, however, the only reasons why his person became the subject of controversies. In his many sermons delivered in Czech, German, and Latin, Milíč openly criticized the corruption of the clergy and the morals of the mendicant orders. He did not refrain from accusing priests of neglecting their duties, drinking too much, visiting brothels, practicing simony, and so on, and he was subsequently accused of accusing too many. Once again, what we can maintain about the content of his sermon is no more than that clerics *were* actually *criticized* for their magical activity and for abusing the liturgy for superstitious practices. It

---

16. BJ 1396, fol. 273v; quoted in Kowalczyk, "Wróżby, czary i zabobony," 9: "Sunt et alii sacerdotes vel clerici, qui sacramentis abutuntur in suis vel mulierum coniuracionibus, incantationibus, sortilegiis. Sunt qui in missis suis novis vel primis amorem mulierum vel precio vel pecunia conducti cingunt se cingulis ad supersticiones faciendas. Sunt qui scribunt contra febres vel infirmitates super hostia, super lauri baca, super cedula, vel scribunt illud Ihesus autem transiens etc. vel Lutum fecit Dominus ex sputo etc. quando evangelium legitur ac si illa verba evangelii non valerent alio tempore scripta, quam cum evangelium legitur, quia hoc est supersticiosum, quod tempore illi creditur, vel incidunt cruces infra passionis leccionem in die Palmarum vel ligaturam faciunt. . . . Hi sacerdotes, qui hec supersticiosa faciunt vel fieri permittunt et non prohibent, non sunt sacerdotes Domini sed Baal, non Christi sed Belial. Vertunt enim letanias sanctorum in invocaciones demonum, Ioviniani sunt non Christiani."

17. See Morée, *Preaching in Fourteenth-Century Bohemia*. On the particular problem of Milíč and the Prague prostitutes, see David C. Mengel, "From Venice to Jerusalem and Beyond: Milíč of Kroměříž and the Topography of Prostitution in Fourteenth-Century Prague," *Speculum* 79 (2004): 407–42.

remains an open question whether all his accusations were entirely authentic. What we can still claim with confidence, however, is that associations of clerics performing magic was a current theme.

Instead of proceeding now in the direction of the involvement of local priests in popular practices, let us remain within the field of learned magic and concentrate on the evidence for an interest in magic among monks. Unfortunately, at the present stage of research, no Central European monastery can rival the reputation of St. Augustine's of Canterbury, where the concentration of magic books in the library—copied and collected by the monks—was so high that David Pingree simply called it a "center for magical studies." The modern historian of this library is in an enviable position indeed: not only did a large portion of the magical codices survive, but even the specific donors and owners can be identified, their role in the history of St. Augustine's described, and their attraction toward magic in the framework of the monks' interest in sciences and religion contextualized.[18]

No Polish, Bohemian, or Hungarian monastic collection can be compared to the library in Canterbury, either with regard to a well-definable magical interest, or to the abundance of the evidence that has come down to us. Even though their codices usually did not survive, cloister libraries of the region can be reconstructed to a certain extent: often the lists of manuscripts survived even when the manuscripts themselves did not.[19] And as far as one can judge from a mere list of titles, these libraries in Central Europe rarely included magical items. Here, however, serious methodological problems arise. First of all, in such lists, most manuscripts are indicated by a single title, even when they contain from two or three to fifty or sixty distinct works. Sometimes manuscripts are not even mentioned by title but by a description, such as "medical texts" or even simply "various texts." Did such manuscripts contain treatises on talismanic or divinatory magic scattered among the scientific tracts, as many of the codices thus far examined did, or not? And the manuscripts described only as containing "liturgical texts"? Is it not often in such volumes that copies of the *Liber visionum* have survived? A second problem is that the Dominicans, for example, unlike the Cistercians, often traveled together with

---

18. Pingree, "Diffusion," 94; Page, "Magic at St. Augustine's."
19. For medieval monastic book-inventories from Bohemia and Hungary, see Ivan Hlaváček, "Nachträge zu den böhmischen mittelalterlichen Bücher- und Bibliotheksverzeichnissen," *Mediaevalia Bohemica* 1 (1969): 306–15; Hlaváček, "O studiu středověkých knižních katalogů" (On the Study of Medieval Book Catalogs), *Acta Universitatis Carolinae, Philosophica et Historica* 2 (1958): 179–93; Hlaváček, *Středověké soupisy knih a knihoven v českých zemích* (Medieval Lists of Books and Libraries in Bohemia), Acta Universitatis Carolinae, Philosophica et Historica—Monographia 11 (Prague: Univerzita Karlova, 1965); and Edit Madas and István Monok, *A könyvkultúra Magyarországon a kezdetektől 1730-ig* (Book Culture in Hungary from the Beginnings to 1730) (Budapest: Balassi Kiadó, 1999), esp. 82–84.

their books and did not keep them in the monastic library. Thus, the historian who tries to reconstruct their book collections on the basis of the extant booklists is faced with serious difficulties, and will have to concentrate his research after all on the extant codices.

In spite of the methodological complications, and the meager information provided by the sources, some traces of a Central European monastic interest in magic can be tracked down. Among the positive examples one can mention the ample evidence for the considerable role that alchemy played in the life of certain monks (a question explored in detail in Chapter 5), and also a few manuscripts containing divinatory practices that once belonged to the Augustinians in Brno.[20] A bit more surprising perhaps, is a Bible found in the library of the Franciscans in Gyöngyös (Hungary) that betrays an interest in treasure hunting quite out of character for a mendicant order. On the blank pages of this printed Latin Bible, someone recorded an "*experimentum*," in fact, an incantation in Hungarian, sometime between 1529 and 1541. The addressee of this charm is no other than a divining rod, over which the operator first makes the sign of a cross, then orders and obliges it—in the name of God, the Father, the Son, and the Holy Spirit—not to become a "struggler" in what is asked from it, and to reveal the locations of all hidden treasures. It is further specifically commanded to point at neither iron, nor copper, nor tin, but only to gold, silver, and pure treasure. This is followed by a second, considerably shorter incantation, also in Hungarian, addressed to an arrow, instructing it to do the same thing.[21] Unfortunately, we cannot be sure whether this printed Bible was already in the possession of the Gyöngyös Franciscans when these texts were copied,[22] but the single fact that someone chose specifically a Bible for recording such methods is rather expressive about how charms and religious texts could have been associated in the minds of certain scribes.

Equally problematic is the origin of another source prepared during the same decades, the so-called *Peer Codex*.[23] Scattered in various places in that codex—which

---

20. Vladislav Dokoupil, *Catalogus codicum manu scriptorum bibliothecae Monasterii Eremitarum S. Augustini Vetero-Brunae* (Brno: Univerzitní knihovna, 1957), MS A 48, fols. 2r–70v (*Prognosticon*), fols. 71v–149r (*Practica geomantiae*). For a detailed overview of the Moravian monastic libraries whose collections can be found today in the Moravian Library of Brno, see Dokoupil, *Dejiny moravských klášterních knihoven* (History of the Moravian Monastic Libraries) (Brno: Univerzitní knihovna, 1972).

21. Gábor Döbrentei, ed., *Régi magyar nyelvemlékek* (Old Hungarian Sources), vol. 2 (Buda, 1840), 45–46; Éva Pócs, ed., *Magyar ráolvasások* (Hungarian Incantations), vol. 2 (Budapest: MTAK, 1986), 342–43; Ágnes Bolgár, ed., *Magyar bájoló imádságok a XV–XVI. századból* (Hungarian Incantations from the Fifteenth and Sixteenth Centuries) (Budapest, 1934), 19–21.

22. In fact, as a note in the binding seems to indicate, in the mid-sixteenth century the codex was probably in the possession of a certain Michael in Buda, and made its way to the Franciscan library some time before 1662.

23. *Peer-kódex: a nyelvemlék hasonmása és betűhű átirata* (The *Peer Codex*: The Facsimile and

consists mainly of pious texts, legends, prayers, hymns, and poems—we find shorter charms and exorcism formulas to protect their user against weapons and to arrest arrows in flight.[24] In one of these texts, divine names, such as *Elÿ, Elon, Tetragrammaton, Agla, Alpha et O* are also included.[25] Against epilepsy ("contra caducum morbum"), the book explains, a whole mass is to be celebrated over a piece of paper put on the altar and containing the following text-picture:

> *almagondis*
> *almagondi*
> *almagond*
> *Almagon*
> *Almago*
> *Almag*
> *Alm*
> *A*
> *Iesus*
> *In nomine patris et filij et spiritus sancti amen*
> *Iesus maria augustinus*
> [on the right side of the page, written upside down:]
> *A*
> *ab*
> *aba*
> *abar*
> *abarg*
> *abargu*
> *abargul*
> *abargula*
> *abargulan*
> *abargulans*[26]

The manuscript was most probably prepared in the circles of the Hungarian Pauline Order in the opening decades of the sixteenth century, and contains

---

Transcription of a Literary Monument), ed. Andrea Kacskovics-Reményi and Beatrix Oszkó (Budapest: Argumentum Kiadó, 2000).
24. Ibid., 250–78.
25. Ibid., 254–55.
26. Ibid., 740–41. For further medical charms in Hungarian, see Bolgár, *Magyar bájoló imádságok*. For the same in the European medical literature, see McVaugh, "Incantationes in Late Medieval Surgery." On the use of the text of the Mass for healing, see Olsan, "Appropriation of Liturgy" (see Chap. 5, n. 1).

therefore a rather strong indication on how seriously the monks took medical charms. However, just as in the case of the Gyöngyös Bible, this attribution is not unchallenged.[27]

Besides these singular and isolated examples, when neither the scribes nor the precise readership of the texts can be identified, there is basically one single monastic community in the region that shows a relatively coherent interest in learned magic,[28] the Augustinian monastery of Třeboň (Wittingau), in southern Bohemia, founded by the early Rožmberks in 1367.[29] This Bohemian aristocratic family was always generous with its monastic libraries as far as book donations were concerned. Reports indicate that since the mid-fourteenth century, the erudite members of the family had enriched their monasteries scattered all around South Bohemia, namely Český Krumlov, Zlatá Koruna, Písek, and first of all Třeboň, with manuscripts written and decorated in their own scriptoria.[30]

Among those Prague manuscripts that were surely in Třeboň in the fifteenth century, we have already mentioned the *Confundarius* (A Compilation, or A Mixture of Things) written and collected by Mattheus Beran, as containing the only long *Ars notoria* text in the region. Mattheus Beran was a medical doctor.[31] He was a member of the Augustinian monastery in Rudnicz (Roudnice) and educated at the universities of Paris, Vienna, and Erfurt. He became a medical doctor at some point before 1418, after which he returned to his monastery. Like John of Morigny, he was both a student and a monastic, and was explicitly interested in the notory art, but unlike John, he incorporated it openly in his medical manual. For reasons unknown to us, this manual went later to the cloister of Třeboň, and arrived finally at the private library of the Rožmberk family. It is difficult to say whether the *Flores aurei*, that is, the first section of the *Ars notoria* copied in the last part of the *Confundarius*, was consulted by the monks in any of these monasteries. What makes the case interesting, nevertheless, is that both Třeboň and Rudnicz were Augustinian cloisters, just like the Canterbury monastery, so it seems that the relatively

27. On the arguments concerning the history of the codex, see *Peer-kódex*, 15–18.
28. The present-day collection of the National Library of the Czech Republic (formerly the University Library in the Klementinum), the history of which starts with the foundation of Charles University in 1348, includes a considerable number of manuscripts that once belonged to the library of the Rožmberk family in Třeboň. Petr Voit, *Pražské Klementinum* (The Klementinum in Prague) (Prague: Národní knihovna, 1990); for the list of codices coming from Třeboň, see Truhlář 399–400.
29. Karl Bosl, ed., *Handbuch der Geschichte der Böhmischen Länder*, vol. 1 (Stuttgart: Anton Hiersemann, 1967), 444–49.
30. Jitka Šimáková, ed., *Castle Library of Český Krumlov* (Prague: Mezinárodní asociace bibliofil, 1995).
31. František Šmahel, "Mistři, licenciáti, bakaláři a studenti pražské lékařské fakulty do počátků husitské revoluce" (Masters, Licentiates, Bachelors, and Students of the Prague Medical Faculty until the Beginnings of the Hussite Revolution), *Acta Universitatis Carolinae, Historia Universitatis Carolinae Pragensis* 20–22 (1980): 35–68, esp. 39.

less rigorous Augustinian rules provided a more encouraging context for collecting magical texts than the stricter life of various other orders.

But Beran's codex is far more interesting than a simple book containing a copy of the *Ars notoria*. It is an anthology of useful tracts compiled and written by its owner. Beran repeatedly claims in various points of the codex that he collected the texts with considerable effort, carefully choosing them on the basis of their efficacy. In the *explicit* of the whole codex, at the end of the text of the *Ars memorativa*, he further adds that the selection and the copying were carried out through many years in many places from many exemplars, and his aim was to include the texts in one single book, the *Confundarium maius*.[32] He is so confident about the utility of the content of his book that in the beginning of his own lapidary text he even feels obliged to explain that when he had put this knowledge of stones into practice, it proved so effective that those who saw the result, believed it was genuine necromancy.[33]

The table of contents on the first page, which lists the titles in alphabetical order and gives their page numbers, reinforces the impression that he meant his codex to be used as a handbook. Finally, the practicability of the manual was also served by the fact that the compiler included the Czech translation of many Latin terms (for example, the name of herbs) in the margins, and also that he consistently arranged his inventories of stones, plants, trees, animals, and their influence on the health of men in alphabetical order.

The codex contains texts from different disciplines of the science of nature, most of them concentrating on medical issues. We find for example Beran's own *lapidarius* and *antidotarius*, texts on waters, herbs, urine, the pulse, poisons, letting blood, the vein from which it is let (including a drawing of a human body with the points indicating the appropriate places), the medical evaluation of all this method, and a calendar with prognostications and the appropriate time for specific medical activities. This overall medical interest includes astrological elements, too; we are provided with data on celestial bodies and their influence on men, as well as a calendar and various astronomical calculations. Discussion of the applicability of the flesh of animals, especially of snakes, is not missing either. In most cases it is hard to distinguish what he wrote himself from what he copied from other sources. Divination is not completely missing from this collection either; preceding the *Ars notoria*, for example, there is a *Chiromantia cum delineatione*

32. PNK I F 35, fol. 484r.: "Et hec breviter collecta sufficiant pro nostro Confundario supplendo, per me fratrem M. Ber. exulem canonicum regularem de Rudnic manu mea propria scripta per multa annorum tempora, per diversas terras et loca per varia et mira exemplaria ad laudem et gloriam Dei omnipotentis et Omnium Sanctorum et utilitatem omnium christianorum."
33. Ibid., fol. 43r. "Diversa legens hoc labore in uno collegi et expertus sum que dum operarer quia tam sublimis erat efficacie, quod videntes nigromancie ascribebant."

manuum with full-page, left (feminine) and right (masculine) hands indicating the major lines, and somewhat earlier we may admire a great and sophisticated *Sphera Pythagorae* (Plate 23). In several places we also find long lists of geomantic and other prognostic tables with the help of which various practical questions of the future can be answered.[34] The last twenty folios are reserved for texts that are not concerned any longer with the natural world and with the human body, but offer a certain "meta-science," the *Ars notoria* text explaining how all this knowledge can be learned, and the *Ars memorative* text on how it can be remembered and recalled when necessary. All in all, it was not too frequent in the Middle Ages that a manuscript contained such a coherently chosen selection of texts, forming a well-structured unity.[35]

Beran's codex is not the only evidence that Třeboň's library collected texts on astronomy, medicine, natural science, natural magic, and mnemotechnics: a set of scientific manuscripts was left to the monastery by one of its monks, Ulricus Crux of Telcz (Oldřich Kříž z Telče, 1435/40–1504).[36] He copied and collected a great number of works by Johannes Regiomontanus and Gerardus Cremonensis, on the computus, on calendars, and an anonymous *Ars memorativa*. Two of his codices, still in the library of Třeboň, contain an anonymous text on physiognomy, Pseudo-Aristotle's *Physiognomia* and the *Secreta mulierum* ascribed to Albertus Magnus, in the context of various historical and theological works, and some shorter tracts, among which we find one on a magic lamp that is supposed to be consecrated so that hidden treasure may be explored with its help (*De candela ad inveniendum thesaurum*), another one explaining how to use a cane for the same purpose (*Ad inveniendum thesaurum: De virgulis*), and furthermore a collection of alchemical truths excerpted from the writings of various philosophers (*Tractatus de alchimia excerpti plurimum philosophorum*—this last piece is inserted between tracts on agricultural questions, namely on bees and trees), and finally various practical recipes on alchemy, medicine, beer, and wine.[37] Ulricus Crux of Telcz was also interested

---

34. For example, fols. 13v–23r and fols. 420r–444r.

35. That this collection of texts was not the result of some copying coincidence but that of conscious selection is further attested to by another manuscript compiled by Beran, kept today in the Metropolitan Library of Prague, KMK N LIII (Podlaha 1577). The codex is an anthology of medical writings to which Beran added his own texts compiled on the basis of the books of many doctors (fols. 109r–280v and 281r–326v). The codex also contains a number of sermons, and—more important for our present interest—approximately forty folios, that is, one tenth of the whole book, is occupied by geomantic and other divinatory texts, including chiromancy and a sphere of life and death (fols. 56r–96v).

36. Among others, PNK XI C 8, I G 11a and XIII C 17. On Ulricus Crux de Telcz, see Pavel Spunar, "Vývoj autografu Oldřicha Kříže z Telče" (On the Development of the Autograph of Ulricus Crux de Telcz), *Listy filologické* 81 (1958): 220–26.

37. MS 6: A4, and 9: A7. See Jaroslav Weber, Josef Tříška, and Pavel Spunar, *Catalogus codicum manu scriptorum Trzebonae Crumloviique asservatorum* (Prague: Nakladatelství Československé Akademie věd, 1958), 29–52 and 63–94.

in the theological conflicts of religion, philosophy, and science: he listed errors condemned by various authorities of the medieval church. He copied a considerable selection of such condemnations in his manuscript: those of Étienne Tempier in 1277, the theological mistakes that "Wilhelm," the bishop of Paris (William of Auvergne), condemned, the articles condemned by Robert Kilwardby, and those censured in Paris in 1398.[38] Considering the wide range of themes that he copied, it would be misleading to conclude that Ulricus was particularly interested in science and magic; he was basically involved in every intellectual issue from medicine to theology, from natural magic to philosophy, and from alchemy to astronomy.

This list of manuscripts can be continued with a book already discussed in the chapter on image magic (PNK adlig. 14. H. 208). On the last eleven pages of the printed edition of Messahalah's (Nuremberg, 1504) and Ficino's (no year is given) works there is a concise handwritten selection of talismanic texts, among them, the *Liber de 15 stellis, herbis et lapidibus* of Hermes, Pseudo-Ptolemy's *Liber de lapidibus,* and finally the *De septem quadraturis planetarum,* which describes the effects and depicts the structure of the seven magic squares associated with the seven planets, and a set of spirits, which are applicable for all benign and destructive aims.[39] Although the book does not come from Třeboň, but from the library of the Franciscans in Krumlov, since the Krumlov monastery was also a usual beneficiary of the book donations of the Rožmberks, the codex adds one more piece of evidence characterizing the intellectual interests of the aristocratic family and its cloisters.

Unfortunately, the fifteenth-century history of the library (or libraries) of Třeboň and the Rožmberks is much more obscure than we would wish it to be. In the absence of further evidence we cannot even tell whether all the works we have listed characterize the interest of the donators, the Rožmberk family, or that of the monks in Třeboň, Krumlov, and Rudnicz. Apparently, we are very far from having such a detailed image as we had of the activity of the Canterbury monks; what information we have is not enough for even a rough reconstruction of the original picture.

To conclude this chapter, we can describe two ways in which magical literature arrives in a monastic library. The less frequent and more direct way is that of Benedictus, a monk who was himself formerly a practicing necromancer. He simply brought his demonic books (whether they include the *Liber visionum* or not) to the scene of his new life. The less direct but more frequent way is that of Mattheus Beran and Ulricus Crux of Telcz, monks who have the opportunity to travel and to consult codices in various other libraries. They copied a great many texts on a wide variety of topics, and among these texts they included works on magic. The difference between the two ways does not necessarily coincide with a difference in

---

38. Třeboň MS 6, fols. 198r–253v.
39. On the content of the text on the seven magic squares, see Chapter 3.

the genres of magic, that is, ritual magic texts may end up on a library by either route. While it is true in general that alchemy, natural, and image magic have a tendency to travel with medical and scientific texts on the natural world and that works of ritual magic usually occur alone or with other pieces of the same genre, there are exceptions to this rule. The case of Beran, for example, does not support this correlation: his *Ars notoria* appears in a simple medical context. So although it would be tempting to conclude that the arrival of ritual magic texts in a monastic library was usually more noticeable and raised certain anxiety about magic while other genres had more of a chance to be left unnoticed in the company of scientific texts, it seems that the patterns of copying and importing magical works are more complex.

8
Magic in the Courtly Context

The Queen, the Pope, and the Hangman

A curious parchment letter has survived in the binding of a Kraków manuscript. The author of the letter was the queen of Poland, Anna Cilly, wife of Wladislas Jagiello, its addressee the pope, John XXIII, and its date December 10, 1410. Queen Anna, probably responding to a letter of inquiry from Rome, explains the details of the case of a certain Nicholas who had been tried for and found guilty of necromancy by the Kraków city councilors. We learn that Nicholas had often taken part in the torturing and interrogating of criminals and had performed the executions: he was a hangman. Later on, however, he seems to have changed his profession and become a magician. As a layperson, he fell under the jurisdiction of the city council, but a Dominican inquisitor cooperating with the city authorities was also involved in the investigations. The queen furthermore informs us—or more precisely, the pope—that during the search in the house of Nicholas, they had found crystals and a mirror that he had supposedly used to foretell the future, and he had also had in his possession a book with talismans and seals in it. Nicholas's activities seem to involve two interesting themes: he was a hangman on the one hand, and convicted necromancer, as Anne had mentioned in her letter, on the other. His case is important also because this is the earliest proof for crystallomantic activity in Central Europe. From the letter it becomes obvious that Nicholas was not simply practicing magic in secret, but was a well-equipped magician with a rich inventory of texts and equipment for practicing image magic and crystallomancy.[1]

---

1. Dipl. BJ 610. On the letter of Queen Anna, preserved in the codex BJ 1934, see Zathey, "Per la storia," 104–5 (see Chap. 6, n. 10); for a reproduction of the letter itself, see ibid., figs. 3–4. See also Kowalczyk, "Wróżby, czary i zabobony," 14. The most recent and most detailed description of the case is given in Hanna Zaremska, *Niegodne rzemiosło: kat w społeczeństwie Polski 14–16 w.* (Undignified Craft: Hangmen in Polish Society from the Fourteenth to the Sixteenth Century) (Warsaw: PWN, 1986), 102–3. See also Ryszard Ganszyniec, "Krystalomancja" (Crystallomancy), *Lud* 41 (1954): 256–339.

But who was this Nicholas, accused of practicing necromancy and crystallomancy, who was such an intriguing personality that the queen had written a letter about him to the pope himself? As many of the details of his story are unknown, we cannot promise a definitive answer to this question. Yet, indirectly, we may be able to explore the circumstances of such an obscure case by surveying what learned magic had to do with royal courts, and what place books of magic occupied in royal book collections.

The royal court as a genuine place for magical practices and divination was already a central theme in the second book of John of Salisbury's *Policraticus* (1159). During his long career at various courts of the twelfth century, John had the opportunity personally to observe the temptation magic posed for the ambitious courtiers whose insecure life depended too much upon the quickly changing will of their *seigneurs,* and who in consequence often consulted magicians in order to learn their futures or turned to magic to further their careers.[2] Indeed, magic was always ready to offer the appropriate means: pleasing the king, gaining his benevolence, changing the attitude of one's lord, influencing the opinion of others, gaining the love of one's mistress, that is, all the objectives that a courtier may have wanted to reach, were among the usual motives that the basic texts of image magic promised to their readers. The permanent needs of the courtiers in these fields provided stable employment for court magicians. Not less decisive might have been the rulers' own desires: to foresee the outcome of complicated political conflicts, to reveal the hidden intentions of the subjects, or simply to know the most appropriate moment to establish a university were issues belonging to the competence and "research field" of a court astrologer or a personal magician.[3]

The next two sections focus on specific actors of the courtly life who can be viewed as magicians and divinators satisfying the needs listed above. This will be followed by an *excursus* on such cases when these magicians, such as Nicholas the Hangman, found themselves in front of a tribunal. The final section investigates the extent to which the book collections of royal libraries reflected the interests of rulers and courtiers in magic.

The King and the "Magician"

Learned magic was available in royal courts in the form of written texts in the libraries on the one hand, but it was also present in the activity of its practitioners,

---

2. C. I. Webb, ed., *Ioanis Saresberiensis episcopi Carnotensis Policratici* (Oxford: Clarendon Press, 1909), 49–169.

3. For a helpful overview on the topic, see Peters, *The Magician, The Witch, and the Law,* 46–57. For specific cases from the French court around the turn of the fourteenth century, see Veenstra, *Magic and Divination,* 59–96.

operators, and alleged and real authors, on the other. These personalities can be viewed—with serious reservations—as "magicians." Because of these reservations, whenever I use the term "magician," quotation marks are implied. The term thus constructed will not denote an obscure, black-clothed figure with a peaked cap who hung around royal courts invoking demons and telling futures, but rather a learned man whose political or scientific activity or literary production was in some way related to the topic of magic.

The interaction of the two actors, the sovereign and the magician, can be described in various ways, with the help of a wide variety of terms. The magician offers his intellectual service, for which he gets certain political power and influence, and he is bestowed with financial backing and protection. The scene has usually more than two actors; we have to take into account the group of courtiers who seek the same privileges, though perhaps by different means, and whose envy may turn them against the successful magician. The accusation—into which this envy might develop—offers itself as a solution to the problem on both a psychological and a political level: the success of the magician is obviously due to the secret, dangerous, and forbidden magical tools he uses to secure the king's good will. In many cases, magic appears only in the phase of the accusation; the high respect of a simple scientist or a court doctor can be easily undermined with the accusation of *maleficium* by the jealous opponents even if the doctor in question was never interested in this topic.

The history of Central Europe provides abundant examples of such cases. As an example of the magician offering his intellectual abilities to his sovereign, we have seen the case of the author of Wladislas's prayer book. One can only speculate about the influence such a learned man could have had at his disposal, a person who compiled a book of a most intimate and devotional nature for his king, a book which promised superhuman power to its reader. It is probably not an exaggeration to suppose that the knowledge possessed by such an individual might have seemed fairly precious for his lord. In other cases, the magician's intellectual contribution had not only religious but also political overtones: Melchior, the author of the alchemical Mass, the *Processus sub forma missae*, dedicated a book to his king that contained not only alchemical elements and liturgy but also exhortations against the military threat of the Turks.

Magic, when something went wrong, could cause the magician flee from the court. The alchemist John of Laz had to escape the wrath of the Empress Barbara, the reasons being precisely related to the practice of alchemy. Conrad Kyeser was also exiled. His intellectual services must have been as precious as those of the author of Wladislas's prayer book: his expertise in technology, medicine, and magic was unusual for his day. The great military handbook, which he dedicated to Ruprecht of Pfalz, was an important work, copied for several bibliophile rulers later on, including Sigismund and Matthias. The reasons why Kyeser had to leave the court where he enjoyed supposedly great respect were political: the changes that the future emperor, Sigismund, brought, who deposed his brother, Wenceslas, and who marked a new era in Prague. However, there might have been other reasons for Kyeser's dismissal. As his masterpiece, the *Bellifortis*, testifies at several points, Kyeser consciously played the role of the court magician. Besides the technical mechanisms, his handbook contains magical recipes, amulets, methods to cause the enemy to see visions, and devices against demonic activity. In one of the pictures he himself appears in a castle tower invoking spirits (Plate 4). Even the engines and machinery that he describes have a terrifying appearance, one looking like a marvelous cat, the other like a monster. In an epitaph composed for himself, his fate seems to anticipate that of Faust: his fame has shone forth everywhere, and his *Bellifortis* overcame whole armies, but as a price for his mastery in this science, his death will be most horrible, and he will be "cast down to Wrath."[4] The inspiring (although far from being proven) theory put forward by Eamon is nothing other than the idea that it was Kyeser himself who was responsible for his own expulsion. "Deliberately projecting an image of himself as a powerful sorcerer," he became the victim of this image, which could have been used against him in a politically motivated trial.[5] Proficiency in magic could have lead to royal appreciation at one point, and to banishment from the court at another.

In other cases, it was not any actual magical interest, but only rumors and gossip about alleged practices, that forced someone into the role of the magician. It was rather easy to accuse someone that he abused magic in order to gain political influence when there was no other visible reason why a simple, non-noble university doctor had advanced suddenly from obscurity to a high position in the political hierarchy. At the court of Emperor Wenceslas, there were two such cases, that of Conrad of Vechta and Albicus of Uniczow, two scientists who subsequently (and consecutively) became archbishops of Prague.

Conrad of Vechta (originally from Westphalia) appeared in the circles of King Wenceslas in 1395, in three years he became a member of the royal council, between 1401 and 1405 he was chancellor, after 1408 bishop of Olomouc, and finally in 1413 archbishop of Prague.[6] His swift ascent to a position of power and influence had caused considerable amazement and envy: contemporary political pamphlets suggested that Conrad's good reputation in the eyes of the king was simply due to

---

4. Kyeser, *Bellifortis*, fol. 137a. For a translation and discussion of this epitaph, see Eamon, "Technology as Magic," 186–94.
5. Eamon, *Science and the Secrets of Nature*, 68–69; Eamon, "Technology as Magic," 190.
6. Josef Krása, *Die Handschriften König Wencels IV* (Vienna: Forum, 1971), 60.

his alchemical and necromantic knowledge.[7] Probably it was a consequence of these rumors that Conrad appeared as the author of an alchemical recipe in a German alchemical handbook.[8]

Albicus of Uniczow (Albicus of Moravia), archbishop of Prague in 1411–12, had an even greater reputation as a magician than his successor. He was born around 1360, earned a master's degree from the Faculty of Arts of the University of Prague in 1386, and three years later further degrees both in law and medicine.[9] He advanced very quickly at the royal court, and earned the respect of two emperors: he became the personal physician of Wenceslas IV in 1404, and probably kept this position under Wenceslas's successor, Sigismund. When the previous archbishop died in 1411, and there was an urgent need for a successor, Albicus's appointment provoked some shock; nevertheless, he held the office for only a year.[10] A few years later, when Wenceslas died in 1419, Albicus left Prague and went to Buda, where he died in 1427.[11] His literary output is ample: he wrote a great variety of medical tracts, more than fifty health regimens, recipes, descriptions on illnesses and bodily problems, treatises on the plague, and so on.[12] His Latin and German writings were widespread in medieval handbooks; several of the manuscripts discussed in this book contain them,[13] and three of his works were even printed.

Albicus was involved in political intrigues, and his enemies were numerous. Among them, we find his own pupil, the famous court astrologer and future university rector, Christian of Prachatitz.[14] All in all, it is not surprising that Albicus was accused of a number of crimes: simony in order to earn the archiepiscopal position, avarice, and disqualification. Certain stories went as far as accusing him of practicing necromancy in the company of his king and protector. Although

---

7. F. M. Bartoš, *Čechy v dobe Husove* (Prague: Česke dějiny, 1947), 220, 232, and 470; Ivan Hlaváček, "Konrad von Vechta: Ein Niedersachse im spätmittelalterlichen Böhmen," *Beiträge zur Geschichte der Stadt Vechta* 1 (1974): 17.

8. British Library, MS Sloane 3457. See Chapter 4.

9. Walther Koerting, *Die deutsche Universität in Prag: Die letzten 100 Jahre ihrer medizinischen Fakultät* (Munich: Bayerische Landesärztekammer, 1968), 574. He was also in contact with the University of Óbuda, the second attempt to found a university in Hungary. See György Székely, "Hungarian Universities in the Middle Ages: The University of Óbuda," in *Studies on the History of the University of Óbuda 1395–1995* (Budapest: Eötvös University Press, 1995), 34, and Petr Svobodný, "Contacts between Bohemian and Hungarian Medical Faculties (14th–20th Centuries)," in Szögi and Varga, *Universitas Budensis*, 251–60.

10. A. Frind, *Geschichte der Bischöfe und Erzbischöfe von Prag* (Prague, 1873), 116.

11. Šmahel, "Mistři," 49. The most detailed study on Albicus is a doctoral dissertation (available in German libraries in manuscript form): Hans-Joachim Weitz, "Albich von Prag: Eine Untersuchung seiner Schriften" (Universität Heidelberg, 1971).

12. See Spunar, *Repertorium*, 1:103–15, and Weitz, "Albich von Prag," 23–39.

13. SLB N 100, fol. 161r; CLM 125, fol. 299r–v; BJ 774, fol. 61v–80v.

14. Weitz, "Albich von Prag," 57. Christian de Prachatitz was to become the court astrologer for Wenceslas IV.

these charges remained informal as long as Wenceslas was alive, the rumors might have forced Albicus to leave Prague after the king's death.[15] Interestingly, although he expressly opposed alchemy,[16] because he wrote recipes on the *aqua vitae*,[17] a subject which belonged rather to medicine than alchemy at the time, his posterity saw him as an alchemist.[18]

TREASURE HUNTING AND CRYSTALLOMANCY: THE CASE OF HENRY THE BOHEMIAN

From the legal action brought against Henry the Bohemian, a whole secret story of a circle of learned magicians emerges.[19] In 1429 in Kraków, Henry was accused of conjuring up demons, necromancy, and the propagation of Hussite ideas. Since this was not the first time he had brought to trial on such charges, his life was in serious danger, his execution a real possibility.

Henry was not an average personality of Polish history. "Magister Henricus genere Bohemus" (Master Henry from the Bohemian nation)—as Jan Długosz, the great Polish historian, reports—was a talented astronomer residing at the royal court of Wladislas Jagiello from 1423 to the autumn of 1427. He was held in high respect and was close to Queen Sophie. This is shown, *inter alia*, by the fact that he was allowed to be present at the births of the king's three sons and even cast their horoscopes.[20] In spite of this high esteem, in 1429 Henry was accused of Hussitism, using astrology and magic to find hidden treasure (apparently with demonic assistance), and possession of forbidden necromantic books.

15. Weitz, "Albich von Prag," 17.
16. Ibid., 29.
17. CLM 14526, fol. 138r; see also Weitz, "Albich von Prag," 58.
18. See, for example, Vladimír Kuncitr, "Alchemy in the Czech Lands," in *Opus Magnum* (Prague: Trigon, 1997), esp. 277.
19. BJ 2513 and BJ 2014. For Henry and his legal process, see also Zathey, "Per la storia," esp. 105–6; Aleksander Birkenmajer, "Sprawa Magistra Henryka Czecha" (The Case of Master Henry the Bohemian), *Collectanea Theologica* 17 (1936): 207–24; and Birkenmajer, "Henryk le Bohémien," in *Études d'histoire des sciences en Pologne*, 497–98 (this article is the French translation of Birkenmajer's contribution on Henry the Bohemian to the *Polski Słownik Biograficzny*, 9:419. For a reconstruction of the process and a critical edition of the *Consilia Stanislai de Scarbimiria contra astrologum Henricum Bohemum*, based on BJ 2014, fols. 120r–129v (ca. 1432), and BJ 2513, fols. 261r–269v (1435), see Stanisław Wielgus, "*Consilia* de Stanislas de Scarbimiria contre l'astrologue Henri Bohemus," *Studia Mediewistyczne* 25 (1988): 145–72. The Polish philosopher Andreas de Kokorzyn participated in and transcribed Henry's trial; his text survives in the two codices. On him, see Mieczysław Markowski, "Poglądy filozoficzne Andrzeja z Kokorzyna" (The Philosophical Opinions of Andreas de Kokorzyn), *Studia Mediewistyczne* 6 (1964): 55–136. On the whole case, see finally, Láng, "Angels Around the Crystal."
20. Johannis Długosz, "Annales seu cronicae incliti Regni Poloniae," in *Opera Omnia*, vol. 13 (Kraków, 1877), 349–50.

The court case was conducted by Stanislas of Skalbimierz (d. 1431). In his person, a rather important figure of the Polish Middle Ages undertook the duty of the investigations. He was the first rector of the renewed University of Kraków and a severe polemist in matters related to the Hussite movement. He had also participated at the Council of Constance, and he was—at the time of Henry's trial—the vicar-general of the archbishop of Kraków.[21] He was a most adequate person for this task, not only because of his proficiency in theological issues related to Hussitism, but also thanks to his competence in magical issues, primarily concerning popular practices.[22] In Henry's case, however, Stanislas was faced with a slightly different set of problems: instead of folk charms and spells, instead of agricultural magic and divination from the candle, instead of midwives and superstitious women who walked around their fields with crosses,[23] here he was faced with learned ritual magic and its usual inventory: necromantic books, magic circles, a crystal, and a young boy. He was in the position of handling Henry over to lay authorities as a heretic and irrecoverable backslider, which would have meant the end of the astrologer's life. However—as Stanislas diplomatically implied—the royal dynasty was also involved in the trial thanks to Henry's good standing at the court and his popularity in Kraków as an astrologer, and this protection saved his life: he was "only" imprisoned for life.[24]

---

21. Bożena Chmielkowska, "Stanislas de Skarbimierz—Le premier recteur de l'Université de Cracovie après le renouveaux de celle-ci," *Mediaevalia Philosophica Polonorum* 24 (1979): 73–112; see also Jerzy Wyrozumski, "L'Idée de la tolérance à l'Université de Cracovie," in *Société et l'Église: Textes et discussions dans les universités de l'Europe Centrale*, ed. Sophie Włodek (Turnhout: Brepols, 1995), 133–44.

22. Stanislas's sermons and theoretical treatises show a great interest in popular magical practices that violated the sanctity of the liturgy. He devoted one of his many sermons (*Magistris non inclinavi aurem meam*) to the question of superstitions, and he also advanced some original theological arguments against the popular practices of magic. It is significant that these arguments are not borrowed from Nicolaus Jawor's *De superstitionibus*, which was already a classic antimagical text by his time. See BJ 192, fols. 104r–106r; BJ 193, fols. 118v–121v; Kowalczyk, "Wróżby, czary i zabobony"; Bracha, *Teolog, diabeł i zabobony*; and Krzysztof Bracha, "Magie und Aberglaubenskritik in den Predigten des Spätmittelalters in Polen," in *Religion und Magie in Ostmitteleuropa (Spielräume theologischer Normierungsprozesse in Spätmittelalter und Frühe Neuzeit)*, ed. Thomas Wünsch (Berlin: LIT Verlag, 2006), 197–215.

23. On folk practices of these times mentioned in Polish and Bohemian theological discourse, see Bylina, "La prédication"; Stanisław Bylina, "Magie, sorcellerie et culture populaire en Pologne aux XVe et XVIe siècles," *Acta Ethnographica, A Periodical of the Hungarian Academy of Sciences* 37 (1991): 173–90; Bracha, *Teolog, diabeł i zabobony*; Krzysztof Bracha, "Katalog magii Rudolfa," in *Cystersi w społeczeństwie Europy Środkowej* (Poznan: Wydawnictwo Poznańskie, 2000), 806–20; Beata Wojciechowska, "Magic in Annual Rites in Late Medieval Poland," in Wünsch, *Religion und Magie in Ostmitteleuropa*, 225–38; and František Šmahel, "Stärker als der Glaube: Magie, Aberglaube und Zauber in der Epoche des Hussitismus," *Bohemia: Zeitschrift für Geschichte und Kultur der böhmischen Länder* 32 (1991): 316–37.

24. Wielgus, "*Consilia*," 147.

The indictment specifies that Henry attempted to search for treasures in the earth with demonic help.[25] He possessed forbidden books that contained heretical teachings and texts of diviners, astrologers, and sorcerers, among them divinatory procedures, invocations of demons, conjurations, interrogations, and consultations in order to find treasure and various hidden objects.[26] One of these books was written by a certain Matthias, a necromancer.[27] Unfortunately, neither the books nor this Matthias have as yet been identified.

A further source, a confession made by Henry the Bohemian, complements our picture with some new details. Here Henry admits that he invoked demons and searched for treasure with his companions in the garden of Zwierzyniec, the zoological garden of the Polish king. On the methods of how to conjure and bind demons, they found the instructions in necromantic books. In addition, they also practiced crystallomancy with the help of a young boy medium—again for the purpose of finding treasure.[28] Interestingly, the confession is the only source related to Henry where the child and the crystal appear: they were not mentioned in Stanislas of Skalbimierz's report on the trial.

The sources inform us that Henry had not performed this magic alone, and even name three of his companions.[29] One of them was Monaldus de Luca, an Italian

---

25. "Quidam astrologus, vehementer de haeresi suspectus, generaliter omnem haeresim abiuravit; qui tamen, post abiurationem in iudicio in debita forma factam, maleficis invocantibus daemonia pro inveniendis thesauris in terra defossis per astra ad eosdem inveniendos indicavit, custodemque socii, sperans se fieri lucri participem, se fecit, bisque maleficiis illorum, qui daemonia invocabant, ut occultos thesauros invenirent, interfuit." BJ 2014, fol. 120r; Wielgus, "*Consilia,*" 153.

26. "Quartus articulus, quod post promulgacionem sentencie episcopi et inquisitoris libros hereticos et magicos non manifestasti nec restituisti." BJ 2513, fols. 272r–278r.; Birkenmajer, "Sprawa Magistra Henryka Czecha," 221. "Librosque tam continentes haereses, quam artes magicas aut alias divinaciones vel invocaciones demonum." BJ 2513, fol. 261r; Birkenmajer, "Sprawa Magistra Henryka Czecha," 210; BJ 2014, fol. 120r; Wielgus, "*Consilia,*" 154. "Necnon variae et multiplices daemonum invocationes, coniurationes, interrogationes et consultationes pro thesauris et aliis occultis inveniendis et diversi errores divinationum, astrologorum et sortilegorum." BJ 2014, fol. 125r; Wielgus, "*Consilia,*" 163.

27. "Nonnullos cartas et libellos cuiusdam Mathie nigromantici clam in quodam hospicio receptos." BJ 2513, fol. 261r; Birkenmajer, "Sprawa Magistra Henryka Czecha," 210; BJ 2014, fol. 120r; Wielgus, "*Consilia,*" 154.

28. "Nam ex confessione tua habetur, quod presens fuisti, cum in Kazimiria quidam negromanticus Stanislaus sedente quodam iuvene et inspiciente cristallum demones invocabat et coniurabat et responsa eorum inquirebat pro thesauris occultis in terra defossis inveniendis. Et postea in nocte ultra Zwierzyniec presens fuisti dum nigromantici similiter per nigromanciam demones adiurabant, invocabant et coniurabant, pro eidem thesauris inveniendis, et vidisti bene iuvenem sedentem et in cristallum inspicientem sed tunc invocaciones nigromanticorum non adiuvisti, quia in alia parte stetisti custodiendo, ne aliqui de villa venientes impedirent fodientes thesauros in terra quorum tu partem habere voluisti, prout habetur ex tua confessione. Scivisti eciam in libellis dicti nigromantici contineri adiuraciones, per quas demon esset compellendus ad ostendendum thesauros absconditos, prout habetur ex tua recognicione." BJ 2014, fol. 138; quoted in Zathey, "Per la storia," 105.

29. "Quis dicet"—writes Stanislaus—"hanc frequentationem non in uno, sed in pluribus, ad minus in duobus locis (quia coram teste certo et certis familiaribus magistri Nicolaus Hinczonis ac

who was a professor at the University of Kraków who specialized in, among other things, mining and minting.[30] He was a friend of the family that produced the famous Martin Bylica of Olkusz, the court astrologer of King Matthias of Hungary.[31] His medical recipes and his short treatise on the plague have been preserved in a codex of the Jagiellonan Library.[32] The second companion was Nicolaus Hinczonis, originally from Kazimierz, a quarter of present-day Kraków, who was also a master of the University of Kraków: he earned his master's degree in 1403, he was elected as rector in the winter of 1412, and he died around 1434.[33] Finally, a last person is mentioned in the confession of Henry, a certain Stanislas, who also participated in the treasure hunts; he can be probably identified with Stanislas Johannis of Casimiria, who was a student in Kraków in 1408, and later a schoolmaster in Kazimierz.[34]

In short, three university masters were involved in magical activities together with Henry the Bohemian. It is logical to ask now whether he himself was a university person. Henry appears both in the *Annales* of Długosz and in the official sentence of his legal case as "Magister Henricus de Brega, vocatus astrologus, laicus."

---

magistro Monaldo et quibusdam suis consociis) maxime iunctis aliis suspicionibus, esse modicam sive levem suspicionem, cum simplices ad credulitatem vel idiote seu minus eruditi scandalizari poterant vel infirmari in fide?" BJ 2513, fol. 266v; Birkenmajer, "Sprawa Magistra Henryka Czecha," 214; BJ 2014, fol. 126v; Wielgus, "*Consilia*," 166.

30. His name occurs in the list of the Kraków professors, but his subject is not indicated. Pauly, Ulanowski, and Chmiel, *Album studiosorum*, 1:6. Monaldus appears also in the list of the medical doctors of the university ("Hii sunt doctores et magistri," BJ 258, fols. 130r–131v). For a published version of this text, see Mieczysław Markowski, "Les manuscrits des listes de docteurs en médecine à l'Université de Cracovie entre 1400 et 1611," *Mediaevalia Philosophica Polonorum* 20 (1974): 121–40; for Magister Monaldus medicus, see 137.

31. Jerzy Zathey, "Marcin Bylica of Olkusz," in Gierowski, *Cracow Circle*, esp. 79–80.

32. Monaldus de Luca, *Medicinalia praecepta*, in BJ 792, fols. 33r–42r; Monaldus de Luca, *De pestilentia*, in BJ 849, fols. 161r–162v. He is also mentioned as a victim of a robbery. Concerning the trial of the robber, see Karl August Fink, ed., *Repertorium Germanicum. Verzeichnis der in Päpstlichen Registern und Kameralakten vorkommenden Personen* (Berlin: Weidmannsche Verlagsbuchhandlung, 1957), vol. 4, pt. 2, pp. 1417–31, col. 1876. On Monaldus's earlier life and conflict with the law, see Jan Ptaśnik, ed., *Cracovia Artificum, 1300–1500* (Kraków, 1974), 24.

33. See Antoni Gąsiorowski, ed., *Liber promotionum facultatis artium in universitate cracoviensi saeculi decimi quinti* (Kraków: Nakładem Polskiej Akademii Umiejętności, 2000), 8, and Maria Kowalczyk, "Mikołaj Hinczowicz z Kazimierza" (Nicolaus Hinczonis of Kazimierz), *Polski Słownik Biograficzny*, 21:113–14. Jerzy Zathey raised the idea that this Nicolaus Hinczonis may have been the Nicholas accused of necromancy about whom Anna Cilli wrote in her letter to the pope. See Zathey, "Per la storia," 104. Indeed, the fact that both persons are mentioned as participating in crystallomantic practices in Kraków in more or less the same period argues that they were the same person; however, the first Nicholas was a *tortor*, a marginal figure who tortured prisoners and performed executions, whereas Nicolaus Hinczonis was a university master. This difference undermines Zathey's theory considerably. See Zaremska, *Niegodne rzemiosło*, 102–3.

34. BJ 2014, fol. 138; quoted in Zathey, "Per la storia," 105. On Stanislas Johannis of Casimiria, see also Pauly, Ulanowski, and Chmiel, *Album studiosorum*, 1:27.

The title *magister* implies that he did indeed have a university background. However, Henry is not mentioned either in the *Album studiosorum* or in the *Liber promotionum* of the University of Kraków, and even Stanislaus of Skalbimierz implies that Henry was not actually a *magister*.[35] Whether he brought his title from Prague is dubious and depends greatly upon which of the many astronomers of Bohemian history called Henricus he might have been.[36] Since there is no consensus on this question, we can only claim that at least three, but possibly four, persons in this company of magicians had university educations.

Henry's crystal-gazing and treasure-hunting methods, as well as his books, indicate an expertise in magic as elaborate as, and in many respects similar to, that which we find in the prayer book of Wladislas (see Chapter 6). These two examples of Polish crystallomancy are strikingly close to each other in time. Thus it remains now to examine whether there is any evidence supporting our earlier conjecture that Henry was the author of Wladislas's prayer book.

First of all, we should remember that King Wladislas Warnenczyk, whom we have identified as a possible owner of the prayer book, was one of the three princes whose birth Henry had attended. We furthermore see that at the end of his trial Henry avoided capital punishment, and even though he was finally jailed, somewhat later he managed to leave prison, and lived freely in Kraków.[37] In the *Acta Officialia Cracoviensis* several notes report that *Henricus Bohemus astronomus* was alive in 1440.[38] It seems that he did not give up his magical interest completely: Johannes of Dobra, a medical doctor, reports in one of his medical handbooks that Henricus Bohemus talked to him about an Armenian who lived for four hundred years thanks to a special medicine.[39]

Being experienced in the field of crystallomancy, possessing books of magical content, a good friend of King Wladislas, and living freely in the early 1440s, Henry the Bohemian could easily have been commissioned to produce a special prayer book on an omniscient crystal and on "clarifying" angels in order to satisfy the "magico-devotional" purposes of the king. Taking into consideration the fact that the extant text of the prayer book was written in the 1430s or 1440s, one could even reverse the question: who else, experienced enough in these fields, could have

---

35. Wielgus, "*Consilia*," 149; for the text, see 166. In the text Stanislas mentions that Henry "magister est, ut asserit, in artibus."

36. For the possibilities, see Birkenmajer, "Sprawa Magistra Henryka Czecha," 222, and Wielgus, "*Consilia*," 149.

37. Kowalczyk, "Przyczynki."

38. Bolesław Przybyszewski, ed., *Cracovia artificum*, vol. 1 (Wrocław: Zakład Narodowy im. Ossolińskich, 1985), 91–92; Przybyszewski, ed., *Cracovia artificum*, supplementa 2 (Wrocław: Zakład Narodowy im. Ossolińskich, 1988), 119, 120, and 127.

39. BJ 778, fol. IIIv. This example was already quoted in Chapter 2. See also Kowalczyk, "Przyczynki," 88.

been commissioned for this task when Henry was at court? Even though the author cannot be identified with complete certainty, at the moment Henry the Bohemian is the most plausible contender for this role. He was a most learned man in medieval magic: he possessed the texts of the *Ars notoria* and the *Liber visionum* and had a close acquaintance with crystals. What is more, his interest was apparently not limited to the field of theory: he and his friends put their magical knowledge into practice as well.

Excursus: The Criminalization of Learned Magic

Courtrooms and prisons were certainly among the places where magicians could be found in the Middle Ages. Imprisonment and execution were real dangers threatening those interested in magical practices. One of the most paradigmatic instances for the condemnation and execution of an intellectual involved in learned magic in Western Europe was the famous case of Cecco d'Ascoli. Cecco d'Ascoli was a university master and an astrologer burned at the stake by the Inquisition in Florence in 1327.[40] As his commentary to the otherwise strictly cosmographical and astronomical *Sphera* by Sacrobosco shows, he was seriously interested in various fields of image magic and astral necromancy; his knowledge testifies to a deep acquaintance with books of magic.[41] Although it sounds logical that Cecco's magical interests were responsible for his execution, the real reasons of his prosecution are still unknown. Executing a university professor, however much he had been interested in learned magic and judicial astrology, and even if he went as far as casting Christ's horoscope, was rather exceptional at the time. Political reasons and struggles for courtly influence, or simply personal conflicts, may have also accounted for his somber end. Cecco's magical teachings might have been among the reasons indeed, but they were certainly not the only ones. If magic or astrology alone had been enough, not many astrologers would have avoided capital punishment in the Middle Ages, and his example would not be so exceptional. The main moral of the case of Cecco d'Ascoli for our present investigations is that the relationship between the condemnation of someone and the magic that he practiced is far more complicated than a simple causal nexus.

The mechanism of criminalization, the relationship of the practice of magic and its prosecution, was no less complex in Central Europe. At first glance, nevertheless, it might seem that there are in fact no complications in this issue: possessing

---

40. On Cecco d'Ascoli, see *HMES*, 2:948–68; Stephano Caroti, *L'astrologia in Italia* (Rome: Newton Compton, 1983), 206–8; WP 398–406, and Nicolas Weill-Parot, "I demoni della Sfera: La 'nigromanzia' cosmologico-astrologica di cecco d'Ascoli" in Antonio Rigon, ed. Cecco d'Ascoli: Cultura scienza e politica nell' Italia del Trecento. (Roma: Istituto storico italiano per il medio eva, 2007) 105–128.
41. Lynn Thorndike, *The "Sphere of Sacrobosco" and Its Commentators* (Chicago: Chicago University Press, 1949).

books of magical content and putting this content into practice led directly and necessarily to trial and imprisonment, if not to execution. A number of examples seem to support this opinion. First of all, Henry the Bohemian was found guilty of possessing necromantic books and looking for treasure with a boy medium, and he was thus imprisoned. Second, Nicholas the Hangman had a whole arsenal of magical tools and books, and as a result he too had to stand trial. Third, Conrad Kyeser was interested in (and perhaps practiced) certain kinds of magic, and—probably because of this—he had to leave the Imperial court and go into exile.

To this fairly consistent list, we can add one more university professor, Paulus de Praga or Paul the Jew. In the early modern times, Paul had the fame of a magician, he was considered to have been in contact with the Devil, and his life was associated with the Faust legend.[42] What we actually know about him is that he obtained a doctor's degree from the University of Padua in medicine, and before he came to lecture in Kraków in 1451, he had taught at several other universities, and had spent some time in Bohemia as a gynecologist. He was finally imprisoned in the bishop's jail in Kraków, where (or slightly after which) he wrote his famous compendium, an extensive encyclopedic handbook, the *Liber viginti artium* (The Book of the Twenty Arts). This book was even more notorious than its author; it was often called the *Book of Twardowski*—after the diabolical figure of that name in Polish myth. It was, reportedly, either locked away in a separate chamber in Vilnius chained to the wall, or—as other reports claim—hidden under a pavement stone so that nobody could read it. It was also believed to bear the trace of the Devil's touch. Indeed, with minor philological research we can discover the black spots on folio 151r in the surviving codex, which gave ample opportunity for speculations.[43]

Taking all these cases into consideration, it does not seem too hasty to conclude that practicing magic had legal consequences. To confirm this argument, we can also compare these cases to cases in Western Europe involving treasure hunting, crystallomancy, the invocation of demons, and the possession of magical books.

A little-known English text on crystal scrying resembles documents from the case of Henry the Bohemian so closely that it could have been copied from a Polish original. The text is again a confession, this time made by William Byg, alias

---

42. Josephus Muczkowski, *Pauli Paulirini olim Paulus de Praga vocati viginti artium manuscriptum librum cuius codex Twardovio vulgo tribuitus descripsit vitamque auctoris adjecit* (Kraków, 1835); Josef Reiss, "Das Twardowski-Buch: Opus magicum des polnischen Faust," *Germanoslavica* 2 (1933): 90–101; Zathey, "Marcin Bylica of Olkusz," esp. 86–87. See also Roman Bugaj, *Nauki tajemne w Polsce w dobie odrodzenia* (Secret Sciences in Poland in the Renaissance) (Wrocław: Ossolineum, 1976), 157–61.

43. Paulus de Praga, *Liber viginti artium*, in BJ 257. Also see Zathey, *Historia Biblioteki Jagiellońskiej*, 1:121–22, and Alena Hadravova, ed., *Paulerinus (Pavel Žídek) "Liber viginti artium"* (f. 185ra–190rb) (Prague: KLP, 1997).

Lech.[44] This magician arrived in South Yorkshire in 1465, and for the following two or three years he lived on recovering stolen property with the help of a crystal. As his fame grew, he was soon standing before the vicar-general of the archbishop of York accused of heresy—just as Henry was accused by the vicar-general of the archbishop of Kraków, Stanislas of Skalbimierz. In his confession made in front of the Commissary Poteman in 1467, William Byg admitted how he had performed his practices with the help of a sixteen-year-old boy, with a crystal stone, and through prayers to Christ and the angels.[45] As a result of all the preparations, the boy could see one or two angels thus invoked appearing in the crystal, and these angels were willing to answer questions about the location of numerous precious stolen properties belonging to various noblemen.[46] The question to be asked of the conjured angel is spelled in English in the otherwise Latin confession: "Say me trewe, chylde, what man, what woman, or what childe hase stolne yis thyng, and shewe me thing in his hand." Like the confession of Henry the Bohemian, this text also ends with a statement that all these methods were learned from magical handbooks, and that the angels appeared while reading these books.[47]

Confessing all the experiments he had done, William finally avoided being executed and was merely forced to walk around with a torch in his right hand and a rod in his left with his books dangling from it. Inscriptions were also attached to his body announcing that he was a *sortilegus* and an *invocator spirituum*. He was also required to secure his abjuration of magic by throwing his books into the flames. This embarrassing but relatively moderate punishment was probably due to the fact that some noblemen of the area were also involved in Byg's practices. As in Henry's case, the magician avoided his well-deserved death thanks to his aristocrat protectors.

A fairly analogous picture of crystallomantic procedures involving a similar magical apparatus emerges from the documentation of a somewhat earlier legal proceeding against a real or alleged magician; this is the well-known and often cited

---

44. For the background of this case, see James Raine, "Divination in the Fifteenth Century by the Aid of a Magical Crystal," *Archaeological Journal* 13 (1856): 372–74.

45. For the text of the confession of William Byg, see ibid., 373–74: "Et dicit interogatus quod cencies, a tempore quo ipse primo pervenit ad villam de Wombewell, ad reducendum bona furtive, artem que sequitur occupavit, viz. primo juvenem quemdam annorum etatis citra xij usitavit statuere super scabellum coram ipso Willelmo, et in manu pueri sive juvenis hujusmodi posuit, ut dicit, unum lapidem cristallum, ipsum cogendo dicere Pater Noster, Ave et Credo."

46. "Et tunc, ut dicit, fecit juvenem hujusmodi prospicere in lapidem, et petiit ab eo quid viderit, . . . juvenis hujusmodi vidit in lapide praedicto bona subtracta et quandoque subtractores bonorum in eodem lapide, et quandoque unum angelum, et quandoque duos angelos, et nunquam ultra, etc." Ibid.

47. "Et dicit quod premissam artem didicit a quodam Arthuro Mitton a Leycistre, circiter annos tres ultra elapsos, sed habuit libros suos apud Greynwiche cito post mortem ducis quondam Gloucestre in camera ejusdem apud Greynwich, et dicit quod credit firmiter angelos predictos cicius apparuisse per lecturam suam super libros predictos." Ibid., 374.

case of Jean de Bar.⁴⁸ From Jean de Bar's famous confession of 1398 (again a confession!), we learn that he consecrated a crystal stone in order to trap a devil in it, whom he mistook for a benign angel, and during these events a child was also present.⁴⁹ While Henry the Bohemian performed his invocations in the royal zoological garden of Kraków, Jean chose the Bois de Brie as a site for his secret practices. He describes the ritual components of his practices in great detail: how he (ab)used the elements of Christian liturgy (wearing consecrated clothes, singing the Mass), and how he applied figures, characters, images, the holy names of God, and foreign words (*estranges paroles*) during the invocations.⁵⁰ These latter elements—especially the strange, unfamiliar words, the *verba ignota*—may imply that the confessor had used magical texts belonging to the genre of the *Ars notoria*. The demons invoked through these rituals enter a consecrated mirror later on, and tell the operator all the secrets and answer honestly whatever is asked from them,⁵¹ just as the angels in the prayer book of Wladislas do. Finally, like Henry and William, Jean speaks about his magical books: "En mes livres sont plusieurs erreurs contre nostre foy, comme dire que aucuns dyables soient bons et benign, aucuns tous puissans et tout saichant, aucuns n'en enfer, n'en paradis, et que bons angelz ont revelé teles sciences et que les sains prophetes et autres ont fait les miracles et dit leurs prophecies par telz arts."⁵² It is worth pausing for a moment with the eventful history of the books collected by these two magician-owners: William Byg left his codices to the library of the late Humphrey, duke of Gloucester (d. 1446), who was himself suspected of an interest in magic, and whose collection formed the main core of the Bodleian,⁵³ while it is highly possible that Jean de Bar's handbooks of ritual magic were confiscated by the library of King Charles VI.⁵⁴ To put it shortly: noblemen, kings, and ultimately university libraries inherited the written inventory of condemned magicians.

Having arrived at this point in this comparative analysis, we are sorely tempted

---

48. From the vast literature available, see, for example, Veenstra, "The Confession of Master Jehan de Bar," and Boudet, "Les Condamnations de la magie."

49. "J'ay conjuré ou consacré une pierre de cristal pour y enclore un dyable que je cuidoye estre bon angel. Et disoit un petit enfent qu'il voeit une figure d'evesque qui signoit les choses que je vouloye consacrer." Veenstra, "The Confession of Master Jehan de Bar," 352.

50. "J'ay usé de vestements conjurés tandis que on chantoit messe, et fait user prestres en invocant dyables. Et estoient plusieurs figures et caracteres et estranges paroles, la estoient avec ce bonnes paroles des euvangiles, de sains et sainctes et leurs ymages . . . et mesprisement des sains noms de Dieu et des sains et sainctes." Ibid.

51. "J'ay voulu par plusieurs foiz consacrer aucuns miroirs d'acier a certains dyables et creoie que ilz deüssent entrer dedens et reveler les choses secretes et respondre a ce que on leurs demanderoit veritablement et sans decevoir. Et pour venir a ceste j'ay fais invocacions de dyables, fais cercles, figures, espees, vestements, et autres choses abhominable et deffendues et contre nostre foy." Ibid., 353.

52. Ibid., 354.
53. Raine, "Divination in the Fifteenth Century," 372.
54. Boudet, "Les Condamnations de la magie," 14.

to claim with utmost confidence that possessing magical books and following their instructions led necessarily to condemnation in the Middle Ages, both in Western and in Central Europe. But let us not yield to this temptation so easily!

As scholars dealing with these issues have pointed out, both Jean's and Henry's cases are far more complicated than simple condemnations of simple magicians. As for Jean de Bar, in the same year when he confessed his errors, the Faculty of Theology of the University of Paris issued twenty-eight articles on condemned magical arts,[55] which correspond structurally, thematically, and occasionally even word for word to the declared sins of Jean de Bar.[56] Among these condemned superstitious beliefs and activities, we find virtually all the elements confessed to by the magician: the conviction that demons may be good, benign, and omniscient; that God constrains demons through the art of magic; the use and consecration of rings, magic mirrors, books, and clothes; the charting of figures on given days and at given hours; the use of the blood of the hoopoe; and the proclamation that the use of magic is good.

Were these articles inspired by the trial? Was the confession inspired by the articles? What was the role of Jean Gerson, the chancellor of the university, in the accusations, who inserted some years later the whole list of the condemned articles in his *De erroribus circa artem magicam* (The Errors Concerning the Art of Magic),[57] and whose codex contains the only extant copy of Jean de Bar's confession?[58] Gerson's role is still under research, but it seems that Jean de Bar's condemnation was a result of a very complicated political situation.[59] While Henry the Bohemian and William Byg survived the legal process thanks to their influential connections, Jean de Bar—perhaps because he was *too* influential at the royal court—was executed. His case was not the only one prosecuted against magicians in Paris in those years, and apparently his confession was influenced by many other factors besides his actual crystallomantic practices.

Similar complications arise in the Central European cases. It would be most reasonable to suggest that the practice of magic was the main reason for Kyeser's dismissal from the court and Paul of Prague's imprisonment. However, when we examine these examples more closely, we see that unless we enter into adventurous conjectures and plausible but unfounded speculations, we cannot establish such

---

55. For the text, see Denifle and Chatelain, *Chartularium Universitatis Parisiensis*, 4:32–35 (see Chap. 1, n. 21). For an English translation, see Thorndike, *University Records*, 260–66 (see "In Search of Magician Schools," n. 10). For a new, critical edition, see Boudet, "Les Condamnations de la magie," 27–31.

56. This parallel was discovered by Jan Veenstra and Jean-Patrice Boudet simultaneously.

57. Gerson, "De erroribus circa artem magicam."

58. BnF lat. 22552, fols. 313r–315v.

59. For a discussion of this issue, see Veenstra, "The Confession of Master Jehan de Bar," 350, and Boudet, "Les Condamnations de la magie."

causal connections with confidence. Paul's codex of the *Liber viginti artium*, which has come down to us, is no more than a general encyclopedia, incorporating a mixture of medieval and new scientific knowledge, including grammar, medicine, and music. For those readers who are inspired by the wicked fate of the book, its contents will be fairly disappointing; it does not involve any special magical matter. Considering the strong conviction about Paul's contact with black magic, it is fairly plausible that there were originally two books, the surviving one containing the description of sciences in alphabetical order, and another one which provoked the bad rumors. But it is even more plausible to suppose that there was no other codex at all, and the stories about it were forged later. As the written sources mentioning the magical fame of the codex and its author are not contemporary, but date from as late as the eighteenth century, Paul's imprisonment might have had nothing to do with magic at all, and everything to do with political or personal conflicts.[60]

We have even less grounds to examine the mechanism of criminalization in the cases of Conrad of Vechta and Albicus of Uniczow, since there is no record that formal charges were ever brought against either of them. These accusations—as we have seen—remained on the level of slander and innuendo.

The accusation and rumor of magic as a means for getting rid of rivals in courtly conflicts had considerable future in Central European courts. Erotic magic may have seemed especially useful for undermining the political influence of a female protagonist.[61] Queen Beatrix of Hungary accused a woman called Borbála—who just happened to be the lover of Beatrix's husband, King Matthias, and the mother of the king's natural son, John of Corvin—of bewitching her in order to make her barren.[62] The king managed to smooth down the quarrel, but somewhat later, interestingly, the rumors spread by the queen came back to haunt her. Her claim to have been rendered incapable of bearing children gave the next king, Wladislas II, an excuse not to marry her. In the sixteenth-century history of the Polish kings, there are three cases—all related to Augustine Sigismund (1520–72)—of royal lovers and queens being accused of using love potions and poisons, abusing their womanly and political influence on the king, and practicing love magic.[63] Thanks to their

---

60. Reiss, "Das Twardowski-Buch." The argument that two books might have existed was made already in the eighteenth century. See ibid., 91.

61. For a general discussion, see Kieckhefer, "Erotic Magic."

62. Ágnes Ritoókné Szalai, "Borbála" (Barbara), in *Ámor, álom és mámor: a szerelem a régi magyar irodalomban és a szerelem ezredéves hazai kultúrtörténete*, ed. Géza Szentmártoni Szabó (Amor, Dream and Inebriety: Love in the Old Hungarian Literature and the Millennial Vernacular Cultural History of Love) (Budapest: Universitas Kiadó, 2002), 369–84.

63. See Anna Brzezinska, "Political Significance of Love Magic Accusations at the Jagiellonian Court" (master's thesis, Central European University, 1995), and Brzezinska, "Female Control of Dynastic Politics in Sixteenth-Century Poland," in *The Man of Many Devices, Who Wandered Full Many Ways—: Festschrift in Honor of János M. Bak*, ed. Balázs Nagy and Marcell Sebők (Budapest: CEU Press, 1999), 187–94.

privileged position, these ladies were invulnerable, so the best tools to destroy their good fame and to stigmatize them were plots and gossip. All these developments constitute important chapters in the history of the criminalization of magic, they are not, however, very informative about the actual practice of magic in royal environments, since they follow rather the logic of courtly plots and intrigues.

The case of Henry the Bohemian provide more details and better insight into the role magic played in the course of a condemnation, and yet the complications are still there. Did Henry really perform crystallomantic treasure hunts, or should we rather suspect that the mention of necromantic books and the invocation of demons in the accusations served mere argumentative purposes? Were they not simply means of stigmatizing him and some further suspicious figures and university persons of Kraków?

A careful reading of the sources shows that we should not be that skeptical. Henry's magical practices played only a secondary role in his condemnation; the judges did not need the charge of necromancy to inflate the indictment: Hussitism was quite enough.[64] Stanislas of Skalbimierz put more emphasis on Henry's contacts with Hussite thought; magic is left in the background, and he explicitly specified that Hussitism was the main reason behind the sentence. Of course, he discussed magic as well, and going through a detailed argumentation, referring to the Bible, Aristotle, Augustine, Aquinas, Albertus Magnus, Pope John XXII, and various further authorities, Stanislas concluded that invoking demons in order to find hidden treasure is a heretical activity. It seems that the accusations had some real foundation, and Henry had indeed put his knowledge of crystallomancy and the invocation of spirits into actual practice. To be sure, we cannot rule out categorically that the trial was a result of a conflict among the various political powers, in which an astrologer's freedom was sacrificed on the altar of the fight for courtly influence; however, it is more probable that magic was not a major concern for the judges and that we should view the case as a regular condemnation of someone involved in the teachings of the Hussite movement who was actually also a magician.

This is not to deny that the practice of magic *was* a crime in late medieval Kraków just as it was elsewhere. Even though it played a secondary role in Henry's case, we have seen, for example, that in the case of Nicholas the Hangman, who was not in such a good position, magic was treated as a criminal activity, and that the mere possession of magical handbooks, crystals, and mirrors was enough to indict him. Still, while magic was criminalized both in Central and Western Europe, there seem to have been differences in the extent of its condemnations.

In Paris, magical handbooks accessible for the students interested in the field were already a major worry for William of Auvergne. William, himself a former

---

64. Birkenmajer, "Sprawa Magistra Henryka Czecha," 221; Wielgus, "*Consilia*," 147.

student and a master in Paris, writes in his *De legibus* that he himself had a look in *libris magorum atque maleficiorum* in his youth.[65] The availability of these books provoked serious concern on the part of the authorities in the following centuries; the prologue of the famous condemnations of Etienne Tempier in 1277 explicitly mentions a book of geomancy and books and booklets containing texts on necromancy, the invocation of demons, and conjurations.[66] While magic played a relatively minor role in the 219 condemned articles in 1277, in 1398—as we have just seen—it became a major concern, being the subject of 28 condemned articles issued by the same university. In the following three decades, the chancellor of the university, Jean Gerson, dedicated a series of treatises to the problem of magic, divination, medical astrology, judicial astrology, medical amulets, lullism, and similar topics. Around the year 1400, magic caused no little disquiet in theological circles.[67] On German soil, Johannes of Francofordia, Nicolaus Jawor, and Henricus of Gorkum all dedicated theoretical works to the question of popular superstitions, the issue of demons, and that of magical practices.[68] While all these decisions and treatises were being produced, the royal court of France saw a number of executions of alleged and real magicians, one of whom was Jean de Bar.[69]

Generally speaking, in comparison with the Western developments, less emphasis seems to have been laid on the criminal nature of magic in Central Europe, and condemning learned magic had a more modest tradition in this region. In the history of the universities of Central Europe, no list of condemned magical practices and books was issued: in the absence of sources, we cannot tell whether the magical books provoked a similar concern or not.

In various records there is some mention of persons practicing magic, divination or alchemy, and that some of these concern instances in which the person was accused or condemned for doing so. Caspar, an assistant priest in Poznań is mentioned several times as a practitioner of alchemy.[70] The *Acta Rectoralia* of the Kraków University reports of university students practicing chiromancy, necromancy, and possessing a book called the *Speculum necromancie*.[71] The punishment, if mentioned, is no more than a moderate fine. There is furthermore a note in the same records

65. William of Auvergne, *De legibus*, chap. 25, 78aF.
66. Denifle and Chatelain, *Chartularium Universitatis Parisiensis*, 1:543.
67. See also Gerson, "Dossier," in *Oeuvres complètes*, 10:73–76.
68. Françoise Bonney, "Autour de Jean Gerson, Opinions de théologiens sur les superstitions et la sorcellerie au début de XVe siècle," *Le Moyen Age* 77 (1971): 85–98.
69. See also Boudet, *Le "Recueil,"* 2:240–91.
70. See also Bolesław Ulanowski, ed., *Acta capitulorum nec non iudiciorum ecclesiasticorum selecta* (Kraków, 1902), nos. 1470 and 1603.
71. Władysław Wisłocki, ed., *Acta rectoralia Almae Universitatis studii Cracoviensis* (Kraków, 1893–97), vol. 1, no. 1988 (necromancy in 1504), no. 2052 (chiromancy in 1505), and no. 2598 (mentioning a book entitled "Speculj nigromancie" [sic] in 1522). See also Bugaj, *Nauki tajemne w Polsce*, 81–82, 102–4.

from 1517–18, claiming that chiromancy is a forbidden art, and this may perhaps account for why, in the Kraków manuscript BJ 551, a chiromantic text and a human hand were crossed out, while on the previous folios Latin and German magical recipes and a short version of the *Ars notoria*—involving explicit invocations to spirits—were left intact. The reader found only the *chiromantia* so wicked and forbidden that he felt obliged to destroy it.[72] We can add finally an interesting case to this list, in which the Franciscan author, the German Thomas Murner (1475–1537) was suspected of "transmitting" magic in the University of Kraków. His inventive work in logic and mnemotechnics, the *Logica memorativa: Chartiludium logice, sive totius dialectice memoria* (Memorative Logic, Cardplaying, or the Memory of Logic and the Entire Dialectics), published first in Kraków in 1507 (and then in Strassburg in 1509), was found so successful in making illiterate men erudite and efficient in logic and memory in an unlikely short period, that suspicion emerged that it had something to do with magic. As we remember, surprisingly quick learning was also among the reasons the methods of *Ars notoria* were found suspicious. Murner's book was soon in front of the academic body of the Kraków University, and—as it is reported by a member of the college, Johannes of Glogovia—the professors found quickly that the work reflected not so much magical, as divine talent, and enthusiastically recompensed the author.[73] All in all, mention of instances (and "noninstances") of magic are relatively rare in the history of Central European universities; moreover, no serious denunciation of the practice of magic by students or professors has survived.

While astrology for example was a topic of scientific and theological discourse in Kraków,[74] branches of learned magic did not become the subject of such open

72. Wisłocki, *Acta rectoralia*, vol. 1, no. 2445. On the manuscript, see Chapter 4.
73. Thomas Murner, *Logica memorativa. Chartiludium logice, sive totius dialectice memoria & novus Petri hispani textus emendatus: cum iucundo pictasmatis exercitio* (Argentine: J. Gruninger, 1509), next to last page: "Testimonium magistrale Cracoviensium. Ego magister Ioannes de Glogovia: Universitatis Cracoviensis Collegiatus: & ad sanctum Florianum in Clepardia Canonicus: testimonium do veritatis: que eum audivimus & vidimus: non possumus non protestari: Venerabilem patrem Thomam Murner Alemannum: Civitatis Argentinensis filium: nostre universitatis Cracoviensis, sacre theologie baccalaurium: hanc chartiludiorum praxim: apud non finxisse: legisse: & non sine grandi omnium nostrorum ammiratione: usque adeo profecisse: quod in mensis spacio etiam rudes & indocti: sed in rebus logicis: sic evaserint memores & eruditi: q(uae) grandis nobis suspicio: de predicto patre oriebatur: quiddam magicarum rerum infudisse potius: quam precepta logica tradidisse: Auditores eum suos: iuramento sed nec cuiq(uem) viventi communicare: de qua suspicione nostra: ad expurgationis responsa vocatus: hoc presens obtulit chartiludiorum memoramentum: sic a nobis approbatum: sic laudatum: ita q(ue) non modo magicum: sed divinum potius ingenium habuisse: unanimi voce iudicaremus: virum laudavimus: & in nostrum numerum: insigniter promovimus: nec suo labore frustratus: viginti quattuor ungaricos florenos: mercedis titulo recepit: quibus ego interfui: que & vidi: & hisce auribus hausi: ob q(ue) veritatis testimonium prebui: in fidem omnium & singulorum premissorum."
74. In the first half of the century, astrology, especially the effect of the stars on the human intellect and free will, was rejected in the theological literature of the Kraków *magistri;* however, by the end of the same century, new attempts were made to reconcile astrology with Christian teaching,

discussion. In Prague, issues related to this field—such as foretelling the future, practicing "piromancia, hydromancia, geomancia, nigromancia, spatulamancia," or the use of amulets, herbs, and stones against demons—could serve occasionally as themes for university *quodlibets*,[75] however, there seems to have been no need to condemn such practices in statutes. Meanwhile, a growing intellectual interest in the magical arts is detectable in various informal groups related to the courts and universities, but while works on natural, image, and demonic magic, as well as divination and alchemy, could be found on the shelves of the Central European book collectors, such interest did not provoke the great anxiety it did in Paris.

Besides legal prosecution against magicians, their subsequent confession, and university statutes, there are of course further sources on the prohibition of magic: penitentials, preachers' postilles, tracts of theologians, and inquisitorial sources.[76] Penitentials are less useful for the present inquiry: on the one hand, they are less explicit on the actual practices of courtly and university intellectuals than on the convictions and fears of canon lawyers, and on the other, their Central European copies show little specificity and no originality: they mainly repeat the beliefs, practices, and folk customs listed in their Western sources, and are subsequently rather uninformative for us.[77] Examples of this genre in medieval Kraków and Prague, confession handbooks, and lists of questions to be put at the visitation of the bishop, show the same general patterns as the Western penitentials, including the use of amulets, baptizing of images, invocation of demons, divinations, incantations, healing practices, and so on.[78]

---

prognostications became widely accepted, and professors of theology, such as Johannes of Glogovia, viewed astrology as a useful art. See Mieczysław Markowski, "Stanowisko średniowiecznych przedstawicieli uniwersytetu Krakowskiego wobec astrologii" (The Attitudes of Representatives of Kraków University in the Middle Ages Toward Astrology), *Biuletyn Biblioteki Jagiellońskiej* 49 (1999): 95–102

75. Jiří Kejř, *Kvodlibetní disputace na pražské univerzitě* (Quodlibet Disputations at the Prague University) (Prague: Universita Karlova, 1971). "Utrum omnes species sciencie iudiciorum sive pronosticacionum et derivacionum ut interrogacionum, nativitatum, revolucionum, eleccionum, piromancie, aerimancie, ydromancie, geomancie, nigromancie, spatulamancie et ciromancie et aliis habeant radices firmas naturales." Magister Simon de Tišnov around 1416, see ibid., 157. "Utrum herbe, lapides preciosi, caracteres, ymagines et armonie [*sic*] habeant virtute sua vexaciones demonum impedire." Magister Prokop de Kladrau, around 1417, see ibid., 163. See also Šmahel, "Stärker als der Glaube," 329.

76. For overviews on the history of legal prosecutions, ecclesiastical condemnations, and prohibitions of magic, see Peters, *The Magician, the Witch and the Law*; Norman Cohn, *Europe's Inner Demons: An Enquiry Inspired by the Great Witch-Hunt* (New York: Meridian, 1975); and Kieckhefer, *Magic in the Middle Ages*, 176–201.

77. On magic appearing in medieval penitentials, see Peters, *The Magician, the Witch and the Law*, 78–81.

78. See, for example, BJ 2397, fol. 279v: "Ad episcopum mittuntur . . . maiores sorciarii maxime qui baptizant ymagines et qui ymolant demonibus"; BJ 2415, fol. 232v: "Item an sunt aliqui sacrilegi, incantatores vel divinatores cum invocacione demonum, aut aliorum nominum, aut aliquas supersticiones facientes et servantes"; and BJ 2213, fol. 199r: "Sortilegiis auguriis aut divinationibus

As for the concerns of preachers and theologians, we have already touched upon such examples in the cases of Jan Milíč and Stanislas of Skalbimierz. This kind of source is most useful when we try to provide an ethnographical analysis of magical folk customs. However, when it comes to the question of how far learned magic was criminalized, they are usually less helpful.[79]

Finally, inquisitors were occasionally involved in legal actions against magicians, as they were in the cases of Nicholas the Hangman and Henry the Bohemian, and thus we would expect that they expressed their views on such cases in their handbooks. However, when inquisitorial sources have something to say about magic, they remain on a rather general level of prohibiting every divinatory and magical practice as a whole, mentioning *divinatio, incantationes,* and *sortilegii* in general, and are mainly concerned with the illiterate masses rather than with learned magicians.[80]

There are several factors behind the relative tolerance of the Central European universities as compared with the Western ones. The Central European institutions were significantly younger, and no similar need to openly condemn the teachings of professors had had time to emerge. Because of the relatively late arrival of the magical texts in the region, the entire process of using and condemning them seems to have been somewhat belated.

Debates were probably solved in other, less official ways, which had to do with the fact that these institutions were not only relatively young but also relatively small: the number of professors and students working in the institution was considerably smaller than in Paris. While we have enough evidence to prove that certain masters were interested in magic, there is no sign that their interest was enough to disquiet the authorities. The silent reading of the professors could have provoked less threat than the public political activity of, say, Jean de Bar.

I am not suggesting that Central Europe was a particularly magical environment compared with the West. Nor am I suggesting that Johannes Manlius's claim, that

---

intendere. Karacteres, scripturas, in plumbo aut in aliquo alio coligaturas plumbi fusi vel cere vel alicuius alterius non medicionalis differe atque in his contra preceptum Domini et ecclesie spem ponere." For further examples, see Kowalczyk, "Wróżby, czary i zabobony," 12–13. For cases in Bohemia, see Šmahel, "Stärker als der Glaube," 326–28.

79. Šmahel, "Stärker als der Glaube," 328–30. See also Bracha, "Magie und Aberglaubenskritik in den Predigten," and Zdeněk Uhlíř, "Texte über den Aberglauben in den tschechischen Handschriftensammlungen des Mittelalters," in Wünsch, *Religion und Magie in Ostmitteleuropa,* 85–120.

80. See, for example, the instructions of the archbishop of Prague to the Dominican inquisitor Rudolf, in Alexander Patschovsky, *Die Anfänge einer ständigen Inquisition in Böhmen: Ein Prager Inquisitoren-Handbuch aus der ersten Hälfte des 14. Jahrhunderts* (Berlin: Walter de Gruyter, 1975), 26–27, 194–95. On the Polish inquisitors considerably less information is available; since they did not leave any records, their activity can be reconstructed only with the help of external sources. See Paweł Kras, "Inkwizycja papieska w walce z husytyzmem na ziemiach polskich" (The Papal Inquisition and the Persecution of Hussites in Poland), in *Polskie echa husytyzmu* (Polish Echoes of Hussitism), ed. Stanisław Bylina and Ryszard Gładkiewicz (Warsaw: Wydawnictwo Instytutu Historii PAN, 1999), 88–115.

230   PART THREE: READERS AND COLLECTORS

magic had been publicly instructed in Kraków, should be taken seriously.[81] What is clearly visible from the source material, however, is that authors, scribes, and collectors of learned magic did not feel any need to preserve their anonymity, nor did authors of magic classifications feel any need to fear the consequences of arguing for the benefits of certain branches of magic. In consequence, these authors, scribes, and collectors can be identified today as members of a relatively respectable social stratum.

Magic in Royal Book Collections

The last strategy to be followed here to explore the role magic played in courtly milieus is to examine how it might be reconstructed on the basis of the royal book collections.

If we take a look first at the most renowned royal bibliophiles of Western history, we observe that learned magic was a recurrent object of curiosity. Although bibliophilism became a central characteristic of courtly culture only in the fourteenth century, it had its roots in some thirteenth-century royal collections. The courts of Emperor Frederick II in Sicily and of Alfonso X (the Wise) (1252–84) in Castile were famous for the respect books enjoyed, and this respect was inspired not least by the Arabic model. Both courts were places of important translating activity, which gave open access to the Arabic learning entering Europe, and—accordingly—both were responsible for the import of learned magic (the *Picatrix*, for example, was translated at Alfonso's court). The library of another thirteenth-century collector, King Louis IX (Saint Louis) of France, developed into the largest royal collection by the fourteenth century. Under Charles V (the Wise) (d. 1380), this library contained more than nine hundred volumes, it was as rich as the collection of the Sorbonne, and—as we would expect from a proper institutional library—it had its own permanent librarian.[82] Approximately one-third of this large collection was on science and medicine, and more than one-tenth of the books indicates the king's interest in astrology, divination, and magic. As far as ritual magic is concerned, four copies of the *Ars notoria* could be found on the royal bookshelves, one of them in the vernacular: "en langaige espagnol ou lombart."[83]

---

81. As I mentioned in "In Search of Magician Schools," Manlius claimed in the sixteenth century that magic had been widely used and publicly practiced in Kraków a century earlier

82. Joan Cadden, "Charles V, Nicole Oresme, and Christine de Pizan: Unities and Uses of Knowledge in Fourteenth-Century France," in *Texts and Contexts in Ancient and Medieval Science: Studies on the Occasion of John E. Murdoch's Seventieth Birthday*, ed. Edith Sylla and Michael McVaugh (Leiden: Brill, 1997), 208–44. For the library and the astrological interests of Charles V, see 211–16.

83. Léopold Delisle, *Recherches sur la librairie de Charles V et Charles VI (1364–1422)*, vol. 2 (Paris: Champion, 1907), 117, nos. 710–13.

Central European evidence does make the historians' lives easy when they try to reconstruct royal libraries and find the place for an interest in learned magic in these libraries. We have already seen, for example, that an illuminated copy of the Pseudo-Aristotelian *Secretum secretorum* was among the books prepared for the Hungarian king Louis I of Anjou (1342–82), but we also saw that it would be too hazardous to suppose that this is a proper evidence indicating certain magical interests: the *Secretum* was such a widespread book that it was present in virtually all the larger libraries, and it was so rich in various other kinds of material—not to mention that it was viewed as a king's mirror—that its mere presence says very little about the curiosity of the collector, especially if he is a king.[84]

One of the oldest courtly libraries, which may be—even though only partially—reconstructed, is that of the last Přemyslids, the Bohemian royal house that died out in the early fourteenth century. According to the supposition of Karel Fischer, among those items that Nicolaus Cusanus purchased in 1444 in Nuremberg, a number of astronomical tools—an astrolabe, an armillary sphere, and a torquetum—and sixteen astronomical and astrological manuscripts originated from the Bohemian royal court of Ottokar II (1253–78) and his son, Wenceslas II (1278–1305). These items—the hypothesis goes—entered the possession of the newly founded University of Prague (1348) but were physically left in the royal castle in the possession of court astrologers. It was Emperor and king of Bohemia Sigismund who brought them with him to Germany in 1420, where Cusanus had the opportunity to buy them.[85]

As a result of thorough and detailed codicological research, Alois Krchňák proved that only five manuscripts, the Codices Cusani (and indeed the astronomical instruments), were demonstrably from the collection of the Bohemian kings.[86] These books, prepared in a Prague scriptorium, contain a wide range of readings in the Arabic and Greek celestial sciences, written by (or ascribed to) Alfraganus, Al-Kindi, Ptolemy, Hippocrates, Hali, Messahallah, Albumasar, Alkabicius, and so forth, mostly translated in the twelfth and thirteenth centuries.[87] From these sources,

---

84. Oxford, Bodleian Library, MS Hertford College 2 (E. N. 2.). For more details on this codex, see Chapter 2.

85. Karel Fischer, "Najstarsze słowańskie przedstawienia konstelacji gwiezdnych" (The Oldest Slavonic Representations of Stellar Constellations), *Problemy* 16 (1960): 878–90. Fischer's theory is summarized in Alois Krchňák, "Die Herkunft der astronomischen Handschriften und Instrumente des Nikolaus von Kues," *Mitteilungen und Forschungsbeiträge der Cusanus-Gesellschaft* 3 (1963): 108–80.

86. Namely, the codices Cusani 207, 208, and 210, of the Cusanus Bibliothek at Kues. Cusani 207 and 208 each contain two, originally separate, manuscripts. Krchňák, "Die Herkunft der astronomischen Handschriften."

87. For a description of the codices, see Jakob Marx, *Verzeichnis der Handschriften-Sammlung des Hospitals zu Cues* (Trier: Schaar und Dathe, 1905), 193–202. MS 207 contains, furthermore, a text on constellations (fols. 88v–114v, see also Thorndike [1947], 266–67), with an interesting set of depicted planetary figures made in a Czech workshop of miniature painters (fols. 115r–116r). For

Krchňák deduces that there was a cultural relationship between Bohemia and Spain at the time of the last Přemyslids, a relationship grounded already in the times of Ottokar II and Alfonso X. Moreover, this connection was an intellectual cooperation as well; the manuscripts testify that several Spanish astrologers were active at the court of Wenceslas II around 1300.[88]

It would be reasonable to expect that interest in the celestial sciences at the Bohemian court emerged—similarly to the Arabic history of science and to the preference of the Spanish translators—in close connection with divination and image magic. Since there is also a human aspect in the relationship between the two courts involved (the Spanish astrologers), this joint interest could have been transmitted easily from Toledo to Prague. Disappointingly, however—apart from the fact that a magico-therapeutic lapidary dedicated to King Wenceslas II claimed to have been a translation from Greek[89]—the very little knowledge we have on the library of the Přemyslids does not satisfy these expectations. For such a satisfaction we have to wait another hundred years, for the library of Wenceslas IV, Holy Roman Emperor and king of Bohemia.

The reconstruction of the library of Wenceslas IV is only slightly more developed than that of the Přzemislid book collections: only eight extant manuscripts can be identified with complete certainty as once belonging to the emperor.[90] Just like the earlier kings of Bohemia, Wenceslas showed a considerable interest in astrology.[91]

---

the figures, see Krchňák, "Die Herkunft der astronomischen Handschriften," 121–23. For other miniatures prepared by the same workshop, see Karel Fischer, "Some Unpublished Astrological Illustrations from Central and Eastern Europe," *JWCI* 27 (1964): 311–12.

88. This intellectual relation was also the reason—in Krchňák's opinion—why an astrological manuscript written in Toledo (London, British Museum, Cod. Harl. 3734) was brought to Prague (this manuscript was also among those bought by Cusanus in 1444). Krchňák, "Die Herkunft der astronomischen Handschriften," 144–45 and 176.

89. See *HMES*, 2:266, and TK 160. The lapidary was printed in Merseburg in 1473. A copy of it can be found in BJ 778, fols. 200r–209r: "Abesten, abstratus, adamas> <verenius, zemech, zirgutes; fol. 200v: Abesten, lapis Latine dictus, qui in Greco odolfanus dicitur, fetularinus perisces in Caldeo nuncupatur. Hic est coloris ferrei et invenitur sepissime in Arabia> <aut sinistre manus, cum qua aliquis libenter ludit, ad taxillos desiderium ludendi repremit et refrenat et cetera. Sequitur." An interesting detail that might help the dating of this text appears on fol. 201v: "Audivimus enim a quodam viro veridico in Stiria, quod cum excellentissimus princeps dominus Ottokarus, pie recordacionis pater domini Wenceslai secundi regis Bohemorum, cum exercitu intrasset regnum Ungarie, transivit quandam silvam." Ottokar became king of Bohemia in 1253 and fought against the Hungarians in 1253, 1260, 1270, and 1278.

90. On the library of Wenceslas IV, see Krása, *Die Handschriften*, and by the same author, *Rukopisy Václava IV* (Praha: Odeon, 1971). For a survey and interpretation of the astrological, alchemical, and magical emblems in Wenceslas's library, see Milena Bartlová, "The Magic of Image: Astrological, Alchemical and Magical Symbolism at the Court of Wenceslas IV," in *The Role of Magic in the Past: Learned and Popular Magic, Popular Beliefs and Diversity of Attitudes*, ed. Blanka Szeghyová (Bratislava: Pro Historia, 2005), 19–28. See also *HMES*, 3:590–92.

91. Krása, *Die Handschriften*, 48–58.

He employed court astrologers, among them Christian of Prachatitz (1368–1439), a well-known master and rector of the University of Prague,[92] and he probably inherited (and his astrologers made use of) the astrological manuscripts and the astronomical instruments of the earlier kings of Bohemia. Among the eight extant codices written in the last years of the fourteenth century for the emperor, three are devoted specifically to astrology.[93] These contain once again the Latin translations of basic Late Antique and Arabic works of astrology. One of them, ÖNB Cod. lat. 2271, exclusively reproduces the Greek "Bible" of astrology, the *Tetrabiblos* (*Quadripartitus*) of Ptolemy, while the two others, CLM 826 and ÖNB Cod. lat. 2352, are collections of shorter treatises, mainly of basic Arabic works on this science.[94] One of the astrological works is the *De noticia ordinum stellarum fixarum celi* (On the Order of the Fixed Stars of the Sky),[95] an excerpt from the *Liber introductorius* by Michael Scot, the court astrologer, scientist, and translator of Frederick II, an excerpt which also appears in one of the Cusanus codices, originating from the library of the last Přemyslids.[96] ÖNB Cod. lat. 2352 incorporates, besides the astrological tracts, texts of divination and ritual magic. It contains a *rota fortunae*,[97] preceded by divinatory circles and geomantic charts, and followed by a text on name magic, and a set of answers to questions concerning one's fate.[98] In addition, on the last folios of the codex, we find prayers with magical characters and divine names (Adonay, Joseph, Messias, Sother, Emanuel, and Sabaoth), and further prayers to God for attaining wisdom and conjuring spirits.[99]

Besides these eight manuscripts, the emblems of Wenceslas IV appear in some further codices that (or the original copies of which) were in all probability written and illuminated in the scriptoria of the emperor's court. One of these is the *Bellifortis* by Conrad Kyeser, the book on military technology, the magical elements of

92. Spunar, *Repertorium*, 1:116–31; Šmahel, "Mistři," 52; Renata Bicherl, "Die Magister der Artistenfakultät der Hohen Schule zu Prag und ihre Schriften im Zeitraum von 1348 bis 1409" (Ph.D. diss., Friedrich-Alexander Universität, 1971), 138–40.
93. ÖNB Cod. lat. 2271; ÖNB Cod. lat. 2352; CLM 826.
94. For a description of these codices, see Krása *Die Handschriften*, 52–58 and 206–15.
95. ÖNB Cod. lat. 2352, fols. 1r–4v.
96. Codex Cusani 207, fols. 108r–114v.
97. ÖNB Cod. lat. 2352, fol. 86r.
98. Ibid., fols. 95r–96r, fol. 101v.
99. Ibid., fol. 101v, fols. 101v–102r, and fol. 102r. Fritz Saxl, *Verzeichnis astrologischer und mythologischer illustrierter Handschriften des lateinischen Mittelalters II: Die Handschriften der National-Bibliothek in Wien* (Heidelberg: Carl Winters, 1927), 86–90. On this manuscript, see also Werner Abraham, ed., *Losbuch in deutschen Reimpaaren. Vollständige Faksimile- Ausgabe im Originalformat des Codex Vindobonensis*, series nova 2652 der Österreichischen Nationalbibliothek ("Codices selecti" 38) (Graz: Akademische Druck- und Verlagsanstalt, 1973); Josef Krása, "Astrologické rukopisy Václava IV" (Astrological Manuscripts of King Wenceslas IV), *Umeni* 12 (1964): 466–86; and Paul Kunitzsch, *Der Almagest. Die Syntaxis Mathematica des Claudius Ptolomäus in arabisch-lateinischer Überlieferung* (Wiesbaden: Harrassowitz, 1974).

which—alchemy and astrology, magic lamps and fires, demons, and the grease of a hanged man—were described in greater detail in Chapter 2. There were copies of Kyeser's book in several royal libraries, among them the libraries of Sigismund and King Matthias.

The Corvinian Library

Let us conclude this survey on royal libraries with the most ambitious Central European book collection of the fifteenth century, the Bibliotheca Corviniana of King Matthias (1458–90). It is important to underline first of all that Matthias played a rather particular role in the succession of Hungarian rulers. He was the only king of the country who was not born of royal blood, but belonged to the lesser nobility. His father, Johannes Hunyadi (ca. 1407–56), was a real "newcomer," a talented politician and general, a legendary hero in the eyes of the Christians, who defeated the Turks many times in various spectacular battles, and who—as a result of his victories—became a powerful baron, and the regent of Hungary (1446–53) while the previous king was young. Johannes's prestige was a primary reason why his younger son, Matthias, was proclaimed king in 1458, at the age of eighteen. Matthias became a real Renaissance king, leading a particularly active foreign policy, attacking virtually all the countries surrounding Hungary. Wishing to become emperor, he even occupied Vienna for a few years. Despite the continuous warfare, his reign is remembered as one of the most glorious periods of Hungarian history.

Matthias himself received a humanist education, and one of his chief goals was to establish his court as a center of humanism comparable to those of Cosimo (1389–1464) and Lorenzo (1449–92) de Medici, where the greatest Italian humanists participated in huge banquets during which they listened to music and engaged in philosophical discussions. Hungary was probably never so "up-to-date" as far as cultural life is concerned; the intellectual relations between the country and the rest of Europe were never so close as in those days. Matthias's Renaissance court became the first humanist center outside Italy, and thus an integral part of the culture of Western Europe. The Italian humanists were present in Hungary not only through their books: they were in correspondence with the Hungarian elite, and some of them—if Ficino himself could not be convinced, Galeotto Marzio and Francesco Bandini and other members of the humanist generation—even visited the king's court in person.

The appreciation of astrology in this Neoplatonic milieu is well known and thoroughly researched.[100] Although the patronage of cultural life was centralized in

---

100. See, for example, József Huszti, "Platonista törekvések Mátyás király udvarában" (Platonist Efforts at King Matthias's Court), pts. 1 and 2, *Minerva* 8 (1924): 153–222, and 9 (1925): 41–76;

Matthias's time, the places where traces of astrological interest are to be found are scattered. The celestial sciences were not exclusively the king's fascination; they played a crucial role also in the life of Johannes Vitéz (1408–72),[101] first bishop of Várad, later archbishop of Esztergom, as well as in the life of his nephew Janus Pannonius (1434–72), the famous Hungarian poet, whose astrological knowledge and even his own natal chart can be reconstructed from his poems.[102] Vitéz, who had tutored the young Matthias, invited humanists and astrologers to his court from abroad, which became, in turn, a model for the future king. Vitéz also arranged an astronomical center and observatory in Várad, which was later transferred to Esztergom. From his archiepiscopal court, there is also pictorial evidence for his fascination with the celestial sciences: a fresco on a surviving archway was decorated with the signs of the zodiac.[103]

Pozsony (Pressburg, Istropolis, today's Bratislava) and the newly founded university, the so-called Academia Istropolitana,[104] was another crucial intellectual center for a short period (1467–72). Vitéz and Matthias invited the most prominent practitioners of astronomy and astrology to the quadrivial chair of the university: Johannes Regiomontanus (1436–76), Martin Bylica of Olkusz (1433–93), and supposedly even Galeotto Marzio (ca. 1427–ca. 1497).[105] The astrologers, who were requested

---

Zoltán Nagy, "Asztronómia a Mátyás-korabeli Magyarországon" (Astronomy in Hungary, in the Age of Matthias), *Világosság* 17 (1976): 775–81; Péter Kulcsár, "Az újplatonizmus Magyarországon" (Neoplatonism in Hungary), *Irodalomtörténeti Közlemények* 87 (1983): 41–47; Lajos Bartha, "Régi magyar csillagászok" (Early Hungarian Astronomers), pts. 1 and 2, *Technikatörténeti szemle* 8 (1976): 71–113, and 11 (1979): 169–81; and Tibor Klaniczay and József Jankovics, eds., *Matthias Corvinus and the Humanism in Central Europe,* Studia Humanitatis 10 (Budapest: Balassi, 1994).

101. Klára Csapodiné Gárdonyi, *Die Bibliothek des Johannes Vitéz,* Studia Humanitatis 6 (Budapest: Akadémiai Kiadó, 1984); Tibor Klaniczay, "Das Contubernium des Johannes Vitéz: Die erste ungarische Academie," in *Forschungen über Siebenbürgen und seine Nachbarn: Festschrift für Attila T. Szabó und Zsigmond Jakó,* ed. Kálmán Benda (Munich: Trofenik, 1988), 241–55.

102. It is worth adding that Janus Pannonius is considered to be the first Hungarian poet, but he was actually Croatian by birth, and wrote in Latin. On his astrology, see József Huszti, "Janus Pannonius asztrológiai álláspontja" (The Astrological Position of Janus Pannonius), *Minerva* 11 (1927): 43–58; Lajos Bartha, "Janus Pannonius két csillagászati verse" (Two Astronomical Poems by Janus Pannonius), *Irodalomtudományi Közlemények* 82 (1978): 340–45; and János Bollók, *Asztrális misztika és asztrológia Janus Pannonius költészetében* (Astral Mysticism and Astrology in the Poetry of Janus Pannonius) (Budapest: Argumentum, 2003).

103. Zoltán Nagy, "Ricerche cosmologiche nella corte umanistica di Giovanni Vitéz," in *Rapporti veneto-ungheresi al'epoca del Rinascimento,* ed. Tibor Klaniczay (Budapest: Akadémiai Kiadó, 1975), 65–93.

104. The widespread name of the new university, Academia Istropolitana, was probably first used in the eighteenth century. In those days, the university was never referred to as *academia,* but rather as *universitas, studium generale,* or *universale gymnasium;* the word *academia* (still without the adjective Istropolitana) appears first at the end of the fifteenth century. Whatever the university was called, it was a real institution with faculties, scholarships, and a building.

105. The secondary literature of this Hungarian attempt to found a university is very extensive; it suffices here to mention Xystus Schier, *Memoria Academiae Istropolitanae seu Posoniensis* (Vienna:

to cast a horoscope for the university, predicted a flourishing future for the new institution.[106] Unfortunately, this prophecy turned out to be wrong, and the Academia Istropolitana could not avoid the fate of the earlier Hungarian attempts to establish universities in Pécs and in Óbuda: after a very short golden period it began to break up. The dissolution of the university is a sad story; conflict arose between the humanist king and his humanist prelates—Archbishop Vitéz and Bishop Janus Pannonius—who organized a plot against their ruler. They were deposed and forced to flee, and died soon after. Their deaths discouraged the rest of the professors, the students left Pozsony, and the university began a long and painful decline. Simultaneously, the somewhat disappointed king removed the Hungarian humanists from his court and surrounded himself with humanists from abroad, mainly Italians, among them his second wife, Beatrix of Aragon. Matthias was also aware that a real Renaissance king was expected not only to support scientists and artists but also to found a library as a source of mental nourishment and a site of learned debate.

If we consider a library as the mirror of its collector's literary and scientific interests, we have every right to expect that a significant portion of Matthias's books would be on astrology and a lesser but still significant part of them on learned magic. King Matthias's enthusiastic interest in the sciences, including astrology and the occult arts, and the scientific orientation of his Corvinian library was widely admired by his contemporaries and has been widely studied by scholars.[107] Reports left by the actors of Matthias's court contain a variety of exciting hints regarding the intellectual attitudes of the king. The famous Italian humanist Galeotto Marzio, who spent long years in Hungary as a guest of the court, gave an enthusiastic account of Matthias's Neoplatonic, scientific, and astrological interests.[108] Another Italian humanist and guest of the court, Antonio Bonfini (1427–1502), specifies in his *Symposium* that the intellectual debates held in the court were often organized around the topic of Neoplatonism and focused on such authors as Plato, Hermes Trismegistos, Zoroaster, Plotinus, and Pythagoras.[109]

Kurzbök, 1774); Leslie S. Domonkos, "The Origins of the University of Pozsony," *New Review: A Journal of East-European History* 9 (1969): 270–89; and Tibor Klaniczay, "Egyetem Magyarországon Mátyás korában" (The University in Hungary in the Age of Matthias), *Irodalomtörténeti Közlemények* 94 (1990): 575–612.

106. The nativity is extant; see Schier, *Memoria Academiae Istropolitanae*.

107. See, for example, Csaba Csapodi, "Medical and Scientific Manuscripts of the Corvinian Library," *Orvostörténeti közlemények* 109–12 (1985): 37–45.

108. "Tenebat preterea astrologiam et in operibus Apulei Platonoci ita detritus, ut eius dogma omnino calleret, unde et apud eum theologi, philosophi, medici, poetae et oratores et astrologi et qui omnes disciplinas profitebantur, frequenter erant." Galeottus Martius Narnensis, *De egregie, sapienter,* 3:9.

109. Bonfini, *Symposium de virginitate et pudicitia coniugali,* 119–200. For general overviews on the question, see Kulcsár, "Az újplatonizmus"; Jolán Balogh, *Mátyás király és a művészet* (King Matthias and the Arts) (Budapest: Magvető, 1985); and Balogh, *Adattár*.

To what extent does the Corvinian book collection reflect these themes?[110] Among the approximately two hundred extant codices, twenty items—that is, one-tenth—can be related to Neoplatonism.[111] We find works by Plato, Victorinus, Cicero, Porphyry, Synesius, Pseudo-Dionysius, Calcidius, Theophrastus, William of Conches, and Ficino. Another considerable portion of the collection is devoted to works of astrology by Ptolemy, Firmicus Maternus, Regiomontanus, Peuerbach, and so forth. In addition, the library included a book originally prepared for Emperor Wenceslas IV, the *Commentarius in Ptolomaei quadripartitum* (Commentary to the Tetrabiblos of Ptolemy) by Haly Aberudiam Heben Rodan (translated into Latin at the court of Alfonso the Wise), and a number of calendars and forecasts.[112] This selection would have been extremely useful material for any medieval astrologer.[113] The astrological nature of the library is also stressed on the vault of one room of the library, where a starry sky was painted with the horoscope of Matthias and a short Latin poem catching the attention of the visitors:

> Aspice Matthiae micuit quo tempore regis
> Natalis coeli qualis imago fuit
>
> [Look! Such is the image that shone in the heavens
> at the time of the birth of Matthias the king.][114]

The observatory of the library was rich in astronomical instruments, including gnomons, astrolabes, and horologiums, most of them made by a Viennese metallurgist, Hans Dorn.[115]

Three Corvinae contain works and letters by Marsilio Ficino (1433–99), who corresponded faithfully with members of the royal court.[116] The Florentine philosopher

---

110. For a reconstruction of the library, see Csapodi, *Corvinian Library* (see Chap. 6, n. 68), and Csapodi and Csapodiné Gárdonyi, *Bibliotheca Corviniana*.

111. Kulcsár, "Az újplatonizmus," 44.

112. Katalin Barlai and Ágnes Boronkai, "Astronomical Codices in the Corvinian Library," *Memorie della Societa Astronomica Italiana* 65 (1994): 533–46; the same article was published in Hungarian as Katalin Barlai and Ágnes Boronkai, "Csillagászati kódexek a Corvina könyvtárban" (Astronomical Codices in the Corvinian Library), *Meteor Csillagászati Évkönyv 1997-re* (1996): 192–99. For the scientific codices of the library, see also Csapodi, "Medical and Scientific Manuscripts."

113. For the library of a hypothetical astrologer, see Maxime Préaud, *Les astrologues à la fin du Moyen Age* (Paris: J. C. Lattès, 1984), esp. "Annexe: La bibliothèque d'un astrologue."

114. Balogh, *Mátyás király,* 105. For descriptions on the library and the observatory, see Balogh, *Adattár,* 62–65.

115. Balogh, *Mátyás király,* 418; Balogh, *Adattár,* 447–49, on astronomical tools and clocks, and 583–84, on mechanics. The most beautiful pieces of this collection were given to the University of Kraków, after the death of King Matthias's court astrologer, Martin Bylica of Olkusz.

116. Besides the king, Janus Pannonius, and Vitéz, Ficino sent letters to Nicholas Báthory, the bishop of Vác, Péter Váradi, and János Váradi. For those, see Valery Rees, "Ad vitam felicitatemque:

dedicated a copy of his commentary on Plato's *Symposium* to Janus Pannonius,[117] and books 3 and 4 of his collected letters to King Matthias.[118] (To this famous work Ficino attached a lesser-known writing against those astrologers who did a different kind of astrology from the one practiced by Ficino. This note is entitled *Quantum astronomi metiuntur, tantum astrologi mentiuntur,* or in other words, "as much as astronomers measure, that much astrologers lie.")[119] Last but not least, Ficino dedicated the third book of his masterpiece *De vita libri tres* (Three Books of Life), *De vita coelitus comparanda* (On Obtaining Life from the Heavens), to the Hungarian king.[120] In *De vita coelitus comparanda* Ficino discusses not only such topics as the effect of the sky on earthly beings, but also the secret virtues of herbs, animals, and stones and the effect they exercise on human life. He argues that not only natural beings but even artificial objects may receive occult virtue from the stars, and that images are able to serve the aims of the operator. He furthermore explains how the human operator can make use of these occult powers and how by manipulating them influence nature.[121] Among the "three books of life," this is the only one containing magical elements, and these elements—the virtue of words, stones, talismans, planetary images, and the power of spirits involved—resemble mostly those of medieval image magic.[122]

This magical content, however, was never consulted by the learned courtiers of Hungary; the book did not reach Buda. The manuscript was not completed in Matthias's lifetime. It was dedicated on July 10, 1489, but the king died in 1490. Thus, it remained in Florence, where it still is, with Matthias's coat of arms covered by that of the Medicis.[123]

Marsilio Ficino to his Friends in Hungary," *Budapest Review of Books* 8 (1998): 57–63, and Marsilio Ficino, *The Letters of Marsilio Ficino* (London: Shepheard-Walwyn, 1975). See also Jolán Balogh, "Néhány adat Firenze és Magyarország kulturális kapcsolatainak történetéhez" (Some Data on the History of the Cultural Relations of Florence and Hungary), *Archeologiai Értesítő* 50 (1923–26): 189–209.

117. Ficino, *Commentarius in Platonis Convivium,* dedicated to Janus Pannonius around 1470, in ÖNB Cod. lat. 2472, M C 38.

118. Wolfenbüttel, Cod. Guelf. 12, Aug. 4°.

119. Csaba Csapodi, "Die Corvinische Codices in Wolfenbüttel," *Wolfenbüttel Beiträge* 1 (1972): 29–44; for the text, see also *Zeitschrift von und für Ungarn* (1804): 162–67 and 207–16.

120. Florence, Bibliotheca Medicea Laurenziana, Plut. 73, Cod. 39.

121. Marsilio Ficino, *Three Books on Life,* ed. Carol V. Kaske and John R. Clark, Medieval and Renaissance Texts and Studies 57 (Binghamton, N.Y.: Renaissance Society of America, 1989).

122. Ibid., 45–55.

123. Together with Ficino's *De vita,* several dozens of codices have been identified recently in Florence that were commissioned by King Matthias, but because of his death in 1490, were not sent to his Buda court. See Angela Dillon Bussi, "Ancora sulla Biblioteca Corviniana e Firenze," in *Uralkodók és corvinák: Az Országos Széchényi Könyvtár jubileumi kiállítása alapításának 200. évfordulóján* (Potentates and Corvinas: Anniversary Exhibition of the National Széchényi Library), ed. Orsolya Karsay (Budapest: Országos Széchényi Könyvtár, 2002), 63–70. For the Ficino manuscript, see 186.

What we are concerned with here, however, is not the dissemination of *Renaissance* Hermetism, nor the reception of practical image magic in the philosophy of *Italian* humanists such as Galeotto and Ficino,[124] but the distribution of manuscripts of *medieval genres* of learned magic in *Central European* royal collections. Surprisingly, we see no such manuscripts in Matthias's library: as the genres of magic were defined in the first and second parts of the present work, they are simply not represented in the Corvinian library. I want to emphasize this against the claims of the Hungarian historian, László Szathmáry, who thought that he could identify a number of elements of practical magic in Matthias's environment.[125] What he found was primarily pure astrological material—which falls outside the realm of magic in this study, and physiognomy—which I would rather classify under the field of medicine in those times. There is simply no trace of texts of medieval natural, image, and ritual magic in the king's book collection; the Hermes who was held in great respect at the royal court was clearly not the medieval Hermes of the Arabs, but the Renaissance Hermes Mercurius, introduced into the intellectual discourse by Ficino's translations. I do not want to argue here against the continuity of medieval and Renaissance magic—this issue deserves, and in fact it has deserved, separate studies.[126] I only conclude that learned magic was present in the royal library, but primarily through its contemporary Neoplatonic sources and not in the kind of texts discussed in the previous chapters.

On a final note, it should be added that although the Corvinian library has been a continuously researched topic in the last century, only about ten percent of the original codices have been identified.[127] Scholars estimate the original number of the *Corvinae* at two or two and a half thousand, of which slightly more than two hundred have been found. This ratio makes every claim about the nature of the Corvinian library necessarily conjectural. In consequence, I cannot exclude the

---

124. On Galeotto and Ficino, see *HMES*, 4:399–405 and 562–73, and WP 723–30 and 639–75. For an exhaustive study on Galeotto Marzio, see the series of articles by Gabriella Miggiano, "Galeotto Marzio da Narni," pts. 1–5, *Il Bibliotecario: rivista di biblioteconomia, bibliografia e scienze dell'informazione* 32 (1992): 45–96; 33–34 (1992): 65–154; 35 (1993): 61–108; 36–37 (1993): 83–193; 38 (1993): 27–122.

125. László Szathmáry, "Az asztrológia, alkémia és misztika Mátyás király udvarában" (Astrology, Alchemy and Mysticism at King Matthias' Court), in *Mátyás király emlékkönyv* (Memorial Book of King Matthias), ed. Imre Lukinich (Budapest: Franklin, 1940), 415–51.

126. Richard Kieckhefer, "Did Magic Have a Renaissance? An Historiographic Question Revisited," in Burnett and Ryan, *Magic and the Classical Tradition*, 199–212. On Ficino's debts to medieval sources, primarily to the *Picatrix* and Al-Kindi's *De radiis stellarum*, as compared to his Late Antique sources (Plotinus, Iamblichos, Proclus, and Hellenistic Hermetism), see Ficino, *Three Books on Life*, 46–51. On Galeotto's reception of astral magic, medical astrology, and divination, see Miggiano, "Galeotto Marzio da Narni," pt. 4.

127. Nonetheless, thanks to the recent discovery of the Florentine Corvina codices, the proportion of the identified codices drastically increased. See Karsay, *Uralkodók és corvinák*.

possibility that handbooks of medieval practical magic were present on the bookshelves of King Matthias, but I do not think that the emergence of new sources would change the general consensus that the king was interested in the new philosophical Hermetism, not in the "old" practical methods.

King Matthias died in 1490, and under the reign of the Jagiellos and during the Turkish occupation of the country, the codices of the library were scattered across Europe or were taken to Constantinople. No further humanists arrived from Italy, but some of those who spent so many years in the court remained in Hungary for their entire lives. The story of Hungarian humanism did not end here, in the following years it became less centralized, and spread downward from the royal court. This however, is not a medieval story anymore.

9
Magic in the University Context

A Magician's Calling Card

In the early years of the sixteenth century, a magician's fairly bizarre calling card was circulating in German territories, and it had also reached an alumnus of the University of Kraków, Johannes Virdung of Hassfurt. On this card the magician listed all the titles he wished to call himself:

> *Magister Georgius Sabellicus Faustus iunior, fons necromanticorum, astrologus, magus secundus chyromanticus agromanticus pyromanticus in hydra arte secundus.*

> [Magister Georgius Sabellicus Faustus junior, the inspiration of necromancers, astrologer, the second magus, palmist, practitioner of divination with the use of high places and fire, and second in the art of divination with the use of water.][1]

Virdung was the sort of person such an individual would most want to meet: his library included an impressive selection of magical texts copied when he was a university student in Kraków, and he had remained fascinated by the topic of magic ever since. He was always willing to meet personally the chief representatives of occult studies of his time, whether they were of a practical or a philosophical bent. Before examining Virdung's reaction to this card, we will first survey the Central European universities where one had excellent opportunities to get acquainted with the literature of astrology and magic, then look at some Polish and Bohemian professorial libraries that contained magical items, and make an attempt

---

1. For an English translation, see Baron, *Doctor Faustus*, 29–30; for the Latin original, see 96–97.

to reconstruct the magical interest and library of one such master, Johannes Virdung of Hassfurt, who remained faithful to the occult studies throughout his life. In a closing *excursus,* we will take a look at those contemporaries of Virdung who chose magic as a full-time profession.

The Making of Universities in Central Europe

Universities appeared in Central Europe one and a half or even two centuries later than in the western part of the Latin world.[2] In the first wave of foundations, universities were founded in Prague (1348),[3] Kraków (1364),[4] Vienna (1365),[5] and Pécs (1367),[6] and this was followed by a second wave, leading to the reorganization of the University of Vienna (1384), that of Kraków (1397–1400), and the founding and refounding of the University of Óbuda (1395 and 1410),[7] and the founding of a great number of universities in Germany.

---

2. For a helpful overview of the historiography of Central European universities, see the overview by Klaniczay, "Late Medieval Central European Universities." For general surveys on the history of these new institutions, see Adam Vetulani, "Les origines et le sort des universités de l'Europe Centrale et orientale fondées au cours du XIVe siècle," in *The Universities in the Late Middle Ages,* ed. Jozef Ijsewijn and Jacques Paquet (Leuven: Leuven University Press, 1978), 148–67, and György Székely, "Fakultät, Kollegium, akademische Nation—Zusammenhänge in der Geschichte der mitteleuropäischen Universitäten des 14. und 15. Jahrhunderts," *Annales Universitatis Scientiarum Budapestiensis, Sectio Historica* 13 (1972): 47–78.

3. The classic work on the University of Prague is Václav Chaloupecký, *The Caroline University of Prague* (Prague: Orbis, 1948). For more recent literature, see Peter Moraw, "Die Universität Prag im Mittelalter. Grundzüge ihrer Geschichte im europäischen Zusammenhang," in *Die Universität zu Prag,* ed. Richard W. Eichler (Munich: Verlagshaus Sudetenland, 1986). A most useful, detailed, and structured bibliography on the history, students, and masters of the university can be found on 127–34. See also Moraw, "Die Prager Universitäten des Mittelalters," in *Spannungen und Widersprüche: Gedenkschrift für František Graus,* ed. Susanna Burghartz (Sigmaringen: Jan Thorbecke, 1992).

4. Two general works on the university are Casimir Morawski, *Histoire de l'Université de Cracovie* (Paris: Pickard et fils, 1900–1903), and Adam Vetulani, "Les origines de l'Université de Cracovie," *Acta Poloniae Historica* 13 (1966): 14–40. For recent literature, see Jerzy Wyrozumski, ed., *The Jagiellonian University in the Evolution of European Culture* (Kraków: Secesja, 1992), esp. Wyrozumski, "L'université de Cracovie à l'époque conciliaire," and Leszek Hajdukiewicz, "Der Krakauer Universität zur Zeit der frühen Renaissance."

5. Franz Uiblein, ed., *Acta facultatis Artium Universitatis Vindobonensis (1365–1416)* (Vienna: Hermann Böhlaus, 1968); Uiblein, "Zu den Beziehungen der Wiener Universität zu anderen Universitäten im Mittelalter," in Ijsewijn and Paquet, *Universities in the Late Middle Ages,* 168–89. See also Kurt Mühlberger, "Das Wiener Studium zur Zeit des Königs Matthias Corvinus," in Szögi and Varga, *Universitas Budensis,* 89–116.

6. Tibor Klaniczay, "Megoldott és megoldatlan kérdések az első magyar egyetem körül" (Solved and Unsolved Questions Around the First Hungarian University), in Klaniczay, *Hagyományok ébresztése* (The Awakening of Traditions) (Budapest: Szépirodalmi Könyvkiadó, 1976), 136–65.

7. László Domonkos, "The Founding (1395) and Refounding (1410) of the University of Óbuda," in Szögi and Varga, *Universitas Budensis,* 19–34.

Although these new universities were largely modeled after the Western educational institutions like the universities of Bologna and Paris, their foundation and functioning had some major peculiarities. First, the typical Western universities (but not the Spanish ones, or the University of Naples) emerged gradually from previous educational structures: their birth was a result of spontaneous development in the course of which masters and students tried to secure their privileges and obtain legal protection. In contrast, their fellow institutions in Central Europe were founded from above, as fruits of the will and the conscious educational program of a given ruler, who wanted to satisfy his administrative needs, or to create an intellectual elite educated inside the country, or to enhance his personal prestige.

Second, and as a sad consequence of the previous point, the continued existence of these newly founded institutions depended too much on the quickly changing intentions of their protectors and on unpredictable economic and political circumstances: they usually fell into a state of decline (or even ceased to exist) after a few decades, unless they were refounded and reorganized by another royal benefactor. Hungary, for example, seems to enjoy a rather privileged position on any map representing university foundations. With its three universities (Pécs, Óbuda, and Pozsony—today's Bratislava),[8] to which we can add a second foundation at Óbuda (1410) and a last attempt in the 1470s (by King Matthias in Buda), Hungary outshone all the other countries of the region. What this imaginary map cannot express is that as the result of an unfortunate combination of many factors—lack of persistence, unreliable financial backing, and so on—none of these attempts at establishing a *studium generale* in Hungary attained any sort of permanence: three universities disappeared after a short period of existence from the history of learning and the fourth never even opened.

The third peculiarity of Central European universities is their relatively national character. While in Oxford and Paris, both the *ius ubique docendi* and the system of the academic nations around which education was organized expressed the international and privileged position of the masters and also the independence of the institution from the given monarchy, Central European universities depended more on dynastic and national factors, bore generally a greater amount of national

8. Schier, *Memoria Academiae Istropolitanae*; Mihály Császár, *Az Academia Istropolitana: Mátyás király pozsonyi egyeteme* (The Academia Istropolitana: The Pozsony University of King Matthias) (Bratislava: Eder, 1914); Karol Rebro, "Istropolitana a Bologna" (Istropolitana and Bologna), in *Humanizmus a renesancia na Slovensku v 15–16. storočí* (Humanism and the Renaissance in Slovakia in the Fifteenth and Sixteenth Centuries), ed. Ľudovít Holotík and Anton Vantuch (Bratislava: Slovenská akadémia vied, 1967), 5–24; Domonkos, "Origins of the University of Pozsony"; Asztrik Gabriel, *The Medieval Universities of Pécs and Pozsony: Commemoration of the 500th and 600th Anniversary of Their Foundation, 1367–1467–1967* (Notre Dame: The Medieval Institute, University of Notre Dame, 1969); Klaniczay, "Egyetem Magyarországon Mátyás korában."

traits, and several of them—Kraków and Pécs, for example—functioned without the system of nations.⁹

A fourth specific feature is that three—Kraków, Vienna, and Pécs—of the four universities belonging to the first wave of foundations were not immediately allowed to establish faculties of theology: in Vienna this was finally permitted in 1384, while in Kraków this came with the reorganization in 1400. The reasons for this are manifold and have been frequently discussed: it reflects not only a certain cautiousness of papal policy, but also a practical orientation of their founders: monarchs needed jurists and administrative personnel, and did not feel particularly short of doctors of theology.

As it has been just pointed out, the emergence of the new universities was inconceivable without a strong royal support. Central European universities did not just appear; on the contrary, they were planned consciously by the greatest national monarchs of the area: Emperor Charles IV was the founder of Charles University in Prague;¹⁰ Casimir the Great, king of Poland, established the University of Kraków,¹¹ which was later reorganized by Wladislas Jagiello (and in 1817 renamed Jagiello University); and the names of the Hungarian university founders—Louis the Great, Sigismund of Luxembourg, and King Matthias Corvinus—are no less prominent in the history of the region.

Not just kings but queens as well took an active role in the foundations. Jadwiga (Hedvig), queen of Poland, was an important benefactress of the reorganized University of Kraków, while her sister, Maria, queen of Hungary, became enthusiastically involved in the 1395 project of establishing a university in her own city, Óbuda, even though both of them died before their respective universities actually opened. Was this queenly enthusiasm a compensation for their bad conscience, felt because of the negligence of their father, Louis of Anjou, who had let both of his universities fall into decline? At any rate, Jadwiga left generous endowments to the University of Kraków; she even bequeathed to the university her personal jewels, the famous Angevin collection—one of the largest in Europe at that time. As a consequence, Kraków became the best-funded university in Central Europe. The participation of queens was important for one more reason: the new universities, which appeared late and were organized artificially from above, had no organic place in

---

9. For the national aspect of Central European universities, see Gábor Klaniczay, "National Saints on Late Medieval Universities," in *Die ungarische Universitätsbildung und Europa*, ed. Márta Font and László Szögi (Pécs: Pécsi Tudományegyetem, 2001), 87–108, and Klaniczay, "Late Medieval Central European Universities."

10. Harrison Thomson, "Learning at the Court of Charles IV," *Speculum* 25 (1950): 1–20.

11. For the role of Casimir the Great and for scholarly debates around the foundation of the University of Kraków, see Paul W. Knoll, "Casimir the Great and the University of Cracow," *Jahrbücher für Geschichte Osteuropas* 16 (1968): 232–49; for the Polish culture of the age, see Knoll, "Learning in Late Piast Poland," *Proceedings of the American Philosophical Society* 120 (1976): 136–57.

the already saturated medieval cities, new territories and new buildings had to be freed for them. Two methods presented themselves: obtaining a property of the queen (this happened in the cases of Óbuda and Kraków) or buying—or rather appropriating and confiscating—the possessions of expelled Jews (as happened in Prague, Vienna, Heidelberg, and Kraków).[12]

The organizing ability of powerful ecclesiastical or state officials should also be mentioned as a crucial factor: the bishop of Pécs, Lucas Demetrius, was the provost of Óbuda, and Archbishop Johannes Vitéz was the organizer of the Academia Istropolitana. However, when (respectively) Louis of Anjou, Sigismund, and King Matthias no longer had enough energy, power, or motivation to support their newly founded institutions, they perished quickly. The reasons for the royal negligence could be various: (1) the given university was in a remote city of southern Hungary (Pécs) and the king (Louis of Anjou) concentrated rather on his wars; (2) the sovereign's attention turned toward dynastic and political conflicts (Sigismund); (3) the king broke with his almost omnipotent archbishop, whose educational project was no longer appreciated, and the disgrace extended to the university as well (as was the case with Matthias, Vitéz, and the University of Pozsony); or (4) most prosaically, the king simply died (Casimir the Great in 1370) and the successors did not pay much attention to the development of his cultural program.

Regardless of the energetic beginnings of the universities of Prague, Vienna, and Kraków, in spite of the fact that the organizers of the Academia Istropolitana invited all the notable scientists of the region, no matter that the *studium generale* of Óbuda could be represented in a considerable delegation of professors in the Council of Constance (1414–18)—in the absence of consistent support, the students migrated toward other centers, and the universities of Central Europe fell into obscurity (as the Hungarian institutions) or suffered a period of stagnation until they got a new stimulus (as Vienna in 1384, and Kraków around 1400).

A last peculiarity common to Central European universities that we address here at some length is a surprising blossoming and even dominance of the natural sciences in the intellectual production of the universities:[13] among them physics, medicine, but first of all astronomy and astrology. Organizers and professors in Vienna and Pozsony, but above all in Kraków, paid unexpected attention to the celestial sciences.

12. On the practice of building a university or establishing a college by occupying properties seized from Jews, see Hanna Zaremska, "Jewish Street (*Platea Judeorum*) in Cracow: The 14th–the First Half of the 15th c.," *Acta Poloniae Historica* 83 (2001): 27–57.

13. For a history of science at the University of Kraków with special regard to physics, see Mieczysław Markowski, *Burydanizm w Polsce w okresie przedkopernikańskim* (Buridanism in Poland in the Pre-Copernican Times) (Wrocław: Zakład Narodowy im. Ossolińskich, 1971), and Pawel Czartoryski, "La Notion d'université et l'idée de la science à l'université de Cracovie dans la première moitié du XVe siècle," *Mediaevalia Philosophica Polonorum* 14 (1970): 23–39.

The University of Vienna, following the usual destiny of the universities of the area, was founded twice, both times by masters from the University of Paris. In 1365, the Parisian Master Albert of Saxony became the first rector of the university, and after a twenty-year period of half-existence, it was reorganized by the German Heinrich von Langenstein (Henry of Hesse 1325–97), another master who studied in Paris.[14] Interest in astrology was prevalent from this second foundation onward. Although Langenstein himself denied the validity of judicial astrology, the influence of the Habsburg family as founder and patron of the university encouraged the study of astrology considerably. A number of professors became involved in the celestial sciences and astrological medicine during Langenstein's career. The Habsburg courts—the imperial court of Frederick III (1440–93) and the royal court of Wladislas Posthumous (1452–57), king of Hungary and Bohemia—created a demand for skilled astrologers, and the astrologers trained at the University of Vienna were available to satisfy that demand.[15]

Among the astronomers/astrologers appearing at the university and in the Habsburg courts, one can name Johannes Gmunden[16] and Johannes Nihili of Bohemia,[17] as well as the two leading scientists of the time: Georgius Peuerbach and Johannes Regiomontanus.[18] While becoming the protagonists of a new chapter in the history of astronomy,[19] they also became involved in astrological affairs, Peuerbach becoming the court astrologer of Wladislas Posthumous, and Regiomontanus casting the horoscope of Maximilian, the son of Frederick III and Empress Eleanor of Portugal. In the next generation, the prophet-astrologer Johannes Lichtenberger should be mentioned, whose predictions were highly esteemed in the Habsburg courts.[20]

Pozsony—being halfway between Vienna and Kraków—served as a convenient meeting point for German and Polish astronomers.[21] During the short existence

---

14. On Henry of Hesse, see *HMES,* 3:472–511, and Michael H. Shank, "Academic Consulting in 15th-Century Vienna: The Case of Astrology," in Sylla and McVaugh, *Texts and Contexts,* 245–70.

15. For the role of astrology in Vienna, see Shank, "Academic Consulting"; and for a different opinion on the importance of astrology in the university, see Claudia Kren, "Astronomical Teaching at the Late Medieval University of Vienna," *History of Universities* 3 (1983): 15–30.

16. Shank, "Academic Consulting," 255–57.

17. Ernst Zinner, *Leben und Wirken des Johannes Müller von Königsberg genannt Regiomontanus,* 2nd ed. (Osnabrück: O. Zeller, 1968), 29–31.

18. Ibid.; Ernst Zinner, *Regiomontanus, His Life and Work* (Amsterdam: Elsevier Science, 1990).

19. On their scholarly production, see Georg von Peuerbach, *Theoricae nouae planetarum* (Cologne: Apud haeredes Arnoldi Birckmanni, 1581), and Johannes Regiomontanus, *Tabulae directionum profectionumque* (Wittemberg: Mattheus Welach, 1648).

20. Dietrich Kurze, "Popular Astrology and Prophecy in the Fifteenth and Sixteenth Centuries: Johannes Lichtenberger," in Zambelli, *Astrologi Hallucinati,* 177–93.

21. Margit Waczulik, *A táguló világ magyarországi hírmondói, XV–XVII. század* (The Messengers of the Widening World in Hungary, Fifteenth–Seventeenth Centuries) (Budapest: Gondolat, 1984).

of the newly founded university, the Academia Istropolitana—as we have seen in the previous chapter—Johannes Vitéz and King Matthias invited some of the most active professors of astronomy and astrology to the quadrivial chair: the above-mentioned Regiomontanus and the Polish astrologer Martin Bylica of Olkusz.[22] With this beginning, the University of Pozsony had a serious, albeit aborted, chance to become an intellectual center of mathematics and celestial studies, comparable to Kraków. An indication of the high esteem astrology enjoyed in the new institution is the fact that astrologers were officially commissioned to cast the university's own horoscope.

Finally, as far as the University of Kraków is concerned, its reorganization in 1400 was the start of a golden age that lasted for more than a century.[23] From the present point of view, the history of two special private chairs is to be underlined. The first was founded in the first decade of the fifteenth century through the generosity of Johannes Stobner, a citizen of Kraków (1360–1405),[24] and was designated particularly for the study of geometry, arithmetic, the theory of music, optics, and astronomy. The *collegae Stobneriani*, however, were mainly concerned with mathematical and astronomical studies.

One of them, Martin Król of Żurawica (1422–53),[25] moved first to Prague while still a young *magister*, then traveled to Vienna, Leipzig, and Padua, to finally reach Bologna, where he studied medicine and taught astronomy. It was probably in Italy that he became deeply involved in astrological studies. Later he appeared in Hungary as a physician at the court of János Hunyadi (the father of King Matthias), and finally returned to Prague to take over the chair of Stobner. Some years later, just before his death, he founded another chair especially for astrological studies. This chair started functioning in the late 1450s.[26] In this new department of the university, the lectures were based on such astrological and astronomical works

---

22. Zathey, "Marcin Bylica of Olkusz." A brief work by Regiomontanus, the *Disputationes inter Viennensem et Cracoviensem super Cremonensis in "Planetarum theoricas" deliramenta,* provides a personalized report of Regiomontanus's discussions on planetary theories with Martin Bylica of Olkusz. See Johannes Regiomontanus, *Disputationes Joannis de monte regio contra cremonensia in planetarum theoricas deliramenta praefatio* (Venice: Petrus Liechtenstein, 1518).

23. For the early history of the institution, see Bozena Chmielowska, "Stanislaus de Skarbimierz, le premier recteur de l'Université de Cracovie après le renouveau de celle-ci," *Mediaevalia Philosophica Polonorum* 24 (1979): 73–131, and Maria Kowalczyk, *Krakowskie mowy uniwersyteckie z pierwszej polowy XV wieku* (Kraków University Speeches of the First Half of the Fifteenth Century) (Wrocław: Zakład Narodowy im. Ossolińskich, 1970).

24. On the question whether Johannes or Nicolaus Stobner (both citizens of Kraków) was the founder of the chair, see Lemay, "Late Medieval Astrological School," esp. 338–39 (see Chap. 3, n. 16).

25. Born in 1422, he became a *magister artium* in Kraków in 1445, was awarded a *doctor medicinae* in Bologna in 1449, and died in 1453. On his life, see Grażyna Rosińska, "Traité astronomique inconnu de Martin Rex de Zurawica," *Mediaevalia Philosophica Polonorum* 18 (1973): 159–66; see also Martin Zurawica, *Tractatus de astrologia,* in BJ 2497.

26. Birkenmajer, *Études d'histoire des sciences en Pologne;* Gierowski, *Cracow Circle.*

as the *Quadripartitum* (Four Books) and the *Centiloquium* attributed to Ptolemy, the *Liber introductorius* (Introductory Book) by Alkabicius, the *De magnis coniunctionibus* (Great Conjunctions) by Albumasar,[27] the *De sphaera* of Johannes de Sacrobosco,[28] and the *Tabulae Alphonsi* (Aphonsine Tables).[29]

By the middle of the century, therefore, the university possessed two chairs devoted to the study of the stars. These chairs yielded many new astronomical and astrological works and gave several generations of astronomers to the history of science.[30] The intense astrological preoccupation produced not only written results, but also a set of spectacular astronomical instruments and celestial globes that can be still seen today in Kraków, in the museum of the Collegium Maius.[31] Thanks to this proliferation, the University of Kraków became an international center of astronomy as well as of astrology, and it had an extensive relationship with other centers in Bologna, Prague, Paris, Vienna, and the royal court of Matthias, king of Hungary.[32] It provided various European universities and royal, episcopal, and papal courts with astrologers. Martin Król of Żurawica, the founder of the chair

---

27. Because it was used in university courses, Albumasar's *De magnis coniunctionibus* was printed at an early stage of book production in Augsburg in 1489.

28. Sacrobosco's work was printed (among others) in Venice by various publishers in 1482, 1490, and 1491.

29. See, for example, the *Tabulae Alphonsinae*, in BJ 570 (c. 1467), pp. 31–74. On the sources of the education, see Markowski, "Astronomie und der Krakauer Universität im XV. Jahrhundert," in *Les universités à la fin du Moyen Age, Actes du congrès international du Louvain (26–30 mai, 1975)*, ed. Jozef Ijsewijn and Jacques Paquet (Leuven: Leuven University Press, 1978), esp. 258–61, and *A et A* 22–23.

30. Mieczysław Markowski, "Die Mathematischen und Naturwissenschaften an der Krakauer Universität im XV. Jahrhundert," *Mediaevalia Philosophica Polonorum* 18 (1973): 121–31; Markowski, "Die Astrologie an der Krakauer Universität in den Jahren 1450–1550," in Szczucki, *Magia, astrologia e religione*, 83–89.

31. Concerning the astronomical tools of the University of Kraków, see Grażyna Rosińska, *Instrumenty astronomiczne na uniwersytecie krakowskim w XV wieku* (Astronomical Instruments at the University of Kraków in the Fifteenth Century) (Wrocław: Zakład Narodowy im. Ossolińskich, 1974); Danuta Burczyk-Marona, *Scientific and Teaching Instruments in the Jagiellonian Museum* (Kraków: POW Exartim, 1993); Karol Estreicher, *Copernican Relics in Jagiellonian University* (Kraków: Jagiellonian University, 1980); and Flóris Rómer, "A krakkói, Corvin Mátyás korabeli magyarországi csillagászati készletekről" (On Kraków Astronomical Tools From the Age of Matthias Corvinus), *Archeológiai Értesítő* 8 (1876): 274–76.

32. Asztrik Gábriel, "Intellectual Relations Between the University of Paris and the University of Cracow in the Fifteenth Century," *Studia Źródłoznawcze* 25 (1980): 37–63; Endre Kovács, *A krakkói egyetem és a magyar művelődés* (The University of Kraków and Hungarian Education) (Budapest: MTA Történettudományi Intézete, 1964). For Polish works in Vienna (by Andrzej Grzymala, Wojciech of Brudzewo, Adalbertus de Opatów, Johannes Glogoviensis, and so on) and German works in Kraków (by Johannes Regiomontanus and Georgius Peuerbach), see Mieczysław Markowski, "Beziehungen zwischen der Wiener Mathematischen Schule und der Krakauer Astronomischen Schule im Licht der erhaltenen mathematisch-astronomischen Schriften in den Manuscripten der Österreichischen Nationalbibliothek in Wien und der Jagellonischen Bibliothek in Kraków," *Mediaevalia Philosophica Polonorum* 18 (1973): 133–58.

of astrology, was also the astrologer of the Hungarian magnate János Hunyadi; Martin Bylica of Olkusz spent many years at the court of King Matthias;[33] Johannes Stercze (1433–93) was also invited to Hungary, and became the astrologer of the Rozgonyi family;[34] Adalbertus of Opatow (1454–56), Jacobus of Zalesie (1469–70), and Johannes Bossis (1471–75) held lectures at the University of Bologna while in the service of Miklós Stolz, the bishop of Nagyvárad in Hungary (Oradea in present-day Romania); Gregorius of Nowa Wies was the astrologer of Pope Paul II (1464–68); and Nicolaus Wodka of Kwidzyn (1442–94) was in the service of the prince of Urbino.[35] Wojciech of Brudzewo (1445–95)[36] and Johannes of Glogovia (1445–1507),[37] who belonged to the second generation of the professors of the astrological chair, also wandered throughout Europe but finally returned to their homelands. Reading this list of names, which could be easily lengthened, it is not surprising that the general impression of the contemporaries of the city was that "Kraków is stuffed with astrologers."[38]

Mathematicians and scientists in Central Europe studiously collected each other's works and had frequent opportunities to meet. They traveled throughout the region without regard to political boundaries: the journeys of Martin Król of Żurawica to Vienna, Prague, Bologna, and Padua, followed by his return to Kraków, can be viewed as typical. These centers, as well as Pozsony and Buda, were in direct scientific contact at this time.[39] Among the "Western" influences, the impact of Italy is

33. Leslie Domonkos, "The Polish Astronomer Martinus Bylica de Ilkusz in Hungary," *Polish Review* 13 (1968): 71–79.
34. See BJ 1839 (ca. 1485), pp. 306–12, for Jan Stercze, *Iudicium anni 1467*, and BJ 1839, pp. 312–14, for Stercze's *Iudicium eclipsis Solis anni 1463*.
35. Markowski, "Die Astrologie," 85–88.
36. Zofia Pwlikowska Brozek, "Wojciech of Brudzewo," in Gierowski, *Cracow Circle*, 61–76; Mieczysław Markowski, "Repertorium bio-bibliographicum astronomorum cracoviensum medii aevi," pt. 2, *Studia Mediewistyczne* 27, no. 1 (1990): esp. 117–32.
37. Zwiercan, "Jan of Glogów"; see also Markowski, "Repertorium bio-bibliographicum," pt. 1.
38. "Cracovia astrologis referta est." See Birkenmajer, *Études d'histoire des sciences en Pologne*, 491. For more Polish astrologers, such as Andreas de Cracovia, Jakub de Zalesie, Jan de Bossis Polonus, Jan Ilkowski, Jan Stercze, Jerzy de Drohobycz, Jan Gmunden, and Jan de Dondis, see Birkenmajer, *Études d'histoire des sciences en Pologne*, and *A et A*.
39. Adorján Divéky, "Lengyelország magyar vonatkozású kéziratanyaga" (Manuscripts of Hungarian Interest in Poland), *Levéltári Közlemények* 3 (1927): 45–46; Endre Kovács, *Magyar-cseh történelmi kapcsolatok* (Hungarian-Bohemian Historical Relations) (Budapest: MTA Történettudományi Intézet, 1952); Lajos Szádeczki, "Lengyel földi levéltárakból, magyar történeti szempontból" (From Polish Archives, from a Hungarian Historical Aspect), *Századok* 15 (1881): 313–31 and 414–30; Jan Dąbrowski, "Krakkó és a krakkói egyetem szerepe a magyar kultúra történetében" (The Role of Kraków and Its University in the History of Hungarian Culture), in *Tanulmányok a lengyel magyar irodalmi kapcsolatok köréből* (Studies on Hungarian-Polish Literary Relations), ed. István Csapláros and Lajos Hopp (Budapest: Akadémiai Kiadó, 1969); Dąbrowski, "A krakkói és a magyar reneszánsz kapcsolatai" (The Relations of the Kraków and Hungarian Renaissance), *Művészettörténeti értesítő* (1969): 31–36.

to be emphasized: most of the astrologers went to the universities of Bologna or Padua; some came back but remained in correspondence with Italian intellectuals, while some stayed there as court astrologers.[40] This phenomenon will provide us a general explanation of how scientific and magical literature arrived from Italy in the library of the professors but—since virtually everybody had Italian contacts—will also make it difficult to specify the exact routes of the intellectual import in the case of those texts that do not have an identified owner.

Professors' Libraries

The holdings of university libraries developed primarily through the donations and legacies of the masters teaching at the institution. Virtually all of the medieval manuscripts kept today in the Biblioteka Jagiellońska originally belonged to fifteenth-century university professors.[41] Meanwhile, although the collection of the National (earlier University) Library of Prague underwent a serious expansion thanks to donations, purchases, and the incorporation of monastic libraries, a considerable portion of the codices kept today in the Klementinum goes back to the collections of the professors of Charles University.[42] This means that most of the Kraków and Prague codices discussed in the second part of this study were originally copied, collected, and owned by university masters.

We have already seen in the case of Henry the Bohemian how university people were involved in magical practices, treasure hunting, the invocation of demons, and crystallomancy: Monaldus of Luca, Nicolaus Hinczonis, and perhaps even Henry himself graduated in a *studium generale,* and—as the sources testify—they possessed necromantic books. (Unfortunately, however, none of the manuscripts kept in the present-day collection of the Biblioteka Jagiellońska can be identified as having belonged to this group.) In Chapter 5, we met Mattheus Beran, an Augustinian brother from Rudnicz, who copied with his own hands a number of natural

---

40. Bronislaw Bilinski, *Tradizioni italiane all'università Jagellonica di Cracovia* (Wrocław: Zakład Narodowy im. Ossolińskich, 1967); Sante Graciotti and Cesare Vasoli, *Italia e Ungheria all'epoca dell'umanesimo corviniano,* Civiltà veneziana, Studi 45 (Florence: Leo S. Olschki, 1994); Balogh, "Néhány adat." For Polish works appearing in Padua, see Mieczysław Markowski, "Krakowskie dzieła astronomiczne w zbiorach rękopiśmiennych Biblioteki Uniwersyteckiej w Padwie jako świadectwo ich recepcji przez naukę włoską" (The Works of Kraków Astronomers in the Manuscript Collection of the University Library of Padua Witnessing That They Were Known in Italy), *Biuletyn Biblioteki Jagiellońskiej* 29 (1979): 43–53.

41. Szczepan K. Zinamer, *The Jagellonian University Library in Cracow* (New York: Czas Publishing, 1963).

42. Voit, *Pražské Klementinum.* On book donations in Bohemia, see also Hlaváček, *Středověké soupisy,* and Thomas Krzenck, "Books in Late Medieval Wills in Bohemia," *Annual of Medieval Studies at CEU* 7 (2001): 187–208.

magic and divinatory texts together with the *Flores aurei* (a part of the *Ars notoria*) into his codices. But before becoming a monk, Beran studied at the universities of Paris, Erfurt, and Vienna until he became a doctor of medicine. The historian is more fortunate in Beran's case than in that of Henry: not only the person but also his books can be identified. What these two cases can teach us is that university masters played a central role in the dissemination of texts of learned magic. The main objective of the present section is to take a second look at those magical manuscripts already discussed which once were part of the collection of a student or a professor.

In our surveys of natural magic, but first of all in that of image magic, we examined a number of codices that were copied or owned by Kraków *magistri*. Among them, the Dresden manuscript deserves special attention because of the number of magical texts it contains. As it can be recalled, in an extensive collection of astrological works written by the Kraków professors there were included some geomantic texts, a copy of the rare *Liber runarum*, the Hermetic *Liber de stellis beibeniis*, a bibliographical list of magical books, and other astrological and divinatory literature.[43] The errors and idiosyncrasies[44] in the *Liber runarum* attest that the book was copied from the same model as another copy of the same text copied by Johannes Virdung of Hassfurt in Kraków in 1488.[45] We know, furthermore, that the Dresden manuscript was copied at the same time by a certain Egidius of Corintia, student of Kraków, but unfortunately nothing is known about this person: his name does not appear in the lists of Kraków students.[46]

No less frustrating is the lack of evidence concerning another book of image magic, BJ 793. This codex, which contains an early copy of the *Picatrix* and an outstanding set of images of the planetary and decanic figures, as well as the two basic texts of image magic accepted by the *Speculum astronomiae*, that is, the *Opus imaginum* of Pseudo-Ptolemy and Thebit's *De imaginibus*, along with a representative selection of geomantic books of fate, is one of the most interesting handbooks of magic in Kraków. It has survived without its first page, and while it is obvious that it was owned and copied by a Kraków master, we cannot say for sure who this master was. Even the supposition about possible Italian sources is conjectural, since the codex or codices that served as the archetype(s) of this manuscript do not seem to have survived. And even if it was really copied from Italian examples, it is impossible to specify who the actual scribe or owner was, since

---

43. For a more detailed study of this codex, see Chapter 3, and Markowski, "Krakowskie dzieła astronomiczne w zbiorach rękopiśmiennych Biblioteki Uniwersyteckiej w Padwie."
44. For a discussion of the parallels of the two texts, see Chapter 3.
45. On Virdung and his codices, see the next section.
46. See, however, *A et A* 6–7.

most of the Kraków professors showed up in Northern Italy in the course of their careers.[47]

The supposition that Petrus Gaszowiec, astronomer and rector of the university, brought the sources of these manuscripts from Perugia or Cologne, where he traveled as a student, and that the two scribes who accompanied him copied the texts, is plausible but not proven.[48] It is true that Gaszowiec, on coming back from his travels in 1456, brought manuscripts of contemporary Italian astronomers to Poland, namely the astronomical tables of Johannes Bianchini,[49] but there is no decisive sign that BJ 793 originally belonged to him.

The problem of ownership cannot be solved decisively, and Gaszowiec's role in the history of the codex is only a supposition; however, the intellectual circle to which such a book belonged can be identified. Some of the texts contained in BJ 793 are identical with various parts of some other codices of the Jagiellonian Library, such as BJ 566, 805, and 813. All three belong to the library of a Kraków professor, Andrzej Grzymala, and attest to a similar interest in magic, medicine, and astrology.

BJ 813 is a handbook on medical and astrological texts composed of two parts.[50] The first is a curriculum handbook containing standard texts on medicine by Hippocrates, Galen, and Philaretus, and probably served the needs of a medical student. The second contains some classic texts on natural magic and astrological divination, the *Secretum secretorum* attributed to Aristotle, *Introductio in iudicia astrologiae* (Introduction to Astrological Judgments) by Arnald of Villanova, and Messahala's *De occultis* (On Occult Things),[51] and *De occultatione annuli* attributed to the first-century astrologer, Dorotheus Sidoneus. As for the two other codices, BJ 805 contains among other pieces the *Centiloquium* of Hermes, a treatise on geomancy,[52] and the *Experimenta* (or *Liber aggregationis*) attributed to Albertus Magnus,[53] while BJ 566 is a simple reader in medical astrology.[54]

Among these books, BJ 813 and 805 belong to the earliest collections of university professors; they were collected around 1364 and owned first by the professor Herman z Przeworska. A century later, these precious handbooks on medicine

---

47. About the content of this manuscript, on the suppositions on its ownership, and on the curriculum of Gaszowiec, see Chapter 3.

48. *CBJ*, 6:136, "Codicis origo et fata"; see also Chapter 3.

49. See BJ 555, fols. 1r–24v, and BJ 557 fols. 1ra–12va and 13r–131v. Gaszowiec did, in fact, own both of these codices.

50. See also Zathey, *Historia Biblioteki Jagiellońskiej*, 15–21, and *CBJ*, 6:213–23.

51. For this text and its diffusion, see Carmody, *Astronomical Works*, 28–29, and Lynn Thorndike, "The Latin Translations of Astrological Works by Messahala," *Osiris* 12 (1956): esp. 56–62.

52. See fols. 405r–409v. Following Rosińska, the library catalog incorrectly identifies this work as *De constellationibus*.

53. *CBJ*, 6:178–85.

54. *CBJ*, 5:9–20.

came into the possession of Andrzej Grzymala, and when he died in 1466, his older fellow Jan Oswiecim (d. 1488) purchased them.[55] We know Oswiecim originally as a professor of theology, but his later acquisitions (after 1466), such as BJ 830, which had originally belonged to Grzymala, show an interest in medicine. Also among those ancient and precious books that he obtained from Grzymala, we find BJ 839, which contains the *Liber geomantiae* (Book of Geomancy) of Hugo of Santalla, and another *Experimenta Alberti*. It is worth mentioning that Oswiecim prepared a table of contents for both BJ 805 and 813, and in these lists he omitted the geomantic text, the *De occultis* by Messahala, the *De occultatione annuli* attributed to Dorotheus Sidoneus, and the *De aqua ardente*. Therefore, it seems likely that the magical contents of these medical codices reflects Grzymala's interests rather than Oswiecim's.[56]

Andrzej Grzymala of Posnania (ca. 1425–66)[57] graduated from the University of Kraków, and just like Gaszowiec, he spent some years in Italy (1460–61), partly in Rome and perhaps also in Perugia. In 1453 and 1458 he was the dean of the Faculty of Arts, in 1464 dean of the Medical Faculty, and finally in the winter term of 1465/66 the rector of the university. Taking into consideration the fact that Petrus Gaszowiec was the dean of the Medical Faculty in 1459 and 1462, and the rector of the university in 1464 and in the summer term of 1465, it is plausible to suppose that they knew each other quite well.[58] Grzymala was an important donor to the university library; two dozen manuscripts of the Biblioteka Jagiellońska have survived from his collection, including the three codices just discussed.[59] The extant copies indicate that Grzymala consciously and persistently built up his professorial library mainly by purchasing medical manuscripts, some of them rather expensive.[60]

One more person can be related to the group of Grzymala, Gaszowiec, and Oswiecim: Mikołaj Wodka of Kwidzyn or Nicolaus Marienwerder[61] (ca. 1442–94),

---

55. Zathey, *Historia Biblioteki Jagiellońskiej*, 106–7.

56. On Oswiecim's scientific interests and the reconstruction of his library, see Wacława Szelińska, *Biblioteki profesorów uniwersytetu krakowskiego w XV początkach XVI wieku* (The Libraries of the Professors of the University of Kraków in the Fifteenth and Sixteenth Centuries) (Wrocław: Zakład Narodowy im. Ossolińskich, 1966), 101–14.

57. *Polski Słownik Biograficzny*, 9:114–16; *A et A* 25–27; Markowski, "Repertorium bio-bibliographicum," pt. 2, 111–63.

58. On the medical doctors of the University of Kraków, see Renata Mikołajczyk, "Examples of Medieval Plague Treatises from Central Europe," *Annual of Medieval Studies at CEU* 3 (1996–97): 229–35.

59. Markowski, "Repertorium bio-bibliographicum," pt. 2, 144.

60. On his notes left in the manuscripts purchased and on the prices of these codices, see Anna Z. Kozłowska, "Ceny książek ręcznie pisanych" (Prices of Handwritten Books), *Biuletyn biblioteki Jagiellońskiej* 49 (1999): 45–65.

61. Kwidzyn is a town situated on an island in the Vistula called *Insula Mariae* in Latin, hence the name Marienwerder.

doctor of philosophy and medicine.[62] He started his studies at the University of Kraków in 1462, and concentrated primarily on astronomy and mathematics. The fruit of these studies was a little astronomical treatise, the *Calendarium cyclicum* (Cyclical Calendar), composed in 1464. Around 1468, he—supposedly—went to the new Hungarian university, the Academia Istropolitana.[63] In the following decades we find him in Bologna where he studied medicine, later in Urbino, and finally in Poland again, where he was probably one of the teachers of Nicolaus Copernicus.

From our point of view, his early years are more interesting, because we have from that period a codex on logic, philosophy, and astronomy (ÖNB Cod. lat. 4007), part of which is in his own hand.[64] Besides Marienwerder's *Calendarium cyclicum*, this book also contains a four-folio long treatise on chiromancy, with the drawings of two hands.[65] Taking into consideration both his interest testified by his codex and his curriculum, and the chronological data (Marienwerder was a student at University of Kraków when Gaszowiec and Grzymala were professors), it seems likely that there was some sort of a connection among these three persons.[66]

We have, therefore, a group of university individuals related in one way or another to handbooks also containing magical practices. The evidence at hand enables us neither to determine to what extent they were interested in natural and image magic, nor to decide whether they simply read or even practiced any branch of

---

62. Ludwik Antoni Birkenmajer, "Mikołaj Wodka de Kwidzyn, médecin et astronome polonais du XVe siècle," *Bulletin de l'Academie Polonais des Sciences et des Lettres* (1924): 783–86; Birkenmajer, "Mikołaj Wodka z Kwidzyna zwany Abstemius, lekarz i astronom polski XV-go stulecia" (Mikołaj Wodka of Kwidzyn, Polish Doctor and Astronomer in the Fifteenth Century), *Roczniki Towarzystwa Naukowego w Toruniu*, 1926, 110–250; *A et A* 158–61.

63. On the supposition that Marienwerder was one of the students of this university, see Birkenmajer, "Mikołaj Wodka z Kwidznyna," 145.

64. See Csaba Csapodi, *A budai királyi palotában 1686-ban talált kódexek és nyomtatott könyvek* (The Codices and Printed Books Found in the Royal Castle of Buda in 1686) (Budapest: MTA, 1984), 24; Csapodi, "Codices, die im Jahre 1686 von Buda nach Wien geliefert wurden," *Codices Manuscripti* 7 (1981): 121–27; Franz Unterkircher, Heidelinde Horninger, and Franz Lackner, eds., *Die datierten Handschriften der Österreichischen Nationalbibliothek von 1501 bis 1600*, vol. 4 (Vienna: Österreichische Akademie der Wissenschaften, 1976), 189; and *A et A* 320. For a short study on the codex, see also Birkenmajer, "Mikołaj Wodka z Kwidznyna," 232–36. For a microfiche copy of the manuscript, see Magyar Tudományos Akadémia Könyvtára (Library of the Hungarian Academy of Sciences), Mf. 3437/II.

65. *Introduction in chiromantiam*, in ÖNB Cod lat. 4007 (1449), fols. 73r–77r; *Calendarium cyclicum*, ibid., fols. 77v–128r.

66. Birkenmajer, "Mikołaj Wodka z Kwidznyna," 129–34. It is worth noting that on the first folio of this manuscript, some Hungarian names appear, probably as the result of someone testing his pen: Symon Cardus de Karachonfalva, Stephanus de Bordus, and later Nyaradtew. The place names (Karácsonyfalva, Bordus, and Nyárádtő) indicate Transylvania as a possible origin of these individuals, who, in turn, seem to be Hungarian university masters related to Marienwerder's career either in Kraków or Pozsony. A certain Johannes Valentini de Karachonfalva, for example, was a student in Kraków in Marienwerder's time. Pauly, Ulanowski, and Chmiel, *Album Studiosorum*, 1:179.

magic. There are, however, general tendencies that can be identified. The codices owned by Andreas Grzymala, Johannes Oswiecim, and Nicolaus Marienwerder undeniably contain texts that may be classified as natural magic and divination, but the general nature of these manuscripts does not indicate more than that these works were considered as being thematically close to the main topics of the codices, medicine, astronomy, and astrology. Taking an overall look at these sources, nothing supports the idea that the inclusion of such texts, as the *Experimenta Alberti*, the *Secretum secretorum*, and the texts on geomancy and palmistry, are due to a particular interest in magic, and I would suggest that they rather constituted an integral part of the general medical theme in the library of professors.[67]

In contrast, the two previous manuscripts, the Dresden SLB N. 100 and BJ 793, even though oriented generally toward astrology, show a consistent interest in image magic and divination. Apart from the short bibliographical note on necromantic books in the Dresden codex,[68] no explicit sign indicates that the scribes *consciously* went beyond the realm of mere astrology, or that they ever actually manufactured the talismans of Thebit's *De imaginibus* or those of the *Picatrix*, but we can claim with confidence that the systematic incorporation of such texts in the two books indicate an awareness of the genre of talismanic magic, and that the presence of magical texts on the bookshelves of some, although not always identified, masters of the University of Kraków in the fifteenth century was definitely not accidental.

THE HERMETIC COLLECTION OF JOHANNES VIRDUNG OF HASSFURT

By far the most impressive group of magical texts copied in the Central European region can be found in the library of a Kraków *magister*, but these texts are no longer in Poland. The Palatine collection at the Vatican Apostolic Library includes half a dozen manuscripts[69] that were in the possession of, and to a great extent even copied by, Johannes Virdung of Hassfurt (ca. 1463–1538).[70] These codices contain primarily astronomical and astrological works of the leading scientists of

---

67. For a helpful reconstruction and analysis of the professorial libraries of University of Kraków, see Szelińska, *Biblioteki profesorów uniwersytetu krakowskiego*.
68. See Chapter 1.
69. BAV Pal. lat. 1369, 1375, 1385, 1391, 1396, 1439. For a description of the manuscripts, see Schuba, *Die Quadriviums-Handschriften*, and Włodek, *Polonica*, 83–105.
70. On Virdung, see Gustav Bauch, *Deutsche Scholaren in Krakau der Zeit der Renaissance, 1460–1520* (Breslau: M. & H. Marcus, 1901), 33–34, and Alexander Birkenmajer, "Formula," *Isis* 19 (1933): 364–78. On the dates of Virdung's birth and death, see Lynn Thorndike, "Johann Virdung of Hassfurt: Dates of Birth and Death," *Isis* 37 (1947): 74. Birkenmajer puts these dates at 1465 and 1535; see "Formula," 365.

the Central European region, such as Johannes of Glogovia, Albertus of Brudzewo, Georgius Peuerbach, Johannes of Gmunden, and Johannes Regiomontanus, but other basic texts of the celestial sciences by Albumasar, Richardus of Wallingford, and Johannes Bianchini are also included.[71] Sandwiched between the scientific tracts, Virdung reproduced a considerable number of magical works, belonging generally to the field of image magic. His Pal. lat. 1439—as we have already seen—contains one of the few extant copies of the *Liber runarum*, a text on manipulating planetary spirits for all kinds of benign and malign aims with the help of talismans, in which the spirits' names are to be engraved on metal plates in a runic alphabet. Unique to this copy of the *Liber runarum* is a sophisticated circular diagram showing the correspondences between the letters of runic and Latin alphabets (fol. 199r; see Plate 17). Since this *rota runarum* does not strictly belong to the main text of the *Liber runarum*, it is possible that Virdung himself composed it in order to facilitate the understanding of the complicated relations of runes and spirits detailed in the text.

Virdung was apparently also interested in practical Hermetic texts. His copy of the *Liber runarum* in Pal. lat. 1439 follows the *Liber de stellis beibeniis*, an astrological work on the fixed stars attributed to Hermes, while another of his Vatican manuscripts, Pal. lat. 1375, contains two magical Hermetic texts copied with his own hands in Kraków: *De imaginibus sive annulis septem planetarum* of Hermes, and *De imaginibus septem planetarum* of Belenus (Plate 18).[72] These classical works of talismanic magic are preceded in the manuscript by an otherwise unknown tract on imprisoning spirits of the planets in rings with the help of animal sacrifice, pieces of metal, exorcisms, characters, and engravings on gems.[73] The fourth item of this series on magical images is a so far unidentified text attributed to "Master Thomas," which contains similar elements to the previous ones, together with explicit conjurations addressed to the spirits. Against the background of this explicit interest in talismans, it is not surprising that Virdung acquired a codex in 1500 containing a copy of the relatively widespread *De imaginibus* of Thebit.[74]

Finally, Virdung's manuscripts also contain a range of divinatory material: the *summa* of the basic rules of chiromancy collected by him from various texts of palmistry (Plate 20),[75] the *Sphera Pythagorae*, which is also called the sphere of life and death (Plate 21),[76] geomantic figures,[77] and, on numerous folios of his manuscripts,

71. Thorndike, "Giovanni Bianchini in Italian Manuscripts."
72. On these texts, see Chapter 3.
73. "Incipit liber de spiritibus inclusis," in BAV Pal. lat. 1375, fols. 269v–270r. See also Thorndike, "Johann Virdung of Hassfurt Again."
74. BAV Pal. lat. 1369, fols. 127v–129v.
75. *Chyromantia ex diversis libris collecta*, in BAV Pal. lat. 1396, fols. 91r–93r.
76. BAV Pal. lat. 1375, fol. 44r.
77. Ibid.

lists of several sets of secret alphabets (Plate 22).[78] Except for *De imaginibus*, Virdung copied this far from everyday selection of magical texts when he was a student in Kraków.

Johannes Virdung of Hassfurt is first known in the secondary literature for his astrological works, printed at the beginning of the sixteenth century when he was already living in Germany.[79] We can get a clear picture of his earlier life too, because, fortunately, he gives many details about his education here and there throughout Pal. lat. 1439.[80]

On the basis of this "curriculum vitae" (and other bits of information he left in his manuscripts), we can reconstruct his scholarly itinerary quite precisely.[81] He attended the university in Leipzig in 1481; in 1482 he entered the University of Kraków, where he studied for four years,[82] and attended the lectures of (and worked together with) the two most important professors of astrology of Poland, Johannes of Glogovia and Albertus of Brudzewo, whose texts are well represented in Virdung's codices. Later he became the *mathematicus*, that is, the court astrologer, of the elector palatine,[83] he produced yearly prognostications, and taught mathematics, astronomy, and medicine at the University of Heidelberg.[84] After his death, his manuscripts passed into the library of the elector palatine, and in 1622, in the military whirl of the Thirty Years' War, the whole manuscript collection of Heidelberg, including the codices of Virdung, was taken to the Vatican, where it forms today the Palatinus latinus collection.[85]

Did such a career in the field of astrology predestine Virdung to be fascinated by the magical sciences? Comparing his curriculum and interest with another person with similar dispositions, the answer seems to be negative. Virdung was not the only German student of University of Kraków who studied astrology and copied the crucial texts of the professors. In the university library of Jena, eight manuscripts

---

78. BAV Pal. lat. 1375, fols. 19r, 284r, 285r, and 1391, fol. 288r.
79. *HMES*, 4:456–57; for a list of Virdung's *Judicia* and *Practica*, see *A et A* 94–104. For a study on Virdung's prognostications, see Max Steinmetz, "Johann Virdung von Hassfurt, sein Leben und seine astrologischen Flugschriften," in Zambelli, *Astrologi Hallucinati*, 195–214.
80. BAV Pal. lat. 1439, fols. 8r, 39r, 331v–335r, 350v.
81. Thorndike, "Johann Virdung"; Lynn Thorndike, "Another Virdung Manuscript," *Isis* 34 (1942–43): 291–93.
82. His name appears in the *Liber promotionum*, under the year 1486, when he earned his bachelor's degree at the University of Kraków. See Gąsiorowski, *Liber promotionum*, 79.
83. He served first Philip (1476–1508), and then his successor, Ludwig (1508–44).
84. For more details, see Schuba, *Die Quadriviums-Handschriften*, 236–37.
85. For the history of the Palatinus latinus manuscripts of the Biblioteca Apostolica Vaticana, see Elmar Mittler and Wilfried Werner, *Mit der Zeit: Die Kurfürsten von der Pfalz und die Heidelberger Handschriften der Bibliotheca Palatina* (Wiesbaden: Ludwig Reichert, 1986), and Ludwig Schuba, *Quadriviumshandschriften—Referat* (Wützburg: n.p., 1970).).

have survived that are strikingly similar to the codices of Virdung.[86] These codices were owned, copied, and brought to Jena by Johannes Volmar of Villingen.[87] In many respects, Volmar's case is similar to that of Virdung: he also studied in Kraków, just a few years later than Virdung, he also subsequently became a court astrologer in a German court, namely in Wittenberg, and he copied virtually the same texts by Glogovia, Brudzewo, Gaszowiec, and Regiomontanus. The only difference is that Volmar did not include in his manuscripts magical and Hermetic material. Apparently—and not surprisingly—the milieu of the University of Kraków gave ample opportunities to copy talismanic texts (an opportunity used by Virdung, Egidius of Corintia, and the scribe of BJ 793), but as the entirely similar astrological, and the complete lack of magical, interests of another student, Johannes Volmar indicate, copying texts about astrology did not necessarily result in collecting texts about image magic.

Searching for further traces and evidence of Virdung's interest in learned magic, I was faced with a striking absence of such material in his printed works. Besides his countless prognostications, Virdung also published a few books on astrological medicine, but these works do not contain the slightest sign of their author's interest in talismans and planetary spirits.[88] However, turning back to the manuscripts and consulting other sources, one can see that Virdung's interest in image magic texts was consistent and long term. The Pal. lat. 1375, for example, was written by Virdung in Kraków, but contains later additions from Heidelberg. One of these additions is a note on a flyleaf recording his meeting in 1510 with a certain "Nicolaus de Pulchro Monte vulgaliter Schonberg," an excellent British astrologer and necromancer, also a provost and a doctor of law.[89] No further data is known about this enigmatic Nicholas, and even his origin is problematic. Several places exist in Europe with the name *Mons Bellus* or *Pulcher Mons*,[90] and Schönberg is indeed the vulgar form of this name, but if Nicholas is from England, why is the place name in German?[91]

---

86. MS El. f. 64, 70, 71, 72, 73, 74, 77, and MS El. phil. q. 3. For a description of the manuscripts, see Elzbieta Burda and Anna Kozlowska, eds., *Handschriftliche Polonica in den Sammlungen der Universitätsbibliothek Jena* (Jena: Universitätbibliothek Jena, 1989).

87. On Volmar, see Bauch, *Deutsche Scholaren in Krakau*, 56–57, and Ernst Zinner, *Verzeichnis der astronomischen Handschriften des deutschen Kulturgebietes* (Munich: C. H. Beck, 1925), 528–29.

88. These works are the *Nova medicinae methodus curandi morbos* (Haganoae: Kobian, 1533), and *De cognoscendis, et medendis morbis ex corporum coelestium* (Venetia: Zenarius, 1584). I consulted the copies kept in the Herzog August Bibliothek in Wolfenbüttel. See Ursula Zachert, ed., *Verzeichnis medizinischer und naturwissenschaftlicher Drucke, 1472–1830* (Munich: Saur, 1990), 1736–37.

89. "Nicolaus de pulchro monte vulgariter Schonberg Britannicus astrologus optimus et nigromanticus fuit mecum Anno 1510 die lune post Jacobi et recessit die Mercurii, erat prepositus et doctor legum."

90. J. G. Th. Graesse, ed., *Orbis Latinus*, vol. 1 (Berlin: Richard Carl Schmidt, 1909), 247.

91. Thorndike was not able either to find more data about Nicholas. See Thorndike, "Johann Virdung," 364.

This was certainly not the first occasion in Virdung's life on which he was to discuss occult studies with an international audience. We learn from a letter of Johannes Werner, astronomer and mathematician from Nuremberg (1466–1522), addressed to the humanist Konrad Celtis (1459–1508) in 1503, that Virdung, after having borrowed a precious astronomical book from Werner, disappeared together with the book, and went to England to learn magic.[92] There is evidence for Virdung returning from England and resuming his activities in Heidelberg: nothing is known, however, about his magical studies in the British Isles, nor do we know whether he finally returned the book.

Konrad Celtis and Johannes Virdung were two members of a circle of humanists grouped around the court of Heidelberg. Both of them were alumni of the University of Kraków, and both were interested in magic and Hermetism. Celtis spent three years as a student in Kraków (1489–91), where he participated in the meetings of leading humanists grouped around Filippo Buonaccorsi, *alias* Callimachus Experiens.[93] When he moved to Heidelberg, he founded another circle of learned humanists, which included intellectuals such as Johannes Reuchlin (1455–1522), the famous Hebrew scholar, and Johannes Trithemius (1462–1516), abbot of Sponheim. The Heidelberg humanists were under the influence of the Neoplatonic and Hermetic writings of Ficino and Pico della Mirandola; interest in Hermetism, cabbalist philosophy—especially in its christianization à la Reuchlin—, natural magic, and numerology played a fairly important role in their intellectual lives.[94] In Heidelberg, Virdung found a most convenient place to consummate his academic interest.

That Trithemius and Virdung were friends is further attested to by their correspondence, which included occult issues. This intellectual contact can answer a question about the dissemination of the *Liber runarum* (raised in Chapter 3). On the one hand, one of the four extant copies of this rare text was copied in Virdung's own hand; on the other hand, one of the scarce medieval reports on the magical

---

92. Hans Rupprich, ed., *Der Briefwechsel des Konrad Celtis* (Munich: Beck, 1934), 548–49: "In tanta igitur mentis perturbatione saepe consolatur me libellus ille Graecus, Laertius videlicet Diogenes, quem sua dignatio tanquam pro pignore mihi relinquit; nam eius iussu quempiam alium libellum et in re astronomica satis pretiosum atque in orbe terrarum rarissimum accomodavi Johanni Hasfurt, artium doctori atque illustris ducis ac principis palatini mathematico. Hic autem cum ipso libro est proditus; haud vanus rumor est magicae dicendae gratia in Angliam profectum esse."

93. Konrad Celtis was in contact with not only the Heidelberg and Kraków groups of humanists, but also the royal court of Buda. On these issues, see Tibor Klaniczay, "Celtis und die Sodalitas Litteraria per Germaniam," in *Respublica Guelpherbytana: Wolfenbütteler Beiträge zur Renaissance- und Barockforschung, Festschrift für Paul Raabe*, ed. August Buck (Amsterdam: Rodopi, 1987), 79–105, and *A magyarországi akadémiai mozgalom előtörténete* (The Pre-History of the Hungarian Academic Movement), Humanizmus és reformáció 20 (Budapest: Balassi, 1993), 47–77.

94. Martina Backers, *Das literarische Leben am kurpfälzischen Hof zu Heidelberg im 15. Jahrhundert* (Tübingen: Max Niemeyer, 1992), 150–57; Mittler and Werner, *Mit der Zeit*, 15–18.

use of the runes was Trithemius's *Antipalus Maleficiorum,* the list of magic books, where the abbot mentions it as a vain and superstitious text containing names of malign sprits.[95] In addition, Virdung's codex, the Pal. lat. 1375, contains the same four Hermetic texts on talismans and enclosed spirits that Trithemius lists one after another in his *Antipalus.* It seems highly possible that the library of Johannes Virdung of Hassfurt, being easily accessible to his friend Trithemius, offered the abbot the opportunity to consult magical texts, among them a copy of the *Liber runarum* and the talismans of "Master Thomas," about which we only have two testimonies, the astrologer's codex and the abbot's book list.

One of the issues related to magic that Virdung and Trithemius discussed in their letters concerned another practitioner of magic, Georgius Sabellicus. Virdung must have asked Trithemius's opinion on this strange character, but his letter is no longer extant, and we have only the addressee's answer, dated August 20, 1507.[96] The abbot calls *Magister Sabellicus Faustus iunior* a charlatan and impostor. Faustus—writes Trithemius—dared to call himself the foremost of the necromancers, and he even composed a calling card in order to send it to the important personalities of his time.[97] Trithemius further suggests that Faustus is not only an unstable character and a vagabond, but is also sexually perverted, being an active admirer of young boys.[98] These harsh words have enjoyed great scholarly attention in modern times, because Trithemius's letter contains the first mention of the historical person called Georgius Faustus, whose notorious life and constantly growing legend furnished material for so many literary texts. Trithemius is the first of Faustus's contemporaries to provide bibliographical data on the basis of which Faustus's life, his early career as a student at the University of Heidelberg, and his later activity as a magician can be reconstructed.[99]

From the letter it appears that Virdung had received Faustus's card, and was keenly interested in meeting the magus who called himself the prince of necromancers, but before they met, he had cautiously inquired of the abbot whether he knew anything about this person. It is not known whether the scandalous details that Trithemius shared with him discouraged Virdung, or that he finally encountered Faustus. At any rate, it seems that Virdung had a conscious program of personally

95. For the original passage in Busaeus, *Paralipomena opusculorum,* see Chap. 3, n. 87.
96. On the letter and its background, see Lynn Thorndike, "Faust and Johann Virdung of Hassfurt," *Isis* 26 (1937): 321, and Dieter Harmening, "Faust und die Renaissance-Magie: Zum ältesten Fauszeugnis: Johannes Trithemius an Johannes Virdung, 1507," *Archiv für Kulturgeschichte* 55 (1973): 56–79. Baron, *Doctor Faustus,* esp. 23–39, is the most reliable secondary source on the historical Faust.
97. See the introduction of this chapter.
98. "Qui mox nefandissimo fornicacionis genere cum pueris videlicet voluptari cepit, quo statim deducto in lucem, fuga penam declinavit paratam." Baron, *Doctor Faustus,* 30 and 97. This is probably the most unfounded of Trithemius's accusations.
99. For a reconstruction, see Baron, *Doctor Faustus.*

meeting all the magicians of his time, including Nicolaus de Pulchro monte, Georgius Sabellicus Faustus, and the English magicians whom he visited in 1503 when traveling to Britain to study the occult arts.

Trithemius mentions Virdung's name once more, when he describes the uncommon arrival of the Italian magician Johannes Mercurius (another charlatan, in his view) to Lyon, and his success at the French royal court. In these lines, Virdung appears as a "mathematician of the Count Palatine, who is living today at Budoris with his prince Ludwig."[100] (That Virdung was in Lyon is also attested to by a letter written by the kapellmeister of the court of Elector Ludwig, in which he informs his lord that Virdung brought some music from Lyon, where the French royal court was residing.)[101] Reading Trithemius, we can see that the foolishness and haughtiness of Mercurius was no smaller than that of Faustus.[102] He arrogantly wished to be called Mercury, his wife, his children, his servants, and himself were clothed in linen, and they all wore iron chains around their necks.[103] Although illiterate and uneducated, he claimed not only to possess all the science, mystery, and arcana of the ancient sages, but also to surpass them. All this happened—he stated—not with demonic help, but through the art of natural magic.[104] He was amicably accepted in the French court, and when the doctors of the king examined him, they found that he was indeed proficient in all fields of human knowledge even though he was without an adequate knowledge of Latin.[105]

The parallel of the descriptions of these two magicians, the explicit wish to discredit them, and the hatred Trithemius expresses are manifest, and seem to be surprising at first glance. Trithemius, when collecting nearly two thousand volumes for his abbey at Sponheim, included numerous magical items in this impressive library. In addition, as his literary production attests, the abbot himself was deeply involved in the field of Hermetism and learned magic, and thus his criticism of magicians should not be seen as the disapproval of a furious outsider, but as the wrath of a rival. It belongs to the background of his attitude that Trithemius himself was accused of practicing black magic. This happened thanks to a confidential

---

100. Trithemius, *Annales Hirsaugiensis*, 2:584–85: "Testem adduco tertium Johannem Virdungem de Hasfurt, Comitis Palatini Mathematicum, qui & ipse apud Budoras hodie vivit . . . cum suo Principe Ludovico." See also Thorndike, "Another Virdung Manuscript," 292–93.
101. Backers, *Das literarische Leben am kurpfälzischen Hof*, 158.
102. On Mercurius, see *HMES*, 4:557–58, and W. B. McDaniel, "An Hermetic Plague-Tract by Johannes Mercurius Corrigiensis," *Transactions and Studies of the College of Physicians of Philadelphia*, 4th ser., 9 (1941–42): 217–25.
103. Trithemius, *Annales Hirsaugiensis*, 2:584: "per arrogantiam ipse Mercurium se voluit appellari, uxorem habens et liberos, servos et ancillas, qui una cum ipso lineis duntaxat erant induti, singuli singulas catenas ad collum ferreas portantes."
104. Ibid.
105. On Johannes Mercurius, see Wouter J. Hanegraaff, "Giovanni da Correggio," in Hanegraaff et al., *Dictionary of Gnosis and Western Esotericism*, 273–75.

letter he wrote on March 25, 1499, to Arnold Bostius, in which he spoke about his future book on secret writing, the *Steganographia*, and also about a revelation he experienced while dealing with magic. This letter was accidentally read by hostile eyes instead of those of the actual addressee, who had died in the meantime, and as a result of this accident, Trithemius spent the rest of his life defending himself against hostile rumors. His intention to discredit Faustus and Mercurius should be situated in this context, where it appears as a pure and well-known argumentative technique of defending one's reputation: "What I do is serious philosophy; what you do is foolish magic."[106] The abbot wrote to Virdung about Faustus, "When he comes to you, you will find that he is not a philosopher but rather a very rash fool."[107] Trithemius saw himself not as a magus, but as a philosopher concerned with magic at a high spiritual level, and however close his interest seemed to be to the occult practices of Faustus and Mercurius—or exactly because of this closeness—he saw a most dislikable phenomenon in the emergence of these figures.

Excursus: The Self-Fashioning of Magicians

In a final brief digression, a new phenomenon should be emphasized, one which can be called the "self-fashioning" of Renaissance magicians.[108] Through various sophisticated techniques and extravagant self-promotion, Mercurius and Faustus consciously built up the image of the magician and shaped their public identities to conform to it.

This is reflected first of all by the names they used. They took Latin names, as was fashionable in the circles of humanists. One of them called himself Mercurius after the magical figure of Hermes Trismegistos, while the other adopted the symbolic name Sabellicus. With this choice, he implied that he came from the land of

---

106. For a fuller account of Trithemius and his ambivalent attitude toward learned magic, see Frank L. Borchardt, "Trithemius and the Mask of Janus," in *Traditions and Transitions: Studies in Honor of Harold Jantz*, ed. Liselotte E. Kurth (Munich: Delp, 1972), 37–49, and Noel L. Brann, *Trithemius and Magical Theology* (New York: SUNY Press, 1999); on Faust and Mercurius, see 64–67.

107. Baron, *Doctor Faustus*, 29–30, and 97: "Cum venerit ad te, non philosophum sed hominem fatuum et nimia temeritate agitatum invenies."

108. The expression was made famous by the renowned book of Stephen Greenblatt, *Renaissance Self-Fashioning: From More to Shakespeare* (Chicago: University of Chicago Press, 1980). Here, however, I do not make full use of Greenblatt's complex theory, but rather refer to self-fashioning in the everyday meaning of the expression, implying freedom of self-determination. See the "horizontal scale" of personal development in Thomas Greene's discussion of self-fashioning, "The Flexibility of the Self in Renaissance Literature," in *The Disciplines of Criticism*, ed. Peter Demetz, Thomas Greene, and Lowry Nelson Jr. (New Haven: Yale University Press, 1968), 241–64. See also Jan Veenstra, "Self-Fashioning and Pragmatic Introspection: Reconsidering the Soul in the Renaissance (Some Remarks on Pico, Pomponnazzi and Macchiavelli)," in *Self-Fashioning—Personen(selbst)darstellung*, ed. Rudolf Suntrup and Jan Veenstra (Frankfurt a. M.: Peter Lang, 2003), 285–308.

the Sabines, famous for the practice of the occult from the time of Roman Antiquity up to the sixteenth century. Faustus furthermore called himself the *princeps necromanticorum* and the *fons necromantiae*. Both Faustus and Mercurius manipulated their public: by sending around calling cards and generating rumors, they constructed their fame, which outshone their actual personalities. In an age when the media were not yet invented, a calling card listing all the titles by which one wanted to be remembered was a useful way of propagating one's fame and to become the main subject of gossip. Provoking the public, both persons risked acquiring enemies: when Faustus sent his card to Virdung and Trithemius, and when Mercurius marched gloriously into Lyon, they were certainly aware that their reception would not be unanimously positive. However, attaining fame is a greater achievement than becoming popular.

Fame and legend became superior to historical reality. The image of Faust was formed by Luther, Melanchton, and posterity in general: new details were added to the life and especially the death of this magician, new opinions emerged about his relations with the Devil. Even his name changed through the decades of the sixteenth century: from Georgius Faustus to Johann Faust. By the time of Goethe, hardly anybody remembered that a real historical figure stood behind all these beliefs.

But the shift in favor of the legend can be demonstrated even more expressively in the case of Mercurius: according to certain modern theories, his legend was so much more essential than his reality that we can even suppose that the magician did not exist altogether. An argument was put forth in 1938 that Johannes Mercurius was a fictive character, his fame being simply constructed by a contemporary, Lodovico Lazzarelli (ca. 1450–1500).[109] Lazzarelli wrote three prefaces in which he claimed that Mercurius had been his master.[110] Lazzarelli either invented the figure of this genius magician or magnified an otherwise insignificant person, spreading rumors about him, in order to cover his own authorship of some Hermetic texts by attributing them to this Mercurius. Now, it is true that the stylistic analysis of Lazzarelli's and Mercurius's texts reveal a strong similarity, and that the second

---

109. Kurt Ohly, "Johannes 'Mercurius' Corrigiensis," *Beiträge zur Inkunabelkunde*, n.s., 2 (1938): 133–41. See also McDaniel, "An Hermetic Plague-Tract."

110. On Lazzarelli and his literary production, see Paul Oskar Kristeller, "Marsilio Ficino e Ludovico Lazzarelli," in Kristeller, *Studies in Renaissance Thoughts and Letters* (Rome: Edizioni di Storia e Letteratura, 1984), 221–46; Kristeller, "Lodovico Lazzarelli e Giovanni da Correggio, due Ermetici del Quattrocento," in *Biblioteca degli Ardenti della Città di Viterbo*, 1960; Eugenio Garin, Minella Brini, and others, eds., *Testi umanistici sull' Ermetismo* (Rome: Bocca, 1955), 24–50; Wouter Hanegraaff and R. M. Bouthoorn, eds., *Lodovico Lazzarelli (1447–1500): The Hermetic Writings and Related Documents* (Tempe: Arizona Center for Medieval and Renaissance Studies, 2005); and Wouter J. Hanegraaff, "Lodovico Lazzarelli," in Hanegraaff et al., *Dictionary of Gnosis and Western Esotericism*, 679–83.

group of sources could not have been written by an illiterate author. It can be also argued that the contemporary reports on Mercurius depend in one way or another on the information spread by Lazzarelli, one piece of gossip nourishing the other. The only person whose testimony does not depend on Lazzarelli—and this is the weak point of the skeptical argument—is Johannes Virdung of Hassfurt, cited by Trithemius.

Whatever truth there may be in that argument, we see the rise of a new magician figure, who—by complex techniques of self-fashioning—forms a way of life in which magical interest becomes primary, and constructs his own fame by which he lives. Johannes Virdung of Hassfurt was present at the birth of this new type of self-appointed magician.[111] He himself, however, remained a passive witness to this process: magic was always one of his main interests, but it was never his primary interest. He was a typical member of the Central European circle of medical doctors, university members, and courtly astrologers concerned with magic, one who copied, read, and collected the magical and Hermetic techniques and who personally met the exponents of these fields. We are quite fortunate to have all these traces that Virdung left us about his occult interests. In the case of the Dresden manuscript, however, we know only the name of the copyists, while in the case of BJ 793, even less. Although we cannot identify each owner, each copyist, and each magician of late medieval Kraków or Prague, we can describe the university context where the students and professors became acquainted with learned magic and Hermetism, and we can refer to academic travels that advanced the import of the basic texts.

111. On the question whether Renaissance magic and Renaissance magicians differed substantially from the medieval ones, see Kieckhefer, "Did Magic Have a Renaissance?"

Conclusion: Seven Questions

My inquiries have had a twofold objective. First, I intended to provide a catalog and an analysis of the texts of learned magic that have survived in Central Europe, and second, I wished to characterize the circle of those persons who can be related to these magical texts. These two objectives can be divided into two sets of questions.

To provide a catalog and an analysis of the texts of learned magic that have survived in Central Europe, it was necessary to ask:

1. What texts of magical content (belonging to the fields of natural, image, and ritual magic, as well as to those of alchemy and divination) can be found and identified in the manuscript collections of Central Europe?

2. What texts that have not survived, but which surely existed, since we have evidence of their fifteenth-century existence from the extant source material, can be identified?

3. And to what extent does this group of magical texts represent an "original" intellectual production of this region? In other words, were these texts written in this region by local authors, or were they simply imported from the West by local scribes?

To characterize the circle of those persons who can be related to these magical texts, it was necessary to ask:

4. Who are those persons who were in one way or another responsible for the emergence of the magical sources, that is, who were their authors, scribes, owners, readers, and users? How can we describe the circle of these persons? Were they magicians, outsiders, marginal figures living on the periphery of society, or ordinary monks, average courtiers, and everyday university people?

5. What was the place of learned magic in their interest: primary or accidental? Why were these sources copied or written: to put them into practice or just for contemplation? Did any reader wish to apply the divinatory methods, talismanic instructions, and ritual invocations? Or did magic simply belong to a pure "academic interest" of the collectors?

6. Remaining still with the issue of the collectors' fascination for magic, one can ask a question that might be considered both anachronistic and naive, and yet everyone dealing with medieval texts of magic will sooner or later ponder on it. Why didn't these collectors see that it was impossible to learn the seven liberal arts through the prayers of the *Ars notoria,* that it was impossible to expel scorpions from Bath or destroy cities with the help of Thebit's *De imaginibus,* and that the magnet does not say anything about the chastity of their wives? Or should we rather suppose that the methods did actually work in their time?

7. And finally, did the scribes, collectors, and authors of magic texts form a coherent group of practitioners, or a company of interested friends? Did they copy the texts from each other's codices, did they discuss the content, did they put this content into practice together, or were they isolated intellectuals with no visible connections?

Let us see systematically what the answers to these questions are, as offered by my research.

1. I believe that my study has convincingly shown that Central European manuscript collections offer fewer, but an equally rich variety of, magical texts as Western European libraries. Polish, Bohemian, and Hungarian scribes and collectors included natural and image magic, alchemy and divination, as well as various types of ritual magic in their codices not just by mere chance. This is the region which preserved, *inter alia,* the first long version of the famous handbook of magic, the *Picatrix,* which is also the only illustrated copy we have, and two of the four extant copies of the *Liber runarum,* a short tract combining Hermetic talismans with Scandinavian runes. In addition, this part of Europe gave birth to the following: a unique version of ritual magic, the prayer book of King Wladislas, which incorporates crystallomancy, and long paragraphs of the *Liber visionum* of John of Morigny; the *Bellifortis* of Conrad Kyeser, a source of technology and military engineering that is rich in magical elements; the *Antipocras* of Nicholas of Poland, a theoretical work on the borderline of medicine and natural magic, which recommends its reader to consume snake flesh for medicinal purposes; and Nicolaus Melchior's *Processus,* which combines the text of the Christian Mass with the alchemical process. These four texts of "local authorship" inspired wide interest among Western scholars, too.

The only category of texts missing from these manuscripts was necromancy *per se,* the genre which contains long invocations to benign and malign spiritual agents, offers explicitly demonic procedures, and operates with an inventory of magic circles, animal sacrifices, suffumigations, summoned and bound demons, and so on. (To be sure, texts of image magic may also contain such elements, although in different contexts and in different concentrations.) However, demonic magic was fairly rare even in the West; texts such as the Munich manuscript published by Richard

Kieckhefer and the MS Rawlinson 252 are considered singular survivors, and it is by no means surprising that no such examples have been found so far in Central European manuscript collections.

2. Some of the extant source materials contain clear indications that certain other magical works were in use and had been read in late medieval Central Europe. Precise textual borrowings in the *Bellifortis* attest that Conrad Kyeser, when writing and compiling his work, had in front of him a copy of the *Liber vaccae,* and two texts attributed to Albertus Magnus, the *Experimenta,* and the *De mirabilibus mundi.* We have every right to suppose that the latter two texts were consulted with great attention also by Nicholas of Poland, the doctor from Montpellier. The *Liber visionum* of John of Morigny, a (perhaps incomplete) copy of the *Ars notoria,* and some further magical and crystallomantic texts were without doubt on the table of the author of the prayer book of Wladislas, who incorporated long paragraphs from these sources in his handbook. Nicholas the Hangman and Henry the Bohemian were both accused in Kraków of possessing magical books (one of these was written by a certain Matthias, a necromancer); and even though these books cannot be identified today, we may suppose that they belonged to the field of ritual magic. Finally, the author of the short book list of the Dresden manuscript—whom I believe to have been the scribe of the codex, Egidius of Corintia—was well acquainted with the eleventh chapter of the *Speculum astronomiae,* where the author of the *Speculum* establishes the classifications of Hermetic, Solomonic, and natural literature; he must have also read the *Picatrix;* and he seems to have had firsthand information about at least some of the magical and necromantic books he lists, such as the *Clavicula Salomonis,* the *Liber Semphoras,* the *Liber quattuor annulorum Salomonis,* the *De arte eutonica,* the *Liber ad demoniacos,* the *Liber machometi de septem nominibus,* the *Liber institutionis Raziel,* the *Liber lunae,* and the *Liber Almandel.* Even though these texts have no trace in the extant book collections, we can plausibly suppose that they were accessible for a Kraków student at the end of the fifteenth century.

3. It is perhaps naive but certainly reasonable to inquire about the originality of this wide range of magical texts. Bearing in mind that discerning between original authorship and mere compilation has little relevance in a medieval context in general, and therefore any answer to such a question is necessarily misleading, we can say that in the fields of medicine and astronomy, Central European scholars proved to be most fruitful and "original," and their scientific outcome constitutes an important chapter of the history of science, but their texts on natural and image magic as well as on divination were, as a rule, mere reproductions of the well-known Western material. We have only a few, albeit striking, examples when a text is not a simple copy of an Italian, French, or German codex. Such examples are the *Bellifortis* of Kyeser and the royal prayer book of Wladislas—even though this book

is at least ninety-five percent compiled from other texts, the act and the aspects of the compilation can be regarded as "original," which is the usual type of originality in the genre of ritual magic. Interestingly, alchemy proved the most inspiring topic for the authors of this region: besides reproducing Western texts, such as the works of Johannes of Rupescissa, Central European scribes had the opportunity to copy local products, too, whether they were the Latin works by Johannes Ticinensis, the Czech *Rightful Way* of John of Laz, or the alchemical process in the form of a Christian Mass by Nicolaus Melchior. While we have less reason to speak about Central Europe's own group of *magician*-authors, the region certainly had a considerable number of practicing *alchemist*-authors.

4. Having identified the individuals who can be related to magic, we can observe that virtually none of them can be seen as a real outsider, that is, a marginal figure of the society. In Poland, Bohemia, and Hungary, we find mainly insiders related to manuscripts of magic: university professors, monastic figures, ecclesiastical and courtly officers, medical doctors, and engineers—that is, intellectuals whose activity was not monopolized by the topic of magic. Even Nicholas of Poland, whose medical methods and obsession with snake flesh shocked and terrified many, and caused no little scandal around Kraków, was a doctor trained in the best schools of his time, and nobody considered him an obscure magician.

Among the three places where readers of magic gathered—the monastery, the university, and the court—the monastic milieu yielded the least evidence for a reconstruction of some magical interest. Alchemy was certainly a recurrent concern for the monks of Central Europe (as it was for monks in the West), and so was natural magic (probably as a form of medical knowledge), but no monastery of the region can rival the richness of magic sources in St. Augustine's in Canterbury. As far as one can judge from the extant list of titles, monastic libraries in Central Europe rarely included explicitly magical items. The courtly context was a much more fertile soil for a curiosity about learned magic, and this curiosity was not limited to telling the future. Courtly intellectuals were in the position of being able to read a wide range of magical materials, as it is attested by Wladislas's prayer book, Kyeser's military handbook, and the court case of Henry the Bohemian, who was accused of invoking spirits in order to find treasure.

The greatest number of tracts, however, appears in the codices of the masters of the newly founded Central European universities, especially in the milieu of the chair of astrology in Kraków. The *Picatrix*, the *Liber runarum*, the *Experimenta Alberti*, and a variety of other magical works may be found in the late medieval professorial libraries of the region. To be sure, the predominance of university masters in the role of the collectors and scribes of magical texts might have several other reasons than their greater interest in magic. First, professors usually owned more books than other readers in the Middle Ages. Second, compared to other medieval book collections, their libraries enjoyed the best chances of survival, and are consequently the easiest to reconstruct. Modern national libraries, such as the Biblioteka Jagiellońska in Kraków and the National Library of Prague, which were the main "suppliers" of this study, were originally based on private and institutional medieval book collections related to the university.

5. The fact that most texts of magic survived from the libraries of university people explains their codicological context, too. Generally speaking, works on natural magic and talismans became integral constituents of medical and astronomical manuscripts without being considered particularly magical or problematic, and this reflects the fact that they had an equally organic place in the scientific interest of the collectors. Analysis of the library of a Kraków student, Johannes Virdung of Hassfurt, has proven that a clear awareness of the magical character of talismans did not discourage some masters from including image magic in their books. Virdung's collection of Hermetic and talismanic texts is especially rich even by Western standards. While we do not know whether he practiced the methods that he studiously copied on the blank folios between the scientific tracts, the great number of these texts, along with his later interest in the magicians of Europe, indicates that he was an attentive reader of image magic, and that he thus turned to the talismans with deep intellectual interest.

The scientific context of magical works is almost universal: texts of philosophy and theology rarely occur together with magic. Perhaps related to this fact, the theoretical reflections on magic, such as Al-Kindi's *De radiis stellarum* and the *Speculum astronomiae*, also occur separately, never in the company of texts of practical magic. An exciting exception from this rule is the book list of magical works in the Dresden manuscript, which is copied in the company of astronomical, astrological, talismanic, and divinatory texts. This difference of codicological context is one of the reasons why I think that the book list was the scribe's own intellectual production, with the purpose of orienting the reader in the mass of magical texts partly contained by the same manuscript.

In most cases, we are simply not in the position to decide whether the occurrence of a magical text in a codex indicates actual practices or simple curiosity. The *Picatrix* or Thabit's *De imaginibus* contain no indication whether their readers constructed talismans. Some sources are, fortunately, more talkative. The long list of successive manuscript pages representing geomantic charts in BJ 793 among other examples, the sophistication with which these charts are elaborated, the indications and cross-references in the margins, and the omission of theoretical introductions to the methods of divination not only point to a general, theoretical interest in divinatory methods, but indicate expertise in their concrete application. In a word, I am convinced that at least some sections of BJ 793 were copied with the definite purpose of fortune telling. More interesting perhaps, actual use of ritual magic, crystallomancy, and the invocation of angels may also be revealed. External evidence—legal documents and confessions—is not the only way to prove that someone attempted to apply the methods of crystallomancy and demon invocation; but internal evidence left in the magical texts may also show such application. As we have seen, in the case of the royal prayer book of Wladislas, the consequent substitution of the name of the operator implies that the text was prepared with the intention of making it suitable and ready for real use, and it was in all probability even consecrated.

6. Once we identified the collectors of natural magic, talismanic, divinatory, alchemical, and ritual magic texts as learned monks, court intellectuals, and university masters, that is, as intelligent individuals capable of reflection, it is rather obvious to inquire: how can we account for the fact that these persons were never faced with the problem that the methods they copied did not work in practice? Did they not see that the mechanism of magic is obviously false, and that its falsity can be easily shown with the help of simple experiments? Or did the methods perhaps actually work?

While such questions about the past might seem somewhat present-minded and thus illegitimate, the real danger is not to ask *questions* inspired by the concerns of the present (such important research fields as the history of women, childhood, or everyday life are typically inspired by the concerns of the present), but to give *answers* distorted by these concerns. We can therefore freely raise our naive questions, even though there is something anachronistic in such inquiries, we only have to be careful when answering them.

In fact, we are not looking for one single answer to explain why the methods of magic could have been seen as effective, but rather a group of interconnected answers. What we can claim in general, however, is that those magic practices surveyed in this book fitted quite well into the scientific-religious conceptual framework of the Middle Ages.

We have already touched upon the issue of efficacy in the case of talismanic magic in Chapter 3. There is no point in doubting that belief in the *general* protective power of talismans was prevalent in the Middle Ages, and, in addition, a number of stories support the idea that the same talismans were believed to have sufficient virtue for *concrete*—for instance military—purposes, too. It happened that women started feeling affection for someone, that castles were occupied, and that scorpion populations decreased. Success in such cases might have been attributed to magic. In other words: magic in some cases actually seemed to work. And this was closely related to the fact that processes of natural and talismanic magic were not as alien from the contemporary natural philosophy as they are from our modern natural science. The underlying assumptions behind the mechanism of talismans and magic stones, the occult virtue of herbs, and the healing power of animal substances formed part of the same correspondential worldview that was typical of many fields of medieval science. Our first answer to the initial questions is therefore that in many cases users certainly regarded magic as effective.

But what happened when such a technique manifestly did not work? Here, we have to differentiate according to the type of magic we are discussing. Taking ritual magic first: to ask why its practitioner did not get disappointed when his prayers to the angels did not lead to success is quite the same as to ask religious persons whether they become atheists if God does not accomplish what is asked in the prayers. Faith needs obviously different kinds of proof—if it needs any. To construct scientific experiments with the intention of testing what percentage of prayers turns out to be successful—even though such an experimental approach was subject of fairly heated debate in late nineteenth-century England[1]—sounds bizarre both in the fifteenth century and today.

To continue with the *experimenta* literature and the talismans, we see a more basic disagreement between the medieval and the present attitudes. The self-criticism and the readiness to exclude those methods which repeatedly failed to produce the expected results was not a particularly central idea in the natural philosophy of those times. As we have seen in Chapter 2, what counted as an experiment was not what was tested in a number of controlled experimental situations, but what the old philosophers and authorities described, and what was generally accepted about nature. Even for those philosophers who taught that demons—having exclusively spiritual and not corporal existence—are not perceivable, it was the experience, that is, the general conviction, that proved their existence.[2]

Against such a background, it is not surprising that relatively fantastic convictions could be considered through the centuries as sufficiently confirmed scientific facts.[3] An instructive example is the conviction that magnets will loose their power of attraction if they are rubbed with garlic. This "fact" was repeated many times as a self-evident "proof" for the theory of antipathies by authors over fifteen centuries, from Plutarch to the sixteenth century. A convenient worldview (in this case the theory of sympathies and antipathies) and a sufficiently strong textual tradition became more efficient means for this conviction to gain epistemological status than practical tests. And—to complicate the problem—those who believed in the

---

1. Frank M. Turner, "Rainfall, Plagues, and the Prince of Wales: A Chapter in the Conflict of Religion and Science," *Journal of British Studies* 13 (1974): esp. 64; quoted in Thomas F. Gieryn, "Boundary-Work and the Demarcation of Science from Non-Science: Strains and Interests in Professional Ideologies of Scientists," *American Sociological Review* 48 (1983): 781–95.

2. On the modern history of the word experience, see Peter Dear, *Discipline and Experience: The Mathematical Way in the Scientific Revolution* (Chicago: University of Chicago Press, 1995), esp. 11–25.

3. I would, however, definitely not wish to imply that this was true only in the Middle Ages and that modern science is free of theories that will someday seem fantastic and ridiculous.

magnet-garlic antipathy claimed to have tried it in practice. The same empirical argument that seems to us to disprove the theory became its actual proof. This changed only when the generally accepted ontology of the world was transformed and magnets and garlic were no longer seen as having antipathies and sympathies, but one of them as having magnetic force, and the other as being completely irrelevant as far as magnetism is concerned. Things are proved to be nonexistent and theories are proved to be false when they change their status in the classification of a new worldview.[4]

Finally, we hasten to add that in a number of cases experiments must have produced results that were seen as negative by the contemporaries, too. Even in such cases, however, it would be anachronistic to expect them to abandon the given theory; various strategies less drastic than rejecting the core hypotheses of magic were available to explain the failure. One could always argue that the operator had not sufficiently or correctly prepared to perform the given magical task: he had not fasted enough or attained a satisfactory level of bodily and spiritual purity. It was also possible to argue that the constellation at the moment of the experiment was not favorable. Or perhaps everything happened as it was described in the handbooks, only the person was not right one. Such experiments were not conceived in the democratic way of the modernity (according to which an experiment carried out under the same specified conditions can be repeated by anyone, anywhere, regardless of gender, race, and origin): only the initiated, the adepts, could perform them, and the pupils were not necessarily in the possession of such abilities. If the given result was expected from a helping angel or demon, the argument could have been made that the spirits were able, just not willing, to do what had been required from them. Finally, one could always say that the instructions—originating usually from texts written several hundred years earlier—were not understood properly (just as we have serious problems in understanding Galileo's descriptions of experiments), or that the text was simply not transmitted—copied or translated—correctly (as the talismans of the magic squares were copied indeed with many errors).

All in all, there are many reasons why the methods of magic described in the handbooks could not be falsified, and even though I do not exclude that there may have been some skepticism about some methods, in general, there is no reason to doubt that most of these texts were copied with a fairly strong conviction that the methods written in them would work.

7. The last issue to be addressed here concerns the relations and links of the persons who can be associated in one way or another with learned magic. To put it differently, the question is whether any cooperation, correspondence, or intellectual contact of magicians is detectable. If so, it remains for us to speculate whether we

---

4. Daryn Lehoux, "Tropes, Facts, and Empiricism," *Perspectives on Science* 11 (2003): 326–44.

can claim that any of the intellectual centers—courts, cloisters, or universities—of the region were particularly magical in nature, and with this we have returned to the initial question of the book: could Faustus have studied magic in Kraków, if he had turned up there?

The historical Faustus probably never went to Kraków not only because magic was not studied publicly there in the late fifteenth century, but also because that city did not yet have the same magical fame it was to have one hundred years later. The pieces of evidence collected during my research do not support the assertion that Kraków offered an intense magical milieu to its visitors at that time—while it undeniably offered a particularly strong astrological environment. My conclusion is that however ample the evidence we have concerning an intellectual interest in learned magic in Central Europe, and especially in Kraków, there is no sufficient reason to call any of the intellectual foci and institutions a "center for magical studies," and no coherent and institutional study of magic is detectable in the region.

Still, although there was no public chair of learned magic in the heart of the University of Kraków, we can point to the presence of some important cooperation related to magic. It can be reconstructed in detail that in the early fifteenth century Henry the Bohemian worked together with other university people, a certain Stanislas, the Italian professor Monaldus of Luca, and the Polish Nicolaus Hinczonis of Casimiria, on his crystallomantic treasure-finding projects in the royal gardens.

Sixty years later, Johannes Virdung of Hassfurt copied talismanic texts in the same year and from the same sample book as another student of the university, Egidius of Corintia. Whether they were acquainted cannot be proven, but the similarities of their interests and the resemblance of their manuscripts suggest at least some intellectual contact, and one can easily imagine how they got involved in the discussion of the content of the *Liber runarum* or of the Hermetic *Liber de stellis beibeniis*. Virdung's manuscripts and Egidius's Dresden codex both contain representative selections of texts on image magic and Hermetism and surprisingly similar collections of astrological texts. In addition, Egidius's list of magical titles testifies to a certain theoretical interest in the issue of classifying magical texts, which may have also easily been a topic discussed among the students of the University of Kraków. We cannot reconstruct the rest of Egidius's life, but we know that Virdung, upon returning to Germany, took steps to become acquainted with all of his contemporaries who were interested in magic on a technical or on a spiritual level. Thus, he was in contact with Abbot Trithemius, the English necromancer Nicolaus de Pulchro Monte Schonberg, and the humanist Konrad Celtis (who had also been a student at Kraków). He probably also met Johannes Mercurius and Georgius Faustus.

If we remain with the question of the cooperation among "magicians" and the transmission of magical ideas and texts, we cannot discount the effects of Italy and

Germany. The Bohemian alchemist John of Laz claimed to be a pupil of a certain Antonio of Florence, killed in Bohemia because of his alchemical practices. In Kraków, the Italian Monaldus of Luca took part in the treasure-hunting practices of a circle of university masters around Henry the Bohemian. In Hungary King Matthias was in correspondence with Marsilio Ficino, whose pupil and fellow in the Florentine Academia Platonica, Francesco Bandini, even visited the royal court of Buda; another Italian Platonist, Callimachus spent several years at the University of Kraków. Last but not least, the mysterious BJ 793, containing many texts on image magic and divination, as well as the *Picatrix,* is probably a copy of an Italian codex. Italian masters and manuscripts seem to have played a crucial role as external factors promoting the Central European reception of learned magic, which reception was also facilitated by the fact that students of the region often visited Italian universities. The role of Germans was somewhat different, rather modeled by the Faust legend. Konrad Celtis and Johannes Virdung of Hassfurt as young students went to Kraków, and although they did not study magical arts at the university, they clearly got involved in learned magic, and the manuscripts they found in Kraków became a source of their fascination with certain genres of magic.

One of the reasons why Central Europe could have seemed an adequate place for a student to satisfy his interest in magic, and why especially the University of Kraków could have been an institution where magical texts were frequently copied, could be the relative tolerance of magical activity in the region. I am still not arguing that Central Europe provided the students and courtiers with a particularly magical milieu as compared to Western Europe; however, it is undeniable that it was a relatively calmer place with regard to criminalization. The practice of magic *did* lead to court cases in several occasions—as we have seen in the cases of Nicholas the Hangman and Henry the Bohemian—but there were no such severe condemnations on the part of the university or other authorities as we can observe in contemporary Paris.

A second—rather global—reason for the emergence of magical texts in the fifteenth century might be a general European tendency, namely that from the twelfth century on certain forms of magic had more and more opportunity to cross the borderlines of legitimate science. It seems that the notions of both science and magic were (and are) historically changing, dynamic constructions, and it was not *ahistorically* given what counted as scientific knowledge teachable at universities and what was excluded as dangerous and harmful, and what was seen as rational enterprise and what was considered irrational. While arguments against certain practices and ideas related to magic reflect a growing severity, more and more frequently other forms of magic in other sources were labeled as scientific. This tendency—called the "positivization of magic"[5]—can be well exemplified by such classifications

---

5. I am quoting again Claire Fanger's terminology, as I did in Chapter 1. See also Chapter 7.

as that of Conrad Kyeser or the author of the Dresden book list, where alchemy, theurgy, and certain forms of natural and image magic appeared as respectable elements of science.

It was due to this process that leading intellectuals were provided with ample opportunity to find a legitimate and scholarly approach to dealing with magical methods. As a result, the readers of magic in Central Europe are not to be looked for primarily within the circles of the Faustus or Mercurius-type of full-time, semi-literate, and self-made magicians, nor in that of anonymous university members whose number "outran the demand" and who remained without jobs. Partly because local higher education started functioning in the Central European area relatively late, there was no time in the fifteenth century for the emergence of a surplus of university masters and an "underemployed and largely unsupervised clerical underworld," as had happened in the West.[6] As nearly as we can reconstruct the picture, the late medieval collectors and readers of magical manuscripts of the region belonged to a high and respected intellectual stratum, benefited from the tolerant milieu of the Central European universities and courts, and apparently did not feel obliged to lock the door of the room in which they kept their books of secrets.

6. Kieckhefer, *Forbidden Rites*, 12.

Epilogue: When Central Europe Was Finally Close to Becoming a Center for Magical Studies

According to the popular story, the sixteenth-century Polish physician, magician, and alchemist Piotr Twardowski engaged Satan's help in order to learn necromancy and satisfy his worldly ambitions. Besides his pact with the Devil, his unusual end as well makes him a real precursor of the legendary Faust-figure: in line with the contract he signed with the magician, the Devil finally came for his soul. However—as some version of the legend says—an angel, fairly incorrectly, interfered, and helped the magician violate the contract, thereby saving him from hell. Since no one with a past like Twardowski's could have been allowed to enter heaven, the most convenient solution seemed to be to confine him to the Moon, where he still resides, gazing down at Kraków.

The story is less realistic than famous, but it may have definitely been among the reasons why Kraków could have seemed a particularly magical town at the end of the sixteenth century for such authors as Manlius. By this time a number of Western European intellectuals—among them the famous English scientist, mathematician, and angel-invoker magus John Dee—had somehow been convinced that Central Europe was a place where practitioners of the magical arts and alchemy were particularly welcome. In fact, several centers provided some basis for such aspirations, offering generous "research opportunities" and fairly good financial support to individuals studying those arts. What these centers had in common was that they were not located at universities, but rather at the courts of kings and noblemen, and that in all cases the emphasis had shifted toward alchemy, whether practical or spiritual.

One of these noblemen was the Hungarian magnate Boldizsár Batthyány (Balthasar Batthyany), a great book collector, patron of book printing, fervent devotee of the natural sciences, and not least an active student of practical alchemy. Batthyány (ca. 1537–90) developed a real humanist court in Németújvár (today's Güssing in Austria) at the time when—under the reign of the Habsburg family—

the royal court moved out from the territory of the Hungarian kingdom, settled down in Vienna, and the country was left without an intellectual center. Batthyány's court did welcome wandering scholars persecuted in the West for their religious convictions, among them Johannes Manlius, the printer from Laibach, the same person who recorded for the posterity the commonplace that Kraków hosted a school of magical studies, and the Flemish botanist Carolus Clusius, who transformed the count's rosary into an exceptional botanical garden, which was the first one in the region where paprika and perhaps even potatoes were grown, a garden where vegetables were cultivated systematically not for their use but on account of their exotic nature.

Batthyány's intellectual relations reached far beyond the boundaries of his court; he was in correspondence with a large number of humanists, medical doctors, booksellers, and alchemists of Western and Central Europe (among them Elias Corvinus, the Viennese professor, and Augerius de Busbeq), the chief preoccupation of his letters being the natural sciences, in particular: alchemy. His library—the fifth largest in Hungary at the time—was a result of a conscious selection process in which both the count and his book collectors played important roles. These collectors, scattered all over Europe, had to make serious efforts on some occasions to find a certain book at the request of the count. Thanks to his book collection, Batthyány was fairly up-to-date as far as Hermetic philosophy and the literature of alchemy were concerned. He was a follower of the new, Paracelsian methods, and he himself performed alchemical experiments in the laboratory of Németújvár.[1]

Batthyány's laboratory did not survive, but we can reconstruct how it might have looked like from the documentation of the archeological findings from a contemporary and fairly close alchemical laboratory, the one excavated in the chapel of the castle of Oberstockstall (Kirchberg am Wagram), in Lower Austria. Over eight hundred objects were recovered from the dig, among them ceramic and glass apparatuses, alembics, receivers, crucibles, and cupels. Active in the second half of the sixteenth century, this laboratory was built, sponsored, and run by a sequence of local parish priests. But these were not ordinary priests, Urban von Trenbach for example, during whose priesthood (1552–61) the laboratory was already active,

---

1. Szabolcs Ö. Barlay, "Boldizsár Batthyány und sein Humanisten Kreis," *Magyar Könyvszemle* 95 (1979): 231–51; István Monok, Péter Ötvös, and Edina Zvara, eds., *Balthasar Batthyány und seine Bibliothek,* special issue, *Burgenländische Forschungen* 26 (2004); Dóra Bobory, "Qui me unice amabat. Clusius and Boldizsar Batthyany," in *Carolus Clusius: Towards a Cultural History of a Renaissance Naturalist,* ed. Florike Egmond, Paul Hoftijzer, and Robert Visser (Amsterdam: Edita, 2007); Robert John Evans, *The Wechel Presses. Humanism and Calvinism in Central Europe, 1572–1627,* Supplement 2 (Oxford: The Past and Present Society, 1975). György Endre Szőnyi brings arguments for the case that Boldizsár Batthyány may have been the mysterious Hungarian nobleman whom John Dee mentions as the magnate who invited him to Hungary. See Szőnyi, *John Dee's Occultism,* 243–45.

and who was also interested in geomancy, chiromancy, and astronomy according to the sources, was a rather influential personality in church politics: when he left Oberstockstall, he became the prince-primate of Passau. He was definitely too busy to remain involved in the alchemical experiments, but he certainly continued to support the activities of the laboratory through his followers, among them members of the famous Fugger family.[2]

A third center was the court of the last Rožmberks. The Rožmberks were the most important Bohemian magnates, the highest representatives of the aristocracy in the sixteenth century, their court second only to that of Rudolf II. Their interests were very similar to the emperor's: they were great collectors, educated humanists, and patrons of culture, and they also shared the enthusiasm of Rudolf for the occult arts. The last two members of the family, Peter Vok (1539–1611) and his elder brother Vilém (1535–92), were both practicing alchemists; cabalists and magicians gathered together at their court (which traveled around in South Bohemia, the last stops being Krumlov and Třeboň). Distinguished guests were invited: Heinrich Khunrath was Vilém's court physician, while John Dee and his medium, Edward Kelley, organized séances in the Rožmberk household.[3] The magical aura of Třeboň was further accentuated by the occult nature of the Rožmberk book collection: this library, which contained more than ten thousand printed and manuscript volumes—according to Václav Březan (d. 1618), the archivist and librarian of the family who was instructed to prepare its catalog—was enriched by a great deal of cabalistic and alchemical manuscripts and early printings purchased by the two brothers.[4]

Count Albert Łaski, Polish aristocrat, politician, humanist, and patron of artists, was yet another host of the traveling John Dee. Just like his Hungarian and Bohemian fellow aristocrats, Batthyány and the Rožmberks, he was fascinated by the philosophy of Paracelsus, and he maintained an alchemical laboratory in his birthplace,

---

2. For the literature on the laboratory, see Chapter 5.

3. On the Rožmberks, see Robert John Evans, *Rudolf II and His World: A Study in Intellectual History, 1576–1612* (Oxford: Clarendon Press, 1973), 140–43 and 223–27. The most complete bibliography on the family can be found in the modern edition of Březan's history on the Rožmberks: Václav Březan, *Životy posledních Rožmberků* (Prague: Svoboda, 1985), 2:730–45.

4. Theodor Wagner, "Wissenschaftlicher Schwindel im südlichen Böhmen (Alchymie, Magie u. ä. aus dem Wittingauer Archiv und den Correspondenzen des W. Březan 1570–91)," *Mitteilungen des Vereines für Geschichte der Deutschen in Böhmen* 16 (1878): 112–23, and 19 (1880): 133–40; Adolf Berger, "Die Rosenbergische Bibliothek und Wenzel Březan," *Mitteilungen des Vereines für Geschichte der Deutschen in Böhmen* 20 (1881–82): 193–211; Svatopluk Samek, "O Rožmberské knihovně" (On the Rožmberk Library), *Jihočeský sborník historický* 19 (1950): 11–14. This library was disseminated after the death of the last Rožmberk, Peter Vok. It went into the possession of the crown and was moved to Prague from where an important portion of the collection was captured by the Swedes in the middle of the Thirty Years' War, while other parts traveled to the University Library of Prague, or were returned to the monastic library of Třeboň.

the town of Késmárk in Upper Hungary (Kežmarok in today's Slovakia). A sign of his interest in the magical arts is that during his trip to England he participated in Dee's famous conversations with angels in the magician's home at Mortlake.[5]

All these centers are, nonetheless, of secondary significance when compared with the splendid court of Emperor Rudolf II (1552–1612). A most controversial personality, Rudolf is certainly not remembered as an energetic and talented politician; however, the cultural, scientific, and magical bustle of his Prague court has given sufficient material for a number of illustrious expositions in our times. This was the court where Arcimboldo the artist, Giordano Bruno the philosopher, the astronomers Tycho Brahe and Johannes Kepler, Johannes Jesensky the physician, and magicians like John Dee and Edward Kelley preferred to spend as much time as possible. Just this short list of names shows how international Rudolf's court was—even by Renaissance standards: local, Italian, German, Danish, Polish, and English scholars and artists populated it. Most of them were deeply involved in Hermetic, Neoplatonic, and magical philosophy in one way or another; all were searching for the lost ancient wisdom. If we follow the career of the inner circle of physicians, astrologers, and librarians grouping around Rudolf, we will see that most of them shared the emperor's enthusiasm for the occult arts, the Kabbalah (Johann Pistorius), emblems (Jacopo and Octavio Strada), astrology (Kepler), and alchemy (Michael Maier, Tadeus Hájek, and Martin Ruland).[6]

John Dee's expectations concerning the prestige of magical arts and his own prospects in Central Europe may have been somewhat overoptimistic, and in fact it was not without frustration that he traveled back to England after his five-year sojourn. On the other hand, even though not everything happened according to his intentions, and he was not granted the title of "Royal Mathematician" in Prague, the English doctor by no means spent this period as an outcast magician, but enjoyed considerable support and respect from the local aristocracy.[7] Although there is no evidence that the region hosted public schools of magic in Faustus's time, we can easily understand why a century later people believed that it had.

    5. On John Dee's Central European patrons, see Szőnyi, *John Dee's Occultism*, 242–70.
    6. Evans, *Rudolf II;* György Endre Szőnyi, "Scientific and Magical Humanism at the Court of Rudolf II," in *Rudolf II and Prague: the Court and the City,* ed. Eliška Fučiková, James Bradburne, Beket Bukovinská, et al. (London: Thames and Hudson, 1997), 223–30.
    7. Szőnyi, *John Dee's Occultism*, 249–50.

Appendix 1: Bibliographical Essay on Current Debates

The Eleventh Chapter of the *Speculum astronomiae* and the *Biblionomia* of Richard of Fournival

The *Speculum astronomiae* presents the world of medievalist scholars with two sets of questions. The first concerns the identification of the textual references scattered throughout the work, but especially condensed in the eleventh chapter; the second, the origin, the authorship, and the date of birth of this exceptional book.

The first attempt to identify the references of the eleventh chapter is a long and oft-cited article by Lynn Thorndike, in which he introduces a number of medieval Latin texts of legendary attribution (to Hermes, Belenus, Toz Graecus, Solomon, Muhammed, Aristotle, Raziel, Thebit ben Corat, and Ptolemy), defining his material as an intermediary category between books of purely magical content and sources that are exclusively astrological and astronomical. These texts—according to Thorndike—deal with engraved operative images, rings, and seals related to planets, signs, or constellations.[1] After a gap of several years, David Pingree added further manuscripts on talismans, lapidaries, and amulets to Thorndike's list, and a few crucial examinations of the manuscript tradition that enriched the secondary literature of the *Speculum*.[2] Pingree's articles on image magic were followed by a thousand-page study by Nicolas Weill-Parot, who systematically identified the works mentioned in the eleventh chapter of the *Speculum* with specific texts in surviving codices.[3] He relied mainly on the earlier research of Thorndike and Pingree, but he also added his own discoveries, thereby complementing and occasionally correcting the two masters.

As for the question of authorship, the *Speculum* had long been attributed to Albertus Magnus (starting with mid-fourteenth-century testimonies and manuscripts), until Pierre Mandonnet questioned this assumption in 1910, and proposed Roger Bacon as an alternative possibility. The debate continued throughout the major part of the twentieth century, and a number of medievalists contributed to it (including Lynn Thorndike and Richard Lemay, as well as Dominican and Franciscan scholars who tried to clear the names of Albert and Roger respectively from the authorship

1. T (1947) 217–74.
2. Pingree, "Learned Magic"; Pingree, "Diffusion."
3. WP 40–62.

of that suspicious work), until Paola Zambelli reconstructed the arguments in her historiographical study and seemed to resolve the question once and for all, in favor of Albertus Magnus.[4] The solution, however, did not prove satisfactory for long. Recent research by Agostino Paravicini Bagliani, Paolo Lucentini, and Bruno Roy—working independently from one another—has shed new light on the issue, indicating once again that it is unlikely that Albertus Magnus authored the book in question.

Agostino Paravicini Bagliani compiled a catalog of all the surviving manuscripts of the *Speculum astronomiae,* and for the first time systematically checked their attribution.[5] He found that the first manuscript ascribed to Albertus Magnus was written in the middle of the fourteenth century (more precisely, after 1339), seventy or eighty years after the *Speculum* was composed, which Lemay places as early as 1245, Madonnet as late as 1277, and Zambelli and Weill-Parot in the 1260s. Paravicini Bagliani's codicological research showed that the fifteen earliest manuscripts contain neither any attribution nor the title *Speculum astronomiae,* and consequently, the text should be referred to as the *Nomina librorum astronomiae.* Thus, neither the earliest manuscript evidence nor the literary testimonies (the first of them dating back to the mid-fourteenth century) supports the authorship of Albertus Magnus.

Paolo Lucentini followed a different method.[6] In the early 1980s, Loris Sturlese noticed that the hostile references in the *Speculum* to Hermes contradict the opinions Albertus Magnus expressed in his authenticated texts.[7] Lucentini went further, systematically comparing the attitude of the genuine works by Albertus Magnus toward Hermes with the rather negative standpoint of the *Speculum.* He found that it was highly doubtful that the same person produced both these works and the *Speculum*; however—he maintained—Albertus might have read (and his later works could have been influenced by) the *Speculum.*[8]

To understand Bruno Roy's argument, we have to go back in time. Thanks to the research of Paola Zambelli and David Pingree, it has been sufficiently proven that the author of the *Speculum* consulted the books kept in the fairly rich library of Richard of Fournival. In 1241, when Richard of Fournival became the chancellor of the cathedral of Amiens, he compiled a catalog of his library, the *Biblionomia.* This source was published in the nineteenth century by Léopold Delisle, who

---

4. Zambelli, *The "Speculum Astronomiae" and Its Enigma,* 1–125. For a shorter and more recent summary of the issue, see WP 27–32.
5. Bagliani, *Le "Speculum Astronomiae" une énigme?*
6. Lucentini, "L'Ermetismo magico."
7. Loris Sturlese, "Saints et magiciens: Albert le Grand en Face d'Hermès Trismegiste," *Archives de philosophie* 43 (1980): 632.
8. Lucentini, "L'Ermetismo magico," 437.

expressed his doubts whether there had been a real book collection behind the text, and suggested that it was simply a catalog of a utopian library.[9] Half a century later, however, Aleksander Birkenmajer proved that the *Biblionomia* was a description of an actual library; he identified a number of codices in the medieval booklists and in the present library of the Sorbonne that had surely belonged to the real—and exceptional—library of Richard of Fournival, which had originally comprised approximately three hundred items.[10] To complicate the question further, the *Biblionomia* also mentioned that a special section of the library contained books of secrets. Regrettably, the catalog was silent about this section, and this silence forced modern scholars to try to find these books of secrets.[11] Pingree, who managed to identify some of the *libri secretorum,* argued that these texts were precisely those that were consulted by the author of the *Speculum* and described in detail in the eleventh chapter.[12] According to Bruno Roy, instead of postulating two authors for the two catalogs, the *Biblionomia* and the *Speculum,* we should think of one single writer, Richard of Fournival, who described his collection twice, in two different ways for two different purposes.[13]

The question of who authored the *Speculum* has been so controversial that nobody knows what the scholarly consensus (if any) will be in five years. This is the reason why Nicolas Weill-Parot calls the author simply *Magister Speculi.*[14]

Image Magic

The list of secondary literature on image magic starts with one medieval and one Renaissance book: the *Speculum astronomiae* and the *Opus preaclarum de imaginibus astrologicis* of Hieronymus Torrella. The *Speculum,* as we have seen, classifies the texts on talismans according to internal criteria (involvement of ritual elements, demons, and suffumigations) by examining the methods applied. It is not just the

---

9. Delisle, *Le Cabinet,* 2:518–35 (see Chap. 1, n. 47).
10. Aleksander Birkenmajer, "La Bibliothèque de Richard de Fournival, poète et érudit français du début du XIIIe siècle et son sort ultérieur," in *Études d'histoire des sciences et de la philosophie du Moyen Age,* Studia Copernicana 1 (Wrocław: Zakład Narodowy im. Ossolińskich, 1970), 118–210. The study was originally written in 1919. See also Richard H. Rouse, "Manuscripts Belonging to Richard de Fournival," *Revue d'histoire des textes* 3 (1973): 253–69.
11. Delisle, *Le Cabinet,* 2:521: "Ceterum, preter illa quorum fecimus mentionem, est et aliud genus tractatuum secretorum, quorum profunditas publicis oculis dedignatur exponi. Ac proinde non est intentionis nostre ut inter prehabitos ordinentur; sed eis deputandus est certus locus, neminem preter dominum proprium admissurus. Quare nec eorum descriptio pertinet ad hunc librum."
12. Pingree, "Diffusion," 80–102.
13. Bruno Roy, "Richard de Fournival, auteur du *Speculum Astronomiae?*" *AHDLMA* 67 (2000): 159–80.
14. WP 32.

eleventh chapter of the *Speculum* that touches upon the field of image magic: Thebit's *De imaginibus,* for example, is repeatedly quoted with great approval throughout the whole work, while other great authorities on astronomy and astrology, such as Ptolemy, Albumasar, and Alkabicius are also much-favored references. A few centuries later, Hieronymus Torrella gives the first systematic overview of the literature of talismans, proceeding from the *verbum nonum* of the *Centiloquium* and its commentary by Haly, through Thebit, Bacon, and Aquinas, to finally arrive at Albertus Magnus's *De mineralibus* and his *Speculum "scientiae."*[15] In modern times, Joan Evans made the first important reference to engraved gems and talismans in the context of the history of lapidaries. In her discussion, Evans relies on archaeological material, and she also edited some of the medieval texts on the use of stones and seals, including Thetel's *De lapidibus.*[16] Later in the twentieth century and quite understandably, secondary literature on image magic overlapped with that of the *Speculum astronomiae.* Thorndike compiled the first inclusive bibliography of image magic, and Pingree researched the transmission of these texts—their arrival in Europe and their circulation in the Latin libraries.[17] Francis J. Carmody's bibliography of Arabic astronomical and astrological works in Latin translation serves as a helpful starting point for further research on image magic texts, thanks to the list of manuscripts and the added bibliographical guide.[18] It was also Carmody who published the astronomical works of Thābit ibn Qurra, including his *De imaginibus* translated by John of Seville.[19] Although his edition is somewhat outdated and is not lacking in errors, it is still often consulted, as the only edition of this text.

A detailed analysis can be found on the structure of image magic texts, the transmission of the manuscripts, and the intentions of the scribes and the owners collecting them, in Frank Klaassen's forthcoming *Religion, Science, and the Transformations of Magic*. In her unpublished study, Sophie Page reviews and analyzes the talismanic and Hermetic texts belonging to the monastic library of St. Augustine's in Canterbury (especially MS Oxford, Corpus Christi 125, fols. 69–174).[20] The most comprehensive book on this topic was written by Nicolas Weill-Parot, who provided fuller descriptions of the texts than Thorndike, and placed the question of astrological images in the philosophical and scientific production of medieval and Renaissance times.

15. Hieronymus Torrella, *Opus praeclarum* (see Chap. 3, n. 33).
16. Joan Evans, *Magical Jewels of the Middle Ages and the Renaissance, Particularly in England* (Oxford: Clarendon Press, 1922).
17. T (1947); Pingree, "Diffusion"; Pingree, "Learned Magic."
18. Frances J. Carmody, *Arabic Astronomical and Astrological Sciences in Latin Translation: A Critical Bibliography* (Berkeley and Los Angeles: University of California Press, 1956).
19. Carmody, *Astronomical Works.*
20. Klaassen, *Religion, Science,* chaps. 2 and 3; Page, "Magic at St. Augustine's," chap. 4.

For the time being, it seems impossible for me to say where the term "image magic" comes from. It became a primary category in Page's and Klaassen's works, but neither of them coined it (Klaassen uses the expression "scholastic image magic," which is his invention). Kieckhefer does not use it consistently as a technical term,[21] while Thorndike, Pingree, and Burnett apply the category of "talismanic texts" without showing special preference for this expression.

Regarding finally the specific research questions related to the field of image magic, I would like to emphasize three fields that have been in constant development in recent years. The first of them is the issue of Hermetic texts, which is at the center of scholarly interest and editorial practice, as it is described in Chapter 3. The second concerns a specific text, the *Picatrix*, which, because of its complexity, cannot be viewed as a simple practical talismanic text, but rather as a compendium of natural, talismanic, and ritual methods. The wide scholarly interest in the *Picatrix*, dating at least from the time of Aby Warburg, did not result in a critical edition of the Latin version to accompany the Arabic original[22] until Vittoria Perrone Compagni published parts of the text in 1975.[23] In 1986 David Pingree published an edition of the complete Latin text.[24] Perrone Compagni and Pingree have gone on to produce studies on the sources, compiled elements, and medieval diffusion of the *Picatrix* that have proved indispensable for any understanding and research of the text.[25]

The third developing field in contemporary research concerns the most basic text of image magic, Thebit's *De imaginibus*.[26] Thābit ibn Qurra, this productive translator of Aristotle, mathematician and astronomer, lived in Baghdad in the ninth century. Thābit's work on manufacturing talismans, the Arabic version of which is lost, survived in two Latin translations, one by John of Seville (*De imaginibus*) and one by Adelard of Bath (*Liber prestigiorum*).[27] (The medieval translators used *prestigium* as the equivalent for the Arabic word meaning "talisman.") Translations of the same text cannot differ more than these two: it is rather instructive that the author of the *Speculum*, while accepting John of Seville's version as nondemonic,

---

21. However, the term does pop up occasionally in his article on erotic magic. See Kieckhefer, "Erotic Magic," 41.
22. For the Arabic original (edited by Ritter in 1933) and a German translation, see H. Ritter and M. Plessner, *"Picatrix" Das Ziel des Weisen von Pseudo-Magrîtî* (London: The Warburg Institute, 1962).
23. Perrone Compagni, "*Picatrix latinus*."
24. See the bibliography.
25. Perrone Compagni, "*Picatrix latinus*"; Perrone Compagni, "La magia ceremoniale"; Pingree, "Some of the Sources"; Pingree, "Between the *Ghâya* and *Picatrix*."
26. As mentioned in Chapter 1, I use the form "Thebit" to denote the ascribed author of the Latin translation, and "Thābit" to denote the historical personality.
27. See Burnett, "Talismans"; Charles Burnett, "Adelard, Ergaphalau and the Science of the Stars," in Burnett, *Magic and Divination*, II, 133–45; and Burnett, "Thābit ibn Qurra the Harrānian."

classified Adelard's text as an abominable one, which involves illicit ritual elements.[28] Whether John of Seville translated the text selectively, omitting certain dangerous elements, or whether Adelard added new interesting details (inscriptions of rings, suffumigations, and prayers to spirits) to his text, is still debated. Charles Burnett, who also prepared an edition of the *Liber prestigiorum* of his own, has researched the sources of Adelard and the reasons for the differences between the two versions.[29] Most recently, Vittoria Perrone Compagni identified new sources of Adelard's version, the Hermetic *Liber lunae* and the *Liber solis* from the collection entitled *Liber planetarum ex scientia Abel*, which were supposedly translated by Adelard himself (as terminological parallels between the three texts indicate). With this discovery and supposition, she seemed to refute the idea that Adelard's version is closer to the Arabic original text of Thābit.[30] The question still remains: were the elements of the *Liber prestigiorum* borrowed from other Hermetic works inserted by Adelard (as Perrone Compagni claims), or did he translate a version of Thābit's text on talismans which already contained these additions (in accordance with Burnett's theory)? This debate does not have a direct effect on our present research, since as far as it can be judged at the moment, no manuscript of the *Liber prestigiorum* (which had a more modest circulation than the *De imaginibus*) is preserved in any of the Central European countries. Ultimately, however, it does concern us, since the local success and survival of magical texts depended greatly on the role they played in the Western textual tradition, and on whether they were deemed as natural and tolerable, or demonic and abominable.

Ritual Magic

Modern scholarship divides the literature of ritual magic into two subgenres: the demonic and the angelic. The difference lies not only in whether the spirits invoked are malign or benign in nature, but also in the purposes of the given art and in the techniques applied.[31] In the absence of Central European examples for the demonic category,[32] we will limit the present discussion to the second type, and particularly to the notory art—a branch of magic performed in a Christian framework.[33]

28. Zambelli, *The "Speculum Astronomiae" and Its Enigma*, 240–42 and 248.
29. See the articles cited in note 27 and Burnett, "Arabic Hermes" and "The *Liber Prestigiorum Thebidis secundum Ptolomeum et hermetem* Translated by Adelard of Bath" (forthcoming).
30. Vittoria Perrone Compagni, "*Studiosus incantationibus*. Adelardo di Bath, Ermete e Thabit," *Giornale critico della filosofia Italiana* 82 (2001): 36–61.
31. See the considerations in Fanger, *Conjuring Spirits*, vii–viii.
32. For an instructive published example of this category, see CLM 849 in Kieckhefer, *Forbidden Rites*, where extensive references can be found concerning another text of demonic magic, the Bodleian MS Rawl. 252.
33. This expression is used both in Fanger, *Conjuring Spirits*, vii, and in Page, "Magic at St. Augustine's," chap. 6.

Long after Thorndike's old, very brief, and mostly surpassed paragraphs on the *Ars notoria*,[34] J. Dupèbe reexamined the issue in his 1987 article, where he collected medieval reports—mainly condemnations—of this type of magico-devotional text.[35] Though focusing primarily on image magic, divination, and on different examples of ritual magic (first of all, on a derivation of the *Ars notoria*, the *Liber visionum* by John of Morigny), the articles published in the *Conjuring Spirits*, edited by Claire Fanger, clarified a great number of research issues regarding the notory art. Proceeding along the paths of Dupèbe and the *Conjuring Spirits*, the next comprehensive article on this issue was published by Jean-Patrice Boudet, who situated the *Ars notoria* in the context of the genre of theurgy, admitting that no direct relation can be detected between this kind of magic and Late Antique Neoplatonic theurgy.[36] Three works can be added to these studies. Both Sophie Page and Frank Klaassen devoted considerable portions of their dissertations to the *Ars notoria*. Page situates it in the context of its Christian audience, in particular, the monks of St. Augustine's Abbey in Canterbury;[37] Klaassen studies its circulation in Western Europe.[38] Julien Véronèse's *L'Ars notoria* offers a thorough introduction to and finally a critical edition of this important text.[39]

As far as earlier text editions are concerned, the *Ars notoria* remained for a long time a manuscript phenomenon; it first appears in print in a seventeenth-century edition of Cornelius Agrippa's *Occult Philosophy*,[40] on the basis of which Robert Turner published an English translation in 1657.[41]

Before we turn to the research problems and textual derivatives of this text, it might be instructive to copy three descriptions of the *Ars notoria* in three languages, one after the other, put forward by two modern scholars and a medieval practitioner, which emphasize different aspects of the text. In chronological order, we start with the definition of John of Morigny: "Liber enim ille notoria prima facie, scilicet exterius, apparet quod sit sanctus, et omnium librorum pulcherrimus et

---

34. *HMES*, 2:279–89. Although the whole ten-page long chapter is titled "Solomon and the Ars Notoria," strictly speaking, only two pages (281–82) deal with this text.
35. Dupèbe, "L'«Ars Notoria» et la polémique."
36. Boudet, "L'*Ars notoria* au Moyen Age."
37. Page, "Magic at St. Augustine's," chap. 6. See also Sophie Page, *Magic in Medieval Manuscripts* (London: The British Library, 2004).
38. Klaassen, "Religion, Science," chap. 4.
39. Julien Véronèse, *L'Ars notoria au moyen age;* Véronèse, "Les anges dans l'*Ars notoria*"; and Véronèse, "Magie, théurgie et spiritualité dans le rituel de l'*Ars notoria* au Moyen Âge," forthcoming in a collection of essays edited by Claire Fanger.
40. Agrippa, *Opera Omnia*, 2:603–60.
41. *Ars Notoria: The Notory Art of Solomon*, trans. Robert Turner (London: F. Cottrel, 1657; repr., Seattle: Trident Books, 1987). This text can be also found on the following website: www.esotericarchives.com/notoria/notoria.htm

utilissimus, et eciam sanctissimus, quia in eo scriptura debet de diuersis coloribus scribi. In eo sunt pulcherrime figure diuersis coloribus colorate. Breuissimus liber est, et omnium scienciarum scripturarum et arcium adempcionem breui tempore Deus omnipotens per ipsum operantibus promittit et tribuit."[42] The next definition is from Jean-Patrice Boudet: "Sorte de théurgie fondée sur une ascèse sévère, des prières et des invocations de noms divins et angéliques, et qui promet à son adept un savoir total, l'*ars notoria* . . . connaît un réel succès dans l'Occident chrétien, du XIIIe au XVIIe siècle."[43] Finally, there is that of Claire Fanger: "The *Ars Notoria* of Solomon is a late medieval ritual text whose goal is to strengthen the operator's memory, eloquence, understanding and perseverance, and to obtain knowledge of the seven liberal arts, all of which are sought in various sequences of prayers and rituals, and directly infused into the operator via angels and the holy spirit."[44]

An important peculiarity of this text, and a chief reason given for condemning it, is that it contains a long list of foreign words, the so-called *verba ignota* (Greek, Hebrew, Chaldean, Arabic, and even incomprehensible divine and angelic names), and a set of artistic diagrams filled with text, which are called *notae,* and which provided the name "notoria" for the whole art. The *notae* scattered in the art have received limited scholarly attention.[45] These complex drawings, each devoted to one of the liberal or other arts, and to theology, chastity, peace, and similar domains, are integral parts of the *Ars notoria*. Their function has been explained by modern scholars in several ways: (1) as splendidly organized schemata surrounded by benign angels, intended to systematize the main body of the text in a diagrammatic form; (2) as contributing to the air of mystery about the art through the use of secret characters; (3) as mnemotechnic devices; and (4) especially, as tools for meditation and contemplation.

An important issue related to the text of the *Ars notoria* is its origin: its theurgy bears considerable resemblance to Late Antique Neoplatonic conceptions. However, at the moment no evidence supports the idea that these theories could have been transmitted in any indirect ways (through Greek, Byzantine, or Arabic-Spanish mediation); therefore, in the absence of any bridge over the gap between the Late Antique Greek and the medieval Latin theurgy, two possibilities remain: either the *Ars notoria* is an endogenous phenomenon with no direct influence from Neoplatonic philosophy as Boudet suggests,[46] rejecting the argument on the resurgence of

---

42. Fanger and Watson, "Prologue," 133–34 (see Chap. 6, n. 18).
43. Boudet, "L'*Ars notoria* au Moyen Age," 173.
44. Fanger, "Plundering the Egyptian Treasure," 216.
45. Virtually all the quoted articles mention the *notae,* but only one—fairly preliminary—study is devoted exclusively to this issue: Camille, "Visual Art."
46. Boudet, "L'*Ars notoria* au Moyen Age," 187–91.

Late Antique theurgy put forward by Dupèbe,[47] or it is rooted in Jewish traditions as Kieckhefer proposes.[48]

The rejection of the *Ars notoria* by theologians, among them Aquinas and Oresme, is a recurrent topic in secondary literature;[49] here it suffices to mention one living issue that concerns a source that, in contrast to the theologians, does not condemn the notory art, even though we would expect it to do so. As we remember, the eleventh chapter of the *Speculum astronomiae* condemned a set of texts as detestable for a number of reasons, and on the basis of the attribution of the texts referred in this section, David Pingree labeled this category as Solomonic magic. It would be logical to expect the author of the *Speculum* to include the *Ars notoria* in this category, since it is the most famous magical text attributed to Solomon, but he does not, it is left to us to decide whether or not he should have. Nicolas Weill-Parot's answer is positive: the *Ars notoria* is ascribed to Solomon, as it contains unintelligible words and obscure language in the prayers, as well as images for contemplation, that is, all the basic traits characterizing Solomonic magic.[50] In contrast, one could argue that while the author of the *Speculum* makes it clear that the detestable texts bind and compel spirits (as opposed to the Hermetic texts, which persuade them), the orations and prayers to God and his angels in the *Ars notoria* do not actually contain any constraint; instead, they are humble appeals similar to the attitude of Christian liturgy. The adept of the art does not conjure spirits, but modestly addresses divine power through holy and mystical techniques; so, according to the terminology of the *Speculum*, the *Ars notoria*, paradoxically, is Hermetic rather than Solomonic. Finally and most important, the question of why the author of the *Speculum astronomiae* neglects the *Ars notoria* may be seen as misleading altogether: why should he mention it at all? As Frank Klaassen stresses, there is no reason to expect the eleventh chapter of the *Speculum* to include the notory art, since the *Speculum* concentrates on texts involving *imago astronomica*, which the *notae* in the *Ars notoria* are not.[51] The *Speculum* is concerned with texts on astronomy and astrology (mostly of Arabic origin), while the *Ars notoria* simply does not belong to this category.

While it does not strictly concern the medieval circulation of the *Ars notoria*, the research carried out by Stephen Clucas is worth mentioning. Clucas suggests that the Pseudo-Solomonic *Ars notoria* served as a primary source for the angelic

---

47. Dupèbe, "L'«Ars Notoria» et la polémique," 124.
48. Kieckhefer, "Devil's Contemplatives."
49. See Dupèbe, "L'«Ars Notoria» et la polémique," and Klaassen, *Religion, Science*, chap. 4.
50. WP 59.
51. Frank Klaassen, "Medieval Ritual Magic in the Renaissance," *Aries: Journal for the Study of Western Esotericism* 3 (2003): 166–99.

conversations of John Dee, and that, in addition, the visual iconography of the notory art exercised a considerable influence on the English scholar-magus.[52]

Several further medieval texts containing beatific visions derive from the tradition of the *Ars notoria,* and two of these are of particular interest to scholars. The *Liber iuratus* (*Liber sacratus*), or the "Sworn Book" attributed to a certain Honorius of Thebes, describes the conflict of (blameless) magicians and the pope and his (wicked) theologians; following this curious apology of practicing magicians it contains textual borrowings of prayers and orations from an early version of the *Ars notoria.* The text has been studied by Robert Mathiesen and Richard Kieckhefer, both examining its content and suggesting a date for its composition, and more recently by Jean-Patrice Boudet, who included in his findings extensive abstracts of the Latin original as well as two magical sigils reproduced from the manuscripts.[53] The Swedish Latinist Gösta Hedegård has prepared a critical edition of it. Joseph H. Peterson has prepared a noncritical, sometimes inaccurate but more easily accessible transcription as well.[54]

Even more attention is paid to the *Liber visionum* compiled by the French Benedictine monk, John of Morigny. Although the *Ars notoria* presented itself in a Christian framework, John of Morigny found it demonically inspired, and purifying it by the Virgin's help, he gave birth to an exceptional collection of Marian visions, the *Liber visionum beate Marie.* Even though it has been discovered just recently, and was virtually unknown to earlier scholarship, a number of accurate studies published since the 1990s seem to make up for this previous disregard considerably.

Dupèbe had already discussed an incomplete version of this text and its early condemnation,[55] but Sylvie Barnay was the first scholar to show a deeper interest in the text, and who had access to the whole text including its autobiographical prologue.[56] While Barnay examined the *Liber visionum* from the point of view of medieval Mariology and situated it in the history of the apparitions of the Blessed Virgin, several of the studies in Claire Fanger's book dedicated to the questions

---

52. Stephen Clucas, "*Non est legendum sed inspiciendum solum:* Inspectival Knowledge and the Visual Logic of John Dee's *Liber Mysteriorum,*" in *Emblems and Alchemy,* ed. Alison Adams and Stanton J. Linden (Glasgow: Glasgow Emblem Studies, 1998); Clucas, "John Dee's Angelic Conversations."
53. Mathiesen, "A Thirteenth-Century Ritual"; Kieckhefer, "Devil's Contemplatives"; Boudet, "Magie théurgique." See also *HMES,* 2:281–89.
54. Hedegård, *Liber iuratus Honorii* (see Chap.1, n. 81); Joseph H. Peterson ed., *Liber Juratus, or the Sworne Booke of Honorius,* www.esotericarchives.com/juratus/juratus.htm/.
55. Dupèbe, "L'«Ars Notoria» et la polémique," 127. The condemnation and burning of the text of a certain monk from Morigny was known even to Thorndike (*HMES,* 3:21), but Dupèbe was the first who found this condemnation to correspond to a manuscript of the *Liber visionum,* CLM 276.
56. Barnay, "La mariophanie"; Sylvie Barnay, "Désir de voir et interdits visionnaires ou la 'mariophanie' selon Jean de Morigny (XIVe siècle)," in *Homo Religiosus,* ed. Giuseppe Alberigo (Paris: Fayard, 1997), 519–26. See also Barnay's *Le ciel sur la terre: les apparitions de la Vierge au Moyen Age* (Paris: Éditions du Cerf, 1999), 154–60.

raised concerning this source find its place rather in the genre of ritual magic.[57] One of the foci of the research on this text has been the content and the functions of the *Liber visionum* as compared to the *Ars notoria:* that is, the way in which—and the aspects according to which—John revised the notory art. However, the geographical dissemination of the *Liber visionum* manuscripts and the casual reinterpretations and recontextualisations of its text are domains still waiting to be researched.

As scholarship on this text develops, new manuscripts turn up continually, in which full, partial, or adapted versions of the prayers of John the monk occur.[58] In the meantime, Claire Fanger and Nicholas Watson are preparing an edition of the *Liber visionum.* So far, however, only its autobiographical prologue is accessible.[59]

But even this prologue has proven to be a particularly rich source of information. In it, Brother John describes in great detail that before redacting his own version, he used to practice the *Ars notoria,* and what is more, he even composed a necromantic book.[60] Therefore—as Fanger observes—when he condemns this magical practice, his attitude is not merely academic, and his standpoint not simply theological: he speaks through personal experience.[61] John goes on to inform us that when he finally realized the wickedness of the *Ars notoria,* he gave up its practice. He had no fewer than three reasons to do so: personal, angelic, and theological ones. The personal reason is presented in the autobiographical prologue: John's sister, called Gurgeta, was also an active practitioner of the *Ars notoria,* in order to learn to read and write with extra speed. But after she started this accelerated method of learning, she had horrible visions and malign spirits haunted her, which—as John concludes—is a sign indicating demonic involvement in the notory art.[62] As a result, she renounced the *Ars notoria,* and the devils consequently withdrew. John's angelic reasons were no less explicit: in a number of visions, he heard the voice of supernatural powers, especially the Virgin Mary, telling him that he should not let himself be persuaded about the most holy nature of this art—which it claims to be—because it is deeply evil, and should be abandoned.[63]

John's third worry in relation to the art may be called theological: on the basis

---

57. Watson, "John the Monk's *Book of Visions*"; Fanger, "Plundering the Egyptian Treasure"; Kieckhefer, "Devil's Contemplatives."
58. For a list of the extant copies of the *Liber visionum* (not all containing the autobiographical account), see the appendix in Fanger and Láng, "John of Morigny's *Liber visionum*, and Fanger and Watson, "Some Further Manuscripts" (see Chap. 6, n. 75).
59. Fanger and Watson, "Prologue."
60. Fanger and Watson, "Prologue," 145.
61. Fanger, "Plundering the Egyptian Treasure," 217.
62. Ibid., 247; Fanger and Watson, "Prologue," 152–53.
63. Among other places, Fanger and Watson, "Prologue," 145.

of what he omitted from the notory art when purifying it, we can observe that he agreed with Thomas Aquinas on a number of points. Aquinas condemns the notory art for its use of figures and unknown words (*verba ignota*)[64]—assuming that these components are means of communication between the practitioner and demons. These are exactly those elements that John got rid of in his revision. Two surprising conclusions may be drawn here—and are indeed drawn by Claire Fanger.[65] On the one hand, Aquinas was unexpectedly well prepared in the topic he is condemning; he knew very well the aims of the notory art (acquisition of earthly knowledge in a very short period), and the arguments with which the practice defends itself (it is a holy practice, acknowledged by God, presenting no demonic danger). On the other hand, John, a practitioner of ritual magic, was well aware of the theological problems his methods can raise, and was careful enough to remove the elements responsible for these problems. In other words, there is more intellectual contact between the official Christian orthodoxy and those involved in magical practices than scholarship had believed. It is also possible that this contact actually turned into a theological debate, in which the *Liber visionum* was an attempt at creating the genre of a nondemonic ritual magic.[66]

Finally, it should be mentioned that Jean-Patrice Boudet and Julien Véronèse have collaborated on an article that provides a helpful overview on the whole genre of ritual magic.[67] In it they survey all of the basic texts of the genre, such as the *Clavicula Salomonis,* the *Liber Almandal,* the *Liber Raziel,* the *Ars Notoria,* the *Liber Juratus,* and the *Liber visionum.*

64. Thomas Aquinas, *Summa Theologiae,* 2a–2ae, q. 96.
65. Fanger, "Plundering the Egyptian Treasure," 223–25.
66. Ibid., 234: "My point is that John's *Liber visionum* is, among other things, part of an active and ongoing theological conversation about an occult ritual practice, in which he argues that the practice of the Ars Notoria (if not the Solomonic text itself) is defensible."
67. Jean-Patrice Boudet and Julien Véronèse, "Le secret dans la magie rituelle médiévale," *Micrologus* 14 (*Il Segreto*) (2006): 101–50. See also Jean-Patrice Boudet, *Entre science et "nigromance": Astrologie, divination et magie dans l'Occident médiéval (XIIe–XVe siècle).* Paris: Publications de la Sorbonne, 2006.

Appendix 2 A Comparison of the Contents of SLB N. 100 and BAV Pal. lat. 1439

	Dresden N. 100 (Egidius of Corintia, 1487)	Pal. lat. 1439 (Johannes Virdung of Hassfurt, 1488)
Petrus Gaszowiec, *De mutatione aeris*	fols. 174r–185r, 223r–225v	fols. 336r–344r
Johannes of Glogovia, *Summa astrologiae*	fols. 192v–196v, 230r–266r, 268v–288r	fols. 122r–152r, 211r–239v
Johannes of Glogovia, *Tractatulus ex intentione sapientium*	fols. 192v–196v	fols. 155r–160r
Albertus of Brudzewo, *De iudicio configurationis*		fols. 314r–316v
Albertus of Brudzewo (?), *rectificatio geniture sec. verbum 51 Ptolomei*	fols. 222r–222v	fol. 40r–v
Albertus of Brudzewo, *Iudicium anni 1487*		fols. 323v–330v
Albertus of Brudzewo, *Commentariolum in theoricas planetarum Purbachii*	fols. 121r–149v	
Commentary on Sacrobosco's *Sphera*	fols. 27r–82v	fols. 78v–102v
Johannes of Sacro Bosco, *Sphera*	fols. 27r–82r	fols. 293r–304v
Ps-Ptolemy, *Compositio et operatio astrolabii*	fols. 11v–19v	fols. 279r–285r
Ps-Ptolemy, *Compositio et operatio astrolabii*	fols. 1r–11r	fols. 317r–323r
De invencione orbis magni	fols. 288r–288v	
Albicus of Uniczow, *Pronosticationes infirmo secundum dies incensionis*	fol. 161v	fol. 198r
Albertus Magnus, *Secretum de leonis sigillum*	fol. 201v	
Sphera Pythagorae	fol. 203v	
Liber de stellis beibeniis	fols. 228r–229r	fols. 344v–345v
Liber runarum	fols. 198r–200v	fols. 346r–347v; *rota runarum*, fol. 199r

SELECTED BIBLIOGRAPHY

Printed Editions of Primary Sources

Agrippa, Cornelius. *Ars Notoria.* In *Opera Omnia,* vol. 2, pp. 603–60. Lyons: Beringos Fratres, c.1620.
Al-Kindi. *De radiis.* Edited by Marie-Thérèse d'Alverny and Françoise Hudry. *AHDLMA* 41 (1974): 139–260.
Ars Notoria: The Notory Art of Solomon. Translated by Robert Turner. London: F. Cottrel, 1657. Reprint, Seattle: Trident Books, 1987. The text can be also found at http://www.esotericarchives.com/notoria/notoria.htm.
Bernacki, Ludwik, and Ryszard Ganszyniec, eds. *Modlitewnik Władysława Warneńczyka w zbiorach Bibljoteki Bodlejańskiej* (Wladislas Warnenczyk's Prayer Book Kept in the Bodleian Library). Kraków: Anczyc i Spółka, 1928.
Bernardus Silvestris. *Experimentarius.* In Maria Brini Savorelli, "Un manuale di geomanzia presentato da Bernardo Silvestre da Tours (XII secolo): l'*Experimentarius.*" *Rivista Critica di Storia della Filosofia* 14 (1959): 282–342.
Bolgár, Ágnes, ed. *Magyar bájoló imádságok a XV–XVI. századból* (Hungarian Incantations from the Fifteenth and Sixteenth Centuries). Budapest: Mérnökök Nyomda, 1934.
Bonfini, Antonius. *Symposium de virginitate et pudicitia coniugali.* Edited by Stephanus Apró. Budapest: K. M. Egyetemi Nyomda, 1943.
Bos, Gerrit, Charles Burnett, Thérèse Charmasson, Paul Kunitzsch, Fabrizio Lelli, and Paolo Lucentini, eds. *Hermes Trismegistus: Astrologica et divinatoria.* Turnhout: Brepols, 2001.
Carmody, Francis J., ed. *The Astronomical Works of Thabit ben Qurra.* Berkeley and Los Angeles: University of California Press, 1960.
De septem herbis et septem planetis. In *Textes latins et vieux français relatifs aux Cyranides,* ed. Louis Delatte, 209–33. Liège-Paris: Droz, 1942.
Döbrentei, Gábor, ed. *Régi magyar nyelvemlékek* (Old Hungarian Sources). Vol. 2. Buda, 1840.
Draelants, Isabelle. *Le Liber de virtutibus herbarium, lapidum et animalium* (Liber aggregationis), Florence: Sismel, 2007.
Fanger, Claire, and Nicholas Watson, eds. "The Prologue to John of Morigny's *Liber Visionum:* Text and Translation." *Esoterica: The Journal of Western Esoteric Studies* 3 (2001): 108–217. http://www.esoteric.msu.edu.
Ficino, Marsilio. *Three Books on Life.* Edited by Carol V. Kaske and John R. Clark. Medieval and Renaissance Texts and Studies 57. Binghamton, N.Y.: Renaissance Society of America, 1989.
Galeottus Martius Narnensis. *De egregie, sapienter, iocose dictis ac factis regis Mathiae.* Edited by Ladislaus Juhász. Vol. 3. Budapest: Egyetemi nyomda, 1934.
Ganszyniec, Ryszard, ed. *Brata Mikołaja z Polski pisma lekarskie* (The Medical Writings of Brother Nicolaus of Poland). Poznan: Czcionkami Drukarni Zjednoczenia, 1920.
Gerson, Jean. *De erroribus circa artem magicam.* In *Oeuvres complètes,* ed. Palémon Glorieux, vol. 10, *L'oeuvre polémique,* 77–90. Paris: Desclée, 1973.

Giralt, Sebastià, ed. *Arnaldi de Villanova, Opera medica omnia, VII.1, Epistola de reprobacione nigromantice ficcionis (de improbatione maleficiorum)*. Barcelona: Fundació Noguera, Universitat de Barcelona, 2005.

Hartlieb, Johann. *Das Buch aller verbotenen Künste des Aberglaubens und der Zauberei*. Edited by Falk Eisermann and Eckhard Graf. Ahlerstedt: Param, 1989.

Herner, János, and László Szörényi. "A Tudás Könyve. Hasznos útmutató haladó kincsásóknak" (The Book of Knowledge: Useful Guide for Treasure-Diggers). In *Collectanea Tiburtiana: tanulmányok Klaniczay Tibor tiszteletére* (*Collectanea Tiburtiana*: Studies in Honor of Tibor Klaniczay), ed. Bálint Keserű, 9–33. Szeged: József Attila Tudományegyetem, 1990.

Joannes de Lasnioro. "Tractatus secundus aureus de lapide philosophorum." In *Theatrum Chemicum*, vol. 4, edited by the heirs of Eberhard Zetzner, 579–84. Argentorati: Zetzner, 1659.

Johannes Trithemius. *Annales Hirsaugiensis*. 2 vols. St. Gall: Georgius Schleger, 1690.

———. "Antipalus Maleficiorum." In *Paralipomena opusculorum Petri Blesensis et Joannis Trithemii aliorumque*, ed. Ianus Busaeus, 273–313. Mainz: Balthasar Lippius, 1605.

———. "Antipalus Maleficiorum." In Paola Zambelli, "Pseudepigrafia e magia secondo l'abate Johannes Trithemius." In *Ratio et Superstitio: Essays in Honor of Graziella Federici Vescovini*, ed. Giancarlo Marchetti, Orsola Rignani, and Valeria Sorge, 347–68. Louvain-la-Neuve: Fédérations Internationales des Instituts d'Études Médiévales, 2003.

Johnsson, John W. S., ed. "Les Experimenta magistri Nicolai." *Bulletin de la société française d'histoire de la médicine* 10 (1911): 269–90.

Kyeser, Conrad. *Bellifortis*. Edited by Götz Quarg. 2 vols. Düsseldorf: Verlag des Vereins Deutscher Ingenieurie, 1967.

Kyranides. In *Textes latins et vieux français relatifs aux Cyranides*, ed. Louis Delatte, 4–206. Liège-Paris: Droz, 1942.

Liber de Angelis. In "The Book of Angels, Rings, Characters and Images of the Planets: Attributed to Osbern Bokenham," ed. Juris Lidaka. In Fanger, *Conjuring Spirits*, 32–75.

Liber de stellis beibeniis, ed. Paul Kunitzsch. In Bos et al., *Hermes Trismegistus*, 7–81.

Liber runarum. Edited by Paolo Lucentini. In Bos et al., *Hermes Trismegistus*, 401–49.

Melchior Cibinensis, Nicolaus. "Addam et Processum Sub Forma Missae a Nicolao Melchiore Cibinensi Transiluano, ad Ladislaum Ungariae et Bohemiae Regem olim missum." In *Theatrum Chemicum*, vol. 3, ed. Lazarus Zetzner, 758–61. Ursel, 1602.

Nicolaus de Polonia. *Antipocras*. In Karl Sudhoff, "Antipocras, Streitschrift für mystische Heilkunde in Versen." *Archiv* 9 (1916): 31–52.

Peer-kódex: a nyelvemlék hasonmása és betűhű átirata (The *Peer-Codex*: The Facsimile and Transcription of a Literary Monument). Edited by Andrea Kacskovics-Reményi and Beatrix Oszkó. Budapest: Argumentum Kiadó, 2000.

Picatrix: The Latin Version of the Ghāyat al-hakīm. Edited by D. Pingree. Studies of the Warburg Institute 39. London: The Warburg Institute, University of London, 1986.

Pócs, Éva, ed. *Magyar ráolvasások* (Hungarian Incantations). 2 vols. Budapest: MTAK, 1985–86.

Przybyszewski, Bolesław, ed. *Cracovia artificum*. Vol. 1. Wrocław: Zakład Narodowy im. Ossolińskich, 1985.

———, ed. *Cracovia artificum*. Supplementa 2. Wrocław: Zakład Narodowy im. Ossolińskich, 1988.

Pseudo Albertus Magnus. *The Book of Secrets of Albertus Magnus of the Virtues of Herbs, Stones and Certain Beasts; also, A Book of the Marvels of the World*. Edited by Michael R. Best and Frank H. Brightman. Oxford: Clarendon Press, 1973.

———. *De secretis mulierum. De virtutibus herbarum, lapidum et animalium*. Amsterdam: Iodocus Ianssonius, 1648.

Selected Bibliography   297

———. *Liber aggregationis seu liber secreto[rum]; de virtutibus herba[rum] lapidum [et] animalium quorumd[am].* London: Wilhelmus de Mechlinia, 1483.
———. *Speculum astronomiae.* In Zambelli, *"Speculum astronomiae,"* 208–73.
Pseudo Aristoteles. *Secretum secretorum cum glossis et notulis.* In *Opera hactenus inedita Rogeri Baconi,* ed. R. Steele, vol. 5, *Secretum secretorum.* Oxford: Typographeo Clarendoniano, 1920.
Richard de Fournival. *Biblionomia.* In *Le Cabinet des manuscrits de la Bibliothèque Nationale,* ed. Léopold Delisle, vol. 2, pp. 518–35. Paris: Imprimerie Nationale, 1876.
Stanislas de Scarbimiria. *Consilia contra astrologum Henricum Bohemum.* In Stanisław Wielgus, "Consilia contre l'astrologue Henri Bohemus." *Studia Mediewistyczne* 25 (1988): 145–72.
Toral-Niehoff, Isabel, ed. *Kitāb Ġirānīs: Die arabische Übersetzung der ersten Kyranis des Hermes Trismegistos und die griechischen Parallelen herausgegeben, übersetzt und kommentiert.* München: Herbert Utz Verlag, 2004.
William of Auvergne. *Opera Omnia.* Paris: Andraeas Pralard, 1674. 2 vols. Reprint, Frankfurt am Main: Minerva, 1963.
Witelo. *De natura daemonum.* In Aleksander Birkenmajer, *Études d'histoire des sciences en Pologne,* 122–36. Studia Copernicana 4. Wrocław: Zakład Narodowy im. Ossolińskich, 1972.
Zathey, Jerzy, ed. "Modlitwa z XIV wieku o charakterze zaklęcia, mająca zapewnić żonie miłość męża" (A Fourteenth-Century Magical Prayer Which Is to Guarantee the Love of a Husband to His Wife). *Biuletyn Biblioteki Jagiellońskiej* 34–35 (1984–85): 63–64.

Catalogs, Handbooks, and Other Reference Material

Ameisenowa, Zofia. *Rękopisy i pierwodruki iluminowane Biblioteki Jagiellońskiej* (Illuminated Manuscripts in the Biblioteka Jagiellońska). Wrocław: Zakład Narodowy im. Ossolińskich, 1958.
Bauch, Gustav. *Deutsche Scholaren in Krakau der Zeit der Renaissance, 1460–1520.* Breslau: M. & H. Marcus, 1901.
Bicherl, Renata. "Die Magister der Artistenfakultät der Hohen Schule zu Prag und ihre Schriften im Zeitraum von 1348 bis 1409." Ph.D. diss., Erlangen-Nürnberg, 1971.
Burda, Elzbieta, and Anna Kozlowska, eds. *Handschriftliche Polonica in den Sammlungen der Universitätsbibliothek Jena.* Jena: Universitätsbibliothek Jena, 1989.
Carmody, Francis J. *Arabic Astronomical and Astrological Sciences in Latin Translation: A Critical Bibliography.* Berkeley and Los Angeles: University of California Press, 1956.
von Carolsfeld, Franz Schnorr, and Ludwig Schmidt, eds. *Katalog der Handschriften der Königlichen Öffentlichen Bibliothek zu Dresden.* Vol. 3. Lepzig: B. G. Teubner, 1906.
Csapodi, Csaba. *A budai királyi palotában 1686-ban talált kódexek és nyomtatott könyvek* (The Codices and Printed Books Found in the Royal Castle of Buda in 1686). Budapest: MTA, 1984.
———. "Codices, die im Jahre 1686 von Buda nach Wien geliefert wurden." *Codices Manuscripti* 7 (1981): 121–27.
Csapodi, Csaba, and Klára Csapodiné Gárdonyi. *Bibliotheca Corviniana: The Library of King Matthias Corvinus of Hungary.* 4th ed. Budapest: Helikon, 1990.
———, eds. *Bibliotheca Hungarica: kódexek és nyomtatott könyvek Magyarországon 1526 előtt* (*Bibliotheca Hungarica:* Codices and Printed Books in Hungary Before 1526). Budapest: Magyar Tudományos Akadémia Könyvtára, 1993.
Dokoupil, Vladislav, ed. *Catalogus codicum manu scriptorum bibliothecae Monasterii Eremitarum S. Augustini Vetero-Brunae.* Brno: Universitní knihovna, 1957.

Gąsiorowski, Antoni, ed. *Liber promotionum facultatis artium in universitate cracoviensi saeculi decimi quinti*. Kraków: Nakładem Polskiej Akademii Umiejętności, 2000.

Hlaváček, Ivan. "Nachträge zu den böhmischen mittelalterlichen Bücher- und Bibliotheksverzeichnissen." *Mediaevalia Bohemica* 1 (1969): 306–15.

———. "O studiu středověkých knižních katalogů" (On the Study of Medieval Book Catalogs). *Acta Universitatis Carolinae, Philosophica et Historica* 2 (1958): 179–93.

———. *Středověké soupisy knih a knihoven v českých zemích* (Medieval Lists of Books and Libraries in Bohemia). Acta Universitatis Carolinae, Philosophica et Historica—Monographia 11. Prague: Univerzita Karlova, 1965.

Keussen, Hermann, ed. *Die Matrikel der Universität Köln*. Vol. 1. Bonn: P. Hanstein, 1928–81.

Lucentini, Paolo, and Vittoria Perrone Compagni, eds. *I Testi e i codici di Ermete nel Medioevo*. Florence: Polistampa, 2001.

Markowski, Mieczysław, ed. *Astronomica et astrologica Cracoviensia ante annum 1550*. Studi e testi / Istituto nazionale di studi sul Rinascimento 20. Florence: L. S. Olschki, 1990.

———. "Les manuscrits des listes de docteurs en médecine à l'Université de Cracovie entre 1400 et 1611." *Mediaevalia Philosophica Polonorum* 20 (1974): 121–40.

———. "Repertorium bio-bibliographicum astronomorum cracoviensum medii aevi." Pts. 1, 2, and 3. *Studia Mediewistyczne* 26 (1989): 103–62; 27, no. 1 (1990): 111–63; and 27, no. 2 (1990): 159–73.

Marx, Jakob, ed. *Verzeichnis der Handschriften-Sammlung des Hospitals zu Cues*. Trier: Schaar und Dathe, 1905.

Muczkowski, J., ed. *Statuta nec non liber promotionum philosophorum ordinis in universitate studiorum Jagellonica*. Kraków: Uniwersytet Jagielloński, 1849.

Pauly, Z., B. Ulanowski, and A. Chmiel, eds. *Album studiosorum Universitatis Cracoviensis*. 3 vols. Kraków: typis, C. R. Universitatis, 1887–1904.

Podlaha, Antonín, ed. *Soupis rukopisů knihovny metropolitní kapituly pražské* (Catalog of Manuscripts of the Metropolitan Chapter Library of Prague). Prague: Česká Akademie věd, 1922.

Polski Słownik Biograficzny (Polish Biographical Dictionary). Edited by Władysław Konopczyński et al. Kraków: Polska Akademia Nauk, 1935– .

Rosińska, Grażyna, ed. *Scientific Writings and Astronomical Tables in Cracow: A Census of Manuscript Sources (XIVth–XVIth Centuries)*. Studia Copernicana 22. Wrocław: Zakład Narodowy im. Ossolińskich, 1984.

Schuba, Ludwig, ed. *Die Quadriviums-Handschriften der Codices Palatini Latini in der Vatikanischen Bibliothek*. Wiesbaden: Reichert, 1992.

Selecká Mârza, Eva. *A középkori lőcsei könyvtár* (The Medieval Library of Lőcse). Szeged: Scriptum Kft, 1997.

Šmahel, František. "Mistři, licenciáti, bakaláři a studenti pražské lékařské fakulty do počátků husitské revoluce" (Masters, Licentiates, Bachelors, and Students of the Prague Medical Faculty until the Beginnings of the Husssite Revolution). *Acta Universitatis Carolinae, Historia Universitatis Carolinae Pragensis* 20–22 (1980): 35–68.

Sopko, Július, ed. *Codices Ac Fragmenta Codicum Bibliothecarum Slovaciae*. Martin: Matica Slovenská, 1986.

Spunar, Pavel. *Repertorium auctorum bohemorum provectum idearum post universitatem Pragensem conditam illustrans*. 2 vols. Studia Copernicana 25 and 35. Wrocław: Ossolineum, 1985, 1995.

Szentiványi, Robertus. *Catalogus concinnus librorum manuscriptorum Bibliothecae Batthyányanae*. Szeged: Hungaria, 1958.

Thorndike, Lynn, and Pearl Kibre, eds. *A Catalogue of Incipits of Mediaeval Scientific Writings in Latin*. Revised and augmented edition. Cambridge, Mass.: Mediaeval Academy of America, 1963.
Truhlář, Josef, ed. *Catalogus codicum manu scriptorum latinorum, qui in c. r. bibliotheca publica atque universitatis Pragensis asservantur*. 2 vols. Prague: Regia Societas Scientiarum, 1905–6.
Uiblein, Franz, ed. *Acta facultatis Artium Universitatis Vindobodensis (1365–1416)*. Vienna: Hermann Böhlaus, 1968.
Unterkircher, Franz, H. Horninger, and Franz Lachner, eds. *Die datierten Handschriften der Österreichischen Nationalbibliothek von 1501 bis 1600*. Vol. 4. Vienna: Österreichische Akademie der Wissenschaften, 1976.
Weber, Jaroslav, Josef Tříška, and Pavel Spunar, eds. *Catalogus codicum manu scriptorum Trzebonae Crumloviique asservatorum*. Prague: Nakladatelství Československé Akademie věd, 1958.
Wisłocki, W., ed. *Katalog rekopisów Biblioteki Uniwersytetu Jagiellońskiego* (Catalog of the Manuscripts of the Jagiellonian University Library). Kraków: Uniwersytet Jagielloński, 1877–81.
Włodek, Zofia. "Inventaire des manuscrits médiévaux latins, philosophiques et théologiques de la bibliothèque des pères dominicains de Cracovie." *Mediaevalia Philosophica Polonorum* 14 (1970): 155–86.
———, ed. *Polonica w średniowiecznych rękopisach bibliotek niemieckich: Aschaffenburg, Augsburg, Bamberg, Eichstätt, Harburg, Moguncja, Norymberga* (*Polonica* in the Medieval Manuscripts of German Libraries: Aschaffenburg, Augsburg, Bamberg, Eichstätt, Harburg, Mainz, Nürnberg). Wrocław: Zakład Narodowy im. Ossolińskich, 1974.
Włodek, Zofia, Jerzy Zathey, and Marian Zwiercan, eds. *Catalogus codicum manuscriptorum Medii Aevi Latinorum qui in Bibliotheca Jagellonica Cracoviae asservantur*. 8 vols. Wrocław: Zakład Narodowy im. Ossolińskich, 1980–2004.

Secondary Literature

Alverny, Marie Thérèse de. *La transmission des textes philosophiques et scientifiques au Moyen Âge*. Edited by Charles Burnett. Aldershot: Variorum, 1994.
Ameisenowa, Zofia. "Średniowieczne ilustracje alchemiczne w rękopisie Biblioteki Jagiellońskiej" (Medieval Alchemical Illustrations in a Manuscript of the Biblioteka Jagiellońska). *Kalendarz ilustrowango kurjera codziennego na rok 1938* (1939): 216–18.
Baczkowska, Wanda. "Die internationalen Beziehungen der Krakauer Akademie in der Zeit vom 15. bis zum Anfang des 16. Jahrhunderts." In Szögi and Varga, *Universitas Budensis*, 79–88.
Bailey, Michael D. *Battling Demons: Witchcraft, Heresy, and Reform in the Late Middle Ages*. University Park: Pennsylvania State University Press, 2003.
———. "From Sorcery to Witchcraft: Clerical Conceptions of Magic in the Later Middle Ages." *Speculum* 76 (2001): 960–90.
Balogh, Jolán, ed. *A művészet Mátyás király udvarában: Adattár* (Art in the Court of Matthias: Database). Budapest: Akadémiai Kiadó, 1966.
———. *Mátyás király és a művészet* (King Matthias and the Arts). Budapest: Magvető, 1985.
———. "Néhány adat Firenze és Magyarország kulurális kapcsolatainak történetéhez" (Some Data on the History of the Cultural Relations of Florence and Hungary). *Archeologiai Értesítő* 50 (1923–26): 189–209.
Barlai, Katalin. "Csillagászati kódexek a Corvina könyvtárban" (Astronomical Codices in the Corvinian Library). *Meteor Csillagászati Évkönyv 1997-re* (1996): 192–99.

Barlai, Katalin, and Ágnes Boronkai. "Astronomical Codices in the Corvinian Library." *Memorie della Societa Astronomica Italiana* 65 (1994): 533–46.
Barnay, Sylvie. *Le ciel sur la terre: les apparitions de la Vierge au Moyen Age*. Paris: Éditions du Cerf, 1999.
———. "Désir de voir et interdits visionnaires ou la 'mariophanie' selon Jean de Morigny (XIVe siècle)." In *Homo Religiosus*, ed. Giuseppe Alberigo, 519–26. Paris: Fayard, 1997.
———. "La mariophanie au regard de Jean de Morigny: Magie au miracle de la vision mariale." In *Miracles, Prodiges et Merveilles au Moyen Age*, 173–90. Paris: Publications de la Sorbonne, 1995.
Baron, Frank. *Doctor Faustus: From History to Legend*. Munich: Wilhelm Fink Verlag, 1978.
Bartha, Lajos. "Janus Pannonius két csillagászati verse" (Two Astronomical Poems by Janus Pannonius). *Irodalomtudományi Közlemények* 82 (1978): 340–45.
———. "Régi magyar csillagászok" (Early Hungarian Astronomers). Pts. 1 and 2. *Technikatörténeti Szemle* 8 (1976): 71–113; 11 (1979): 169–81.
Bartlová, Milena. "The Magic of Image: Astrological, Alchemical and Magical Symbolism at the Court of Wenceslas IV." In *The Role of Magic in the Past: Learned and Popular Magic, Popular Beliefs and Diversity of Attitudes*, ed. Blanka Szeghyová, 19–28. Bratislava: Pro Historia, 2005.
Beckers, Hartmut. "Eine spätmittelalterliche deutsche Anleitung zur Teufelsbeschwörung mit Runenschriftverwendung." *Zeitschrift für deutsches Altertum und deutsche Literatur* 113 (1984): 136–45.
Berger, Adolf. "Die Rosenbergische Bibliothek und Wenzel Březan." *Mitteilungen des Vereines für Geschichte der Deutschen in Böhmen* 20 (1881–82): 193–211.
Birkenmajer, Aleksander. "La Bibliothèque de Richard de Fournival, poète et érudit français du début du XIIIe siècle et son sort ultérieur." In *Études d'histoire des sciences et de la philosophie du Moyen Age*. Studia Copernicana 1. Wrocław: Zakład Narodowy im. Ossolińskich, 1970.
———. *Études d'histoire des sciences en Pologne*. Studia Copernicana 4. Wrocław: Zakład Narodowy im. Ossolińskich, 1972.
———. "Formula." *Isis* 19 (1933): 364–78.
———. "Henryk le Bohemien." In *Études d'histoire des sciences en Pologne*, 497–98. Studia Copernicana 4. Wrocław: Zakład Narodowy im. Ossolińskich, 1972.
———. "Sprawa Magistra Henryka Czecha" (The Case of Master Henry the Czech). *Collectanea Theologica* 17 (1936): 207–24.
Birkenmajer, Ludwik Antoni. "Mikołaj Wodka de Kwidzyn, médecin et astronome polonais du XVe siècle." *Bulletin de l'Academie Polonais des Sciences et des Lettres* (1924): 783–86.
———. "Mikołaj Wodka z Kwidzyna zwany Abstemius, lekarz i astronom polski XV-go stulecia" (Mikołaj Wodka of Kwidzyn, Polish Doctor and Astronomer in the Fifteenth Century). *Roczniki Towarzystwa Naukowego w Toruniu* (1926): 110–250.
Bollók, János. *Asztrális misztika és asztrológia Janus Pannonius költészetében* (Astral Mysticism and Astrology in the Poetry of Janus Pannonius). Budapest: Argumentum, 2003.
Bolte, J. "Zur Geschichte der Losbücher." In *Georg Wickrams Werke*, ed. J. Bolte, vol. 4, pp. 276–341. Tübingen: Litterarischen Verein in Stuttgart, 1903.
Bonney, Françoise. "Autour de Jean Gerson: Opinions de théologiens sur les superstitions et la sorcellerie au début de XVe siècle." *Le Moyen Age* 77 (1971): 85–98.
Borkowska, Urszula. *Królewskie modlitewniki* (Royal Prayer Books). Lublin: Towarzystwo Naukowe Katolickiego Uniwersytetu Lubelskiego, 1999.
Boudet, Jean-Patrice. "L'*Ars notoria* au Moyen Age: une résurgence de la théurgie antique?" In *La Magie: Actes du colloque internatonal de Montpellier 25–27 Mars 1999*, vol. 3, pp. 173–91. Montpellier: Université Paul-Valéry, Montpellier III, 2000.
———. "Les Condamnations de la magie à Paris en 1398." *Revue Mabillon*, n.s., 12 (2001): 121–57.

———. *Entre science et "nigromance": Astrologie, divination et magie dans l'Occident médiéval (XIIe–XVe siècle)*. Paris: Publications de la Sorbonne, 2006.

———. "La Genèse médiévale de la chasse aux sorcières: Jalons en vue d'une relecture." In *Le mal et le diable: leurs figures à la fin du Moyen Age*, ed. Nathalie Nabert, 35–52. Paris: Beauchesne, 1996.

———. "Magie théurgique, angélologie et vision béatifique dans le *Liber sacratus sive juratus* attribué à Honorius de Thèbes." In Bresc and Grévin, "Les Anges et la magie," 851–90.

Boudet, Jean-Patrice, and Julien Véronèse. "Le secret dans la magie rituelle médiévale." *Micrologus* 14 (*Il Segreto*) (2006): 101–50.

Boureau, Alain. "Une épisode central dans la construction de la magie noire du livre: de la rivalité des exégèses à la crémation du Talmud (1144–1242)." In Ganz, *Das Buch*, 137–58.

Braarvig, Jens. "Magic: Reconsidering the Grand Dichotomy." In *The World of Ancient Magic: Papers from the First International Samson Eitrem Seminar at the Norwegian Institute at Athens, 4–8 May, 1997*, ed. David R. Jordan, Hugo Montgomery, and Einar Thomassen, 21–54. Bergen: The Norwegian Institute at Athens, 1999.

Bracha, Krzysztof. "Magie und Aberglaubenskritik in den Predigten des Spätmittelalters in Polen." In Wünsch, *Religion und Magie*, 197–215.

———. "Pismo, słowa i symbole" (Writing, Words, and Symbols). In *Inskrypcje toruńskie* (Toruń Inscriptions), ed. Irena Sawickiej, 7–25. Toruń: UMK, 1999.

———. *Teolog, diabeł i zabobony: Świadectwo traktatu Mikołaja Magni z Jawora "De superstitionibus"* (The Theologian, the Devil and the Superstitions: The Testimony of the Treatise of Nicolaus Jawor, *De superstitionibus*). Warsaw: Instytut Historii PAN, 1999.

Braekman, W. L. *Middeleeuwse witte en zwarte magie in het Nederlands taalgebied: Gecommentarieerd compendium van incantamenta tot einde 16de eeuww*. (Medieval Black and White Magic in Dutch-Speaking Regions: Compendium of Incantations until the End of the Sixteenth Century). Ghent: Koninklijke Academie voor Nederlandse Taal- en Letterkunde, 1997.

———, ed. *Middelnederlandse geneeskundige recepten* (Middledutch Medical Prescriptions). Ghent: Koninklijke Vlaamse Academie voor Taal- en Letterkunde, 1970.

———. "A Unique Magical Mirror from the Sixteenth Century." *Societas Magica Newsletter* 8 (2001): 5–6.

Brashear, William. "Magical Papyri: Magic in Bookform." In Ganz, *Das Buch*, 25–58.

Bremmer, Jan N., and Jan R. Veenstra. "Appendix: Magic *and* Religion." In Bremmer and Veenstra, *Metamorphosis of Magic*, 267–71.

———, eds. *The Metamorphosis of Magic from Late Antiquity to the Early Modern Period*. Leuven: Peters, 2002.

Bresc, Henri, and Benoît Grévin, eds. "Les Anges et la magie au Moyen Âge: Actes de la table ronde, Nanterre, 8–9 décembre 2000." *Mélanges de l'École Française de Rome, Moyen Âge* 114 (2002): 851–90.

Bridges, John Henry. *The Life and Work of Roger Bacon: An Introduction to the Opus Majus*. Merrick, N.Y.: Richwood Publishing, 1976.

Brozek, Zofia Pwlikowska. "Wojciech of Brudzewo." In Gierowski, *Cracow Circle*, 61–75.

Brzezinska, Anna. "Female Control of Dynastic Politics in Sixteenth-Century Poland." In *The Man of Many Devices, Who Wandered Full Many Ways—: Festschrift in Honor of János M. Bak*, ed. Balázs Nagy and Marcell Sebők, 187–94. Budapest: CEU Press, 1999.

———. "Political Significance of Love Magic Accusations at the Jagiellonian Court." Master's thesis, Central European University, Budapest, 1995.

Bugaj, Roman. *Nauki tajemne w Polsce w dobie odrodzenia* (Secret Sciences in Poland in the Renaissance). Wrocław: Ossolineum, 1976.

Buntz, Herwig. "Alchemy III: 12th/13th–15th Century." In *Dictionary of Gnosis and Western Esotericism*, ed. Wouter J. Hanegraaff et al., 34–41. Leiden: Brill, 2005.
Burchardt, Jerzy. *List Witelona do Ludwika we Lwówku Śląskim* (Vitelo's Letter to Ludwig in Lwówek). Studia Copernicana 19. Wrocław: Zakład Narodowy im. Ossolińskich, 1979.
Burnett, Charles. "The Arabic Hermes in the Works of Adelard of Bath." In Lucentini, Parri, and Perrone Compagni, *Hermetism*, 369–84.
———. "The Conte de Sarzana Magical Manuscript." In Burnett, *Magic and Divination*.
———. "The Establishment of Medieval Hermeticism." In *The Medieval World*, ed. Peter Linehan and Janet L. Nelson, 111–30. London: Routledge, 2001.
———. "A Group of Arabic-Latin Translators Working in Northern Spain in the Mid-Twelfth Century." *Journal of the Royal Asiatic Society*, 1977, 62–108.
———. "Innovations in the Classification of the Sciences in the Twelfth Century." In *Knowledge and the Sciences in Medieval Philosophy. Proceedings of the Eighth International Congress of Medieval Philosophy*, ed. S. Knuuttila, vol. 2, pp. 25–42. Helsinki: Yliopistopaino, 1990.
———. *Magic and Divination in the Middle Ages: Texts and Techniques in the Islamic and Christian Worlds*. Collected Studies Series. Aldershot: Variorum, 1996.
———. "The Prognostications of the Eadwine Psalter." In *The Eadwine Psalter*, ed. T. A. Heslop, R. W. Pfaff, and M. Gibson, 165–67. London: Modern Humanities Research Association, 1992.
———. "Scandinavian Runes in a Latin Magical Treatise. Postscript by M. Stoklund." *Speculum* 58 (1983): 419–29. Reprinted in Burnett, *Magic and Divination*.
———. "The *Sortes Regis Amalrici:* An Arabic Divinatory Work in the Latin Kingdom of Jerusalem?" *Scripta Mediterranea* 19–20 (1998–99): 229–37.
———. "Talismans: Magic as Science? Necromancy Among the Seven Liberal Arts." In Burnett, *Magic and Divination*.
———. "Thābit ibn Qurra the Harrānian on Talismans and the Spirits of the Planets." Forthcoming in R. Rashed and R. Morelon, eds., *The Proceedings of the al-Furqān Conference on Thābit ibn Qurrah, November 2001*.
———. "What Is the *Experimentarius* of Bernardus Silvestris? A Preliminary Survey of the Material." *AHDLMA* 44 (1977): 62–108.
Burnett, Charles, and William Francis Ryan, eds. *Magic and the Classical Tradition*. London: The Warburg Institute, 2006.
Burnett, Charles, Keiji Yamamoto, and Michio Yano. "Al-Kindi on Finding Buried Treasure." *Arabic Sciences and Philosophy* 7 (1997): 57–90.
Bylina, Stanisław. "Magie, sorcellerie et culture populaire en Pologne aux XVe et XVIe siècles." *Acta ethnographica, A Periodical of the Hungarian Academy of Sciences* 37 (1991): 173–90.
———. "La prédication, les croyances et les pratiques traditionnelles en Pologne au bas Moyen Age." In *L'Église et le peuple chrétien dans les pays de l'Europe du Centre-Est et du Nord (XIVe–XVe siècles)*, 301–13. Rome: École française de Rome, 1990.
Byliński, Bronisław. *Tradizioni italiane all'università Jagellonica di Cracovia*. Wrocław: Zakład Narodowy im. Ossolińskich, 1967.
Cadden, Joan. "Charles V, Nicole Oresme, and Christine de Pizan: Unities and Uses of Knowledge in Fourteenth-Century France." In McVaugh and Sylla, *Texts and Contexts*, 208–44.
Camille, Michael. "Visual Art in Two Manuscripts of the *Ars Notoria*." In Fanger, *Conjuring Spirits*, 110–43.
Cammann, Schuyler. "Islamic and Indian Magic Squares." *History of Religions* 8 (1969): 271–99.
Cavallo, Guglielmo, and Roger Chartier, eds. *Histoire de la lecture dans le monde occidentale*. Paris: Editions du Seuil, 1997.

Chaloupecký, Václav. *The Caroline University of Prague.* Prague: Orbis, 1948.
Charmasson, Thérèse. "Divinatory Arts." In *Dictionary of Gnosis and Western Esotericism,* ed. Wouter J. Hanegraaff et al., 313–19.
———. "Les premiers traîtés latins de géomancie." *Cahiers de civilisation médiévale* 21 (1978): 121–36.
———. *Recherches sur une technique divinatoire: la géomancie dans l'Occident médiéval.* Centre de Recherches d'Histoire et de Philosophie de la IVe Section de l'École Pratique des Hautes Études 44. Geneva: Librarie Droz, 1980.
Chmielowska, Bozena. "Stanislaus de Skarbimierz, le premier recteur de l'Université de Cracovie après le renouveau de celle-ci." *Mediaevalia Philosophica Polonorum* 24 (1979): 73–131.
Cierny, Michal. *Medizin und Mediziner an der Prager Karls-Universität von der Gründung bis 1654.* Zürich: Juris, 1973.
Clucas, Stephen. "John Dee's Angelic Conversations and the *Ars notoria:* Renaissance Magic and Mediaeval Theurgy." In *John Dee: Interdisciplinary Essays in English Renaissance Thought,* ed. Clucas, 231–73. Dordrecht: Springer, 2006.
———. "*Non est legendum sed inspiciendum solum:* Inspectival Knowledge and the Visual Logic of John Dee's *Liber Mysteriorum.*" In *Emblems and Alchemy,* ed. Alison Adams and Stanton J. Linden. Glasgow: Glasgow Emblem Studies, 1998.
Cohn, Norman. *Europe's Inner Demons: An Enquiry Inspired by the Great Witch-Hunt.* New York: Meridian, 1975.
Copenhaver, Brian P. "The Power of Magic and the Poverty of Erudition: Magic in a Universal Library." In Ganz, *Das Buch,* 159–80.
Csapodi, Csaba. "Ein Bellifortis Fragment von Budapest." *Gutenberg Jahrbuch,* 1974, 18–28.
———. "Die Corvinische Codices in Wolfenbüttel." *Wolfenbütteler Beiträge* 1 (1972): 29–44.
———. "Medical and Scientific Manuscripts of the Corvinian Library." *Orvostörténeti Közlemények* 109–12 (1985): 37–45.
———. "Az úgynevezett 'Liber de septem signis': Kyeser 'Bellifortis'-ának töredékéről" (The So-Called *Liber de septem signis*: About the Fragment of Kyeser's *Bellifortis*). *Magyar Könyvszemle* 82 (1966): 217–36.
———. "Mikor szűnt meg Mátyás király könyvfestőműhelye?" (When Did King Matthias's Miniaturist Workshop Cease to Be Active?). *Magyar Könyvszemle* 79 (1963): 24–42.
———. "Quando cessò l'attività della bottega di miniatura di Mattia?" *Acta Historiae Artium Academiae Scientiarum Hungaricae,* 1968, 223–33.
Csapodiné Gárdonyi, Klára. *Die Bibliothek des Johannes Vitéz.* Studia Humanitas 6. Budapest: Akadémiai Kiadó, 1984.
Császár, Mihály. *Az Academia Istropolitana: Mátyás király pozsonyi egyeteme* (The Academia Istropolitana: The Pozsony University of King Matthias). Bratislava: Eder, 1914.
Csontosi, János. "Corvin János két horoszkópja" (Two Nativities of János Corvin). *Magyar Könyvszemle,* 1880, 381–89.
Czartoryski, Pawel. "La Notion d'université et l'idée de la science à l'université de Cracovie dans la première moitié du XVe siècle." *Mediaevalia Philosophica Polonorum* 14 (1970): 23–39.
Dabrowski, Jan. "Krakkó és a krakkói egyetem szerepe a magyar kultúra történetében" (The Role of Kraków and Its University in the History of Hungarian Culture). In *Tanulmányok a lengyel magyar irodalmi kapcsolatok köréből* (Studies on Polish-Hungarian Literary Relations), ed. István Csapláros and Lajos Hopp. Budapest: Akadémiai Kiadó, 1969.
———. "A krakkói és a magyar reneszánsz kapcsolatai" (The Relations of the Kraków and Hungarian Renaissance). *Művészettörténeti értesítő,* 1969, 31–36.

Delatte, Armand. *La Catoptromancie grecque et ses dérivés*. Paris: Librairie Droz, 1932.
Divéky, Adorján. "Lengyelország magyar vonatkozású kéziratanyaga" (Manuscripts of Hungarian Interest in Poland). *Levéltári Közlemények* 3 (1927): 45–46.
Dokoupil, Vladislav. *Dejiny moravských klášterních knihoven* (History of the Moravian Monastic Libraries). Brno: Univerzitní knihovna, 1972.
Domonkos, László. "The Founding (1395) and Refounding (1410) of the University of Óbuda." In Szögi and Varga, *Universitas Budensis*, 19–34.
———. "The Origins of the University of Pozsony." *New Review: A Journal of East-European History* 9 (1969): 270–89.
———. "The Polish Astronomer Martinus Bylica de Ilkusz in Hungary." *Polish Review* 13 (1968): 71–79.
Draelants, Isabelle. "Une mise au point sur les oeuvres d'Arnoldus Saxo." *Bulletin de Philosophe Médiévale* 34 (1992): 163–80; 35 (1993): 130–49.
———. "La virtus universalis: un concept d'origine hermétique?" In Lucentini, Parri, and Perrone Compagni, *Hermetism*, 157–88.
Draelants, Isabelle, and Antonella Sannino. "Albertinisme et hermétisme dans une anthologie en faveur de la magie, le *Liber aggregationis*: prospective." In *Mélanges d'histoire des sciences offerts à Hossam Elkhadem à l'occasion de son 65e anniversaire par ses amis et ses élèves*, ed. Fr. Daelemans, J. M. Duvosquel, Robert Halleux, and David Juste, 223–55. Archives et Bibliothèques de Belgique, numéro spècial 83. Brussels: n.p., 2007.
Dupèbe, Jean. "L'«Ars Notoria» et la polémique sur la divination et la magie." In *Divination et Contreverse Religieuse en France au XVIe siècle*, 123–34. Paris: Centre V. L. Saulnier, 1987.
Düwell, K. "Runen als magische Zeichen." In Ganz, *Das Buch*, 87–100.
Eamon, William. *Science and the Secrets of Nature: Books of Secrets in Medieval and Early Modern Culture*. Princeton: Princeton University Press, 1994.
———. "Technology as Magic in the Late Middle Ages and the Renaissance." *Janus* 70 (1983): 171–212.
Eamon, William, and Gundolf Keil. "*Plebs amat empirica*: Nicholas of Poland and His Critique of the Medieval Medical Establishment." *Sudhoffs Archiv* 71 (1987): 180–96.
Edwards, Glenn Michael. "The *Liber Introductorius* of Michale Scot." Ph.D. diss., University of Southern California, 1978.
Estreicher, Karol. *Copernican Relics in Jagiellonian University*. Kraków: The Jagiellonian University Press, 1980.
Evans, Joan. *Magical Jewels of the Middle Ages and the Renaissance, Particularly in England*. Oxford: Clarendon Press, 1922.
Evans, Michael. "The Geometry of the Mind." *Architectural Association Quarterly* 12 (1980): 32–55.
Evans, Robert John. *Rudolf II and His World: A Study in Intellectual History, 1576–1612*. Oxford: Clarendon Press, 1973.
Fanger, Claire, ed. *Conjuring Spirits: Texts and Traditions of Medieval Ritual Magic*. University Park: Pennsylvania State University Press, 1998.
———. "Plundering the Egyptian Treasure: John the Monk's *Book of Visions* and Its Relation to the *Ars notoria* of Solomon." In Fanger, *Conjuring Spirits*, 216–49.
———. "Things Done Wisely by a Wise Enchanter: Negotiating the Power of Words in the Thirteenth Century." *Esoterica* 1 (1999): 97–132. http://www.esoteric.msu.edu/esoteric.msu.edu/Fanger.html.
Fanger, Claire, and Frank Klaassen. 'Magic III: Middle Ages." In *Dictionary of Gnosis and Western Esotericism*, ed. Wouter J. Hanegraaff et al., 724–31. Leiden: Brill, 2005.

Fanger, Claire, and Benedek Láng. "John of Morigny's *Liber visionum* and a Royal Prayer Book from Poland." *Societas Magica Newsletter* 9 (2002): 1–4.
Fischer, Karel. "Some Unpublished Astrological Illustrations from Central and Eastern Europe." *JWCI* 27 (1964): 311–12.
Flint, Valerie. *The Rise of Magic in Early Medieval Europe.* Oxford: Clarendon Press, 1991.
Flowers, Stephen E. *Runes and Magic: Magical Formulaic Elements in the Older Runic Tradition.* New York: Peter Lang, 1986.
Friedman, John B. "Les images mnémotechniques dans les manuscrits de l'époque gothique." In *Jeux de mémoire: aspects de la mnémotechnic médiévale,* ed. Bruno Roy and Paul Zumthor, 169–83. Paris: Librairie philosophique J. Vrin, 1985.
Fürbeth, Frank. *Johannes Hartlieb: Untersuchungen zu Leben und Werk.* Tübingen: Max Niemeyer Verlag, 1992.
Gabriel, Asztrik. "Intellectual Relations Between the University of Paris and the University of Cracow in the Fifteenth Century." *Studia Zródloznawce* 25 (1980): 37–63.
———. "Magyar diákok és tanárok a középkori Párizsban" (Hungarian Students and Masters in Medieval Paris). *Archivum Philologicum* 48 (1938): 41–49.
———. *The Medieval Universities of Pécs and Pozsony: Commemoration of the 500th and 600th Anniversary of Their Foundation, 1367–1867–1967.* Notre Dame: The Medieval Institute, University of Notre Dame, 1969.
Ganszyniec, Ryszard, ed. *Brata Mikołaja z Polski pisma lekarskie* (The Medical Writings of Brother Nicolaus of Poland). Poznan: Czcionkami Drukarni Zjednoczenia, 1920.
———. "Krystalomancja" (Crystallomancy). *Lud* 41 (1954): 256–339.
———. "O Modlitewniku Władysława" (Wladislas's Prayer Book). In Bernacki and Ganszyniec, *Modlitewnik Władysława Warneńczyka,* 25–93.
Ganz, Peter, ed. *Das Buch als magisches und als Repräsentationsobjekt.* Wiesbaden: Otto Harrassowitz, 1992.
Gierowski, Józef, ed. *The Cracow Circle of Nicholas Copernicus.* Copernicana Cracoviensia 3. Kraków: The Jagiellonian University Press, 1973.
Gieysztor, Aleksander. *L'Europe nouvelle autour de l'An Mil. La Papauté, l'Empire et les "nouveaux venus."* Rome: Unione internazionle degli Istituti di Archeologia, 1997.
Graciotti, Sante, and Cesare Vasoli. *Italia e Ungheria all'epoca dell'umanesimo corviniano.* Civiltà veneziana. Studi 45. Florence: Leo S. Olschki, 1994.
Grant, Edward. *Planets, Stars, and Orbs: The Medieval Cosmos, 1200–1687.* Cambridge: Cambridge University Press, 1994.
Greene, Thomas. "The Flexibility of the Self in Renaissance Literature." In *The Disciplines of Criticism,* ed. Peter Demetz, Thomas Greene, and Lowry Nelson Jr., 241–64. New Haven: Yale University Press, 1968.
Grmek, Mirko Dražen. "La lettre sur la magie noire et les autres manuscrits d'Arnaud de Villeneuve dans les bibliothèques yougoslaves." *Archives Internationales d'Histoire des Sciences* 42 (1958): 21–26.
———. "Rasprava Arnalda iz Villanove o crnoj magiji" (The Letter of Arnaldus de Villanova on Black Magic). *Starine Jugoslavenska Akademija Znanosti i Umjetnosti* 48 (1958): 217–29.
Halleux, Robert. *Les textes alchimiques.* Turnhout: Brepols, 1979.
Hansen, Bert. *Nicole Oresme and the Marvels of Nature: A Study of His "De Causis Mirabilium" with Critical Edition, Translation and Commentary.* Wetteren: Pontifical Institute of Mediaeval Studies, 1985.
———. "Science and Magic." In *Science in the Middle Ages,* ed. David Lindberg, 483–505. Chicago: University of Chicago Press, 1978.

Hansen, Joseph, ed., *Quellen und Untersuchungen zur Geschichte des Hexenwahns und der Hexenverfolgung im Mittelalter.* Bonn: Carl Georgi, 1901.
Hansmann, Liselotte, and Lenz Kriss-Rettenbeck, eds. *Amulett und Talisman: Erscheinungsform und Geschichte.* Munich: Verlag Georg D. W. Callwey, 1966.
Harmening, Dieter. "Faust und die Renaissance-Magie: Zum ältesten Faustzeugnis: Johannes Trithemius an Johannes Virdung, 1507." *Archiv für Kulturgeschichte* 55 (1973): 56–79.
Hubicki, Włodzimierz. "Chemistry and Alchemy in Sixteenth-Century Cracow." *Endeavour* 17 (1958): 204–7.
———. "Fuitne olim alchimia in Academia Cracoviensi lecta?" *Kwartalnik historii nauki i techniki* 9 (1964): 199–210.
Huszti, József. "Janus Pannonius asztrológiai álláspontja" (The Astrological Attitude of Janus Pannonius). *Minerva* 11 (1927): 43–58.
———. "Magyar királyok horoszkópjai egy vatikáni kódexben" (Nativities of Hungarian Kings in a Vatican Codex). *Magyar Könyvszemle* 35 (1928): 1–10.
———. "Platonista törekvések Mátyás király udvarában" (Platonistic Efforts in King Matthias's Court). Pts. 1 and 2. *Minerva* 8 (1925): 153–222; 9 (1925): 41–76.
Jacoby, P. "Hochschulen der Zauberei." In *Handwörterbuch des deutschen Aberglaubens,* ed. Hanns Bächtold-Stäubli, 10 vols. Berlin-Leipzig: Gruyter, 1927–42.
Juste, David. *Les Alchandreana Primitifs: Etudes sur les plus anciens traités astrologiques latins d'origine arabe (Xe siècle).* Leiden: Brill, 2007.
Karpenko, Vladimir. "Between Magic and Science: Numerical Magic Squares." *Ambix* 40 (1993): 121–28.
———. "The Chemistry and Metallurgy of Transmutation." *Ambix* 39 (1992): 47–62.
———. "Greek Fire in a Czech Alchemical Manuscript." *Centaurus* 30 (1987): 240–44.
———. "Magic Squares in European Mysticism." *Hamdard Medicus* 34 (1991): 39–51.
———. "The Oldest Alchemical Manuscript in the Czech Language." *Ambix* 37 (1990): 61–73.
———. "Two Thousand Years of Numerical Magic Squares." *Endeavour,* n.s., 18 (1994): 147–53.
Keil, Gundolf. "*Virtus occulta:* Der Begriff des 'empiricum' bei Nikolaus von Polen." In *Die okkulten Wissenschaften in der Renaissance,* ed. August Buck, 159–96. Wolfenbütteler Abhandlungen zur Renaissanceforschung 12. Wiesbaden: Otto Harrassowitz, 1992.
Kieckhefer, Richard. "The Devil's Contemplatives: The *Liber Iuratus,* the *Liber visionum* and the Christian Appropriation of Jewish Occultism." In Fanger, *Conjuring Spirits,* 250–65.
———. "Did Magic Have a Renaissance? An Historiographic Question Revisited." In *Magic and the Classical Tradition,* ed. Charles Burnett and W. F. Ryan, 199–212. London: The Warburg Institute, 2006.
———. "Erotic Magic in Medieval Europe." In *Sex in the Middle Ages,* ed. Joyce E. Salisbury, 30–55. New York and London: Garland Publishing, 1991.
———. *European Witch Trials: Their Foundations in Popular and Learned Culture, 1300–1500.* London: Routledge & K. Paul, 1976.
———. *Forbidden Rites: A Necromancer's Manual of the Fifteenth Century.* Stroud: Sutton, 1997.
———. "The Holy and the Unholy: Sainthood, Witchcraft, and Magic in Late Medieval Europe." *Journal of Medieval and Renaissance Studies* 24 (1994): 355–85.
———. *Magic in the Middle Ages.* Cambridge Medieval Textbooks. Cambridge: Cambridge University Press, 1989.
———. "The Specific Rationality of Medieval Magic." *American Historical Review* 99 (1994): 813–36.
Kiss, Gábor Farkas, Benedek Láng, and Cosmin Popa-Gorjanu. "The Alchemical Mass of Nicolaus Melchior Cibinensis: Text, Identity and Speculations." *Ambix* 53 (2006): 143–59.

Klaassen, Frank. "English Manuscripts of Magic, 1300–1500: A Preliminary Survey." In Fanger, *Conjuring Spirits,* 3–31.
———. "Medieval Ritual Magic in the Renaissance." *Aries: Journal for the Study of Western Esotericism* 3 (2003): 166–99.
———. "Religion, Science, and the Transformations of Magic: Manuscripts of Magic, 1300–1600." Ph.D. diss., Department of History, University of Toronto, 1999 (forthcoming in the Magic in History series by the Pennsylvania State University Press).
Klaniczay, Gábor. "Bûchers tardifs en Europe centrale et orientale." In *Magie et sorcellerie en Europe du Moyen Age à nos jours, ed.* Robert Muchembled, 215–33. Paris: Armand Colin, 1994.
———. "Late Medieval Central European Universities: Problems of Their Comparative History." In Szögi and Varga, *Universitas Budensis,* 171–82.
———. "Medieval Central Europe: An Invention or a Discovery?" In *The Paradoxes of Unintended Consequences,* ed. Lord Dahrendorf, Yehuda Elkana, et al., 251–64. Budapest: CEU Press, 2000.
———. "National Saints on Late Medieval Universities." In *Die ungarische Universitätsbildung und Europa,* ed. Márta Font and László Szögi, 87–108. Pécs: Pécsi Tudományegyetem, 2001.
———. "The Process of Trance, Heavenly and Diabolic Apparitions in Johannes Nider's *Formicarius.*" Discussion Paper Series 65, June 2003. http://www.colbud.hu/main/PubArchive/DP/DP65-Klaniczay.pdf.
———. "Witch-Hunting in Hungary: Social or Cultural Tensions." *Acta Ethnographica Academiae Scientiarum Hungariae* 37 (1991–92): 67–91.
Klaniczay, Gábor, and Ildikó Kristóf. "Écritures saintes et pactes diaboliques. Les usages religieux de l'écrit au moyen âge et temps modernes." *Annales, Histoire, Sciences Sociales* 56 (2001): 947–80.
Klaniczay, Tibor. "Celtis und die Sodalitas Litteraria per Germaniam." In *Respublica Guelpherbytana: Wolfenbütteler Beiträge zur Renaissance- und Barockforschung. Festschrift für Paul Raabe,* ed. August Buck, 79–105. Amsterdam: Rodopi, 1987.
———. "Das Contubernium des Johannes Vitéz: Die erste ungarische Academie." In *Forschungen über Siebenbürgen und seine Nachbarn: Festschrift für Attila T. Szabó und Zsigmond Jakó,* ed. Kálmán Benda, 241–55. Munich: Trofenik, 1988.
———. "Egyetem Magyarországon Mátyás korában" (The University in Hungary in the Age of Matthias). *Irodalomtörténeti Közlemények* 94 (1990): 575–612.
———. *A magyarországi akadémiai mozgalom előtörténete* (The Prehistory of the Hungarian Academic Movement). Humanizmus és reformáció 20. Budapest: Balassi, 1993.
———. *Mattia Corvino e l'umanesimo italiano: conferenza tenuta nella seduta del 9 marzo 1974.* Roma: Accademia nazionale dei Lincei, 1974.
———. "Megoldott és megoldatlan kérdések az első magyar egyetem körül" (Solved and Unsolved Questions Around the First Hungarian University). In Klaniczay, *Hagyományok ébresztése* (The Awakening of Traditions), 136–65. Budapest: Szépirodalmi Könyvkiadó, 1976.
———, ed. *Rapporti veneto-ungheresi all'epoca del Rinascimento.* Budapest: Akadémiai Kiadó, 1975.
Klaniczay, Tibor, and József Jankovics. *Matthias Corvinus and the Humanism in Central Europe.* Studia Humanitatis 10. Budapest: Balassi Kiadó, 1994.
Knoll, Paul W. "Casimir the Great and the University of Cracow." *Jahrbücher für Geschichte Osteuropas* 16 (1968): 232–49.
———. "Learning in Late Piast Poland." *Proceedings of the American Philosophical Society* 120 (1976): 136–57.
Koerting, Walther. *Die deutsche Universität in Prag: Die letzten 100 Jahre ihrer medizinischen Fakultät.* Munich: Bayerische Landesärztekammer, 1968.

Kovács, Endre. *A krakkói egyetem és a magyar művelődés* (The University of Kraków and Hungarian Education). Budapest: MTA Történettudományi Intézete, 1964.

———. *Magyar-cseh történelmi kapcsolatok* (Hungarian-Bohemian Historical Relations). Budapest: MTA Történettudományi Intézete, 1952.

Kowalczyk, Maria. *Krakowskie mowy uniwersyteckie z pierwszej połowy XV wieku* (Kraków University Speeches of the First Half of the Fifteenth Century). Wrocław: Zakład Narodowy im. Ossolińskich, 1970.

———. "Mikołaj Hinczowicz z Kazimierza" (Nicolaus Hinczonis of Kazimierz). In *Polski Słownik Biograficzny* (Polish Biographical Dictionary), vol. 21, 113–14. Kraków: Polska Akademia Nauk, 1976.

———. "Przyczynki do biografii Henryka Czecha i Marcina Króla z Żurawicy" (Appendices to the Biography of Henry the Czech and Marcin Król of Żurawica). *Biuletyn Biblioteki Jagiellońskiej* 21 (1971): 87–91.

———. "Wróżby, czary i zabobony w średniowiecznych rękopisach Biblioteki Jagiellońskiej" (Divinations, Superstitions, and Sortileges in the Medieval Manuscripts in the Biblioteka Jagiellońska). *Biuletyn Biblioteki Jagiellońskiej* 29 (1979): 5–18.

Kras, Paweł. "Inkwizycja papieska w walce z husytyzmem na ziemiach polskich" (The Papal Inquisition and the Persecution of Hussites in Poland). In *Polskie echa husytyzmu* (Polish Echoes of Hussitism), ed. Stanisław Bylina and Ryszard Gładkiewicz, 88–115. Warsaw: Wydawnictwo Instytutu Historii PAN, 1999.

Krása, Josef. "Astrologické rukopisy Václava IV" (Astrological Manuscripts of King Wenceslas IV). *Umění* 12 (1964): 466–86.

———. *Die Handschriften König Wencels IV.* Vienna: Forum, 1971.

———. *Rukopisy Václava IV.* Prague: Odeon, 1971.

Krchňák, Alois. "Die Herkunft der astronomischen Handschriften und Instrumente des Nikolaus von Kues." *Mitteilungen und Forschungsbeiträge der Cusanus-Gesellschaft* 3 (1963): 108–80.

Kren, Claudia. "Astronomical Teaching at the Late Medieval University of Vienna." *History of Universities* 3 (1983): 15–30.

Kulcsár, Péter. "Az újplatonizmus Magyarországon" (Neoplatonism in Hungary). *Irodalomtörténeti Közlemények* 87 (1983): 41–47.

Kunitzsch, Paul. "Origin and History of *Liber stellis beibeniis*." In Lucentini, Parri, and Perrone Compagni, *Hermetism*, 449–60.

Kurze, Dietrich. "Popular Astrology and Prophecy in the Fifteenth and Sixteenth Centuries: Johannes Lichtenberger." In Zambelli, *"Astrologi Hallucinati,"* 177–93.

Láng, Benedek. "Angels Around the Crystal: The Prayer Book of King Wladislas and the Treasure Hunts of Henry the Bohemian." *Aries: Journal for the Study of Western Esotericism* 5 (2005): 1–32.

———. "The Criminalization of Possessing Necromantic Books in Fifteenth Century Krakow." In Wünsch, *Religion und Magie*, 257–71.

———. "Demons in Krakow, and Image Magic in a Magical Handbook." In *Demons, Spirits, Witches / II: Christian Demonology and Popular Mythology*, ed. Gábor Klaniczay and Éva Pócs, 13–44. Budapest: CEU Press, 2006.

———. "The Kraków Readers of Hermes: Magical and Hermetic Manuscripts in Kraków." In Lucentini, Parri, and Perrone Compagni, *Hermetism*, 577–600.

———. "Research Problems of Magical Texts in Central Europe." In *The Role of Magic in the Past. Learned and Popular Magic, Popular Beliefs and Diversity of Attitudes*, ed. Blanka Szeghyová, 11–17. Bratislava: Pro Historia, 2005.

Lemay, Richard. "The Late Medieval Astrological School at Cracow and the Copernican System."

In *Science and History: Studies in Honor of Edward Rosen*, ed. Pavel Czartoryski et al., 337–54. Studia Copernicana 16. Wrocław: The Polish Academy of Sciences Press, 1978.

———. "Origin and Success of the Kitāb Thamara of Abū Ja'far Ahmad ibn Yūsuf ibn Ibrāhīm: From the Tenth to the Seventeenth Century in the World of Islam and the Latin West." In *Proceedings of the First International Symposium for the History of Arabic Science*, 91–107. Aleppo: Aleppo University, 1978.

———. "The Teaching of Astronomy in Medieval Universities, Principally at Paris in the Fourteenth Century." *Manuscripta* 19 (1975): 197–217.

———. "The True Place of Astrology in Medieval Science and Philosophy: Towards a Definition." In *Astrology, Science and Society: Historical Essays*, ed. Patrick Curry, 57–73. Woodbridge: Boydell, 1987.

Leng, Rainer. *Ars belli: Deutsche taktische und kriegstechnische Bilderhandschriften und Traktate im 15. und 16. Jahrhundert*. Wiesbaden: Reichert Verlag, 2002.

Lidaka, Juris. "The Book of Angels, Rings, Characters and Images of the Planets: Attributed to Osbern Bokenham." In Fanger, *Conjuring Spirits*, 32–75.

Lucentini, Paolo. "L'Asclepius ermetico nel secolo XII." In *From Athens to Chartres. Neoplatonism and Medieval Thought. Studies in Honour of Edouard Jeauneau*, ed. Haijo Jan Westra, 398–420. Leiden: Brill, 1992.

———. "L'edizione critica dei testi ermetici latini." In *I moderni ausili all'Ecdotica (Atti del Convegno internazionale di studi, Fisciano—Vietri sul Mare—Napoli, 27–31 Ottobre 1990)*, ed. Sebastiano Martelli and Vincenzo Placella, 265–85. Naples: Edizioni scientifiche italiane, 1994.

———. "L'Ermetismo magico nel sec. XIII." In *Sic itur ad astra: Studien zur mittelalterlichen, insbesondere arabischen, Wissenschaftgeschichte. Festschrift für Paul Kunitzsch zum 70. Geburtstag*, ed. Menso Folkerts and Richard Lorch, 409–50. Wiesbaden: Harrassowitz Verlag, 2000.

Lucentini, Paolo, Ilaria Parri, and Vittoria Perrone Compagni, eds. *Hermetism from Late Antiquity to Humanism: La tradizione ermetica dal mondo tardo-antico all'umanesimo*. Turnhout: Brepols, 2003.

Madas, Edit, and István Monok. *A könyvkultúra Magyarországon a kezdetektől 1730-ig* (Book Culture in Hungary from the Beginnings to 1730). Budapest: Balassi Kiadó, 1999.

Marchetti, Giancarlo, Orsola Rignani, and Valeria Sorge, eds. *Ratio et Superstitio: Essays in Honor of Graziella Federici Vescovini*. Louvain-La-Neuve: Fédérations Internationales des Instituts d'Études Médiévales, 2003.

Markowski, Mieczysław. "Die Astrologie an der Krakauer Universität in den Jahren 1450–1550." In Szczucki, *Magia*, 83–89.

———. "Astronomie und der Krakauer Universität im XV. Jahrhundert." In *Les universités à la fin du Moyen Age, Actes du congrès international du Louvain (26–30 mai, 1975)*, ed. Jozef Ijsewijn and Jacques Paquet, 256–75. Leuven: Leuven University Press, 1978.

———. "Beziehungen zwischen der Wiener Mathematischen Schule und der Krakauer Astronomischen Schule im Licht der erhaltenen mathematisch-astronomischen Schriften in den Manuscripten der Österreichischen Nationalbibliothek in Wien und der Jagellonischen Bibliothek in Kraków." *Mediaevalia Philosophica Polonorum* 18 (1973): 133–58.

———. "Krakowskie dzieła astronomiczne w rękopiśmiennych zbiorach Saskiej Biblioteki Krajowej w Dreźnie" (Kraków Astronomical Works in the Manuscript Holdings of the Saxon Library in Dresden). *Studia Mediewistyczne* 22 (1983): 19–28.

———. "Marcin Biem of Olkusz." In Gierowski, *Cracow Circle*, 7–21.

———. "Die Mathematischen und Naturwissenschaften an der Krakauer Universität im XV. Jahrhundert." *Mediaevalia Philosophica Polonorum* 18 (1973): 121–31.

———. "Poglądy filozoficzne Andrzeja z Kokorzyna" (The Philosophical Opinions of Andreas de Kokorzyn). *Studia Mediewistyczne* 6 (1964): 55–136.
Markus, Robert A. "Augustine on Magic: A Neglected Semiotic Theory." *Revue des Études Augustiniennes* 40 (1994): 375–88.
Marrone, Steven P. "William of Auvergne on Magic in Natural Philosophy and Theology." In *Was ist Philosophie im Mittelalter?* (Akten des X. Internationalen Kongresses für mittelalterliche Philosophie der Société Internationale pour l'Étude de la Philosophie Médiévale 25. bis 30. August 1997 in Erfurt), ed. Jan Aertsen and Andreas Speer, 741–48. Berlin: Walter de Gruyter, 1998.
Mathiesen, Robert. "A Thirteenth-Century Ritual to Attain the Beatific Vision from the *Sworn Book of Honorius of Thebes.*" In Fanger, *Conjuring Spirits*, 143–62.
McDaniel, W. B. "An Hermetic Plague-Tract by Johannes Mercurius Corrigiensis." *Transactions and Studies of the College of Physicians of Philadelphia*, 4th ser., 9 (1941–42): 217–25.
McVaugh, Michael R. "Incantationes in Late Medieval Surgery." In *Ratio et Superstitio: Essays in Honor of Graziella Federici Vescovini*, ed. Giancarlo Marchetti, Orsola Rignani, and Valeria Sorge, 319–46. Louvain-La-Neuve: Fédérations Internationales des Instituts d'Études Médiévales, 2003.
McVaugh, Michael R., and Edith Dudley Sylla, eds. *Texts and Contexts in Ancient and Medieval Science: Studies on the Occasion of John E. Murdoch's Seventieth Birthday.* Brill's Studies in Intellectual History 78. Leiden and New York: Brill, 1997.
Mikołajczyk, Renata. "Examples of Medieval Plague Treatises from Central Europe." *Annual of Medieval Studies at CEU* 3 (1996–97): 229–35.
———. "*Non sunt nisi phantasiae et imaginationes:* A Medieval Attempt at Explaining Demons." In *Communicating with the Spirits*, ed. Éva Pócs and Gábor Klaniczay, 40–52. Budapest: CEU Press, 2005.
Miodońska, Barbara. "Historyk sztuki o datowaniu tzw. Modlitewnika Władysława Warneńczyka w Oksfordzie" (Art Historian's Dating of the So-called Władysław Warneńczyk Oxford Prayerbook). In *Kultura średniowieczna i staropolska* (Medieval and Early Modern Polish Culture), 703–14. Warsaw: PWN, 1991.
Miśkowiec, Marta. "Związki aniołów z magicznym znaczeniem kryształów." (Angels and the Magical Meaning of Crystals). In *Księga o aniołach* (The Book on Angels), ed. Herbert Oleschko, 440–49. Kraków: Wydawnictwo WAM, 2002.
Mittler, Elmar, and Wilfried Werner. *Mit der Zeit: Die Kurfürsten von der Pfalz und die Heidelberger Handschriften der Bibliotheca Palatina.* Wiesbaden: Ludwig Reichert, 1986.
Moraw, Peter. "Die Prager Universitäten des Mittelalters." In *Spannungen und Widersprüche: Gedenkschift für František Graus*, ed. Susanna Burghartz, 109–23. Sigmaringen: Jan Thorbecke, 1992.
———. "Die Universität Prag im Mittelalter. Grundzüge ihrer Geschichte im europäischen Zusammenhang." In *Die Universität zu Prag*, ed. Richard W. Eichler, 9–134. Munich: Verlagshaus Sudetenland, 1986.
Morawski, Casimir. *Histoire de l'Université de Cracovie.* Paris: 1900–1903.
Mossakowski, Stanisław. "La non più esistente decorazione astrologica del castello reale di Cracovia." In Szczucki, *Magia*, 90–98.
Muczkowski, Josephus. *Pauli Paulirini olim Paulus de Praga vocati viginti artium manuscriptum librum cuius codex Twardovio vulgo tribuitus descripsit vitamque auctoris adjecit.* Kraków, 1835.
Mühlberger, Kurt. "Das Wiener Studium zur Zeit des Königs Matthias Corvinus." In Szögi and Varga, *Universitas Budensis*, 89–116.
Murdoch, John, ed. *Album of Science: Antiquity and the Middle Ages.* New York: Charles Scribner's Sons, 1984.

Murray, Alexander. "Missionaries and Magic in Dark-Age Europe." Review of *The Rise of Magic in Early Medieval Europe* by Valerie Flint. *Past and Present* 136 (1992): 186–205.
———. *Reason and Society in the Middle Ages.* Oxford: Clarendon Press, Oxford University Press, 1978.
Nagy, Zoltán. "Asztronómia a Mátyás-korabeli Magyarországon" (Astronomy in Hungary in the Age of Matthias). *Világosság* 17 (1976): 775–81.
———. "Ricerche cosmologiche nella corte umanistica di Giovanni Vitéz." In *Rapporti veneto-ungheresi al'epoca del Rinascimento,* ed. Tibor Klaniczay, 65–93. Budapest: Akadémiai Kiadó, 1975.
Neagu, Cristina. "The *Processus sub forma missae:* Christian Alchemy, Identity and Identification." *Archaeus: Études d'Histoire des Religions* 4 (2000): 105–17.
Newman, William R. *Promethean Ambitions: Alchemy and the Quest to Perfect Nature.* Chicago: University of Chicago Press, 2004.
———. *The "Summa Perfectionis" of Pseudo-Geber.* Leiden: Brill, 1991.
———. "Technology and Alchemical Debate in the Late Middle Ages." *Isis* 80 (1989): 423–45.
North, John D. "Celestial Influence: The Major Premiss of Astrology." In Zambelli, *"Astrologi Hallucinati,"* 45–100.
Nováček, V. J. "Amulet ze XIV. století, nalezený v chrámu sv. Jiří na hradě pražském" (A Fourteenth-Century Amulet from the Saint George Basilica of the Prague Castle). *Český lid* 10 (1901): 353–54.
Ohly, Kurt. "Johannes 'Mercurius' Corrigiensis." *Beiträge zur Inkunabelkunde,* n.s., 2 (1938): 133–41.
Osten, Sigrid von. *Das Alchemistenlaboratorium Oberstockstall: Ein Fundkomplex des 16. Jahrhunderts aus Niederösterreich.* Innsbruck: Universtitätsverlag Wagner, 1998.
Pack, R. A. "A Pseudo-Aristotelian Chiromancy." *AHDLMA* 36 (1969): 189–241.
Page, Sophie. *Astrology in Medieval Manuscripts.* London: The British Library, 2002.
———. "Image-Magic Texts and a Platonic Cosmology at St Augustine's, Canterbury, in the Late Middle Ages." In *Magic and the Classical Tradition,* ed. Charles Burnett and W. F. Ryan, 69–98. London: The Warburg Institute, 2006.
———. "Magic at St. Augustine's, Canterbury, in the Late Middle Ages." Ph.D. diss., The Warburg Institute, University of London, 2000.
———. *Magic in Medieval Manuscripts.* London: The British Library, 2004.
Paravicini Bagliani, Agostino. *Le "Speculum Astronomiae" une énigme? Enquête sur les manuscrits.* Micrologus Library. Turnhout: Brepols, 2001.
Paschetto, Eugenia. "Witelo et Pietro d'Abano à propos des demons." In *L'homme et son univers au Moyen Age,* ed. Christian Wenin, vol. 2, pp. 675–82. Louvain-la-Neuve: Editions de l'Institut supérieur de philosophie, 1986.
Patschovsky, Alexander. *Die Anfänge einer ständigen Inquisition in Böhmen: Ein Prager Inquisitoren-Handbuch aus der ersten Hälfte des 14. Jahrhunderts.* Berlin: Walter de Gruyter, 1975.
Perger, Richard. "Schwarzkünstler und Ordensmann: Aus dem Leben des Schottenpriors und Seitenstettner Abtes Benedikt." *Wiener Geschichtsblätter* 32 (1977): 167–76.
Perrone Compagni, Vittoria. "La magia ceremoniale de *Picatrix* nel Rinascimento." *Atti dell'Accademia di scienze morali e politiche di Napoli* 88 (1977): 279–330.
———. *"Picatrix latinus.* Concezioni filosofico-religiose e prassi magica." *Medioevo* 1 (1975): 237–77.
———. *"Studiosus incantationibus:* Adelardo di Bath, Ermete e Thabit." *Giornale critico della filosofia italiana* 80 (2001): 36–61.
Peters, Edward. *The Magician, the Witch, and the Law.* Philadelphia: University of Pennsylvania Press, 1978.

Pingree, David. "Between the *Ghâya* and *Picatrix*, 1: The Spanish Version." *JWCI* 44 (1981): 27–56.
———. "The Diffusion of Arabic Magical Texts in Western Europe." In *La diffusione delle scienze Islamiche nel Medio Evo Europeo*, ed. B. Scarcia Amoretti, 57–102. Rome: Accademia Nazionale dei Lincei, 1987.
———. "From Hermes to Jābir and the *Book of the Cow*." In *Magic and the Classical Tradition*, ed. Charles Burnett and W. F. Ryan, 19–28. London: The Warburg Institute, 2006.
———. "Learned Magic in the Time of Frederick II." In *Le scienze alla corte di Federico II, Sciences at the court of Frederick II*, 39–56. Micrologus Library 2. Turnhout: Brepols, 1994.
———. "Plato's Hermetic *Book of the Cow*." In *Il Neoplatonismo nel Rinascimento*, ed. Pietro Prini, 133–45. Roma: Istituto della Enciclopedia Italiana, 1993.
———. "Some of the Sources of the Ghayat al-Hakim." *JWCI* 43 (1980): 1–15.
Podlacha, Władysław. "Miniatury modlitewnika Warneńczyka" (On the Miniatures of the Prayer Book). In Bernacki and Ganszyniec, *Modlitewnik Władysława Warneńczyka*, 93–141.
Pomian, Krzystof. "Astrology as a Naturalistic Theology of History." In Zambelli, *"Astrologi Hallucinati,"* 29–43.
Porreca, David. "Hermes Trismegistos: William of Auvergne's Mythical Authority." *AHDLMA* 67 (2000): 143–58.
Potkowski, Edward. "Gott, Teufel und Schrift. Vorstellungen zu den heiligen und dämonischen Wirkungen der Schrift im Polen des 15.–16. Jahrhunderts. In Wünsch, *Religion und Magie*, 273–85.
Préaud, Maxime. *Les astrologues à la fin du Moyen Age*. Paris: J. C. Lattès, 1984.
Price, Derek. "Pseudo-Aristoteles: Chiromantia." *AHDLMA* 39 (1972): 289–320.
Raine, James. "Divination in the Fifteenth Century by the Aid of a Magical Crystal." *Archaeological Journal* 13 (1856): 372–74.
Rebro, Karol. "Istropolitana a Bologna" (Istropolitana and Bologna). In *Humanizmus a renesancia na Slovensku v 15.–16. storočí* (Humanism and Renaissance in Slovakia in the Fifteenth and Sixteenth Centuries), ed. Ľudovít Holotík and Anton Vantuch, 5–24. Bratislava: Slovenská akadémia vied, 1967.
Rees, Valery. "Ad vitam felicitatemque: Marsilio Ficino to His Friends in Hungary." *Budapest Review of Books* 8 (1998): 57–63.
Reiss, Josef. "Das Twardowski-Buch: Opus magicum des polnischen Faust." *Germanoslavica* 2 (1933): 90–101.
Ritoókné Szalai, Ágnes. "Borbála" (Barbara). In *Ámor, álom és mámor: a szerelem a régi magyar irodalomban és a szerelem ezredéves hazai kultúrtörténete* (Amor, Dream and Inebriety: Love in the Old Hungarian Literature and the Millennial Vernacular Cultural History of Love), ed. Géza Szentmártoni Szabó, 369–84. Budapest: Universitas Kiadó, 2002.
Rómer, Flóris. "A krakkói, Corvin Mátyás korabeli magyarországi csillagászati készletekről" (About Kraków Astronomical Tools from the Age of Matthias Corvin). *Archeológiai Értesítő* 8 (1876): 274–76.
Rosińska, Grażyna, ed. *Instrumenty astronomiczne na uniwersytecie krakowskim w XV wieku* (Astronomical Instruments in Kraków University in the Fifteenth Century). Studia Copernicana 11. Wrocław: Zakład Narodowy im. Ossolińskich, 1974.
———. "Traité astronomique inconnu de Martin Rex de Zurawica." *Mediaevalia Philosophica Polonorum* 18 (1973): 159–66.
Roy, Bruno. "Richard de Fournival, auteur du *Speculum Astronomiae*?" *AHDLMA* 67 (2000): 159–80.
Ryan, William Francis. *The Bathhouse at Midnight: An Historical Survey of Magic and Divination in Russia*. Stroud: Sutton, 1999.

———. "Magic and Divination: Old Russian Sources." In *The Occult in Russian and Soviet Culture*, ed. Bernice Glatzer Rosenthal, 35–58. Ithaca: Cornell University Press, 1997.
Samek, Svatopluk. "O Rožmberské knihovně" (On the Rožmberk Library). *Jihočeský sborník historický* 19 (1950): 11–14.
Sannino, Antonella. "Ermete mago e alchimista nelle biblioteche di Guglielmo d'Alvernia e Ruggero Bacone." *Studi medievali* 40 (2000): 151–209.
———. "La tradizione ermetica a Oxford nei secoli XIII e XIV: Ruggero Bacone e Tommaso Bradwardine." *Studi filosofici* 18 (1995): 23–56.
Schmitt, Charles B., and Dilwyn Knox. *Pseudo-Aristoteles Latinus: A Guide to Latin Works Falsely Attributed to Aristotle Before 1500.* Warburg Institute Surveys and Texts XII. London: The Warburg Institute, University of London, 1985.
Seńko, Władisław. *Les tendances préhumanistes dans la philosophie polonaise au XVe siècle.* Wrocław: Zakład Narodowy im. Ossolińskich, 1973.
Ševčenko, Ihor. "Remarks on the Diffusion of Byzantine Scientific and Pseudo-Scientific Literature Among the Orthodox Slavs." *Slavonic and East European Review* 59 (1981): 321–45.
Shank, Michael H. "Academic Consulting in 15th-Century Vienna: The Case of Astrology." In McVaugh and Sylla, *Texts and Contexts,* 245–70.
Sigerist, Henry. "The 'Sphere of Life and Death' in Early Mediaeval Manuscripts." *Bulletin of the History of Medicine* 11 (1942): 292–303.
Skeat, T. C. "An Early Mediaeval 'Book of Fate': The Sortes XII Patriarcharum, with a Note on 'Books of Fate' in General." *Mediaeval and Renaissance Studies* 3 (1954): 41–54.
Skemer, Don C. *Binding Words: Textual Amulets in the Middle Ages.* University Park: Pennsylvania State University Press, 2006.
Šmahel, František. "Die Prager Judengemeinde im hussitischen Zeitalter (1389–1485)." In *Jüdische Gemeinden und ihr chlistlicher Kontext in kulturräumlich vergleicher Betrachtung (5.–18. Jahrhundert),* ed. Christoph Cluse, Alfred Haverkamp, and Israel J. Yuval, 341–63. Hannover: Verlag Hahnsche Buchhandlung, 2003.
———. "Stärker als der Glaube: Magie, Aberglaube und Zauber in der Epoche des Hussitismus." *Bohemia: Zeitschrift für Geschichte und Kultur der böhmischen Länder* 32 (1991): 316–37.
Śnieżyńska-Stolot, Ewa. *Astrological Iconography in the Middle Ages: The Decanal Planets.* Kraków: Jagiellonian University Press, 2003
Soukup, Rudolf Werner, and Helmut Mayer. *Alchemistisches Gold—Paracelsistische Pharmaka: Laboratoriumstechnik im 16. Jahrhundert.* Vienna: Böhlau, 1997.
Stapleton, H. E. "The Antiquity of Alchemy." *Ambix* 5 (1953): 1–43.
Steinmetz, Mauritz. "Johann Virdung von Hassfurt, sein Leben und seine astrologischen Flugschriften." In Zambelli, *"Astrologi Hallucinati,"* 195–214.
Sturlese, Loris. "Saints et magiciens: Albert le Grand en Face d'Hermès Trismegiste." *Archives de philosophie* 43 (1980): 632.
Svobodný, Petr. "Contacts Between Bohemian and Hungarian Medical Faculties (14th–20th Centuries)." In Szögi and Varga, *Universitas Budensis,* 251–60.
Szádeczki, Lajos. "Lengyel földi levéltárakból, magyar történeti szempontból" (From Polish Archives, from a Hungarian Historical Aspect). *Századok* 15 (1881): 313–31 and 414–30.
Szathmári, László. "Az asztrológia, alkémia és misztika Mátyás király udvarában" (Astrology, Alchemy, and Misticism in King Matthias's Court). In *Mátyás király emlékkönyv* (Memorial Book of King Matthias), ed. Imre Lukinich, vol. 2, pp. 415–51. Budapest: Franklin, 1940.
———. *Magyar alkémisták* (Hungarian Alchemists). Budapest: Könyvértékesítő vállalat, 1986.

Szczucki, Lech, ed. *Magia, astrologia e religione nel Rinascimento: convegno polacco-italiano, Varsavia, 25–27 settembre 1972.* Wrocław: Zakład Narodowy im. Ossolińskich, 1974.
Székely, György. "Fakultät, Kollegium, akademische Nation—Zusammenhänge in der Geschichte der mitteleuropäischen Universitäten des 14. und 15. Jahrhunderts." *Annales Universitatis Scientiarum Budapestiensis, Sectio Historica* 13 (1972): 47–78.
Szelińska, Wacława. *Biblioteki profesorów uniwersytetu krakowskiego w XV początkach XVI wieku* (The Libraries of the Professors of the University of Kraków in the Fifteenth and Sixteenth Centuries). Wrocław: Zakład Narodowy im. Ossolińskich, 1966.
Szende, Katalin, ed. *A magyar iskola első évszázadai: 996–1526* (The First Centuries of the Hungarian School, 996–1526). Győr: Sylvester János Kiadó, 1996.
Szögi, László, and Júlia Varga, eds. *Universitas Budensis, 1395–1995.* Budapest: Bak-Fisch, 1997.
Szőnyi, György Endre. *John Dee's Occultism: Magical Exaltation Through Powerful Signs.* Albany: SUNY Press, 2005.
———. "Scientific and Magical Humanism at the Court of Rudolf II." In *Rudolf II and Prague: The Court and the City,* ed. Eliška Fučíková et al., 223–30. London: Thames and Hudson, 1997.
Theisen, W. "The Attraction of Alchemy for Monks and Friars in the Thirteenth to Fourteenth Centuries." *American Benedictine Review* 46 (1995): 239–53.
Thomassen, Einar. "Is Magic a Subclass of Ritual?" In *The World of Ancient Magic: Papers from the First International Samson Eitrem Seminar at the Norwegian Institute at Athens, 4–8 May, 1997,* ed. David R. Jordan, Hugo Montgomery, and Einar Thomassen, 55–66. Bergen: The Norwegian Institute at Athens, 1999.
Thorndike, Lynn. "Another Virdung Manuscript." *Isis* 34 (1942–43): 291–93.
———. "Chiromancy in Medieval Latin Manuscripts." *Speculum* 40 (1965): 674–706.
———. "Faust and Johann Virdung of Hassfurt." *Isis* 26 (1937): 321.
———. "Further Consideration of the *Experimenta, Speculum astronomiae,* and *De secretis mulierum* Ascribed to Albertus Magnus." *Speculum* 30 (1955): 413–43.
———. "Giovanni Bianchini in Italian Manuscripts." *Scripta Mathematica* 19 (1953): 5–17.
———. *A History of Magic and Experimental Science.* New York: Macmillan, 1923–58.
———. "Johann Virdung of Hassfurt: Dates of Birth and Death." *Isis* 37 (1947): 74.
———. "Johann Virdung of Hassfurt Again." *Isis* 25 (1936): 363–71.
———. "The Latin Translations of Astrological Works by Messahala." *Osiris* 12 (1956): 49–72.
———. *Michael Scot.* London: Nelson, 1965.
———. "Some Little-known Astronomical and Mathematical Manuscripts." *Osiris* 8 (1949): 41–72.
———. "Some Medieval Conceptions of Magic." *Monist* 25 (1915): 107–38.
———. *The "Sphere of Sacrobosco" and Its Commentators.* Chicago: University of Chicago Press, 1949.
———. "A Study in the Analysis of Complex Scientific Manuscripts: Sloane 3457: An Important Alchemical Manuscript." *Isis* 29 (1938): 377–92.
———. "Traditional Medieval Tracts Concerning Engraved Astronomical Images." In *Mélanges Auguste Pelzer: études d'histoire littéraire et doctrinale de la scholastique médiévale offertes à Auguste Pelzer à l'occasion de son soixante-dixième anniversaire,* 217–74. Leuven: Institut Supérieure de Philosophie, 1947.
———. "Vatican Latin Manuscripts in the History of Science and Medicine." *Isis* 13 (1929): 53–102.
Toth, Ladislaus. "Savoir et pouvoir par les livres de magie." *Aries* 15 (1993): 13–25.
Uhlíř, Zdeněk. "Texte über den Aberglauben in den tschechischen Handschriftensammlungen des Mittelalters." In Wünsch, *Religion und Magie,* 85–120.
Uiblein, Franz. "Zu den Beziehungen der Wiener Universität zu anderen Universitäten im Mittelalter."

In *The Universities in the Late Middle Ages,* ed. Jozef Ijsewijn and Jacques Paquet, 168–89. Leuven: Leuven University Press, 1978.

Vasoli, Cesare. *I miti e gli astri*. Naples: Guida, 1977.

———. *Spiritualita e lettere nella cultura italiana e ungherese del basso medioevo*. Florence: Olschki, 1995.

Veenstra, Jan. "The Holy Almandal: Angels and the Intellectual Aims of Magic." In Bremmer and Veenstra, *Metamorphosis of Magic,* 189–230.

———. *Magic and Divination at the Courts of Burgundy and France: Text and Context of Laurens Pignon's "Contre les devineurs" (1411)*. Leiden: Brill, 1998.

———. "Self-Fashioning and Pragmatic Introspection: Reconsidering the Soul in the Renaissance (Some Remarks on Pico, Pomponnazzi and Macchiavelli)." In *Self-Fashioning—Personen-(selbst)darstellung,* ed. Rudolf Suntrup and Jan Veenstra, 285–308. Frankfurt a. M.: Peter Lang, 2003.

Veress, Endre. *Olasz egyetemeken járt magyarországi diákok anyakönyve és iratai, 1221–1864* (The Enrollment Records and Transcripts of Hungarian Students in Italy). Budapest: Magyar Tudományos Akadémia, 1941.

Véronèse, Julien. *L'Ars notoria au moyen age: introduction et édition critique*. Micrologus Library 21. Florence: Sismel, 2007.

———. "Les anges dans l'*Ars notoria:* Révélation, processus visionnaire, et angélologie." In Bresc and Grévin, "Les Anges et la magie," 813–49.

———. "Magie, théurgie et spiritualité dans le rituel de l'*Ars notoria* au Moyen Âge." Forthcoming in a collection of essays edited by Claire Fanger.

Versnel, Henk. "Some Reflections on the Relationship Magic-Religion." *Numen* 38 (1991): 177–97.

Vetulani, Adam. "Les origines de l'Université de Cracovie." *Acta Poloniae Historica* 13 (1966): 14–40.

———. "Les origines et le sort des universités de l'Europe Centrale et orientale fondées au cours du XIVe siècle." In *The Universities in the Late Middle Ages,* ed. Jozef Ijsewijn and Jacques Paquet, 148–67. Leuven: Leuven University Press, 1978.

Vezin, Jean. "Les livres utilisés comme amulettes et comme reliques." In Ganz, *Das Buch,* 101–16.

Vickers, Brian. "On the Rise of Magic in Early Medieval Europe." *History of European Ideas* 18 (1994): 275–87.

Vizkelety, András. "Ismeretlen magyar vonatkozású kódexek Münchenben" (Unknown Munich Codices of Hungarian Interest). *Magyar Könyvszemle* 95 (1979): 198–202.

Voigts, Linda Ehrsam. "The Character of the *Carecter:* Ambiguous Sigils in Scientific and Medical Texts." In *Latin and Vernacular: Studies in Late Medieval Texts and Manuscripts,* ed. A. J. Minnis, 91–109. Cambridge: Brewer, 1989.

———. "The Latin Verse and Middle English Prose Texts on the Sphere of Life and Death in Harley 3719." *Chaucer Review* 21 (1986): 291–305.

Voit, Petr. *Pražské Klementinum* (The Clementinum in Prague). Prague: Národní knihovna, 1990.

Wade, Elizabeth I. "A Fragmentary German Divination Device: Medieval Analogues and Pseudo-Lullian Tradition." In Fanger, *Conjuring Spirits,* 87–109.

Wagner, Theodor. "Wissenschaftlicher Schwindel im südlichen Böhmen (Alchymie, Magie u. ä. aus dem Wittingauer Archiv und den Correspondenzen des W. Březan 1570–91)." *Mitteilungen des Vereines für Geschichte der Deutschen in Böhmen* 16 (1878): 112–23; 19 (1880): 133–40.

Waley Singer, Dorothea. "Alchemical Texts Bearing the Name of Plato." *Ambix* 2 (1946): 115–28.

Watson, Nicholas. "John the Monk's *Book of Visions of the Blessed and Undefiled Virgin Mary, Mother of God:* Two Versions of a Newly Discovered Ritual Magic Text." In Fanger, *Conjuring Spirits,* 163–215.

Weill-Parot, Nicolas. "Causalité astrale et 'sciences des images' au Moyen Age: Éléments de réflexion." *Revue d'histoire des sciences* 52 (1999): 205–40.

———. "Encadrement et dévoilement: l'occulte et le secret dans la nature chez Albert le Grand et Roger Bacon." *Micrologus* 14 (*Il Segreto*) (2006): 151–70.

———. *Les "images astrologiques" au Moyen Âge et à la Renaissance: Speculations intellectuelles et pratiques magiques (XIIe–XVe siècle)*. Paris: Honoré Champion, 2002.

White, Lynn. "Kyeser's 'Bellifortis': The First Technological Treatise of the Fifteenth Century." *Technology and Culture* 10 (1969): 436–41.

———. "Medical Astrologers and Late Medieval Technology." *Viator: Medieval and Renaissance Studies* 6 (1975): 295–307.

Wickersheimer, Ernest. "Figures médico-astrologiques des IXe, Xe, XIe siècles." *Janus* 19 (1914): 1–21.

Wielgus, Stanisław. "*Consilia* de Stanislas de Scarbimiria contre l'astrologue Henri Bohemus." *Studia Mediewistyczne* 25 (1988): 145–72.

Williams, Steven J. "The Early Circulation of the Pseudo-Aristotelian *Secret of Secrets* in the West: The Papal and Imperial Courts." *Micrologus* 2 (*Sciences at the Court of Frederick II*) (1994): 127–44.

———. "Esotericism, Marvels, and the Medieval Aristotle." *Micrologus* 14 (*Il Segreto*) (2006): 171–91.

———. *The "Secret of Secrets": The Scholarly Career of a Pseudo-Aristotelian Text in the Latin Middle Ages*. Ann Arbor: University of Michigan Press, 2003.

Wojciechowska, Beata. "Magic in Annual Rites in Late Medieval Poland." In Wünsch, *Religion und Magie*, 225–38.

Wood, Juliette. "Virgil and Talesin: The Concept of the Magician in Medieval Folklore." *Folklore* 94 (1983): 91–104.

Wünsch, Thomas, ed. *Religion und Magie in Ostmitteleuropa (Spielräume theologischer Normierungsprozesse in Spätmittelalter und Frühe Neuzeit)*. Berlin: LIT Verlag, 2006.

Wyrozumski, J. "L'Idée de la tolérance à l'Université de Cracovie." In *Société et l'Église: Textes et discussions dans les universities de l'Europe Centrale*, ed. Sophie Włodek, 133–44. Turnhout: Brepols, 1995.

———, ed. *The Jagiellonian University in the Evolution of European Culture*. Kraków: Secesja, 1992.

Yates, Frances Amelia. *Giordano Bruno and the Hermetic Tradition*. London: Routledge and Kegan Paul, 1964.

———. "The Hermetic Tradition in Renaissance Science." In *Art, Science and History in the Renaissance*, ed. Charles S. Singleton. Baltimore: John Hopkins University Press, 1968.

Zambelli, Paola. "Astrologers' Theory of History." In Zambelli, *"Astrologi Hallucinati,"* 1–28.

———, ed. *"Astrologi Hallucinati": Stars and the End of the World in Luther's Time*. Berlin: Walter de Gruyter, 1986.

———. "Le problème de la magie naturelle à la Renaissance." In Szczucki, *Magia*, 48–82.

———. "Pseudepigrafia e magia secondo l'abate Johannes Trithemius." In *Ratio et Superstitio: Essays in Honor of Graziella Federici Vescovini*, ed. Giancarlo Marchetti, Orsola Rignani, and Valeria Sorge, 347–68. Louvain-La-Neuve: Fédérations Internationales des Instituts d'Études Médiévales, 2003.

———. *The "Speculum Astronomiae" and Its Enigma: Astrology, Theology, and Science in Albertus Magnus and His Contemporaries*. Boston Studies in the Philosophy of Science 135. Boston: Kluwer Academic Press, 1992.

Zaremska, Hanna. "Jewish Street (*Platea Judeorum*) in Cracow: The 14th–the First Half of the 15th c." *Acta Poloniae Historica* 83 (2001): 27–57.

Zathey, Jerzy. *Historia Biblioteki Jagiellońskiej* (The History of the Biblioteka Jagiellońska). Vol. 1. Kraków: Uniwersytet Jagielloński, 1966.

———. "Marcin Bylica of Olkusz." In Gierowski, *Cracow Circle,* 77–94.

———. "Per la storia dell'ambiente magico-astrologico a Cracovia nel Quattrocento." In Szczucki, *Magia,* 99–109.

Zinamer, Szczepan K. *The Jagellonian University Library in Cracow.* New York: Czas Publishing, 1963.

Zinner, Ernst. *Leben und Wirken des Johannes Müller von Königsberg genannt Regiomontanus.* 2d ed. Osnabrück: O. Zeller, 1968.

———. "Regiomontanus Magyarországon" (Regiomontanus in Hungary). *Matematikai és természettudományi értesítő* 55 (1936): 280–87.

Zwiercan, Marian. "Jan of Glogów." In Gierowski, *Cracow Circle,* 95–110.

Description of Selected Manuscripts

The Collection of the Augustinian Monastery, Moravská zemská knihovna (Brno)

A 48. Scribe unknown, 1526.
    fols. 2r–70v *Prognosticon*
    fols. 71v–149r *Practica geomantiae*

Magyar Tudományos Akadémia Könyvtára (Budapest)

MTAK Cod. lat. K 465. Scribe unknown, 1414–15. Owned by Emperor Sigismund and King Matthias.
    Conrad Kyeser, *Bellifortis*, fragment

Sächsische Landesbibliothek (Dresden)

SLB N 100. Inscribed by Egidius of Corintia, ca. 1487–88.
    fols. 1r–11r Pseudo-Ptolemaeus, *Compositio et operatio astrolabii*
    fols. 11v–19v Pseudo-Ptolemaeus, *Compositio et operatio astrolabii*
    fols. 20r–24v *De compositione quadrantis*
    fols. 27r–86v Sacrobosco's *Sphera* and its commentaries
    fols. 87r–120v Georgius Purbach, *Theorica nova*, and its commentary by Egidius of Corintia
    fols. 121r–149v Albert of Brudzewo, *Commentariolum in theoricas planetarum Purbachii*
    fols. 151r–158, 161v–171v Excerpta medico-astrologica
    fols. 159r–161v Arnaldus of Villanova, *De cautelis medicorum*
    fol. 161v Sigismundus Albicus, *Pronosticationes infirmo secundum dies incensionis*
    fols. 172r–173r *De duodecim imaginibus Hermetis*
    fol. 173v List of magical book titles
    fols. 174r–185r, 223r–225v Petrus Gaszowiec, *De mutatione aeris*
    fols. 192r–196v, 230r–266r, 268v–288r Johannes of Glogovia, *Summa astrologiae*
    fols. 198r–200v *Liber Runarum*
    fol. 201v Albertus Magnus, *Secretum de leonis sigillo*
    fol. 203r Geomantic treatise
    fol. 203v *Sphera Pithagorae*
    fols. 214r–218 Messahala, *Astrologia*
    fol. 222r–v Albertus of Brudzewo (?), *rectificatio geniture sec. verbum 51 Ptolomei*
    fols. 228r–229r *Liber de Stellis Beibeniis*
    fol. 288r–v *De invencione orbis magni*
    fols. 297v–306v *Tractatulus de stellis fixis in octava spera*

Biblioteka Jagiellońska (Kraków)

BJ 257. Inscribed (in part) by Paulus of Praga, ca. 1463. Owned by Ioannis Welsz of Posznania.
    fols. 1r–356v Paulus of Praga, *Liber viginti artium*

BJ 551. Scribe unknown, 1388 and the fifteenth century.
    fols. 1r–22v *Tabulae Alphonsinae*
    fols. 23r–30v Ioannes Danco of Saxonia, *Canones Tabularum Alphonsinarum et eclipsium*
    fols. 30v–31v *De usu astrolabii cum tabula*
    fols. 32r–34v Messahala, *De usu astrolabii*
    fols. 35r–42r Pseudo-Gerardus of Cremona, *Theorica planetarum*
    fols. 42v–44r Iannes Eligerus of Gunderslauen, *De utilitate quadrantis*
    fols. 44v–49r *De compositione astrolabii*
    fols. 49v–52r *Tabula coniunctionum Solis et Lunae*
    fols. 52v–56r Ioannes of Lineriis, *Algorismus de minutiis vulgaribus*
    fols. 56r–57r Messahala, *Canones astrolabii*
    fol. 57v *Nota de experimento*
    fols. 58r–70v Ioannes of Lineriis, *Canones Tabularum*
    fols. 71r–73v Medical notes
    fols. 74r–96v Ioannes of Lineriis, *Tabulae astronomicae*
    fols. 97r–108v *Tabulae astronomicae*
    fol. 109r *Medicinalia praescripta*
    fols. 109v–111r Excerpt from the *Ars Notoria*
    fol. 111r–v *Alchemica praescripta*
    fols. 112r–115r Ioannes of Plauen, *Oycreper*
    fol. 115r Magical recipe
    fols. 115v–116r Pseudo-Albertus Magnus, *Secreta Mulierum*
    fol. 116r Magical recipes in Latin and German
    fols. 116v–117r Magical recipes
    fol. 117r *De chiromantia*
    fols. 117v–118r Excerpt from the *Ars Notoria*
    fols. 118v–120r *De imbribus*
    fol. 120r–v *De colore eclipsis Solis et Lunae*
    fols. 120v–121r *Excerpta ex Ptolemaei Centiloquio*
    fols. 121v–122r Al-Kindi, *De pluviis*
    fols. 122r–124r Guilelmus Anglicus, *De urina*
    fols. 124r–125v Thebit ben Chorat, *De motu octavae sphaerae*
    fols. 126r–127r *De horologio*
    fols. 127v–128v *De alchemia*
    fol. 129r–v *Tabulae Solis*
    fol. 129v *Alchemica praescripta*
    fol. 129v *Proverbia cum notis*

BJ 793. Scribe unknown, 1458–59.
    fols. 1r–33v Albubather, *De nativitatibus*
    fols. 33v–42r *Tractatus de nativitatibus*
    fols. 44r–46r Guilelmus Anglicus, *De urina non visa cum tabula*

Description of Selected Manuscripts 321

fols. 46v–47v *De aegritudine*
fols. 47v–48v Pseudo-Alkindus, *De planetis sub radiis*
fols. 48v–50r *De potestate planetarum*
fols. 50r–51r *Introductio in astrologiam medicam*
fol. 51r–v *De signis et planetis*
fols. 51v–52r *De naturis planetarum*
fols. 52r–53v *De divisione signorum*
fols. 53v–59r Albumasar, *Electiones planetarum*
fols. 60r–61r *De septem quadraturis planetarum seu quadrati magici*
fols. 61r–63r Thebit ben Chorat, *De imaginibus*
fol. 63r–v Pseudo-Albertus Magnus, *Secretum de Sigillo Leonis*
fol. 63v *De figura Leonis*
fols. 63v–67r *Sortilegium geomanticum*
fols. 67v–69r *Sortilegium geomanticum*
fols. 69v–71r *Sortilegium geomanticum*
fols. 71v–73r *Sortilegium geomanticum*
fols. 73v–81r Socrates Basileus, *Prognostica*
fols. 81r–85v Albedatus, *Geomantia*
fol. 86r–v *Figurae astrologicae cum canonibus*
fols. 87v–103v *Sortes Regis Amalrici*
fols. 105r–106v *Tabula aequationum duodecim domorum caeli*
fols. 107v–109v Pseudo-Hippocrates, *De medicorum astrologia*
fols. 109v–115v Alkindus, *De mutatione temporum*
fol. 115v *Nota de dispositione aeris*
fol. 116r–v *Tabula mansionum planetarum*
fols. 116v–120v Petrus Gaszoviec, *De mutatione aeris (Absque fine)*
fol. 121v *De nonnullis experimentis*
fols. 127r–138r Ioannes of Rupescissa, *De consideratione quintae essentiae*
fols. 138r *De aqua ardenti seu Excerpta De aqua vitae*
fol. 139r–v Pseudo-Ptolemaeus, *Opus imaginum*
fols. 139v–140v Ptolemaeus, *De lapidibus pretiosis*
fol. 140v *Lapidarius Mercurii*
fols. 140v–143v Thebit ben Chorat, *De imaginibus*
fols. 143v–148v Pseudo-Albertus Magnus, *Experimenta*
fols. 149r–151r Hermes, *Centiloquium a Stephano de Messana translatum*
fols. 151r–152v Albategni, *Centiloquium*
fol. 153r Leopoldus de Austria, *Compilatio de astrorum scientia*
fols. 153r–154r *De mutatione aeris*
fol. 154r–v *De re certa vel desperata*
fols. 154v–155r *De pestilentia*
fols. 155r–156r Petrus Gaszowiec, *De mutatione aeris*
fol. 156r–v Robertus Grosseteste, *De impressionibus aeris seu de prognosticatione*
fol. 156v *Nota de aspectibus*
fols. 157r–158r Messahala, *De revolutione annorum mundi*
fol. 158r–v *Secreta astrologorum*
fol. 158v *Notae ad astrologiam spectantes*
fols. 158v–160r *De coniunctionibus planetarum*

fols. 160r–161r *De proprietatibus duodecim signorum zodiaci*
fols. 165r–167v *Introductio in astrologiam medicam*
fols. 167v–169v Alexander, *De quattuor complexionibus hominum*
fols. 171r–197r *Picatrix, Versio Latina, cum figuris*

BJ 805. 1398–99. Owned by Andreas Grzymala.
    fols. 9r–154r *Expositio et commentum in Aphorismos Hippocratis*
    fols. 154r–164v *Expositio prognosticorum Hippocratis*
    fols. 165r–219r Gentilis of Fulgineo, Various medical writings
    fols. 225r–238v *De calculis renum et vesicae*
    fols. 239r–243r Pseudo-Albertus Magnus, *Experimenta*
    fols. 243r–250v *Experimenta alia*
    fols. 251r–274v Gilbertus Anglicus, *Commentum in carmen Aegidii Corboliensis "De urinis"*
    fols. 299r–310v Thomas of Wratislavia, *Antidotarium*
    fols. 335r–360r Zael, astrological writings
    fols. 360v–361r Gentilis of Fulgineo, *De venenis*
    fols. 361v–364v *De anatomia*
    fol. 367v *De balneis naturalibus*
    fols. 368r–371v Petrus Hispanus, *Thesaurus pauperum*
    fols. 372r–382v Alcabitius, *Introductorius*
    fols. 392r–393v Hermes, *Centiloquium*
    fols. 393v–396v Pseudo-Ptolemaeus, *Centiloquium*
    fols. 396v–398r Albategni, *Centiloquium*
    fols. 398r–400r *De planetis*
    fols. 401v–404v *De utilitate astrolabii*
    fols. 405r–409v *Geomantia*
    fols. 410r–415v Ioannes of Saccis, *Iudicium nativitatis*
    fols. 416r–477v Mundinus of Foro Iulii, *Synonyma medicinae*

BJ 813. Scribe unknown, fourteenth century. Owned by Andreas Grzymala.
    fols. 1r–5r Ioannitus, *Introductio in artem parvam Galeni*
    fols. 5r–10v Hippocrates, *Liber aphorismum*
    fols. 10v–15v Theophilus, *Liber de urinis*
    fols. 15v–19v Hippocrates, *Liber prognosticorum*
    fols. 19v–21r Philaretus, *Liber de pulsibus*
    fols. 21r–37r Galenus, *Ars parva*
    fols. 39r–79v, 85r–90r Bartholomaeus Anglicus, *De proprietatibus rerum*
    fols. 79v–82v *Introductio in astrologiam seu de cursu Lunae*
    fols. 82v–83v *Da aqua ardente*
    fols. 91r–108v, 111r–122v Matthaeus Platearius, *De simplici medicina*
    fol. 108v *Nota de signis zodiaci*
    fols. 109v–110v Hugo Ripelin of Argentina, *De physionomia*
    fol. 124r–v *Interpretationes somniorum*
    fols. 124v–130r Arnaldus of Villa Nova, *Introductio in iudicia astrologiae*
    fols. 130r–134r *De consideratione dierum criticorum*
    fols. 134r–136v Pseudo-Hippocrates, *De medicorum astrologia*
    fols. 136v–137r *De aspectu planetarum*

fol. 137r *De natura aeris*
fol. 137r *De temporibus aptis phlebotomiae*
fols. 137v, 138r–139r Messahala, *De occultis*
fols. 137v–138v Dorotheus Sidonius, *De occultatione anuli*
fols. 141r–152r Aegidius Corboliensis, *De urinis*
fols. 153r–173v Pseudo-Aristoteles, *Secretum secretorum*
fols. 173v–174r Henricus Langenstein of Hassia, *De cometa*
fols. 174r–178v *Canones de usu astrolabii*
fols. 178v–181r *De cylindro*

BJ 817. 1483. Owned by Matthias of Miechów.
    pp. 1–2 Beda Venerabilis, *De tonitruis libellus ad Herefridum*
    pp. 3–5 Thebit ben Chorat, *De imaginibus*
    pp. 6–8 *Parvus tractatus de lunationibus*
    pp. 8–10 *De temporibus anni, considerationes astrologicae*
    pp. 10–28 *Questio de medicina et astronomia*
    pp. 28–42 Rasis, *De sexaginta animalibus*
    pp. 43–79 *Kiranides, libri I–IV*
    pp. 80–90 Petrus Hispanus, *Questiones de medicinis laxativis*
    pp. 90–92 Hugo Ripelin of Argentina, *Phisionomia*
    pp. 11–103 Guilelmus, *De aegritudinibus renum et vesicae*
    pp. 103–9 Hippocrates, *Liber de aere*
    pp. 109–19 Richardus Anglicus, *De urinis*
    p. 119 *De epilepsia*
    pp. 121–40 *Recommendationes et principia in Universitate habita*
    pp. 140–43 Iannes of Parma, *Practicella*
    pp. 144–45 *Schemata et notae de urinarum coloribus*
    pp. 146–47 Gualterus Agilon, *Liber de pulsibus*

BJ 839. Ca. 1457. Owned by Andreas Grzymala.
    fols. 1r–10r Moses Maimonides, *De venenis*
    fols. 10r–12r Ioannes Iacobi, *Medicinalia praecepta*
    fols. 12v–16v Gerardus of Solo, *De febribus*
    fols. 16v–19r *Regulae de urinis secundum Aegidium Corboliensem*
    fol. 19r Henricus de Wintonia, *Carmen de coloribus urinarum*
    fols. 20v–21v Ioannes Iacobi, *De calculo*
    fols. 21v–23r *Medicinalia praecepta*
    fols. 23r–36v *Liber de Geomantia, translatus a Hugo de Santalla*
    fols. 37r–47v Raymundus Lullus, *De arte medicinae compendium*
    fols. 48r–219v Ionnes Serapion, *Liber aggregationum in medicinis simplicibus*

BJ 2496. Inscribed by Michael of Wratislavia, fifteenth century.
    pp. 1–70 *De nativitatibus*
    pp. 73–88 Messahala, *De revolucionibus*
    pp. 89–120 Albumasar, *De experimentis*
    pp. 121–54 Albumasar, *De floribus*
    pp. 155–64 Valentinus of Zathor, *significatio comete*

pp. 165–68 *De cometis*
pp. 169–90 *Speculum astronomiae*
pp. 190–91 *Epistola b. Thome De impressionibus et iudiciis astrorum*
pp. 193–11 Messahala, *De significacione planetarum*
pp. 212–68 *Fragmenta astrologica*

Universitätsbibliothek (Munich)

2° Cod. ms. 738. Inscribed by Stephanus of Rivulo Dominarum., 1406.
    fols. 1r–175r Guido of Columna, *Historia Destructionis Troiae*
    fols. 175r–176r *Regimen sanitatis, De conservatione corporis* (Pseudo-Aristoteles, *Secretum secretorum)*
    fol. 176v *Regimen sanitatis salernitanum*
    fol. 177v *Medicina recepta*
    fols. 178v–184v *Liber similitudinum*
    fols. 184v–189r *De cursu lunae*
    fols. 191v–192r Bernardus Sylvestris, *Prognosticon*

Germanisches Nationalmuseum (Nuremberg)

Hs 168. Inscribed by Michael Harsch of Geppingen alias Furndow, 1427 (Buda, Felhévíz). Owned by the Carthausians of Aggsbach.
    fols. 2r–47r Albertus Magnus, *De mineralibus*
    fols. 47v–48r Ademar Parisiensis, *Dialogus cum Guilelmo fratri suo*
    fols. 48v, 50v Plague recipes
    fols. 51r–97r Rogerius Bacon, *Epistola de retardatione accidentium senectutis, et sermo de conservatione iuventutis*
    fols. 99r–136r *De compositione quarundam medicinarum*
    fols. 137r–148v *Tractatus ex alchimia* (Theodericus Cervensisi, *De aqua vitae*)
    fols. 149r–153v *Regimen sanitatis*
    fols. 153v–160r Bruno Longoburgensis, *Chirurgia Magna*
    fols. 160v–165r *Remedia*
    fols. 165r–169v Zacharias, *De passionibus oculorum*
    fols. 169v–198r *Remedia et regimina*
    fols. 199r–201r *Regimen sanitatis quotidianum*
    fols. 201v–206v Alchemical and medical recipes

Bodleian Library (Oxford)

Rawl. liturg. d. 6. Scribe unknown, fifteenth century.
    fols. 1r–80v *The Prayer Book of Wladislas*

Hertford College 2 (E N 2). Scribe unknown, 1371–82. Owned by Louis the Great, king of Hungary.
    fols. 1r–66v Pseudo-Aristoteles, *Secretum secretorum*

Národní knihovna (Prague)

PNK I F 35 (267). Written and collected by Mattheus Beran, 1426–31.
    fols. 3r–42v *Calendarium astronomicum cum praenosticatione et practica medicinali*
    fols. 43r–55v *Lapidarius fratris M. Berani*
    fols. 56r–57v *Proprietates et virtutes lapidum*
    fols. 58r–60r *De aquis*
    fols. 60v *Spera pittagorica, quam Appulegius descripsit*
    fols. 61r–89r *Herbarius*
    fols. 89v–92v *Registrum herbarii* (Latin-Bohemian bilingual)
    fols. 93r–136r *Divina ars scilicet Essencia quinta ex diversis philosophis collecta*
    fols. 136r–138r *Supplementum Lapidarii superioris*
    fols. 138v–156r *Lignarius*
    fols. 156r–174v *De animalibus*
    fols. 175r–244v *Antidotarius fratris Mathei Beran*
    fols. 245r–251r *Practica, Ars saccellacionis*
    fols. 251r–257r *De neutralitate*
    fols. 257r–259r *Tabula sive Flores Antidotarii*
    fols. 259v–261v *Vocabula antidotarii*
    fols. 261v–390v *Practica de morbis et remediis humane nature*
    fols. 390v–391v *De odoribus et saporibus*
    fols. 392r–401r *Dieta communis*
    fols. 401r–410v *Tractatus de urinis*
    fols. 410v–414v *De serpente et de venenis*
    fols. 414v–417r *De pulsibus*
    fols. 417r–420r *Cautele medicorum contra deceptores*
    fols. 420r–444r *Tabula narracionis fortune cum sua practica*
    fols. 444v–447v *Chiromantia cum delineatione manuum*
    fols. 448r–458v *Biblia pauperum: Versus mnemotechnici*
    fols. 458v–464v *Libri iuris canonici*
    fols. 464v–476v *Liber Eirohtonsitra—vetis notorie—sanctissime* (Apollonius, *Flores aurei*)
    fols. 477r–484r *Ars avitaromem (evitaromem)—ars memorativa fratris Beran*

PNK XI C 2 (2027). Scribe unknown, 1420–40.
    fols. 1r–6r *Calendarium a mense Martio usque ad Decembrem*
    fols. 7r–10v *Notae astronomicae et computisticae*
    fols. 11r–17v *Tractatus astrologicus de nativitatibus*
    fols. 17v–31r *Astronomia Regis Johannis presbiteri de maiori Indya* (In Czech and Latin)
    fols. 31r–45v Text on astrological medicine in Czech with Latin insertions
    fols. 45v–49r Text on balsams in Czech
    fols. 49r–53r *Tractatus de cursu lunae*
    fols. 53r–55r *Tractatus de naturis septem planetarum*
    fols. 55r–56v *De VI imaginibus stellarum et lunae*
    fols. 56v–64v *Tractatus de mensibus*
    fols. 64v–68r *De signis duodecim*
    fols. 68r–70r *Versus medicinales*
    fols. 70r–71r *Cursus fortunae (geomantia)*

fols. 72v–77r *Tractatus geomanticus*
fols. 78r–85r *Tractatus geomanticus*
fol. 86r–v *Sphera Pythagorae*
fols. 87r–88v *Sortes Regis Amalrici*
fols. 88v–104v *Practica astrologica*
fols. 105r–133v *Herbarium cum interpretatione bohemica*
fols. 134r–146v Petrus Hispanus, *Thesaurus pauperum*
fols. 146v–147r *Formulae magicae*
fols. 147v–155r *Herbarium cum interpretatione bohemica*
fols. 155r–160r *De febribus, de lepra, de urina*
fols. 160r–167r *Herbarium cum interpretatione bohemica*
fols. 167r–211v Text in Czech on urines
fols. 212r–226r Recipes in Czech and Latin
fols. 226r–228v *Notae de urinis cum tabula de iudiciis urinarum*
fols. 228v–238v Medical texts
fols. 238v–250r Arnaldus of Saxo, *De virtutibus lapidum*
fols. 250r–255v Pseudo-Albertus Magnus, *Experimenta*
fols. 256r–264r Medical recipes
fols. 264v–272r Johannes Boboniensis, *De vino*
fols. 272r–273r *De aceto*
fols. 272r–283v *Consecrationes antidotarii*
fols. 283v–286v *Medicinae contra colicam*
fols. 286v–288v *Epistola Bernardi ad Johannem militem*
fols. 289r–291v Medical text in Czech
fols. 292r–295r Lapidarium in Czech
fols. 295v–298v *Regulae sanitatis*
fol. 299r–v *Remedia pestilentia*

PNK adlig. 14 H 208 (2764). Scribe unknown, after 1504.
    14 H 208. *Liber Messahala De scientia motus orbis,* Nuremberg, 1504. Ficino, *De triplici vita* (n.p., n.y.)
    N 2 *Tractatus de duodecim signis zodiaci et effectibus eorum* (3 fols.)
    N 3 *Hermetis Liber de quindecim stellis, herbis et lapidibus* (5 fols.)
    N 4 *Liber Ptolomei de lapidibus preciosis et sigillis eorum* (1 fol.)
    N 5 *De septem quadraturis planetarum* (3 fol.)

Biblioteca Apostolica Vaticana (Vatican City)

BAV Pal. lat. 1375. Inscribed and owned by Johannes Virdung of Hassfurt, 1482–88,
    fol. ar "Nicolaus de pulchro monte vulgaliter Schonberg Britannicus astrologus optimus et nigromanticus fuit mecum Anno 1510 die lune post Jacobi et recessit die Mercurii, erat prepositus et doctor legum."
    fols. 1r–8v Johannes Blanchinus, *Canones Tabularum*
    fols. 8r–10v Johannes of Lineriis, *abbreviatio aequatorii*
    fols. 11r–17r *Figurae planetarum*
    fols. 18r–43r Astronomical tables

fol. 44r *Sphera Pythagorae*
fols. 44v–53r Astronomical tables
fols. 55r–106r Georgius Peuerbach, *Tabulae coniunctionum*
fols. 106v–171r Johannes Regiomontanus, *Tabulae directionum*
fols. 171v–176r Astronomical tables
fols. 177v–178r, 181r–182v *Compositio quadrantis*
fols. 180r–181r Philo Byzantinus, *De spiritualibus ingeniis*
fol. 183r–v *De compositione cylindri*
fols. 185r–262v Johannes Blanchinus, *Tabulae*
fols. 263r–269r *Figurae astronomicae*
fols. 269v–270r *Liber de spritibus inclusis*
fol. 270r–v *Liber Belemich de ymaginibus septem planetarum*
fol. 270v *Hermes de imaginibus sive annulis septem planetarum*
fols. 271v–272r *Mansiones Lunae*
fol. 272r Anonymous text on talismanic magic
fols. 272v–273v *Investigationes astronomicae*
fols. 274v–275v Arzachel, *Canones*
fols. 277v–283v Planetary tables for the years 1470–1601
fol. 285r Secret alphabets

BAV Pal. Lat. 1439. Inscribed and owned by Johannes Virdung of Hassfurt, 1487–88.
    fols. 1r–8r Georg Peuerbach, *Canones eclipsum solis et lune*
    fols. 8r, 39r, 331v–335r, 350v Notes concerning Virdung's life and studies
    fols. 9v–11r *Regimen mensium*
    fols. 13r–39r Johannes of Monteregio, *praefatio tabulae directionum*
    fol. 39r Secret alphabet
    fols. 40r–40v Albertus of Brudzewo (?), *rectificatio geniture sec. verbum 51 Ptolomei*
    fols. 41r–49v Albertus of Brudzewo, *De nativitatibus*
    fols. 50r–66r *Canones de nativitatibus collecti ex canonibus directionum Johannis de Monte Regio*
    fols. 67r–77r *Horologium diei et noctis*
    fol. 76r *De baculo Jacob*
    fol. 76v *Arithmetica*
    fols. 78v–102v Johannes of Sacro Bosco, *Sphera*
    fols. 103r–116v *Kalendarium solis et lunae cum tabulis*
    fols. 117r–121v *Canones kalendarii*
    fols. 122r–152r, 211r–239v Johannes of Glogovia, *Summa astrologiae*
    fols. 155r–160r Johannes of Glogovia, *Tractatulus ex intentione sapientium*
    fols. 160v–163r Johannes of Glogovia, *De astrologia respectu doctrinae Christiana*
    fols. 165r–194r Johannes of Glogovia, *Introductio in tabulas resolutas*
    fols. 194v–198r Pseudo-Hippocrates, *De astronomia*
    fol. 198r Sigismundus Albicus, *Pronosticationes infirmo secundum dies incensionis*
    fol. 199r *Rota runarum*
    fols. 189v–202r *Excerpta e Guidonis Bonati libro astronomico*
    fols. 204v–207r *De aeris mutatione prognostica*
    fols. 239v–244r *Instrumentum: Theorica planetarum*
    fols. 244v–247v *De modo computandi eclipses*

fols. 260r–265r *Prognostica nativitatis*
fols. 268r–277r *Instrumentum iuvans artem computisticam*
fols. 279r–285r Pseudo-Ptolemaeus, *Compositio et operatio astrolabii*
fols. 285v–289v Guido Bonatus, *Excerpta*
fols. 293r–304v Pseudo-Ptolemaeus, *Compositio et operatio astrolabii*
fols. 305r–308r *Figurae caeli*
fols. 308v–313v Albertus of Brudzewo, *De iudicio eclipsis*
fols. 314r–316v Albertus of Brudzewo, *De iudicio configurationis*
fols. 317r–323r *De invencione orbis magni*
fols. 323v–330v Albertus of Brudzewo, *Iudicium anni 1487*
fols. 336r–344r Petrus Gaszowiec, *De mutatione aeris*
fols. 344v–345v *Liber de Stellis Beibeniis*
fols. 346r–350r *Liber Runarum*

Österreichische Nationalbibliothek (Vienna)

ÖNB Cod Lat. 4007. Ca. 1449. Owned by Nicolaus of Marienwerder.
   fols. 1r–29v Eypheus, *Commentarius in Aristotelis praedicamenta*
   fols. 30r–31r Augustinus, *Praedicabilia*
   fols. 31r–44v Augustinus, *Praedicamenta*
   fols. 44r–48v *Articuli Avicenne*
   fols. 48v–59r *Distinctiones communes usitatae Parisiis*
   fol. 60v *Tentamen conceptus signis quibuslibet fixandi*
   fols. 61r–69r *De arte praedicandi*
   fols. 73r–77r *Introductio in chiromantiam*
   fols. 77v–90v, 122v–128r Nicolaus of Marienwerder, *Calendarium Cyclicum*
   fols. 91r–122r *Praelectiones Parisiis factae de arte praedicandi*
   fols. 131r–161v Laurentius Aquilegiensis, *Ars dictandi ad tabelliones Bononiae*
   fols. 163r–220v *Tractatus de philosophia naturali*
   fols. 221r–239v *Tractatus de ente*
   fols. 245r–281r *Tractatus de logica*
   fols. 281v–286v Thomas Aquinas, *De generibus scientiarum*
   fols. 286v–301v Thomas Aquinas, *Tractatus de dimensionibus*

Index

Adelard of Bath, 31, 94, 285–86
Albertus Magnus, 24, 36, 55–57, 61, 94, 128, 145, 147, 151, 186, 206, 225, 252, 267, 281–82, 284
    Ps-Albertus Magnus, *Experimenta Alberti, Liber aggregationis, De virtutibus herbarum, lapidum et animalium*, 36, 55–65, 67, 72, 85, 252–55, 267–68, 271
    Ps-Albertus Magnus, *Speculum astronomiae*. See *Speculum astronomiae*
Albertuse of Brudzewo, 108, 249, 256–57
Albicus of Uniczow, 115 n. 91, 212–14, 224
alchemical laboratory in Oberstockstall, 151–52, 277–78
alchemy, 4, 8, 10, 38, 41.–42, 59, 70, 144–61, 187, 198, 202, 206–8, 211–14, 226, 228, 234, 268
    in the 16th century, 276–79
    and clerics, 147–55
    and the Holy Trinity, 152–55
Alfonso the Wise (king of Castile), 81, 96, 230, 232, 237
Al-Kindi, 23–24, 80, 83, 108 n. 70, 126, 231, 269
amulets, 110, 120, 200, 212, 226–28
Andrzej Grzymala of Posnania, 62, 85, 192, 252–55
Anna Cilly, 209–10
Aristotle, 5, 31, 56, 58–60, 69, 105, 119, 128, 206, 225, 252, 281, 285
Arnald of Villanova, 62, 151, 198–99, 252
Arnaldus Saxo, 67–68
Ars notoria, 2, 33–34, 40–41, 48–49, 81, 118, 125, 140, 148, 183–97, 204, 205–6, 208, 222, 227, 230, 251, 266–67
    and the prayer book of king Wladislas, 165–87
    research on, 287–92
Asclepius, 26, 68, 105, 119
astrology, 2, 4–5, 10–12, 20, 25–27, 36, 59, 70, 78, 80, 105–6, 121, 142, 147, 149, 187, 219, 226, 241, 245–46, 284–89
    in Kraków, 10–12, 33, 115, 192, 214, 227, 248–55, 257–58, 268
    in Buda, 230, 234–39
    in Prague, 232–34

Augustine, St., 20, 25–26, 35, 39, 124, 225
    St. Augustine's Abbey in Canterbury, 11 n. 31, 184, 201, 268, 284, 287
Augustine Sigismund, king of Poland, 224

Bacon, Roger, 70, 145, 147, 149, 281, 284
Barbara of Cilly, wife of emperor Sigismund, 156–57, 211
Batthyány, Boldizsár, 276–77
Beatrix, queen of Hungary, 224, 236
Benedictus, former necromancer, monk in Schottenkloster, 194–98
Boldizsár Batthyány. See Batthyány
Bonfini, Antonio, 11, 236

Cardano, Girolamo, 91–92
Casimir the Great, king of Poland, 10, 244–45
Caspar, assistant priest on Poznań, 226
Central Europe, the definition of, 7–10
Charles IV, Holy Roman Emperor, 200, 244
chiromancy, 123, 127–31, 148, 186–87, 226–27, 254, 256, 278
Christian of Prachatitz, 213, 233
Conrad of Vechta, 151, 159, 161, 198, 212–13, 224
Conrad Kyeser, author of *Bellifortis*, 36, 49, 71–78, 136, 149, 182, 211, 220, 233, 266–67, 275
Correggio, Giovanni da. *See* Johannes Mercurius Corrigiensis
cryptography, 110, 130–32, 137
crystallomancy, 3, 124, 162–64, 168, 170–83, 209–10, 215–25, 250, 266–67, 270, 273

decanic figures, 79–80, 97–98, 101–2, 104, 251
Dee, John, 181, 276–79, 290
De imaginibus septem planetarum (Belenus), 82, 116–18, 256, 327
De imaginibus, sive annulis septem planetarum (Hermes), 27, 82, 115–16, 118, 256, 327
demons, 20–25, 26, 29–31, 34, 38–40, 48, 60, 65, 68, 71, 75–76, 79–80, 95, 125, 140, 167, 181, 194–97, 199, 211, 214, 216, 220, 22–26, 228, 266, 272. *See also* magic, demonic

330　Index

De septem quadraturis planetarum, 83–84, 91–94, 207, 321, 326
De virtutibus herbarum, lapidum et animalium. *See* Albertus Magnus, Ps-Albertus Magnus
diagrams, 135–43
divination, 2, 4, 11, 20, 26, 33–34, 38, 64, 76, 86–89, 123–35, 137–38, 172, 175, 210, 226, 228, 232–33, 241, 252, 255, 266–67, 274. *See also* geomancy, chiromancy, sphere of life and death
Divine names. *See* God, names of
Dürer, Albrecht, 91–92

Egidius of Corintia, 33–35, 103, 107, 109, 251, 258, 267, 273
Etienne Tempier, 125, 191, 207, 226
Experimenta Alberti. See Albertus Magnus, Ps-Albertus Magnus

Faustus, Gregorius, 1–3, 12, 212, 220, 241, 260–63, 273–75, 276, 279
Ficino, Marsilio, 11, 82, 103–6, 119, 207, 234, 237–39, 259, 274

Galen, 53, 60, 62, 252
Galeotto Marzio, 11, 234–39
geomancy, 4, 38, 76, 85–90, 109, 124–27, 130–35, 137, 206, 226, 228, 233, 251–56, 269, 278
Georgius Peuerbach, 237, 246, 256
Gerbert d'Aurillac (Pope Sylvester II), 70
Gerson, Jean, 22, 60 n. 27, 95, 223, 226
God, names of, 165, 169–73, 175, 181, 186–87, 203, 222, 233, 288

Harpocration of Alexandria, 57
Hartlieb, Johannes, 38, 124, 172–73
Heinrich von Langenstein (Henry of Hesse), 246
Henry the Bohemian, 47, 182, 214–23, 225, 229, 250–51, 267–68, 273–74
Hermes Trismegistus, 11, 26, 30, 33, 35, 38, 57, 63, 79, 82–83, 85, 94, 104–9, 114–16, 118–20, 127, 145, 155, 192, 207, 236, 239, 252, 256, 262, 281–82
hermetic talismans, 104–19
hermetism, the two kinds of, 104–6, 239
Hippocrates, 52–54, 60, 62, 231, 252
Hugh of Santalla, 126, 128
Hugh of St. Victor, 38, 124

Inquisition, 200, 219

Jacobus of Piacenza, 198
Jadwiga, queen of Poland, 10, 244

Jan Milíč (Johannes Milicius) 199–200, 229
Janus Pannonius, 235–38
Jean de Bar, 173, 222–23, 226, 229
Jean Gerson, 22, 60 n. 27, 95, 223, 226
Johannes Bianchini, 108, 252, 256
Johannes Faustus. *See* Faustus
Johannes Hartlieb. *See* Hartlieb
Johannes Hunyadi, 234
Johannes Lasnioro (John of Laz), 155–57, 211, 268, 274
Johannes Manlius. *See* Manlius
Johannes Mercurius Corrigiensis, 261–64, 273
Johannes Nider, 194–97
Johannes of Dobra, 68–69, 152, 218
Johannes of Francofordia, 21, 226
Johannes of Glogovia, 107, 227, 249, 256–58
Johannes of Ragusio, 69
Johannes of Rupescissa, 95, 147, 149, 268
Johannes of Sacrobosco, 108, 219, 248
Johannes of Transylvania, 150
Johannes Regiomontanus, 11, 108, 206, 235, 237, 246–47, 256, 258
Johannes Ticinensis, 149, 151, 268
Johannes Trithemius. *See* Trithemius
Johannes Virdung of Hassfurt, 107, 109, 115, 118, 128, 130, 241–42, 251, 255–64, 269, 273, 274
Johannes Vitéz, 235–36, 245, 247
Johannes Volmar of Villingen, 258
John of Laz. *See* Johannes Lasnioro
John of Morigny, author of the *Liber visionum*, 40–41, 167–69, 180–84, 197, 267, 287, 290–92
John of Salisbury, 173, 210

Konrad Celtis, 259, 273–74
Kyranides, 55, 57, 59, 61–63, 68, 106

Łaski, Albert, 278–79
Laz, John of. *See* Johannes Lasnioro
Lazzarelli, Lodovico, 263–64
Liber aggregationis. *See* Albertus Magnus, Ps-Albertus Magnus
Liber de spiritibus inclusis, 80, 116–18, 256, 327
Liber de stellis beibeniis, 108–9, 114, 251, 256, 273
Liber de xv stellis, xv lapidibus, xv herbis, et xv imaginibus, 82, 207
Liber iuratus Honorii, 2, 39–40, 48, 290
Liber lunae, 26, 30, 33, 34, 82, 114, 267, 286
Liber runarum, 3, 33, 83, 109–15, 118, 137–38, 251, 256, 259–60, 266, 268, 273, 293
Liber vaccae, 28, 62 n. 37, 72, 267

Index

Louis the Great, king of Hungary and Poland, 58, 244
Lullus, Raimundus, 136, 145, 149, 151

magic
  classifications of, 24–43
  criminalization of, 219–30
  definitions of, 17–20
  demonic, 2, 20–22, 30, 37, 39–40, 104, 199, 266
  image, 26–27, 29–33, 35–38, 79–122, 138, 193, 207–10, 251, 256–58, 266–67, 283–86
  natural, 25–27, 35–38, 51–78, 170–71, 251–52, 261, 266
  "positivization" of, 22, 35, 274
  ritual, 2–4, 20, 37–41, 48, 116, 140–43, 162–88, 208, 222, 230, 265–70, 286–92
magic squares. *See De septem quadraturis planetarum*
Maiolus, Simon, 1–2
Manlius, Johannes, 1, 229, 277
Marcus Graecus, *Liber ignium*, 72, 149
Martin Bylica of Olkusz, 11, 217, 235, 247
Martin Król of Żurawica, 247–49
Martin, Túrócszentmárton, town in Slovakia, 96–97
Mattheus Beran, 185–86, 192, 204–8, 250–51
Matthias Corvinus, king of Hungary, 10–11, 77–78, 119, 180, 217, 224, 234–40, 243–49
Matthias, necromancer, 216, 267
Mercurius. *See* Johannes Mercurius Corrigiensis
Michael Harsch of Geppingen, 148
military engineering, 70–76, 233, 266
mirror, magical, 138–39, 170–73, 175, 181, 209, 222–23, 225
Monaldus of Luca, 157, 216–17, 250, 273–74

necromancy, 3, 7, 24–27, 29–30, 33–37, 41–42, 48, 69, 71, 97, 114, 118, 138, 167, 172–75, 182, 194–98, 209–10, 214–17, 219–26, 241, 260, 266–67, 273
Nicholas of Marienwerder, 128, 253–55
Nicholas of Poland (Nicholas of Montpellier), author of *Antipocras* and *Experimenta*, 36, 51–55, 60–61, 266–68
Nicholas, the Kraków hangman, 47, 209–10, 220, 225, 229, 267, 274
Nicolaus Cusanus, 231, 233
Nicolaus de Pulchro Monte, 258, 261, 273
Nicolaus Magni of Jawor, 124, 173, 226
Nicolaus Melchior Cibinensis, author of the *Processus sub forma missae*, 144–46, 158–61, 211, 268
Nicolaus Olah, 158–60, 198
notory art. *See Ars notoria*

Oberstockstall. *See* alchemical laboratory in Oberstockstall
Ottokar II, king of Bohemia, 231–32

palmistry. *See* chiromancy
Paul of Prague, 48, 220–24
Peer Codex, 67 n. 54, 148 n. 1, 202–4
Petrus Gaszowiec, 98, 103, 107, 108, 152, 252–54, 258
Picatrix, 3, 23, 34, 35, 41, 43, 80–81, 83, 94, 96–106, 115, 117, 120, 136, 138, 230, 251, 255, 266–69, 274, 285
Plato, 11, 28, 62, 119, 161, 236, 237, 238
Ptolemy, 5, 37, 82–83, 85, 95, 106, 231, 233, 237, 281, 284
  Ps-Ptolemy, *Centiloquium*, 32, 63, 80, 83, 121, 248
  Ps-Ptolemy, *Opus imaginum*, 31, 34, 36, 82, 94, 251

Regiomontanus. *See* Johannes Regiomontanus
Richard of Fournival, 19, 28–29, 35, 191, 281–83
Rota Pythagorae. *See* sphere of life and death
Rožmberk family, 204, 207, 278
Rudolf II (Holy Roman Emperor), 10, 145, 278–79
runes. *See Liber runarum*

Secretum de sigillo leonis, 94
Secretum secretorum, 55–60, 61–64
self-fashioning, 262–64
Sigismund, Holy Roman Emperor, king of Hungary, 49, 71, 77, 97, 151, 156, 212–13, 224, 231, 234, 244–45
Solomon, 29, 34–35, 39, 163, 165, 167, 175, 281, 288–89
  Rings of, 141, 185
  Solomonic magic, 29, 120, 169, 175, 267, 289–90
Sortes regis Amalrici, 64, 132 n. 27, 134 n. 28
Speculum astronomiae, 19, 24–38, 80–83, 93–94, 103–4, 115–16, 125, 191, 251, 267, 281–84, 289
Sphera Pythagorae. *See* sphere of life and death
sphere of life and death, 90, 109, 130–31, 133–35, 137, 140, 197, 206, 256, 293
Stanislas of Skalbimierz, 215–18, 221, 225, 229
Stevin of Bruges, Simon, 79–80, 98

talismans. *See* magic, image
Thebit ben Corat, Thābit ibn Qurra, 35, 37
  De imaginibus, 23, 30–31, 34, 36, 63–64, 70, 81–82, 93–94, 251, 255–56, 284

Thomas Aquinas, 24, 38, 128, 225, 284, 289, 292
Thomas, author of a work on talismans, 118, 256, 260
Thomas Murner, 227
Thomas of Pisan, 121–22
Thorndike, Lynn, 2, 39, 232
Trithemius, Johannes, 1, 32, 114, 118, 159, 198, 259–64, 273

Ulricus Crux of Telcz, 206–7

Wenceslas II, king of Bohemia, 69, 231–32
Wenceslas IV, Holy Roman Emperor, 71, 77, 212–14, 232–33, 237

William Byg, 173, 220–23
William of Auvergne, 19, 24–27, 29, 30, 32, 35–36, 54, 124, 171, 173, 207, 225
Witelo, 21–22
Wladislas I, of Varna, 178–80, 182, 218
Wladislas II, 144, 159–61, 179–80, 224
Wladislas Jagiello, 209, 214, 244
Wladislas, king, owner of the prayer book, 41, 48–49, 162–83, 185, 211, 218, 222, 266–68, 270
Wladislas Posthumous, 246

Index of Manuscripts

Alba Iulia, *Bibliotheca Batthyányana*
   R I 36   61 n. 34
   R I 64   61 n. 34

Brno, *Moravská zemská knihovna*
   From the Library of the Augustinians in Staré
      Brno: 48, 27 n. 12, 202 n. 20

Budapest, *Magyar Tudományos Akadémia Könyvtára*
   K 465   77 nn. 84 and 86, 319

Jena, *Universitätsbibliothek*
   El. f. 74   258 n. 86
   El. f. 77   258 n. 86
   El. phil. q. 3   258 n. 86

Dresden, *Sächsische Landesbibliothek*
   N. 100   33, 94 nn. 31 and 33, 106,
                       107 n. 66, 108–11, 115, 127
                       n. 12, 131 n. 23, 213 n. 13,
                       255, 293, 319

Kraków, *Biblioteka Jagiellońska*
   257   48 n. 4, 220 n. 43, 320
   551   108 n. 70, 125, 127, 148,
                       166, 186–87, 227, 320
   610   94 n. 31, 96 n. 42, 106 n. 62,
                       138 n. 47
   778   68, 69 nn. 66 and 68, 218 n.
                       39, 232 n. 89
   792   217 n. 32
   793   31, 64, 80, 84–104, 106,
                       108, 119–20, 131–32, 134,
                       147, 251–52, 255, 258, 264,
                       269, 274, 320
   805   62, 63 n. 39, 85, 106 n. 62,
                       127 n. 11, 252–53, 322
   813   62, 63 n. 39, 252, 322
   817   63, 323
   837   152–55
   839   127 n. 12, 253, 323
   1839   249 n. 34
   1970   31 n. 61

   2014   214–17
   2252   106 n. 62, 108 n. 70, 109 n.
                       74
   2496   32 n. 61, 323
   2513   214–17
   5465   149
   Dipl. BJ 610   209–10

London, *British Library*
   Sloane 3457   151, 213 n. 8

Martin, *Literárny archív*
   J 2042   97 n. 43

Munich, *Bayerische Staatsbibliothek*
   CLM 125   108 n. 70, 131 n. 23, 213 n.
                       13
   CLM 826   233

Munich, *Universitätsbibliothek*
   2° Cod. ms. 738   134–35, 324

Nuremberg, *Germanisches Nationalmuseum*
   Hs 168   148 n. 13, 324

Oxford, *Bodleian Library*
   Rawl. Liturg. d. 6. 162–83, 324
   Hertford College
      2 (E.N. 2.)   58 n. 24, 231 n. 84, 324

Prague, *Národní knihovna ČR*
   267 I F 35   131 n. 23, 133, 140 n. 53,
                       141, 185–86, 192 n. 5, 205
                       n. 32, 325
   1144 VI F 7   192 n. 4
   1609 VIII G 27   32 nn. 63 and 65, 33 n. 67,
                       114
   1832 X B 3   94 n. 31
   1998 X H 20   62 n. 37
   2027 XI C 2   64–68, 127 n. 12, 131 n. 23,
                       134 n. 28, 135 n. 36, 137 n.
                       41, 325
   2764 adlig.
      14 H 208   83 n. 12, 91 n. 21, 207, 326

Prague, *Knihovna metropolitní kapituly*
1323 L LXXVII   23 n. 26
1367 M XI   53 n. 8, 55 n. 16
1370 M XVII   149 n. 21
1374 M XXI   63 n. 42
1577 N LIII   206 n. 35

Prague, *Knihovna národního muzea*
III H 11   155 n. 43
V H 21   155 n. 42

Třeboň, *Státní oblastní archiv*
6 (A 4)   206–7
9 (A 7)   206–7

Vienna, *Österreichische Nationalbibliothek*
Cod. lat. 4007   128 nn. 14 and 16, 254, 328
Cod. lat. 2352   233

Cod. lat. 11133   160 nn. 58 and 59
Cod. lat. 11347   160 n. 58

Vatican, *Biblioteca Apostolica Vaticana*
Pal. lat. 1375   83, 106–9, 115–20, 130–32, 138, 256–58, 260, 326
Pal. lat. 1385   255 n. 66
Pal. lat. 1391   130 n. 21, 255 n. 66, 257 n. 78
Pal. lat. 1396   128 n. 18, 129, 199 n. 15, 200 n. 16, 255 n. 66, 256 n. 75
Pal. lat. 1439   106–15, 128, 137 n. 44, 255 n. 66, 256–57, 293, 327

Zagreb, *Knjižnica Metropolitana*
MR lat. 154   198 n. 11